Performance Modeling
for Computer Architects

Performance Modeling
for Computer Architects

C.M. Krishna

IEEE Computer Society Press
Los Alamitos, California

Washington • Brussels • Tokyo

Library of Congress Cataloging-in-Publication Data

Performance modeling for computer architects / [compiled by] C.M. Krishna.
    p.   cm.
   Includes bibliographical references.
   ISBN 0-8186-7094-0
   1. Electronic digital computers—Evaluation—Mathematical models. 2. Computer simulation.
I. Krishna, C.M.
QA76.9.E94P49   1996
004.2 ' 4 ' 011—dc20   95-14981
                                                  CIP

Published by the
IEEE Computer Society Press
10662 Los Vaqueros Circle
P.O. Box 3014
Los Alamitos, CA 90720-1314

IEEE Computer Society Press Order Number BP07094
IEEE Catalog Number EH0422-6
Library of Congress Number 95-14981
ISBN 0-8186-7094-0

Additional copies can be ordered from

IEEE Computer Society Press	IEEE Service Center	IEEE Computer Society	IEEE Computer Society
Customer Service Center	445 Hoes Lane	13, avenue de l'Aquilon	Ooshima Building
10662 Los Vaqueros Circle	P.O. Box 1331	B-1200 Brussels	2-19-1 Minami-Aoyama
P.O. Box 3014	Piscataway, NJ 08855-1331	BELGIUM	Minato-ku, Tokyo 107
Los Alamitos, CA 90720-1314	Tel: (908) 981-1393	Tel: +32-2-770-2198	JAPAN
Tel: (714) 821-8380	Fax: (908) 981-9667	Fax: +32-2-770-8505	Tel: +81-3-3408-3118
Fax: (714) 821-4641	mis.custserv@computer.org	euro.ofc@computer.org	Fax: +81-3-3408-3553
Email: cs.books@computer.org			tokyo.ofc@computer.org

Technical Editor: Dharma P. Agrawal
Production Editor: Lisa O'Conner

99 98 97 96   5 4 3 2

The Institute of Electrical and Electronics Engineers, Inc.

Contents

Chapter 5: Disk and Disk Cache Systems 331

About the Author..391

Preface

As computers have become more complex, the number and complexity of the tasks facing the computer architect have increased. The performance of the computer can depend in an often complex way on the design parameters, and intuition must be supplemented and aided by performance studies if design productivity is to be enhanced.

There are three ways for the architect to characterize the performance of a machine as a function of the design parameters. He can (a) develop a performance model based on queuing theory and probability, (b) simulate the machine, or (c) carry out experimental studies on prototypes. These alternatives are arranged in increasing order of cost and accuracy. Performance models are almost always approximate: this is the price that must be paid for tractability. However, they are usually computationally inexpensive, and can usually be executed in a few seconds on a workstation. Simulations require considerable investment of time in programming, but are more accurate. Experimental studies on variations of a prototype are the most expensive of all and require considerable engineering effort, but are the most accurate (provided that representative workloads are available).

These three alternatives complement one another, and are used in different stages of the development process. In the early stages of design, when the architect is searching a parameter space of many dimensions to determine the approximate system configuration, it is impossible to carry out experimental studies on prototypes and very time-consuming to do detailed simulation experiments. During this initial phase, the architect is interested in basic performance tradeoffs and in narrowing the range of parameters to be considered. For example, he might be concerned with how the memory system is to be configured, what the cache structure should be, and what impact incremental changes in cache size can have on the miss rate. It would be a waste of resources to carry out detailed simulations at this stage: all that is required are approximate calculations to indicate the performance tradeoffs. Such approximate—and quick—calculations are provided by performance models.

Over the past decade, much progress has been made in developing performance models for computer systems. The purpose of this volume of readings is to introduce computer architects to such models, and to convince them that these models are relatively simple, inexpensive to implement, and sufficiently accurate for most purposes.

The mathematical prerequisites for reading this book are a knowledge of computer architecture and basic probability theory. As the contents of this book will show, it does not require a particularly deep knowledge of probability theory or any other mathematical field to understand the papers in this volume, or to use them. In this field, a little probability theory goes a very long way.

Acknowledgments: I would like to thank Professor Y.-H. Lee of the University of Florida for his advice regarding some of the papers in this collection. The author was supported by the National Science Foundation under CCR-9119922.

Chapter 1

Probability Theory and Performance Evaluation

In this chapter, we outline the elements of probability theory. Most readers will have taken courses on probability and statistics, and this chapter is meant mainly as a refresher on techniques that are used in the papers collected in this book. Probability is a vast subject, and the Further Reading section contains a brief list of some introductory volumes.

1.1 Introduction

It is possible to make up a rigorous definition of probability, based on sigma algebras and measure theory, but our interests are much more practical. From our point of view, there are some things, called *events*, which have a given probability of occurring. For example, if you have a "fair" coin, the probability of getting a tail upon tossing it is 0.5. This is a way of saying that if you toss a fair coin N times, then

$$\lim_{N \to \infty} \frac{\text{Number of Tails out of } N \text{ Tosses}}{N} = \frac{1}{2} \tag{1.1}$$

Two events that cannot occur at the same time are called *mutually exclusive*. For example, if you have a memory module with one I/O port, you cannot have two simultaneous reads in progress. Suppose that events $e_1, e_2, \cdots, e_n$ are mutually exclusive, and $P(e_i)$ is the probability of e_i occurring. Define E as the event that one of $e_1, e_2, \cdots, e_n$ occurs. Then,

$$\text{Prob}\,\{E \text{ occurs}\} = \sum_{i=1}^{n} P(e_i) \tag{1.2}$$

The probability of any event must lie between 0 and 1. An event that occurs with probability 1 is said to happen *almost surely*. This term points up a common misconception about probabilities: namely, that an event with probability 1 is certain to occur, and an event with probability 0 will never occur. This is not true. For example, suppose we run an experiment which consists of choosing a random point in an interval $[0, 1]$. There is an uncountable infinity of such points, and so the probability that we choose a given point (say, 0.55), is zero. In fact, *every* outcome in this experiment will have probability zero!

Given events $A_1, A_2, \cdots, A_n$ the event that they all occur is expressed by $A_1 \cap A_2 \cap \cdots \cap A_n$, while the event that at least one of them occurs is denoted by $A_1 \cup A_2 \cup \cdots \cup A_n$. The notation arises from the fact that we can denote the event probabilities by area in a Venn diagram. In such a diagram, $\text{Prob}(A_i)$ would be proportional to the area occupied by A_i. The probability of the event that either A_1 or A_2 (or both) occurred is proportional to the area of $A_1 \cup A_2$. Similarly, the probability of both A_1 and A_2 occurring is represented by the area covered by $A_1 \cap A_2$.

We have
$$\text{Prob}\,(A_1 \cup A_2) = \text{Prob}\,(A_1) + \text{Prob}\,(A_2) - \text{Prob}\,(A_1 \cap A_2) \tag{1.3}$$
The $\text{Prob}\,(A_1 \cap A_2)$ term corrects for the double-counting that occurs when both events occur. We can extend Equation 1.3 recursively. For example,

$$
\begin{aligned}
\text{Prob}\,(A_1 \cup A_2 \cup A_3) &= \text{Prob}\,(A_1 \cup A_2) + \text{Prob}\,(A_3) - \text{Prob}\,([A_1 \cup A_2] \cap A_3) & (1.4) \\
\text{Prob}\,([A_1 \cup A_2] \cap A_3) &= \text{Prob}\,([A_1 \cap A_3] \cup [A_2 \cap A_3]) \\
&= \text{Prob}\,(A_1 \cap A_3) + \text{Prob}\,(A_2 \cap A_3) - \text{Prob}\,([A_1 \cap A_3] \cap [A_2 \cap A_3]) \\
&= \text{Prob}\,(A_1 \cap A_3) + \text{Prob}\,(A_2 \cap A_3) - \text{Prob}\,(A_1 \cap A_2 \cap A_3) & (1.5)
\end{aligned}
$$

Thus,

$$
\begin{aligned}
\text{Prob}\,(A_1 \cup A_2 \cup A_3) =\ & \text{Prob}\,(A_1) + \text{Prob}\,(A_2) + \text{Prob}\,(A_3) \\
& -\text{Prob}\,(A_1 \cap A_2) - \text{Prob}\,(A_1 \cap A_3) - \text{Prob}\,(A_2 \cap A_3) \\
& +\text{Prob}\,(A_1 \cap A_2 \cap A_3)
\end{aligned}
\tag{1.6}
$$

It is probably easier to see this graphically, using a Venn diagram. See Figure 1.1, and relate the area enclosed by the circles to the probabilities in Equation 1.6.

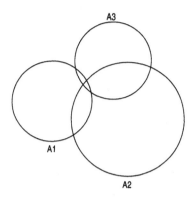

Figure 1.1. Venn Diagram for Prob $(A_1 \cup A_2 \cup A_3)$

If $A_1, \cdots, A_n$ is the set of all possible events (n may or may not be finite), then

$$\text{Prob}\,(A_1 \cup A_2 \cup \cdots \cup A_n) = 1 \qquad (1.7)$$

Two events A and B are said to be *independent* if

$$\text{Prob}\,(A \cap B) = \text{Prob}\,(A) \times \text{Prob}\,(B) \qquad (1.8)$$

For example, if successive tosses of a fair coin are independent, the probability that we have a head followed by a tail is $0.5 \times 0.5 = 0.25$. We can extend Equation 1.8 recursively. If A, B, C are independent events, then

$$\text{Prob}\,(A \cap B \cap C) = \text{Prob}\,(A) \times \text{Prob}\,(B) \times \text{Prob}\,(C) \qquad (1.9)$$

One of the most useful concepts in probability theory is *conditional probability*. We denote by $\text{Prob}\,(B|A)$ the probability that event B occurs, *given that* event A has occurred. The fundamental equation relating to conditional probability is Bayes' law:

$$\text{Prob}\,(B|A) = \frac{\text{Prob}\,(A \cap B)}{\text{Prob}\,(A)} \qquad (1.10)$$

We can rewrite Bayes' law as follows:

$$\text{Prob}\,(A \cap B) = \text{Prob}\,(B|A) \times \text{Prob}\,(A) \qquad (1.11)$$

This leads to the following useful construct

$$\text{Prob}\,(B|A) \quad = \quad \frac{\text{Prob}\,(A \cap B)}{\text{Prob}\,(A)}$$

3

$$= \frac{\text{Prob}\,(A|B) \times \text{Prob}\,(B)}{\text{Prob}\,(A)} \tag{1.12}$$

1.2 Random Variables

A random variable can be formally defined as a mapping from the set of events to the real line. That is, a random variable is a function, which associates a real number with each event. The real number usually denotes some parameter of physical interest. For example, if the event is accessing memory, we can define a random variable t_{access} which is the memory access time. Suppose we are given that an access is to cache with probability p_{cache}, to main memory with probability p_{main}, to disks with probability p_{disks}, and to tape with probability p_{tape}. Denote by $t(cache)$, $t(main)$, $t(disks)$, and $t(tape)$ the access times associated with these various media. We can now write

$$t_{access} = \begin{cases} t(cache) & \text{with probability } p_{cache} \\ t(main) & \text{with probability } p_{main} \\ t(disks) & \text{with probability } p_{disks} \\ t(tape) & \text{with probability } p_{tape} \end{cases} \tag{1.13}$$

Associated with each random variable, X, is a *probability distribution function* (PDF),

$$F_X(x) = \text{Prob}\,\{X \leq x\} \tag{1.14}$$

Assuming that $t(cache) < t(main) < t(disks) < t(tape)$, we can write the PDF of t_{access} as

$$F_{t_{access}}(t) = \begin{cases} 0 & \text{if } t < t(cache) \\ p_{cache} & \text{if } t(cache) \leq t < t(main) \\ p_{main} + p_{cache} & \text{if } t(main) \leq t < t(disks) \\ p_{disks} + p_{main} + p_{cache} & \text{if } t(disks) \leq t < t(tape) \\ 1 & \text{otherwise} \end{cases} \tag{1.15}$$

If the PDF is a differentiable function (that is, it can be differentiated), its derivative is called the *probability density function*, (pdf). If the PDF takes discrete jumps (as was the case with t_{access} in our example), a pdf does not exist and we can define instead a *probability mass function* (pmf),

$$m_X(x) = \text{Prob}\,\{X = x\} \tag{1.16}$$

4

For example, the pmf of t_{access} is given by

$$m_{t_{access}}(t) = \begin{cases} p_{cache} & \text{if } t = t(cache) \\ p_{main} & \text{if } t = t(main) \\ p_{disks} & \text{if } t = t(disks) \\ p_{tape} & \text{if } t = t(tape) \\ 0 & \text{otherwise} \end{cases} \tag{1.17}$$

The *expectation*, $E[X]$, of a random variable, X, is its average or mean. If the random variable takes discrete values from the set $A = \{a_1, a_2, \cdots\}$, it has a pmf, and we have

$$E[x] = \sum_{i \in A} a_i m_X(a_i) \tag{1.18}$$

If X has a pdf, we have

$$E[X] = \int_{x=-\infty}^{\infty} x f_X(x)\, dx \tag{1.19}$$

If the expectation of X is finite, we can also determine it by the expression

$$E[X] = \int_{x=0}^{\infty} (1 - F_X(x))\, dx - \int_{x=-\infty}^{0} F_x(x)\, dx \tag{1.20}$$

If you remember elementary techniques of integration, you might try deriving Equation 1.20 from Equation 1.19.

Expectation is a linear operator. That is a fancy way of saying that

$$E[X_1 + X_2 + \cdots + X_n] = E[X_1] + E[X_2] + \cdots + E[X_n] \tag{1.21}$$

The n'th moment of a random variable X is $E[X^n]$. The first moment is, of course, the mean. The *variance* of X is given by

$$V[X] = E[X^2] - (E[X])^2 \tag{1.22}$$

The *standard deviation* of a random variable is the square root of its variance.

5

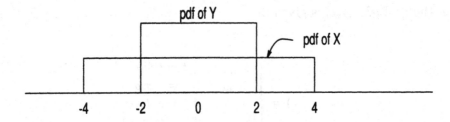

Figure 1.2. Illustrating Variance

While the first moment gives us the average value, the variance tells us how much variation or spread we can expect. For example, consider the random variables X and Y with pdf's shown in Figure 1.2. We have

$$f_X(x) = \begin{cases} 0.125 & \text{if } -4 \leq x \leq 4 \\ 0 & \text{otherwise} \end{cases} \quad ; \quad f_Y(x) = \begin{cases} 0.250 & \text{if } -2 \leq x \leq 2 \\ 0 & \text{otherwise} \end{cases} \tag{1.23}$$

While random variables both have a mean of 0, it is clear that X is more "spread out." This is reflected in the variances: $V[X] = 8$; $V[Y] = 2$.

Let us now turn to the distribution of the sum of independent random variables. This will also give us an opportunity to demonstrate the usefulness of Bayes' law. If X, Y are independent random variables with pdf's, then

$$\begin{aligned} \text{Prob}\,(X + Y < w) &= \int_{x=-\infty}^{\infty} \text{Prob}\,(X + Y < w \cap X = x)\, dx \\[2ex] &= \int_{x=-\infty}^{\infty} \text{Prob}\,(X + Y < w | X = x) f_X(x)\, dx \\[2ex] &= \int_{x=-\infty}^{\infty} \text{Prob}\,(Y < w - x | X = x) f_X(x)\, dx \\[2ex] &= \int_{x=-\infty}^{\infty} f_Y(w - x) f_X(x)\, dx \end{aligned} \tag{1.24}$$

We can apply this expression recursively to the sum of more than two variables. For example,

$$\text{Prob}\,(X + Y + Z < w) = \int_{x=-\infty}^{\infty} f_{Y+Z}(w - x) f_X(x)\, dx \qquad (1.25)$$

where f_{Y+Z} is the pdf of the random variable $Y + Z$.

Let us now look at two important PDFs. Perhaps the simplest is the *uniform* distribution, which we have already encountered in Figure 1.2. For a continuous random variable, the PDF and pdf are

$$F_X(x) = \begin{cases} 0 & \text{if } x < a_1 \\ \dfrac{x - a_1}{a_2 - a_1} & \text{if } a_1 \le x \le a_2 \\ 1 & \text{otherwise} \end{cases} \quad ; \quad f_X(x) = \begin{cases} 1/(a_2 - a_1) & \text{if } a_1 \le x \le a_2 \\ 0 & \text{otherwise} \end{cases} \qquad (1.26)$$

The exponential distribution and density functions are given by

$$F_X(x) = \begin{cases} 1 - e^{-\mu x} & \text{if } x > 0 \\ 0 & \text{otherwise} \end{cases} \quad ; \quad f_X(x) = \begin{cases} \mu e^{-\mu x} & \text{if } x > 0 \\ 0 & \text{otherwise} \end{cases} \qquad (1.27)$$

A random variable which is exponentially distributed is said to be *memoryless*. The reason for this lies in the following computation:

$$\begin{aligned} \text{Prob}\,(X > x \mid X > a) &= \frac{\text{Prob}\,(X > x \cap X > a)}{\text{Prob}\,(X > a)} \\[2mm] &= \begin{cases} \dfrac{\text{Prob}\,(X>a)}{\text{Prob}\,(X>a)} & \text{if } a \ge x \\ \dfrac{\text{Prob}\,(X>x)}{\text{Prob}\,(X>a)} & \text{if } a < x \end{cases} \end{aligned} \qquad (1.28)$$

Since $\text{Prob}\,(X > t) = e^{-\mu t}$, we have

$$\text{Prob}\,(X > x \mid X > a) = \frac{\text{Prob}\,(X > x \cap X > a)}{\text{Prob}\,(X > a)} = \begin{cases} 1 & \text{if } a \ge x \\ e^{-\mu(x-a)} & \text{if } a < x \end{cases} \qquad (1.29)$$

If $a < x$, we have from Equation 1.29 that

$$\text{Prob}\,(X > x \,|\, X > a) = \text{Prob}\,(X > x - a) \tag{1.30}$$

which is a function of the *difference* between x and a. That is, for every $\delta > -a$,

$$\text{Prob}\,(X > x \,|\, X > a) = \text{Prob}\,(X > x + \delta \,|\, X > a + \delta) \tag{1.31}$$

If, for example, a light bulb has an exponentially-distributed lifetime, the probability that it will burn out over the next hour is not a function of how old it is, but only of whether it has yet burned out or not. That is why this distribution is called memoryless. This property is very important in mathematical modeling.

Associated with the exponential distribution is the *Poisson process*. Consider some events, such as memory requests, that occur over a period of time. Let $N(t)$ denote the number of such events over the interval of time $[0, t]$. The event-arrival process is called *Poisson* with rate $\lambda(t)$ if:

- The probability of one or more events occurring in an interval $[a, b]$ is unaffected by what happened outside this interval.

- The probability of an event occurring in an interval $[t, t + dt]$ is $\lambda(t)\,dt$.

- The probability of two events occurring in an interval of length dt is of the order of $(dt)^2$ or less.

If $\lambda(t) = \lambda$ for all t, we have a *homogeneous* Poisson process. We can show that

$$\text{Prob}\,(N(t) = n) = e^{-\int_{x=0}^{t} \lambda(x)\,dx} \frac{\left\{\int_{x=0}^{t} \lambda(x)\,dx\right\}^n}{n!} \tag{1.32}$$

If $\lambda(t) = \lambda$ for all t, we have

$$\text{Prob}\,(N(t) = n) = e^{-\lambda t} \frac{\{\lambda t\}^n}{n!} \tag{1.33}$$

That there is a relationship between the Poisson process and the exponential distribution is demonstrated as follows. Denote by τ the time between two successive event occurrences. We have

$$\begin{aligned}
\text{Prob}\,(\tau > t) &= \text{Prob}\,(N(t) = 0) \\
&= e^{-\lambda t} \tag{1.34}
\end{aligned}$$

Thus, the interarrival time (that is, the time between successive event arrivals) of a Poisson process is exponentially distributed.

Another important process is the *Bernoulli process*. Consider a set of random variables, $X_1, X_2, \cdots, X_n, \cdots$, which can take only two values: 0 and 1. The sum $S_n = X_1 + X_2 + \cdots + X_n$, $n = 1, 2, \cdots$, is called a Bernoulli process.

Suppose $\text{Prob}\,(X_i = 1) = p$, and $\text{Prob}\,(X_i = 0) = 1 - p$ for all $i = 1, 2, \cdots$. Then,

$$\text{Prob}\,(S_1 = k) \;=\; \begin{cases} p & \text{if } k = 1 \\ 1 - p & \text{if } k = 0 \\ 0 & \text{otherwise} \end{cases} \tag{1.35}$$

$$\begin{aligned} \text{Prob}\,(S_2 = k) &= \text{Prob}\,(S_1 + X_2 = k) \\ &= \text{Prob}\,([S_1 = k - 1 \cap X_2 = 1] \cup [S_1 = k \cap X_2 = 0]) \\ &= \text{Prob}\,(S_1 = k - 1)p + \text{Prob}\,(S_1 = k)(1 - p) \end{aligned} \tag{1.36}$$

$$\vdots$$

$$\text{Prob}\,(S_n = k) \;=\; \text{Prob}\,(S_{n-1} = k - 1)p + \text{Prob}\,(S_{n-1} = k)(1 - p) \tag{1.37}$$

It is easy to show (try it) that this series of equations yields

$$\text{Prob}\,(S_n = k) = \binom{n}{k} p^k (1 - p)^{n-k} \tag{1.38}$$

where $\binom{n}{k}$ is the number of combinations of n things, taken k at a time. You will no doubt remember from elementary algebra that

$$\binom{n}{k} = \begin{cases} \dfrac{n!}{k!(n - k)!} & \text{if } k \le n \\ 0 & \text{otherwise} \end{cases} \tag{1.39}$$

As an aside, perhaps the best way to compute these functions is to use the recursion

$$\binom{n}{k} = \binom{n-1}{k-1} + \binom{n-1}{k}$$

(1.40)

As an elementary exercise, try proving this result.

1.3 Markov Chains

Markov chains are perhaps the most important tool in the development of mathematical performance models. In this section, we will provide an informal (well, almost informal) treatment. We will make no claims of rigor, restricting ourselves to some common sense observations and basic mathematics.

Everyone is familiar with the idea of a finite-state machine (FSM). It consists of a finite set of *states* and *transition rules*. At any time, the system must be in exactly one state. The transition rules govern how the system moves from state to state, usually in response to a clock and other inputs. The next state thus depends only on

- The present state;

- The input(s), if any; and

- The transition rules.

An FSM is deterministic (if it weren't, computing would be impossible!). In other words, if you have two identical FSMs, start them in the same initial state, and provide them with identical inputs, you will get identical outputs. Markov chains are very similar to FSMs, except in two crucial respects:

- They may have a finite or a countably infinite number of states.[1]

- Their state transitions are usually not deterministic: it is possible to have *probabilistic* transition rules. That is, we can specify that the system will move from, say, state 1 to state 2, with probability $p_{1,2}(i)$ in response to an input, i.

---

[1]By "countably infinite," we mean that it is possible to set up a one-to-one mapping between the states of the Markov chain and the set of integers. For example, the set of rational numbers is countably infinite, while the set of real numbers is not. Consult any book on real analysis for further information.

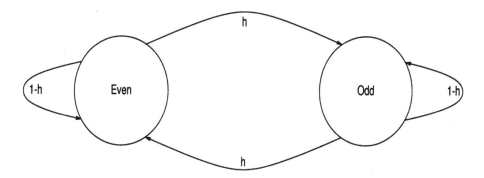

Figure 1.3. Markov Chain for First Coin-Tossing Example

Because their state transitions can be probabilistic, it is possible to take two identical Markov chains, start them in the same initial state, apply identical inputs, and yet end up in different states. When dealing with Markov chains, we are interested in finding the probability of the chain being in a particular state.

A Markov chain may be either *discrete-* or *continuous-*time. A discrete-time chain only undergoes state changes at integral multiples of some time granule (that is, a clock), while continuous-time chains can undergo state changes at any time.

Let us consider a few toy examples of discrete-time chains. Consider a situation where we toss an unfair coin once every clock period. We are not concerned with the total number of heads and tails that result: only with whether that total number is odd or even. Given that we start with even parity at time 0, what is the probability of having even parity at time n, for any $n = 1, 2, \cdots$? Let the probability of having a head be h; that of a tail is $1 - h$.

There are only two states: odd and even. At any time, the next state that the system goes to depends only on the present state, and the outcome of the present coin toss. It is therefore a Markov chain.

Figure 1.3 shows the Markov chain associated with this example. The arcs are labelled with the transition probabilities, which are calculated from the following table:

Present State	Event	Next State	Probability
Odd	Head	Even	h
Odd	Tail	Odd	1-h
Even	Head	Odd	h
Even	Tail	Even	1-h

11

We can write the probability of the system being in a state at time i as a function of its state at time $i - 1$. That is,

$$p_{odd}(i) = p_{odd}(i - 1) \cdot (1 - h) + p_{even}(i - 1) \cdot h \qquad (1.41)$$

$$p_{even}(i) = p_{odd}(i - 1) \cdot h + p_{even}(i - 1) \cdot (1 - h) \qquad (1.42)$$

Note that $p_{even}(i) + p_{odd}(i) = 1$, since the chain must be in one of its states at any one time. Thus, one of these equations is redundant. Let us drop Equation 1.42 from consideration, and limit ourselves to Equation 1.41. We therefore have:

$$
\begin{aligned}
p_{odd}(i) &= p_{odd}(i - 1) \cdot (1 - h) + (1 - p_{odd}(i - 1)) \cdot h \\
&= p_{odd}(i - 1) \cdot (1 - 2h) + h, \quad i > 0
\end{aligned}
\qquad (1.43)
$$

If $h = 0$, every toss of the coin will turn up tails, and there will be no state change, that is, the system will be frozen at its initial state. If $h = 1$, every toss will turn up heads and there will be a state change every clock period. In both cases, the memory of the initial state will propagate to eternity. If $h = 0$, we will have $\lim_{i \to \infty} p_{odd}(i) = p_{odd}(0)$, and if $h = 1$, $\lim_{i \to \infty} p_{odd}(i)$ does not exist. Now, if $0 < h < 1$, the limit $\lim_{i \to \infty} p_{odd}(i)$ exists, and is independent of the initial state (that is, $p_{odd}(0)$): we can see this by inspection, and will not show this formally. How can we obtain this limit? The easiest way of doing this (once we are assured that such a limit exists) is to take limits in Equation 1.43 as follows:

$$\lim_{i \to \infty} p_{odd}(i) = \lim_{i \to \infty} p_{odd}(i - 1)(1 - 2h) + h \qquad (1.44)$$

But, $\lim_{i \to \infty} p_{odd}(i) = \lim_{i \to \infty} p_{odd}(i - 1)$. For brevity, write $\lim_{i \to \infty} p_{odd}(i) = \pi_{odd}$. We therefore have from Equation 1.44,

$$\pi_{odd} = \pi_{odd} \cdot (1 - 2h) + h \qquad (1.45)$$

$$\Rightarrow \pi_{odd} = 1/2 \qquad (1.46)$$

Equations such as Equation 1.46 are commonly referred to as *balance equations*. They can usually be written down by inspection of the Markov chain, by balancing the "flow" out of a state with the "flow" into it. The intuitive argument is that if the probability of being in a state does not change with time (which is the case here in the limit as time goes to infinity), there must be an equality of flow into, and out of, each state. In our example, the "flow" out of state **odd** was given by $\pi_{odd}h$, and the flow into state **even** was given by $(1 - \pi_{odd})h$. Equating, we obtain

$$\pi_{odd}h = (1 - \pi_{odd})h \qquad (1.47)$$

which yields the result $\pi_{odd} = 1/2$.

In general, the flow out of a state in a discrete-time chain is the product of the probability of being in that state and the transition probability.

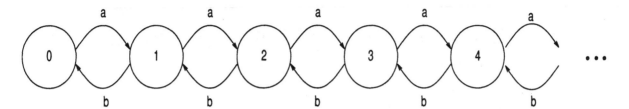

Figure 1.4. Markov Chain for Second Example: Birth-Death Process

Probabilities of the form $\lim_{i \to \infty} p_{odd}(i)$ are called *steady-state* probabilities for obvious reasons.

As a second example, consider the discrete-time chain in Figure 1.4. If the system is in state i, at each clock tick, the probability of a transition to state $i+1$ is a, and for all $i > 0$ the probability of a transition to $i-1$ is b. This Markov chain represents a *birth-death* process: the term arose from considering each move to the right a birth, and each move to the left a death. The balance equations can be written down by inspection. Once again, denote by π_i the steady-state probability of being in state i.

$$
\begin{aligned}
a\pi_0 &= b\pi_1 \\
(a+b)\pi_i &= a\pi_{i-1} + b\pi_{i+1}, \quad i > 0
\end{aligned}
\tag{1.48}
$$

We also have the boundary condition that all the probabilities must add to one:

$$
\pi_0 + \pi_1 + \cdots + \pi_n + \cdots = 1
\tag{1.49}
$$

To obtain the value of π_i, $i = 0, 1, \cdots$, we use Equation 1.48 to express all the π_i in terms of π_0, and then use Equation 1.49 to solve for π_0. We have from Equation 1.48 and some algebra,

$$
\begin{aligned}
\pi_1 &= (b/a)\pi_0 \\
\pi_2 &= (b/a)^2\pi_0 \\
&\vdots \\
\pi_n &= (b/a)^n\pi_0 \\
&\vdots
\end{aligned}
\tag{1.50}
$$

From Equations 1.49 and 1.50, we have

$$
(1 + (b/a) + (b/a)^2 + \cdots + (b/a)^n + \cdots)\pi_0 = 1
$$

$$
\Rightarrow \pi_0 = \frac{1}{1 - (b/a)}
\tag{1.51}
$$

13

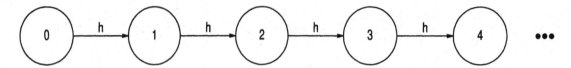

Figure 1.5. Markov Chain for Third Example: Coin Tossing

Note that we have $\pi_i > 0$ only if $b/a > 1$, that is, if $b > a$. It is only if $b > a$ that steady-state exists.

Let us now construct a third example of Markov chains. This time, let us count the number of heads that are generated by n coin tosses, for $n = 1, 2, \cdots$. The Markov chain for this system is shown in Figure 1.5. Note that this chain has an infinite number of states. State i represents the situation where i heads have been obtained. Let $p_i(n)$ denote the probability of obtaining i heads after n tosses. We have

$$p_i(n) = hp_{i-1}(n-1) + (1-h)p_i(n-1) \tag{1.52}$$

Note that unless $h = 0$, the limit $\lim_{n\to\infty} p_i(n) = 0$, for all $i = 0, 1, 2, \cdots$. A state whose probability goes to zero in the limit as time goes to infinity is called a *transient* state. In this chain, every state is transient.

1.4 Queues

A *queue* is a waiting area where jobs are held, awaiting service. They are served in first-come-first-served, or some other prespecified order. There is a vast literature on queues, and we restrict ourselves here to providing the bare minimum needed to understand the papers in this volume.

Let us begin with some notation. An A/B/C/D/E queue means the following:

- A refers to the arrival process.

- B refers to the service process.

- C is the number of servers.

- D is the maximum number of jobs for which the queue has room. The default value is ∞.

- E is the maximum number of jobs. The default value is ∞.

For example, the queue A/B/1 refers to a queue with arrival process denoted by A, service process denoted by B, and having a single server. Since the fourth and fifth fields are not specified, the default values are assumed for the waiting room and the maximum number of jobs.

We denote by M a Poisson arrival process or an exponentially distributed service process; by D a deterministic arrival or service process, and by G a general arrival or service process. For example, the queue M/M/1 means that:

- Jobs arrive according to a Poisson process.

- The service time of each job is exponentially distributed.

- There is one server.

- There is infinite waiting room and no limit on the number of jobs.

Similarly, the queue M/G/1 means that:

- Jobs arrive according to a Poisson process.

- The service time of each job is generally distributed (that is, there is no restriction on the form the service-time distribution may take).

- There is one server.

- There is infinite waiting room and no limit on the number of jobs.

and the queue M/D/1 means that:

- Jobs arrive according to a Poisson process.

- The service time of each job is *deterministic*, that is, each job takes exactly the same service time.

- There is one server.

- There is infinite waiting room and no limit on the number of jobs.

We shall not go into how to analyze these queues, but content ourselves with pointing out some basic formulas. If the mean arrival rate into a queue is λ, the expected waiting time in the queue, W, and the mean number of jobs in the queue, L, are related by Little's Law[2]:

$$L = \lambda W \tag{1.53}$$

The Pollaczek-Khinchine (PK) formulas apply to M/G/1 queues. Let $W^*(s)$ and $B^*(s)$ denote the Laplace transforms of the pdfs of the job waiting and service times, let the arrival rate be λ, and let the mean job service time be τ. Further, let $N(z) = \sum_{i=0}^{\infty} \pi_i z^i$, where π_i is the probability of i jobs in the queue. $N(z)$ is called the z-transform of π_i, $i = 0, 1, cdots$. The PK formulas are as follows:

$$N(z) = B^*(\lambda - \lambda z) \frac{(1 - \tau\lambda)(1 - z)}{B^*(\lambda - \lambda z) - z} \tag{1.54}$$

$$W^*(s) = \frac{s(1 - \rho)}{s - \lambda + \lambda B^*(s)} \tag{1.55}$$

The Laplace and z transforms can be used to find the moments of the waiting time and number in the queue. It is easy to show that if $A^*(s)$ is the Laplace transform of a pdf $a(x)$, the n'th moment of that pdf is given by

$$(-1)^n \left. \frac{d^n A^*(s)}{ds^n} \right|_{s=0} \tag{1.56}$$

and if $N(z)$ is the z-transform of the pmf of random variable X, given by

$$E[X] = \left. \frac{dN(z)}{dz} \right|_{z=1} \tag{1.57}$$

$$E[X(X - 1)] = \left. \frac{d^2 N(z)}{dz^2} \right|_{z=1} \tag{1.58}$$

Equations 1.56 and 1.58 are easy to verify. We can use them to find an expression for the mean waiting time in an M/G/1 queue:

$$W = \frac{\lambda}{2(1 - \lambda\tau)} \left\{ \tau^2 + \sigma_s^2 \right\} \tag{1.59}$$

---

[2]There are some types of queues which do not follow Little's law, but these will not be encountered in this volume.

16

where σ_s is the standard deviation of the service time. The mean number in the queue is given by

$$L = \lambda\tau + \frac{\lambda^2 + \sigma_s^2}{2(1 - \lambda\tau)} \qquad (1.60)$$

Equations 1.59 and 1.60 are also sometimes referred to as the Pollaczek-Khinchine formulas.

1.5   The Role of Analytical Performance Models

It is important to understand where analytical models can, and cannot, be used. To ensure that they are tractable, almost all analytical performance models are approximate. Also, there is often no way to tightly bound the accuracy of such models. That is, one cannot guarantee that the real performance measure is within $x\%$ of that predicted by the model, for some finite $x\%$. Usually, the only way to assess the accuracy of the model is to run a few simulations and compare the simulation and model outputs.

The approximate nature of performance models is often acceptable for two reasons. First, the models themselves might be used to explore design alternatives, and it is sufficient to have approximate estimates to correctly rank the alternatives. Second, it may be impossible to accurately estimate the input parameters for the model. For example, we may have only an approximate idea of the workload. In such cases, approximate estimates are all that is theoretically possible.

If more accurate performance characterization is needed (and we have sufficiently accurate workload information to make it possible), the designer must turn to simulation or experiments on a prototype. Of course, one has to pay for the additional accuracy: writing simulation models and developing prototypes are neither easy nor inexpensive tasks.

One should also realize that the quality of the output of a performance model depends also on the quality of the input data, and on the appropriateness of the chosen performance measure. No matter how good the model may be, it cannot be expected to give accurate results if the input data are wrong or not representative of the workload that the system will be subjected to in practice. Collecting representative workload data is critical to accurate performance prediction.

The appropriateness of the performance measure is a more subtle factor than the accuracy of the model or the representative nature of the input data, but is no less important. A good performance measure will have the following characteristics:

(a) The measure will be relevant or meaningful in the context of the application.

(b) The measure will allow an unambiguous comparison to be made between machines.

(c) It will be possible to develop models to estimate this performance measure.

(d) The model to estimate this performance measure will not be very difficult to collect or estimate.

It is usually impossible to meet all four requirements. (c) and (d) are essential if the measure is to be practically meaningful, and we try to do the best we can with respect to (a) and (b).

This introductory chapter contains one paper. This is an excellent survey of performance evaluation techniques. In addition, the authors also discuss the gathering of workload data and simulation techniques.

1.6 Suggestions for Further Reading

1. L. Kleinrock, *Queuing Systems, Vols. 1 and 2*, New York: Wiley, 1975 and 1976.

   This is an excellent, if slightly dated, introduction to performance evaluation using queuing theory. It is meant for readers with a fair background in probability theory, and is highly recommended.

2. K.S. Trivedi, *Probability & Statistics with Reliability, Queuing, and Computer Science Applications*, Englewood Cliffs: Prentice-Hall, 1982.

   This is a very good introduction to probability techniques used in performance evaluation. It requires no prior knowledge of probability.

3. W. Feller, *An Introduction to Probability Theory and its Applications*, (2 vols.), New York: John Wiley, 1968, 1971.

   This book is a classic. Many regard this as the best book on probability theory they have ever read. Not only does it provide an excellent introduction to probability theory, but it includes a wealth of examples which illustrate the applicability of probability to a wide range of fields.

4. D.E. Knuth, R.L. Graham, and O. Patasnik, *Concrete Mathematics*, Reading: Addison-Wesley, 1989.

   This is a well-written book containing much of the mathematics that computer scientists should know.

Other useful sources include:

- A.O. Allen, *Probability, Statistics, and Queuing Theory with Computer Science Applications,* New York: Academic Press, 1978.

- D. Ferrari, *Computer Systems Performance Evaluation,* Englewood Cliffs: Prentice-Hall, 1978.

- H. Kobayashi, *Modeling and Analysis: An Introduction to System Performance Evaluation Methodology,* Reading: Addison-Wesley, 1978.

- E.A. MacNair and C.H. Sauer, *Elements of Practical Performance Modeling,* Englewood Cliffs: Prentice-Hall, 1985.

Computer Performance Evaluation Methodology

PHILIP HEIDELBERGER, MEMBER, IEEE, and STEPHEN S. LAVENBERG, MEMBER, IEEE

(Invited Paper)

Abstract — The quantitative evaluation of computer performance is needed during the entire life cycle of a computer system. We survey the major quantitative methods used in computer performance evaluation, focusing on post-1970 developments and emphasizing trends and challenges. We divide the methods used into three main areas, namely performance measurement, analytic performance modeling, and simulation performance modeling, which we survey in the three main sections of the paper. Although we concentrate on the methods per se, rather than on the results of applying the methods, numerous application examples are cited. The methods to be covered have been applied across the entire spectrum of computer systems from personal computers to large mainframes and supercomputers, including both centralized and distributed systems. The application of these methods has certainly not decreased over the years and we anticipate their continued use as well as their enhancement when needed to evaluate future systems.

Index Terms — Computer performance measurement, computer performance modeling, computer workload characterization, discrete event simulation, queueing networks.

I. INTRODUCTION

PERFORMANCE is one of the key factors that needs to be taken into account in the design, development, configuration, and tuning of a computer system. Hence, the quantitative evaluation of computer performance is required during the entire life cycle of a system. (The evaluation of a computer system can also involve such factors as function, ease of use, cost, availability, reliability, serviceability, and security but we will not consider these factors here.) In this paper we will survey the major quantitative methods used in computer performance evaluation. We will focus on post-1970 developments and emphasize trends and challenges for the future. We will concentrate on the methods per se, rather than on the results of applying the methods, but will also cite numerous application examples. The methods to be covered have been applied across the entire spectrum of computer systems from personal computers to large mainframes and supercomputers, including both centralized and distributed systems. (Although the methods have also been applied in evaluating the performance of communication networks, we will not consider network performance evaluation.) The main challenge to be faced in computer performance evaluation is that the development of the required performance evaluation methods keep pace with the explosion of new system designs brought on by rapid technological advances.

Manuscript received March 7, 1984; revised August 8, 1984.
The authors are with the IBM T. J. Watson Research Center, Yorktown Heights, NY 10598.

As we will see, a broad spectrum of skills is needed in computer performance evaluation. The skills range from designing and implementing measurement instrumentation to mathematically analyzing queueing models of computer performance. While computer performance evaluation is of great practical importance to computer manufacturers and computer installation managers, it is also an area of considerable research activity both in industry and universities. The number of recent books which deal with aspects of computer performance evaluation attests to the interest in this area. Recent books include [57], [61], [69], [110], [117], [127], [163], and [197]. Computer performance evaluation papers regularly appear in computer science journals as well as in more practically oriented publications and there are journals that are devoted exclusively to the topic (e.g., *Performance Evaluation*). In addition there are regularly held conferences devoted exclusively to computer performance evaluation including the highly practical conferences sponsored by the Computer Measurement Group, Inc. and the more research oriented conferences sponsored by ACM SIGMETRICS and by IFIP.

We have divided computer performance evaluation methods into three main areas, namely performance measurement, analytic performance modeling, and simulation performance modeling. We will survey these areas in the remaining three sections of the paper. Performance measurement is possible once a system is built, has been instrumented, and is running. However, modeling is required in order to otherwise predict performance. Performance modeling is widely used not only during design and development, but also for configuration and capacity planning purposes. Performance models span the range from simple analytically tractable queueing models to very detailed trace driven simulation models. One of the principle benefits of performance modeling, in addition to the quantitative predictions obtained, is the insight into the structure and behavior of a system that is obtained by developing a model. This can be particularly valuable during system design and can result in the early discovery and correction of design flaws. Finally, it is common that performance measurement and both analytic and simulation performance models are used during the life cycle of a system. As more information about the design of a system becomes available, more detailed models can be developed. Once the system can be measured, previously developed models can be validated and modified if necessary. The models can then be used with greater confidence to investigate the performance effects of design enhancements and configuration changes.

Reprinted from *IEEE Trans. Computers*, Vol. C-33, No. 12, Dec. 1984, pp. 1195–1220.

II. Performance Measurement

A. Introduction

The measurement of system performance is of great practical importance to computer installation managers and to computer manufacturers. For example, in order to effectively manage a computer installation performance measurement is required to do the following.

1) Identify current performance problems and correct them, e.g., by tuning or workload balancing.

2) To identify potential future performance problems and prevent them, e.g., by upgrading system resources in a timely manner.

These measurement activities are typically carried out in an uncontrolled live user environment. Computer manufacturers typically measure performance in a controlled environment using benchmarks which may be real workloads or synthetic executable workloads. For interactive systems remote terminal emulators are commonly used to provide a reasonable approximation of an interactive environment. The purposes of a computer manufacturer's measurement activities include assessing the performance of a new system as soon as a prototype is running, providing performance data for competitive bidding, and helping customers configure their systems to meet performance objectives.

Performance measurement is also a fundamental part of research activities conducted at universities and elsewhere in which new system designs are not simply proposed or studied on paper but are implemented, tested, and studied empirically. An early example of a system that was heavily instrumented for performance measurement as part of research activities is the Multics system, an advanced (for its time) time sharing operating system developed at the Massachusetts Institute of Technology in the 1960's [157]. Other early examples are the C.mmp multiprocessor system developed at Carnegie-Mellon University in the 1970's [65], [100], and the PRIME multiprocessor system developed at Berkeley in the 1970's [56]. More recent examples are the Cm* multiprocessor system developed at Carnegie-Mellon University starting in the 1970's [67], [173], and the Erlangen General Purpose Array currently being developed at the University of Erlangen-Nurnberg [64]. The increasing support for experimental computer science at universities will increase the research use of performance measurement.

Another use of performance measurement is to obtain input parameter values for and to validate performance models. A discussion of such performance measurement in the context of analytical queueing network models can be found in [156] and in the context of a trace driven simulation model of C.mmp in [134].

The advantage of performance measurement over performance modeling is, of course, that the performance of the real system is obtained rather than the performance of a model of the system. Interactions may be present in a system that affect performance and are difficult to capture in a model. If they can be captured, say in a very detailed simulation model, the model may take extremely long to program and run. An example illustrating this is a recent paper on cache performance [42] where measured cache hit ratios differed considerably from those in comparable trace driven simulation studies due to such effects as operating system references, task switching, and instruction prefetching which are not normally represented in simulation studies of cache performance. Among the disadvantages of performance measurement are the need for a running system, not just a design, the measurement instrumentation required, the need for a dedicated system if controlled measurements are to be taken, the time consumed to set up and make a measurement run, and the difficulty of modifying the system so that the effect of system changes can be studied.

A method that has recently been used to evaluate performance that lies somewhere between system measurement and detailed simulation modeling is virtual machine emulation. A virtual machine is an execution environment that is functionally the same as a target system other than the actual physical system on which the environment runs. One use of virtual machines is to do functional prototyping. Although the functional properties of the target system are maintained, real-time properties and hence performance are not. IBM's VM/370 control program supports multiple virtual machines on a single physical system. Canon *et al.* [31] describe an enhancement to VM/370 that adds timing simulation via a virtual clock in order to closely approximate the real-time properties of a target system. The user specifies the processor and I/O device timing characteristics of the target system. Executable workloads can be run on the emulated system and performance measured. Virtual machine emulation does not exactly reproduce the performance of the target machine since the timing characteristics of the target machine's devices are only approximated. For more detail and validation results see [31] and for a discussion in the context of emulating distributed systems and networks see [202]. Emulation capabilities are not widely available and this approach, while interesting, does not appear to be widely used.

Numerous measurement studies have been reported on in the literature although their number is dwarfed by the number of analytic or simulation modeling studies. For example, Schwetman and Browne [172] reported on experiments on a large multiprogrammed computer system at the University of Texas. The experiments were conducted in a controlled environment using an artificial batch workload and had the purpose of studying the variations in performance produced by changes in resource availability and scheduling. Recent examples include measurement studies of the speedup achieved when running algorithms on a multiprocessor [67], performance enhancements to a relational database system [188], cache performance of a minicomputer [42], the performance of a new virtual memory management technique [146], the computational speed of supercomputers [26], the degree of parallelism achieved by a processor array [64], and the paging characteristics of a virtual memory system for an object oriented personal computer [15]. In addition to measurements aimed at evaluating some aspect of system performance, the measurement of program performance has received considerable attention. The importance of measuring program performance was demonstrated in [108]. It is particularly important for programs written in very high level languages where there is no simple mapping between source code and machine operations so that performance is difficult to predict. This point is discussed and illustrated in detail in [46]. Our concern, however, will be aspects of system performance rather than program performance.

The focus of the remainder of this section is not on the applications of performance measurement but rather on the methods and tools that are used in performance measurement. The measurement of new systems often requires new tools and techniques as we will see. The topics we will cover are measurement instrumentation, workload characterization, and statistical aspects of performance measurement including design of experiments and analysis of results.

B. Instrumentation

We will review some of the principles of measurement instrumentation, present an early important example, and then several recent examples that illustrate trends and challenges. A thorough discussion of measurement instrumentation principles can be found in [57, chapter 2] and in [61, chapter 5].

The basic means of instrumenting a system for performance measurement purposes are hardware probes and software (or microcode) probes. Hardware probes are high-impedance electrical probes that are connected to the hardware device being measured. They can be used to sense the state of hardware components of the system, e.g., registers, memory locations, and data transfer paths. The term hardware monitor refers to a measurement device that uses hardware probes. A hardware monitor is typically external to the measured system and does not interfere with the measured system or alter its performance. The sensed signals can be combined in order to sense more complex states than those measured directly. The resulting signals together with the output of a real-time clock can be processed to detect events (state changes) of interest which can then be counted or recorded as a trace (time stamped sequence of events). In addition, times between events can be obtained by counting clock pulses between events. Hardware monitors are commonly implemented using both high-speed hardwired logic and slower speed stored program logic. A mini- or microcomputer may interface with the monitor to set up and control a measurement session and reduce, analyze, and display the collected data. Hardware monitors usually do not have access to software related information such as which process caused an event, although there are exceptions as discussed later in the examples. This is a disadvantage of hardware monitors along with their cost and often their lack of ease of use.

Software probes are instructions added to the measured system (i.e., to the operating system or to application programs) to gather performance data. They may gather data by reading memory locations or otherwise sensing status. A measurement device that uses software probes is called a software monitor. (Microcode probes may also be used.) Since the monitor's instructions run on the measured system and hence use system resources they alter, possibly significantly, the performance of the system. In some cases this

effect is straightforward to compensate for, e.g., by subtracting out the CPU utilization and other resource usage due to the monitor, but in other cases it may not be. Thus, software monitors produce performance estimates that may differ from the true performance of the system running without the monitor.

A software monitor can be either event driven or timer driven or both. In event driven monitoring the probes detect events, e.g., instruction executions, storage accesses, I/O interrupts, and then collect data. In timer driven monitoring data are collected (sampled) at specified time instants. This sampling is typically accomplished by generating interrupts based on a hardware clock or interval timer and then passing control to a data collection routine. Sampling typically requires less code and that code is executed less frequently than event driven monitoring. Hence, it interferes less with the measured system. However, sampling introduces additional errors in the performance estimates since status is only sampled periodically. These sampling errors can be decreased by increasing the sampling frequency, and hence the interference. Other errors can occur using sampling if care is not taken. For example, if certain system routines are not interruptable then their contribution to CPU utilization will not be measurable by sampling as described above. Hardware monitors need not produce true performance values either, e.g., due to the resolution of the real-time clock (see [61, chapter 5]). However, they are typically much more accurate than software monitors. It is therefore important that the accuracy of a software monitor be tested, perhaps by comparing its measurements to those of a hardware monitor. One such study of accuracy and methods for correcting the software measurements can be found in [19].

It is possible to combine the advantages of hardware monitors (speed and accuracy) with those of software monitors (flexibility and easy access to software related data) by judiciously combining hardware and software probes in a so-called hybrid monitor, examples of which will be given below. The software causes of hardware events can be readily measured with a hybrid monitor.

An early important example of measurement instrumentation was that done for the Multics system at the Massachusetts Institute of Technology [157]. Multics was an innovative multiprogrammed time sharing operating system that supported multiprocessing, demand paging, and sharing, among other features. Measurement instrumentation was integrated into the system at the early design phase and software probes were an integral part of the operating system. Measurement was directed towards a detailed understanding of operating system performance and was very successful in revealing unsuspected performance problems. The hardware (GE 645) on which Multics ran provided features that were exploited by the measurement facilities. These hardware features were a program readable clock and program loadable clock comparison register for generating timer interrupts, a memory cycle counter for each processor, and an externally drivable I/O channel via which a separate computer could externally monitor memory contents. The many software monitor facilities that were implemented are discussed in detail in [157].

Included were timer and counter facilities for selectable operating system modules and limited tracing facilities. The performance interference caused by these facilities was found to be acceptably small. A remote terminal emulator was implemented to simulate interactive users but due to physical limitations the number of simulated users was small. Therefore, an internal driver was also implemented to generate heavier loads. Real-time graphical displays of performance were generated using the separate computer that served as an external monitor.

We next briefly discuss recent examples of monitors that illustrate trends in this area. Each monitor is described in detail in the references that are given. DIAMOND [90] is a hybrid monitor developed by DEC for internal use. Hardware probes sense the program counter, the CPU mode, channel and I/O device activity, and a system assigned task id which is contained in a special register. A software probe senses the user's id which is also contained in a special purpose register. All sensed signals are buffered in a digital interface and then analyzed by a microcoded machine to obtain traces and histograms of various kinds. A separate minicomputer controls the measurement. Emphasis was placed on ease of use. There is a natural language interface with interactive dialogs for new users. The interface facilitates the set up of a measurement session, replication of experiments, maintenance of a measurement log, and report preparation.

XRAY [14] is a low overhead event and timer driven software monitor developed by TANDEM for networks of TANDEM/16 computer systems. It is integrated into the GUARDIAN network operating system. Networkwide measurements are controlled from a single node with data collected and analyzed locally at each node. The emphasis is on measuring hardware utilizations and access rates, both in total and the contributions by specified processes. Counters are employed that are incremented using microcoded instructions in order to keep the overhead low. The counters are periodically written to files. The primary use of the monitor is for bottleneck detection. A language is provided for the selection of hardware components and processes to be measured and this selection can be changed online while data are being collected. The language also facilitates browsing through the data and real-time displays are provided. There is no time synchronization between nodes so that typically no attempt is made to correlate data from different nodes.

A hybrid monitor was developed by Olivetti for its S6000, a single-bus architecture minicomputer, and similar machines [60]. Data are captured by hardware probing of the bus's address and data lines. Additional general hardware probes were provided as well as a clock pulse signal from the measured system. Low overhead software probes were inserted in the operating system. Event traces, event counts, and times between events were obtained from the measured signals using hardwired logic. However, this processing is controlled via the contents of registers that are loadable by the user via a controlling minicomputer. This separate computer both controls the measurements and analyzes the results.

The Erlangen General Purpose Array is a tightly coupled hierarchically organized multiprocessor being developed at the University of Erlangen-Nurnberg. It is an extensible array of elementary "pyramids," each pyramid consisting of a top control processor and four bottom working processors. The control processor is multiprogrammed and the working processors can execute in parallel on behalf of one program at a time. Both hardware and software monitors were implemented to study in detail the dynamic behavior of the parallelism achieved by the system as well as more traditional performance measures [64], [86]. The hardware monitor, Zahlmonitor III, records event traces as well as event counts and elapsed times. Software events can be measured by probing a register that contains system assigned process numbers, as well as by other hardware means. The trace for a single processor consists of a time ordered sequence of the pairs (process executing, execution time). The asynchronous traces from the different processors are merged by the hardware into a single well-ordered trace. (So far measurements have been reported for only a single pyramid.) Such detailed trace information has been used, for example, to compare different methods of process synchronization [64]. Traces of I/O activity are also obtained and can be related to the processor traces. In addition to the hardwired logic used to implement the above functions a minicomputer is used to control the measurements, analyze the traces, and provide graphical displays. A software monitor for tracing software events on each processor was also implemented and graphical methods were developed for dynamically displaying parallel activities.

A general trend is illustrated by these examples. In terms of applications the measurement of multiple processor systems, ranging from tightly coupled to geographically distributed systems, is of increasing interest. In order to understand the complex interactions that occur in such systems when they run parallel or distributed programs and the effect of these interactions on performance, special instrumentation will be required. Flexible and easy to use monitors, either hardware monitors that can access software related data, hybrid monitors, or low overhead software monitors, are fundamental tools that will aid in gaining this understanding. Hardware and hybrid monitors are being made flexible and easy to use by the use of a controlling computer that provides a user friendly interface including real-time graphics capabilities for displaying measurement results. A further discussion of using a separate computer for controlling distributed system experiments can be found in [63], which includes a description of a distributed system experimental testbed developed at Honeywell.

C. Workload Characterization

The performance of a system obviously depends heavily on the demand for hardware and (application and system) software resources of the workload being processed. Therefore, the quantitative characterization of the resource demands of workloads is an important part of computer performance evaluation studies. This is true for both measurement and modeling studies. Workload characterization provides a basis for constructing representative synthetic executable workloads to drive a system being measured or for obtaining representative parameter values for analytic or simulation performance models. A comprehensive discussion of workload characterization can be found in [61, chapter 2]. We will focus on methods used to characterize workloads for performance measurement studies. However, much of what we will say is also applicable to workload characterization for analytic or simulation models.

We can distinguish three types of workloads suitable for performance measurement studies, namely, live workloads, executable workloads consisting of portions of real workloads, and synthetic executable workloads. By live workloads we mean real workloads generated and executed in a live user environment. Live workloads are not suitable for controlled and reproducible measurement experiments and will not be considered here. The other two types of workloads are not executed in a live user environment. They are generated and submitted for execution using a program called a driver that simulates a live user environment. A driver that runs external to the system being measured and simulates interactive users is called a remote terminal emulator. Remote terminal emulators have been used for many years in performance measurement studies. A portion of a real interactive workload that is suitable for driving an interactive system using a remote terminal emulator can be obtained by tracing the sequences of think times and commands generated by each user logged on to a system as the system executes. However, traces can be expensive to obtain and store and are not flexible in terms of the workload characteristics they represent. Synthetic executable workloads have the advantage that they can be made parametric and hence flexible in representing workload characteristics. For example, parameters can control the amount of computation a program does and the number of files and records it reads or writes. They have the disadvantage of possible lack of realism, i.e., they may not adequately represent features of real workloads that can significantly affect system performance.

We next summarize the steps that comprise a common approach to characterizing an existing real workload. Examples of workload characterization studies in which several, if not all, of these steps are applied can be found in [1], [3], [18], [61, chapter 2], [75], [76], [130], [174], and [184]. If a system has a mixed workload, e.g., batch, interactive, and database, then this approach can be applied separately to each such distinct part of the workload. The five steps that comprise this approach are as follows.

1) Selection of the workload component to be characterized. For example, when characterizing a batch workload the component may be a job or a job step, when characterizing an interactive workload it may be a session, a sequence of commands or a single command, and when characterizing a database workload it may be a transaction.

2) Selection of the features (parameters) used to characterize a component. The features may be hardware resource demands [1], [3], e.g., processor instructions or time, memory space used, number of I/O's to various devices, or software resource demands [75], [76], e.g., number of calls to compilers, editors, file handlers. An advantage of using hardware resource features is that hardware resource demands directly impact system performance. An advantage of using software resource features is that the resulting characterization may be more system independent.

3) Workload measurement. The real workload is measured while executing to obtain the feature values for each measured workload component. Typically, data are obtained for a large number of components. For example, measurements collected over a period of a month or more yielded data on over 10 000 job steps in the studies reported on in [3], [174]. The result is a large collection of multivariate data.

4) Exploratory data analysis. In this step empirical distributions and sample moments of each of the features may be obtained. In order to obtain comparable ranges for feature values, features with highly skewed distributions may be transformed, e.g., by taking the log of the values. Components having feature values that are outliers may be deleted and different features may be scaled to lie in a common interval. The deletion of outliers requires great care since outliers may have very large resource demands and hence strongly influence system performance. Transformations and/or scaling are often applied to the data if the next step is performed.

5) Cluster analysis. The measured components (perhaps after transformation and/or scaling), or a random sample of the measured components, are partitioned into clusters such that components in the same cluster have similar feature values. The purpose is to treat all components in a cluster as being effectively identical so that a compact workload characterization can be obtained. For example, in studying workloads from over 100 systems Artis [3] found that in each case many thousands of job steps could be partitioned into 15–20 clusters based on eight hardware resource oriented features. Cluster analysis was originally developed in the context of biological taxonomy and has been applied in a wide variety of disciplines. A large number of clustering algorithms exist (e.g., [78], [143]). The algorithms most commonly applied to workload characterization are variants of the K-means (also called nearest centroid) algorithm. The basic algorithm and some of its variants are presented in [78, chapter 4]. The basic algorithm partitions the components into a specified number of clusters in order to locally minimize the partition error, defined to be the sum over all components of the Euclidean distance between a component and the centroid (center of mass) of the cluster to which it has been assigned. An initial partition is chosen and components are moved one at time between clusters in order to reduce the partition error until a local minimum is achieved. Criteria for choosing the number of clusters are presented in [78]. Variants applied to workload characterization can be found in [1], [3], [174]. Issues in applying cluster analysis to workload characterization are discussed in [2], [61, chapter 2].

It is possible to construct synthetic executable workloads based on the above type of workload characterization. The components of the synthetic workload can be parameterized and the parameter values chosen to match the feature values of a cluster, specified for example by the cluster's centroid. An interesting example of this is given in [3] where the clusters also provide a basis for workload forecasting. Reports on the construction and use of parametric workloads can also be found in [172], [184]. (Cluster analysis was not used in these studies and representative feature values were obtained by sampling.) Unfortunately, most papers on workload characterization using cluster analysis do not report on the actual construction and use of parametric workloads and it is not clear how widely this is done.

Most workload characterization studies have used hardware oriented features. In [75] and [76], software resource demands were used instead. The workload component was an interactive job (sequence of tasks) and seven software resource demands were used to characterize each component. After clustering was performed the sequence of software resources used by each job in a cluster was modeled by an absorbing Markov chain. The purpose was to obtain a more realistic workload model than one which assumes that successive resource demands are statistically independent. The data indicated that the Markov chain had to be either nonhomogeneous or higher than first order (i.e., the current resource demand depends on the past several resource demands) in order to provide a statistically adequate model. (Details of the statistical tests used are given in [76].)

The type of workload characterization we have described also provides a basis for determining representative parameter values for analytic and simulation performance models. For example, cluster analysis can be used to determine the job classes to be used in a product form queueing network model (see Section III) and to assign representative values to the mean service demands in the model. (Only the means of the service demands affect the performance of such models.) The number of jobs in each class in the model can be chosen to be proportional to the number of jobs in each cluster. If service demand distributions were needed, e.g., for nonproduct form models or simulation models, they could be obtained from the empirical distributions of the feature values within each cluster.

One of the main challenges in workload characterization is to develop synthetic executable workloads that yield approximately the same system performance as the real workloads they represent. Despite considerable activity in workload characterization there is little published evidence of success in this regard. An approach in which workload components are directly characterized by the system performance they yield rather then by their resource demands is described in [58], [61, chapter 2]. Although this approach may prove successful in meeting the above challenge it yields a highly system dependent workload characterization. Issues related to the adequacy of resource demand oriented workload characterizations are discussed in [59] where queueing network models are used to show that simple characterizations can yield the same model performance as more complex ones. Most workload characterization has involved batch and to a lesser extent interactive workloads. Therefore, a key area that needs to be addressed is characterization of database

workloads. Another challenge is to develop synthetic executable workloads to drive new systems when relevant real workloads are nonexistent. This is the case for multiprocessor systems that support parallel processing and for distributed systems. A facility to generate synthetic executable workloads for the Cm* multiprocessor system is described in [178]. A high-level language is provided for representing a synthetic parallel program as a type of data flow graph. The processing activities specified by the nodes of the graph are realized using a library of system specific routines. There is clearly a continuing need for synthetic workload generation in the performance evaluation of new systems.

D. Statistical Methods

It is important that sound experimental methods be employed in performance measurement studies. The purpose of a study should be clearly formulated, the measurement experiments should be carefully designed, and the resulting data should be carefully analyzed so that meaningful conclusions can be made. This is true whether measurement is done in a live user environment or in a controlled environment. While common sense can play an important role in this regard, so can statistical methods. Statistical methods have been discussed in some detail in performance evaluation books, e.g., [57, chapter 2], [110, chapter 5], and articles written for the performance evaluation community, e.g., [9], [166]. Application examples are discussed in these books and articles. We will first discuss the random nature of performance measurement data and will advocate that confidence intervals be obtained in order to account for this randomness when producing performance estimates. We will then discuss regression analysis and statistical design of experiments and representative applications of these methods. We will conclude with a discussion of why these two methods have rarely been used in performance measurement studies.

1) The Random Nature of Measurement Data: Random fluctuations are often present in performance measurement data. This is the case when synthetic executable workloads are at least in part probabilistically generated. For example, successive think times and successive command types may be probabilistically chosen when generating a synthetic interactive workload. Even without this obvious source of randomness, repetitions of a measurement session can yield nonidentical data due to factors that are uncontrollable or too difficult to control from session to session. Such data can also be considered to fluctuate randomly. This is the case when measurement is conducted in a live user environment due to the uncontrolled nature of the workload. Therefore, a measured data sequence, e.g., a sequence of measured response times, should be viewed as a random sequence. Any performance estimate produced from such a sequence, e.g., the sample average, should be viewed as a random variable. The same situation arises in discrete event simulation when a probabilistic model is simulated. Many methods have been developed for statistically analyzing simulation outputs, e.g., see Section IV-B of this paper and [117, chapter 6]. Typically, the methods are used to obtain confidence intervals in addition to point estimates. (The definition of a confidence interval is given in Section IV-B.) Confidence intervals should also be obtained when dealing with system measurements, particularly when synthetic probabilistic workloads are used. In practice they very rarely are.

An application to a performance measurement study of a broadly applicable method for obtaining confidence intervals that was originally developed for simulation output analysis can be found in [85]. The method was applied to estimating steady state characteristics of transaction response time sequences in a database system. Measurement was done in a controlled environment using synthetic workloads with probabilistically selected transaction types and transaction arrival times. Confidence intervals for the mean response time and for quantiles of the response time distribution were obtained at several transaction rates for two system variants and used to compare the two variants. The method used, called the spectral method (see Section IV-B), obtains a confidence interval for a steady state parameter from a single output sequence, i.e., repeated measurement sessions are not necessary. The method is broadly applicable since it makes only weak probabilistic assumptions about an output sequence. For example, it does not assume members of the sequence are independent or normally distributed. An alternative broadly applicable method of obtaining confidence intervals is independent replications which requires statistically independent and identical repetitions of a measurement session. While this is feasible when synthetic probabilistically generated workloads are used, it may not be possible in a live user environment.

2) Regression Analysis: Regression analysis can be used to approximate the functional dependence of one or more variables (called dependent variables) on another collection of variables (called independent variables). The approximate functional relationship can then be used to predict values of the dependent variables from values of the independent variables. Each dependent variable is expressed as a postulated function of the independent variables and a collection of parameters plus a random error term. While the form of the function is assumed known, the parameter values are not. Usually, a linear relationship is postulated (linear regression), i.e.,

$$y = a_0 + a_1 x_1 + \cdots + a_k x_k + \varepsilon \qquad (2.1)$$

where y is a dependent variable, x_j's are the independent variables, a_j's are the parameters, and ε is the random error. The parameter values are estimated from n observed values of all the variables, i.e., from $y_i, x_{1i}, \cdots, x_{ki}, i = 1, \cdots, n$, and an informal measure of goodness of fit is obtained. If the errors for different observations are assumed to be independent and normally distributed with zero mean and identical variances then confidence intervals for the parameters can be obtained and formal statistical tests of goodness of fit can be applied. Details and further discussion can be found in the concise presentations in [9], [110, chapter 5], and in standard texts on regression analysis, e.g., [50]. In an example due to Bard [6], which is discussed in [9], the CPU time consumed by an

operating system (the dependent variable) is linearly related to the number of calls to certain operating system services (the independent variables). The parameters have a physical interpretation, i.e., they are the CPU times per call for each of the services represented. These overhead parameters could not readily be measured but the number of operating system calls of each type and the total operating system CPU time could be measured. Estimates for the overheads were obtained using linear regression. A subsequent study [10] revealed inadequacies in this linear model which were corrected to some degree. This illustrates that the application of statistical methods may not be straightforward.

3) Design of Experiments: Statistical design of experiments is used to design experiments whose purpose is to estimate the effects of multiple controllable factors on measured responses. Separate sets of measurements are made with the factors set at different specified levels. A key aspect of the designs is that the factors are varied simultaneously rather than one at a time in order to facilitate estimating the effects of interactions between the factors. Typically, a linear model with additive random error is used to approximate the relationship between a measured response and the effects of the factors. For example, for a two-factor experiment where factor 1 has I levels and factor 2 has J levels, the linear model would be

$$y_{ij} = m + a_i + b_j + c_{ij} + \varepsilon_{ij} \qquad (2.2)$$

where m is the overall mean, and for factor 1 at level i and factor 2 at level j, y_{ij} is the measured response, a_i is the main effect of factor 1, b_j is the main effect of factor 2, c_{ij} is the interaction effect of factors 1 and 2, and ε_{ij} is the error term. The errors for measurements at different levels are assumed to be independent random variables with zero mean and identical but unknown variances. If measurements are obtained for all combinations of the factor levels the experiment is called a full factorial experiment. The measured responses at the different combinations of factor levels (including, if possible, replicated measurements at each combination) are used to estimate the overall mean and the main and interaction effects in the linear model. A technique called analysis of variance is used to determine the significance of the effects. If the errors are assumed to be normally distributed then formal statistical tests can be applied. If the number of factors and levels is so large that a full factorial experiment is too costly then a fractional factorial experiment can be conducted. In such an experiment measurements are obtained for only certain combinations of factor levels. Although all interaction effects cannot be estimated with fractional experiments, all main effects and some interactive effects can be. More detail on design of experiments can be found in [110, chapter 5], [166], [197, chapter 11], and in standard texts on design of experiments, e.g., [20], [43].

An often cited application of design of experiments to performance measurement studies can be found in [198], [199]. (The first paper reports on the application and conclusions while the second describes the statistical methods used.) The effects of four factors (e.g., paging algorithm, main memory size) on various measures of paging performance were estimated by varying each factor at three levels using a full factorial design resulting in 81 different combinations of factor levels. For one performance measure the conclusion was that three main effects and one interaction effect predominated. Bard and Schatzoff [9] discussed this example and showed that the same conclusions could have been obtained with a fractional factorial design using only 16 combinations instead of 81.

The above experiments were performed in a controlled environment. An application in a live environment due to Margolin *et al.* [131] is discussed in [9]. The purpose was to compare the effects on performance of two different free storage management algorithms. Measurements were taken on eight days in two consecutive weeks (Mondays–Thursdays only). Rather than run algorithm *A* the first week and algorithm *B* the second week the algorithms were assigned to days so that each algorithm was run twice each week and once on each of the corresponding days of the weeks. The purpose was to eliminate as much as possible the otherwise uncontrollable effects of day of the week and week-to-week workload variations. Clearly, this is good common sense and formal methods are not necessary to arrive at this design. Bard and Schatzoff [9] give a formal description of the design as well as the analysis of variance results. It turned out that the effects of day and week were so small and of algorithm so large that the careful design was not required. However, in other cases it might be.

An interesting application of design of experiments to simulation model validation is given in [167]. Identical multi-factor experiments were carried out for performance measurements of a system and for a trace driven simulation model of the system. The criterion for model validity was that the same significant effects be identified from both experiments.

4) Conclusion: The application of regression analysis and statistical design of experiments to performance measurement studies has been rare. This was noted by Grenander and Tsao [74], who tried to motivate their increased use, and it remains true today. While their lack of use may be due to lack of familiarity with these methods by performance analysts, it is also true that these methods are not straightforward to apply in performance measurement studies. This is partly because they are based on assumptions about the data, e.g., independent errors with common means and variances, that may be far from true for performance data. Also, there is typically a large number of variables that can affect performance and their effect may be more complex than can be explained by standard statistical models. Published work on the application of regression analysis and statistical design of experiments in performance measurement studies indicates that successful application of the methods requires the involvement of both experienced applied statisticians and experienced computer performance analysts. It is rare that both skills reside in one person. Nonetheless, by carefully applying these methods more meaningful conclusions can be drawn from performance measurement studies than would otherwise be possible. Therefore, we recommend their increased use in such studies.

III. ANALYTIC PERFORMANCE MODELING

Computer systems can generally be characterized as consisting of a set of both hardware and software resources and a set of tasks, or jobs, competing for and accessing those resources. Examples of hardware resources include main memory and devices such as CPU's, channels, disks, tape drives, control units, and terminals. An example of a software resource is a lock for a database item. Because there are multiple jobs competing for a limited number of resources, queues for the resources are inevitable and with these queues come delays.

It is therefore natural to represent, or model, the system by a network of interconnected queues. The purpose of the model is to predict the performance of the system by estimating characteristics of the resource utilizations, the queue lengths and the queueing delays. Analytic performance models are queueing network models for which these characteristics may be found mathematically (or analytically). Therefore, research in performance modeling methodology has essentially been research in queueing theory. Key advances in computer performance modeling have also been seen as fundamental breakthroughs in queueing theory. Queueing theory has attained new relevance because of the computer performance modeling application. Furthermore, to a great extent, the direction of queueing theory has been influenced and driven by this application.

Queues are also inevitable in communications systems and a closely related topic is performance evaluation of communications systems. Indeed, the telephone system provided motivation for the earliest work on queueing theory [54]. Communications systems consist of messages accessing hardware resources such as switches, channels, buffers, and computers. Software resources in a communications system result from the system's communications protocols. Such a software resource might be a message passing token in a ring network or a limit on the number of messages on a route imposed by a window flow control scheme. The distinction between computer and communications systems is diminishing. However, the focus of this paper is on computer systems. Analytic models have also had substantial impact in performance evaluation of communications systems (e.g., [106], [107], [170]).

In this section we will give an overview of the role of analytic modeling in computer performance evaluation and highlight the major methodological advances that have taken place over the last decade. These advances are threefold.

1) Identification of a broad class of models, called product form queueing networks, having a mathematically tractable solution.

2) Development of computationally efficient and numerically stable algorithms for product form queueing networks.

3) Development of accurate and computationally efficient algorithms to approximate the solution of large product form queueing networks and queueing networks that do not fall into the product form class.

We will close the section by indicating what we believe are the key challenges which performance modeling and queueing theory must meet in order to maintain relevance in computer science throughout the next decade.

A. *The Role of Analytic Models*

Analytic performance modeling has become widely accepted as being a cost effective evaluation technique for estimating the performance of computer systems. Analytic models are cost effective because they are based on efficient solutions to mathematical equations. However, in order for these equations to have a tractable solution, certain simplifying assumptions must be made regarding the structure and behavior of the queueing network model. As a result, analytic models cannot capture all of the detail that can be built into simulation models. Nevertheless, for many types of systems the key resources and workload requirements can be analytically modeled with sufficient realism to provide insight into the bottlenecks and key parameters affecting system performance. It is generally thought that carefully constructed analytic models can provide estimates of average job throughputs and device utilizations to within 10 percent accuracy and estimates of average response time to within 30 percent accuracy [127, p. 14]. We cite three areas where this level of accuracy is usually considered sufficent and where analytic models have had substantial impact, namely capacity planning, I/O subsystem performance evaluation, and as a preliminary design aid in development of new systems.

1) Capacity Planning: Analytic models play a key role in capacity planning. Capacity planning is the process of determining future computing system hardware needs based on projections of the growth in the workload and hence in the demand for processing power, memory space, and I/O activity. Capacity planning generally consists of three steps.

1) Measurement and data reduction of the current system.

2) Construction and validation of a queueing model of the current system.

3) Extending the model to incorporate new devices and running the model against projected future workloads.

The system is parameterized by key factors such as the speeds and numbers of the CPU's, disks, and channels and the size of main memory (which affects paging rates). The rate of transactions arriving to the system (or the number of users and the users' think times) and the transaction workload requirements are also parameters of the model. The key parameters are varied until a configuration meeting both the cost and performance objectives of the organization is determined. Because the queueing models can be solved efficiently, a large number of model runs can be made allowing a thorough search of the parameter space. Due to the uncertainties in future workloads, the accuracy of the queueing model is more than sufficient for this purpose.

There are a number of commercial capacity planning packages currently available including BEST/1 (from BGS Systems) for IBM MVS systems [29] and the VM Performance Planning Facility (from IBM) for IBM VM systems (based on a model described in [7]). In addition to a queueing component, these packages both contain interfaces to measurement facilities and data reduction capabilities.

2) I/O Subsystem Modeling: Because of the vast difference between I/O access times and main memory access times, I/O subsystem performance has become a dominant factor affecting overall system performance. This is expected to continue in the future as processors and main memories become faster whereas access times for mechanically activated disks are not expected to decline much further. Memory hierarchies have been constructed to mask this speed difference and I/O subsystems have been constructed to get the best possible performance out of the memory hierarchy.

Analytic models are widely used to predict the performance of I/O subsystems. They have been successfully used to analyze the performance of proposed changes in I/O subsystem architecture. Examples include modeling buffered, or cached, disk units and dynamic path selection both of which attempt to reduce I/O service times. Buffered disks attempt to reduce the probability of a seek while dynamic path selection tries to reduce the probability of the additional rotation that occurs because the transfer path is busy when a disk attempts to reconnect to a channel for data transfer [21], [23]. More detailed discussions of I/O subsystem models, with additional references, may be found in [117], [127].

3) Preliminary Design Aid: Analytic models have been successfully applied to study the performance of proposed future computer architectures or systems. An analytic model can provide insight into the key factors affecting performance of a proposed system, and determine the sensitivity of performance to parameter changes. Such a model can provide guidance into the overall design of the system and also be useful in the development of more detailed simulation models as the design matures. For example, the analytic model could determine where effort should placed in building the simulation model; if performance is not a problem in some subsystem, then that subsystem need not be modeled in great detail. The analytic model could also be used to limit the range of parameters to be used in the more expensive runs of the simulation model.

An example of such a study can be found in [73]. This model studies the overall design considerations and technology tradeoffs for the memory interconnection structure of several hypothetical future multiprocessor systems. One of the systems consists of a few high performance processors, each with its own local memory. There is also a large semiconductor memory that is shared by all processors. Upon a page fault to the local memory, a page must be transferred from the shared memory. Contention occurs for both the modules of the shared memory and for transfer buses between the shared and local memories. The system is parameterized by the numbers of processors, memory modules, and buses, the memory access and bus transfer times, and the page fault rate. The purpose of the model is to determine the bus bandwidth required to support the processors at a reasonable performance level.

B. *Product Form Queueing Networks*

Queueing theory has a long history beginning with the work of Erlang [54]. It is not our intention to give a history of queueing theory, but rather to highlight recent methodological advances that have had a significant impact on computer performance evaluation. We start with a simple example.

Fig. 1 represents a simple model of a computer system, called a central server model with terminals. There is a fixed number N of users, each with his own terminal, submitting transactions to the system. Each user is represented by a job in the network. When a transaction is submitted it goes through a number of CPU–I/O cycles; it executes on the CPU, performs I/O on one of the I/O devices, and returns to the CPU, repeating this process until the transaction is completed. Between transactions the user is in the think state. Let the node in Fig. 1 representing the terminals be service center 1, the CPU be service center 2, and the I/O devices be service centers $3, \cdots, M$. In order to completely define the model, the following must be specified.

1) The queueing disciplines at each of the centers.
2) The service requirements of jobs at the centers.
3) The routing of jobs between centers.

When the above are appropriately defined, the evolution of the system can frequently be modeled by a continuous time Markov chain. For example, suppose that the service disciplines at the devices are all first come first served (FCFS), that the think times and the service times at each device are independent random variables with a common exponential distribution, and that when a job leaves center i, it proceeds to center j with probability p_{ij}. Let $Q_i(t)$ denote the queue length at center i at time t. Then $Q = \{Q(t) = (Q_1(t), \cdots, Q_M(t)), t \geq 0\}$ forms a continuous time Markov chain. Let $n = (n_1, \cdots, n_M)$ and define $p(n, t) = \text{Prob} \{Q(t) = n\}$.

Finding $p(n, t)$ requires solving a system of linear differential equations with constant coefficients. However, the limiting, or stationary, distribution $p(n) = \lim_{t \to \infty} p(n, t)$ can be found by solving a system of linear equations, called the global balance equations, which, for each state, equates the rate of flow into the state to the rate of flow out of the state. In this application, we are usually interested in the stationary distribution not only for reasons of mathematical convenience but also because a time average converges to its stationary value. There is one linear equation for each state of the system. In the above example there are

$$\binom{N + M - 1}{M - 1} \tag{3.1}$$

equations since that is the size of the set $\{n : n_1 + \cdots + n_M = N\}$. Thus, the number of states becomes unmanageably large as N and M increase.

For a restricted class of networks called product form networks, including the above example, the solution to the global balance equations can be shown to be a product of terms where the form of each term is explicitly given. More specifically,

$$p(n) = (1/G(N)) \prod_{i=1}^{M} p_i(n_i) \tag{3.2}$$

where $G(N)$ is a normalization constant chosen to make the probabilities sum to one. Performance measures such as the

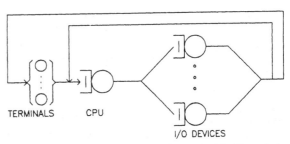

Fig. 1. Queueing diagram of the central server model with terminals.

mean response time, mean queue lengths, and device utilizations can be computed once $G(N)$ is known. The importance of the product form solution is not only that it gives the form of the stationary distribution, but also that efficient algorithms exist to compute $G(N)$ and the relevant performance metrics (in order $M(N + 1)$ operations). The existence of computationally efficient algorithms for a broad class of models makes analytic queueing models an attractive tool for applied performance modeling studies of computer systems.

Jackson [97] was the first to show a product form solution in a general network of queues. He was motivated by job-shop, or manufacturing, applications. Jackson considered an open network, meaning a network in which jobs arrive from an external source, pass through some sequence of service centers, and eventually depart from the system. The class of Jackson networks allows only a single type, or chain, of jobs with a Markovian arrival process dependent on the total population of the network. Service disciplines are FCFS, service demands are exponential with queue length dependent service rates, and routing is Markovian. The routing probabilities appear in the solution only through terms relating the relative number of visits jobs make to the centers, called visit ratios. Gordon and Newell [72] extended Jackson's results to cover closed networks; networks such as the central server model with terminals in which there are neither external arrivals nor departures but rather a fixed number jobs circulating indefinitely.

1) The Convolution Algorithm and BCMP Networks: Buzen [27], [28] was the first to develop a computationally efficient algorithm, the convolution algorithm, for Gordon and Newell's class of closed networks. Let $G_j(n)$ denote the normalization constant for a network with n jobs and centers $1, \cdots, j$. In this notation $G(N) = G_M(N)$. Buzen's algorithm computes $G(N)$ by convolving arrays according to the recursion

$$G_j(n) = \sum_{i=0}^{n} G_{j-1}(i) X_j(n - i) \tag{3.3}$$

where $X_j(i)$ is defined in terms of the relative visit ratio and the service rates of center j and $G_1(i) = X_1(i)$.

Baskett, Chandy, Muntz, and Palacios-Gomez [11] greatly extended the class of product form networks. Their generalization allowed for the following.

1) Multiple types, or chains, of jobs. Jobs in different chains can have different routing probabilities and different service demand distributions (at non-FCFS service centers).

2) Mixed networks, meaning networks with both open and closed chains.

3) New service disciplines including infinite servers (IS), processor sharing (PS, a limiting case of round robin as the quantum size goes to zero), last come first served preemptive resume (LCFSPR, of little importance in practice), in addition to FCFS.

4) General service demand distributions at IS, PS, and LCFSPR service centers.

The service demand distribution at any FCFS center must be exponential and all jobs receiving service at that center must have the same mean service demand regardless of type. These networks have come to be called BCMP networks.

For a network consisting of only closed chains, the product form is as follows. Define n_{ji} to be the number of chain j jobs at center i, $n_i = (n_{1i}, \cdots, n_{Mi})$, $|n_i| = n_{1i} + n_{2i} + \cdots + n_{Mi}$ and let ρ_{ji} be the relative visit ratio of chain j jobs to center i times the mean service demand of chain j jobs at center i. Let $\mu_i(n)$ be the service rate at center i when there are n jobs at center i and let $A_i(n) = \mu_i(1) \mu_i(2) \cdots \mu_i(n)$. The stationary distribution is given by

$$p(n_1, \cdots, n_M) = (1/G(N)) \prod_{i=1}^{M} p_i(n_i) \qquad (3.4)$$

where

$$p_i(n_i) = A_i(|n_i|) |n_i|! \prod_{j=1}^{K} (\rho_{ji}^{n_{ji}}/n_{ji}!) \qquad (3.5)$$

where M is the number of sevice centers and K is the number of closed chains. In the above, only those states for which $n_{j1} + \cdots + n_{jM} = N_j$ for each chain j have nonzero probability where $N = (N_1, \cdots, N_K)$, and N_j is the population of closed chain j.

Kelly [102] has a somewhat different, but in many ways equivalent, formulation of queueing networks yielding product form. The BCMP formulation has become the most widely used in practice. Although the class of product form networks has been somewhat extended beyond the BCMP networks, e.g., certain types of state dependent routing in [196], these extensions have not been found to be particularly useful in applications. It is now generally thought that the class of product form networks will not be significantly extended beyond the BCMP networks.

Reiser and Kobayashi [154] developed a generalization of the convolution algorithm for BCMP networks. The computational complexity of this and other algorithms depends essentially on the number of service centers, the number of closed chains, and the populations of the closed chains. This assumes that the extent of any population dependent arrival rates for open chains is limited [117], [160]. For closed networks with queue length independent service rates the convolution algorithm requires on the order of

$$MK \prod_{k=1}^{K} (1 + N_k) \qquad (3.6)$$

operations to compute $G(N)$. This is again a considerable savings compared to the computational cost of solving the set of linear balance equations of the underlying continuous time Markov chain; there would be at least

$$\prod_{k=1}^{K} \binom{N_k + M - 1}{M - 1} \qquad (3.7)$$

equations.

2) *The Mean Value Analysis Algorithm:* Reiser and Lavenberg [155] developed a new algorithm, the Mean Value Analysis (MVA) algorithm, for product form networks. This algorithm computes mean performance measures such as utilizations, throughputs, mean queue lengths, and mean response times directly without explicit computation of the normalization constant $G(N)$. The algorithm was first developed for closed networks with fixed rate and queue length dependent rate servers only, but has been extended to cover a broader range of product form networks including state dependent routing and more general forms of state dependent service rates [153], [160]. For networks with either IS or fixed rate service centers, MVA has an intuitively appealing justification, making it easier to teach than the convolution algorithm. MVA also provides a basis for approximations for either large product form networks or nonproduct form networks. It is also easier to program than the convolution algorithm and it avoids certain numerical instabilities present in the convolution algorithm. MVA is based on two simple principles.

1) Little's formula $L = \lambda W$ which is a generally applicable theorem relating the mean queue length L to the throughput λ and the mean waiting time W.

2) The "Arrival Theorem" [120], [175] which states that in a stationary product form network, the state distribution that a job sees upon arrival to a service center is equal to the stationary distribution of the network with that job removed.

In this paper we will describe MVA for a closed product form network with either IS or fixed rate service centers. The key equation of the MVA algorithm relates, according to the Arrival Theorem, the mean response time of a job at a service center to the mean queue length of a network with one job removed. For a network with fixed rate service centers define μ_i to be the rate at service center i, S_{ji} to be the mean service demand of chain j jobs at center i, y_{ji} be the relative visit ratio of chain j jobs at center i, and let $R_{ji}(n)$, $L_{ji}(n)$, and $\Lambda_{ji}(n)$ be the mean response time, mean queue length, and throughput, respectively, of chain j jobs at center i in a network having $n = (n_1, \cdots, n_K)$ jobs. For fixed rate service centers, the key MVA equation is

$$R_{ji}(n) = (S_{ji}/\mu_i)(1 + \sum_{k=1}^{K} L_{ki}(n - e_j)) \qquad (3.8)$$

where e_j is a vector of zeros except for a one in position j. By the Arrival Theorem, $L_{ki}(n - e_j)$ is the mean chain k queue length when a chain j job in a network with population n arrives at center i. For FCFS service centers (3.8) says that a job's response time consists of waiting for those jobs in front of it on arrival plus its own service time. For IS service centers

$$R_{ji}(n) = S_{ji}/\mu_i . \qquad (3.9)$$

An application of Little's formula to the mean cycle time (time between arrivals of the same job) of center i yields

$$\Lambda_{ji}(\boldsymbol{n}) = \frac{n_j}{\displaystyle\sum_{m=1}^{M} (y_{jm}/y_{ji})R_{jm}(\boldsymbol{n})} \tag{3.10}$$

and an application of Little's formula to the mean queue length at center i yields

$$L_{ji}(\boldsymbol{n}) = \Lambda_{ji}(\boldsymbol{n})R_{ji}(\boldsymbol{n}). \tag{3.11}$$

Equations (3.8)–(3.11) define a recursion allowing one to proceed from populations $\boldsymbol{n} - \boldsymbol{e}_j$ for $j = 1, \cdots, K$ to population $\boldsymbol{n}$.

For the above networks, the computational complexity for MVA is comparable to that of convolution for both single and multiple chain networks. For these networks MVA requires on the order of $MN_1N_2\cdots N_K$ storage locations as opposed to $2N_1N_2\cdots N_K$ storage locations for the convolution algorithm. For networks with queue length dependent rate service centers, the computational and storage requirements of both algorithms are greater than those listed above; see [117], [160], [204] for more complete discussions of the computational complexity of these two major algorithms for product form networks. Lavenberg [117], Sauer [160], Reiser [153], and Chandy and Sauer [39] describe several other algorithms for solving product form networks.

C. Algorithms for Large Product Form Networks

The computational complexity given in (3.6) and the storage requirements for solving product form networks become prohibitive for multiple chain networks having a large number of closed chains or a few closed chains with large populations. Such networks are becoming increasingly important with the advent of distributed processing. For example, Goldberg et al. [70] consider a model of the LOCUS local area distributed operating system. Their model contains sites connected by a communications network. Each site is essentially a central server model with terminals and the users logged on at each site are modeled by a separate closed chain. In today's environment there could easily be 50 sites with, say, 5 users per site. The operations count to exactly solve such a product form network would be larger than 6^{50}. A number of algorithms has been developed to solve, either exactly or approximately, networks of this size.

1) The Tree Convolution Algorithm: Lam and Lien [113] developed the Tree Convolution algorithm to exactly solve networks in which each chain visits only a few centers (sparseness) that are clustered in certain parts of the network (locality). Such networks are common in models of communications systems. Because of the sparseness and locality properties, many states have probability zero. The Tree Convolution algorithm tries to avoid summing over states with probability zero. The algorithm builds trees of centers representing the order in which subnetworks are convolved together. The trees are carefully chosen in an attempt to minimize a cost function capturing space–time complexity. Spectacular savings can occur. Lam and Lien considered a model of window flow control in a communications system. The model had 64 channels (service centers), 32 virtual

routes (chains), and a widow size of 3 for each route ($N_k = 3$). They report a decrease from 10^{22} operations for both Convolution and MVA to 10^6 operations for the Tree Convolution algorithm. Similar savings in storage were obtained. A tree version of MVA has also been developed [200].

2) Bounds for Product Form Networks: A number of algorithms that produce upper and lower bounds on the performance measures in product form networks has been developed. The bounds are produced with much less computational effort than would be required to solve the model exactly. A discussion of simple bounds for queueing networks may be found in [127]. We next discuss two recently developed methods that allow a tradeoff between the computational effort and the tightness of the bounds. The limiting case (in a sense to be made precise below) of both of these methods yields an exact solution.

The first method, based on a multiple integral representation and asymptotic expansion of $G(N)$, has been developed by McKenna et al. [137], McKenna and Mitra [135], Ramakrishnan and Mitra [150], and McKenna and Mitra [136]. Currently, the method applies to mixed networks with at least one IS center visited by each closed chain, single-server fixed rate service centers, and an assumption of "normal usage" which states roughly that the utilizations are not too close to one. The requirement for an IS center will frequently be met in practice since a set of users at terminals is modeled by an IS center.

The integral representation of $G(N)$ comes about by using the integral representation for the factorial terms in (3.5)

$$n! = \int_0^\infty e^{-x}x^n dx, \tag{3.12}$$

and by applying the multinomial theorem to simplify terms in the sum over all possible states. The multiple integral is then expressed in terms of a "large parameter" N, i.e., $G(N) = I(N)$. It is suggested to choose N to be the maximum over i and j of the ratio of the sum over k of the ρ_{jk}'s for IS centers visited by chain j to ρ_{ji} for non-IS centers visited by chain j. An asymptotic expansion for $I(N)$ is developed

$$I(N) \sim \sum_{n=1}^{\infty} A_n/N^n. \tag{3.13}$$

The coefficients A_n turn out to be related to the normalization constants of certain product form networks, called pseudonetworks, with small populations. $I(N)$ is estimated by taking the first m terms in (3.13). Bounds on the difference between $I(N)$ and its m term estimate are also obtained. These bounds become tighter as m increases and converge to the exact result as $m \to \infty$.

Ramakrishnan and Mitra [150] report that, in practice, usually less than four terms are required in the expansion to obtain satisfactory results. They report solving some very large networks, including a one-term expansion of a network with 23 service centers, 17 chains, and 1000 jobs in each chain. Different expansions are required for "heavy usage"; these have been worked out completely for some particular networks [137] and are anticipated for general networks.

The second bounding technique is the Performance Bound Hierarchy (PBH) developed in [51], [52]. We first consider a network with a single chain and single server fixed rated centers. The level i bounds are produced by obtaining optimistic and pessimistic bounds on the performance measures of a network with $N - i$ jobs, and then applying the MVA equations (or a slight modification of them for the optimistic bounds) until population N is reached. The initial bounds at population $N - i$ are trivially obtained from simple asymptotic bounds (e.g., [127]). Letting $\lambda_{\text{opt}}^i(N)$ and $\lambda_{\text{pess}}^i(N)$ denote the optimistic and pessimistic level i bounds on the throughput at some center in a network with population N, then the PBH produces a nested hierarchy of bounds in the sense that

$$\lambda_{\text{pess}}^{i-1}(N) \le \lambda_{\text{pess}}^i(N) \le \lambda(N) \le \lambda_{\text{opt}}^i(N) \le \lambda_{\text{opt}}^{i-1}(N) \qquad (3.14)$$

where $\lambda(N)$ is the exact throughput. Nested bounds for mean queue lengths and mean response times are also obtained. The level N bounds correspond to exact application of MVA. For single-chain networks, the bounds are of theoretical interest only since it is not very costly to solve such networks exactly.

The methodology has been extended to multiple chain networks in [51], although the procedure is significantly more complicated. A nested hierarchy of bounds is also obtained in this case. The computational complexity to obtain the level i bounds is order

$$MK\binom{K + i}{i}. \qquad (3.15)$$

Algorithms, called looping algorithms, to improve the initial bounds are also described; it was found empirically that the level i looping bounds are usually about as tight as the ordinary level $i + 2$ bounds.

In practice, the bounds produced by both methods tend to loosen as congestion in the network increases. A limited comparison between the PBH bounds and the integral representation bounds showed that, for comparable computational effort, neither method dominated the other [51].

3) Approximation Algorithms for Large Product Form Networks: Approximation methods provide a still cheaper alternative to solving product form networks consisting of single-server fixed rate and IS centers. The decreased cost is offset by the fact that bounds on the errors introduced by the approximate solution method are usually not available. The analyst must rely on experience gained in validation studies to judge whether or not the approximation method is reliable. For a given network, it is impossible to judge the quality of the approximation other than to compare it to a result obtained by a more costly method (exact solution, bounding technique, or simulation).

There have been a number of methods suggested for approximately solving large product form networks. These methods typically rely on MVA for motivation. In a multi-chain product form network the key MVA equation for single-server fixed rate centers given in (3.8) implies a recursion over all possible populations n for which $0 \le n \le N$. The approximate MVA methods eliminate the need for this recur-

sion by estimating $L_{ki}(n - e_j)$. Bard [8] and Schweitzer [171] proposed estimating

$$L_{ki}(n - e_j) = \begin{cases} L_{ki}(n) & k \ne j \\ L_{ji}(n)(n_{ji} - 1)/n_{ji} & k = j. \end{cases} \qquad (3.16)$$

The MVA equations can then be reduced to a set of K nonlinear equations which are typically solved by successive substitution [117]. Existence of a physically meaningful solution has been shown in [48] but uniqueness and convergence have not been shown except for the case of single-chain networks [51]. The algorithm has been shown empirically to be fairly accurate for most networks (errors greater than 20 percent are rare) and is known to yield exact results in the limit as the chain populations increase to infinity.

Chandy and Neuse [37] describe the Linearizer approximation algorithm which is designed to improve the accuracy of the Bard–Schweitzer algorithm for smaller populations. Linearizer is basically an iterative technique to improve estimates of $F_{jki}(n)$ where

$$F_{jki}(n) = \begin{cases} (L_{ki}(n - e_j)/n_{ki}) - (L_{ki}(n)/n_{ki}) & k \ne j \\ (L_{ji}(n - e_j)/(n_{ji} - 1)) - (L_{ji}(n)/n_{ji}) & k = j. \end{cases}$$
$$(3.17)$$

and the Bard–Schweitzer algorithm assumes $F_{jki}(n) = 0$. The iteration begins by applying Bard–Schweitzer at populations N and $(N - e_k)$ for all k. At each iteration, values of $F_{jki}(N)$ obtained from the previous iteration are used to calculate new estimates of $F_{jki}(N)$. Neither existence, uniqueness, nor convergence has been shown, although this has not been a problem in practice and the method provides quite accurate results for most models (errors greater than 2 percent are extremely rare).

Another approach to dealing with large closed chain populations is to replace a closed chain by an open chain with an appropriately chosen arrival rate. In a closed product form network with an IS center having mean service times S_k, Lavenberg [116] has shown that as the populations N_k increase in such a way that N_k/S_k converges to a constant λ_k, then the stationary distribution converges to that of a network having open chains with Poisson arrival rates λ_k. He also gives adjustments to compensate for the finite populations N_k. In related work, Zahorjan [205] showed that replacing a closed chain by an open chain (in certain classes of single-chain product form networks) with the same throughput yields pessimistic results in the sense that mean response times are larger in the open chain representation and can, in fact, be substantially larger.

The model of LOCUS described earlier has been solved approximately by a method described in [48]. The method as applied to the LOCUS model assumes that most of the work done by a job is processed at its local site and only occasionally does a job visit a foreign site. The method loops through the sites representing the effect of foreign jobs at a local site by an open chain and representing the processing at foreign sites by an IS delay. This method was somewhat less accurate, but significantly faster than Linearizer on large LOCUS models.

D. Nonproduct Form Networks

Although the class of product form networks has proven quite useful, there are many important features which, when incorporated into a model, lead to queueing networks violating the product form assumptions. Such features include priority scheduling disciplines, general service time distributions at queues with FCFS disciplines, and certain blocking phenomena. In models of computer systems, the blocking frequently arises because a job requires more than one resource before it can be processed. Examples include the following.

1) Holding a channel and a disk drive before data transfer can occur.

2) Obtaining a memory partition before job processing can occur.

3) Obtaining a database lock before the data item can be read from disk.

Increasing model realism often leads to models without product form. There are three ways to solve such networks: exactly, approximately, or by simulation. Unless the model has very special structure, the computational cost of exact solution techniques quickly gets out of hand due to the explosion in the size of the state space. However, in general, such structure is hard to find and exact solution is, for all practical purposes, impossible. The main focus of this section is on approximation methods; simulation will be discussed in Section IV. However, before discussing approximations, we will describe several general classes of nonproduct form models for which special structures do exist along with relatively efficient computational algorithms.

1) Models Having a Matrix Geometric Solution: Neuts [145] has studied a general class of Markovian models, arising frequently in applications, for which computationally efficient algorithms can be constructed. Neuts calls this class "Models of the GI/M/1 Type" since they are a two-dimensional generalization of the GI/M/1 queue. The form of the solution to this class is called the "Matrix Geometric Solution." We discuss the solution for discrete time Markov chains; an analogous treatment for continuous time Markov chains is also given in [145]. The state space consists of the set of two-dimensional pairs (i, j) where $i \geq 0$ and $1 \leq j \leq B$ for some finite constant B. Transitions can occur from state (i, j) to states (i', j') where $0 \leq i' \leq i + 1$. Although a somewhat more general structure can be accommodated, the basic structure of the transition matrix of the Markov chain is

$$P = \begin{bmatrix} B_0 & A_0 & 0 & 0 & 0 & \cdots \\ B_1 & A_1 & A_0 & 0 & 0 & \cdots \\ B_2 & A_2 & A_1 & A_0 & 0 & \cdots \\ \cdot & \cdot & \cdot & \cdot & \cdot & \cdots \end{bmatrix} \qquad (3.18)$$

where A_k and B_k are square B-by-B matrices. Letting x_k be the stationary distribution of the kth block, i.e., states of the form $\{(k, j), 1 \leq j \leq B\}$, then, assuming irreducibility and a stability condition,

$$x_k = x_0 R^k \qquad (3.19)$$

where R is the minimal nonnegative solution to the nonlinear matrix equation

$$R = \sum_{k=0}^{\infty} R^k A_k \qquad (3.20)$$

and x_0 is a left eigenvector (corresponding to the eigenvalue one) of the matrix

$$B[R] = \sum_{k=0}^{\infty} R^k B_k, \qquad (3.21)$$

i.e., $x_0 = x_0 B[R]$ with $x_0(I - R)^{-1}e = 1$ where e is a vector of ones. Recursive algorithms to compute R exist and are particularly simple for quasi-birth and death processes in which transitions can only occur from (i, j) to (i', j') for $i' = i - 1, i, i + 1$. In general, the algorithms should be computationally efficient provided B is not too large, $A_k = 0$ for large values of k, or the spectral radius of R is not too close to one.

A computer performance evaluation example is given by Latouche [115] who considers a system consisting of C CPU's and J I/O devices. There is a single queue for the CPU's and another queue for the I/O devices. There is a total of M memory partitions and arriving jobs can only enter the system if a partition is free, otherwise it queues for the next available partition. This is an example of simultaneous resource possession since jobs must simultaneously own both a memory partition and a device before receiving service. Nelson and Iyer [144] applied the Matrix Geometric approach to study performance tradeoffs in a model of a replicated database. A variety of other applications can be found in [145].

2) Matrix Methods for Nearly Decomposable Models: A number of matrix iterative methods, called aggregation/disaggregation methods, which converge to the exact solution of nearly decomposable Markovian models has been recently studied by Cao and Stewart [32]. A Markovian model is termed nearly completely decomposable if the state space can be partitioned in such a way that the transition matrix P can be written as

$$P = \begin{bmatrix} P_{11} & P_{12} & P_{13} & \cdots \\ P_{21} & P_{22} & P_{32} & \cdots \\ P_{31} & P_{32} & P_{33} & \cdots \\ \cdot & \cdot & \cdot & \cdots \end{bmatrix} \qquad (3.22)$$

where the off diagonal block matrices P_{ij} for $i \neq j$ are nearly zero. Thus, transitions are most likely to occur within blocks and transitions between blocks are infrequent. Models of this type arise frequently in applications as will be discussed in the section on approximations. In aggregation/disaggregation methods, the states within a block are lumped together to form a single aggregate state. These methods then compute the stationary probabilities of the aggregate states and the conditional state probabilities given the aggregate state. These quantities are computed exactly in the limit as the number of iterations tends to infinity. Cao and Stewart [32] showed that a number of previously described such procedures can be placed in the same framework of being related to block matrix iterative methods. They also established convergence criteria and determined the convergence rates of the methods. At each step of the iteration, a set of linear equations must be solved for each of the aggregate states of the model. In addition, a set of equations describing the rate of flow between aggregate states must be solved. The methods avoid working directly with the original transition matrix P and their efficiency is thus related to the number of aggregate states and the number of states in each of the aggregate states. These methods appear promising for moderate sized problems, but we know of no reports in the literature in which these methods have been used to solve the kind of very large scale models that arise in performance modeling applications.

3) Approximation Methods: We will not give a comprehensive survey of approximation methods, but rather describe the general approaches that are used and comment on the validation of approximations. Surveys of approximation techniques along with more detailed descriptions can be found in [38], [48], [117], [162]. In addition, Lazowska *et al.* [127] describe a number of approximation techniques for modeling specific subsystems.

For product form networks, both exact solution techniques and bounding techniques have been developed as discussed earlier. Due to both the complexity and the explosion in size of the multidimensional state spaces that arise, neither exact solution techniques nor bounding techniques for general classes of nonproduct form networks have been forthcoming. The bounding techniques for product form networks have been based on the special nature of those networks, either through the convolution or MVA equations. Since these equations do not apply to nonproduct form networks, the bounding techniques cannot be applied. Approximation techniques (based on either limit theorems or heuristics) are thus the only viable alternative to simulation. Because error bounds are usually not available with an approximation technique, the accuracy of the method in any particular case can only be determined by comparison to simulation (or the exact solution if the state space is small enough). In order to develop generally applicable and reliable approximation techniques that can be incorporated into a package for, say, capacity planning, it is necessary to thoroughly validate the approximation over a wide range of parameter values by comparison to simulations. While it is relatively easy to suggest approximations, it is difficult, tedious, and computationally expensive to validate them.

Thus, although there is a plethora of methods for approximating the solutions to nonproduct form networks incorporating a variety of features, very few of these techniques have been thoroughly validated. An ideal validation study identifies a practically important class of models and key parameters of that class. Validations are then performed over the entire range of the parameter space and errors are quantified in terms of the parameters. A qualitative interpretation of the errors is then given, identifying where (in the parameter space) the approximation performs well and where it fails. Bryant *et al.* [25] performed such a validation for networks

incorporating priority scheduling. They considered a set of two queue networks and parameterized the model in terms of the total utilization of the priority server ρ and the fraction of that utilization devoted to the high-priority jobs f. Contour plots of errors over the parameter space were given showing that several of the proposed methods were reliable as long as both ρ and f were not too close to one. The implication of the validation studies is that the approximation can be applied in practice with confidence provided these parameters are kept out of the extreme region where the method fails. There are few other such systematic validation studies reported in the literature. This type of comprehensive study becomes more difficult to design and expensive to perform in networks having more than two queues for which there may be more than two key parameters.

The major approaches to developing approximations are based on either limit theorems or heuristics. The limit theorems provide theoretical justification for an approximation whereas the heuristics are based on common sense and experience. There are two general classes of limit theorems used to justify approximations.

1) Heavy traffic limit theorems which lead to diffusion approximations.

2) "Nearly Completely Decomposable System" limit theorems which lead to a class of approximations called hierarchical decomposition, or aggregation, approximations.

Heavy traffic limits were originally obtained for classical queueing problems such as the waiting time process in a GI/G/1 queue as the traffic intensity approaches one [103]. They have been extended to both open networks of queues with high traffic intensities and general service times (e.g., [66], [94], [95], [151]) as well as to closed networks with large populations (e.g., [91]). The heavy traffic limit theorems show that as the traffic intensity approaches one, a properly scaled version of the queue length process converges in distribution to a diffusion process. Kobayashi [109] and Gelenbe [68] have applied diffusion approximations to queueing network models of computer systems. However, in practice, diffusion approximations have not been widely used because most systems do not operate with all service centers at or near full capacity. Furthermore, proper treatment of the boundary conditions of the multidimensional diffusions generally leads to an intractable system of partial differential equations [77].

The theory behind hierarchical decomposition is treated in Courtois [45]. A nearly completely decomposable Markov transition matrix Q can be rewritten in the form $Q = A + \varepsilon B$ where A is a stochastic block diagonal matrix with, say, M blocks and ε is small. For such systems, interactions between states within a block are much greater than those between blocks. This allows an accurate approximation to the stationary distribution of the Markov chain defined by Q to be computed by solving for the stationary distribution of each of the blocks of A and then computing the stationary distribution of an M-by-M transition matrix P which approximates the transition rates between blocks. This method is exact as $\varepsilon \to 0$. Whereas decomposition finds approximations for the stationary probabilities of the aggregate states and the conditional state probabilities given the aggregate state, these quantities are computed exactly (in the limit as the number of iterations → ∞) for the matrix iterative aggregation/disaggregation methods that were discussed in the previous section. However, the aggregation/disaggregation methods will generally involve substantially more computational effort than decomposition. In computer performance examples, if M is small and the blocks are chosen to correspond to product form networks, then a computationally efficient solution procedure results. Although error bounds are, in principle, possible to compute [45], [186], this does not seem to have been done for any very large scale applications.

We now consider an example of how decomposition has been used to model simultaneous resource possession in single chain networks [4], [44], [117], [159]. In the central server model with terminals pictured in Fig. 1, suppose that there is a limited number of memory partitions P. A job must acquire one of these partitions before its processing can begin and queueing is FCFS for the partitions. A block, or aggregate state, corresponds to the number of jobs using or waiting for partitions. This leads one to consider fixed multiprogramming levels in the (product form) CPU–I/O central server "inner" model. For each possible multiprogramming level, $n = 1, \cdots, P$, let $\alpha(n)$ be the throughput of jobs at the CPU divided by the average number of visits a job makes to the CPU before returning to the terminals; this corresponds to the rate of jobs leaving the CPU–I/O complex when the multiprogramming level is n. These throughputs are then used as queue length dependent rates for an aggregate server representing the CPU–I/O complex in a cyclic two service center "outer" model consisting of the terminals and the aggregate server. The aggregate server has rates $\mu(n)$ defined by

$$\mu(n) = \begin{cases} \alpha(n) & 0 \le n \le P \\ \alpha(P) & n \ge P. \end{cases} \quad (3.23)$$

Selection of these rates models limiting the maximum multiprogramming level to P. The two service center outer model also has product form and in this particular case reduces to a birth and death process. Thus, the approximate solution to the nonproduct form network is efficiently obtained by solving two related product form networks.

There is also a second justification for this method that is provided by a theorem due to Chandy, Herzog, and Woo [34] which states that the above procedure yields exact results in product form networks. In the above example, this corresponds to not having a limit on the multiprogramming level, i.e., P equals the total population of the network. The theorem states that a product form network can be solved exactly by replacing a subnetwork of service centers by a single service center with queue length dependent service rates. The rates are determined by solving, for each population, a network in which the service times of all service centers outside the subnetwork are set to zero, in effect "shorting" out the rest of the network. This theorem is sometimes called Norton's theorem since it is a queueing analog to Norton's theorem in analysis of electrical circuits. The theorem has been extended to multiple chain networks in [111].

Hierarchical decomposition has been used to model a variety of features in nonproduct form networks including the simultaneous resource possession example given above, priority scheduling disciplines [161] and certain types of parallelism [82]. In practice it has been found to be a highly accurate approximation technique and is a cornerstone of much applied modeling work.

However, decomposition has limitations for multiple chain models. For example, suppose the central server model with terminals has K chains and a limited number of memory partitions P_k for each chain k. Then throughput rates for each chain $\mu_k(n_1, \cdots, n_K)$ must be computed for each possible multiprogramming level $(n_1, \cdots, n_K)$ where $0 \le n_k \le P_k$ for $k = 1, \cdots, K$. Assuming the inner model still has product form, these could (at least in theory) be calculated in one pass of MVA. However, the outer model no longer satisfies product form and its solution requires solving the global balance equations for a K-dimensional birth and death process. The size of the state space is $(N_1 + 1) \cdots (N_K + 1)$ where N_k is the number of jobs in chain k. The transition matrix is sparse and can be solved by matrix iterative methods provided the product of the N_k's is not too large. Sauer [159] considered this model for two chains and $N_1 = 40$ and $N_2 = 4$ and found that decomposition provided quite accurate results. However, for models with more than two chains the method becomes computationally infeasible because of the explosion in the size of the state space. A method proposed independently by Brandwajn [22] and Lazowska and Zahorjan [126] attempts to circumvent this problem by iteratively solving a sequence of K one-dimensional birth and death processes rather than one K-dimensional birth and death process. The rates used for chain k are essentially obtained by setting the populations of the other chains to estimates of their mean values. Only limited validations of this approach have been done; it is generally less accurate than complete decomposition but is obtained at much lower cost.

It is sometimes possible to prove limit theorems for particular models allowing theoretically justified approximations. Salza and Lavenberg [158] prove a theorem showing that the sojourn time in a central server model converges to an exponential distribution as the feedback probability converges to one. This result is used, along with decomposition, to approximate the response time distribution in a central server model with terminals; the response time distribution in queueing networks is not analytically tractable except in special cases (e.g., [165], [201]). Other examples of special limit theorems are given by Mitra and Weinberger [142] and Lavenberg [118] who have used asymptotic expansions to estimate the probability of lock contention in a model of a database system as the size of the database increases.

Approximations based on heuristics have been used to model a wide variety of features in queueing networks. There are two major approaches upon which such heuristics are based.

1) The MVA equations and the Arrival Theorem.
2) Iterative methods.
Some approximation methods are based on a combination

of approaches, for example, iteration and decomposition [22], [126]. Still other approximations use specially tailored techniques.

A primary use of the MVA approach has been to model service disciplines and distributions other than those allowed in product form networks [8], [25], [152]. For some service disciplines or distributions, if the distribution of the number of jobs seen upon arrival of a job to a service center is known, then the mean response time at that service center can be calculated either exactly or approximately. In the MVA based approach, the distribution of jobs seen on arrival is assumed to be given by the Arrival Theorem; namely, it is the stationary distribution of a network with that one job removed. Because the Arrival Theorem is not valid except in product form networks, the method is an approximation. Reiser [152] considers an approximation to model the FCFS discipline for centers having exponential distributions with different means. If center i is FCFS, then the requirement for product form is that the mean service demands S_{ji} are independent of j. For distinct S_{ji}'s the suggested approximation is to modify (3.8) as follows:

$$R_{ji}(n) = (1/\mu_i)(S_{ji} + \sum_{k=1}^{K} S_{ki}L_{ki}(n - e_j)), \quad (3.24)$$

which states that a job's average response time is its own average service time plus the mean queue length of jobs found on arrival times the average service time of each job. If all the service times are identical, (3.24) reduces to (3.8). A modification using the mean residual life (from renewal theory) for distributions other than exponential was also suggested by Reiser [152] and approximations for priority queueing disciplines have been proposed by Bryant et al. [25] and Chandy and Lakshmi [36].

A second general heuristic approach to analyzing non-product form networks is iteration. In this approach, a sequence of simplified networks is solved so that, upon convergence, the solution closely approximates the solution of the network of interest. If each network in the sequence has product form, the overall method is computationally efficient provided convergence is obtained in a reasonable number of iterations. This approach can often be shown to be equivalent to finding the fixed point of a multidimensional set of nonlinear equations $x = f(x)$ [41], [48], [81], [82]. Existence of a solution can frequently be shown by applying the Brouwer fixed point theorem [147]. The equations are typically solved by successive substitutions, i.e., $x^{n+1} = f(x^n)$. If the function f can be shown to be a contraction mapping, then convergence and uniqueness are guaranteed. However, in performance applications f usually cannot be shown to be such a mapping. The function f is generally a complicated function usually involving the solution of a product form network and the variables x represent performance measures of the network.

Heidelberger and Trivedi [81] consider a model of parallel processing in which a primary job spawns an asynchronous task whenever it passes through a particular node in the network. The primary jobs are represented by a closed chain. The overall model does not have product form but it is ap-

proximated by a product form network having an extra open chain representing the spawned tasks. The Poisson arrival rate of the spawned tasks is set equal to the throughput of the primary jobs at the spawning node. The throughput of primary jobs depends on the arrival rate of spawned jobs and the fixed point problem reduces to finding that arrival rate for which the primary job throughput equals the spawned task arrival rate. Uniqueness and convergence were proven for this example and an extensive validation study was performed.

Iterative methods have also been applied to analyzing networks incorporating a wide variety of features including simultaneous resource possession [98], [99], general service time distributions [132], database lock contention [194], and parallel processing systems in which tasks requiring synchronization are spawned [82]. Selection of the approximating simplified networks is still an art form.

E. Operational Analysis—An Alternative Viewpoint

We have presented the analysis of queueing networks from the stochastic process point of view. For example, using the theory of Markov processes, product form can be shown formally to hold provided certain assumptions on service time distributions, arrival processes, stochastic routing and queueing disciplines are met. A recently developed alternative viewpoint is Operational Analysis which relates measurable quantities in queueing networks [30], [47], [127]. The measurable quantities are not assumed to be random variables. The operational viewpoint is that if a system is measured during an interval $[0, T]$, say, then certain relationships between variables must hold provided the system satisfies certain operational assumptions during the interval. For example, if a queue length can only change by either plus or minus one job when there is an arrival or departure, then the number of arrivals must equal the number of departures provided T is chosen so that the queue length at time zero equals the queue length at time T. More subtle relationships can be shown as well including an operational analog of Little's result $L_T = \lambda_T W_T$ provided the queue is empty at times zero and T [53], [128]. In this equation $L_T = (1/T)\int_0^T L(s)\,ds$ where $L(s)$ is the queue length at time s, $\lambda_T = N(T)/T$ where $N(T)$ is the number of arrivals (and departures) from the queue in $[0, T]$, and $W_T = (1/N(T))\sum_{i=1}^{N(T)} W(i)$ where $W(i)$ is the waiting time of customer i. In fact, this sample path version of Little's result predates the first papers on operational analysis by about 15 years. In the operational framework, the fraction of time spent in a state is the analog of a state probability. Using this analog, product form can also be shown to be an operational law provided certain operational assumptions are satisfied during the measurement period. These include homogeneity assumptions on routing and devices. For example, device homogeneity assumes that the departure rate from a center depends only on the queue length of that center and not on the state of any other center. Operational versions of MVA and the Arrival Theorem have been derived as well.

The obvious question is how the operational assumptions are related to the stochastic assumptions. This has not been investigated in much detail. However, there is an interesting analysis by Bryant [24] showing that, in the limit as the length of the measurement period $T \to \infty$, the only M/G/1 queue satisfying the operational assumption of homogeneous service times is the M/M/1 queue, i.e., the queue with exponential service times. The assumption of homogeneous service times is thus analogous to the assumption of a fixed (queue length independent) rate server with exponential service times. We conjecture that there are similar results for networks relating operational to stochastic assumptions. For example, one can show (using ergodic properties of finite state space continuous time Markov chains) that the operational assumptions necessary for product form hold in the limit with probability one (along an appropriate sequence of regeneration points) for the class of single chain closed product form networks with queue length dependent exponential centers. Furthermore, the homogeneous service time assumption can be shown to hold in the limit for such networks with queue length independent exponential centers. For such closed single chain models, no other general class of well-defined stochastic queueing models has been identified for which the operational assumptions hold, with probability one, in the limit. Whether or not such a class exists is an open question.

One claimed advantage of the operational viewpoint is that it allows one to test the assumptions and to provide bounds on errors induced when the operational assumptions are violated. Indeed, although it is possible to formally test in a statistical sense the stochastic assumptions, there are few quantitative sensitivity results in queueing theory. However, the sensitivity results for operational analysis can frequently be interpreted in the stochastic setting. For example, Suri [190] provides sensitivity results, in the form of gradients, for deviations from the homogeneous service time assumption. The gradients can be used to obtain error bounds for performance measures predicted by assuming homogeneous service times in networks in which this assumption is slightly violated (the bounds are valid only in an appropriately defined neighborhood about the homogeneous point). These results can also be interpreted as being gradients and bounds on stochastic queueing networks when service rates are not constant.

Operational analysis thus provides a different set of assumptions on which to base and interpret certain results primarily about product form queueing networks. It has broadened the appeal of queueing networks to include those who feel uncomfortable making stochastic assumptions such as independence, stationarity, and exponential distributions. A challenge for operational analysis is to provide major new results, rather than (as has been the case) to merely provide operational versions of existing theorems which were originally derived using stochastic analyses.

F. Future Challenges

Analytic performance modeling has been an extremely useful tool for evaluating the performance of computing systems of the 1970's and early 1980's. However, computing systems are rapidly advancing and analytic modeling techniques must advance with them in order to maintain relevance in the late 1980's and into the 1990's. Distributed processing, parallel processing, and radically new computer architectures present significant modeling challenges and opportunities.

Distributed processing systems will become commonplace. These systems will serve large numbers of users, consist of many devices, and will incorporate large databases, both centralized and distributed. High levels of performance will be key. Performance needs to be designed into these systems, not only in determining the number of devices and their speeds, but also in designing operating system algorithms to dynamically manage the system. Optimization of queueing networks will thus become more important both in terms of distributed system design and load balancing. Some optimal load balancing results for queueing networks are beginning to emerge [192], however, major new advances in this area are required. Further work is needed in database modeling where satisfactory methods for analyzing lock contention are also just starting to emerge [71], [118], [142], [148], [193], [195]. Particular attention needs to be paid to modeling distributed databases.

Parallel processing systems will also become widespread as hardware costs continue to decline. By parallel processing we mean multiple subtasks running concurrently and cooperating to solve some larger task. Parallel processing will come about as a result of new computer architectures, such as data flow and multiple microprocessor architectures, which are explicitly designed to take advantage of parallelism. Parallel processing will also arise as the result of distributed databases and the requirement for highly reliable and available systems. There have been very few techniques developed to analyze such systems [55], [81], [82], [87] and much work remains to be done.

In meeting these challenges approximations will play a key role. If possible, computable error bounds need to be developed, although this looks extremely difficult for nonproduct form networks. Improved methods for applying hierarchical decomposition in multiple chain models need to be developed. A consistent and comprehensive framework for validating approximations needs to be developed and applied. The validations need to include stress cases to identify when approximations fail as well as when they are successful. Finally, there has been very little work on validating combinations of approximations. Most approximation studies have focused on introducing a single nonproduct form feature into an otherwise product form network. Exceptions to this are the previously mentioned capacity planning tools [7], [29] which incorporate a variety of approximations simultaneously and have been validated against measurements.

IV. Simulation Performance Modeling

Simulation is an extremely versatile and useful tool in computer performance evaluation. Whereas analytic techniques have limitations on the range of features that can be modeled, a simulation model can be constructed to an almost arbitrary level of detail. This allows one to model extremely complex situations that are analytically intractable. Furthermore, whereas analytic models typically provide only mean values, simulations can provide estimates of distributions and higher moments. In addition, dynamic, or transient, behavior can be studied using simulation while analytic models can usually be used to study only steady state behavior. In fact, a major application of simulation is to validate analytic models.

There are two distinct types of simulation that have become widespread in computer performance evaluation.

1) Trace Driven Simulation: This is a simulation of a deterministic model that is driven by a sequence, or trace, obtained from measurements of an existing system. The model often does not have a queueing structure. Trace driven simulations have been primarily used to study the performance of storage hierarchies and of processor pipelines.

2) Stochastic Discrete Event Simulation: This is typically a simulation of a queueing model that is driven by sequences of random (or pseudorandom) numbers with user specified distributions. These random sequences are used for obtaining service times, routing, etc. Occasionally, trace data are used (possibly in conjunction with random sequences) to drive queueing model simulations, e.g., [177]. Discrete event simulations have extremely broad applicability and have been used extensively in computer performance evaluation.

In this section, we will discuss these two types of simulation. Since stochastic discrete event simulations are statistical experiments, their outputs are random and require careful statistical interpretation. We will describe some of the statistical problems that arise in analysis of simulation output data, including confidence interval generation and simulation run length control.

A. Trace Driven Simulation

In the design of storage hierarchies, trace driven simulation has been used to study the performance effects of paging algorithms (e.g., [5], [12]), cache management algorithms [182], database buffering strategies [179], buffered, or cached, disks [180], and long-term file migration policies [181].

An appropriate trace, or script, is obtained by measuring a system. For example, in studies of cache performance a job is run and the sequence of memory address (page and line) references is recorded. A software model of the cache organization and its management algorithms is constructed. These management algorithms determine how data are brought into and removed from the cache. The software cache model takes the address reference sequence as input and simulates the behavior of the cache. The model can be easily changed to reflect different cache organizations and management algorithms. The key performance measure of interest in such studies is usually the cache miss ratio, the fraction of references not found in the cache. The miss ratio is critically dependent on the size of the cache and it is common to plot the miss ratio as a function of the cache size. These curves can be efficiently generated in one pass through the address trace using a "stack processing algorithm" [133] for a broad class of demand paging algorithms, including the

Least Recently Used replacement algorithm. Stack processing is applicable to performance evaluation of multilevel memory hierarchies, not just a single-level cache.

The combination of a flexible software model and repeatable workloads enables one to study a variety of cache organizations under identical workloads without having to build hardware. Using a set of representative measurement traces increases model realism and avoids the necessity of constructing possibly complicated stochastic workload models. However, obtaining representative traces for multiprogramming environments may be difficult in practice. Consider a page reference trace from a multiprogramming system which includes references from the operating system dispatcher which is invoked upon page faults. When such a trace is run against a model simulating different paging algorithms, a reference from the trace that caused a page fault in the measured system may not cause a page fault in the simulated system. However, the trace still consists of the references from the dispatcher which should not be invoked in the simulator. As a result of this type of consideration, many traces are taken from single jobs running in uniprogramming environments. Smith [182] simulated task switching by switching between traces of different jobs at periodic intervals. As noted in Section II-A, Clark [42] observed differences between measurement and trace driven simulation results for these reasons among others.

Trace driven simulation is also a powerful tool in the performance analysis of processor pipeline design. Instruction traces, obtained from measurements, are used to drive a software model of the pipeline. The model may be of arbitrary detail. For example, the model may or may not include the effects of a finite size cache. The key performance measure in pipeline studies is usually the instruction throughput, the number of instructions per machine cycle. Lang *et al.* [114] describe in more detail a general approach to modeling pipelines. Pipeline simulators, which tend to be built by manufacturers for use in machine development, are often proprietary. However, examples of pipeline simulators in the open literature include those by Kumar and Davidson [112] who modeled the IBM 360/91, Smith [183] who studied branch prediction strategies for the CDC CYBER 170 architecture, Srini and Asenjo [185] who considered a variety of changes in the Cray-1S architecture, and MacDougall [129] who considered the IBM 370 architecture.

B. Stochastic Discrete Event Simulation

Stochastic discrete event simulations are driven by sequences of pseudorandom numbers generated by the computer. In addition to specifying the model structure, the analyst must also specify the distributions of these sequences. The term discrete event refers to the fact that events in the simulation can only occur at a countable number of points in simulated time and not continuously. Discrete event simulations are much more widespread in computer performance evaluation than are continuous simulations and we not will discuss continuous simulation at all.

The development of simulation models is greatly facilitated by the use of general purpose simulation modeling languages, such as GPSS, SIMSCRIPT, GASP, and SLAM, overviews and examples of which are given in [125]. These and other simulation languages ease development of simulation models by providing high-level constructs and features common to all simulations, such as random number generation, event scheduling, queue management, and statistics gathering and reporting. A number of these and other simulation languages are beginning to appear on microcomputers [149]. Simulation modeling packages specifically designed for computer performance evaluation have also been developed, e.g., RESQ [164], PAWS [96], and QNAP [140]. These packages provide higher level modeling constructs particularly well suited for simulation of queueing network models of computer performance. Even higher level packages exist for modeling particular computer systems; e.g., SNAP/SHOT [187], used in capacity planning, includes built in models of certain IBM devices and control programs.

General texts on simulation include [62], [125]. These texts treat basic simulation modeling concepts, random number generation, statistical analysis of simulation output data, and give overviews of simulation languages. References [110] and [117] contain sections on various aspects of simulation as applied to computer performance evaluation.

1) Statistical Analysis of Simulation Output: Discrete event simulation is controlled statistical experimentation. Models are driven by random input sequences, such as service times, and produce random output sequences, such as response times, from which estimates of the response time distribution and/or its moments are obtained. If the simulation is rerun under identical conditions (but driven by different statistically independent input sequences), the output estimates will be different, often dramatically so. Thus, as in the case of measurements, sound statistical methods are required to interpret the results of simulation models. We will give an overview of some of the statistical aspects of simulation output analysis. More complete discussions are in [104], [105], [117, chapter 6], [123].

Because simulation outputs are random, it is important to assess the amount of variability in estimates that is due purely to random sampling effects. In addition to assessing statistical accuracy, it is important to be able to adjust the length(s) of the simulation run(s) so as to obtain estimates of specified accuracy. These two problems of accuracy assessment and run length control can be addressed through the use of confidence intervals. Suppose μ is some unknown output characteristic of the model to be estimated, e.g., the mean steady state response time. An interval (L, U) with random endpoints L and U is said to be a $100(1 - \alpha)$ percent confidence interval for μ if Prob $\{L \leq \mu \leq U\} = 1 - \alpha$. For $(1 - \alpha)$ close to one, there is a high probability that the unknown parameter μ is between L and U. The confidence interval is usually formed in such a way that a point estimate $\hat{\mu}$ of μ lies in the interval and is frequently the midpoint of the interval. Formation of such a confidence interval generally requires an estimate of the variance of $\hat{\mu}$. The width of the interval $U-L$ is then a measure of the accuracy of $\hat{\mu}$. The narrower the interval, the more confidence can be placed in the estimate. Simulation run length control algorithms have been developed that allow a model to be run until confidence intervals of suitable accuracy (as defined by the analyst) have been obtained or until a CPU time limit is exceeded [83], [121].

Classical statistical techniques can be applied when estimating transient characteristics since multiple independent replications can be performed thereby generating iid (independent and identically distributed) observations. However, simulation studies of queueing network models of computer performance often involve estimating steady state characteristics. There are a variety of procedures for generating confidence intervals for steady state characteristics. Standard statistical approaches based on iid observations cannot be directly applied since simulation output sequences are usually both autocorrelated and nonstationary. The autocorrelation arises because of queueing; if the waiting time of a job at a device is large, then it is likely that the waiting time of the next job will also be large. Nonstationarity is a consequence of the model's initial conditions; if all jobs in the model of Fig. 1 are started in the think state at the terminals, then the first job arriving to the CPU experiences no queueing whereas subsequent arrivals may require queueing.

Suppose we let $X_1, \cdots, X_N$ be the response time output sequence generated by the simulation and that we are interested in estimating the mean steady state response time $\mu = \lim_{n \to \infty} E(X_n)$. The usual estimate for μ is the sample average

$$\hat{\mu} = (1/N) \sum_{n=1}^{N} X_n . \tag{4.1}$$

The problem of nonstationarity is that for small n, $E(X_n) \neq \mu$ which in general means that $E(\hat{\mu}) \neq \mu$. The typical approach for dealing with this problem, which is also called the problem of the initial transient, is to determine an N_0 such that $E(X_n) \simeq \mu$ for $n \geq N_0$, delete the observations before N_0, and then estimate μ by

$$\hat{\mu} = (1/(N - N_0)) \sum_{n=N_0+1}^{N} X_n . \tag{4.2}$$

This will be an approximately unbiased estimate of μ. Schruben [169] has proposed statistical tests for stationarity that can be used to test the adequacy of an N_0.

The other difficult problem is dealing with the autocorrelation. Suppose that a satisfactory N_0 is found so that $\{X_n, n \geq N_0\}$ is approximately a (covariance) stationary sequence. Then the central limit theorem states that, for large N, $(\hat{\mu} - \mu)/\sigma(\hat{\mu})$ is approximately normally distributed with mean zero and variance one where $\sigma^2(\hat{\mu})$ is the variance of $\hat{\mu}$. If the X_n's are iid, then $\sigma^2(\hat{\mu}) = \sigma^2(X)/(N - N_0)$ where $\sigma^2(X)$ is the variance of X_n. However, this equation is not valid for correlated observations. For large sample sizes, the correct expression for the variance of correlated observations is

$$\sigma^2(\hat{\mu}) \simeq (\sigma^2(X)/(N - N_0)) \left(\sum_{k=-\infty}^{\infty} \rho_k \right) \tag{4.3}$$

where ρ_k is the autocorrelation between X_n and X_{n+k}. Thus, the variance of a correlated sequence equals the variance of an independent sequence times an expansion factor (the sum of the autocorrelation function) which measures the amount of correlation in the sequence. This expansion factor is usually positive in simulations of queueing networks, and it can easily be much larger than one. For example, in the M/M/1 queue with traffic intensity 0.90, the expansion factor is 367 [16]. It cannot be ignored in generating confidence intervals since assuming positively correlated observations are independent leads to severe underestimation of the variance and confidence intervals which are much too narrow.

There are two general approaches to dealing with the correlation when generating confidence intervals.

1) Avoid it by organizing the simulation output into iid observations.

2) Estimate the correlation and compensate for it.

There are three methods to avoid the correlation. The first method is to use independent replications. This has the advantage of simplicity but the disadvantages of being sensitive to the effects of the initial transient and wasteful of data if the transient portion is discarded from the beginning of each replication. The second method is called batch means (e.g., [124], [138]) which operates on a single run. The sequence is divided into long blocks, or batches, of length B so that the means of the batches are approximately iid. If B is so chosen, then classical statistical methods can be applied. However, selection of an adequate B is a difficult statistical problem and there is currently no completely satisfactory method. The third method is called the regenerative method (e.g., [93]) which is based on the fact that some stochastic sequences, called regenerative processes, contain regeneration points which delimit the sequence into iid blocks of random length. However, the method is not generally applicable since most processes arising in computer performance evaluation are either not regenerative or contain too few regeneration points to produce valid confidence intervals unless the run is extremely long.

A single-run method, called the spectral method, that estimates the correlation in the sequence is described in [83]. This method uses the fact that $\sigma^2(\hat{\mu}) \simeq p(0)/(N - N_0)$ where $p(0)$ is the spectral density of the process at zero frequency. The spectral density is the Fourier cosine transform of the covariance function $\{\gamma_k\}$ of the process defined by

$$p(f) = \sum_{k=-\infty}^{\infty} \gamma_k \cos(2\pi fk). \qquad (4.4)$$

Spectral estimation techniques are applied to estimate $p(0)$. This method has been shown empirically to produce satisfactory results for a variety of computer performance models and has been incorporated into a run length control procedure.

The problems of combining initial transient detection and deletion, confidence interval generation, and run length control into one automatic procedure have been investigated by Heidelberger and Welch [84]. Procedures combining the transient tests in [169] with the spectral method were tested. Although generally acceptable results were obtained, there were extreme cases of slowly developing transients in which the methods failed. Further work is needed in this area.

The above procedures are used to place a confidence inter-val on a single parameter which can be expressed as a mean. Both moments and points on a probability distribution can be expressed as means. Analogous techniques also exist for generating confidence intervals for quantiles [80], [92]. Multivariate statistical procedures can be applied to place simultaneous confidence intervals on more than one parameter (e.g., [125], [168]), although this is rarely done in practice. Regression and design of experiments are potentially useful techniques in simulation modeling. For example, Jones [101] used design of experiments and analysis of variance to design and analyze simulation experiments investigating factors affecting disk subsystem performance. However, because of the difficulties in identifying key parameters and specifying a functional form and the requirement for independent observations with identical variances, these techniques have not been widely used by simulation practitioners. These are essentially the same reasons that were cited in Section II-D for why such techniques have not been applied frequently in measurement studies.

The variance expansion due to the autocorrelation in the output sequences [see (4.3)] poses another difficulty besides variance estimation; it implies that quite a long simulation run may have to be performed before a reasonable level of accuracy is attained. Variance reduction techniques attempt to decrease the variance of an estimate by using known information about the system being simulated. For example, Lavenberg et al. [119] propose using known information about service times and job routing in a variance reduction technique known as control variables. While variance reduction techniques are an attractive possibility for cutting down on simulation run lengths and have been much studied in the literature, they have been rarely successful in real applications [122].

Ho et al. [89] and Suri [189] have proposed an interesting technique called perturbation analysis for estimating the gradient of a performance measure with respect to some input parameter of the simulation, e.g., a mean service time. The gradient estimate is obtained from a single run by carrying along certain ancillary information which measures the effect of an infinitesimal change in the parameter on the sample path. The gradient estimates can be used in sensitivity analysis or optimization procedures. Questions of the unbiasedness and ergodicity properties (convergence with probability one) of the gradients estimates have been addressed in some specific instances [88], [191]. General conditions for these properties to hold have been given in [33], although these conditions appear difficult to verify in practice. The method has also been proposed to study the effects of finite changes in parameters, e.g., increasing a buffer size. Although some empirical validations have been done, little is known about the statistical properties of such estimates. Perturbation analysis should also prove applicable in trace driven simulations and measurements of real systems.

C. Future Challenges

As computer systems become larger and more complicated, analytic modeling will become more difficult and simulation will play an increasingly important role in performance evaluation. A key challenge is to be able to devise computationally efficient techniques to simulate models of increasingly complex systems. Effective generally applicable variance reduction techniques need to be developed, although this appears unlikely. Innovative approaches, such as perturbation analysis, need to be developed, refined, and applied in practice. Hierarchical modeling techniques should be applicable in simulation modeling as well as in analytic modeling. However, some preliminary studies [17] indicate that such an approach is not always computationally attractive and there are difficult statistical issues to be faced. However, hybrid modeling techniques that contain both analytic and simulation components, often in a hierarchical structure, have occasionally been successfully applied in practice (e.g., a model of IBM's MVS operating system by Chiu and Chow [40]) and should prove to be an effective approach in the future. Shanthikumar and Sargent [176] survey hybrid modeling techniques.

Parallel processing holds promise for increasing simulation efficiency. A potentially attractive approach is to coordinate the activities of multiple microprocessor systems. However, control of distributed simulation is analagous to ensuring consistency in distributed databases. Therefore, synchronization and deadlock detection algorithms are required (e.g., [35]) for distributed simulations just as concurrency control algorithms [13] are required for distributed databases. The challenge is to be able to effectively partition models in such a way that both the overhead for these algorithms is small and that high levels of parallelism can be achieved. Prototype systems and languages are beginning to appear (e.g., [203]).

Computer graphics will also play an increasingly important role in simulation. Graphics can be used to facilitate model input [49]. Data analysis, both in general and in simulation applications, will employ graphical techniques and these are starting to appear [79], [117, chapter 6]. Real-time graphic animation of simulation is an intriguing possibility [139], [141]. Such real-time graphics present exciting opportunities for interactive control and analysis of simulation models.

Acknowledgment

The authors are grateful to D. Ferrari, D. Mitra, R. Suri, and W. White for conversations that were helpful in the preparation of this paper. We thank K. Trivedi for inviting us to write this paper. We also thank E. Zoernack for her help in preparing the manuscript.

References

[1] A. K. Agrawala, R. M. Bryant, and J. M. Mohr, "An approach to the workload characterization problem," *Computer*, vol. 9, pp. 18–32, 1976.

[2] A. K. Agrawala and J. M. Mohr, "The relationship between the pattern recognition problem and the workload characterization problem," in *Proc. SIGMETRICS/CMG VIII*, 1977, pp. 131–139.

[3] H. P. Artis, "Capacity planning for MVS computer systems," in *Performance of Computers Installations*, D. Ferrari, Ed. Amsterdam, The Netherlands: North-Holland, 1978, pp. 25–35.

[4] B. Avi-Itzhak and D. P. Heyman, "Approximate queueing models for multiprogramming computer systems," *Oper. Res.*, vol. 21, pp. 1212–1229, 1973.

[5] O. Babaoğlu and D. Ferrari, "Two-level replacement decisions in paging stores," *IEEE Trans. Comput.*, vol. C-32, pp. 1151–1159, Dec. 1983.

[6] Y. Bard, "Performance criteria and measurement for a time-sharing system," *IBM Syst. J.*, vol. 10, pp. 193–216, 1971.

[7] ——, "The VM/370 performance predictor," *Comput. Surveys*, vol. 10, pp. 333–342, 1978.

[8] ——, "Some extensions to multiclass queueing network analysis," in *Performance of Computer Systems*, M. Arato, A. Butrimenko, and E. Gelenbe, Eds. Amsterdam, The Netherlands: North-Holland, 1979, pp. 51–61.

[9] Y. Bard and M. Schatzoff, "Statistical methods in computer performance analysis," in *Current Trends in Programming Methodology, Vol. III: Software Modeling*, K. M. Chandy and R. T. Yeh, Eds. Englewood Cliffs, NJ: Prentice-Hall, 1978, pp. 1–51.

[10] Y. Bard and K. Suryanarayana, "On the structure of CP-67 overhead," in *Statistical Computer Performance Evaluation*, W. Freiberg, Ed. New York: Academic, 1972, pp. 329–346.

[11] F. Baskett, K. M. Chandy, R. R. Muntz, and F. Palacios-Gomez, "Open, closed, and mixed networks of queues with different classes of customers," *J. Assoc. Comput. Mach.*, vol. 22, pp. 248–260, 1975.

[12] L. A. Belady, "A study of replacement algorithms for a virtual storage computer," *IBM Syst. J.*, vol. 5, pp. 78–101, 1966.

[13] P. A. Bernstein and N. Goodman, "Concurrency control in distributed database systems," *Comput. Surveys*, vol. 13, pp. 185–221, 1981.

[14] R. Blake, "Instrumentation for multiple computers," in *Perform. Eval. Rev. 9, Proc. PERFORMANCE '80*, 1980, pp. 11–25.

[15] R. Blau, "Paging on an object-oriented personal computer," in *Perform. Eval. Rev., Special Issue, Proc. 1983 ACM SIGMETRICS Conf. Meas. Modeling Comput. Syst.*, pp. 44–54.

[16] N. Blomqvist, "The covariance function of the M/G/1 queueing system," *Skand. Akt. Tidskr.*, vol. 50, pp. 157–174, 1967.

[17] A. Blum, L. Donatiello, P. Heidelberger, S. S. Lavenberg, and E. A. MacNair, "Experiments with decomposition of extended queueing network models," IBM, Yorktown Heights, NY, Res. Rep. RC 10213, 1983.

[18] M. L. Bolzoni, M. Calzarossa, P. Mapelli, and G. Serazzi, "A package for the implementation of static workload models," in *Perform. Eval. Rev. 11, Proc. 1982 ACM SIGMETRICS Conf. Meas. Modeling Comput. Syst.*, pp. 58–67.

[19] P. Bourret and P. Cros, "Presentation and correction of errors in operating system measurements," *IEEE Trans. Software Eng.*, vol. SE-6, pp. 395–398, 1980.

[20] G. E. P. Box, W. G. Hunter, and J. S. Hunter, *Statistics for Experiments, An Introduction to Design, Data Analysis and Model Building*. New York: Wiley, 1978.

[21] A. Brandwajn, "Multiple paths versus memory for improving DASD subsystem performance," in *PERFORMANCE '81*, F. J. Kylstra, Ed. Amsterdam, The Netherlands: North-Holland, 1981, pp. 415–434.

[22] ——, "Fast approximate solution of multiprogramming models," in *Proc. 1982 ACM SIGMETRICS Conf. Meas. Modeling Comput. Syst.*, pp. 141–149.

[23] ——, "Models of DASD subsystems with multiple access paths: A throughput-driven approach," *IEEE Trans. Comput.*, vol. C-32, pp. 451–463, 1983.

[24] R. M. Bryant, "On homogeneity and on line-off-line behavior in M/G/1 queueing systems," *IEEE Trans. Software Eng.*, vol. SE-7, pp. 291–299, 1981.

[25] R. M. Bryant, A. E. Krzesinski, and P. Teunissen, "The MVA pre-empt resume priority approximation," in *Perform. Eval. Rev., Special Issue, Proc. 1983 ACM SIGMETRICS Conf. Meas. Modeling Comput. Syst.*, pp. 12–27.

[26] I. Y. Bucher, "The computational speed of supercomputers," in *Perform. Eval. Rev., Special Issue, Proc. 1983 ACM SIGMETRICS Conf. Meas. Modeling Comput. Syst.*, pp. 151–165.

[27] J. P. Buzen, "Queueing network models of multiprogramming," Ph.D. dissertation, Div. Eng. Appl. Phys., Harvard Univ., Cambridge, MA, 1971.

[28] ——, "Computational algorithms for closed queueing networks with exponential servers," *Commun. ACM*, vol. 16, pp. 527–531, 1973.

[29] ——, "A queueing network model of MVS," *Comput. Surveys*, vol. 10, pp. 319–331, 1978.

[30] J. P. Buzen and P. J. Denning, "Measuring and calculating queue length distributions," *Computer*, vol. 13, pp. 33–44, 1980.

[31] M. D. Canon, D. H. Fritz, J. H. Howard, T. D. Howell, M. F. Mitoma, and J. Rodriquez-Rosell, "A virtual machine emulator for performance evaluation," *Commun. ACM*, vol. 23, pp. 71–80, 1980.

[32] W. Cao and W. J. Stewart, "Iterative aggregation/disaggregation techniques for nearly uncoupled markov chains," North Carolina State Univ., Tech. Rep., 1984; also *J. Assoc. Comput. Mach.*, to be published.

[33] X. R. Cao, "Convergence of parameter sensitivity estimates in a stochastic environment," in *Proc. 23rd IEEE Conf. Decision and Control*, Las Vegas, NV, to be published.

[34] K. M. Chandy, U. Herzog, and L. Woo, "Parametric analysis of queueing networks," *IBM J. Res. Develop.*, vol. 19, pp. 36–42, 1975.

[35] K. M. Chandy, V. Holmes, and J. Misra, "Distributed simulation of networks," *Comput. Networks*, vol. 3, pp. 105–113, 1979.

[36] K. Chandy and M. S. Lakshmi, "An approximation technique for queueing networks with preemptive priority queues," Dep. Comput. Sci., Univ. Texas, Austin, TX, Tech. Rep., 1983.

[37] K. M. Chandy and D. Neuse, "Linearizer: A heuristic algorithm for queueing network models of computer systems," *Commun. ACM*, vol. 25, pp. 126–134, 1982.

[38] K. M. Chandy and C. H. Sauer, "Approximate methods for analysis of queueing network models of computer systems," *Comput. Surveys*, vol. 10, pp. 263–280, 1978.

[39] ——, "Computational algorithms for product form queueing networks," *Commun. ACM*, vol. 23, pp. 573–583, 1980.

[40] W. W. Chiu and W. M. Chow, "A performance model of MVS," *IBM Syst. J.*, vol. 17, pp. 444–462, 1978.

[41] W-M. Chow, "Approximations for large scale closed queueing networks," *Perform. Eval.*, vol. 3, pp. 1–12, 1983.

[42] D. W. Clark, "Cache performance in the VAX-11/780," *ACM Trans. Comput. Syst.*, vol. 1, pp. 24–37, 1983.

[43] W. G. Cochran and G. M. Cox, *Experimental Designs (second edition)*. New York: Wiley, 1957.

[44] P. J. Courtois, "Decomposability, instabilities and saturation in multiprogramming systems," *Commun. ACM*, vol. 18, pp. 371–377, 1975.

[45] ——, *Decomposability: Queueing and Computer System Applications*. New York: Academic, 1977.

[46] C. A. Coutant, R. E. Griswold, and D. R. Hanson, "Measuring the performance and behavior of icon programs," *IEEE Trans. Software Eng.*, vol. SE-9, pp. 93–103, 1983.

[47] P. J. Denning and J. P. Buzen, "The operational analysis of queueing network models," *Comput. Surveys*, vol. 10, pp. 225–261, 1978.

[48] E. de Souza e Silva, S. S. Lavenberg, and R. R. Muntz, "A perspective on iterative methods for the approximate analysis of closed queueing networks," in *Mathematical Computer Performance and Reliability*, G. Iazeolla, P. J. Courtois, and A. Hordijk, Eds. Amsterdam, The Netherlands: North-Holland, 1984, pp. 225–244.

[49] M. C. Dewsnup, "Using graphics to build simulation models," in *Proc. 1983 Winter Simulation Conf.*, pp. 279–280.

[50] N. R. Draper and H. Smith, *Applied Regression Analysis (second edition)*. New York: Wiley, 1981.

[51] D. L. Eager, "Bounding algorithms for queueing network models of computer systems," Ph.D. dissertation, Dep. Comput. Sci., Univ. Toronto, Toronto, Ont., Canada, 1984.

[52] D. L. Eager and K. C. Sevcik, "Performance bound hierarchies for queueing networks," *ACM Trans. Comput. Syst.*, vol. 1, pp. 99–115, 1983.

[53] S. Eilon, "A simpler proof of $L = \lambda W$," *Oper. Res.*, vol. 17, pp. 915–917, 1969.

[54] A. K. Erlang, "The theory of probabilities and telephone conversations," *Nyt Tidsskrift Matematik*, vol. 20, pp. 33–39, 1909.

[55] G. Fayolle, R. Iasnogorodski, and I. Mitrani, "The distribution of sojourn times in a queueing network with overtaking: Reduction to a boundary problem," in *PERFORMANCE '83*, A. K. Agrawala and S. K. Tripathi, Eds. Amsterdam, The Netherlands: North-Holland, 1983, pp. 477–486.

[56] D. Ferrari, "Architecture and instrumentation of a modular interactive system," *Computer*, vol. 6, pp. 25–29, 1973.

[57] ——, *Computer Systems Performance Evaluation*. Englewood Cliffs, NJ: Prentice-Hall, 1978.

[58] ——, "A performance-oriented procedure for modeling interactive workloads," in *Experimental Computer Performance Evaluation*, D. Ferrari and M. Spadoni, Eds. Amsterdam, The Netherlands: North-Holland, 1981, pp. 57–78.

[59] ——, "On the foundations of artificial workload design," in *Perform. Eval. Rev. 12, Proc. 1984 ACM SIGMETRICS Conf. Meas. Modeling Comput. Syst.*, pp. 8–13.

[60] D. Ferrari and V. Minetti, "A hybrid measurement tool for mini-

computers," in *Experimental Computer Performance Evaluation*, D. Ferrari and M. Spadoni, Eds. Amsterdam, The Netherlands: North-Holland, 1981, pp. 217–233.

[61] D. Ferrari, G. Serazzi, and A. Zeigner, *Measurement and Tuning of Computer Systems*. Englewood Cliffs, NJ: Prentice-Hall, 1983.

[62] G. S. Fishman, *Principles of Discrete Event Simulation*. New York: Wiley, 1978.

[63] W. R. Franta, H. K. Berg, and W. T. Wood, "Issues and approaches to distributed testbed instrumentation," *Computer*, vol. 15, pp. 71–81, 1982.

[64] H. Fromm, U. Hercksen, U. Herzog, K.-H. John, R. Klar, and W. Kleinoder, "Experiences with performance measurement and modeling of a processor array," *IEEE Trans. Comput.*, vol. C-32, pp. 15–31, Jan. 1983.

[65] S. H. Fuller, R. J. Swan, and W. A. Wulf, "The instrumentation of C.mmp, a multi-(mini) processor," in *Proc. COMPCON 73*, pp. 173–176.

[66] D. P. Gaver, "Diffusion approximations and models for certain congestion problems," *J. Appl. Prob.*, vol. 5, pp. 607–623, 1968.

[67] E. F. Gehringer, A. K. Jones, and Z. Z. Segall, "The Cm* testbed," *Computer*, vol. 15, pp. 40–53, 1982.

[68] E. Gelenbe, "On approximate computer system models," *J. Assoc. Comput. Mach.*, vol. 22, pp. 261–269, 1975.

[69] E. Gelenbe and I. Mitrani, *Analysis and Synthesis of Computer Systems*. New York: Academic, 1980.

[70] A. Goldberg, G. Popek, and S. S. Lavenberg, "A validated distributed system performance model," in *PERFORMANCE '83*, A. K. Agrawala and S. K. Tripathi, Eds. Amsterdam, The Netherlands: North-Holland, 1983, pp. 251–268.

[71] N. Goodman, R. Suri, and Y. C. Tay, "A simple analytic model for performance of exclusive locking in database systems," in *Proc. 2nd ACM Symp. Database Syst.*, 1983, pp. 203–215.

[72] W. J. Gordon and G. F. Newell, "Closed queueing systems with exponential servers," *Oper. Res.*, vol. 15, pp. 254–265, 1967.

[73] A. Goyal and T. Agerwala, "Performance analysis of future shared storage systems," *IBM J. Res. Develop.*, vol. 28, pp. 95–108, 1984.

[74] U. Grenander and R. F. Tsao, "Quantitative methods for evaluating computer system performance: A review and proposals," in *Statistical Computer Performance Evaluation*, W. Freiberger, Ed. New York: Academic, 1972, pp. 3–24.

[75] G. Haring, "On state-dependent workload characterization by software resources," in *Perform. Eval. Rev. 11, Proc. 1982 ACM SIGMETRICS Conf. Meas. Modeling Comput. Syst.*, pp. 51–57.

[76] ——, "On stochastic models of interactive workloads," in *PERFORMANCE '83*, A. K. Agrawala and S. K. Tripathi, Eds. Amsterdam, The Netherlands: North-Holland, 1983, pp. 133–152.

[77] J. M. Harrison and M. I. Reiman, "On the distribution of multidimensional reflected Brownian motion," *SIAM J. Appl. Math.*, vol. 41, pp. 345–361, 1981.

[78] J. A. Hartigan, *Clustering Algorithms*. New York: Wiley, 1975.

[79] P. Heidelberger and P. A. W. Lewis, "Regression-adjusted estimates for regenerative simulations, with graphics," *Commun. ACM*, vol. 24, pp. 260–273, 1981.

[80] ——, "Quantile estimation in dependent sequences," *Oper. Res.*, vol. 32, pp. 185–209, 1984.

[81] P. Heidelberger and K. S. Trivedi, "Queueing network models for parallel processing with asynchronous tasks," *IEEE Trans. Comput.*, vol. C-31, pp. 1099–1108, 1982.

[82] ——, "Analytic queueing models for programs with internal concurrency," *IEEE Trans. Comput.*, vol. C-32, pp. 73–82, Jan. 1983.

[83] P. Heidelberger and P. D. Welch, "A spectral method for confidence interval generation and run length control in simulations," *Commun. ACM*, vol. 24, pp. 233–245, 1981.

[84] ——, "Simulation run length control in the presence of an initial transient," *Oper. Res.*, vol. 31, pp. 1109–1144, 1983.

[85] P. Heidelberger, P. D. Welch, and P. C. Yue, "Statistical analysis of database systems measurements," in *PERFORMANCE '81*, F. J. Kylstra, Ed. Amsterdam, The Netherlands: North-Holland, 1981, pp. 335–344.

[86] U. Hercksen, R. Klar, W. Kleinoder, and F. Kneissl, "Measuring simultaneous events in a multiprocessor system," in *Perform. Eval. Rev. 11, Proc. 1982 ACM SIGMETRICS Conf. Meas. Modeling Comput. Syst.*, pp. 77–88.

[87] U. Herzog, W. Hoffmann, and W. Kleinoder, "Performance modeling and evaluation for hierarchically organized multiprocessor computer systems," in *Proc. 1979 Int. Conf. Parallel Processing*, pp. 103–114.

[88] Y. C. Ho and X. Cao, "Perturbation analysis and optimization of queueing networks," *J. Optimization Theory Applications*, vol. 40,

pp. 559–582, 1983.

[89] Y. C. Ho, X. Cao, and C. Cassandras, "Infinitesimal and finite perturbation analysis for queueing networks," *Automatica*, vol. 4, pp. 439–445, 1983.

[90] J. H. Hughes, "DIAMOND — A digital analyzer and monitoring device," in *Perform. Eval. Rev. 9, Proc. PERFORMANCE '80*, 1980. *Oper. Res.*, pp. 27–34.

[91] D. L. Iglehart, "Limiting diffusion approximations for the many server queue and the repairman problem," *J. Appl. Prob.*, vol. 2, pp. 429–441, 1965.

[92] ——, "Simulating stable stochastic systems. VI. Quantile estimation." *J. Assoc. Comput. Mach.*, vol. 23, pp. 347–360, 1976.

[93] ——, "The regenerative method for simulation analysis," in *Current Trends in Programming Methodology, Vol. III: Software Modeling*, K. M. Chandy and R. T. Yeh, Eds. Englewood Cliffs, NJ: Prentice-Hall, 1978, pp. 52–71.

[94] D. L. Iglehart and W. Whitt. "Multiple channel queues in heavy traffic. I.," *Adv. Appl. Prob.*, vol. 2, pp. 150–177, 1970.

[95] ——, "Multiple channel queues in heavy traffic. II: Sequences, networks, and batches." *Adv. Appl. Prob.*, vol. 2, pp. 355–369, 1970.

[96] *PAWS/A User Guide*, Information Research Associates, Austin, TX, 1983.

[97] J. R. Jackson. "Jobshop-like queueing systems." *Mgmt. Sci.*, vol. 10, pp. 131–142, 1963.

[98] P. A. Jacobson and E. D. Lazowska. "Analyzing queueing networks with simultaneous resource procession." *Commun. ACM*, vol. 25, pp. 142–151, 1982.

[99] ——, "A reduction technique for evaluating queueing networks with serialization delays." in *PERFORMANCE '83*, A. K. Agrawala and S. K. Tripathi, Eds. Amsterdam, The Netherlands: North-Holland, 1983, pp. 45–59.

[100] A. K. Jones and P. Schwarz. "Experience using multiprocessor systems — A status report." *Comput. Surveys*, vol. 12, pp. 121–165, 1980.

[101] D. A. Jones. "Statistical investigation of factors affecting filestore performance," in *PERFORMANCE '81*, F. J. Kylstra, Ed. Amsterdam, The Netherlands: North-Holland, 1981, pp. 315–333.

[102] F. P. Kelly, *Reversibility and Stochastic Networks*. New York: Wiley, 1980.

[103] J. F. C. Kingman. "The heavy traffic approximation in the theory of queues," in *Proc. Symp. Congestion Theory*, W. Smith and W. Wilkinson, Eds. Chapel Hill, NC: Univ. North Carolina Press, 1965, pp. 137–159.

[104] J. P. C. Kleijnen. *Statistical Techniques in Simulation, Part I*. New York: Marcel Dekker, 1974.

[105] ——, *Statistical Techniques in Simulation, Part II*. New York: Marcel Dekker, 1975.

[106] L. Kleinrock, *Queueing Systems, Volume 1, Theory*. New York: Wiley, 1975.

[107] ——, *Queueing Systems, Volume 2, Computer Applications*. New York: Wiley, 1976.

[108] D. E. Knuth. "An empirical study of FORTRAN programs." *Software — Practice and Experience*, vol. 1, pp. 105–133, 1971.

[109] H. Kobayashi. "Application of the diffusion approximation to queueing networks I: Equilibrium queue distributions." *J. Assoc. Comput. Mach.*, vol. 21, pp. 316–328, 1974.

[110] ——, *Modeling and Analysis: An Introduction to System Performance Evaluation Methodology*. Reading, MA: Addison-Wesley, 1978.

[111] P. Kritzinger, S. van Wyk, and A. Krzesinski, "A generalization of Norton's theorem for multiclass queueing networks." *Perform. Eval.*, vol. 2, pp. 98–107, 1982.

[112] B. Kumar and E. S. Davidson. "Performance evaluation of highly concurrent computers by deterministic simulation." *Commun. ACM*, vol. 21, pp. 904–913, 1978.

[113] S. S. Lam and Y. L. Lien. "A tree convolution algorithm for the solution of queueing networks." *Commun. ACM*, vol. 26, pp. 203–215, 1983.

[114] D. E. Lang, T. K. Agerwala, and K. M. Chandy. "A modeling approach and design tool for pipelined central processors." in *Proc. 5th Annu. Symp. Comput. Arch.*, 1979, vol. 7, pp. 122–129.

[115] G. Latouche. "Algorithmic analysis of a multiprogramming-multiprocessor computer system." *J. Assoc. Comput. Mach.*, vol. 28, pp. 662–679, 1981.

[116] S. S. Lavenberg. "Closed multichain queueing networks with large population sizes." in *Applied Probability — Computer Science: The Interface, Volume I*, R. L. Disney and T. J. Ott, Eds. Boston, MA: Birkhauser, 1982, pp. 219–249.

[117] *Computer Performance Modeling Handbook*, S. S. Lavenberg, Ed. New York: Academic, 1983.

[118] S. S. Lavenberg. "A simple analysis of exclusive and shared lock contention in a database system," in *Perform. Eval. Rev. 12, Proc. 1984 ACM SIGMETRICS Conf. Meas. Modeling Comput. Syst.*, pp. 143–148.

[119] S. S. Lavenberg, T. L. Moeller, and P. D. Welch. "Statistical results on control variables with application to queuing network simulation," *Oper. Res.*, vol. 30, pp. 182–202, 1982.

[120] S. S. Lavenberg and M. Reiser, "Stationary state probabilities at arrival instants for closed queueing networks with multiple types of customers." *J. Appl. Prob.*, vol. 17, pp. 1048–1061, 1980.

[121] S. S. Lavenberg and C. H. Sauer. "Sequential stopping rules for the regenerative method of simulation." *IBM J. Res. Develop.*, vol. 21, pp. 545–558, 1977.

[122] S. S. Lavenberg and P. D. Welch. "A perspective on the use of control variables to increase the efficiency of Monte Carlo simulations," *Mgmt. Sci.*, vol. 27, pp. 322–335, 1981.

[123] A. M. Law. "Statistical analysis of simulation output data," *Oper. Res.*, vol. 31, pp. 983–1029, 1983.

[124] A. M. Law and J. S. Carson. "A sequential procedure for determining the length of a steady-state simulation," *Oper. Res.*, vol. 27, pp. 1011–1025, 1979.

[125] A. M. Law and W. D. Kelton, *Simulation Modeling and Analysis*. New York: McGraw-Hill, 1982.

[126] E. D. Lazowska and J. Zahorjan. "Multiple class memory constrained queueing networks." in *Perform. Eval. Rev. 11, Proc. 1982 ACM SIGMETRICS Conf. Meas. Modeling Comput. Syst.*, pp. 130–140.

[127] E. D. Lazowska, J. Zahorjan, G. S. Graham, and K. C. Sevcik. *Quantitative System Performance — Computer System Analysis Using Queueing Network Models*. Englewood Cliffs, NJ: Prentice-Hall, 1984.

[128] J. D. C. Little. "A proof of the queueing formula, $L = \lambda W$," *Oper. Res.*, vol. 9, pp. 383–387, 1961.

[129] M. H. MacDougall. "Instruction-level program and processor modeling." *Computer*, vol. 17, pp. 14–24, 1984.

[130] S. A. Mamrak and P. D. Amer. "A feature selection tool for workload characterization." in *Proc. SIGMETRICS/CMG VIII*, 1977, pp. 113–120.

[131] B. H. Margolin, R. P. Parmelee, and M. Schatzoff. "Analysis of free storage algorithms," *IBM Syst. J.*, vol. 10, pp. 283–304, 1971.

[132] R. A. Marie. "An approximate analytical method for general queueing networks." *IEEE Trans. Software Eng.*, vol. SE-5, pp. 530–538, 1979.

[133] R. L. Mattson, J. Gecsei, D. R. Slutz, and I. L. Traiger. "Evaluation techniques for storage hierarchies," *IBM Syst. J.*, vol. 9, pp. 78–117, 1970.

[134] P. F. McGehearty. "Performance evaluation of a multiprocessor under interactive workloads." Ph.D. dissertation, Dep. Comput. Sci., Carnegie-Mellon Univ., Pittsburgh, PA, 1980.

[135] J. McKenna and D. Mitra. "Integral representations and asymptotic expansions for closed Markovian queueing networks: Normal usage." *Bell Syst. Tech. J.*, vol. 61, pp. 661–683, 1982.

[136] ——, "Asymptotic expansions and integral representations of moments of queue lengths in closed Markovian networks." *J. Assoc. Comput. Mach.*, to be published.

[137] J. McKenna, D. Mitra, and K. G. Ramakrishnan. "A class of closed Markovian queueing networks: Integral representations, asymptotic expansions, and generalizations." *Bell Syst. Tech. J.*, vol. 60, pp. 599–641, 1981.

[138] H. Mechanic and W. McKay. "Confidence intervals for averages of dependent data in simulations II." IBM Corp., Yorktown Heights, NY, Tech. Rep. ASDD 17-202, 1966.

[139] D. J. Medeiros and J. T. Larkin. "Animation of output applied to manufacturing capacity analysis." in *Proc. 1983 Winter Simulation Conf.*, S. Roberts, J. Banks, and B. Schmeiser, Eds. pp. 283–286.

[140] D. Merle, D. Potier, and M. Veran. "A tool for computer system performance analysis," in *Performance of Computer Installations*, D. Ferrari, Ed. Amsterdam, The Netherlands: North-Holland, 1978, pp. 195–213.

[141] R. R. Miller. "Simulation and graphics on microcomputers," *Byte*, vol. 9, pp. 194–200, 1984.

[142] D. Mitra and P. J. Weinberger. "Probabilistic models of database locking: Solutions, computational algorithms and asymptotics." Bell Labs., Tech. Rep., 1984; also *J. Assoc. Comput. Mach.*, to be published.

[143] F. Murtagh. "A survey of recent advances in hierarchical clustering algorithms," *Comput. J.*, vol. 26, pp. 354–359, 1983.

[144] R. D. Nelson and B. R. Iyer. "Analysis of a replicated data base." IBM Corp., Yorktown Heights, NY, Res. Rep. RC 10148, 1983.

[145] M. F. Neuts, *Matrix-Geometric Solutions in Stochastic Models, An Algorithmic Approach*. Baltimore, MD: The Johns Hopkins Univ. Press, 1981.

[146] T. Nishigaki, "Experiments on the knee criterion in a multiprogrammed computer system," *IEEE Trans. Software Eng.*, vol. SE-9, pp. 79–86, 1983.

[147] J. M. Ortega and W. C. Rheinboldt, *Iterative Solution of Nonlinear Equations in Several Variables.* New York: Academic, 1970.

[148] D. Potier and P. Leblanc, "Analysis of locking policies in database management systems," *Commun. ACM*, vol. 23, pp. 584–593, 1980.

[149] C. A. Pratt, "Going further," *Byte*, vol. 9, pp. 204–208, 1984.

[150] K. G. Ramakrishnan and D. Mitra, "An overview of PANACEA, A software package for analyzing Markovian queueing networks," *Bell Syst. Tech. J.*, vol. 61, pp. 2849–2872, 1982.

[151] M. I. Reiman, "The heavy traffic diffusion approximation for sojourn times in Jackson networks," in *Applied Probability—Computer Science, The Interface, Vol. II*, R. L. Disney and T. J. Ott, Eds. Boston, MA: Birkhauser, 1982, pp. 409–422.

[152] M. Reiser, "A queueing network analysis of computer communication networks with window flow control," *IEEE Trans. Commun.*, vol. COM-27, pp. 1199–1209, 1979.

[153] ——, "Mean value analysis and convolutional method for queue-dependent servers in closed queueing networks," *Perform. Eval.*, vol. 1, pp. 7–18, 1981.

[154] M. Reiser and H. Kobayashi, "Queueing networks with multiple closed chains: Theory and computational algorithms," *IBM J. Res. Develop.*, vol. 19, pp. 283–294, 1975.

[155] M. Reiser and S. S. Lavenberg, "Mean-value analysis of closed multi-chain queueing networks," *J. Assoc. Comput. Mach.*, vol. 27, pp. 313–322, 1980.

[156] C. A. Rose, "A measurement procedure for queueing network models of computer systems," *Comput. Surveys*, vol. 10, pp. 263–280, 1978.

[157] J. H. Saltzer and J. W. Gintell, "The instrumentation of Multics," *Commun. ACM*, vol. 13, pp. 495–500, 1970.

[158] S. Salza and S. S. Lavenberg, "Approximating response time distributions in closed queueing network models of computer performance," in *PERFORMANCE '81*, F. J. Kylstra, Ed. Amsterdam, The Netherlands: North-Holland, 1981, pp. 133–145.

[159] C. H. Sauer, "Approximate solution of queueing networks with simultaneous resource possession," *IBM J. Res. Develop.*, vol. 25, pp. 894–903, 1981.

[160] ——, "Computational algorithms for state-dependent queueing networks," *ACM Trans. Comput. Syst.*, vol. 1, pp. 67–92, 1983.

[161] C. H. Sauer and K. M. Chandy, "Approximate analysis of central server models," *IBM J. Res. Develop.*, vol. 19, pp. 301–313, 1975.

[162] ——, "Approximate solution of queueing models," *Computer*, vol. 13, pp. 25–32, 1980.

[163] ——, *Computer Systems Performance Modeling.* Englewood Cliffs, NJ: Prentice-Hall, 1981.

[164] C. H. Sauer and E. A. MacNair, *Simulation of Computer Communication Systems.* Englewood Cliffs, NJ: Prentice-Hall, 1983.

[165] R. Schassberger and H. Daduna, "The time for a round trip in a cycle of exponential queues," *J. Assoc. Comput. Mach.*, vol. 30, pp. 146–150, 1983.

[166] M. Schatzoff, "Design of experiments in computer performance evaluation," *IBM J. Res. Develop.*, vol. 25, pp. 848–859, 1981.

[167] M. Schatzoff and C. C. Tillman, "Design of experiments in simulator validation," *IBM J. Res. Develop.*, vol. 19, pp. 252–262, 1975.

[168] L. W. Schruben, "Control of initialization bias in multivariate simulation response," *Commun. ACM*, vol. 24, pp. 246–252, 1981.

[169] ——, "Detecting initialization bias in simulation output," *Oper. Res.*, vol. 30, pp. 569–590, 1982.

[170] M. Schwartz, *Computer Communication Network Design and Analysis.* Englewood Cliffs, NJ: Prentice-Hall, 1977.

[171] P. Schweitzer, "Approximate analysis of multiclass closed networks of queues," in *Proc. Int. Conf. Stochastic Control and Optimization*, Amsterdam, The Netherlands, 1979.

[172] H. D. Schwetman and J. C. Browne, "An experimental study of computer system performance," in *Proc. ACM Nat. Conf.*, 1972, pp. 693–703.

[173] Z. Segall, A. Singh, R. T. Snodgrass, A. K. Jones, and D. P. Siewiorek, "An integrated instrumentation environment for multiprocessors," *IEEE Trans. Comput.*, vol. C-32, pp. 4–14, Jan. 1983.

[174] G. Serazzi, "A functional and resource-oriented procedure for workload modeling," in *PERFORMANCE '81*, F. J. Kylstra, Ed. Amsterdam, The Netherlands: North-Holland, 1981, pp. 345–361.

[175] K. C. Sevcik and I. Mitrani, "The distribution of queueing network states at input and output instants," *J. Assoc. Comput. Mach.*, vol. 28, pp. 358–371, 1981.

[176] J. G. Shanthikumar and R. G. Sargent, "A unifying view of hybrid simulation/analytic models and modeling," *Oper. Res.*, vol. 31,

pp. 1030–1052, 1983.

[177] S. W. Sherman, F. Baskett, and J. C. Browne, "Trace-driven modeling and analysis of CPU scheduling in a multiprogramming system," *Commun. ACM*, vol. 15, pp. 1063–1069, 1972.

[178] A. Singh and Z. Segall, "Synthetic workload generation for experimentation with multiprocessors," in *Proc. 3rd Int. Conf. Distributed Computing Systems*, 1982, pp. 778–785.

[179] A. J. Smith, "Sequentiality and prefetching in database systems," *ACM Trans. Database Syst.*, vol. 3, pp. 223–247, 1978.

[180] ——, "On the effectiveness of buffered and multiple arm disks," in *Proc. 5th Annu. Symp. Comput. Arch.*, 1978, vol. 6, pp. 242–248.

[181] ——, "Long term file migration: Development and evaluation of algorithms," *Commun. ACM*, vol. 24, pp. 521–532, 1981.

[182] ——, "Cache memories," *Comput. Surveys*, vol. 14, pp. 473–530, 1982.

[183] J. E. Smith, "A study of branch prediction strategies," in *Proc. 5th Annu. Symp. Comput. Arch.*, 1981, vol. 9, pp. 135–148.

[184] K. Sreenivasan and A. J. Kleinman, "On the construction of a representative synthetic workload," *Commun. ACM*, vol. 17, pp. 127–133, 1974.

[185] V. P. Srini and J. F. Asenjo, "Analysis of Cray-1S architecture," in *Proc. 5th Annu. Symp. Comput. Arch.*, 1983, vol. 11, pp. 194–206.

[186] G. W. Stewart, "Computable error bounds for aggregated Markov chains," *J. Assoc. Comput. Mach.*, vol. 30, pp. 271–285, 1983.

[187] H. M. Stewart, "Performance analysis of complex communications systems," *IBM Syst. J.*, vol. 18, pp. 356–373, 1979.

[188] M. Stonebraker, J. Woodfill, J. Ranstrom, M. Murphy, M. Meyer, and E. Allman, "Performance enhancements to a relational database system," *ACM Trans. Database Syst.*, vol. 8, pp. 167–185, 1983.

[189] R. Suri, "Infinitesimal perturbation analysis of discrete event dynamic systems: A general theory," in *Proc. 22nd IEEE Conf. Decision and Control*, San Antonio, TX, 1983.

[190] ——, "Robustness of queueing network formulas," *J. Assoc. Comput. Mach.*, vol. 30, pp. 564–594, 1983.

[191] R. Suri and M. Zazanis, "Perturbation analysis gives strongly consistent estimates for an M/G/1 queue," Harvard Univ., Cambridge, MA, Tech. Rep., 1984.

[192] A. N. Tantawi and D. Towsley, "Optimal load balancing in distributed computer systems," IBM Corp., Yorktown Heights, NY, Res. Rep. RC 10346, 1984.

[193] Y. C. Tay, "A mean value performance model for locking in databases," Ph.D. dissertation, Div. Appl. Sci., Harvard Univ., Cambridge, MA, TR-04-84, 1984.

[194] A. Thomasian, "Queueing network models to estimate serialization delays in computer systems," in *PERFORMANCE '83*, A. K. Agrawala and S. K. Tripathi, Eds. Amsterdam, The Netherlands: North-Holland, 1983, pp. 61–81.

[195] A. Thomasian and I. K. Ryu, "A decomposition solution to the queueing network model of the centralized DBMS with static locking," in *Perform. Eval. Rev., Special Issue, Proc. 1983 ACM SIGMETRICS Conf. Meas. Modeling Comput. Syst.*, pp. 82–92.

[196] D. F. Towsley, "Queueing network models with state-dependent routing," *J. Assoc. Comput. Mach.*, vol. 27, pp. 323–337, 1980.

[197] K. S. Trivedi, *Probability and Statistics with Reliability, Queueing, and Computer Science Applications.* Englewood Cliffs, NJ: Prentice-Hall, 1982.

[198] R. F. Tsao, L. W. Comeau, and B. H. Margolin, "A multi-factor paging experiment: I. The experiment and the conclusions," in *Statistical Computer Performance Evaluation*, W. Freiberger, Ed. New York: Academic, 1972, pp. 103–134.

[199] R. F. Tsao and B. H. Margolin, "A multi-factor paging experiment: II. Statistical methodology," in *Statistical Computer Performance Evaluation*, W. Freiberger, Ed. New York: Academic, 1972, pp. 135–158.

[200] S. Tucci and C. H. Sauer, "The tree MVA algorithm," IBM Corp., Yorktown Heights, NY, Res. Rep. RC 9338, 1982.

[201] J. Walrand and P. Varaiya, "Sojourn times and the overtaking condition in Jackson networks," *Adv. Appl. Prob.*, vol. 12, pp. 1000–1018, 1980.

[202] R. T. Wang and J. C. Browne, "Virtual machine-based simulation of distributed computing and networking," in *Perform. Eval. Rev. 10, Proc. 1981 ACM SIGMETRICS Conf. Meas. Modeling Comput. Syst.*, pp. 154–156.

[203] D. L. Wyatt, S. Sheppard, and R. E. Young, "An experiment in microprocessor-based distributed digital simulation," in *Proc. 1983 Winter Simulation Conf.*, S. Roberts, J. Banks, and B. Schmeiser, Eds. pp. 271–277.

[204] J. Zahorjan, "The approximate solution of large queueing network models," Ph.D. dissertation, Comput. Syst. Res. Group, Univ. Toronto, Toronto, Ont., Canada, Technical Report CSRG-122, 1980.

[205] ——, "Workload representations in queueing models of computer systems," in *Perform. Eval. Rev., Special Issue, Proc. 1983 ACM SIGMETRICS Conf. Meas. Modeling Comput. Syst.*, pp. 70–81.

Chapter 2

Processor Architecture

Modern computers use two key techniques to improve speed: pipelining and parallelism. In a pipelined machine, there can be multiple instructions, each at a different stage of completion, being executed at the same time. For example, consider a machine where instructions go through all, or most, of the following cycle:

1. Instruction Fetch;

2. Instruction Decode;

3. Operand Fetch;

4. Execute Instruction;

5. Write Back Result.

In an ideal world, we might have the situation pictured in Figure 2.1, where once the pipeline fills, there are five instructions in the machine at any one time, each in a different stage of completion. Unfortunately, there are many factors which make pipelining less efficient. All instructions do not take the same time; for example, a floating-point multiply takes much longer than an integer add. There can be competition for the hardware, with the same hardware resources being needed by more than one instruction. For example, if the instruction and operand fetch use the same hardware to access memory, only one of them can be executed at any one time. There may be data dependencies between the instructions, with one instruction producing data to be consumed by another instruction. There can be conditional branches,

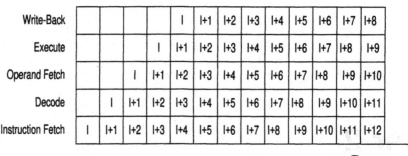

					I	I+1	I+2	I+3	I+4	I+5	I+6	I+7	I+8
Write-Back					I	I+1	I+2	I+3	I+4	I+5	I+6	I+7	I+8
Execute				I	I+1	I+2	I+3	I+4	I+5	I+6	I+7	I+8	I+9
Operand Fetch			I	I+1	I+2	I+3	I+4	I+5	I+6	I+7	I+8	I+9	I+10
Decode		I	I+1	I+2	I+3	I+4	I+5	I+6	I+7	I+8	I+9	I+10	I+11
Instruction Fetch	I	I+1	I+2	I+3	I+4	I+5	I+6	I+7	I+8	I+9	I+10	I+11	I+12

Time

Figure 2.1. An Ideal Five-Stage Pipeline

where the condition is not resolved at the moment of instruction fetch. In such a case, we do not know until we evaluate the condition, which instruction is to be fetched.

Architects have designed a variety of ways to get around these inefficiencies. Let us look at three of them.

- *Buffering:* Buffers can be used in front of the various functional units to smooth the effects of nonuniform execution times. For example, the instruction fetch unit can continue to fetch instructions sequentially and put them in a buffer, to be consumed by the instruction issuing unit at its own pace. (This will need some modifications when the system encounters a branch. See below.) Buffers can also be placed in front of adders, multipliers, etc.

- *Tagging and Forwarding:* If there is a data dependency between instructions, with instruction i producing output to be consumed by instruction j, then instruction j cannot be executed before i's output is available. The instruction issuing unit can nevertheless pick a functional unit to execute instruction j and send that unit a tag in place of the instruction i output. When the latter becomes available, it can be forwarded directly to the functional unit to replace the tag, and execution can take place. For example, if we had the following instructions

```
I1:   a := b+c;
I2:   d := a*q;
```

the instruction issuing unit can assign a multiplier to I2 even before I1 has completed. It will send the multiplier the value q and a tag as a place-holder for a. When I1 completes, the output a will replace the tag, and execution of I2 can commence.

- *Branch Prediction:* Conditional branches are a major problem for the architect. The difficulty is that before the condition is evaluated, we do not know whether the branch is going to be taken or not. For example, consider the following instructions:

48

```
I1    a := d - q;
I2    if (a .gt.  0) go to I10;
I3    ...
```

Then, until I1 completes execution and a is available, we will not be able to resolve the condition in I2. Thus, we will not know until I1 completes whether it is I3 or I10 that is to be executed after executing I2, and we will therefore not know whether to fetch I3 or I10 next.

To reduce the impact of conditional branches on performance, we can guess at whether the conditional branch will be taken or not, and fetch the next instruction based on this guess. If the guess is wrong, then some instructions will have been fetched unnecessarily, and time will have been lost. The fraction of times that the guess is right therefore affects system performance.

There are many mechanisms for guessing whether a conditional branch will be taken or not. The simplest is to use a static scheme, and guess that all branches will either be taken or not. This can be based on an analysis of the type of workload that runs on the machine. A more complex approach is to base the guess on the history of the program so far. For example, if we have encountered one particular conditional branch before, we can guess whether it will be taken or not based on how often it was taken during the past few times it was encountered.

The second approach to increasing performance is parallelism. One can have multiple processors, or multiple functional units, such as adders and multipliers. Or one can have arrays of processors (for example, linear arrays or rectangular meshes) for solving well-structured problems such as matrix multiplication, Fourier transforms, and so on. Array algorithms are characterized by an orderly flow of multiple data streams, with the spacing and delay of each stream being specified by the algorithm. The performance of the array in carrying out a given array algorithm can be estimated directly from these delays and spacings. In the former case, which applies to many mainframes, performance prediction is not easy. The performance is adversely affected by data dependencies and communication between units.

The papers included in this chapter show how to evaluate the performance of machines that use pipelining or multiple functional units.

The paper by Peuto and Shustek provides a model for using instruction timing formulas to estimate CPU performance. The model is used to estimate the performance of two mainframe machines. Although very old by computer standards, this paper provides many useful insights into the process of CPU performance evaluation.

The paper by Kleinrock and Huang deals with a generalization of *Amdahl's Law*. Amdahl's law computes the impact of serial code on the speed of parallel machines. Suppose we have software of which a fraction f can be parallelized, and $1 - f$ must be executed sequentially. If the parallelizable portion can be run in time $P(N)$ on an N-processor machine, and the code takes T_s units to run on a serial machine, an N-machine system would take a total of $T_p(N) = P(N) + (1 - f)T_s$. The speedup would then be given by

$$S(N) = \frac{T_s}{T_p(N)} = \frac{T_s}{P(N) + (1 - f)T_s}.$$

Suppose $P(N) = kfT_s/N$, where k is a constant. We will then have

$$S(N) = \frac{T_s}{kfT_s/N + (1 - f)T_s}$$

$$= \frac{N}{kf + N(1 - f)}$$

This formula indicates that when N is large, even a small sequential fraction can seriously impact the speedup. Indeed, we have

$$\lim_{N \to \infty} S(N) = (1 - f)^{-1}.$$

Kleinrock and Huang define a quantity called "power" and show how to choose the optimal number of processors for a parallel program.

The paper by Jouppi considers the effect of nonuniform distribution of parallelism on performance. The average degree of parallelism available within a program is not sufficient to make accurate performance predictions, since it may mask wide variations in parallelism over time. For example, a program which has an average requirement of three adders (because it is possible to do three additions simultaneously on the average) may have a need for just one adder over the first portion of the program and a need for ten over the last portion. This paper contains a model for nonuniform distribution of parallelism which is claimed to be quite accurate for modeling real machines.

The paper by Kurian et al. studies the impact of instruction buffering techniques. A source of constant frustration for computer designers is that there is a substantial disparity in speed between processors and memory. Various caching and buffering techniques have been constructed to reduce the impact of this disparity on overall computer performance.

The next three papers consider pipelining. All large uniprocessor machines are pipelined to improve performance. However, as we have seen, pipelined machines require more complicated control hardware and can be slowed down by conditional branches, data dependencies, resource conflicts, pipeline setup time, and the complexity of the control circuitry. These papers consider such effects and how they affect pipeline design.

The paper by Emma and Davidson looks at how to characterize branch and data dependencies in programs running on pipelined machines. Such dependencies can reduce the ability of the system to keep the pipeline filled. In general, the longer a pipeline, the greater the impact of dependencies and branches on pipeline performance. However, lengthening a pipeline also results in reducing the machine cycle time, thus potentially improving performance. This paper shows how one can resolve this tradeoff and obtain an optimal pipeline length.

The next paper, by Dubey and Flynn, continues this theme of the impact on performance of conditional branches in pipelined systems. To reduce the cost of such branches, designers have turned to loop buffers and to branch prediction. This paper provides a model of the effectiveness of such techniques.

The discussion of pipelining is rounded off by a comprehensive model by Dubey and Flynn of the performance of pipelined machines. This paper shows how to design pipelines to maximize throughput.

AN INSTRUCTION TIMING MODEL OF CPU PERFORMANCE[*]

Bernard L. Peuto[+]
Zilog, Inc.
Cupertino, California

and

Leonard J. Shustek
Stanford Linear Accelerator Center
and
Computer Science Department
Stanford University
Stanford, California

Abstract

A model of high-performance computers is derived from instruction timing formulas, with compensation for pipeline and cache memory effects. The model is used to predict the performance of the IBM 370/168 and the Amdahl 470 V/6 on specific programs, and the results are verified by comparison with actual performance. Data collected about program behavior is combined with the performance analysis to highlight some of the problems with high-performance implementations of such architectures.

Introduction

General Goals

One of the most important tasks for a computer designer is the evaluation of a computer architecture and its implementation. As two specific instances of that task, we consider (1) a comparison of the performance of the IBM 370/168 Model 1 and the AMDAHL 470 V/6, which are two machines with the same architecture but different implementations, and (2) an analysis of some of the properties of the IBM 370 instruction set.

The basic goal is to apportion the time spent by an executing program among the various system components such as the cache memory, the instruction pipeline and the individual instructions, so that resource utilization and system bottlenecks will appear. This is achieved by using models of the CPU of each machine which also provide estimates of the total CPU times. The total time is important insofar as it is used to verify the accuracy of the model, since the predicted times are compared to the actual performance of the machines.

The decision to make implementation dependent measures of CPU performance for two members of a specific architecture family has several advantages: (1) Some of the traditionally difficult problems encountered when comparing two different architectures are not present, since many confounding factors relating to performance evaluation have the same effect on both machines. (2) The success of one of the levels of a complex system can often be measured by the characteristics of the levels below. Performance evaluation which is close to the implementation level

of a computer gives valuable design information at the architecture level. (3) The speed of collection and the precision of the results are greatly enhanced by having tools that are tailored for a specific instruction set. (4) Practical and useful results can be obtained quickly, paving the way for more general studies.

Previous Studies

The evaluation of computer systems from the buyer's point of view has traditionally received a great deal of attention. The system software often requires careful and tender tuning, and bottlenecks which can have dramatic effects on performance must be identified and removed. An abundant literature addresses these problems and provides techniques for solution [AGA75].

The computer system designer has similar problems to solve, but most of the existing literature is not written for his viewpoint. One explanation for this phenomenon is the lack of feedback; users seldom complain about hardware design because they feel that their complaints will have little effect. The result is a scarcity of information for use by the designer. Most of the studies closest to this work deal with the collection of data on instruction frequencies. The most frequent objectives involve (1) benchmark studies, (2) computer design, (3) language design, and (4) general programmer curiosity.

Some studies leave all interpretation to the reader, and become a useful source of primary data [GIB, CON]. The studies most applicable to the computer designer's point of view often provide instruction frequencies, register utilization, opcode pairs, and static vs dynamic frequency comparisons, but little timing or performance information [LUN, FLY, WIN, HAN, AGA73, ANA, FOS71ab]. The language-oriented studies have provided similar information for specific languages, studying the match between the language and the machine code to which they must be translated [ALE72, HEN, ALE75].

When their interest is only in performance evaluation, users have generally been advised to use benchmark runs instead of instruction mixes based only on instruction frequencies. [ARB,SNI]. The use of timing information with these instructions mixes is made difficult by the lack of published information from the manufacturers, in particular for the high-performance machines. (Amdahl is an exception in this regard [AMD]). This has forced users to produce their own documents [LIP, EME]. The manufacturers themselves must have studied these questions, and some expurgated papers reveal glimpses of large-scale

---

[*] Work supported in part by the U.S. Energy and Research Development Administration under contract E(043)515.

[+] Work done while a Visiting Scientist at the Stanford Linear Accelerator Center.

efforts and sophisticated tools but offer little results [VAN, HUG, MUR].

The previous studies have shown that very few instructions (often four or five) represent 50% of those executed, and a few more (often 20 to 30) represent 90%. This would seem to justify the idea that a few instructions will account for most of a program's behaviour and one can neglect instructions whose frequencies are below a certain threshold. Unfortunately this applies only to a specific program. No trend has been shown in the importance of instructions, because the instructions which make up the 50%, 90% and 100% groups of a program are dependent on the program, the programmer, and the language used. The only instructions which seem universally important are the branches, which most often account for about 15-30% of the instruction counts, but which still show wide variation.

The difficulty with the frequency analysis approach is that for performance evaluation the designer needs information about the instructions which account for most of the execution time. Attempting to derive performance conclusions from an instruction frequency list yields poor results because some instructions can hundreds of times slower than others. To obtain acceptable performance results the designer needs to consider machine dependent variables because they are required for precise evaluation of the instruction execution time.

The Instruction Timing Model

The Methodology

The models of the CPUs used here are based on the instruction timing formulas available from the manufacturers' documents which describe their computers [AMD, IBM]. These documents sometimes sacrifice details for ease of exposition (which is not to say that they are easy to read!) and represent only the best efforts of an engineer to describe the existing machine. (In deriving the model for the Amdahl machine we were quite fortunate to get some help from the designers.)

The programs to be measured were traced in user state, and all the information required to compute the instruction execution time from the formulas was collected. A record was made of counts of occurrences, values of instruction variables used in the formulas, and information about memory performance. Typical variables depend on the specific instruction but may also depend on the implementation details. For example, the number of bytes moved is implementation independent, but measures of pipeline interlocks and timing delays are not. Some variables depend on instruction environment and therefore require information about instruction pair and triple distributions.

Two primary constraints caused us to trace only user-state instructions. (1) Tracing system software, with the attendant performance degradation of at least 50 to 1, would modify operating system behavior in timing dependent I/O sections. By tracing only in user mode, which is basically not speed dependent, we eliminate a source of error which would necessitate a complicated interpretation of the results. (2) Tracing the operating system introduces a large number of problems involving the recording of the trace data. One standard solution is the use of samples rather than complete traces, but then the verification of the predicted CPU time is nearly impossible.

Since the timing formulas do not include the effects of cache memory misses, the cache memory is simulated for each machine. The cache penalty is added to the instruction execution time to obtain the expected program execution time. To verify the model the expected time is compared to the operating system accounting time corrected to compensate for the differences between the measurement methods.

The effects of instruction interaction, which can generally be attributed to pipeline resource interlocks, are rather explicitly accounted for in the Amdahl formulas. For IBM, however, the pipeline effects seem to have been averaged into the formulas in a way which was not clearly indicated. This was a potential source of difficulty, but the effort required to obtain this information from the logic diagrams and microcode listings was prohibitive, and unjustified when an error of a few percent is acceptable.

The techniques used here are much more complex than benchmarking, but not as costly as total hardware simulation. The tools are general enough so they can be -- and have been -- used for other studies. The importance, however, lies in the ability to change the model variables to reflect proposed changes to the existing hardware and to accurately predict the performance effects of those changes.

Choice of Factors

The development of the CPU model has been greatly influenced by the idea of an evolving system of tools -- development by successive refinement. A crude model and simple tools were first assembled and by successive iteration new tools, new measurements, and a more refined model were designed. We think this approach reduced the number of false starts and the elapsed time of the whole study by allowing us to concentrate quickly on the most important factors.

The CPU model used is an intermediate one between full simulation at the hardware register level and a machine-independent representation of performance. The decision to include some factors and exclude others was based on our estimation, often supported by experimentation, of the effect of those factors on the final results. Some of the justification for the decisions are presented below.

The accuracy of the model is supported by the match between the program execution time as predicted by the model and the same time measured by the operating system during actual runs. Performance evaluation by benchmarking is repeatable only within 2-3% because of the large number of uncontrollable variables, and this therefore defines the required precision of the model.

An examination of previously published instruction frequencies might suggest that the more frequent instructions are those whose duration is constant and therefore do not heavily depend on execution variables like the length of operands. If this were true, then those variables could be set to program-independent values without introducing a significant error in the result. To test this hypothesis, the program which computes execution times was given three sets of execution variables with which to predict program running time. One was a programmer's best guess of the true values, and the other two were the smallest and largest extremes which could realistically be expected. The results showed that an instruction could jump from 4% to 50% of the total time depending on the value of its variables with all others remaining the same. This is an unacceptable error, especially since errors in the variables for many instructions could combine to form large systematic errors. Most of the variables which affect execution time were therefore measured exactly or estimated from related measurements.

The predicted execution time is composed of the aggregate instruction timing results and a penalty for cache memory misses. The aggregate instruction timing results have already taken into account the instruction counts and basic execution speed, as well as the pipeline interlocks. The cache miss penalty depends on the reference pattern of the program, the cache organization, and the data flow pattern within the machine. The two machines differ rather markedly in those respects: the 370/168 uses aligned doubleword (8-byte) accesses and an associative set size of 8, while the 470 accesses unaligned fullwords (4-bytes), uses a set size of 2, but has the same total amount of data (16K bytes). There are also rather significant differences in the amount and type of instruction lookahead performed. To accurately measure the cache penalty, the trace analysis program has a detailed simulation of the cache and instruction fetch mechanism of both machines.

Although cache memory miss ratios are known to be low [MER], it is easily shown that the contribution of the time penalty for the misses is too large to be neglected. If the miss ratio is 5%, with a 480 nsec penalty for a miss, 2 memory requests per instruction, and an average instruction execution time of 300 nsec (reasonable values for the 370/168) then the time for the cache misses represents 16% of the execution time.

Two other cache organization features must be considered in the cache penalty correction. For IBM, stores always access main memory ("store-through") which may cause extra delays. For Amdahl, there is an extra penalty when a 4-byte access crosses a cache line boundary. These and the other cache corrections are not attributed to the instructions which caused them, but rather accumulated separately.

The execution time reported by the operating system includes all user-state and some supervisor-state instructions [BEN], whereas the trace program measures only user-state instructions. The time attributed to these supervisor-state instructions executed in the processing of user-initiated supervisor calls (SVCs) must be subtracted from the reported CPU time. Measurements were made of the charged time for all the relevent SVCs as the programs were traced. The correction is very significant for almost all programs, since both the number and cost of the SVCs are high. For the 168, for example, the time charged varies from 107 usec for an I/O operation to 26 msec for opening a file.

Although the SVC time correction could have been measured for the original benchmark programs, they were somewhat modified in view of the substantial correction required (as much as 20%). Wherever possible, the number of I/O operations was reduced by increasing the file blocking factors, but we did not otherwise alter the operation of the programs. Despite this effort, the SVC time correction remained the factor which introduced the largest error in the measurements. We also added a FORTRAN numerical analysis program from which the I/O parts were excised, so that few supervisor services were requested.

Since supervisor-state and user-state instructions share the same cache, there will be some displacement of the user's "working set" from the cache in response to an SVC, which will manifest itself as a lower than normal hit ratio when the user's program is resumed. An unpublished note by Rossman suggested that this would have a significant effect [ROS]. To verify this we simulated the cache activity for one job with a large number of SVCs first assuming a 100% cache flush

for each SVC, and then again with no flush; the number of cache misses changed by a factor of 10. Measurements showed that the actual fraction of the cache displaced by an SVC varies from 0.16 to 1.0, and that almost all non-trivial requests completely replace the cache.

Interrupts which occur during the execution of the program do not account for a significant increase in accounted time (since the user-state CPU timer is disabled during interrupt processing) but there could be an effect due to cache displacement caused by the interrupt routine. On a heavily loaded machine interrupt rates as high as 4000 per minute are common, representing 16.4 ms of extra time (1.7% for IBM) to completely refill the cache for each second of CPU time. Since most of those interrupts are due to other jobs, this effect was reduced to a negligible level by running the job on on otherwise idle system, so that only the few interrupts caused by the benchmark job itself could cause interference. This is unlike the SVC correction, for which no change in the number of cache flushes is possible simply by controlling the environment of the benchmark run. Similar calculations for the effect of channel I/O transfers to memory show that they have even less effect on CPU performance. This is true both for IBM, where the channels transfer directly to main memory and invalidate corresponding cache entries, and for Amdahl, where the channels transfer into the cache.

Overview of the Measurement Programs

An interpretive trace program (TRACE) generates a record for each user-state instruction of the measured program. The record contains the instruction type, memory addresses referenced, and the other required information. These records are processed by a trace analysis program (ANALYSIS) which generates instruction counts, variable values, and memory access statistics such as cache memory miss counts, which are stored in a summary file. In order to avoid saving massive amounts of intermediate trace information (25 megabytes per traced second), the TRACE and ANALYSIS programs execute as coroutines. The combined overhead of the trace and trace analysis programs amounts to 300 seconds per second of real time. This compares favorably to other more detailed hardware simulations, where the overhead has been as high as 6000 seconds per second of real time [VAN].

The summary file is converted into a count file by an intermediate program (CONVERT). The count file contains all the information required to compute the timing formulas for both machines condensed into about 500 numbers. An instruction statistics program (INSTAT) uses the count file and files of encoded instruction timing formulas to produce the final timing and performance information.

We devised several test programs for verifying the formulas and understanding the measurement factors. A general instruction timing program (LTIMER) was designed for precise measurements of instruction times, cache memory miss penalties, SVC times, and the effects of SVCs on cache memory contents.

The Instruction Timing Formulas

An instruction may have several timing formulas associated with it, corresponding to different modes of execution. Each individual timing formula may depend linearly on the variables (the most common case) or have a more complicated dependence. In general, three types of linear formulas are encountered.

Some timing formulas reduce to a constant, and

often only one formula is associated with an instruction. Examples of this case are most register-to-register arithmetic or logical instructions.

ADD REGISTER	IBM	.080 usec
(AR)	Amdahl	.065 usec

Many formulas have a simple linear dependency on execution variables. An example is a Load Multiple (LM) instruction which can be expressed as

Load Multiple	IBM	.520+.080*R usec
(LM)	Amdahl	.065+.065*R usec

where R is the number of registers loaded.

Some formulas may involve variables which are concerned with the general environment of the instruction. These are often measures of the effect of pipeline interference which causes a delay in the execution of an instruction. Examples are the Amdahl variables S1 and DWD. S1 accounts for some cases of pipeline interlocks, and ranges from 0 to .065 usec depending on the "number of execution cycles attributable to the three words of the instruction stream following the instruction of interest" [AMD]. DWD, which is either 0 or .0325 usec, compensates for the occurrence of a doubleword result instruction before the subject instruction, because the machine is fundamentally single word oriented.

Store (ST)	Amdahl	.065+S1+DWD

When several formulas are associated with one instruction, each formula applies only to a specific case of its execution. For example, the Move Character instruction execution formulas depend in important ways on the degree of overlap of the two operands. The different cases involve not only different coefficients, but often different variables.

Move	IBM	.760+.040*B usec	(no overlap)
Character		.640+.240*B usec	(any overlap)
(MVC)			

Amdahl .195+S1+.130*WB+MV usec

where	MV = .130*W	(no overlap, or overlap>32 bytes)
	MV = .1625*W	(3<overlap<=32 bytes)
	MV = .130*B	(1<overlap<=3 bytes)
	MV = .195*B	(overlap=1 byte)

and where	B =	number of bytes moved
	W =	number of words moved
	WB =	number of bytes which must be moved to have the destination on a word boundary when b>63.

For all the individual linear formulas, we need only accumulate the counts and average variable values for each of the timing formula cases.

Unfortunately, some formulas are not linear in their variables. Typical examples are the decimal arithmetic instructions, where the duration depends on the product of the lengths or the average value of the digits used. For these we compute the appropriate products of variables at the time the program is analyzed, and average these values for use by the other programs in an equivalent linear form. These cases of non-linear formulas are sufficiently infrequent to justify this special treatment, but the effect on timing values is too important to ignore them. A simpler approach would assume that the product of the averages is a sufficient estimate of the average

product, but the potential error is great.

The formulas are encoded as a string of records, each corresponding to the coefficient of a term in a subcase of a timing formula for a particular instruction; there are a total of 3200 variable names and coefficient values. A numbering and naming scheme was devised that allows variables which are common to many formulas to be propagated to all appropriate places, as well as giving individual identities to variables which are more specific.

Verification of the Model

Measurement of Cache Miss Penalty

Although cache miss penalty information is available from the manufacturers, it was difficult to interpret precisely what the effect on instruction time is. Since measurements are not difficult and the correction could be significant, the values were verified experimentally. To determine the cost of a cache miss, a test program simply fills the cache with known data. A second loop is then timed, in which either the same data is reloaded, or new data displaces the old. The difference in time between the two versions of the second loop, divided by the number of cache misses caused by the loop which displaces the data, provides the cache miss time. The value found for IBM is 480 nsec, which is not inconsistent with information from the hardware manuals. For Amdahl, cache misses are found to cost 650 nsec, which also agrees with information from the designers.

Once the cache miss penalty is established, the effect of a supervisor request on the user data in the cache can be measured easily. In a similar fashion the cache is filled with known data, the SVC is issued, and the cache is refilled with the same data. The second loop is timed, and compared to the identical loop when the SVC is not present. The time difference divided by the cache miss penalty gives the number of cache lines that were displaced by the SVC. Note that the second loop must fill the cache in the opposite order from the first loop, otherwise the LRU replacement algorithm would cause the original data to be removed instead of the data added by the SVC. Table 1 shows the fraction of cache displacement for some of the more common supervisor requests.

****** TABLE 1 -- SVC TIMES AND CACHE EFFECTS (AVERAGED FOR ALL PROGRAMS)

Name	IBM		Amdahl	
	CPU time usec.	% cache displaced	CPU time usec.	%cache displaced
OPEN	26658	100%	17605	100%
CLOSE	16929	100%	13488	100%
EXCP I/O	107	58%	101	24%
WAIT	234	16%	139	7%
REGMAIN	394	30%	219	17%
LINK	3629	100%	1613	41%
OVERLAY	5214	100%	N/A	N/A

One of the most interesting differences of implementation between the two machines is the effect of data stores on the cache. The IBM approach is to always store data directly into main memory, and to update the cache only if the line already exists. The Amdahl machine updates the cache line if the data is present without storing into main memory. If the data is not in the cache, the line will be read from memory. If the replacement algorithm must remove a line which was modified in the cache, the memory is updated at the time the line is replaced. The IBM method, called "store-through", has often been criticized because it requires a main memory access for all stores [KAP]. Although the store can proceed in parallel with subsequent instructions, any subsequent main memory accesses must be suspended until the memory becomes available. Since the timing formulas do not explicitly account for this effect, it is important to determine its magnitude.

There are three factors which combine to minimize the possible deleterious effects of the store-through policy used by IBM. The first is that the memory is organized with four-way interleaving of adjacent doublewords, so that consecutive stores may well reference separate memory banks. The second is simply that based on the opcode pair distribution we have accumulated, consecutive instructions which store data into memory are relatively infrequent. The third is that even for pairs of such instructions, there appears to be a level of buffering for data that must be written to main memory, at least for the case when that data is also in the cache. A penalty appears only for the third consecutive store, and then is 360 nsec. The full write cycle time penalty of 640 nsec occurs only for the fourth and subsequent store. These factors are sufficient to justify not including a difficult-to-compute correction for store-through writes.

SVC Time Measurement

As previously discussed, the CPU time charged for SVCs was measured in order to be able to correct the time given by the operating system. The time charged for each SVC is often large and varies from program to program even for the same SVC type. To account for these variations we measured the time charged to the user for each SVC as the benchmark programs were being traced. The SVC correction computed by summing the measured SVC times is therefore quite accurate for the 168 because it was the machine used for the tracings. For the 470, the timing program LTIMER was used to give estimates of the average SVC costs. This latter method does not take into account the variation from program to program and the SVC corrections are much less accurate than for the 168. Table 1 shows the time charged for some important SVCs averaged over all programs.

It is interesting that the time charged for supervisor services is often comparable to what would be required if there were no operating system. For I/O operations, previous measurement have shown that the hardware I/O instructions (SIO, TIO, etc.) are incredibly expensive; 100 usec is not unusual [JAY]. This is to be compared with, for instance, the measured charge of 107 usec for the request to the operating system for an I/O operation. Note that both of these are more than two orders of magnitude larger than, for example, the 0.61 usec needed for a double precision floating point multiplication. It would seem that improvements in the arithmetic units of computers have not been accompanied by similar improvements in the I/O interface despite the existence of I/O channels.

The Benchmark Jobs

The results presented here are derived from the analysis of seven benchmark jobs written at SLAC. Except for one (LINSY2) they were all production jobs written for purposes other than performance evaluation. To avoid biasing the results with artifacts from specific languages or programs, we purposely chose the three most used language compilers and programs compiled by them.

(1) FORTC is a compilation by the IBM Fortran-H optimizing compiler.

(2) FORTGO is the execution of the FORTRAN program compiled by FORTC. It is a numerical analysis program which solves partial differential equations.

(3) PL1C is a compilation by the IBM PL/I-F compiler.

(4) PL1GO is the execution of a PL/I program which accumulates and prints accounting summaries from computer use information.

(5) COBOLC is a compilation by the IBM ANSI Standard COBOL compiler.

(6) COBOLGO is the execution of a COBOL program which reformats and prints computer use accounting information.

(7) LINSY2 is the execution of a FORTRAN subroutine which solves large-order simultaneous equations. No I/O is done.

Table 2 summarizes some characteristics of the benchmark jobs.

****** TABLE 2 -- PROGRAM CHARACTERISTICS

Program	# Instr.	Data reads per inst	Data writes per inst	Inst/Cache Miss	
				IBM	Amdahl
COBOLC	6,048,476	0.431	0.130	82.57	36.95
FORTGO	23,865,168	0.352	0.204	104.06	28.07
PL1GO	23,863,497	0.473	0.261	73.28	61.16
LINSY2	11,719,853	0.195	0.067	20597	19598
COBOLGO	3,559,533	0.738	0.453	13.42	30.93
FORTC	17,132,697	0.433	0.146	39.86	24.47
PL1C	24,338,101	0.379	0.137	145.33	63.48

Model validation

Verification basically consists of comparing the time predicted by our model for each benchmark job with the corrected real execution time. The time predicted for each benchmark, Tpred, consists of the following terms:

Tins, the total time predicted from the timing formulas, which does not include the cache miss penalty.

M * Tmiss, where M is the number of cache misses as reported by the cache simulator, and Tmiss is the cache miss penalty. The number of cache misses includes the effect of SVC execution on the cache contents.

Tcross, the time penalty, for Amdahl only, paid when references to the cache cross a line boundary. The penalty is two cycles (.065 usec) for reads and three cycles (.0975 usec) for writes, and is computed using numbers provided by the cache simulator. Virtually all the penalty arises from instruction fetch, since none of the programs access unaligned data. There is no equivalent penalty for IBM because its larger instruction buffer prefetches enough so that two successive doublewords can be accessed without introducing an additional delay.

The corrected time for the actual execution, Trun, consists of the following terms:

Tacc, the time as given by the standard IBM accounting routines.

56

Tsvc, the time attributed to the user for the execution of all the supervisor calls, which must be subtracted from Tacc.

Table 3 provides the values for each of these times for each of the benchmarks. For Tpred and Trun, the relative percentage of each of their components is given. The absolute error, Trun-Tpred, and the percent error, (Trun-Tpred)/Trun, appears on the last lines. The verification process points to large discrepancies between raw execution speed (Tins) and the speed as perceived by the user (Tacc).

The results for IBM are generally extremely good; for all except one program the differences between the predicted and actual running time are less than 2%. The agreement for Amdahl is not as good, but we attribute most of the error to the crude method for measuring the SVC time correction. A factor of two in the the SVC correction, which is certainly conceivable when an OPEN as measured on the 168 can vary from 6 to 33 msec, could easily account for all the the error.

****** TABLE 3 -- MODEL AND BENCHMARK TIMES

COBOLC	IBM		Amdahl		RATIO
	Time	%	Time	%	IBM/Amd
Tins	2.213	98.44	1.179	88.45	1.878
M*Tmiss	.035	1.56	.106	7.95	.330
Tcross			.048	3.60	
Tpred	2.248	100.00.	1.333	100.00	1.686
Tacc	2.57	100.00	1.71	100.00	1.503
-Tsvc	.348	13.54	.320	18.71	1.088
Trun	2.222	86.46	1.390	81.29	1.599
Trun-Tpred	-.026		-.057		
% error	-1.170		-4.101		

FORTGO	IBM		Amdahl		RATIO
	Time	%	Time	%	IBM/Amd
Tins	6.176	98.25	3.286	83.81	1.879
M*Tmiss	.110	1.75	.553	14.10	.199
Tcross			.082	2.09	
Tpred	6.286	100.00	3.921	100.00	1.60
Tacc	6.42	100.00	N/A		
-Tsvc	.082	1.28			
Trun	6.338	98.72			
Trun-Tpred	.052				
% error	0.82				

PL1GO	IBM		Amdahl		RATIO
	Time	%	Time	%	IBM/Amd
Tins	4.561	96.69	2.233	85.88	2.042
M*Tmiss	.156	3.31	.254	9.77	.614
Tcross			.113	4.35	
Tpred	4.717	100.00	2.600	100.00	1.814
Tacc	5.45	100.00	3.42	100.00	1.594
-Tsvc	.293	5.38	.206	6.02	1.422
Trun	5.157	94.62	3.214	93.98	1.604
Trun-Tpred	.440		.614		
% error	8.53		19.10		

LINSY2	IBM		Amdahl		RATIO
	Time	%	Time	%	IBM/Amd
Tins	1.970	100.00	1.561	96.48	1.262
M*Tmiss	.000	0.00	.000	0.00	1.000
Tcross			.057	3.52	
Tpred	1.970	100.00	1.618	100.00	1.218
Tacc	1.98	100.00	1.69	100.00	1.172
-Tsvc	.040	2.02	.031	1.83	1.290
Trun	1.940	97.98	1.659	98.17	1.169
Trun-Tpred	-.030		.041		
% error	-1.55		2.47		

COBOLGO	IBM		Amdahl		RATIO
	Time	%	Time	%	IBM/Amd
Tins	4.291	97.13	2.451	95.67	1.751
M*Tmiss	.127	2.87	.075	2.93	1.693
Tcross			.036	1.40	
Tpred	4.418	100.00	2.562	100.00	1.724
Tacc	4.82	100.00	2.92	100.00	1.651
-Tsvc	.428	8.88	.289	9.90	1.481
Trun	4.392	91.12	2.631	90.10	1.669
Trun-Tpred	-.026		-.069		
% error	-0.59		2.62		

FORTC	IBM		Amdahl		RATIO
	Time	%	Time	%	IBM/Amd
Tins	3.711	94.74	1.886	77.62	1.968
M*Tmiss	.206	5.26	.455	18.72	.452
Tcross			.089	3.66	
Tpred	3.917	100.00	2.430	100.00	1.612
Tacc	4.64	100.00	3.10	100.00	1.497
-Tsvc	.652	14.05	.430	13.87	1.62
Trun	3.988	85.95	2.670	86.13	1.494
Trun-Tpred	.071		.239		
% error	1.78		8.95		

PL1C	IBM		Amdahl		RATIO
	Time	%	Time	%	IBM/Amd
Tins	7.372	98.93	3.846	88.94	1.917
M*Tmiss	.080	1.07	.250	5.78	.320
Tcross			.228	5.27	
Tpred	7.452	100.00	4.324	100.00	1.723
Tacc	8.16	100.00	4.93	100.00	1.655
-Tsvc	.794	9.73	.388	7.87	2.046
Trun	7.366	90.27	4.542	92.13	1.622
Trun-Tpred	-.086		.218		
% error	-1.17		4.80		

Analysis of Results

Opcode Distributions

It has been observed many times that very few opcodes account for most of a program's execution. The COBOLC program, for example, uses 84 of the available 183 instructions, but 48 represent 99.08% of all instructions executed, and 26 represent 90.28%. Table 4 gives the opcodes which account for at least 50% of all instructions executed for each of the benchmark jobs. In addition to the frequencies of execution, the table gives the fraction of execution time attributable

57

to each of the instructions listed. Note that it is common for an instruction to have a ratio of 2 to 5 in execution time percentage versus execution frequency. For example, the "Move Chararacter" (MVC) instruction in the COBOLC job represents 3.92% of all instructions executed, but accounts for 14.97% of IBM execution time, and 16.47% of the Amdahl execution time. In contrast, the "load" (L) instruction in the COBOLGO job represents 16.58% of all instructions executed, but accounts only for 1.65% of IBM execution time, and 1.57% of Amdahl execution time.

****** TABLE 4 -- OPCODE FREQUENCY DISTRIBUTIONS

COBOLC

	Inst Name	%of Inst Count	% of Execution Time IBM	Amdahl
1	BC	22.32	18.81	13.83
2	LA	7.10	2.52	2.37
3	L	6.21	2.03	2.07
4	TM	4.87	1.60	1.62
5	CLI	4.19	1.37	1.40
6	MVC	3.92	14.97	16.47
7	BCR	3.31	2.84	2.64
	Totals	51.91	44.15	40.40

FORTGO

	Inst Name	%of Inst Count	% of Execution Time IBM	Amdahl
1	L	14.05	6.54	6.64
2	AR	12.06	3.74	5.70
3	LE	11.12	5.17	5.26
4	STE	10.54	9.80	5.33
5	ST	7.81	7.27	3.95
	Totals	55.58	32.52	26.87

PL1GO

	Inst Name	%of Inst Count	% of Execution Time IBM	Amdahl
1	L	28.17	17.68	19.56
2	MVI	15.86	23.23	12.61
3	AR	14.84	6.21	10.31
	Totals	58.66	47.12	42.48

LINSY2

	Inst Name	%of Inst Count	% of Execution Time IBM	Amdahl
1	LR	17.96	8.55	10.11
2	AR	13.10	6.24	7.39
3	BC	12.46	21.70	12.35
4	SR	7.28	3.46	4.10
	Totals	50.80	39.94	33.94

COBOLGO

	Inst Name	%of Inst Count	% of Execution Time IBM	Amdahl
1	L	16.58	1.65	1.57
2	AP	10.72	15.45	10.63
3	ZAP	8.96	16.03	10.70
4	BCR	9.92	2.20	1.75
5	MVC	7.31	8.48	8.85
	Totals	52.49	43.82	33.49

FORTC

	Inst Name	%of Inst Count	% of Execution Time IBM	Amdahl
1	L	27.47	15.22	16.22
2	BC	13.01	18.76	14.65
3	ST	12.16	13.47	7.60
	Totals	52.64	47.45	38.47

PL1C

	Inst Name	%of Inst Count	% of Execution Time IBM	Amdahl
1	BC	24.40	24.78	19.49
2	LA	7.77	3.34	3.20
3	CLI	6.76	2.68	2.78
4	L	5.26	2.08	2.16
5	MVC	4.31	16.35	19.73
6	BCR	3.96	4.07	3.90
	Totals	52.47	53.30	51.26

The most commonly executed instructions are often not the ones which account for most of the execution time. Table 5 shows the instructions which, for each of the programs, represent at least '50% of the execution time. Some of the more exotic and many of the variable-length instructions of the 370 architecture now demonstrate their influence; Divide

****** TABLE 5 -- OPCODE TIME DISTRIBUTIONS

COBOLC

	------ IBM ------			------Amdahl ------		
	Name	%Inst Time	%Exec Count	Name	%Inst Time	%Exec Count
1	BC	18.81	22.31	MVC	16.47	3.92
2	MVC	14.97	3.92	BC	13.83	22.32
3	STM	11.47	2.19	XC	9.65	0.49
4	LM	8.38	2.77	EX	8.31	2.08
5	CLC	6.07	2.72	LM	7.70	2.77
	Totals	59.70	33.92		55.97	31.58

FORTGO

	------ IBM ------			------Amdahl ------		
	Name	%Inst Time	%Exec Count	Name	%Inst Time	%Exec Count
1	STE	9.80	10.54	BXLE	11.22	5.33
2	BXLE	7.41	5.33	DR	11.13	0.94
3	LM	7.41	1.98	L	6.64	14.05
4	ST	7.27	7.81	LM	6.14	1.98
5	DR	7.16	0.94	AR	5.70	12.06
6	STM	6.66	0.67	DER	5.58	0.87
7	L	6.54	14.05	STE	5.33	10.54
	Totals	52.24	41.32		51.74	45.77

PL1GO

	------ IBM ------			------Amdahl ------		
	Name	%Inst Time	%Exec Count	Name	%Inst Time	%Exec Count
1	MVI	23.23	15.86	L	19.56	28.17
2	L	17.68	28.17	MVI	12.61	15.86
3	BC	9.53	5.37	AR	10.31	14.84
4	ST	8.99	7.16	BC	8.36	5.37
	Totals	59.43	56.55		50.84	64.23

LINSY2

	------ IBM ------			------Amdahl ------		
	Name	%Inst Time	%Exec Count	Name	%Inst Time	%Exec Count
1	BC	21.70	12.46	MDR	17.48	3.10
2	MDR	11.27	3.10	BC	12.35	12.46
3	LR	8.55	17.96	LR	10.11	17.96
4	STD	8.17	5.72	STD	10.02	5.72
5	AR	6.24	13.11	AR	7.38	13.11
	Totals	55.92	52.35		57.34	52.35

COBOLGO

	------ IBM ------			------Amdahl ------		
	Name	%Inst Time	%Exec Count	Name	%Inst Time	%Exec Count
1	DP	18.65	1.47	DP	32.76	1.47
2	ZAP	16.03	8.96	ZAP	10.70	8.96
3	AP	15.45	10.72	AP	10.63	10.72
	Totals	50.14	34.00		54.09	21.15

FORTC

	------ IBM ------			------Amdahl ------		
	Name	%Inst Time	%Exec Count	Name	%Inst Time	%Exec Count
1	BC	18.76	13.01	L	16.22	27.47
2	L	15.22	27.47	BC	14.65	13.01
3	ST	13.47	12.16	ST	7.60	12.16
4	STM	7.64	0.79	LM	5.69	1.21
5	BCR	6.37	4.67	BCR	5.64	4.67
6	LM	6.02	1.21	STM	5.52	0.79
	Totals	67.48	59.31		55.32	59.31

PL1C

	------ IBM ------			------Amdahl ------		
	Name	%Inst Time	%Exec Count	Name	%Inst Time	%Exec Count
1	BC	24.78	24.40	MVC	19.73	4.31
2	MVC	16.35	4.31	BC	19.49	24.40
3	TRT	5.38	1.00	EX	5.42	1.10
4	STM	4.41	0.68	BAL	5.06	3.08
5	BCR	4.07	3.96	TRT	4.13	1.00
	Totals	54.98	34.35		53.82	33.89

Decimal (DP) accounts for 18.65% of the Amdahl time for COBOLGO, and Translate and Test (TRT) accounts for 5.38% of the IBM time for PL1C. The particular strengths and weaknesses of the implementations are apparent; the Amdahl implementation of DR suffers in comparison to IBM (FORTGO), whereas IBM fares rather poorly on STM. Certain dips in performance are clearly evident, and two such examples appear in COBOLC. The Execute (EX) instruction, which the Amdahl designers expected not to be important, is a particularly obvious problem, and has been noted before [EME]. The Exclusive Or Character (XC) instruction, which accounts for 8.31% of the execution time, is almost always a case of overlap discussed later, which IBM optimized but Amdahl did not.

Instruction Length

The 370 architecture has three instruction lengths: 2, 4, and 6 bytes, which loosely correspond to register to register, register to memory, and memory to memory instructions. Table 6 gives the fraction of each type encountered and the average instruction length. The average instruction length does not vary considerably from program to program; the range is 2.92 to 4.49, with most programs around 3.6 bytes. The only exceptions are the COBOL programs, for which 6-byte storage to storage instructions predominate, and the LINSY2 program, for which 2-byte register to register instructions predominate. Although the average does not vary considerably, the proportion of 4-byte instructions varies from 46% to 81%, and similarly 2-byte instructions vary from 15% to 60%. The high fraction of 2-byte instructions for LINSY2 results from the fact that most of the instructions executed are part of a short (26 byte) inner loop that was highly optimized by the compiler.

TABLE 6 -- INSTRUCTION LENGTHS

Program	%2-byte	%4-byte	%6-byte	Average
COBOLC	16.15	75.91	7.94	3.836
FORTGO	29.02	70.69	0.29	3.425
PL1GO	16.99	82.37	0.64	3.673
LINSY2	53.96	46.04	0.00	2.920
COBOLGO	14.74	45.77	39.49	4.495
FORTC	18.52	80.86	0.62	3.642
PL1C	17.20	75.45	7.35	3.803

Branch Opcode Analysis

For most programs studied, branch instructions represent a considerable fraction of all instructions executed (usually 15% to 30%). In five of the seven programs traced, at least one of the branch instructions (usually the simple conditional branch BC) appears in the 50% group.

In Table 7, the column marked '% Count' indicates the fraction of all instructions executed that were potential branch instructions. The column marked '% Success' which follows, shows the fraction of those potential branches that were successful. In the 370 architecture there are two classes of branches: unconditional branches, and conditional branches whose success depends on values at execution time. Each class contains both successful and unsuccessful branches. The only unusual subclass is the unconditionally unsuccessful branch, which is a no-op instruction. The second part of Table 7 shows the fraction of branches in each of these four subclasses as a fraction of all potential branches encountered.

Branch instructions can create difficulties for pipelined implementations of computer architectures. The instruction fetch mechanism is often a stage in the pipeline which is independent of the instruction decoder, and therefore does not recognize branch instructions. A naive implementation results in a large number of unnecessary instruction fetches following a branch instruction, since the recognition of the need to fetch instuctions from the branch target comes too late.

To address this problem the 168 has a rather sophisticated mechanism by which both the instructions following the potential branch and the instructions at the branch target are fetched into two separate sets of instruction buffers. Although the fraction of success for potential branches seems to be a fairly consistent 60-80%, table 8 demonstrates that it depends heavily on the particular type of branch instruction. The designers of the 168 accounted for this fact by having the instruction fetch mechanism use the specific opcode of the branch to estimate the likelihood of success.

TABLE 7 -- ANALYSIS OF BRANCH INSTRUCTIONS

Program	%Brnchs	%Success	Unconditional %Succ	Unconditional %Unsucc	Conditional %Succ	Conditional %Unsucc
COBOLC	31.26	61.75	35.01	6.22	26.74	32.03
FORTGO	13.49	81.81	31.89	6.62	49.92	12.57
PL1GO	6.65	76.04	11.80	9.17	64.25	14.78
LINSY2	14.13	49.34	0.29	0.05	49.64	50.01
COBOLGO	15.78	71.23	35.87	2.75	35.36	26.02
FORTC	21.60	64.41	24.59	3.22	39.82	32.37
PL1C	35.27	67.65	33.50	4.03	34.15	28.32

TABLE 8

INSTRUCTIONS WHICH CAUSED BRANCHES, SORTED BY FREQUENCY

OPCODE		COUNT	% OF BRANCHES	% SUCCESS FOR THIS OPCODE
47	BC	1343374	56.365%	60.260% OF 2229306
07	BCR	555745	23.318%	69.504% OF 799591
87	BXLE	272120	11.418%	92.208% OF 295116
05	BALR	97030	4.071%	53.303% OF 182036
46	BCT	81041	3.400%	96.562% OF 83926
45	BAL	19646	0.824%	100.000% OF 19646
86	BXH	14387	0.604%	25.434% OF 56565
06	BCTR	3	0.000%	0.009% OF 34229
0A	SVC	1	0.000%	0.420% OF 238
		2383347	100.00%	

In contrast, the 470 simply treats branch instructions as if they had memory operands, and uses the normal memory operand fetch mechanism to fetch the first two words at the branch target location. Pipeline complexity is minimized by having the execution unit determine the results required for conditional branches as early as possible. This is consistent with the very successful philosophy of the Amdahl designers to keep the pipeline as simple as possible. Since we generally find that branch instructions represent a smaller percentage of the execution time for the 470 than the 168, it appears as though the decision to use a simpler mechanism was a good one.

Branch and Execution Distances

One of the common criticisms of the 370 architecture involves the absence of program-counter-relative branch instructions. Table 9 is a typical branch distance distribution which supports this attack, since 75-85% of the branch distances are within 2048 bytes of the program counter. The displacement of 12 bits used in RX branch instructions could therefore have been used for most branches so that base registers would have been unnecessary for most program references. The fact that 50–60% of the branch distances are within 128 bytes of the program counter indicates that even an 8-bit displacement could be used to considerable advantage.

Although 95–99% of the longer branch distances are within 32K bytes, there are still a substantial number of longer branches (8M bytes and above) representing calls to supervisor routines far from the user's program area.

Most programs show a few important peaks in the branch distance distribution corresponding to the important program loops. Note that the asymmetry around the program counter is not sufficient to justify other than a symmetric signed displacement for relative branch instructions.

****** TABLE 9

BRANCH DISTANCES FOR SUCCESSFUL BRANCHES

(RELATIVE TO THE ADDRESS OF THE INSTRUCTION
FOLLOWING THE BRANCH INSTRUCTION.)

INTERVAL		COUNT	CUM % FROM -2
-8388608 TO	-16777214	438	36.51%
-4194304 TO	-8388606	0	36.47%
-2097152 TO	-4194302	0	36.47%
-1048576 TO	-2097150	0	36.47%
-524288 TO	-1048574	0	36.47%
-262144 TO	-524286	11	36.47%
-131072 TO	-262142	0	36.47%
-65536 TO	-131070	0	36.47%
-32768 TO	-65534	5797	36.47%
-16384 TO	-32766	36522	35.97%
-8192 TO	-16382	36939	32.85%
-4096 TO	-8190	22100	29.68%
-2048 TO	-4094	23397	27.79%
-1024 TO	-2046	16830	25.79%
-512 TO	-1022	24076	24.35%
-256 TO	-510	36941	22.28%
-128 TO	-254	31159	19.12%
-64 TO	-126	65120	16.45%
-32 TO	-62	69591	10.87%
-16 TO	-30	46926	4.91%
-8 TO	-14	10160	0.90%
-4 TO	-6	292	0.03%
-2 TO	2	43204	3.70%
4 TO	6	109920	13.11%
8 TO	14	119401	23.34%
16 TO	30	97510	31.69%
32 TO	62	38946	35.03%
64 TO	126	44641	38.85%
128 TO	254	36311	41.96%
256 TO	510	45227	45.83%
512 TO	1022	38096	49.10%
1024 TO	2046	41504	52.65%
2048 TO	4094	28314	55.08%
4096 TO	8190	23357	57.08%
8192 TO	16382	30697	59.70%
16384 TO	32766	37796	62.94%
32768 TO	65534	5956	63.45%
65536 TO	131070	0	63.45%
131072 TO	262142	0	63.45%
262144 TO	524286	10	63.45%
524288 TO	1048574	0	63.45%
1048576 TO	2097150	0	63.45%
2097152 TO	4194302	0	63.45%
4194304 TO	8388606	0	63.45%
8388608 TO	16777214	438	63.49%

TOTAL 1167627

Table 10 shows information related to execution distances, which is defined to be the number of bytes of instructions executed between successful branch instructions. The last column gives the equivalent distance in number of instructions, obtained by dividing the average execution distance by the average instruction length for that program. It would seem to be a reasonable estimate of the true average number of instructions between successful branches.

****** TABLE 10 — EXECUTION DISTANCE

Program	Average	Std. Dev.	Avg. # Inst
COBOLC	19.86	17.25	5.18
FORTGO	28.52	31.03	8.33
PL1GO	69.40	34.11	18.89
LINSY2	41.40	25.92	14.17
COBOLGO	33.96	48.07	7.56
FORTC	26.05	25.08	7.15
PL1C	15.94	13.51	4.19

For most programs, the average execution distance is surprisingly small (less than 32 bytes, which is the cache line size) but the standard deviation is large. There are often isolated peaks for relatively large execution distances (see Table 11). With the exception of the PL1GO program, which has the highest average execution distance, 77% to 85% of execution distances are less than 32 bytes. Distances less than 16 bytes account for 40–60% of the execution distances. This tends to justify the choice of 32 bytes for the linesize of the cache on both machines, at least as far as instruction fetch is concerned. This is also consistent with older designs for instruction fetch buffers, such as the IBM 360/91 which has a 64 byte instruction stack.

****** TABLE 11

EXECUTION DISTANCES

AVERAGE LENGTH 33.964 BYTES
(7.556 INSTRUCTIONS OF AVG
LENGTH 4.495 BYTES)

LENGTH (BYTES)	COUNT	CUM %
0	0	0.0 %
2	0	0.0 %
4	12830	3.21%
6	61386	18.55%
8	24800	24.75%
10	18364	29.34%
12	44346	40.43%
14	26190	46.97%
16	12370	50.07%
18	55437	63.92%
20	12826	67.13%
22	12717	70.31%
24	8272	72.38%
26	2931	73.11%
28	15868	77.08%
30	5058	78.34%
32	114	78.37%
34	1926	78.85%
36	3552	79.74%
38	2	79.74%
40	1574	80.13%
42	2886	80.85%
44	1	80.85%
46	8049	82.87%
48	100	82.89%
50	5601	84.29%
52	0	84.29%
54	228	84.35%

Opcode Pairs

The measurement of opcode pair frequencies confirms that the overall frequency of an opcode is not independent of the surrounding instructions. Pair occurrences are also important in performance analysis because of pipeline interlocks and other miscellaneous issues such as memory store-through. Table 12 gives the five most frequent opcode pairs for each program. It is not uncommon for the measured frequency of those pairs to be 4 to 9 times greater than the product of the individual opcode frequencies.

An examination of the frequent opcode pairs fails to discover any pair which occurs frequently enough to suggest creating additional instructions to replace it. Many of the instruction pairs which do occur frequently are those that when combined would save only one opcode field since the other instruction fields would still be

****** TABLE 12 — OPCODE PAIR DISTRIBUTIONS

COBOLC	First Instr	Second Instr	% Pair Count	% Freq. Product	RATIO
1	TM	BC	4.74	1.09	4.36
2	CLI	BC	4.08	0.93	4.36
3	CLC	BC	2.67	0.61	4.40
4	BC	CLI	2.57	0.93	2.75
5	BC	TM	2.00	1.09	1.84

FORTGO	First Instr	Second Instr	% Pair Count	% Freq. Product	RATIO
1	LE	ST	7.37	1.72	6.29
2	ST	AR	5.34	1.27	4.20
3	AR	AR	5.29	1.45	3.64
4	AR	BXLE	5.28	0.64	8.21
5	BXLE	LE	5.13	0.59	8.66

PL1GO	First Instr	Second Instr	% Pair Count	% Freq. Product	RATIO
1	MVI	MVI	7.65	2.51	3.05
2	AR	AR	7.65	2.20	3.47
3	AR	L	7.16	4.18	1.71
4	L	AR	6.67	4.18	1.60
5	L	A	6.00	1.71	3.50

LINSY2	First Instr	Second Instr	% Pair Count	% Freq. Product	RATIO
1	LR	SR	7.26	1.31	5.55
2	BC	LR	6.65	2.24	2.97
3	SLL	LD	5.39	0.40	13.54
4	LR	SLL	5.22	1.01	5.19
5	LR	AR	4.72	2.35	2.00

COBOLGO	First Instr	Second Instr	% Pair Count	% Freq. Product	RATIO
1	L	BCR	5.79	1.48	3.92
2	AP	NI	5.20	0.72	7.28
3	L	CVD	4.21	0.79	5.31
4	NI	L	3.96	1.11	3.58
5	BCR	L	3.73	1.48	2.52

FORTC	First Instr	Second Instr	% Pair Count	% Freq. Product	RATIO
1	BC	L	6.29	3.57	1.76
2	L	L	6.19	7.54	0.82
3	ST	L	4.03	3.34	1.21
4	L	BCR	3.76	1.28	2.94
5	L	ST	3.66	3.34	1.09

PL1C	First Instr	Second Instr	% Pair Count	% Freq. Product	RATIO
1	CLI	BC	6.54	1.65	3.96
2	BC	LA	4.20	1.90	2.22
3	BC	CLI	3.76	1.65	2.28
4	TM	BC	2.93	0.79	3.71
5	CR	BC	2.26	0.58	3.89

required. Examples of this nature are test or compare instructions followed by conditional branches (TM/BC, C/BC). Many other frequent pairs are artifacts of the program structure; a simple example is the pair which consists of a loop branch and its target instruction. Alexander [ALE75] mentions the load-branch pair as an extremly frequent one for the XPL compiler (L-BC is 12.4% of the count). We find no pairs with such high frequencies, and in particular find the load-branch combination to be significant only in two of the seven programs. Frequent pairs often result from peculiarities of software conventions; the subroutine-call instruction (BALR) is often followed by the unconditional branch (BC) because the first instruction in almost all subroutines is a branch around the name of the program. For the FORTGO program, the extra branches (which could be easily eliminated by putting the name before the first instruction of the subroutine) cost 0.70% of the execution time of the entire program. Many of the programs have a similar extra cost of between 0.5% and 1.0% due to the same convention.

The distinction between the distribution of instruction pairs executed and the static distibution of instruction pairs in the program text should be carefully made. Our results do not contradict findings based on static analysis [FOS71a, HEH] that certain pairs of instructions might be frequent enough to justify replacement by a single instruction to improve code density.

Registers and Address Calculation

The 370 architecture expresses addresses as the sum of a 24 bit base value in a register with a 12 bit displacement in the instruction. Some instructions allow an additional 24 bit quantity in another register to be used as an index. In all cases specification of register 0 for the base or index indicates that a value of zero is to be used in lieu of the contents of the register. The hardware does not distinguish between registers which contain addresses and registers which contain index values, so the interpretation of statistics about base and index register utilization are difficult to relate to the program organization. Nevertheless information about the occurrence of zero in the register fields can be easily interpreted. Table 13 shows that it is very infrequent for instructions to specify the use of both index and base registers. Except for the program LINSY2, which is known to have many array references, 80% to 95% of the indexed instructions do not use both base and index registers. A reorganization of the 370 addressing modes could profitably include a non-indexed mode in which the space saved is used for a longer displacement.

****** TABLE 13

REGISTER USE FOR RX-INSTRUCTION
EFFECTIVE ADDRESS CALCULATION

Program	%No Regs	%1 Reg	%2 Reg
COBOLC	0.39	95.51	4.09
FORTGO	0.96	77.25	21.79
PL1GO	0.09	82.05	17.86
LINSY2	0.24	65.04	34.72
COBOLGO	0.01	98.93	1.06
FORTC	4.08	87.95	7.97
PL1C	1.93	92.48	5.59

The distribution of register utilization for address calculation shows that no more than 3 registers account for most of the use. The others are used for address calculation less frequently, or are used for program accumulators.

Operand Lengths

The TRACE program accumulates the distribution of the lengths of all the operands for instructions for which the operand lengths are not implied by the opcode. These operand lengths are either fixed and defined in other fields of the instructions (like the number of registers specified in the Load Multiple instruction), or are data dependent (like the number of bytes which must be referenced before an inequality is detected in a Compare Character instruction). These variables are required to calculate the instruction execution times.

For the purposes of exposition we have divided the variable operand length instructions into three classes: (1) the multiple register load and store instructions (LM and STM), (2) the character manipulation instructions, like Move Character (MVC), and Compare Character (CLC), and (3) the decimal arithmetic instructions like Add Decimal (AP).

LM/STM. The STM and LM instructions save and load a contiguous set of registers designated by a starting and ending register. From one to sixteen registers may be moved by a single instruction. Table 14 shows a typical distribution (from FORTGO) of the number of registers stored and loaded. It is common for there to be two peaks, one for a low value of about 2 to 3 registers for accessing data stored in consecutive words, and another at a high value of 11 to 15 registers for saving and restoring registers across procedure calls. The LM and STM are not used symmetrically: for a given number of registers loaded or stored the frequency counts are often quite different. For the FORTGO program, the average number of registers used for STM is 13.23, and for LM is 5.99. For both machines, the marginal cost of storing one more register is smaller than the execution time of a load or store instruction, but there is a higher overhead for starting each instruction for IBM than for Amdahl. In both cases it is faster to use several store or load instructions when 3 or fewer registers are involved. Despite the fact that these instructions are never among the most frequent, they contribute much more to the CPU time than their frequency would suggest because of their long execution time. For the FORTGO program for example, the 0.67% of instructions which are STM account for 6.66% of the IBM execution time and 4.59% of the Amdahl execution time.

Character Instructions. The second group of storage-to-storage (SS) instructions are those which specify a source and destination location for a character string and a single length for both operands in the range 1 to 256. One of the characteristics of these instructions that makes their implementation very difficult is that overlapped operands are allowed and must be treated a byte at a time. This allows, for example, a single byte to be propagated throughout a string by a move instruction whose destination address is one greater than the source address, since the fields are processed left to right. Lower performance machines in the 370 family implement these instructions in all cases by processing each byte individually, but for high performance machines this would be too slow. Therefore both computers exhibit execution speeds for the non-overlapped cases which are much higher than that for overlapped. For the IBM Move Character instruction, for example, the non-overlapped case takes 40 nsec per byte moved, but 240 nsec per byte of overlapped move.

On jobs for which MVC is a frequent instruction (PL1C and COBOLC) we find that the nonoverlapped case occurs about 50 times more frequently than the overlapped case. However, the average number of bytes

****** TABLE 14

LENGTH DISTRIBUTION FOR STM

#REGS	#TIMES	PERCENT
2	17982	11.223
3	521	0.325
5	1082	0.675
6	839	0.524
8	1	0.001
9	4	0.002
10	3471	2.166
11	77	0.048
12	3741	2.335
15	128589	80.259
16	3911	2.441
AVG:	13.231 REGS	

LENGTH DISTRIBUTION FOR LM

#REGS	#TIMES	PERCENT
2	151704	35.174
3	19726	4.574
4	25302	5.866
5	63802	14.793
6	897	0.208
7	10	0.002
8	30146	6.990
9	1105	0.256
10	3392	0.786
11	127559	29.576
12	3741	0.867
13	1	0.000
14	519	0.120
15	1	0.000
16	3392	0.786
AVG:	5.989 REGS	

moved is less than 8 for the nonoverlapped move, and greater than 50 for the overlapped move. The result is that the 2% of the MVCs which are overlapped are responsible for 20% of the total MVC time.

The overlapped MVC instructions are used primarily to fill a work area with a specific character, and are probably most used to initialize I/O buffers. This is confirmed by the peaks near 80 and 133 which correspond to card and line printer buffers. For programs which don't otherwise use MVC but still do I/O, the overlapped case is an even higher fraction of all occurrences of MVC. For FORTC, for example, the 6% overlapped MVCs account for 52% of the MVC time.

Table 15 is the distribution of operand length for MVC instruction in FORTC. It is representative of the other distributions in the presence of large peaks for small values, and an overall average of 10.06 bytes. Since the startup overhead for these instructions is large, there is almost always a less expensive way to do the equivalent operation for a small number of bytes. For one byte, a IC/STC combination takes less than half the time of a one-byte MVC on both machines.

Most of the other instructions in this variable operand class are much less frequent than MVC. Among them are the instructions for which the number of bytes processed may be much smaller than indicated in the instruction, such as Compare Character (CLC) and Translate and Test (TRT). For these instructions, the distribution of the length specified in the instructions is a poor indicator of the length actually used. A typical examples is COBOLC, where the average CLC instruction specifies 4.53 bytes, but an average of

****** TABLE 15

LENGTH DISTRIBUTION FOR MVC

BYTES	#TIMES	PERCENT
1	24263	52.518
2	2809	6.080
3	957	2.071
4	12871	27.860
5	898	1.944
6	64	0.139
7	10	0.022
8	34	0.074
9	4	0.009
10	3	0.006
11	3	0.006
12	2	0.004
13	1	0.002
14	10	0.022
15	5	0.011
16	5	0.011
17	2	0.004
18	1	0.002
19	1	0.002
20	11	0.024
21	8	0.017
22	9	0.019
23	2	0.004
24	9	0.019
25	14	0.030
26	1	0.002
27	2	0.004
28	9	0.019
29	1	0.002
30	2	0.004
32	6	0.013
33	8	0.017
43	2	0.004
46	1	0.002
48	3	0.006
54	1	0.002
55	447	0.968
70	7	0.015
79	495	1.071
80	1367	2.959
81	872	1.887
89	2	0.004
90	14	0.030
120	21	0.045
132	942	2.039

TOTAL: 46199.
AVG: 10.062 BYTES

only 1.744 bytes are examined by the hardware.

Another instruction of note is the Exclusive Or Character (XC) which is predominately used in total overlap mode in order to zero fields. This fact was used to advantage in the 168, where the total overlap case is specially optimized to be 15 times faster than the other overlap cases. This was not done for the 470, which explains that XC accounts for 9.6% of the COBOLC program for the 470, but only 3.0% for the 168.

Decimal Instructions. The third group of storage-to-storage instructions consist primarily of those for decimal arithmetic. They appear in significant numbers only in the COBOLGO program. For that program, however, they account for 26.29% of the count, and represent 66.39% of the IBM execution time and 64.30% of the Amdahl execution time. These instructions can vary in execution time by as much as 16 to 1 depending on the operand lengths, but the large execution time arises despite the fact that relatively short operands are common. Most operands are 2 to 6

bytes long even though the maximum possible is 16. The average execution time of the Divide Decimal (DP) instruction is about 15 usec for both machines. Not suprisingly, the average instruction execution rate for the COBOLGO program (.810 MIPS for IBM, 1.353 MIPS for Amdahl) is drastically smaller than the average for all the programs (3.519 MIPS for IBM, 5.518 MIPS for Amdahl). Considering the popularity of COBOL as a programming language, these instructions, which require slow serial byte processing, represent a major degradation of the speed of the machines.

In view of the poor performance of many of the variable operand length instructions, their inclusion in the the architecture of a high-performance computer is questionable. The absence of such instructions in machines like the CDC 7600 and the CRAY-1 is indicative of their emphasis on high speed. The arithmetic which must occur before these instructions begin their data transfer suggests that it is quite difficult to optimize them for short operands. A compromise, if the execution of these instructions cannot be optimized, may be to supply simpler instructions from which the more complex character and decimal instructions can be composed, as illustrated by the byte instructions of the PDP-10. An immediate improvement could be obtained if compilers were to replace these instructions by faster equivalents when they are available, but this would require tailoring the compilers to specific models of the computer series.

Cache Effects

The correction due to cache misses ranges from 1% to 5% for IBM, but from 3% to 19% for Amdahl, indicating that the memory subsystem is a major bottleneck for the Amdahl machine. In some sense the memory architecture forces the 470 to lose some of the raw speed advantage of the CPU. There are two factors which contribute to the problem. The cache organization of the Amdahl machine produces from 1.7 to 3 times the number of cache misses, and the penalty for each miss is 1.56 times that for IBM. Thus the overall cache penalty for Amdahl is 2.5 to 4 times more than IBM, whereas the raw execution speed, defined as Tins (the time required to execute the instructions with no cache misses) is 1.9 times faster than IBM. The loss due to the cache organization could have been eliminated, but to maintain the raw speed advantage would have required a cache miss penalty of 250 nsec, which would not have been economically feasible at the time. The dilemma of Amdahl may result from a mismatch between the MOS memory chips available commercially and its proprietary ECL LSI technology which is far more advanced.

Pipeline Effects for the 470

Because the timing formulas for the Amdahl machine include specific pipeline variables, we can assess their effect on the execution. The pipeline is optimized for 4-byte instructions which have single word operands, and any deviation causes potential conflicts with subsequent instructions.

The seven pipeline variables depend upon local instruction sequences (for exammple S1 and DWD described earlier), and therefore cannot be computed from global averages. The exact evaluation of these variables would require a complete and complex simulation of the pipeline at the time the program is traced. As a compromise, we use the pair and triple frequency data collected while tracing to reconstruct instruction sequences and average the variable value for each sequence.

In general, the speed degradation due to pipeline conflicts seems to be quite small. For most programs, each of the variables contributes less than 0.5% to the total execution time. The only cases of a larger contribution are when the variables affect specific instructions which occur frequently. For the COBOLGO job, an average additional 1.1 cycles (35.75 nsec) is added to each decimal instruction. This represents a 1.35% increase in execution time. For PL1GO, the doubleword store instructions result in an additional 1.17%. For LINSY2, the delay caused by late setting of the condition code needed for conditional branches adds 0.3%. Although there are wide variations, these worst case examples demonstrate the overall good design of the pipeline.

Summary

A verifiable model of CPU performance using simple and reusable tools shows that basic CPU speed as seen by the user is significantly degraded by memory and operating system effects. This performance analysis, based on instruction timing rather than frequency data, shows also that a few instructions can be disproportionately costly. Many traditional problem areas for high performance computers seem to be under control. The instruction pipeline functions well and branching has little deliterious effect. Memory can be a bottleneck, but the effects of cache store-through policies are negligible. No popular instruction pairs cause particular difficulties, and they are often program-specific artifacts.

Program usage seems to be inconsistent with high-performance implementations in some areas. Decimal arithmetic may be convenient for some applications but is disastrously slow. Storage to storage instruction operands are almost always short and those instructions have high startup costs. Some special cases allowed by the architecture (such as totally overlapped Exclusive-Or) must be individually optimized or performance will suffer. Interaction with the operating system is not only visible because of the time charged for its services, but also because it seriously affects the program miss ratio by disturbing cache memory contents.

These conclusions suggest that designers of high-performance computers should consider the following items to be important: (1) faster memory, (2) more efficient cache, (3) simple pipelines, (4) avoidance of instructions which require serial processing of small data elements, and (5) high-speed decimal arithmetic if it must be included at all.

Conclusion

The performance evaluation techniques described in this paper allow us to draw conclusions about the architecture and the implementation of two high-perfomance computers with the same architecture. The time spent by an executing program can be apportioned among the various system components. The confidence in the results derives from the verification of the model with actual performance. The accuracy exhibited by these techniques and the ability to change the timing formulas to reflect changes in an implementation allow the designer to predict the performance effects of those changes on future machines.

ACKNOWLEDGEMENTS

The considerable assistance and advice of Forest Baskett was essential to this work. John Banning was very helpful in criticizing an early version of the paper. We thank Amdahl Corporation, and specifically Kornel Spiro, Manager of Computer Architecture, for their cooperation and for the generous use of an early version of the instruction statistics program originally developed at Amdahl. We are indebted to Chuck Gray at the University of Michigan for running benchmark jobs on their Amdahl 470. The original incentive for the analysis of machine traces is due to Harry Saal. It should be emphasized that the results and discussions are strictly unrelated to any current or future architectural efforts of the manufacturers involved.

REFERENCES

[AGA73] Agarwal, D.P., "Design of an Efficient Instruction Set", Carnegie-Mellon, 12/72, 11/73

[AGA75] Agajanian, A.H., "A Bibliography on System Performance Evaluation", Computer, November 1975, pps 63-74.

[ALE72] Alexander, W.G., "How a Programming Language is Used", Computer Systems Research Group, University of Toronto, Report CSRG-10, February 1972.

[ALE75] Alexander, W.G., Wortman, D.B., "Static and Dynamic Characteristics of XPL Programs", Computer, November 1975, Vol 8, 11, pps 41-46.

[AMD] Amdahl 470V/6 Machine Reference Manual, Amdahl Corporation, Form No. MrM 1000-1, 2nd Ed., 1976, Sunnyvale, Calif.

[ANA] Anagnostopoulos, P.C., Michel, M.J., Sockut, G.H., Stabler, G.M., VanDam, "Computer Architecture and Instruction Set Design", NCC 1973, pps 519-527.

[ARB] Arbuckle, R.A., "Computer Analysis and Throughput Evaluation", Computers and Automation, January 1966, pps 12-15.

[BEN] Bencher, D., "OS/VS2 Release 1 Functional Description", SHARE XL Proceedings, March 1973, pps 320-324.

[CON] Connors, W.D., Mercer, V.S., Sorlini, T.A., "S/360 Instruction Usage Distribution", IBM Systems Development Division, Report TR 00.2025, Poughkeepsie, N.Y., May 1970.

[EME] Emery, A.R., Alexander, M.T., "A Performance Evaluation of the Amdahl 470V/6 and the IBM 370/168", CMG IV, October 1975, San Francisco.

[FLY] Flynn, M.J., "Trends and Problems in Computer Organizations", Information Processing 74, North Holland Pub. Co., pps 3-10, 1974.

[FOS71a] Foster, C.C., Gonter, R., "Conditional Interpretation of Operation Codes", IEEE Trans. on Computers, January 1971, pps 108-111.

[FOS71b] Foster, C.C., Gonter, R.H., Riseman, E.M., "Measures of Opcode Utilization", IEEE Transactions on Computers, May 1971, pps 582-584.

[GIB] Gibson, J.C., "The Gibson Mix", IBM System Development Division, Report TR 00.2043, Poughkeepsie, N.Y., 1970. Research done in 1959.

[HAN] Haney, F.M., "Using a Computer to Design Computer Instruction Sets", Carnegie-Mellon, May 1968 PhD Thesis

[HEH] Hehner, E.C.R., "Matching Program and Data Representations to a Computing Environment", Computer Systems Research Group, University of Toronto, Report CSRG-44, November 1974.

[HUG] Hughes, J.H., "A Functional Instruction Mix and Some Related Topics", International Symposium on Computer Performance Modeling Measurement and Evaluation, Cambridge, Mass., March 1976.

[IBM] IBM System/370 Model 168 Theory of Operation / Diagrams Manual, Form No. SY22-6931-6936, Volumes 1-6, IBM Corporation, Poughkeepsie, N.Y., 1974.

[JAY] Jay, R.M., National CSS Inc, Distribution at SHARE, New York, August 1975.

[KAP] Kaplan, K.R, Winder, R.O, "Cache-Based Computer Systems" Computer, March 1973, pps 30-36.

[LIP] Lipps, H., "Instruction Timing for the CDC 7600 Computer", European Organization for Nuclear Research, CERN 75-19, Geneva, December 1975.

[LUN] Lunde, A., "Evaluation of Instruction Set Processor Architecture by Program Tracing", Department of Computer Science, Carnegie-Mellon University, Pittsburgh, Pa., July 1974.

[MER] Merrill, B., "370/168 Cache Memory Performance", SHARE Computer Measurement and Evaluation Newsletter, July 1974, pps 98-101.

[MUR] Murphey, J.D., and Wade, R.M., "The IBM 360/195 in a world of Mixed Job Streams", Datamation, April 1970, pps 72-79.

[ROS] Rossmann, G.E., Palyn Associates, unpublished communication.

[SNI] Snider, D.R., et al, "Comparison of the Amdahl 470 V/6 and the IBM 370/195 Using Benchmarks", Argonne National Laboratory Report ANL-76-50, March 1976.

[VAN] VanTuyl, W.H., "An Engineering View of Performance, IBM System/370 Model 168", SHARE Computer Measurement and Evaluation Selected Papers, Volume II, p 816-829, August 1973

[WIN] Winder, R.O., "A Data Base for Computer Performance Evaluation", Computer, March 1973, pps 25-29.

On Parallel Processing Systems: Amdahl's Law Generalized and Some Results on Optimal Design

Leonard Kleinrock, *Fellow, IEEE,* and Jau-Hsiung Huang

Abstract—We model a job in a parallel processing system as a sequence of stages, each of which requires a certain integral number of processors for a certain interval of time. With this model we derive the speedup of the system for two cases: systems with no arrivals, and systems with arrivals. In the case with no arrivals, our speedup result is a generalization of Amdahl's Law. We extend the notion of "power" (the simplest definition is power = throughput/response time) as previously applied to general queueing and computer-communication systems to our case of parallel processing systems. With this definition of power we are able to find the optimal system operating point (i.e., the optimal input rate of jobs) and the optimal number of processors to use in the parallel processing system such that power is maximized. Many of the results for the case of arrivals are the same as for the case of no arrivals. A familiar and intuitively pleasing result is obtained, which states that the average number of jobs in the system with arrivals equals unity when power is maximized.

We also model a job in a way such that the number of processors required is a continuous variable that changes continuously over time. The same performance indices and parameters studied in the discrete model are evaluated for this continuous model. These continuous results are more easily obtained, are easier to state, and are simpler to interpret than for the discrete model.

Index Terms—Amdahl's Law, multiprocessing, optimal design, parallel processing, power, processor efficiency, speedup, system utilization.

I. INTRODUCTION

AS parallel computing systems proliferate, the need for effective performance evaluation techniques becomes ever more important. In this paper, we study certain fundamental performance indices, namely, *speedup*, *response time*, *efficiency*, and *power*, and solve for the optimal operating point of these systems. Specifically, by maximizing "power," we are able to find the optimal input rate of jobs and the optimal number of processors to use, given a characterization of the workload.

We model a parallel processing system as a system with a single queue of waiting jobs. Our first model (in Section IV) assumes that only a single job needs to be processed. Our second model (in Section V) allows a stream of arrivals to enter the system; however, only one job may be admitted

Manuscript received April 1, 1991; revised September 20, 1991. Recommended by E. Gelenbe. This work was supported by the Defense Advanced Research Projects Agency, Department of Defense under Contract MDA903-87-C-0663.

L. Kleinrock is with the Computer Science Department, University of California, Los Angeles, Los Angeles, CA 90024.

J.-H. Huang is with the Department of Computer Science and Information Engineering, National Taiwan University, Taipei, Taiwan.

IEEE Log Number 9105395.

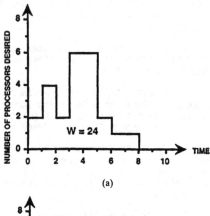

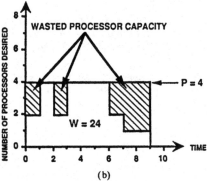

Fig. 1. Job profile. (a) Unlimited number of processors. (b) Limited number of processors ($P = 4$).

into service at a time, following a FCFS discipline, while the others wait in the queue. Both models deal with jobs as follows. While in service, the system provides a maximum of P parallel processors to work on the job. A job is modeled as a sequence of independent stages which must be processed, where the number of processors desired by the job in each stage may be different. If, for some stage, the job in service requires fewer processors than the system provides, then the job will use all that it needs and the other processors will be idle for that stage. If, for some other stage, the job in service requires more processors than the system provides, then it will use all the processors in the system (in a processor sharing fashion [10]) for an extended period of time such that the total work served in that stage is conserved. An example is given in Fig. 1 in which the total processing work required by a job is $W = 24$ s. In this example, if $P \geq 6$, then it takes 8 s to complete the job as shown in Fig. 1(a), whereas if only $P = 4$ processors are provided, then it takes 9 s as shown in

Fig. 1(b), in which case 12 s of processor capacity are wasted.

The model described above has been highly idealized. In particular, we are neglecting some of the following important aspects of the workload. First, we do not allow general precedence relations among the tasks. Our precedence structure is equivalent to a series-parallel task graph with deterministic task service times (see [6] for the definition of the task graph model of computation). Second, we do not separately model the communication times between tasks (i.e., the interprocess communication overhead). We hasten to point out that incorporating this overhead is not simply a matter of adding additional time to each task's processing time, since such overhead only occurs when a task on one processor must pass its results to a task on a different processor; thus to properly include interprocess communication costs, one must model the way in which tasks are assigned to processors (i.e., the task partitioning problem), an assignment that we choose to neglect. Third, we ignore I/O communication overhead related to the management and execution of parallel programs. Lastly, we assume that the program structure is infinitely divisible, in that the time to execute w units of work is equal to max $(w/P, w/P')$, where P is the number of processors that the system provides for execution of this work, and P' is the maximum number of processors that the program is able to use for this work (i.e., the parallelism for this work). These assumptions simplify our analysis and lead to idealized results.

Our workload model was first reported by us in [8]. Later, Gelenbe [6] described a very similar model, as did Sevcik [15]. Gelenbe extended his model, which he referred to as the "Activity Set Model," to include the effect of inefficient use of processors, imbalance of the workload among the processors, and interprocess communication times. Sevcik also described ways in which this idealized model could be extended to include the effect of I/O communications, overhead, and dependencies among parallel threads assigned to different processors.

For such a parallel processing system there are two performance measures which compete with each other: *processor efficiency* and *mean response time*. One can increase the processor efficiency of the system (by reducing the number of processors), but then the mean response time will also be increased. Similarly, one can lower the mean response time (by increasing the number of processors), but then the processor efficiency of the system will also be lowered. In this paper these two performance measures are combined into a single measure, known as *power*, which increases by either lowering the mean response time or by raising the processor efficiency of the system. We seek to find that number of processors which maximizes power.

Power, studied in [5], [11], and [12], was defined for a general queueing system in [12] as

$$\frac{\rho}{T/\overline{x}}$$

where ρ is defined as the system utilization, T is defined as the mean response time, and $\overline{x}$ is defined as the average service time. With this measure we see that an increase in system utilization (ρ) or a decrease in response time (T) increases the power. (Note that this normalized definition is such that since $0 \le \rho < 1$, and since $1 \le T/\overline{x}$, then $0 \le$ power < 1.) The symbol "*" will be used throughout to denote variables which are optimized with respect to power. In [12] it was found that for any M/G/1 queueing system [9], power is maximized when $\overline{N}^* = 1$, where $\overline{N} =$ the average number of jobs in the system. This result says that an M/G/1 system has maximum power when on the average there is only one job in the system. This result is intuitively pleasing, since it corresponds to our deterministic reasoning that the proper operating point for a single-server system is exactly when only one job is being served in the system and no others are waiting for service at the same time. In this paper, our results also show that $\overline{N}^* = 1$ when power is maximized with respect to the job arrival rate (λ).

One might argue that power, as here defined, is an arbitrary performance measure. In response to this argument we point out that one can generalize the definition of power in a way which allows the reader to emphasize delay (or efficiency) in a variety of ways so as to match his or her needs. This issue is discussed below in Section II as well as in [5] and [12]. Moreover, other researchers have seen fit to optimize power for models similar to ours (see, for example [4]). An extensive study of power applied to computer networks is given in [5].

An alternative, and much more familiar, performance measure for parallel processing systems is *speedup*, which describes how much faster a job can be processed using multiple processors, as compared to using a single processor. Specifically, speedup is the ratio of the mean response time of a job processed by a single processor to that of a job executed in a parallel processing system with, say, P processors. Speedup and power are related and we discuss how they interact throughout this paper. Eager *et al.* [4] also discuss issues similar to those in this paper. Their focus is on estimating speedup and efficiency (for the no arrivals case only) simply from the value of the "average parallelism," which is defined as W, the total processing work required by a job, divided by the time it would take to service the job if there were an unlimited number of processors available; in Fig. 1(a) we have $W = 24$, and service time $= 8$, giving an average parallelism equal to 3. They also use the definition of power as we had defined in [11] and [12] and obtain the same result as we obtain in Corollary 7 below. They consider the case of deterministic workloads. Gelenbe [6] introduced an alternate model for the workload for which he also calculates speedup in the case of an infinite number of available processors. He models a job as having a random task graph in which the density of precedence relations between tasks is given by p ($0 \le p \le 1$); he then derives an approximation for an upper bound on the speedup; namely, $(1 + p)/2p$.

II. Definitions

We have already defined the following:

$P =$ Number of (identical) processors in the server;

$W =$ Average number of seconds required to process a job on a single processor; and

$\overline{N} =$ Average number of jobs in the system.

Moreover, we now define the following additional quantities:

$\overline{x}(P) =$ Mean service time of a job in a P-processor system (note that the maximum mean service time is $\overline{x}(1) = W$ and that the minimum mean service time is $\overline{x}(\infty)$);

$T(\lambda, P) =$ Mean response time (queueing time plus service time) of a job in a queueing system with an input rate λ and P processors;

$\lambda =$ arrival rate of jobs;

$\rho =$ system utilization; i.e., the fraction of time when there is at least one job in the system.

$= \lambda\overline{x}(P)$; and

$u(P) =$ processor efficiency in a P-processor system.

Note the difference between $u(P)$, which is the average *processor* efficiency given P processors, and ρ, which is the average *system* utilization. Whenever there is a job in the system, the system utilization is "1," but the processor efficiency need not be "1" in that case, since there may be some idle processors (i.e., it may be that the job in service does not require all the processors). Hence the system utilization is always greater than or equal to the processor efficiency. (Note that $u(1) = \rho$ for a single processor queueing system.)

Two cases regarding the number of jobs in the system are considered in this paper. Case one allows no arrivals of additional jobs (Section IV). That is, there is only one job in the system, and we are concerned with $\overline{x}(P)$, its mean service time in a P-processor system. Case two allows jobs to arrive from a Poisson process at a rate λ, and so queueing effects are considered (Section V).

For the first case, we define the (no arrivals case) *speedup* with P processors, denoted by $S_n(P)$, to be

$$S_n(P) = \frac{\overline{x}(1)}{\overline{x}(P)} = \frac{W}{\overline{x}(P)}.$$

Note that

$$1 = \frac{W}{\overline{x}(1)} \le S_n(P) \le \frac{W}{\overline{x}(\infty)}.$$

Thus it is natural for us to define the maximum value for speedup $S_{n,\max}$ as follows:

$$S_{n,\max} = \frac{W}{\overline{x}(\infty)}.$$

Furthermore, we see that $S_{n,\max} =$ average parallelism.

For the second case, we define the (arrivals case) *speedup* with P processors at system utilization ρ, denoted by $S_a(\lambda, P)$, to be

$$S_a(\lambda, P) = \frac{T(\lambda, 1)}{T(\lambda, P)}.$$

We must distinguish the processor efficiency $u(P)$ in these two cases as follows:

$u_n(P) =$ processor efficiency given P processors in the no arrivals case; and

$u_a(\lambda, P) =$ processor efficiency given job arrival rate λ and P processors in the case with job arrivals.

We now introduce the appropriate definitions of *power*, which we denote by the symbol Q (we would prefer to use the obvious notation P, but P has already been used to denote the number of processors). Let

$Q_n(P) =$ power given P processors in the no arrivals case; and

$Q_a(\lambda, P) =$ power given a job arrival rate λ and P processors in the case with job arrivals.

In this paper we are concerned mostly with power which is defined as processor efficiency divided by the mean response time.

In the case of no arrivals, the mean response time of the (single) job is simply its mean service time $\overline{x}(P)$, and so:

$$Q_n(P) = \frac{u_n(P)}{\overline{x}(P)}.$$

Clearly, power will increase by either raising the processor efficiency or by lowering the mean service time. A more general definition of power (as originally introduced in [12]) is given as

$$Q_n^{(r)}(P) = \frac{[u_n(P)]^r}{\overline{x}(P)}$$

where r is a positive real number whose value may be selected by the system designer. With this generalization, a designer may express a stronger preference for an increase in the processor efficiency at the expense of an increase in the mean service time by simply increasing the value of the parameter r (and vice-versa). Note that $Q_n(P) = Q_n^{(1)}(P)$.

In the case of job arrivals, the definition of power becomes:

$$Q_a(\lambda, P) = \frac{u_a(\lambda, P)}{T(\lambda, P)}$$

and the generalization in this case is

$$Q_a^{(r)}(\lambda, P) = \frac{[u_a(\lambda, P)]^r}{T(\lambda, P)}$$

where again r is a positive real number to be used as a degree of freedom by the system designer. Note that $Q_a(\lambda, P) = Q_a^{(1)}(\lambda, P)$.

With these definitions of power, our goal is to find the optimal number of processors to use in a parallel processing system such that power is maximized. Furthermore, in the case of job arrivals, we also seek the optimal system operating point (i.e., the optimal input rate of jobs).

The rest of this paper is organized as follows. In Section III we present two models of a job: a discrete model, and a continuous model. In Section IV we solve the case when no arrivals are allowed in the system. In this case we find the speedup of the system given P processors. We also find P^*, the number of processors which maximizes power. In Section V we solve the case when job arrivals are allowed in the system. In this case we again solve for the speedup of the system given P processors. We also find λ^* and P^*, which maximize power. One interesting result we get is that the P^* for systems with no arrivals and the P^* for systems with arrivals are equal when power is maximized; this provides a simplification in system design.

68

III. WORKLOAD MODELS

We consider both a discrete as well as a continuous model of job requirements.

A. A Discrete Job Model

Here, we model a job as containing a total of $\widetilde{W}$ tasks. Nonoverlapping subsets of these tasks are collected into *stages*, and these stages are processed sequentially (however, parallelism is exploited *within* each stage—see below). $\widetilde{W}$ is a random variable with mean W and coefficient of variation c_W[1]. We assume that the service time distribution for each task is deterministic, such that each task requires 1 s of work on a processor. For the results we seek in this paper, a job is described by specifying W and c_W along with two other vectors. The first vector is called the *fraction* vector, f', and the second vector is called the *processor* vector, P'. We denote the fraction and processor vectors as

$$f' = [f_1', f_2', f_3', \cdots, f_{n'}']$$
$$P' = [P_1', P_2', P_3', \cdots, P_{n'}']$$

where n' is the number of stages in a job. The ith stage has the pair (f_i', P_i') associated with it. The meaning is as follows: a fraction f_i' of the total tasks in a job can use P_i' processors to concurrently process these tasks. For this definition, it is clear that

$$\sum_{i=1}^{n'} f_i' = 1.$$

The example from Fig. 1 is repeated in Fig. 2(a), where $W = 24$ and $n' = 6$. Stage 4 contains 12 tasks, and so $f_4' = 1/2$; moreover, since $P_4' = 6$ (and if $P \geq 6$), then it will take 2 s to complete stage 4. This stage-type workload model comes directly from the usual task graph model of computation [3] with deterministic task service times. The ith stage corresponds to the ith level in the computation graph.

For convenience, we may rearrange the elements in f' and P' as follows in such a way that neither the mean response time nor the processor efficiency are changed. The elements of P' are rearranged and renumbered so that its elements are nondecreasing; that is, $P_{i-1}' \leq P_i'$. The elements of f' follow the identical permutation and renumbering. We may then merge several stages with the same P_i''s into one stage simply by adding all the corresponding f_i''s. The new vectors will be denoted $P = [P_1, P_2, \cdots, P_n]$ and $f = [f_1, f_2, \cdots, f_n]$, where $n \leq n'$ and $P_{i-1} < P_i$. Since the system admits only one job into service at a time, it can easily be shown that this rearrangement does not affect the performance at all. The example in Fig. 2(a) has been rearranged as shown in Fig. 2(b), where the number of stages is now $n = 4$. Note that $\bar{x}(\infty) = 8$, as it was in Fig. 2(a). One can easily see that if we choose $P = 4$, then $\bar{x}(4)$ will equal 9 in this rearranged case, as was the case for Fig. 1(b).

[1] The coefficient of variation of a random variable is equal to its standard deviation divided by its mean.

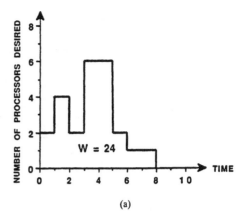

(a)

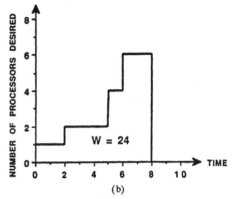

(b)

Fig. 2. Rearranging the job profile. (a) $P = [2, 4, 2, 6, 2, 1]$, $f = [\frac{1}{12}, \frac{1}{6}, \frac{1}{12}, \frac{1}{2}, \frac{1}{12}, \frac{1}{12}]$. (b) $P = [1, 2, 4, 6]$, $f = [\frac{1}{12}, \frac{1}{4}, \frac{1}{6}, \frac{1}{2}]$.

B. A Continuous Job Model

We now describe a continuous version of the above model. In this model we assume that the number of processors required by jobs is a (not necessarily discrete) nondecreasing function of time (recall the rearranging does not affect performance). That is, we permit nonintegral numbers of processors (which could correspond to cases where processors are shared among more than one job). A special model with a deterministic workload per job will be described first, and then a more general model with a random workload per job will be described.

For the special case with a deterministic workload, we define $P(t) = g(t)$, where $g(t)$ is a deterministic function, to be the number of processors that a job desires at time t ($0 \leq t \leq b$) such that $P(b) = B$ (see Fig. 3). For such a model, the workload (seconds of work required) for each job is deterministic with value

$$W = \int_0^b P(t)\, dt.$$

Note that $b = \bar{x}(\infty)$. Moreover, if we limit the number of processors to $P(P < B)$, then A, the (shaded) area of $P(t)$ which lies above the value of P, will be flattened out and extended as a rectangle of area A and of height P beginning

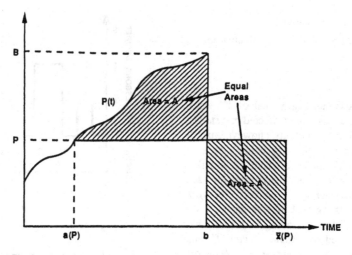

Fig. 3. A continuous job profile and the effect of a limited number of processors.

at the point b on the time axis and extending to the new mean service time $\overline{x}(P)$, as shown in Fig. 3.

For the general case with a random workload, we define

$$\widetilde{P}(t) = g\left(\frac{t}{\widetilde{K}}\right)$$

to be a random function which gives the number of processors desired by the job at time t. $\widetilde{K}$ is a random variable with mean K and coefficient of variation c_K, and g is a function such that it has a fixed maximum value B, with $0 \leq t \leq \widetilde{K}b$. The distribution of $\widetilde{K}$ affects the results given in this paper in the following simple fashion:

i) All time variables should be multiplied by $\widetilde{K}$;
ii) All mean time variables should be multiplied by $\overline{K}$; and
iii) The optimal value of P, namely P^*, is independent of the distribution of $\widetilde{K}$.

Therefore we assume that $\overline{K} = 1$ in the remainder of this paper at no loss of generality. In addition, c_K does affect some of our later expressions, and in those cases it will appear explicitly.

We remind the reader of some of the limitations of this workload model as listed in the introduction. These limitations include: the lack of full generality in the precedence structure among the tasks; the neglect of the interprocess communication overhead; the neglect of I/O processing and communication overhead; and the assumption of the infinite divisibility of the workload.

IV. SYSTEMS WITH NO ARRIVALS

In this section we examine a system of P processors serving a single job with no new arrivals. We wish to find the speedup and the value P^* which maximizes power for the processing of this job. For systems with no arrivals, we have that the processor efficiency is

$$u_n(P) = \frac{W}{P\overline{x}(P)}.$$

This follows from our earlier definition, since the system is busy for $\overline{x}(P)$ s, and in this time P processors could do

$P\overline{x}(P)$ s of work; however, they only accomplish W s of work, since some processors may occasionally be idle. From the definitions of speedup $S_n(P)$ and power $Q_n(P)$, we see that only W, P, and $\overline{x}(P)$ are involved in the definitions. Since W, P, and $\overline{x}(P)$ are not affected by the distribution of the service requirement (but only by the mean W), we conclude that both the speedup and power only depend upon the mean values. Therefore we will not see any higher moments of the job service requirements in this section. Jobs with different random service requirements will give the same results as long as they have the same means. We first study the continuous case, and then apply the results obtained to the discrete case.

A. The Continuous Case

We consider a job profile $P(t)$ such as that shown in Fig. 3. We wish to determine P^*, the optimum number of processors to use with this job, where power is the objective function we seek to maximize. We define:

$a(P) =$ length of the interval from when the job first begins service until it first requires more processors than the system supplies; i.e., $a(P) = \min(t : P(t) > P)$;

$b =$ the service time of the job if the number of processors in the system is always greater than the number of processors required by the job; i.e., $P \geq B$ (note that $b = \overline{x}(\infty)$); and

$$I(P) = \int_{a(P)}^{b} P(t)\, dt.$$

Note from Fig. 3 that $I(P) = [\overline{x}(P) - a(P)]P$. The average service time is

$$\overline{x}(P) = a(P) + \frac{\int_{a(P)}^{b} P(t)\, dt}{P}.$$

The speedup for this system is simply:

$$S_n(P) = \frac{W}{\overline{x}(P)} = \frac{PW}{Pa(P) + \int_{a(P)}^{b} P(t)\, dt}.$$

70

Theorem 1

The power $Q_n(P)$ is maximized with respect to P when $P = P^*$, where P^* is the unique (typically nonintegral) value satisfying

$$P^* = \frac{I(P^*)}{a(P^*)}.$$

Proof: Since

$$u_n(P) = \frac{W}{P\bar{x}(P)}$$

and

$$Q_n(P) = \frac{u_n(P)}{\bar{x}(P)}$$

we have:

$$Q_n(P) = \frac{W}{P[\bar{x}(P)]^2}.$$

Maximizing $Q_n(P)$ with respect to P, we require:

$$\frac{d}{dP} Q_n(P) = 0$$

which leads to the general condition

$$\frac{d\,\bar{x}(P)}{dP} = -\frac{\bar{x}(P)}{2P}.$$

At this point one must consider any problems which might arise in calculating $(d\,\bar{x}(P))/(dP)$, if $P(t)$ has: (i) any non-differentiable points, or (ii) any vertical jumps, or (iii) any horizontal segments. However, it can easily be shown for these three cases that an infinitesimal change in P can only make an infinitesimal change in $\bar{x}(P)$, since the change in the area A must be continuous (see Fig. 3). The only troublesome case is case (iii), since for any $\varepsilon > 0$, $a(P_0 + \varepsilon) - a(P_0 - \varepsilon) = c$ when $P(t)$ has a horizontal segment of length c and height P_0. This is troublesome, since $\bar{x}(P) = a(P) + (I(P))/P$, and thus $\bar{x}(P)$ appears to have a discontinuous jump at $P = P_0$; however, the term $(I(P))/P$ has an equal and opposite jump there as well, which eliminates the problem. Nevertheless, we will indeed run into a problem in uniquely defining $a(P)$ in Corollary 1, below, if $P^* = P_0$, where P_0 is any such horizontal segment height; we settle this problem further below in Corollary 7, case (ii).

From our expression for $\bar{x}(P)$ we find that the general condition given above leads us to the following expression which must be satisfied by the optimal value of P:

$$P = \frac{I(P)}{a(P)} - \frac{2P^2}{a(P)}\left[\frac{da(P)}{dP} + \frac{1}{P}\frac{dI(P)}{dP}\right].$$

Now, since $I(P) = \int_{a(P)}^{b} P(t)\,dt$, we have

$$\frac{dI(P)}{da(P)} = -P(a(P)).$$

But $a(P)$ is such that $P(a(P)) = P$, and so $(dI(P))/(da(P)) = -P$. Using the chain rule, we then have $(dI(P))/(dP) = -P(da(P))/(dP)$; therefore:

$$\frac{da(P)}{dP} + \frac{1}{P}\frac{dI(P)}{dP} = 0.$$

Thus we see that the optimal value P^* must be such that

$$P^* = \frac{I(P^*)}{a(P^*)}.$$

It can easily be shown that $(d^2 Q_n(P)) < 0$; therefore $P^* = (I(P^*))/(a(P^*))$ indeed maximizes power. □

The expression for P^* as given in theorem 1 is not especially illuminating. To help explain the meaning of theorem 1, let us state and then interpret the following corollary:

Corollary 1

Power is maximized if and only if

$$\bar{x}(P^*) = 2a(P^*).$$

Proof: Since $(I(P^*)/P^*) = a(P^*)$, and from the definition of $\bar{x}(P)$ we have that $\bar{x}(P^*) = a(P^*) + a(P^*) = 2a(P^*)$. □

Corollary 1 is one of the principal results of this paper. To interpret this corollary we note from Fig. 3 that $a(P)$ is that portion of the service time when the job has available at least as many processors as it needs. Therefore $\bar{x}(P) = 2a(P)$ implies that the portion of the service time when there are enough processors for a job equals the portion of the service time when there are not enough processors for its needs. Let us define $a(P)$ to be the "unextended service time," and $(I(P))/P$ to be the "extended service time." This corollary states that the optimal number of processors P^* must be selected so that the "unextended service time" exactly equals the "extended service time." Also note that during the unextended service time the processors are not fully utilized ($u < 1$), whereas during the extended service time the processors are fully utilized ($u = 1$). Therefore the time period for $u < 1$ equals the time period for $u = 1$.

At this point we may simplify the proof of the following theorem which appeared in [4, theorem 5]:

Theorem

Under the processor sharing discipline when the number of available processors is equal to P^*, the attained speedup is *at least* 50% of the maximum possible, the efficiency is *at least* 50%, the utilization of the last processor is *at least* 50%, and the utilization of a single additional processor is *no more than* 50%. These bounds can be achieved in the limit as $S_{n,\max} \to (\infty)$.

Proof: For any P we know that $a(P) \leq b \leq \bar{x}(P)$. For $P = P^*$, we know that $\bar{x}(P) = 2a(P)$, and so $\bar{x}(P) \leq 2b = 2\bar{x}(\infty)$. Thus

$$S_n(P) = \frac{W}{\bar{x}(P)} \geq \frac{W}{2\bar{x}(\infty)} = \frac{S_{n,\max}}{2}.$$

That is, $S_n(P)$ is at least half of the maximum achievable speedup. Moreover, all processors are continuously busy in the interval $a(P) \leq t \leq 2a(P)$, and some others may be busy in the interval $0 \leq t \leq a(P)$; thus the processor efficiency is at least 50%. Clearly, the last processor added is busy half the time ($a(P) \leq t \leq 2a(P)$). Any additional processor beyond P^* will be busy only during the interval

$a(P+1) \leq t \leq \bar{x}(P+1)$; but $a(P) < a(P+1)$ and $\bar{x}(P) = 2a(P) > \bar{x}(P+1)$, and so this additional processor efficiency is less than 50%. The attainment of the bounds in the limit is obvious. □

Let us now state the results for the case in which we select $P = P^*$ to optimize the generalized power function $Q_n^{(r)}(P)$.

Theorem 2

Generalized power

$$Q_n^{(r)}(P) = \frac{[u_n(P)]^r}{\bar{x}(P)}$$

is maximized when P^* is selected, such that

$$P^* = \frac{I(P^*)}{ra(P^*)}.$$

Proof: This theorem can easily be derived following the procedure given in the proof for theorem 1. □

Corollary 2

$Q_n^{(r)}(P)$ is maximized when P^* is selected, such that

$$\bar{x}(P^*) = (r+1)a(P^*).$$

Proof: This corollary can easily be derived following the procedure given in the proof for corollary 1. □

From corollary 2 we easily generalize the theorem [4] discussed above in the form of the following:

Theorem 3

When P^* is selected to optimize $Q_n^{(r)}(P)$, then the attained speedup $S_n(P)$ is at least a fraction $1/(r+1)$ of the maximum possible, the processor efficiency is at least $r/(r+1)$, the efficiency of the last processor added is at least $r/(r+1)$, and the efficiency of a single additional processor is no more than $r/(r+1)$.

Proof: This theorem can easily be derived following the procedure given by us in the simplified proof of the theorem [4] above. □

It is instructive to graph the result of theorem 3 as in Fig. 4. In this figure we indicate that when $P = P^*$, then one is guaranteed to lie in the shaded region. As r varies, the shaded rectangle moves from a tall thin rectangle near the right-hand border ($r \to 0$) to a square occupying the upper right-hand quarter of the figure (at $r = 1$) to a wide flat rectangle along the top border of the figure ($r \to (\infty)$). The theorem from [4] basically states the case only for $r = 1$.

Let us consider two examples to show the application of Theorem 2.

Example 1

If $P(t)$ is a linear function—i.e., $P(t) = (B/b)t$ for $0 \leq t \leq b$, and P^* is chosen to maximize the power function $Q_n^{(r)}(P)$, then we have

$$P^* = \frac{B}{\sqrt{2r+a}}$$

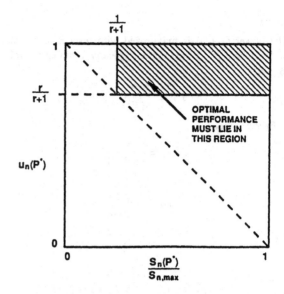

Fig. 4. Region of optimal performance.

or

$$\frac{P^*}{\text{Maximum number of processors required}} = \frac{1}{\sqrt{2r+1}}.$$

Proof: From $P(t)$ we have

$$a(P) = \frac{b}{B}P$$

$$I(P) = \int_{bP/B}^{b} \frac{B}{b}t\,dt = \frac{Bb}{2} - \frac{b}{2B}P^2.$$

Hence, since $P^* = (I(P^*))/(ra(P^*))$, we have

$$P^* = \frac{B^2 - P^{*2}}{2rP^*}.$$

Solving for P^*, we have

$$P^* = \frac{B}{\sqrt{2r+1}}.$$

Note that B is the maximum number of processors required by the job. □

In this example, by setting $r = 1$, we have $P^*/B = 1/\sqrt{3} \cong 58\%$. This is the case that was solved approximately in [13] by numerically solving a 5th-order polynomial; here we have found the *exact* value of P^* analytically.

Example 2

If $P(t) = B/(b^n)t^n$ for $0 \leq t \leq b$, and P^* maximizes $Q_n^{(r)}(P)$, then

$$P^* = \frac{B}{[(n+1)r+1]^{\frac{n}{n+1}}}$$

or

$$\frac{P^*}{\text{Maximum number of processors required}} =$$

$$\frac{1}{[(n+1)r+1]^{\frac{n}{n+1}}}.$$

Proof: This proof is similar to the proof in example 1.
□

We are now in a position to apply some of these results to the simple case of a job with two discrete stages.

B. The Discrete Case: Jobs With Two Stages

In this section a job is modeled as consisting of W tasks, of which a fraction f $(0 < f < 1)$ must be done serially (i.e., each such task can use only one processor), and of which the remaining fraction $(1 - f)$ of the tasks can be done concurrently with at most P processors, where P is the number of processors in the system. Note that this is the model used by Amdahl to derive Amdahl's Law [1], a classic result which we now state.

Amdahl's Law

The speedup of this model, given P processors, is upper bounded as follows:

$$S_n(P) \leq \frac{P}{fP + 1 - f}.$$

Proof: Since Wf of the tasks must be done serially, they will take Wf s; also, since $(1 - f)W$ of the tasks can be done concurrently with at most P processors, they will take at least $((1 - f)W)/P$ s. Therefore the mean service time $\overline{x}(P)$ is at least $Wf + ((1 - f)W)/P$. Moreover, since a single processor working alone will take W s, the speedup is simply W divided by $\overline{x}(P)$, which proves the result. □

This law implies that the speedup of the system depends very strongly on the simple workload measure f, and that the speedup may be much smaller than the number of processors, even for a relatively small f. For example, if $f = 0.1$, then one will, at best, obtain a speedup of less than 10 with 1000 times the processing capacity $(P = 1000)$[2].

For the remainder of this subsection we will make the (optimistic) assumption that $1 - f$ of the tasks can use *exactly* P processors concurrently. For this revised model, the upper bound in Amdahl's Law will be achieved. This corresponds to our discrete model of jobs for which $f = [f, 1 - f]$, and $P = [1, P]$. For a given value of f, we solve for the optimum value of P in the next theorem.

Theorem 4

Power $Q_n(P)$ is maximized when the number of processors

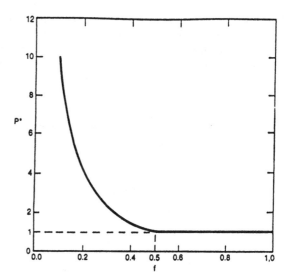

Fig. 5. The optimal number of processors for two stages $(f = [f, 1 - f]$ and $P = [1, P])$.

is selected to be[3]

$$P^* = \begin{cases} 1, & \text{if } f \geq \frac{1}{2} \\ \frac{1-f}{f}, & \text{if } f < \frac{1}{2}. \end{cases}$$

Proof: During the entire service time $\overline{x}(P) = Wf + (W(1 - f))/P$, the processing capability is $P\overline{x}(P)$; the work actually completed is simply W (since the service time for each task is 1). Hence the processor efficiency equals:

$$u_n(P) = \frac{W}{P\overline{x}(P)} = \frac{1}{Pf + 1 - f}.$$

Thus

$$Q_n(P) = \frac{u_n(P)}{\overline{x}(P)} = \frac{1}{W} \cdot \frac{P}{(Pf + 1 - f)^2}.$$

Optimizing $Q_n(P)$ with respect of P, it is easy to show that $P^* = (1 - f)/f$. However, P^* cannot be smaller than 1 (an obvious boundary condition); hence $P^* = 1$, if $(1 - f)/f \leq 1$ (or, $f \geq 1/2$). □

The result given in theorem 4 is intuitively pleasing. Fig. 5 shows the curve for P^* versus f. Note the sharp drop in P^* when f is small, and also note that $P^* = 1$ for $f \geq 1/2$.

Corollary 3

For $P^* = (1 - f)/f > 1$, the interval of time when the system is working on the serial portion of the job exactly equals the interval of time when the system is working on the parallel portion.

Proof: The service time for the serial portion of fW. The service time for the parallel portion is

$$\frac{(1 - f)W}{P^*} = fW. \qquad \square$$

---

[2] As a result of Amdahl's law, one is easily discouraged from using parallel processing. Nevertheless, experience shows in a number of cases that speedups very close to P are quite possible [2]. Gustafson explains this [7] by suggesting that as the number of processors increases, the application problem size also increases in a way such that the parallel portion of the problem grows while the serial portion remains fixed; that is, $f = f(P)$ is a decreasing function of P. In this paper we assume that f is constant, independent of P. Gelenbe [6] provides analytical evidence of this linear growth of the speedup with P by considering a model which includes the effect of a program's inability to effectively use all of the processors assigned to it, as well as the effect of imbalance of the workload across the available processors; Gelenbe shows that this linear dependence on P may be lost, however, when the effect of interprocess communication is included in the model.

[3] In this case we require $P^* \geq 1$.

Corollary 3 is similar to corollary 1, although they each apply to different environments. If we regard the service time for the serial portion as the unextended service time, and regard the service time for the parallel portion as the extended service time, then corollary 3 is exactly the same as corollary 1.

Corollary 4

At the optimal power point, the speedup is as follows:

$$S_n(P^*) = \begin{cases} 1, & \text{if } f \geq \frac{1}{2} \\ \frac{1}{2f}, & \text{if } f < \frac{1}{2} \end{cases}.$$

Proof: From Amdahl's Law and our optimistic assumption, we have

$$S_n(P) = \frac{P}{fP + 1 - f}.$$

From theorem 4 we have

$$P^* = \begin{cases} 1, & \text{if } f \geq \frac{1}{2} \\ \frac{1-f}{f}, & \text{if } f < \frac{1}{2} \end{cases}.$$

Substituting $P = P^*$ in the expression for $S_n(P)$ completes the proof. $\square$

Theorem 5

Generalized power $Q_n^{(r)}(P)$ is maximized when P^* is selected such that

$$P^* = \begin{cases} 1, & \text{if } f \geq \frac{1}{r+1} \\ \frac{1-f}{rf}, & \text{if } f < \frac{1}{r+1} \end{cases}.$$

Proof: It can be shown that

$$Q_n(P) = \frac{[u_n(P)]^r}{\bar{x}(P)} = \frac{1}{W} \cdot \frac{P}{(Pf + 1 - f)^{r+1}}.$$

Optimizing $Q_n^{(r)}(P)$ with respect to P, one finds that $P^* = (1 - f)/(rf)$. However, P^* must not be smaller than 1; hence $P^* = 1$, if $(1 - f)/(rf) \leq 1$ (or $f \geq 1/(r+1)$). $\square$

Corollary 5

For $P^* = (1 - f)/(rf) > 1$, the parallel portion of the job takes exactly r times as long to serve as does the serial portion of the job.

Proof: The service time for the serial portion is fW. The service time for the parallel portion is

$$\frac{(1-f)W}{P^*} = r \cdot fW. \qquad \square$$

Corollary 6

At the optimal power point,

$$S_n(P^*) = \begin{cases} 1, & \text{if } f \geq \frac{1}{2} \\ \frac{1}{(r+1)f}, & \text{if } f < \frac{1}{2} \end{cases}.$$

Proof: This proof is similar to the proof for corollary 4. $\square$

C. The Discrete Case in General

For the general case we assume that a job has W tasks, and that the fraction vector and processor vector (after rearrangement) are

$$f = [f_1, f_2, f_3, \cdots, f_n]$$
$$P = [P_1, P_2, P_3, \cdots, P_n]$$

where $P_i < P_{i+1}$ for $1 < i < n - 1$, and

$$\sum_{i=1}^{n} f_i = 1.$$

Before describing the next theorem we need some more notation. We assume that there are P processors available in the system. We define the index "m" such that; if $P_1 \leq P < P_n$, then m is the integer that satisfies $P_{m-1} \leq P < P_m$; or if $P \geq P_n$, then $m = n + 1$ of if $P < P_1$, then $m = 1$. Once m determined, we may define:

$$\alpha = \sum_{i=1}^{m-1} \frac{f_i}{P_i}$$

and

$$\beta = \sum_{i=m}^{n} f_i.$$

Note that αW is the unextended service time, whereas $(\beta W)/P$ is the extended service time.

Theorem 6

The speedup for any P is given by

$$S_n(P) = \frac{P}{\alpha P + \beta}.$$

Proof: The mean service time is

$$\bar{x}(P) = W\left(\sum_{i=1}^{m-1} \frac{f_i}{P_i} + \frac{1}{P}\sum_{i=m}^{n} f_i\right) = W\left(\alpha + \frac{1}{P}\beta\right).$$

Since a single processor working alone will take W s to serve a job, the speedup with P processors is simply W divided by $\bar{x}(P)$. $\square$

We can easily modify this result to obtain a generalization of Amadahl's Law. Consider a job consisting of W tasks, for which a fraction f_i of these tasks can be done using *at most* P_i processors in parallel ($i = 1, 2, \cdots, n$). Then we have the theorem below.

Theorem 7 (Generalized Amdahl's Law)

For the system just described, the speedup, given P processors, is upper bounded as follows:

$$S_n(P) \leq \frac{P}{\alpha P + \beta}.$$

Proof: This result can easily be derived following the procedure to prove Amdahl's Law and theorem 6. $\quad\square$

The maximum possible speedup $S_{n,\max}$ for the model used in theorem 6 will be achieved when $P \geq P_n$, which gives

$$\alpha = \sum_{i=1}^{n} \frac{f_i}{P_i}$$

and $\beta = 0$. Hence

$$S_{n,\max} = \frac{W}{\sum_{i=1}^{n} \frac{f_i W}{P_i}} = \frac{1}{\sum_{i=1}^{n} \frac{f_i}{P_i}}.$$

In the following two corollaries we derive P^* for the discrete case using the results from corollary 1. Corollary 7 was first obtained in [4, theorem 4].

Corollary 7[4]

Power $Q_n(P)$ is maximized when P^* satisfies either one of the following two conditions:

(i) $\quad P^* = \dfrac{\beta}{\alpha}, \qquad$ if $P_{m-1} < P^* < P_m$

or

(ii) $\quad P^* = P_{m-1}, \qquad$ if $0 \leq \dfrac{\alpha}{2} - \dfrac{\beta}{2P_{m-1}} \leq \dfrac{f_{m-1}}{P_{m-1}}.$

Proof: In case (i) there is no ambiguity in defining the unextended service time. Specifically, the unextended service time $= \alpha W$, and the extended service time $= (\beta W)/P$. From corollary 1 we must have

$$\alpha W = \frac{\beta W}{P^*}.$$

Hence

$$P^* = \frac{\beta}{\alpha}.$$

In case (ii) we encounter an ambiguity in defining the place where the unextended service time ends (and thus the extended service time begins). In order to resolve this, we break the mean service time for stage $m-1$, namely, $t_{m-1} = f_{m-1} W / P_{m-1}$, into two segments: x and $t_{m-1} - x$. We define x to be the interval in stage $m-1$ which we include in the extended service time, and the interval $t_{m-1} - x$ to be the interval in stage $m-1$ which we conclude in the unextended service time, as shown in Fig. 6. To find x, we note from corollary 1 (and assuming $P^* = P_{m-1}$) that

$$\alpha W - x = \frac{\beta W}{P_{m-1}} + x$$

which gives:

$$x = \frac{\alpha W}{2} - \frac{\beta W}{2P_{m-1}}.$$

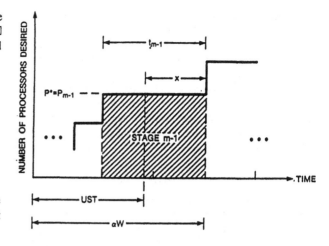

Fig. 6. Segmentation of the service time of stage $m-1$ (UST = Unextended Service Time).

Thus the unextended service time $a(P)$ is simply:

$$a(P) = \alpha W - x$$
$$= \frac{\alpha W + \frac{\beta W}{P_{m-1}}}{2}$$
$$= \frac{\overline{x}(P)}{2}$$

as demanded by corollary 1. Case (ii) will occur whenever, for some m, we have the following two conditions simultaneously true:

$$\alpha W - t_{m-1} < \frac{\beta W}{P_{m-1}} + t_{m-1}$$
$$\alpha W > \frac{\beta W}{P_{m-1}}.$$

These may be rewritten as

$$0 \leq \frac{\alpha W}{2} - \frac{\beta W}{2P_{m-1}} \leq t_{m-1}.$$

But since

$$t_{m-1} = \frac{f_{m-1} W}{P_{m-1}}$$

we have as the condition for case (ii):

$$0 \leq \frac{\alpha}{2} - \frac{\beta}{2P_{m-1}} \leq \frac{f_{m-1}}{P_{m-1}}. \qquad \square$$

Corollary 8

Generalized power $Q_n^{(r)}(P)$ is maximized when P^* satisfies either one of the following two conditions:

(i) $\quad P^* = \dfrac{\beta}{r\alpha}, \qquad$ if $P_{m-1} < P^* < P_m$

or

(ii) $\quad P^* = P_{m-1}, \qquad$ if $0 \leq \dfrac{r\alpha}{r+1} - \dfrac{\beta}{(r+1)P_{m-1}}$
$$\leq \frac{f_{m-1}}{P_{m-1}}.$$

---

[4]It is easy to show that P^* will never be greater than P_n. If $P^* > P_n$ the service time will not be improved, while the processor utilization will be less than when $P^* = P_n$; hence the power will be smaller. A similar argument shows that P^* will never be smaller than P_1.

Proof: This proof is similar to that for corollary 7. □

From corollaries 7 and 8 we develop an interactive procedure in [8] to find P^* for any given f and P. In that procedure the number of iterations is upper bounded by $\log_2 n$, which is reasonably small.

In our results of Sections IV-B and -C we have neglected the physical requirement that P^* be an integer. Clearly, if P^* must be an integer, then P^* should then be rounded up or down to the nearest integer, whichever of the two has a larger value of power.

V. Systems With Arrivals

In this section we study the case when new jobs enter the system according to a Poisson process at rate λ. We now permit random service times. This model corresponds to a parallel processing system which executes one job at a time, but which can accept and enqueue new arrivals which are later served in a first-come-first-served fashion (one at a time). The following theorem describes a property which is useful in finding many results later in this section.

Theorem 8

For all cases (continuous and discrete models), the coefficient of variation of the service time distribution (denoted as c_{x_P} when there are P processors in the system) is not a function of P. That is, for all $P \geq 1$,

$$c_{x_1} = c_{x_P}.$$

Proof: We define $\tilde{x}(P)$ to be the random variable representing the service time when P processors are available. For the continuous model, we can show that

$$\tilde{x}(P) = \tilde{K} \left[a(P) + \int_{a(P)}^{b} \frac{g(t)}{P} \, dt \right].$$

This equation shows that $\tilde{x}(P)$ equals $\tilde{K}$, multiplied by a (deterministic) constant; since this constant multiplies both the standard deviation and the mean of $\tilde{x}(P)$, it will cancel out in their ratio (i.e., the coefficient of variation), and so

$$c_{x_P} = c_K.$$

Hence c_{x_P} is not a function of P, which implies that $c_{x_1} = c_{x_P}$.

For the two-stage discrete case we have

$$\tilde{x}(P) = \widetilde{W} f + \frac{(1-f)\widetilde{W}}{P} = \widetilde{W} \left[f + \frac{(1-f)}{P} \right]$$

where $\widetilde{W}$ is a random variable representing the work brought in by a job. Hence, using a similar argument as above, we have

$$c_{x_P} = c_{x_1} = c_W.$$

Similarly, for the general discrete case we have

$$\tilde{x}(P) = \widetilde{W} \alpha + \frac{\beta \widetilde{W}}{P} = \widetilde{W} \left[\alpha + \frac{\beta}{P} \right].$$

Hence, using the same argument as above, we have

$$c_{x_P} = c_{x_1} = c_W.$$
□

We can show that

$$\widetilde{W} = \int_{0}^{\tilde{K}b} g\left(\frac{t}{\tilde{K}} \right) dt = \tilde{K} \int_{0}^{b} g(t) dt.$$

Since

$$\int_{0}^{b} g(t) dt$$

is a constant, this equation shows that the work brought in by a job is a random variable which has the same coefficient of variation as $\tilde{K}$.

A. Finding the Speedup

In this section we find the speedup for all cases. We discover that the speedup when queueing is allowed is the same as the speedup when queueing is not allowed!

Theorem 9

For all cases (continuous and discrete models), we have

$$S(\lambda, P) = S_n(P).$$

Proof: We have defined ρ to be the system utilization; hence

$$\rho = \lambda \bar{x}(P).$$

Since only one job can be admitted into service at a time, this system can be analyzed as a single-server queueing system. Hence we can apply results from M/G/1 theory [8] to find the average response time for this system. That is,

$$T(\lambda, P) = \bar{x}(P) \left[1 + \rho \frac{1 + c_{x_P}^2}{2(1 - \rho)} \right].$$

In theorem 8 we have shown that $c_{x_1} = c_{x_P}$ for all cases; thus we find the speedup as

$$S_a(\lambda, P) = \frac{T(\lambda, 1)}{T(\lambda, P)} = \frac{\bar{x}(1)}{\bar{x}(P)} = S_n(P).$$
□

Therefore the speedup $S_a(\lambda, P)$ and the speedup $S_n(P)$ are solely determined by the job specification $P(t)$ and P (and not affected by the system's operating point λ) in our models. (Another interesting model studied in [8] has $S_a(\lambda, P) \neq S_n(P)$).

Corollary 9

For the continuous model, we have

$$S_a(\lambda, P) = \frac{P \int_{0}^{b} P(t) \, dt}{P a(P) + \int_{a(P)}^{b} P(t) \, dt}.$$

Proof: This can easily be proved from the expression for $\bar{x}(P)$ and theorem 9. □

76

Corollary 10

For the two-stage discrete model, we have

$$S_a(\lambda, P) = \frac{P}{fP + 1 - f}.$$

Proof: This can easily be proved from the optimistic model of Amdahl's Law and theorem 9. □

Corollary 11

For the general discrete model, we have

$$S_a(\lambda, P) = \frac{P}{\alpha P + \beta}.$$

Proof: This can easily be proved from theorem 6 and 9. □

B. The Optimal Arrival Rate

In this section we find the optimal operating point (λ^*) for both the discrete case and continuous case. Even though the definitions of power in this paper and in [12] are different (since $\rho \neq u_a(\lambda, P)$), the results obtained in both papers are the same. Therefore all the deterministic reasoning given in [12] also applies in this paper.

Theorem 10

Power $Q_a(\lambda, P)$ is maximized when $\lambda = \lambda^*$ (for a given P), such that

$$\lambda^* = \frac{2}{2 + \sqrt{2 + 2c_{x_P}^2}} \cdot \frac{1}{\overline{x}(P)}.$$

Proof: When we allow arrivals we must calculate the processor efficiency over all time. The rate at which seconds of work enter the system is λW, and the maximum rate at which the processors can discharge work is P. Thus

$$u_a(\lambda, P) = \frac{\lambda W}{P}.$$

From M/G/1 theory we have

$$T(\lambda, P) = \overline{x}(P)\left[1 + \rho \frac{1 + c_{x_P}^2}{2(1 - \rho)}\right]$$

$$= \overline{x}(P)\left[\frac{2 + (c_{x_P}^2 - 1)\lambda\overline{x}(P)}{2(1 - \lambda\overline{x}(P))}\right]$$

where $\rho = \lambda\overline{x}(P)$. Defining power as earlier, we have

$$Q_a(\lambda, P) = \frac{u_a(\lambda, P)}{T(\lambda, P)}$$

$$= \frac{\lambda W}{P} \cdot \frac{2(1 - \lambda\overline{x}(P))}{2 + (c_{x_P}^2 - 1)\lambda\overline{x}(P)} \cdot \frac{1}{\overline{x}(P)}.$$

Maximizing power with respect to λ, we have

$$\lambda^* = \frac{2}{2 + \sqrt{2 + 2c_{x_P}^2}} \cdot \frac{1}{\overline{x}(P)}. \qquad □$$

Corollary 12

When power is maximized with respect to λ,

$$\rho^* = \frac{2}{2 + \sqrt{2 + 2c_{x_P}^2}}$$

and

$$\overline{N}^* = 1.$$

Proof: From theorem 10 we trivially show that

$$\rho^* = \lambda^*\overline{x}(P) = \frac{2}{2 + \sqrt{2 + 2c_{x_P}^2}}.$$

Using Little's result [14], it is easy to show that

$$\overline{N}^* = \lambda^*T(\lambda^*, P) = 1. \qquad □$$

The result given above for $\overline{N}^*$ is intriguing. Indeed, $\overline{N}^* = 1$ corresponds to the same deterministic reasoning given in [12] and which is described in our introduction.

Theorem 11

Generalized power $Q_a^{(r)}(\lambda, P)$ is maximized when $\lambda = \lambda^*$ (for a given P) such that

$$\lambda^* = \frac{4r}{(-c_{x_P}^2 + 3)r + (c_{x_P}^2 + 1) + b(r)} \cdot \frac{1}{\overline{x}(P)}$$

where

$$b(r) = \sqrt{(c_{x_P}^4 + 2c_{x_P}^2 + 1)r^2 + 2(-c_{x_P}^4 + 2c_{x_P}^2 + 3)r + (1 + c_{x_P}^2)^2}.$$

Proof: This proof is similar to the proof for Theorem 10. □

Corollary 13

When power is maximized with respect to λ, then

$$\rho^* = \frac{4r}{(-c_{x_P}^2 + 3)r + (c_{x_P}^2 + 1) + b(r)}$$

$$\overline{N}^* = \frac{2r\left[(1 + c_{x_P}^2)r + b(r) + (1 + c_{x_P}^2)\right]}{(c_{x_P}^4 - 1)r^2 + 2(2 - c_{x_P}^2)(1 + c_{x_P}^2)r + \left[(1 - c_{x_P}^2)r + (1 + c_{x_P}^2)\right]b(r) + (c_{x_P}^2 + 1)^2}$$

If $r \gg 1$, we have

$$\lim_{r \gg 1} \rho^* = 1 - \frac{1}{r}$$

and

$$\lim_{r \to \infty} \frac{\overline{N}^*}{r} = \frac{1 + c_{x_P}^2}{2}.$$

Note that the results in Theorem 11 and corollary 13 are the same as in [12].

C. The Optimal Number of Processors (P^*)

In this section we first study the relationship between $Q_n(P)$ and $Q_a(\lambda, P)$. From the result below we show that there are many cases in which P^* for a system with no arrivals and P^* for a system with arrivals are the same!

We may express the utilization $u_a(\lambda, P)$ for systems with arrivals in terms of the utilization $u_n(P)$ for system with no arrivals as follows:

$$u_a(\lambda, P) = (\text{processor utilization})$$
$$= (\text{processor utilization}|\text{system busy})$$
$$\cdot P[\text{system busy}]$$
$$+ (\text{processor utilization}|\text{system idle})$$
$$\cdot P[\text{system idle}]$$
$$= (\text{processor utilization}|\text{system busy})$$
$$\cdot P[\text{system busy}].$$

Thus we come to the simple conclusion that

$$u_a(\lambda, P) = u_n(P) \cdot \rho.$$

Substituting $u_a(\lambda, P) = \rho u_n(P)$ into the definition of power, we find that

$$Q_a(\lambda, P) = \frac{u_a(\lambda, P)}{T(\lambda, P)} = \frac{\rho u_n(P)}{T(\lambda, P)}$$
$$= \frac{\rho}{T(\lambda, P)/\overline{x}(P)} \cdot \frac{u_n(P)}{\overline{x}(P)}.$$

Since $(u(P))/(\overline{x}(P)) = Q_n(P)$ and $\rho/(T(\lambda, P)/\overline{x}(P)) = (2\rho(1-\rho))/(2 - \rho + \rho c_{x_P}^2)$ for M/G/1, we finally have

$$Q_a(\lambda, P) = \frac{2\rho(1-\rho)}{2 - \rho + \rho c_{x_P}^2} \cdot Q_n(P).$$

Note that $\rho/[T(\lambda, P)/\overline{x}(P)]$ is simply the normalized power discussed in [12] and in the introduction.

Let us now discuss the optimal number of processors P^*. When the system is operating at the optimal operating point (λ^*), we have

$$Q_a(\lambda^*, P) = \frac{2\rho^*(1 - \rho^*)}{2 - \rho^* + \rho^* c_{x_P}^2} \cdot Q_n(P).$$

Note that

$$\frac{2\rho^*(1 - \rho^*)}{2 - \rho^* + \rho^* c_{x_P}^2}$$

is only a function of c_{x_P} (since ρ^* is also a function of c_{x_P} only as shown in corollary 12) and, in particular, is not a

function of P; therefore for cases where c_{x_P} is not a function of P, then P^* for $Q_a(\lambda^*, P)$ is the same as P^* for $Q_n(P)$. That is, for c_{x_P} not a function of P, we have systems with

P^*(for systems with no arrivals) =
$$P^*(\text{for systems with arrivals}).$$

For the generalized definition of power, we have

$$Q_a^{(r)}(\lambda, P) = \frac{[u_a(\lambda, P)]^r}{T(\lambda, P)} = \frac{\rho^r [u_n(P)]^r}{T(\lambda, P)}$$
$$= \frac{\rho^r}{T(\lambda, P)/\overline{x}(P)} \cdot \frac{[u_n(P)]^r}{\overline{x}(P)}$$
$$= \frac{2\rho^r(1 - \rho)}{2 - \rho + \rho c_{x_P}^2} \cdot Q_n^{(r)}(P).$$

Using the same argument as above (i.e., for c_{x_P} not a function of P), we have systems with the property

P^*(for systems with no arrivals) =
$$P^*(\text{for systems with arrivals}).$$

Therefore all the results for evaluating P^* obtained in Section IV can be used here. However, not every model has this characteristic. In [8], another model is discussed in which c_{x_P} is indeed a function of P. In that case, a numerical procedure is required to find P^*.

Corollary 14

For the continuous model, power is maximized when P^* is chosen such that

$$P^* = \frac{I(P^*)}{a(P^*)}$$

and

$$\lambda^* = \frac{1}{a(P^*)\left(2 + \sqrt{2 + c_K^2}\right)}.$$

Proof: This is easily derived from theorems 1 and 10. $\square$

Corollary 15

For the two-stage discrete model, power $Q_a(\lambda, P)$ is maximized when

$$\lambda^* = \frac{1}{fW\left(2 + \sqrt{2 + 2c_W^2}\right)}$$

and the optimal number of processors is

$$P^* = \begin{cases} 1, & \text{if } f \geq \frac{1}{2} \\ \frac{1-f}{f}, & \text{if } f < \frac{1}{2} \end{cases}.$$

Proof: This is easily derived from theorems 4 and 10. $\square$

VI. Conclusion

For the model which allows no arrivals we found the speedup $(S_n(P))$ for any P and for the optimal number of processors (P^*) which maximizes power. This $S_n(P)$ was shown to be a generalization of Amdahl's Law. For the model which allows arrivals we found the speedup $(S_a(\lambda, P))$ for any P, the optimal arrival rate (λ^*), and the optimal number of processors (P^*) which maximizes power. It was interesting to find that $S_n(P)$ is the same as $S_a(\lambda, P)$ for the models studied in this paper. It was also interesting to find that P^* for a system with no arrivals is the same as P^* for a system with arrivals when power is maximized. In all cases we found that power is optimized when P^* is chosen so that the unextended service time equals the extended service time. This characteristic makes optimal design (in terms of maximizing power) easier, because the same solution applies to both cases!

Our results apply to an idealized workload model which neglects the degradation to system performance due to certain sources of overhead; consequently, these results must be viewed simply as approximate indicators of choices in any practical system design process.

References

[1] G. M. Amdahl, "Validity of the single processor approach to achieving large scale computing capabilities," *Proc. AFIPS*, vol. 30, 1967.
[2] R. E. Benn, J. L. Gustafson, and R. E. Montry, "Development and analysis of scientific application programs on a 1024-processor hypercube," Sandia Nat. Labs., Albuquerque, NM, Tech. Rep. SAND 88-0317, Feb. 1988.
[3] E. G. Coffman and P. J. Denning, *Operating System Theory*. Englewood Cliffs, NJ: Prentice-Hall, 1973.
[4] D. L. Eager, J. Zahorjan, and E. D. Lazowska, "Speedup versus efficiency in parallel systems," *IEEE Trans. Computers*, vol. 38, pp. 408–423, Mar. 1989.
[5] H. R. Gail, "On the optimization of computer network power," Ph.D. diss., Computer Sci. Dept., UCLA, Sept. 1983.
[6] E. Gelenbe, *Multiprocessor Performance*. New York: Wiley, 1989.
[7] J. L. Gustafson, "Re-evaluating Amdahl's Law," *Commun. ACM*, vol. 31, no. 5, pp. 532–533, May 1988.
[8] J. Huang, "On the behavior of algorithms in a multiprocessing environment," Ph.D. diss., Computer Sci. Dept., UCLA, 1988.
[9] L. Kleinrock, *Queueing Systems*, vol. 1, *Theory*. New York: Wiley-Interscience, 1975.
[10] L. Kleinrock, *Queueing Systems*, vol. 2, *Computer Applications*. New York: Wiley-Interscience, 1976.
[11] L. Kleinrock, "On flow control in computer networks," in *Conf. Rec., Int. Conf. on Communications*, June 1978, vol. 2, pp. 27.2.1–27.2.5.
[12] L. Kleinrock, "Power and deterministic rules of thumb for probabilistic problems in computer communications," in *Conf. Rec., Int. Conf. on Communications*, June 1979, pp. 43.1.1–43.1.10.
[13] K. C. Kung, "Concurrency in parallel processing systems," Ph.D. diss., Computer Sci. Dept., UCLA, 1984.
[14] J. D. C. Little, "A proof of the queueing formula $L = \lambda W$," *Operations Res.*, vol. 9, pp. 383–387, 1961.
[15] K. C. Sevcik, "Characterizations of parallelism in applications and their use in scheduling," *Perform. Eval. Rev.*, vol. 17, no. 1, pp. 171–180, May 1989.

The Nonuniform Distribution of Instruction-Level and Machine Parallelism and Its Effect on Performance

NORMAN P. JOUPPI, MEMBER, IEEE

Abstract—This paper examines nonuniformities in the distribution of instruction-level and machine parallelism. Nonuniformities in instruction-level parallelism include variations between benchmarks, variations within benchmarks, and variations by instruction class. Nonuniformities in machine-level parallelism include variations in latency between different operations, and variations in parallel execution capability depending on the instruction opcode. The results presented in this paper were obtained with a parameterizable code reorganization and simulation system.

The discussion of machine parallelism is based on the concepts of superscalar and superpipelined machines. Superscalar machines can issue several instructions per cycle. Superpipelined machines can issue only one instruction per cycle, but they have cycle times shorter than the latencies of their functional units. These two techniques are shown to be roughly equivalent ways of exploiting instruction-level parallelism. The *average degree of superpipelining* metric is introduced to account for the nonunit operation latencies present in most machines.

In this paper, a methodology for quickly estimating machine performance is developed. A first-order estimate is based on the average degree of machine parallelism. A second-order model corrects for the effects of nonuniformities in instruction-level and machine parallelism and is shown to be accurate within 15 percent for three widely different machine pipelines: the CRAY-1, the MultiTitan, and a dual-issue superscalar machine.

Index Terms—Computer architecture, computer organization, parallel instruction issue, pipelined instruction issue, instruction-level parallelism.

I. INTRODUCTION

THE exploitation of instruction-level parallelism was an active area of research in the late 1960's and early 1970's [14], [12], [2]. Recently, approaches to exploiting instruction-level parallelism have again become increasingly popular areas of research [9], [11], [13], [17], [1], as well as an emerging area of practice [8].

Much of this research has focused on the effects of adding parallel instruction issue capability to a specific pipeline. These results are not necessarily broadly applicable because of the specific machine-dependent timing assumptions made in the context of a specific machine pipeline. For example, in studies which start from a CRAY-1 baseline, the latency of scalar addition is three cycles and the load latency is eleven

Manuscript received February 10, 1989; revised July 25, 1989.

The author is with Digital Equipment Corporation Western Research Laboratory, Palo Alto, CA 94301.

IEEE Log Number 8931171.

cycles. But what do parallel issue studies for these pipeline characteristics imply for a machine with a one-cycle add and a two-cycle load? By fixing the machine latencies and pipeline characteristics, these studies are restricted to a single line of increasing parallelism in what is actually a multidimensional space. In this work, we attempt to present data which cover a large portion of the potential machine design space. Based on these data, a methodology is developed that yields accurate performance estimates for a wide range of machine pipelines.

Another limitation of previous work is that many times the result data are presented in terms of averages. Average parallelism can provide a first approximation to machine performance, but nonuniformities in instruction and machine parallelism can also play a significant part in determining machine performance. For example, consider a machine that requires an average of one addition per cycle for good performance on a benchmark. Is one adder enough for a machine to obtain good performance on this benchmark? If the additions are distributed such that in half the cycles there are no additions required, but in the other half there are two additions required, and such that in the nonaddition cycles there are other instructions which use the results of the additions, then it makes sense to consider machines built with two adders. Thus, the *distribution* of instruction-level parallelism is also an important area of work. In this paper, we consider several nonuniformities in the distribution of instruction-level and machine parallelism and their effects on machine design and the estimation of a machine's performance.

There are also several limitations in the scope of this work. The instruction-level parallelism measured is primarily within basic blocks, except for limited amounts of loop unrolling in the numeric benchmarks. Interblock instruction-level parallelism depends on the particular implementation of branch prediction, trace scheduling, or software pipelining used to make interblock parallelism accessible, and these techniques are beyond the scope of this paper. However, once the interblock instruction-level parallelism made available by these techniques is quantified, the performance estimation techniques developed in this paper are applicable based on the instruction level parallelism present.

Section II describes the parameterizable compilation and simulation environment used to measure the parallelism in benchmarks. In Section III, we present a machine taxonomy[1]

---

[1] An early version of Section III appeared in [6].

helpful for understanding the duality of operation latency and parallel instruction issue. It also presents simulation data showing the duality of superscalar and superpipelined machines. Section IV introduces important nonuniformities in instruction and machine parallelism. Typical distributions of these nonuniformities are presented from simulations using the parameterizable compilation and simulation system. In conjunction with the investigation of these nonuniformities, a methodology for quickly estimating machine performance is developed. Resulting estimates are compared to simulated performance for several machines and differences are discussed. The importance of cache miss latencies and other memory system related effects are briefly considered in Section V. Section VI summarizes the results of the paper.

II. Machine Evaluation Environment

The language system originally designed for the MultiTitan consists of an optimizing compiler (which includes the linker) and a fast instruction-level simulator. The compiler includes an intermodule register allocator and a pipeline instruction scheduler [15], [16]. For this study, we gave the system an interface that allowed us to alter the characteristics of the target machine. This interface allows us to specify details about the pipeline, functional units, cache, and register set. The language system then optimizes the code, allocates registers, and schedules the instructions for the pipeline, all according to this specification. The simulator executes the program according to the same specification.

To specify the pipeline structure and functional units, we need to be able to talk about specific instructions. We therefore group the MultiTitan operations into 14 classes, selected so that operations in a given class are likely to have identical pipeline behavior in any machine. For example, integer add and subtract form one class, integer multiply forms another class, and single-word load forms a third class.

For each of these classes, we can specify an operation latency. If an instruction requires the result of a previous instruction, the machine will stall unless the operation latency of the previous instruction has elapsed. The compile-time pipeline instruction scheduler knows this and schedules the instructions in a basic block so that the resulting stall time will be minimized.

Superscalar machines may have an upper limit on the number of instructions that may be issued in the same cycle, independent of the availability of functional units. We can specify this upper limit. If no upper limit is desired, we can set it to the total number of functional units.

We use our programmable reorganization and simulation system to investigate the performance of various machine organizations. We typically run 18 different benchmarks on each different configuration. All of the benchmarks are written in Modula-2 except for yacc.

ccom	Our own C compiler.
grr	A printed-circuit board router.
linpack	Linpack, double precision, unrolled 4×.
livermore	The first 14 Livermore Loops, double precision, not unrolled.
met	Metronome, a board-level timing verifier.
stan	The collection of Hennessy benchmarks from Stanford (including puzzle, tower, queens, etc).
whet	Whetsones.
yacc	The Unix parser generator.

Unless noted otherwise, the effects of cache misses and systems effects such as interrupts and TLB misses are ignored in the simulations. For more information on the parameterizable compilation and simulation system, see [6].

III. A Machine Taxonomy

There are several different ways to execute instructions in parallel. Before we examine these methods in detail, we need to start with some definitions:

operation latency	The time (in cycles) until the result of an instruction is available for use as an operand in a subsequent instruction. For example, if the result of an Add instruction can be used as an operand of an instruction that is issued in the cycle after the Add is issued, we say that the Add has an operation latency of one.
simple operations	The vast majority of operations executed by the machine. Operations such as integer add, logical ops, loads, stores, branches, and even floating-point addition and multiplication are simple operations. Not included as simple operations are instructions which take an order of magnitude more time and occur less frequently, such as divide and cache misses.
instruction class	A group of instructions all issued to the same type of functional unit.
issue latency	The time (in cycles) required between issuing two instructions. This can vary depending on the instruction classes of the two instructions.

A. The Base Machine

In order to properly compare increases in performance due to exploitation of instruction-level parallelism, we define a base machine that has an execution pipestage parallelism of exactly one. This base machine is defined as follows:

- instructions issued per cycle = 1
- simple operation latency measured in cycles = 1
- instruction-level parallelism required to fully utilize = 1.

The one-cycle latency specifies that if one instruction follows another, the result of the first is always available for the use of the second without delay. Thus, there are never any operation-latency interlocks, stalls, or NOP's in a base machine. A pipeline diagram for a machine satisfying the requirements of a base machine is shown in Fig. 1. The execution pipestage is cross-hatched while the others are unfilled. Note that although several instructions are executing concurrently, only one instruction is in its execution stage at any one

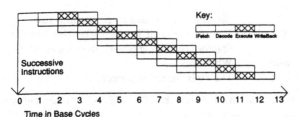

Fig. 1. Execution in a base machine.

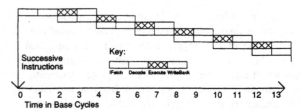

Fig. 3. Underpipelined: issues < 1 instruction per cycle.

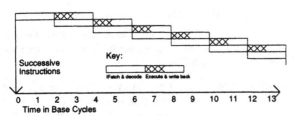

Fig. 2. Underpipelined: cycle > operation latency.

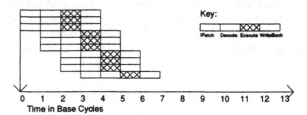

Fig. 4. Execution in a superscalar machine ($n = 3$).

time. Other pipestages, such as instruction fetch, decode, or write back, do not contribute to operation latency if they are bypassed, and do not contribute to control latency assuming perfect branch slot filling and/or branch prediction.

B. Underpipelined Machines

The single-cycle latency of simple operations also sets the base machine cycle time. Although one could build a base machine where the cycle time was much larger than the time required for each simple operation, it would be a waste of execution time and resources. This would be an *underpipelined machine*. An underpipelined machine that executes an operation and writes back the result in the same pipestage is shown in Fig. 2.

The assumption made in many paper architecture proposals is that the cycle time of a machine is many times larger than the add or load latency, and hence several adders can be stacked in series without affecting the cycle time. If this were really the case, then something would be wrong with the machine cycle time. When the add latency is given as one, for example, we assume that the time to read the operands has been piped into an earlier pipestage, and the time to write back the result has been pipelined into the next pipestage. Then the base cycle time is simply the minimum time required to do a fixed-point add and bypass the result to the next instruction. In this sense machines like the Stanford MIPS chip [4] are underpipelined, because they read operands out of the register file, do an ALU operation, and write back the result all in one cycle.

Another example of underpipelining would be a machine like the Berkeley RISC II chip [7], where loads can only be issued every other cycle. Obviously this reduces the instruction-level parallelism below one instruction per cycle. An underpipelined machine that can only issue an instruction every other cycle is illustrated in Fig. 3. Note that this machine's performance is the same as the machine in Fig. 2, which is half of the performance attainable by the base machine.

In summary, an underpipelined machine has worse performance than the base machine because it either has

- a cycle time greater than the latency of a simple operation, or
- it issues less than one instruction per cycle.

For this reason, underpipelined machines will not be considered in the rest of this paper.

C. Superscalar Machines

As their name suggests, superscalar machines were originally developed as an alternative to vector machines. A superscalar machine of degree n can issue n instructions per cycle. Superscalar execution of instructions is illustrated in Fig. 4.

In order to fully utilize a superscalar machine of degree n, there must be n instructions executable in parallel at all times. If an instruction-level parallelism of n is not available, stalls and dead time will result where instructions are forced to wait for the results of prior instructions.

Formalizing a superscalar machine according to our definitions:

- instructions issued per cycle $= n$
- simple operation latency measured in cycles $= 1$
- instruction-level parallelism required to fully utilize $= n$.

A superscalar machine can attain the same performance as a machine with vector hardware. Consider the operations performed when a vector machine executes a vector load chained into a vector add, with one element loaded and added per cycle. The vector machine performs four operations: load, floating-point add, a fixed-point add to generate the next load address, and a compare and branch to see if we have loaded and added the last vector element. A superscalar machine that can issue a fixed-point, floating-point, load, and a branch all in one cycle achieves the same effective parallelism.

1) VLIW Machines: VLIW, or *very long instruction word*, machines typically have instructions hundreds of bits long. Each instruction can specify many operations, so each

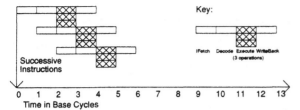

Fig. 5. Execution in a VLIW machine.

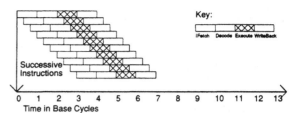

Fig. 6. Superpipelined execution ($m = 3$).

instruction exploits instruction-level parallelism. Many performance studies have been performed on VLIW machines [9]. The execution of instructions by an ideal VLIW machine is shown in Fig. 5. Each instruction specifies multiple operations, and this is denoted in the figure by having multiple cross-hatched execution stages in parallel for each instruction.

VLIW machines are much like superscalar machines, with three differences.

First, the decoding of VLIW instructions is easier than superscalar instructions. Since the VLIW instructions have a fixed format, the operations specifiable in one instruction do not exceed the resources of the machine. However, in the superscalar case, the instruction decode unit must look at a sequence of instructions and base the issue of each instruction on the number of instructions already issued of each instruction class, as well as checking for data dependencies between results and operands of instructions. In effect, the selection of which operations to issue in a given cycle is performed at compile time in a VLIW machine, and at run time in a superscalar machine. Thus, the instruction decode logic for the VLIW machine should be much simpler than the superscalar.

A second difference is that when the available instruction-level parallelism is less than that exploitable by the VLIW machine, the code density of the superscalar machine will be better. This is because the fixed VLIW format includes bits for unused operations while the superscalar machine only has instruction bits for useful operations.

A third difference is that a superscalar machine could be object-code compatible with a large family of nonparallel machines, but VLIW machines exploiting different amounts of parallelism would require different instruction sets. This is because the VLIW's that are able to exploit more parallelism would require larger instructions.

In spite of these differences, in terms of run-time exploitation of instruction-level parallelism, the superscalar and VLIW will have similar characteristics. Because of the close relationship between these two machines, we will only discuss superscalar machines in general and not dwell further on distinctions between VLIW and superscalar machines.

2) Class Conflicts: There are two ways to develop a superscalar machine of degree n from a base machine.

1) Duplicate all functional units n times, including register ports, bypasses, buses, and instruction decode logic.

2) Duplicate only the register ports, bypasses, buses, and instruction decode logic.

Of course, these two methods are extreme cases, and one could duplicate some units and not others. But if all the functional units are not duplicated, then potential class conflicts

will be created. A class conflict occurs when some instruction is followed by another instruction for the same functional unit. If the busy functional unit has not been duplicated, the superscalar machine must stop issuing instructions and wait until the next cycle to issue the second instruction. Thus, class conflicts can substantially reduce the parallelism exploitable by a superscalar machine. (We will not consider superscalar machines or any other machines that issue instructions out of order. Techniques to reorder instructions at compile time instead of at run time are almost as good [2], [3], [16], and are substantially simpler than doing it in hardware.)

D. Superpipelined Machines

Superpipelined machines exploit instruction-level parallelism in another way. In a superpipelined machine of degree m, the cycle time is $1/m$ the cycle time of the base machine. Since a fixed-point add took a whole cycle in the base machine, given the same implementation technology it must take m cycles in the superpipelined machine. Fig. 6 shows the execution of instructions by a superpipelined machine. Note that by the time the third instruction has been issued there are three operations in progress at the same time.

Formalizing a superpipelined machine according to our definitions:

- instructions issued per cycle = 1, but the cycle time is $1/m$ of the base machine
- simple operation latency measured in cycles = m
- instruction-level parallelism required to fully utilize = m.

Superpipelined machines have been around a long time. Seymour Cray has a long history of building superpipelined machines: for example, the latency of a fixed-point add in both the CDC 6600 and the Cray-1 is 3 cycles. Note that since the functional units of the 6600 are not pipelined (two are duplicated), the 6600 is an example of a superpipelined machine with class conflicts. The CDC 7600 is probably the purest example of an existing superpipelined machine since its functional units are pipelined.

E. Superpipelined Superscalar Machines

Since the number of instructions issued per cycle and the cycle time are theoretically orthogonal, we could have a superpipelined superscalar machine. A superpipelined superscalar machine of degree (m, n) has a cycle time $1/m$ that of the base machine, and it can execute n instructions every cycle. This is illustrated in Fig. 7.

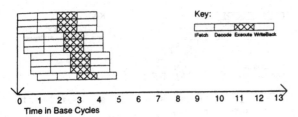

Key:

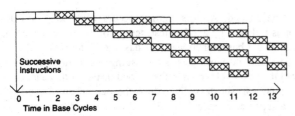

Fig. 7.   A superpipelined superscalar ($n = 3$, $m = 3$).

Fig. 8.   Execution in a vector machine.

TABLE I
AVERAGE DEGREE OF SUPERPIPELINING

Instruction Class	Frequency	MultiTitan Latency	CRAY-1 Latency
logical	6 percent	$\times 1 = 0.06$	$\times\ 1 = 0.06$
shift	9 percent	$\times 1 = 0.09$	$\times\ 2 = 0.18$
add/sub	21 percent	$\times 1 = 0.21$	$\times\ 3 = 0.63$
load	34 percent	$\times 2 = 0.68$	$\times 11 = 3.74$
store	15 percent	$\times 2 = 0.30$	$\times\ 1 = 0.15$
branch	10 percent	$\times 2 = 0.20$	$\times\ 3 = 0.30$
FP	5 percent	$\times 3 = 0.15$	$\times\ 7 = 0.35$
Average Degree of Superpipelining		1.7	5.4

Formalizing a superpipelined superscalar machine according to our definitions:

- instructions issued per cycle $= n$, and the cycle time is $1/m$ that of the base machine
- simple operation latency measured in cycles $= m$
- instruction-level parallelism required to fully utilize $= n \times m$.

F. Vector Machines

Although vector machines also take advantage of (unrolled-loop) instruction-level parallelism, whether a machine supports vectors is really independent of whether it is a super-pipelined, superscalar, or base machine. Each of these machines could have an attached vector unit. However, to the extent that the highly parallel code was run in vector mode, it would reduce the use of superpipelined or superscalar aspects of the machine to the code that had only moderate instruction-level parallelism. Fig. 8 shows serial issue (for diagram readability only) and parallel execution of vector instructions. Each vector instruction results in a string of operations, one for each element in the vector.

G. Supersymmetry

The most important thing to keep in mind when comparing superscalar and superpipelined machines of equal degree is that they have basically the same performance.

A superscalar machine of degree three can have three instructions executing at the same time by issuing three at the same time. The superpipelined machine can have three instructions executing at the same time by having a cycle time 1/3 that of the superscalar machine, and issuing three instructions in successive cycles. Each of these machines issues instructions at the same rate, so superscalar and superpipelined machines of equal degree have basically the same performance.

So far the assumption has been that the latency of all operations, or at least the simple operations, is one base machine cycle. As we discussed previously, no known machines have

this characteristic. For example, few machines have one-cycle loads without a possible data interlock either before or after the load. Similarly, few machines can execute floating-point operations in one cycle. What are the effects of longer latencies? Consider the MultiTitan [5], where ALU operations are one cycle, but loads, stores, and branches are two cycles, and all floating-point operations are three cycles. The MultiTitan is therefore a slightly superpipelined machine. If we multiply the latency of each instruction class by the frequency we observe for that instruction class when we perform our benchmark set, we get the *average degree of superpipelining*. The average degree of superpipelining is computed in Table I for the MultiTitan and the CRAY-1. To the extent that some operation latencies are greater than one base machine cycle, the remaining amount of exploitable instruction-level parallelism will be reduced. In this example, if the average degree of instruction-level parallelism in slightly parallel code is around two, the MultiTitan should not stall often because of data-dependency interlocks, but data-dependency interlocks should occur frequently on the CRAY-1.

To confirm the duality of latency and parallel instruction issue we simulated the eight benchmarks on an ideal base machine, and on superpipelined and ideal superscalar machines of degrees 2–8. Fig. 9 shows the results of this simulation. The superpipelined machine actually has less performance than the superscalar machine, but the performance difference decreases with increasing degree.

Consider a superscalar and superpipelined machine, both of degree three, issuing a basic block of six independent instructions (see Fig. 10). The superscalar machine will issue the last instruction at time t_1 (assuming execution starts at t_0). In contrast, the superpipelined machine will take 1/3 cycle to issue each instruction, so it will not issue the last instruction until time $t_{5/3}$. Thus, although the superscalar and superpipelined machines have the same number of instructions executing at the same time in the steady state, the superpipelined machine has a larger startup transient and it gets behind the superscalar machine at the start of the program and at each branch target. This effect diminishes as the degree of the superpipelined machine increases and all of the issuable instructions are issued closer and closer together. This effect is seen in Fig. 9 as the superpipelined performance approaches that of the ideal superscalar machine with increasing degree.

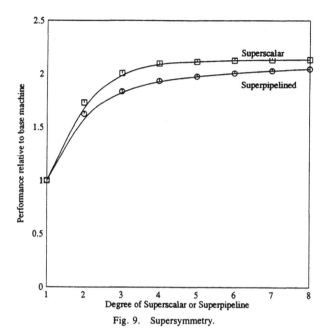

Fig. 9. Supersymmetry.

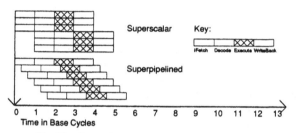

Fig. 10. Startup in superscalar versus superpipelined.

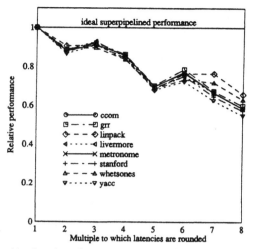

Fig. 11. Loss in performance due to increased latency granularity.

Another difference between superscalar and superpipelined machines involves operation latencies that are noninteger multiples of a base machine cycle time. In particular, consider operations which can be performed in less time than a base machine cycle set by the integer add latency, such as logical operations or register-to-register moves. In a base or superscalar machine, these operations would require an entire clock because that is by definition the smallest time unit. In a superpipelined machine, these instructions might be executed in one superpipelined cycle. Then in a superscalar machine of degree 3 the latency of a logical or move operation might be 3 times longer than in a superpipelined machine of degree 3. Since the latency is longer for the superscalar machine, the superpipelined machine will perform better than a superscalar machine of equal degree. In general, when the inherent operation latency is divided by the clock period, the remainder is less on average for machines with shorter clock periods.

Fig. 11 quantifies the effects of increasing cycle time granularity. A family of superpipelined machines was simulated, with the latencies of the functional units rounded up to the nearest multiple of various numbers. The intrinsic latencies of the functional units were those of the CRAY-1. For example, the CRAY-1 has a load latency of 11 cycles. This results in load latencies of 11, 12, 12, 12, 15, 12, 14, and

16 cycles in machines where the latencies were required to be multiples of 1–8, respectively. Note that the performance of the resulting machines is not monotonically decreasing with increasing cycle time granularity, as the load latency in the previous example decreases from 15 to 12 when going from cycle time multiples of 5 to 6. Since load latency is an important contributor to machine performance, the performance of the benchmarks shown in Fig. 11 also improves when latencies change from multiples of 5 to 6. The difference in performance between the intrinsic superpipelined machine and those machines where functional unit latencies must be a multiple m of the basic cycle time approximates the loss in performance in a superscalar machine of degree m as compared to a superpipelined machine of equal degree due to its increased granularity of functional unit latency. For degrees of 2 and 3, this results in about a 10 percent penalty for the superscalar machine as compared to the superpipelined, and the penalty increases to approximately 15 percent for degree 4. This loss in superscalar performance due to increased latency granularity is larger than that lost by superpipelined machines due to increased startup penalties (see Fig. 9), giving a slight overall preference to superpipelined machines for small degrees of machine parallelism, and a larger preference for increasing degrees of machine parallelism.

Although latency is a dual of parallel instruction issue, latency is often ignored when parallel issue methods are discussed. For example, instruction issue methods have been compared for the CRAY-1 assuming all functional units have 1 cycle latency [1]. This results in speedups of up to 2.7 from parallel issue of instructions, and leads to the mistaken conclusion that the CRAY-1 would benefit substantially from concurrent instruction issue. In reality, since the average degree of superpipelining of the CRAY-1 is 5.4, we would expect the performance of the CRAY-1 to benefit very little from parallel instruction issue. Most of the instruction-level parallelism is absorbed by filling up the long latency functional-unit pipelines in the machine. We simulated the performance of the CRAY-1 assuming single cycle functional unit latency and actual functional unit latencies, and the results are given

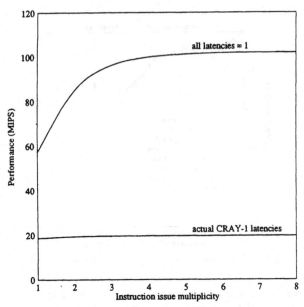

Fig. 12. Parallel issue with unit and real latencies.

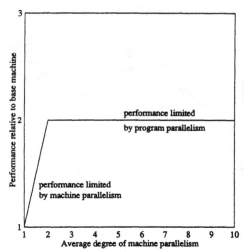

Fig. 13. Piecewise linear approximation to performance versus machine parallelism.

in Fig. 12. As expected, since the CRAY-1 already executes several instructions concurrently due to its average degree of superpipelining of 5.4, there is almost no benefit from issuing multiple instructions per cycle when the actual functional unit latencies are taken into account.

H. A First-Order Performance Approximation

An understanding of the average degree of superpipelining of a machine leads to a simple first-order method of estimating the performance of a machine. First, by multiplying the average degree of superpipelining (S_P) by the degree of parallel issue (i.e., superscalar degree S_S), we get the average degree of machine parallelism (MP).

$$\text{MP} = S_P \times S_S.$$

If the average parallelism in the benchmark (BP) exceeds the average parallelism of the machine, then usually most of the parallelism of the machine will be utilized and the performance will be limited by the parallelism of the machine. Similarly, if the average parallelism in the benchmark is less than the average parallelism of the machine, then the performance will be limited by the parallelism inherent in the benchmark. We can approximate the overall performance as two piecewise linear regions (see Fig. 13). In the region on the left, the performance is limited by the machine parallelism, and on the right the performance is limited by the benchmark parallelism. In other words, relative to a base machine with an equivalent cycle time,

if (BP $\geq$ MP) then performance = MP

if (MP $\geq$ BP) then performance = BP.

The performance given in Fig. 13 is in comparison to a base machine that can only issue one instruction per cycle, with

cycle time S_P times larger than that of the machine in question, on a benchmark with BP equal to 2. From this information, we can derive an estimate of the absolute performance of the processor (neglecting cache misses and other memory system or I/O factors). We can calculate the average CPI (cycles per instruction) of the machine by dividing its average degree of superpipelining by its performance relative to the base machine. For example, if a machine has an average degree of superpipelining of 4 and twice the performance of a base machine, then the machine will have an average CPI of 2. Similarly, if a superscalar machine has an average degree of superpipelining of 1 and outperforms a base machine by a factor of two, then it achieves 0.5 CPI on the average. Finally by dividing the number of cycles per second by the CPI we can get an absolute performance estimate in instructions per second. Since the absolute cycle time is a simple multiplicative factor in our performance comparisons, in the remainder of this paper we will discuss machine performance relative to a base machine with an equivalent cycle time.

Consider three examples using this first-order performance approximation. The MultiTitan has an average degree of superpipelining of 1.7 over the eight-benchmark set. The average instruction-level parallelism within the eight benchmarks is 2.16. Since this is larger than the average machine parallelism of the MultiTitan, the MultiTitan performance will be limited by its machine parallelism. Its performance will be 1.7 times that of a base machine with a cycle time 1.7 times larger than its own. These factors cancel giving an estimated CPI of 1.0 (ignoring cache misses). The relative performance when simulated with zero-cycle cache misses is 1.22 CPI. Thus, the estimate is within 22 percent of the relative performance.

As a second example, consider a dual-issue superscalar machine with the same pipeline latencies as the MultiTitan. Its average machine parallelism would then be twice that of the MultiTitan (assuming no class conflicts), giving MP = 3.4. This machine's performance should be limited by the benchmark parallelism, since its average machine parallelism is larger than the average benchmark parallelism, 2.16. This

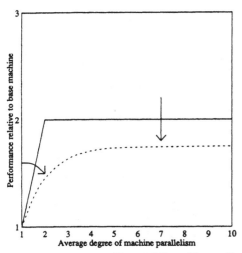

Fig. 14. Performance versus machine parallelism with nonuniformities.

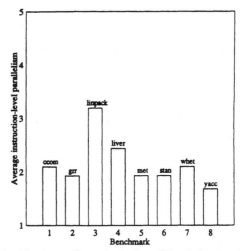

Fig. 15. Average instruction-level parallelism by benchmark.

would give an estimated speedup of 2.16 over a base machine with a cycle time 1.7 times larger. This would make its estimated CPI 0.79 (i.e., 1.7/2.16). The simulated performance was 0.91 CPI when ignoring cache misses. Thus, the estimated performance is about 15 percent less than the simulated performance.

As a third example, consider the CRAY-1. It has an average degree of superpipelining of 5.4 on the eight benchmarks. This is greater than the average instruction-level parallelism present in the benchmarks. This means the performance will be limited by the benchmark parallelism, and a significant amount of the parallelism available in the machine will go unused. The CRAY-1 performance on the benchmarks should be 2.16 times that of a base machine with a cycle time 5.4 times that of the CRAY-1. This means that the average CPI of the CRAY-1 executing the benchmarks is estimated to be 2.50. Actual simulation of the benchmarks on the CRAY-1 yields a CPI of 3.75. This is 50 percent larger than the estimate.

What can cause this large error? Up to now the analysis has only considered averages. Unfortunately machine and instruction-level parallelism within benchmarks is not uniformly distributed. For example, most of the latencies of the CRAY-1 are relatively short compared to the load latency of 11 cycles. Imagine three instructions that can be executed in parallel, and the instructions are a load, an add, and a logical operation. Although we could issue the load followed by the add and the logical operation in successive cycles, a wait for the result of the load would stall the issue of instructions for eight more cycles. Thus, the CPI for these three instructions is 11 (the delay of the load) divided by 3 (the number of instructions executed), or 3.67. This is much closer to the simulated performance.

Significant nonuniformities in machine latency, in instruction-level parallelism, in parallelism by benchmark, and in the distribution of instructions by instruction class all cause the actual performance of the machine to be less than that of the piecewise linear performance estimate. In reality, depending on the range of nonuniformities, the actual performance versus machine parallelism is closer to the dotted line in Fig. 14 than the solid piecewise linear approximation.

The larger the range of nonuniformities from their averages the lower the performance will be for a given machine parallelism. We will examine each of these sources of nonuniformities in detail in the next section. Inclusion of the effects of these nonuniformities into the model will allow us to develop a more accurate second-order performance model. This second-order model will account for nonuniformities in the region limited by benchmark parallelism by lowering its asymptote (see Fig. 14). Similarly, by accounting for the effects of nonuniformities when performance is approximated by the machine parallelism, the asymptote for this region will have a reduced slope.

IV. NONUNIFORMITIES IN INSTRUCTION-LEVEL PARALLELISM

A. Variations in Parallelism by Benchmark

The first nonuniformity in instruction-level parallelism we consider is variation in instruction-level parallelism from benchmark to benchmark. The eight benchmarks introduced in Section II actually have different amounts of instruction-level parallelism. The performance improvement in each benchmark when executed on an ideal superscalar machine of unlimited parallelism is given in Fig. 15. Yacc has the least amount of instruction-level parallelism. Many programs have approximately two instructions executable in parallel on the average, including the C compiler, PC board router (grr), the Stanford collection, Metronome, and Whetstones. The Livermore loops approaches an instruction-level parallelism of 2.5. The official version of Linpack has its inner loops unrolled four times, and has an instruction-level parallelism of 3.2. The total range in average parallelism among the eight benchmarks is almost a factor of two. This range would be further increased if more aggressive loop unrolling was applied to the numeric benchmarks.

B. Variations in Machine Operation Latency

The second nonuniformity in parallelism to consider is the variation in operation latency in real machine designs. For example, in a machine with an average degree of superpipelining

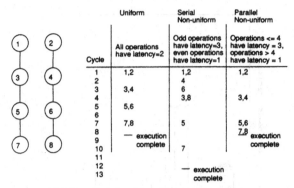

Fig. 16. Variations in machine operation latency.

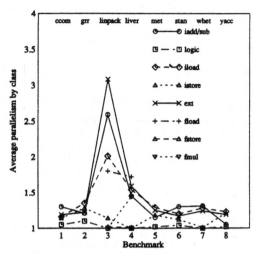

Fig. 17. Average parallelism within instruction classes by benchmark.

of 2, some operations may have single cycle latencies while other operations may have large latencies. Some of the issues to analyze when considering variations in machine operation latency are shown in Fig. 16. In order to better quantify the performance degradation due strictly to machine operation latency nonuniformity, we assume that all other effects are uniform. The sample expression has constant instruction-level parallelism of 2. If a machine with uniform machine latencies equal to 2 and unlimited parallel issue capability executes this expression, the operation latency (e.g., 2) divided by the benchmark parallelism (e.g., 2) will yield the performance relative to a base machine (e.g., 1). However, if the operation latencies are not uniform, the performance of the benchmark is likely to be degraded. Consider the second column where operations with larger latency are in series with each other. Then the performance is limited by the long latency operations because these form a critical path in the expression. The remaining instruction-level parallelism is not enough to fill in the empty slots in the execution of the critical path and sustain the expected performance. Finally, if the long latency operations are executable in parallel with each other, the effects of the long latencies are mitigated. For example, consider the rightmost column of Fig. 16. Here the long latency operations can be executed in parallel with each other. As a result, the total execution time of the expression is the same as if there were uniform operation latencies.

To get a better understanding of the effects of nonuniform latencies, imagine a machine where the latency for one operation is much larger than the others. In the limit, the performance is not given by the long operation latency divided by the benchmark parallelism, but rather by the long latency divided by the parallelism between long latency operations (as was illustrated in Fig. 16). For example, consider a machine where the latency of all operations is 1 except one operation has a latency of 1000. Then the number of short latency instructions in parallel with a large latency instruction is basically insignificant for typical amounts of instruction-level parallelism (e.g., <4). The only important factor is the parallelism of these long latency operations between themselves. The first-order approximation which divides the latency of an operation by the benchmark parallelism (e.g., 2.16) will underestimate the time required for program execution. In the limit, with no long latency operations in parallel with each other, the first-

order approximation underestimates performance by a factor equal to the benchmark parallelism.

How can the effects of nonuniformities in operation latency be accounted for in the performance estimation model? From the previous example, it is clear that the frequency of long latency operations occurring in parallel with each other must be known. Given this information the effects of nonuniform latencies can be approximated as follows. First, we can compute the proper contribution of a long latency operation to performance by dividing its latency by the parallelism of long-latency operations instead of the parallelism of all operations. Then we can subtract the erroneous first-order contribution to performance, which is the latency divided by the parallelism among all operations. This gives a correction to the original first-order performance estimate that properly accounts for the effect of long-latency operations.

Fig. 17 shows the average parallelism within typical instruction classes. These data were obtained by simulating an unlimited issue superscalar machine. For most benchmarks except the unrolled version of linpack, if an operation in a particular instruction class is executed, then the average number of instructions in the same class executable in parallel with the first operation is between 0.1 and 0.25. For example, the data for loads show that on cycles in which there were a nonzero number of loads issued there were 1.25 loads issued on average. Note that this is not saying that on every cycle an average of 1.25 loads were issued, but only that whenever a load was issued there were 0.25 other loads in parallel with the load. The standard version of Linpack used has its inner loop unrolled four times, and so there are many operations of the same class executable at the same time in the inner loop. Similar behavior is expected in other unrolled benchmarks, but has not yet been verified.

Given the data in Fig. 17 we can correct our performance estimate for time that the machine is stalled waiting for the completion of an operation with significantly larger than average latency. For example, consider the performance estimate of the CRAY-1 in Section III-H. The only operations with latency larger than the average degree of superpipelining

88

TABLE II
CALCULATION OF NONUNIFORM LATENCY CORRECTION FACTOR

Instruction Class	Frequency	×	[[Cray-1 Latency] / [Average WCP]]	−	[Cray-1 Latency] / [Average BP]]	= Correction to First-Order Approx.
load	34 percent	×	((11/1.25)	−	(11/2.16))	= 1.26
FP	5 percent	×	((7/1.25)	−	(7/2.16))	= 0.12

Total common-class parallelism correction   1.38

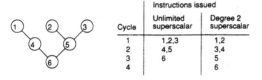

Cycle	Instructions issued Unlimited superscalar	Degree 2 superscalar
1	1,2,3	1,2
2	4,5	3,4
3	6	5
4		6

Fig. 18. Variations in the number of instructions executable in parallel.

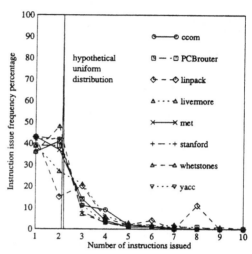

Fig. 19. Distribution of parallel instruction issue frequency.

the CRAY-1 are load and FP operations. Table II shows the result of the correction calculation. (WCP is the within-class parallelism.)

When the CPI correction (1.38) is added to the previous CPI calculation (2.50), an estimate (3.88) much closer to the simulated CPI (3.75) is attained. The CPI correction calculated is based only on the overlap of long operations in the same class. The inclusion of overlaps between different classes will increase the divider to a value larger than the common-class parallelism of 1.25 used in the calculation. This will reduce the magnitude of the overall CPI correction. To the extent that the load latency is much larger than the other latencies, however, the importance of cross-class parallelism within long operations is reduced.

To summarize, when the performance is limited by the benchmark parallelism, nonuniformities in machine parallelism (e.g., latency) can cause errors in the estimated performance. By properly accounting for these nonuniformities in machine parallelism, we can lower the asymptote for this region and improve the accuracy of the performance estimate.

C. Variations in Aggregate Instruction Parallelism

The third nonuniformity we consider is nonuniformity in the cycle-by-cycle amount of instruction parallelism. For example, consider the situation in Fig. 18. Here the average number of instructions executed in parallel is two. A machine with unlimited machine parallelism could execute this expression in three cycles. However, because this parallelism is not uniformly distributed with two instructions in parallel at each level in the expression graph, a machine that can only issue two instructions per cycle would take four cycles to execute the expression. Thus, nonuniformities in instruction-level parallelism will decrease the performance achieved. This is especially true in the region where the machine parallelism is approximately equal to the average benchmark parallelism.

To quantify the scale of variations in the number of instructions executable in parallel, simulations were performed for an ideal superscalar machine with unlimited issue parallelism. Results of this simulation are presented in Fig. 19. This figure shows what percentage of cycles had a given number of

instructions issue in that cycle. For example, the chart shows that all the programs had only one instruction issue in a cycle about 40 percent of the time, even with unlimited issue parallelism. We call this the *single-issue bottleneck*, and will discuss it further. The issue of more than three instructions per cycle is relatively rare. The notable exception to this is linpack which had a cycle with eight instructions issue in the inner loop. There were only a negligible number of cycles where more than ten instructions were issued in a cycle, so they are omitted from the graph.

Averaging the number of instructions executed in parallel for each benchmark from Fig. 19 gives the average parallelism by benchmark shown in Fig. 15. The spike at 2.16 is the hypothetical uniform distribution of parallelism at the average parallelism on the eight benchmarks. If a machine could issue exactly 2.16 instructions per cycle and the benchmark parallelism was a constant 2.16, then the performance would be 2.16 times that obtained by a base machine with the same cycle time. This performance point would be at the intersection of the two piecewise linear approximations.

To better understand the significance of performance degradations due purely to the nonuniformity of instruction-level parallelism, the performance of the benchmarks on superscalar machines of various degrees were simulated. The results of these simulations are shown in Fig. 20. The dotted and dashed lines are the actual performance obtained, while the solid lines are the piecewise linear approximations based on the average parallelism for each benchmark. The largest deviation from the piecewise linear approximation occurs un-

89

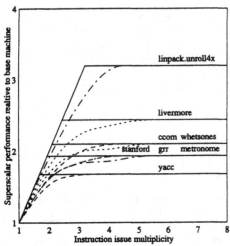

Fig. 20. Instruction-level parallelism by benchmark.

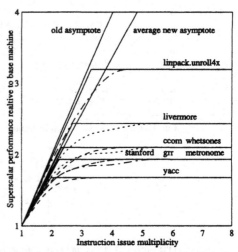

Fig. 22. Single-issue correction for machine-parallelism limited asymptote.

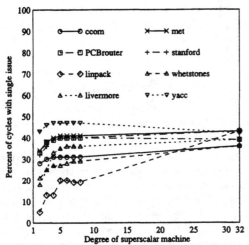

Fig. 21. Frequency of single-issue cycles versus machine parallelism.

der the transition from one approximation to the other. The largest deviation for the machine parallelisms simulated was 27 percent for grr, Metronome and the Stanford benchmarks at an instruction issue multiplicity of 2.

One of the largest components of nonuniformity in instruction-level parallelism are single-issue bottleneck cycles where data dependencies neck down to a single instruction. Based on Fig. 19, in a superscalar machine with unlimited parallel issue capability, single-issue bottlenecking occurs on about 40 percent of all cycles over a wide range of benchmarks. However, if the degree of the superscalar machine is limited, code reorganization will migrate relatively unconstrained instructions to be in parallel with bottlenecks instead of being executed in parallel with earlier instructions. Thus, as the degree of the superscalar machine decreases from an unlimited number down to two, the number of single-issue cycles decreases. (Of course, it becomes 100 percent for superscalar machines of degree 1.) This behavior was observed when superscalar machines of various degrees were simulated (see Fig. 21).

We can compensate the asymptote for the region where the performance is limited by the machine parallelism using the percentage of single-issue cycles. This uses the single-issue bottleneck data from an ideal superscalar machine to improve the accuracy of the estimated performance for a specific machine. Since a certain number of cycles will be single-issue bottlenecks, increases in machine parallelism will only improve the performance of nonbottleneck regions. Based on Fig. 21, 27 percent of the cycles on average in a machine with parallelism 2 will be single-issue cycles. Thus, as the machine parallelism is increased from 1 to 2, only 73 percent (i.e., 100 − 27) of the instructions will benefit from the increased machine parallelism. This has the effect of decreasing the slope of the machine-parallelism limited performance asymptote. Instead of achieving a speedup of 2 at a machine parallelism of 2, the speedup will only be 1.73. Fig. 22 is a version of Fig. 20 where the machine-limited performance asymptote has been adjusted for each benchmark based on the number of single-issue cycles in the benchmark at a machine parallelism of 2. These new asymptotes are much closer upper bounds to the performance of the benchmarks than the old unit slope asymptote.

We can apply a correction for single-issue cycles to the earlier performance estimate for the MultiTitan CPU. In Section III-H, its performance was estimated to be 1.00 CPI because its performance was limited by its own machine parallelism. Correcting just for single-issue cycles would decrease the performance improvement from 1.7 over a base machine to 1 plus 73 percent of the 0.7 extra machine parallelism, or 1.51 times a base machine with a 1.7 times larger cycle time. This is equivalent to a CPI of 1.13 (i.e., 1.7/1.51). Thus, the correction for single-issue cycles reduces the difference between the estimated CPI (1.13) and the simulated CPI (1.22) to less than 10 percent.

To summarize, when the performance is limited by the machine parallelism, nonuniformities in benchmark parallelism can cause errors in the estimated performance. By properly accounting for these nonuniformities in benchmark parallelism, we can lower the slope of the asymptote for this region and improve the accuracy of the performance estimate.

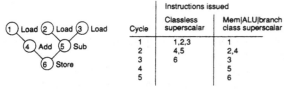

		Instructions issued	
	Cycle	Classless superscalar	Mem|ALU|branch class superscalar
① Load ② Load ③ Load	1	1,2,3	1
④ Add ⑤ Sub	2	4,5	2,4
	3	6	3
⑥ Store	4		5
	5		6

Fig. 23.   Nonuniform distribution by instruction class.

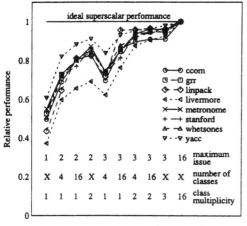

Fig. 24.   The effect of class conflicts on machine performance.

D. Variations in Parallelism by Instruction Class

A fourth important nonuniformity for machines with class conflicts is the distribution of instructions by instruction class. In the example of Fig. 23, the expression can be executed in three cycles by a superscalar machine of degree three with no class conflicts. Consider instead a superscalar machine with three instruction classes: load–store, arithmetic-logical-shift, and branches. If the superscalar machine can only execute at most one instruction of each class each cycle, it will take five cycles to execute the six instructions. This is a reduction of over 50 percent in the speedup obtained as compared to classless multiple issue capability.

Class conflicts can be a significant factor in machine performance. In general, there are a large number of class conflicts and resource conflicts (e.g., limited number of ports to the register file) to be considered. A comprehensive analysis of class and resource conflicts is beyond the scope of this work. However, a simplified analysis of the effect of major class conflicts for ten different machine organizations is given in Fig. 24. The maximum number of instructions issuable (i.e., the superscalar degree) varies from 1 to 16. Each machine has a number of copies of each functional unit specified by the class multiplicity. Most machines have either 4 or 16 different instruction classes. In the case where the machine has its class multiplicity equal to its superscalar degree, the number of classes is irrelevant and is denoted by an "X." Machines with four classes are organized as in Table III. This class structure was chosen to minimize the required machine resources. For example, this four-class structure only requires one data port to the memory system. Similarly, if the machine has separate

TABLE III
THE INSTRUCTION CLASSES OF FIG. 24

TABLE III
THE INSTRUCTION CLASSES OF FIG. 24

Machine Class	Instructions in Class
Load/Store	CPU load, CPU store, transfer, FPU load, FPU store
CPU ALU	CPU (integer) ops: add/sub, logical, shifts, multiply, divide
FPU ALU	FPU (floating-point) ops: add/sub, multiply, divide, conversions
Branch	branch/jump/JSR, trap

floating-point and integer register files, this four-class structure may not require any additional ports to the register file over a nonsuperscalar machine (assuming each register file has one write and two read ports for ALU operations, one independent read/write port for loads and stores, and branches test condition codes). Machines with 16 classes have a class for each of the instruction types listed in Table III. In the remainder of this section, we refer to each machine by the three-tuple of its superscalar degree, number of classes, and class multiplicity. For example, the leftmost machine structure is $(1, X, 1)$.

Fig. 24 shows that class conflicts can have a very significant effect on machine performance. For example, machine $(2, 4, 1)$ only exploits an average of 41 percent of the available instruction-level parallelism, and an average of 61 percent of the parallelism exploited by a machine of the same degree with no class conflicts [e.g., $(2, X, 2)$]. Similarly machine $(3, 4, 1)$ only exploits 51 percent of the parallelism exploited by machine $(3, X, 3)$.

Simply increasing the degree of a superscalar machine has little effect on performance, unless the number of classes or their multiplicity are increased commensurably. For example, machine $(3, 4, 1)$ has on average only 3 percent better performance than machine $(2, 4, 1)$. This is not surprising, since the percentage of floating-point and branch instructions in most programs is lower than that of load/stores or CPU ALU operations to begin with, so even if all floating-point operations or branches could be executed in parallel with load/store and CPU operations, there would still be many cycles with only load/store and CPU operations issuing.

In general, increasing the multiplicity of the functional units is more important than increasing the number of instruction classes. For example, the increase in performance from increasing the multiplicity of functional units from one to two is greater than that from increasing the number of classes from 4 to 16. This is because when there are two copies of a functional unit, it can issue any two instructions of the class, whereas in a machine with many classes two instructions still may conflict. For example, machine $(3, 4, 2)$ can issue any two load instructions in the same cycle, whereas machine $(3, 16, 1)$ can only issue two load instructions if one is a CPU load and the other is an FPU load.

The impact of class conflicts has implications for the choice between superscalar and superpipelined implementations. Since a superpipelined machine is less likely to have class conflicts than a superscalar machine (in general it is cheaper to pipeline a functional unit than to duplicate it), the

TABLE IV
THE COST OF CACHE MISSES

Machine	Cycles per Instruction	Cycle Time (ns)	Memory Time (ns)	Miss Cost (Cycles)	Miss Cost (Instruction)
VAX11/780	10.0	200	1200	6	.6
WRL Titan	1.4	45	540	12	8.6
?	0.5	5	350	70	140.0

effects of class conflicts can give a significant performance advantage to superpipelined machines over superscalar machines. For example, on average the machine (2, 4, 1) only attains 84 percent of the performance of a degree 2 superscalar machine without class conflicts, and machine (3, 4, 1) only attains 79 percent of the performance of a degree 3 superscalar without class conflicts.

V. OTHER IMPORTANT FACTORS

The preceding simulations have concentrated on the nonuniformities in instruction-level and machine parallelism under ideal circumstances. Unfortunately, there are a number of other factors which will have a very important effect on actual machine performance. The most important of these factors is usually cache performance.

Cache performance is becoming increasingly important, and it can have a dramatic effect on speedups obtained from parallel instruction execution. Table IV lists some cache miss times and the effect of a miss on machine performance. Over the last decade, cycle time has been decreasing much faster than main memory access time. The average number of machine cycles per instruction has also been decreasing dramatically, especially when the transition from CISC machines to RISC machines is included. These two effects are multiplicative and result in tremendous increases in miss cost. For example, a cache miss on a VAX 11/780 only costs 60 percent of the average instruction execution. Thus, even if every instruction had a cache miss, the machine performance would only slow down by 60 percent! However, if a RISC machine like the WRL Titan [10] has a miss, the cost is almost ten instruction times. Moreover, these trends seem to be continuing, especially the increasing ratio of memory access time to machine cycle time. In the future, a cache miss on a superscalar machine executing two instructions per cycle could cost well over 100 instruction times!

Cache miss effects decrease the benefit of parallel instruction issue. Consider a 2.0 CPI machine, where 1.0 CPI is from issuing one instruction per cycle, and 1.0 CPI is cache miss burden. Now assume the machine is given the capability to issue three instructions per cycle, to get a net decrease down to 0.5 CPI for issuing instructions when data dependencies are taken into account. Performance is proportional to the inverse of the CPI change. Thus, the overall performance improvement will be from 1/2.0 CPI to 1/1.5 CPI, or 33 percent. This is much less than the improvement of 1/1.0 CPI to 1/0.5 CPI, or 100 percent, as when cache misses are ignored.

VI. CONCLUDING COMMENTS

In this paper, we have shown superscalar and superpipelined machines to be roughly equivalent ways to exploit instruction-level parallelism. The duality of latency and parallel instruction issue was documented by simulations. Ignoring class conflicts and implementation complexity, a superscalar machine will have slightly worse performance than a superpipelined machine of the same degree due to the larger cycle time granularity of the superscalar machine, although this is partially offset by the larger startup transient of the superpipelined machine. For example, reducing the granularity of the functional unit latencies in the CRAY-1 by factors of 2 to 4 results in a 10–15 percent performance loss, respectively. Moreover, if the superscalar machine has significant class conflicts these could further reduce the performance of a superscalar machine by 15–20 percent relative to a superpipelined machine of equal degree without conflicts.

Several nonuniformities in instruction-level parallelism were investigated including variations between benchmarks, within benchmarks, and by instruction class within benchmark. The instruction-level parallelism measured varied by a factor of two from benchmark to benchmark, with most nonnumeric benchmarks close to two in instruction-level parallelism and numeric benchmarks closer to three on average. The range of instruction-level parallelism would be increased further if more aggressive loop unrolling were used in the numeric benchmarks.

Unit-parallelism bottlenecks in benchmarks can have a significant effect on machine performance. The effect of these constrictions in parallelism increases as the machine parallelism increases. For machines that can issue an unlimited number of instructions in parallel, single-instruction issue cycles typically accounted for 40 percent of all cycles.

Variations in machine parallelism (i.e., latency) were also investigated in conjunction with the development of a simple model of machine performance. The model estimates machine performance using a piecewise linear approximation.

In the first region, performance is limited by machine parallelism. The first-order performance estimate is simply the machine parallelism times that of the base machine performance at the equivalent cycle time. The accuracy of this estimate can be improved by considering the effect of nonuniformities in benchmark parallelism. The number of single-issue cycles is a useful correction factor.

In the second region, performance is limited by benchmark parallelism. The first-order performance is simply the benchmark parallelism times the performance of a base machine with the equivalent cycle time. The accuracy of this estimate can be improved by considering the effects of nonuniformities in machine parallelism. A correction factor can be computed using the latency of operations greater than the average degree of superpipelining, their frequency, and their frequency of occurrence in parallel with each other.

Cache misses and other memory system related effects are also very important contributors to machine performance. Much existing excellent work in this area can be used to augment the performance modeling of instruction-level and machine parallelism presented in this paper.

Overall, an understanding of nonuniformities in intrabasic-block instruction-level parallelism and machine parallelism allows the estimation of machine performance to within 15 percent of simulated performance for fully-pipelined machines without significant class or resource conflicts. Finally, a remaining area of research is the exploration of the nonuniformities in the distribution of interbasic-block instruction-level parallelism obtained in code with large amounts of data parallelism transformed into instruction-level parallelism through techniques such as agressive loop unrolling, software pipelining, trace scheduling, or branch prediction.

ACKOWLEDGMENT

D. W. Wall provided the parameterizable compilation and simulation system used in this study, and largely contributed Section II. J. E. Smith provided encouragement to examine the effects of increased cycle time granularity on supersymmetry. R. Swan, D. W. Wall, J. Bertoni, and M. J. Doherty provided valuable comments on an early draft of this paper.

REFERENCES

[1] R. D. Acosta, J. Kjelstrup, and H. C. Torng, "An instruction issuing approach to enhancing performance in multiple functional unit processors," *IEEE Trans. Comput.*, vol. C-35, pp. 815–828, Sept. 1986.

[2] C. C. Foster and E. M. Riseman, "Percolation of code to enhance parallel dispatching and execution," *IEEE Trans. Comput.*, vol. C-21, pp. 1411–1415, Dec. 1972.

[3] T. Gross, "Code optimization of pipeline constraints," Tech. Rep. 83-255, Stanford Univ., Comput. Syst. Lab., Dec. 1983.

[4] J. L. Hennessy, N. P. Jouppi, S. Przybylski, C. Rowen, and T. Gross, "Design of a high performance VLSI processor," in *Proc. Third Caltech Conf. VLSI*, Computer Science Press, Mar. 1983, pp. 33–54.

[5] N. P. Jouppi, J. Dion, D. Boggs, and M. J. K. Nielsen, " MultiTitan: Four architecture papers," Tech. Rep. 87/8, Digital Equipment Corp. Western Res. Lab, Apr. 1988.

[6] N. P. Jouppi and D. W. Wall, "Available instruction-level parallelism for superscalar and superpipelined machines," in *Proc. Third. Int. Conf. Architectural Support Programming Languages Oper. Syst.*, IEEE Computer Society Press, Apr. 1989.

[7] M. G. H. Katevenis, "Reduced instruction set architectures for VLSI," Tech. Rep. UCB/CSD 83/141, Univ. of California, Berkeley, Comput. Sci. Division of EECS, Oct. 1983.

[8] L. Kohn and S.-W. Fu, "A 1,000,000 transistor microprocessor," in *Dig. Int. Solid-State Circuits Conf.*, IEEE, Feb. 1989, pp. 54–55.

[9] A. Nicolau and J. A. Fisher, "Measuring the parallelism available for very long instruction word architectures," *IEEE Trans. Comput.*, vol. C-33, pp. 968–976, Nov. 1984.

[10] M. J. K. Nielsen, "Titan system manual," Tech. Rep. 86/1, Digital Equipment Corp. Western Res. Lab, Sept. 1986.

[11] A. R. Pleszkun and G. S. Sohi, "The performance potential of multiple functional unit processors," in *Proc. 15th Annu. Symp. Comput. Architecture*, IEEE Computer Society Press, May 1988, pp. 37–44.

[12] E. M. Riseman and C. C. Foster, "The inhibition of potential parallelism by conditional jumps," *IEEE Trans. Comput.*, vol. C-21, pp. 1405–1411, Dec. 1972.

[13] G. S. Sohi and S. Vajapeyam, "Instruction issue logic for high-performance interruptable pipelined processors," in *Proc. 14th Annu. Symp. Comput. Architecture*, IEEE Computer Society Press, June 1987, pp. 27–34.

[14] G. S. Tjaden and M. J. Flynn, "Detection and parallel execution of independent instructions," *IEEE Trans. Comput.*, vol. C-19, pp. 889–895, Oct. 1970.

[15] D. W. Wall, "Global register allocation at link-time," in *Proc. SIGPLAN'86 Conf. Compiler Construction*, June 1986, pp. 264–275.

[16] D. W. Wall and M. L. Powell, "The Mahler experience: Using an intermediate language as the machine description," in *Proc. Second Int. Conf. Architectural Support for Programming Languages and Oper. Syst.*, IEEE Computer Society Press, Oct. 1987, pp. 100–104.

[17] S. Weiss and J. E. Smith, "Instruction issue logic for pipelined supercomputers," in *Proc. 11th Annu. Symp. Comput. Architecture*, IEEE Computer Society Press, June 1984, pp. 110–118.

Classification and Performance Evaluation of Instruction Buffering Techniques[*]

Lizyamma Kurian, Paul T. Hulina,
Lee D. Coraor and Dhamir N. Mannai
Department of Electrical and Computer Engineering
The Pennsylvania State University
University Park, PA 16802

Abstract

The speed disparity between processor and memory subsystems has been bridged in many existing large-scale scientific computers and microprocessors with the help of instruction buffers or instruction caches. In this paper we classify these buffers into traditional instruction buffers, conventional instruction caches and prefetch queues, detail their prominent features, and evaluate the performance of buffers in several existing systems, using trace driven simulation. We compare these schemes with a recently proposed queue-based instruction cache memory. An implementation independent performance metric is proposed for the various organizations and used for the evaluations. We analyze the simulation results and discuss the effect of various parameters such as prefetch threshold, bus width and buffer size on performance.

1 Introduction

CPU speeds have increased tremendously in the recent past, but memory speeds have barely kept pace, resulting in a speed disparity between CPU and memory. This disparity has to be bridged in some way and the processing bandwidths matched in order to avoid system bottlenecks. In many existing systems, the speed gap has been bridged by employing memory interleaving or by using a fast memory (cache or instruction buffer) between the CPU and the main memory. Instruction buffers and cache memories are typically 5 to 10 times faster than main memory and hence can reduce the effective memory access time if carefully designed and implemented. As observed by Hill and Smith [9], cache is a time-tested mechanism for improving memory sys-

[*]This research was supported in part by the National Science Foundation under grant MIP-8912455.

tem performance by reducing access time and memory traffic through the exploitation of temporal and spatial locality of reference.

Since the characteristics of access patterns for instructions and data are typically different, a split-cache organization that decouples data access from instruction access has been used to yield more efficient access schemes. This is because the designer can now take advantage of the particular characteristics of the access patterns and design the cache memory systems accordingly. Several recent microprocessors have implemented the split-cache approach (MC 68030, MC 68040); while some have adopted the unified cache scheme as well (Intel 80486).

Cache memory design for mainframes and minicomputers has been extensively studied since IBM introduced the first commercial cache in its System 360, Model 85. Hill and Smith [9] carried out a study on on-chip caches with emphasis on sector cache using miss and traffic ratios as performance metrics, but they performed no studies on prefetching. A performance evaluation of on-chip cache organizations is given by Eickemeyer and Patel [6] where they compare different types of caches such as instruction, data, split, unified, stack, and top-of-stack caches. Farrens and Pleszkun [7] present a combination of an instruction cache, instruction queue and instruction queue buffer and evaluate a set of instruction fetch strategies.

In this paper, we study the instruction buffers and instruction caches of several existing computers and CISC and RISC microprocessors. We first present a classification of the different buffering and caching approaches. Then we describe the prominent features of several existing systems and also of a proposed queue-based instruction cache scheme [4]. We then detail the simulation methodology, propose a performance metric and present the simulation results.

2 A Classification Scheme

The instruction caches/buffers incorporated in various commercial computers and microprocessors share certain characteristics, but differ in several design aspects. Any classification of these buffering or caching schemes will depend to some extent on subjective distinctions and often tend to be vague and overlapping. These classifications may be subject to varying interpretations and it may not always be clear, to which class a particular scheme belongs. Recognizing this, we now turn our attention to classifying instruction buffers/caches of existing machines based on major design aspects. Very broadly, we classify the instruction buffering schemes into three categories:- (i) Instruction Buffers (ii) Instruction Caches and (iii) Prefetch Queues.

The first category in our classification is instruction buffers. By instruction buffers, we mean the traditional instruction buffers as found in the earlier machines such as the IBM 360/91, CDC STAR-100, and CDC 6600 which typically contain one contiguous segment of the program (or a single locality). A recently proposed queue-based cache scheme [4] also shares several characteristics with these buffers and hence we include it also in this category. These instruction buffers are often designed as a queue or stack. Instructions are prefetched in consecutive order and executed until a successful branch occurs. At the point of a successful branch, if the branch target is not in the buffer, then the prefetch buffer is cleared and refilled with instructions which start at the branch address. In most of the traditional instruction buffers, there is an emphasis on prefetching and thus capturing more of spatial locality. The queue-based organization deviates here. It has more emphasis on retaining whatever has already been fetched and thus temporal locality is captured primarily. Also, in the queue-based cache, prefetching is done only when the bus is available and with a lower priority than operand fetch during instruction execution. There are two major factors affecting the success of such instruction buffers, average size of a locality and scattering of localities. The buffer should be larger than the average size of a locality. This is because if the average loop size is greater than that of the buffer, the buffer loses its effectiveness. Since these buffers can contain only one contiguous segment of the program, scattered locality characteristics exhibited by many programs may also cause loss of effectiveness.

The second category in our classification is instruction caches. By instruction caches, we mean buffers that are managed more like a conventional cache, in either a direct-mapped, set-associative, or fully associative mapping scheme. Several recent CISC and RISC microprocessors have this type of fairly conventional instruction cache. We also include the Cray instruction buffers in this class. They are not exactly conventional caches, but since they are managed more similarly to caches than the traditional instruction buffers and since they

can contain more than one contiguous program segment (four in Cray-1, Cray X-MP and Cray Y-MP and eight in Cray-2), it seems more appropriate to include them in this category. At the time the Cray-1 was designed, virtual memory and instruction caches were receiving significant attention. This influence is apparent in the techniques employed in its instruction buffers. Cray 1's instruction buffer design is closer to today's cache memories than it is to the CDC 6600 or the IBM 360/91 buffer designs [16].

The third category in our classification is prefetch queues. The Intel microprocessors 8086, 8088, 80186, 80286 and the Motorola 68000 contain prefetch queues. These prefetch queues are considerably different from the traditional queue-based instruction buffers mentioned before, the major distinction being that these prefetch queues do not capture locality. Instructions are prefetched, whenever the bus is free, and held in the queue, but they are *consumed* by the CPU as they are executed. In other words, the locality is not captured. The MC68010 has an instruction prefetch queue that will support a loop mode of operation, i.e. capture of locality. The queue is two words or four bytes long as in the MC68000, but in the event of a loop that can be contained in the queue, the MC68010 has the ability to enter a loop mode, suppressing all further opcode fetches until an exit loop condition is met. It should be noted that not all instructions are loopable and that only very small loops can be accomodated.

2.1 Instruction Buffers

In this subsection, we describe a few typical implementations of the traditional type of instruction buffers and the recently proposed queue-based instruction cache.

The CDC 6600: The CDC 6600 was the first commercially available computer whose architecture addressed the speed disparity between the central processor, main memory, and I/O devices. One of the techniques used by the CDC 6600 to maximize the rate at which instructions are executed is to employ an *instruction stack* that provides more rapid access to instructions. The instruction stack consists of eight 60-bit registers which hold the instructions most recently executed. As instructions are fetched, they are sent to the stack's *input register*. Immediately upon entering the input register, the first or the leftmost instruction in the 60-bit word is transferred to a series of instruction registers. As this transfer occurs, another instruction fetch is initiated. The condition for this initiation is simply that the left-most instruction is transferred for execution [23]. Instructions continue to be fetched sequentially from central storage until a branch causes transfer of control. When the execution of an instruction causes a branch back to an instruction that is currently in the stack, no refills are allowed after the branch; thereby holding the program loop in the stack. The CDC 7600 instruction buffer is similar to the CDC 6600 buffer, the only difference being that it consists of twelve 60 bit registers instead of the eight in CDC 6600.

The IBM 360 Model 91: The IBM System 360/91 architecture includes an instruction unit that employs an *instruction prefetch* mechanism. The goal of this mechanism is to assure that future instructions are available for processing as required. These instructions are held in an instruction stack that has eight double-word (64 bit) buffers. When the instruction stream is sequential, the instruction fetch mechanism operates as a fetch-ahead unit and attempts to maintain a supply of instructions in the instruction buffer in advance of need. Whenever the number of instructions in the buffer is below three double words beyond the current instruction, a new prefetch is initiated. If storage is not busy with operand fetching, a fetch for a fourth double word is also initiated. If the number of instructions in the buffer is below three double words beyond the current instruction, memory access conflicts are resolved in favor of instruction prefetch; otherwise it favors operand fetch. Thus, generally the buffer holds 24 or 32 bytes beyond the current instruction. The appearance of a branch instruction signals a point in the instruction stream where sequential flow may be altered. A successful branch causes the startup of a new instruction stream sequence; and if the target address is not already in the buffer then the processing of the new stream is delayed until the instruction buffer is replenished. Forward branches with target addresses within the instruction buffer array are satisfied from the instruction buffer. Back branches that are within eight double-words from the current instruction trigger a special processing mode called *loop mode*. In this case, the entire loop can be contained within the instruction buffer array. The instruction buffer array is supplemented by two double-word registers, also called the *branch target buffer*. These two registers are used when a conditional branch is encountered. Both potential instructions to be executed next are thus made available. When the decision is known, one of them is used to supply the instruction and the other is flushed.

The Queue-Based Instruction Cache: The queue-based instruction cache proposed in [4] is based on a RAM queue and a set of registers. The data is loaded from main memory into the RAM queue in a FIFO fashion. However, the CPU may read any of the words currently in the queue and in any order. So the queue approach concerns only the way data is loaded into the cache. Unlike other cache designs, there is no concept of a line (block). The whole RAM is used as one block (or segment) and the address space of the resulting cache is contiguous.

The operation of the cache depends on three load procedures. A *LoadNew* procedure is used to load data into an initially empty cache or to clear an old cache and reload it with new data. To load data sequentially from main memory into a non-empty cache, a *LoadSequential* procedure is used. One major feature of the queue-cache is *preloading*. Preloading means that when the CPU requests information from an address that is not in the queue, but not too far from the last address loaded into the queue, then the referenced data as well as the intermediate addresses are fetched and appended to the queue without clearing the queue. Whenever a forward branch is encountered, the control logic checks to see how far ahead the new branch location is from the last address loaded in the queue. If this distance is within a predefined *preload window*, then the *cache preload procedure* is invoked. Preloading thus prevents unnecessary flushing of the queue, which occurs in the traditional instruction buffers.

2.2 Instruction Caches

In this subsection, we examine the instruction buffers of the Cray computers, the instruction caches in several Motorola processors, and the instruction cache of the Intel RISC processor 80860.

The Cray series: The Cray-1 has four instruction buffers each of which can contain 128 bytes. 128, allowing the buffers to map up to 512 bytes of contiguous memory. Associated with each instruction buffer is a beginning address register (BAR) which holds the address of its first location. When an instruction is referenced, the four BARs are compared with the PC. If there is a match, the next instruction register is loaded from the appropriate instruction buffer. Forward and backward branches are accomodated. There is no storage access delay when instruction sequences are found in the instruction buffers. A two cycle delay ensues when the next instruction is found in a buffer different from the one currently in use. If there is no match, the next instruction must first be fetched from memory and placed in an instruction buffer before instruction processing can proceed. The instruction buffers are used in rotation. The least recently filled instruction buffer is selected for use when the next instruction is not already in a buffer, analogous to a FIFO replacement strategy in caches. The Cray-1 is capable of fetching 128 bytes of data in one memory cycle or 4 processor clock cycles.

Similar to the Cray-1, the Cray X-MP uses four large independent instruction buffers which play the role of an instruction cache. Each buffer contains 32 words of 64 bits, for a total buffer size of 256 bytes. In fact, these buffers are managed like a 1024 byte fully associative cache memory with a FIFO replacement scheme. The operation of these buffers is identical to those of Cray-1, the differences being only in the access times associated with a miss in the buffer. This is due to the difference in the speeds of the memory used in the Cray-1 and the Cray X-MP. The Cray X-MP has a 9.5 ns processor cycle and a 135 ns memory cycle. Hence, 14 clock cycles are required for one memory access whereas 4 cycles would suffice in the Cray-1. If a change of buffer is required, a 2 cycle delay is incurred just as in Cray-1. If the instruction is not in any buffer, then 16 clock cycles are added [15]. The Cray Y-MP also has the same type of buffers as the Cray X-MP. The Cray-2 has 8 instruction buffers, each 128 bytes long.

The Motorola series:

The first 32-bit generation Motorola processor, the MC68020, incorporates a 256-byte on-chip instruction cache memory used to store the instruction stream prefetch accesses from the main memory. It is organized as a direct-mapped cache of 64 long word entries [14]. Each cache entry consists of a tag field, a valid bit, and 32 bits of instruction data.

The MC68030 microprocessor includes a 256-byte on-chip instruction cache organized as a direct mapped cache of 16 lines [14]. This 32-bit processor from Motorola has in addition to this instruction cache, a data cache of equal size. In this study, however, we are interested only in the instruction cache. Each line of the instruction cache consists of four entries and each entry contains four bytes. The tag field for each line contains a valid bit for each entry in the line and each entry is independently replaceable. All four entries in a line have the same tag address. The MC68030 instruction cache operates almost identically to that of the MC68020, except for the cache load/fill procedure. The cache memory can be filled in a single entry mode or as a burst fill, when a miss occurs. In the single entry mode, four longwords are loaded into the cache, one longword at a time. This mode uses asynchronous data transfer requiring four times the time needed to fetch one longword, whereas in the burst mode four long words are transferred in a burst in less than twice the time required to fetch one longword.

The next 32 bit processor from Motorola, the MC68040, contains a 4K-byte on-chip instruction cache configured as a four-way set associative cache of 64 sets of four 16 byte lines [14]. Each cache line contains an address tag, a valid bit and four longwords of instruction data. Since entry validity is provided on per-line basis, an entire line must be loaded from system memory in order for the cache to store an entry. Only burst mode accesses that successfully read four longwords can be cached. Memory devices unable to support bursting forces the processor to complete the access as a sequence of longwords. For prefetch requests that hit in the cache, two longwords are multiplexed onto the internal instruction data bus. When an access misses in the cache, the cache controller requests the memory line containing the required data from memory and places the line in the cache. If all the lines in the set are

already valid, a pseudo random replacement technique is used to select one of the four lines and replace the tag and instruction data contents of the line with the new line information. To implement this replacement algorithm, each cache contains a 2-bit counter which is incremented for each access to the cache. The counter is incremented for each half line accessed in the instruction cache. When a miss occurs and all four lines in the set are valid, then the line pointed to by the current counter value is replaced, and the counter is incremented.

Intel 80860:

Intel's powerful 64-bit RISC microprocessor, the 80860 has both an instruction cache and a data cache. The instruction cache is a two-way, set associative memory of 4 Kbytes, with 32-byte blocks [11]. This processor supports accesses up to a maximum of 64-bits per clock cycle.

2.3 Prefetch Queues

On early microprocessor chips, both Intel and Motorola used prefetch queues since semiconductor technology did not permit integration of on-chip caches at that time. The features and operation of these prefetch queues are discussed below.

The Intel 8086, 80186 and 80286 have a 6-byte first-in-first-out (FIFO) prefetch queue that is continually filled whenever the system bus is not needed for some other operation. This look-ahead feature can significantly increase the CPU's throughput because, much of the time, the next instruction would already be in the CPU when the present instruction completes its execution. If a branch is taken, then the instruction queue is flushed and there is no time saving; but on the average this occurs only a small percent of the time. During the execution of computationally intensive instructions, for instance, the multiplication instruction in the 8086, the CPU will not be using the bus and there are ample clock cycles to fill the instruction queue. When there is a branch to an odd address, the 8086 brings in 1 byte and continues with even address words. After five of the six bytes in the queue are full (when just one byte is left empty), the next fetch will not begin until a word is available in the queue [12].

The 8088 has only a 4-byte instruction queue instead of the 6-byte queue in the 8086. The reason for the smaller queue is that the 8088 can fetch only 1 byte at a time (since it has only an 8-bit data bus) and the longer fetch times mean that the processor cannot fully utilize a 6-byte queue [12]. The prefetching algorithm is different from the 8086 in the sense that instead of waiting for a 2-byte space, the 8088 will initiate a fetch even when a single empty byte in the queue becomes available.

The MC68000 uses a two-word tightly-coupled instruction mechanism to enhance performance. When execution of an instruction begins, the operation word and the word following it would have already been fetched, with the operation word in the instruction decoder. In the case of multi-word instructions, as each additional word of the instruction is used internally, a fetch is made to the instruction stream to replace it. The last fetch from the instruction stream is made when the operation word is discarded and decoding is started on the next instruction. If the instruction is a single-word instruction causing a branch, then the second word is not used. Since this word is fetched by the previous instruction, it is impossible to avoid this superfluous fetch. In the case of an interrupt or trace exception, both words are discarded.

3 Performance Study

The performance models developed in this section are used along with the statistics generated by our simulators to quantify the performance enhancement that can be achieved. The fraction of the total references that result in a hit in the buffer/cache reflects the success of the caching scheme, since the processor infrequently waits for slower main memory references. However, it is observed from our simulations as well as from previous reports [1], that many configurations that provide a higher hit in the cache would actually degrade the performance of the CPU because of higher miss penalties (which is often the case with larger block sizes). Hence hit ratio may not be a good performance measure.

Effective access time is a much better metric to indicate performance. But this parameter depends on the access times of the memory used for the cache and the main memory and thus depends on the particular implementation. In this study, we isolate the implementation dependent parameters and arrive at an implementation independent performance index which we denote as the speed-up factor.

The speed-up that can be obtained by a traditional type of instruction buffer is derived as follows : Let T_{CACHE} denote the cache (instruction buffer) cycle time and T_{MM} denote the access time of the RAM used for main memory. Furthermore, let $p(miss)$ denote the probability of a miss and let $p(prefetch)$ denote the probability of initiation of an *expensive prefetch*. Some prefetches are made only when the bus is free and hence they do not constitute any overhead. However, prefetches made with greater priority than operand fetches do impose severe penalties and we call them *expensive prefetches*. Also let Grain1 represent the number of accesses performed for a miss and Grain2 denote the number of accesses done at a prefetch. The effective access time T_{EFF}^{IB} is

$$T_{EFF}^{IB} = T_{CACHE} + [p(miss) * Grain1$$
$$+ p(prefetch) * Grain2] * T_{MM}. \qquad (3.1)$$

For the CDC 6600 buffer, both Grain1 and Grain2 are

equal to 1 while for the IBM 360/91, Grain1 is 2 and Grain2 is 1.

Speed-up of any cache organization may be defined as the percent improvement in the effective access time by using the cache. In other words, the speed-up is

$$S = \frac{T_{MM} - T_{EFF}}{T_{MM}} = 1 - \frac{T_{EFF}}{T_{MM}} \qquad (3.2)$$

where T_{EFF} is the effective access time of the memory system with a cache. From equations 3.1 and 3.2, the speed-up S_{IB} of the traditional instruction buffer is

$$S_{IB} = 1 - \frac{T_{CACHE}}{T_{MM}} - p(miss) * Grain1$$
$$- p(prefetch) * Grain2 \qquad (3.3)$$

Now if we let R denote the ratio of the access times of the cache to that of the main memory, then equation 3.3 can be rewritten as

$$S_{IB} = 1 - R - p(miss) * Grain1$$
$$- p(prefetch) * Grain2 \qquad (3.4)$$

and

$$S_{IB} = X_{IB} - R \qquad (3.5)$$

where

$$X_{IB} = 1 - p(miss) * Grain1$$
$$- p(prefetch) * Grain2 \qquad (3.6)$$

In equation 3.5, S_{IB} is the speed-up and X_{IB} is the speed-up factor. The speed-up factor is independent of the implementation dependent parameter R. The probability of a miss and that of a prefetch are among the statistics generated by our simulator and hence we calculate the speed-up factor from this equation.

Now we turn to the queue-cache organization. Again, let T_{CACHE} denote the cache cycle time, T_{MAIN}^{QB} denote the time required to retrieve a word from main memory upon a miss, and T_{MM} denote the access time of the main memory. Furthermore, let $p(loadnew)$ denote the probability of a call to the *loadnew* procedure upon a miss and let $AvePreDis$ denote the average preload distance upon a call to the *preload* procedure. (These terms were explained in Section 2.1 where we detailed the operation of the queue-cache.) Then the effective access time T_{EFF}^{QB} is

$$T_{EFF}^{QB} = T_{CACHE} + (1 - H_{QB})T_{MAIN}^{QB} \qquad (3.7)$$

where

$$T_{MAIN}^{QB} = p(loadnew) * T_{MM}$$
$$+ (1 - p(loadnew)) * AvePreDis * T_{MM}. \qquad (3.8)$$

The speed-up of the queue-based cache is

$$S_{QB} = 1 - \frac{T_{CACHE}}{T_{MM}} - (1 - H_{QB})[p(loadnew)$$

$$+ (1 - p(loadnew))\, AvePreDis]. \qquad (3.9)$$

Proceeding as in the case of the traditional buffers,

$$S_{QB} = X_{QB} - R \qquad (3.10)$$

where X_{QB}, the speed-up factor of the queue-cache is,

$$X_{QB} = 1 - (1 - H_{QB})[p(loadnew)$$

$$+ (1 - p(loadnew))\, AvePreDis]. \qquad (3.11)$$

For the next category, instruction caches of the conventional type, let H_{BLOCK} denote the hit ratio for the block cache and K be the block size. Then the effective access time is

$$T_{EFF}^{BLOCK} = T_{CACHE} + (1 - H_{BLOCK})\, K\, T_{MM} \qquad (3.12)$$

The speed up can be calculated from equation 3.2 and 3.12 as

$$S_{BLOCK} = 1 - \frac{T_{CACHE}}{T_{MM}} - (1 - H_{BLOCK})\, K \qquad (3.13)$$

and separating R, the ratio of the cache and main memory access times, the speed-up factor is

$$X_{BLOCK} = 1 - (1 - H_{BLOCK})\, K \qquad (3.14)$$

For our analysis, the hit ratio is obtained from the simulator output and the speed-up factor is calculated using equation 3.14.

Finally we turn to the prefetch queues. Let T_{CACHE} denote the prefetch queue cycle time and $p(miss)$ be the probability of a miss. There are no *expensive prefetches* since all prefetches are made when the bus is free and hence they do not constitute any overhead. Intel literature specifically mentions that prefetches are made only when the bus is free, and even for the MC68000, we make the assumption that operand fetches required during execution take precedence over instruction prefetches. (If this is not the case, the prefetch queue might constitute an overall penalty rather than a performance improvement.) In all the prefetch queues we studied, the fetch granularity is whatever is directly supported by the bus-width. The effective access time T_{EFF}^{PFQ} of these prefetch queues is

$$T_{EFF}^{PFQ} = T_{CACHE} + p(miss) * T_{MM}. \qquad (3.15)$$

From equations 3.2 and 3.15 we obtain the speed-up as

$$S_{PFQ} = 1 - \frac{T_{CACHE}}{T_{MM}} - p(miss) \qquad (3.16)$$

and after isolating the access time ratio as in the above cases, the speed-up factor may be obtained as

$$X_{PFQ} = 1 - p(miss). \qquad (3.17)$$

Thus we observe that the hit ratio in prefetch queues is a direct measure of performance improvement obtained by the scheme. Since the access time ratio R is the same for all systems we can simply compute the speed-up factors and compare them.

4 The Simulation

Trace-driven simulation, which has become the standard cache performance evaluation method, was used in this study. Using a trace permits simulation of caches with many strategies and parameter values in reproducible experiments [1]. A trace-driven simulation is guaranteed to be representative of at least one program in execution [9]. We gathered the address traces used in this study from real programs executed on a VAX 11/785 architecture running the UNIX operating system. The traces were obtained by executing the C Compiler (compiling a program of about 1000 lines of code), the Tex type-setter program (compiling a text file of about 41 Kbytes with several equations) and the Whetstone benchmark. The C Compiler trace has 9222 memory references, the tex trace has 88473 references and the whetstone trace has 528024 references. The C Compiler trace and Tex trace are real program traces and are likely to contain genuine embedded correlations that synthetic benchmarks often lack. For synthetic traces, we observe that the results are extremely sensitive to minor system parameter changes, whereas the range of variation is less wide and more regular for real program traces. We developed trace-driven simulators for the various systems under study.

Simulation Aspects: Our study is an evaluation of the instruction buffering mechanisms only, not of the systems in which they are used. Hence we do not attempt to exercise the various features of the processors or computers, but instead, restrict the evaluation to a general environment with the bus width and access granularity features of the original machine. Any evaluation isolating these features would not be realistic, since for each machine, the cache or buffer size, prefetch threshold, block size and other characteristics were determined by its designers with due concern for these features.

The Cray machines achieve a massive memory bandwidth with the help of interleaving. For instance, the Cray-1 is 16 way interleaved, the Cray X-MP/Model24 is 32 way interleaved and each module has a data width of 8 bytes. The bus width and data transfer granularity of the various processors/computers we studied range from 1 byte to 256 bytes. Considering these aspects, comparing the different schemes in the different

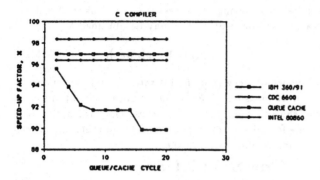

Figure 1: Comparison of Hit Ratios

machines is not a trivial task; only the comparison of systems that operate with an identical bus width would yield meaningful results. Therefore we compare each cache or buffer under study to other caches capable of fetching identical amounts of data in unit access and to a queue-based cache that holds the same amount of data. Thus the IBM 360/91 and CDC 6600 are compared with a queue-cache of size 64 bytes (considering 60 bit words of the CDC as analogous to 8 bytes of others). Similarly, the MC68020 and MC68030 are compared with a 256-byte queue-cache.

Figures 1 to 6 illustrate the various comparisons. The queue-cycle or cache cycle in these plots denotes the number of processor clock cycles needed to perform one memory access. This parameter is significant only for some traditional types of buffers, prefetch queues and the queue-cache. In these schemes, the combination of this parameter with the execution times of instructions determines the amount of possible "free" prefetching. The CDC 6600 and IBM 360/91 buffers consistently exhibit higher hit ratios than the queue-based cache (Figure 1) , but when the speed-up factor is evaluated (Figure 2) the queue-cache displays better performance because the other two buffers perform a number of superfluous prefetches. The branch target buffer of the IBM 360/91 improves the hit ratio, but it also increases the traffic ratio significantly and often detrimentally affects the system. The Intel 80860 RISC processor instruction cache results also appear in Figure 2 along with those of IBM 360/91 and CDC 6600 buffers because of identical access granularity. But it has to be always kept in mind that the Intel 80860's cache is 64 times larger than the other buffers and has a much more complex control circuitry and a higher directory cost than the others. We were not able to plot the results of Cray-1 and Cray X-MP on the same graph because of aforementioned data bandwidth differences, and they appear in Figures 3 and 4 along with queue-caches of equivalent size. Judgements and inferences from Fig-

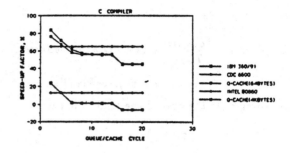

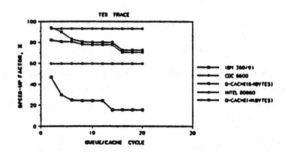

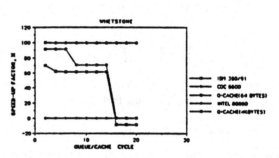

Figure 2: IBM 360/91, CDC 6600 and Intel 80860 instruction buffers/caches

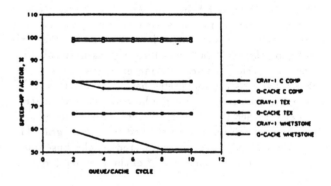

Figure 3: Cray-1 and the Queue-Cache

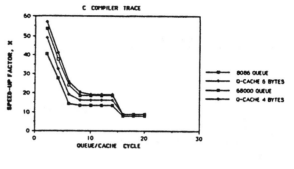

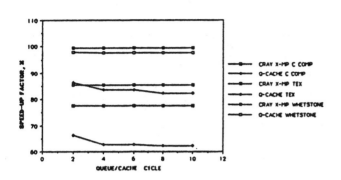

Figure 4: Cray X-MP and the Queue-Cache

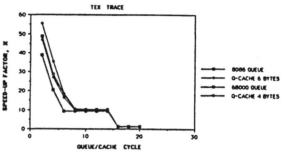

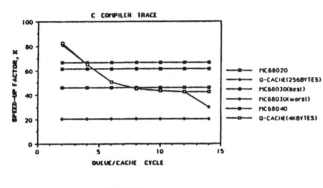

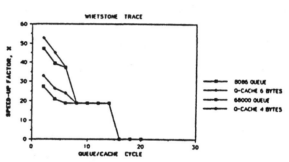

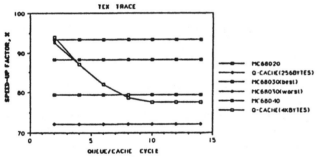

Figure 6: Prefetch Queues of Intel 8086, MC68000 and the Queue-Cache

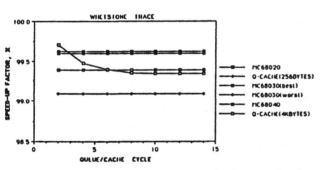

Figure 5: Motorola Processor Caches and the Queue-Cache

ure 5 should be made keeping in mind the fact that the MC68040 cache is 16 times larger than the MC68020 and MC68030 caches.

The best case for the MC68030 is obtained by assuming that all cache fills are done in burst mode and the worst case assumes all fills in single entry mode. The results of MC68040 are obtained without considering burst-mode filling. We observe from Figures 2 and 5, that an increase in size from 256 bytes to 4Kbytes for the queue-cache increases the performance only very nominally. Results from prefetch queue simulations are illustrated in Figure 6.

We also performed studies that detailed how an increase in the buffer size would affect the performance. Figure 7 displays the results. Here we observe that for traditional instruction buffers of the type we studied, an increase in size beyond 256 bytes is only of marginal improvement. This can be explained on the basis of locality characteristics and average loop sizes of programs. Studies of program behaviour [2] show that 60.7% of

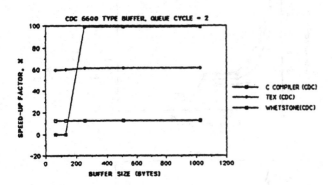

Figure 7: Speed-up factor vs Instruction buffer size

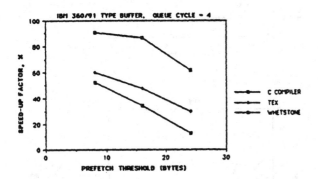

Figure 8: Speed-up factor vs Prefetch Threshold

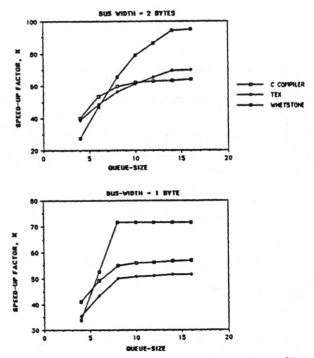

Figure 9: Prefetch Queue Performance vs Queue Size

all branches are within 256 bytes from current point of execution; only 7.2% more jumps fall within 512 bytes, and just 4.0% more in 1024 bytes. Again, since these buffers contain only one contiguous segment of the program, the scattered locality characteristics exhibited by many programs cannot be captured.

The unfavorable effects of excessive prefetching are highlighted by Figure 8. Simulations were performed by changing the prefetch threshold of an IBM360/91 type instruction buffer. The IBM design has a prefetch threshold of three double words or 24 bytes. We varied this threshold and performed simulations. It was observed that prefetching often increases the hit ratio, but when the overall performance of the system is analyzed, excessive prefetching is often detrimental.

We also performed simulations to study the effect of cache size, line size and associativity on conventional instruction caches. The results are in concurrence with published results [18] and hence we do not report them here. Prefetch queues are inherently small in all implementations which is justified from the results in Figure 9 as well. Large prefetch queues tend to be under-utilized. In Figure 9, the performance improvement saturates with fairly small queues, especially for the lower

bus-width case. The queues are better utilized with higher bus-width, however, the speed-up factor still saturates sooner or later. It may be noted that in this figure, a queue-size of 4 bytes for the 1-byte bus-width case represents the Intel 8088 microprocessor queue.

5 Conclusions

In this paper, we have presented a classification and performance evaluation of several on-chip and main-frame/minicomputer instruction caches and buffers. We presented a performance metric that does not depend on implementation dependent parameters and used it in our studies. We compared the existing caches with a proposed queue-based caching approach. Among the three categories we studied, prefetch queues are the simplest and fully associative caches are the most complex. In situations with no restrictions on chip area or directory cost, fully associative or set associative caches that offer better performance than equally large traditional instruction buffers/queue-cache may be used. But larger instruction caches do not necessarily provide a significant improvement in performance, a phenomenon reported by [7] also. The queue-based cache performs better than the implemented approaches when small caches are considered, whereas with larger caches the performance of the queue-cache is either comparable or inferior. Hence this approach is suitable for emerging technologies such as Gallium Arsenide which promise higher speed but currently prohibit reaching high circuit densities. We also conclude that the queue-based cache is not suitable for machines like the Cray which fetch large amounts of data in one access. But such methods of reducing the speed disparity are limited to mainframes and are not feasible in a single-chip environment. Multiple queues can capture scattered locality and might offer good performance in comparison to the large set-associative instruction caches and the Cray buffers. This is an area of study that needs to be investigated. Traditional instruction buffers and the queue-based caches have significantly lower directory overhead compared to equal data area set associative or fully associative caches, and hence consume less chip area. Instruction buffers with less prefetching and the queue-cache offer good performance where constraints of chip area exist and only small caches are feasible. Another conclusion is that prefetching can reduce effective memory access time if carefully designed and implemented, however there is a very good chance that the potential gain in performance is heavily diminished by the disproportionate increase in the number of fetches performed.

References

[1] Alpert, D.B. and M.J. Flynn, "Performance Trade-offs for Microprocessor Cache Memories," IEEE Micro, August 1988, pp. 44-53.

[2] Alexander, W.G. and D.B. Wortman, "Static and Dynamic Characteristics of XPL Programs," Computer, Vol. 8, No. 11, November 1975, pp. 41-46.

[3] Anderson, D.W., Sparacio, F.J., Tomasulo, R.M., "Machine Philosophy and Instruction Handling," IBM Journal of Research and Development, 11, No.1. 8-24, January 1967.

[4] Coraor, L.D., P.T. Hulina, and D.N. Mannai, "A Queue-Based Instruction Cache Memory," Proc. of the Int. Symp. on Computer Architecture and Digital Signal Processing, October 1989, Hong Kong.

[5] Ditzel, D.R., "Program Measurements on a High-Level Language Computer," Computer, Vol. 13, No. 8, August 1980, pp. 62-72.

[6] Eickemeyer, R.J. and Patel J.H. , "Performance Evaluation of On-Chip Register and Cache Organizations", Proc. 15th Int. Symp. on Computer Architecture, 1988, pp. 64-72.

[7] Farrens, M.K. and Pleszkun, A.R., "Improving Performance of Small On-Chip Instruction Caches," Proc. 16th Int. Symp. on Computer Architecture, 1989, pp. 234-241.

[8] Goodman, J.R. and Wei-Chung Hsu, "On the Use of Registers vs. Cache to Minimize Memory Traffic," Proc. 13th Annual Int. Symp. on Computer Architecture, June 1986, pp. 375-383.

[9] Hill, M.D. and A.J. Smith, "Experimental Evaluation of On-Chip Microprocessor Cache Memories," Proc. 12th Annual Int. Symp. on Computer Architecture, June 1985, pp. 55-63.

[10] "i486 Microprocessor Programmer's Reference Manual", Intel Corp., 1989.

[11] "i860 Microprocessor Programmer's Reference Manual", Intel Corp., 1989.

[12] Liu, Y.C and Gibson G.A. , "Microcomputer Systems: The 8086/8088 Family – Architecture, Programming and Design", Prentice Hall, Inc. Englewood Cliffs, N.J. 07632, 1984.

[13] Laha, S., et.al., "Accurate Low-Cost Methods for Performance Evaluation of Cache Memory Systems," IEEE Transactions on Computers, Vol. C-37, No. 11, November 1988, pp. 1325-1336.

[14] MC68xxx Microprocessor User's Manuals, Motorola Inc.

[15] Robbins, K.A. and Robbins, S. , " The Cray X-MP/Model 24," Lecture Notes in Computer Science, no.374, Springer-Verlag, 1989.

[16] Schneck, P.B., "Supercomputer Architecture," Kluwer Academic Publishers, 1987.

[17] Smith, A.J., "Sequential Program Prefetching in Memory Hierarchies," IEEE Computer, December 1978, pp. 7-21.

[18] Smith, A.J., "Cache Memories," ACM Computing Surveys, Vol. 14, No. 3, September 1982, pp. 473-530.

[19] Smith, A.J., "Line (Block) Size Choice for CPU Cache Memories," IEEE Transactions on Computers, Vol. C-36, No. 9, September 1987, pp. 1063-1075.

[20] Smith, A.J., "Cache Memory Design: An Evolving Art," IEEE Spectrum, December 1987, pp. 40-44.

[21] Smith, J.E. and J.R. Goodman, "Instruction Cache Replacement Policies and Organizations," IEEE Transactions on Computers, Vol. C-34, No. 3, March 1985, pp. 234-241.

[22] Strecker, W.D., "Transient Behaviour of Cache Memories," ACM Transactions on Computer Systems, Vol. 1, November 1983, pp. 281-293.

[23] Thornton, J.E.,"Design of a Commmputer: The Control Data 6600," Scott, Foresman and Company, Glenview 1970.

Characterization of Branch and Data Dependencies in Programs for Evaluating Pipeline Performance

PHILIP G. EMMA AND EDWARD S. DAVIDSON

Abstract—The nature by which branches and data dependencies generate delays that degrade pipeline performance is investigated in this paper. We show that for the general execution trace, few specific delays can be considered in isolation; rather, the magnitude of any specific delay may depend on the relative proximity of other delays. This phenomenon can make the task of accurately characterizing a trace tape with simple statistics intractable. We present a set of trace reductions that facilitates this task by simplifying the corresponding data-dependency graph. The reductions operate on multiple data-dependency arcs and branches in conjunction; those arcs whose performance implications are redundant with respect to the dependency graph are identified, and eliminated from the graph. We show that the reduced graph can be accurately characterized by simple statistics. We use these statistics to show that as the length of a pipeline increases, the performance degradation due to data dependencies and branches increases monotonically. However, lengthening the pipeline may correspond to decreasing the cycle time of the pipeline. These two opposing effects are used in conjunction to derive an equation for optimal pipeline length for a given trace tape. The optimal pipeline length is shown to be characterized by $n = \sqrt{\gamma\alpha}$ where γ is the ratio of overall circuit delay to latching overhead, and α is a function of the trace statistics that accounts for the delays induced by data dependencies and branches.

Index Terms—Branch delay, data dependency, performance analysis, pipeline, program trace, trace reduction.

I. INTRODUCTION

IN this paper, a method is developed for deriving performance models of pipelines by using statistics obtained from trace tapes to characterize the workload. This method is presented as an alternative to trace-driven simulation, and it proves to be more flexible in the sense that a single set of trace statistics is sufficient for modeling a large class of pipelines. A set of trace reductions is presented that simplifies the statistics that are collected, and assures that the resulting statistics contain all of the significant information that is required for an accurate model.

Trace-driven simulation has been used by many as a tool for evaluating various aspects of computer design. It has been used to study paging algorithms [1], [2], cache-management algorithms [3], database-buffering strategies [4], buffered disks [5], file-migration policies [6], branch-prediction strate-

gies [7], [8], and CPU design [9]–[11]. Trace-driven simulation facilitates the capture of very detailed information regarding the systems under study; however, the information that is captured tends to be quite specific to the particular systems that are simulated.

Some outstanding work has been done by obtaining measurements from trace tapes, and using these measurements to predict computer performance, thereby "shortcutting" the simulation process. In one of the seminal papers in this area, Peuto and Shustek measure instruction mixes for various benchmarks, and use instruction-timing models to evaluate the relative performance of the IBM 370/168 Model 1, and the Amdahl 470 V/6 [12]. Clark and Levy use a similar form of analysis to evaluate a VAX 11/780 [13]. Blake measures instruction mixes to draw general conclusions about stack machines based on the performance of the HP 3000 [14]. Kobayashi measures dynamic frequencies and nesting levels of loops in trace tapes to characterize program behavior in problem state [15], [16]. MacDougall uses hierarchical measurement to assess the composition of overall system load relative to processes, and characterizes the component processes by examining instruction mixes to arrive at a system-level performance analysis [17].

In this paper, traces are used to measure the nature of interaction between instructions. Namely, the frequency of taken branches and the proximity of data dependencies are measured to assess the degree to which a pipeline machine will suffer performance degradation due to the interlocks inherent to programs. It is demonstrated that due to the complexity of interaction among data dependencies, and between data dependencies and branches, no trace can be fully characterized by simple statistics without specific knowledge of the target pipeline. However, a set of trace reductions is presented that reduce any trace to an equivalent trace that has identical performance characteristics, such that simple statistics exactly characterize the equivalent trace independently of the target pipeline.

This paper shows that as the length of any pipeline is increased, data dependencies and branches monotonically degrade the pipeline performance (in terms of clock cycles per instruction). However, increasing the length of a pipeline for any specific architecture corresponds to reducing the basic instruction cycle, i.e., it corresponds to decreasing the cycle time of the machine. These two opposing effects are used in conjunction to derive a model for determining the pipeline length with optimal performance, given a set of trace statistics and one additional technology parameter that characterizes the

Manuscript received March 15, 1986; revised June 12, 1986. This work was supported in part by the Joint Services Electronics Program under Contract N00014-84-C-0149.

P. G. Emma is with the IBM Thomas J. Watson Research Center, Yorktown Heights, NY, 10598.

E. S. Davidson is with the Center for Supercomputer Research and Development, University of Illinois, Urbana, IL, 61801.

IEEE Log Number 8714103.

Reprinted from *IEEE Trans. Computers*, Vol. C-36, No. 7, July 1987, pp. 859–875. Copyright © 1987 by The Institute of Electrical and Electronics Engineers, Inc. All rights reserved.

time overhead associated with latching between pipeline segments. For an interesting case study of how technology influences the choice of pipeline length, see Doran [18].

In Section II, the effects of data dependencies and branches on pipeline performance are discussed, and a model for these effects is developed. In Section III, the set of trace reductions that are required to obtain simple statistics that characterize the trace is derived, and these reductions are applied to two example traces in Section IV. In Section V, the performance degradation inherent in lengthening the pipeline is traded off against the reduction in cycle time to arrive at a solution for optimal pipeline length for a given set of traces. The application of these same techniques to more complex classes of pipelines is discussed in Section VI.

II. DATA DEPENDENCY AND BRANCH DEGRADATION

Any pipeline that executes the instruction flow of a machine can roughly be separated into two sections, namely, setup and execution. The setup section corresponds to the instruction unit and is responsible for instruction fetch, instruction decode, and operand fetch. The execution section performs a functional operation on one or more input operands and produces an output operand.

If the sink operand (output) of an instruction is the same as a source operand (input) of a latter instruction, then the latter instruction is said to be *data dependent* on the former instruction. The former instruction is said to be the *resolving* instruction, and the latter instruction is said to be the *dependent* instruction. In the case of instruction pipelines, operands can be in memory locations, or in registers, or in condition-code storage-elements (e.g., branch instructions require condition codes for input).

Define the *dependency distance* between a resolving instruction and its dependent instruction as the number of instructions between the two instructions plus 1. That is, if instruction $i + k$ depends on instruction i, then the *dependency distance* is k.

For the purpose of developing the following formal theory, it is assumed that all pipeline segments are constant-time segments with unit service time, and that all instructions in the input stream traverse all pipeline segments in order, i.e., strict execution order is observed. The only reason that these two assumptions are made is that they cause a one-to-one mapping to exist between the dependency distance associated with two instructions and (in the absence of other delays) the difference between the times at which they enter the pipeline. This assumption permits the set of reductions that are developed in Section III to be treated in a simple manner for illustrative purposes. If either assumption does not hold, the validity of the trace reductions is unaltered provided that the definition of dependency distance is broadened. This extension is explained in Section VI.

Whenever a data dependency occurs, the effect that this has on the performance of the pipeline is that the dependent instruction cannot enter the execution section until the resolving instruction leaves the execution section. If out-of-order execution is not permitted, then the dependent instruction blocks the flow of all instructions behind it as well. For a pipelined execution unit having N_E segments, the maximum amount of time that the dependent instruction must wait is given by $(N_E - D)^+$, where D is the dependency distance, and the operator $(x)^+$ maps negative values of x onto the value 0, and positive values of x onto x.

Assume that in the absence of a taken branch, instructions are fetched from sequential locations in memory, and they enter setup in that order. Define a *branch target* as the instruction that follows a taken branch. The effect of a taken branch is to cause a full or partial flush of setup; the associated penalty is attributed to the *branch-target* instruction.

If a branch is not taken, then no penalty is incurred in setup (although conditional branch instructions can incur penalty in the execution section of the pipeline due to data dependencies). Since the target address of a branch instruction is an input operand for the instruction, it is assumed that the target address is known at the end of setup. If the branch is unconditional then it is always taken, and thus, the penalty associated with the target of an unconditional branch is equal to the flush depth. If the branch is conditional, then the penalty associated with it may also have an inherent data-dependency penalty, e.g., the branch may be dependent on a condition that may not have been resolved.

In a pipelined setup section having N_S segments, where each segment of the pipeline takes unit time, the maximum flush penalty is $N_S - 1$, i.e., the target instruction requires time N_S rather than time 1 to reach the end of setup. This is the flush penalty unless the branch target is fewer than N_S instructions past the branch, i.e., the only cases that do not require a full flush of setup are short forward branches.

Thus, it is assumed that unconditional branches do not require execution cycles; when an unconditional branch is encountered, the incurred penalty is equal to the flush depth. For conditional branches, the penalty is twofold: first there is a data dependency that must be resolved between a condition-code setting instruction and the branch, and next, there is a flush penalty if the branch is taken.

If one were to try to predict the performance of a pipeline by looking at the data dependencies and branches in a particular execution trace, the task would be difficult since these effects are not independent, and their associated degradations tend to cancel each other somewhat. Let BW^{-1} denote the *inverse bandwidth* of the pipeline in cycles per instruction. A simple model that does not include branches, and that considers only those data dependencies that do not interfere with each other yields the following solution for inverse bandwidth

$$BW^{-1} = 1 + \sum_{D=0}^{N_E-1} p_D (N_E - D)^+.$$

In this case, it is assumed that: instructions are executed in order, N_E is the length of the execution pipeline, and p_D is the probability that a data dependency exists at distance D for an arbitrarily selected instruction. The case $D = 0$ is included to encompass those branch instructions that compute their own conditions. This simple model assumes that no branches are taken.

A simple model that does not include data dependencies, but

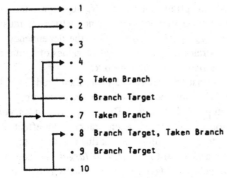

Fig. 1.   A typical data-dependency graph.

assumes that a full flush of setup is required whenever a branch is taken (i.e., short forward branches are not modeled) yields the following solution for inverse bandwidth

$$BW^{-1} = 1 + p_b(N_S - 1).$$

In this case, N_S is the length of the setup pipeline, and p_b is the probability that an arbitrarily selected instruction is a taken branch.

Let all of the data dependencies in a program be represented in a dependency graph. Fig. 1 shows a dependency-graph representation of a typical run of ten instructions. A data dependency is represented by an arc that originates at the dependent instruction and terminates at the resolving instruction. For example, the arc that originates at node 7 and terminates at node 1 represents that the seventh instruction is dependent on the first instruction. Note that in the figure, nodes 6, 8, and 9 are designated as branch targets; thus, instructions 5, 7, and 8 are taken branches.

In general, data-dependency arcs are not isolated from each other; rather, they overlap one another in a complex fashion as shown in Fig. 1. Furthermore, many data-dependency arcs span branch targets, i.e., a taken branch can occur between the resolving instruction and the dependent instruction. If the fact that arcs may overlap is ignored, and the fact that arcs may span branch-target instructions is ignored, then the superposition of the two models above yields the following model.

$$BW^{-1} = 1 + p_b(N_S - 1) + \sum_{D=0}^{N_E - 1} p_D(N_E - D)^+.$$

Recall that dependency distance was defined so as to reflect the actual distance (in time) between instructions in the absence of delay. Whenever a data dependency or a taken branch causes a delay in the pipeline, that delay increases the time between instructions on either side of the delay point by an amount equal to the delay itself. Thus, the "effective distance" associated with an arc that spans a delay point is increased, i.e., the arc is lengthened from a temporal point of view.

In the equation above, the term $(N_E - D)^+$ reflects the delay associated with an arc whose dependency distance is D, under the assumption that the arc does not span other delays. However, if the arc does span other delays, then the delay associated with the effectively lengthened arc is lessened.

Thus, the model above yields a pessimistic estimate of performance. In order to model an execution trace effectively, one must derive a set of sufficient statistics from the trace, i.e., a set of statistics that encompasses all of the necessary information in the trace.

Define an ith-order statistic as a statistic that contains information that characterizes the overlap of i arcs. First-order statistics can be derived from any trace by counting the number of branch targets, and by keeping a histogram of dependency distance for all data dependencies in the trace. For example, the first-order statistics for the trace segment shown in Fig. 1 are

$$p_2 = 2/10, \ p_3 = 2/10, \ p_4 = 1/10, \ p_6 = 1/10, \text{ and } p_b = 3/10,$$

i.e., out of ten instructions, there are two arcs with dependency distance 2, two arcs with dependency distance 3, etc., and three branch-target instructions. The model that was derived above assumes that first-order statistics are sufficient for predicting the performance of a trace for a given N_E and N_S. For example, if $N_E = N_S = 5$, then the model above yields an inverse bandwidth of

$$BW^{-1} = 1 + \frac{3}{10}(5-1) + \frac{2}{10}(5-2)^+ + \frac{2}{10}(5-3)^+$$

$$+ \frac{1}{10}(5-4)^+ + \frac{1}{10}(5-6)^+$$

$$= 1 + 1.2 + 0.6 + 0.4 + 0.1 + 0$$

$$= 3.3.$$

It is simple to demonstrate via hand simulation that this model is pessimistic. For example, let Si represent the setup processing for instruction i, and let Ei represent the execution processing for instruction i. The four dependent nodes and three branch targets in Fig. 1 impose seven constraints:

1) $E5$ cannot start until $E3$ has finished,
2) $E6$ cannot start until $E2$ has finished,
3) $E7$ cannot start until $E1$ and $E4$ have finished,
4) $E10$ cannot start until $E7$ and $E8$ have finished,
5) $S6$ cannot start until $S5$ (and $E3$) have finished,
6) $S8$ cannot start until $S7$ (and $E1$ and $E4$) have finished, and
7) $S9$ cannot start until $S8$ has finished.

The pipeline flow for these ten instructions subject to these seven constraints can then be mapped onto a pipeline for which $N_E = N_S = 5$ in a straightforward manner as shown in Fig. 2. Since the tenth instruction experiences 15 cycles of delay prior to entering setup (i.e., in the absence of delays, it would enter on the tenth cycle), the inverse bandwidth of the pipeline is (10 + 15)/10 = 2.5 cycles per instruction.

Thus, a model that is based on simple first-order statistics is insufficient for accurately predicting performance. A more accurate model can be constructed based on second-order statistics by considering all pairs of arcs that overlap in some way, and by deriving a histogram of the dependency distances of the arcs that reflects the way in which the arcs overlap.

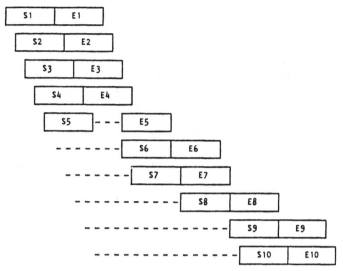

CYCLE

|1|2|3|4|5|6|7|8|9|0|1|2|3|4|5|6|7|8|9|0|1|2|3|4|5|6|7|8|9|0|1|2|3|4|

Fig. 2. Pipeline flow of ten instructions with $N_E = N_S = 5$.

Although such a model would be more accurate than a model that is based on first-order statistics, it would still be a pessimistic model, i.e., it would contain no information about the way in which triples of arcs, quadruples of arcs, etc., interact. Instead, consider reducing the trace prior to taking statistics.

A trace is said to be *separable* at a node if the dependency graph for that trace can be cut at that node without removing any of the dependency arcs. Note that the node at which the trace is separable may appear in both subgraphs. Consider some instruction j in an ordered execution trace of length N whose nodes are $(1, \cdots, j - 1, j, j + 1, \cdots, N)$. If the trace is separable at node j, then there is no dependency arc that originates at any of the nodes $(j + 1, \cdots, N)$ and terminates at any of the nodes $(1, \cdots, j - 1)$. For example, the trace shown in Fig. 1 is separable at node 7.

Any segment of a dependency graph that originates at one separable node and terminates at another separable node is said to be a *chain*. Note that for a trace of length N, the corresponding dependency graph is separable at nodes 1 and N. A chain that contains no separable nodes except at its endpoints is said to be an *inseparable chain*. For an inseparable chain of length i, the only set of sufficient statistics are ith-order statistics.

In general, an entire execution trace may form an inseparable chain. Thus, the only set of sufficient statistics that are guaranteed to characterize a trace of length N are Nth-order statistics, i.e., the sufficient statistics have the same complexity as the trace itself. If one were to use an entire trace in an analytic model, one would be doing simulation rather than analysis. In fact, this is exactly what has been done heretofore when an exact measure of performance was desired.

If simulation is not convenient, then ith-order statistics can be used in an ith-order model for some small value of i (typically $i = 1$). Such an approximation can be fairly good

for short pipelines, since $(N_E - D)^+$ is only sensitive to values of D that are less than N_E. Thus, if N_E is small, then the delays that result do not tend to have global effects. The problem with using small values of i is that the sensitivity to i is unknown, yet it is known that for $i \ll N_E$, the resulting performance estimators can be very inaccurate.

However, the solution to workload modeling that is derived in this paper is an exact solution that uses a first-order model. This is accomplished by using a set of trace reductions that breaks the general complex inseparable chain into small simple chains from which first-order statistics can easily be derived. These reductions preserve the way in which data dependencies and branches interact, and both the static and the dynamic performance characteristics of a reduced trace are identical to those characteristics of the original trace.

Thus, a reduced trace contains all of the relevant performance information, yet the corresponding dependency graph consists of simple chains that are easily characterized. Hence, the set of first-order statistics that is collected from any reduced execution trace is a sufficient set, and a first-order model is thus an exact performance predictor. Since the model must handle branch degradation as well, the statistics are two-dimensional; the first dimension is the dependency distance of an arc, and the second dimension is the number of taken branches that are spanned by the arc. In the next section, the set of reductions that are used is derived, and an algorithm is presented that performs the reductions, and subsequently renders first-order statistics from the reduced trace.

III. EXECUTION-TRACE REDUCTIONS

An execution trace can be considered to be a data-dependency graph, where each node in the graph represents an instruction in the trace, and each directed arc in the graph represents a precedence (ergo *directed* arc) based on an existing data dependency in the trace. A general graph may be

107

an inseparable chain consisting of many arcs. The trace reductions use known precedence information to remove those arcs that do not represent delays, i.e., those arcs that have no performance implications because of their temporal proximity to other delays.

If the removal of arcs is done in the manner specified in this section, then any dependency-graph representation of an execution trace can be reduced to a graph that is composed of simple inseparable chains. Furthermore, this can be done in such a manner that the reduced graph is "equivalent" to the original graph in the sense that all delays inherent to the original graph are present in the reduced graph. The simple chains in the reduced graph can then be analyzed in a straightforward manner to produce a set of first-order statistics that accurately characterizes the original trace.

In Section III-A, a set of three reductions is presented, each being relevant to a specific case in which the removal of an arc is appropriate. The permissibility of arc removal is proved based on the surrounding precedence relationships present in each of these cases. In Section III-B, an algorithm is presented that uses these reductions to break the general data-dependency graph into small simple chains, and it is shown how each of these chains can be rendered into a simple set of first-order statistics.

Preliminary to these subsections, it is helpful to establish a consistent notation as follows. Let the instructions of an execution trace be labeled in temporal order, i.e., instruction i precedes instruction $i + 1$ by exactly one instruction for all i. Define a data-dependency graph that corresponds to the trace, such that each node in the graph has the same label as its corresponding instruction in the trace. Thus, if a data dependency exists between two instructions i and j, then the label of the dependent instruction must have a larger value than the label of the resolving instruction. That is, if $i > j$, then it cannot be the case that instruction j depends on instruction i, but it may be the case that instruction i depends on instruction j. Note that any instruction may be the target of a taken branch, and should be marked as such if this is the case. For example, in Fig. 1, nodes 6, 8, and 9 are nodes that correspond to taken-branch targets. In a trace, taken-branch targets can be identified with specific branches; in an architecture not using the delayed branch, if instruction i is a taken-branch target, then instruction $i - 1$ is a taken branch.

If a data dependency exists such that instruction i is dependent on instruction j, then $i > j$, and the corresponding dependency graph has a directed data-dependency arc that originates at node i and that terminates at node j. Any node may originate zero or more arcs, and may also terminate zero or more arcs. The pipeline through which the instruction stream flows is assumed to have a setup section consisting of N_S segments, and an execution section consisting of N_E segments. Thus, the pipeline comprises $N_S + N_E$ segments.

In the following subsections, all node labels are designated by subscripted letters, e.g., i_1. All label designations with the same letter, but different subscripts, are assumed to be relevant to a particular dependent instruction. In this case, the numbered subscripts dictate the ordering on the nodes, e.g., i_0 precedes i_1 by at least one instruction. If i_0 and i_1 are the only

nodes that have the label i, then because of precedence, it must be the case that i_1 is the dependent node and that i_0 is the resolving node.

If more than two nodes share the same letter label, then the node having the largest subscript represents the dependent instruction, and all other nodes represent resolving instructions for at least that node. Note that any of these nodes can also be dependents or resolvers of other nodes, but the labelings are chosen so as to focus attention on one specific dependent node.

All dependency arcs are given by an ordered pair of labels where the first label represents the dependent node, and the second label represents the resolving node. For example, the pair (i_1, i_0) represents a dependency arc that originates at the dependent node i_1, and terminates at the resolving node i_0. The dependency distance of any arc (i_x, i_y) is denoted by $D(i_x, i_y)$, and it represents the distance in instructions, $i_x - i_y$, between the nodes i_x and i_y. If i_y is the only resolving node of the dependent node i_x, then the dependency distance $D(i_x, i_y)$ can be abbreviated as D_i.

A. Basic Reductions

D_i is a dependency distance (measured in number of instructions) between a dependent instruction, generally i_1, and its resolving instruction, generally i_0, in an execution trace. In the absence of pipeline delays, D_i happens to correspond to the temporal distance (measured in clock cycles) between these two instructions as observed at any fixed segment of the pipeline. Since the goal of trace reduction is to obtain statistics that characterize the temporal aspects of the trace in the presence of delays, a method that infers accurate time delays based on the D_i is required.

Let Δ_x denote the *delay of instruction x*, defined as 1 less than the difference in machine cycles between the time that instruction $x - 1$ enters the first segment of the execution section of the pipeline and the time that instruction x enters the same segment of the pipeline. (The quantity 1 is subtracted since the nondelayed time between these events is 1 cycle.) Define the *effective dependency distance, δ_i,* as the temporal distance associated with the scalar distance D_i. Since in the absence of delays, the scalar distance D_i is equal to the temporal distance δ_i, then in the presence of delays,

$$\delta(i_1, i_0) = D(i_1, i_0) + \sum_{x = i_0 + 1}^{i_1} \Delta_x.$$

Thus, in general, the temporal distance δ associated with an arc i is equal to the scalar distance D of the arc plus the sum of all Δ delays associated with nodes x that are spanned by dependency arc i. This definition is broadened in Section VI.

Reduction 1: In a dependency graph, if there exists a node i_n such that $n > 1$, where i_n depends on n nodes, $i_0, i_1, \cdots, i_{n-1}$, then regardless of any other delays that are inherent to the graph, arcs (i_k, i_n) can be removed from the graph for all $0 \leq k \leq n - 2$. (See Fig. 3 for a depiction of this reduction.)

Proof: Since i_n is dependent on $i_0, i_1, \cdots, i_{n-1}$, instruction i_n cannot begin execution until all instructions i_x, $0 \leq x < n$, have completed execution. Since the instruction

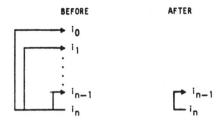

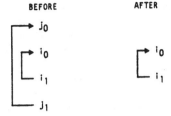

Fig. 3. Depiction of Reduction 1.

Fig. 4. Depiction of Reduction 2.

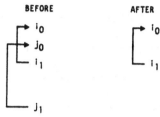

Fig. 5. Depiction of Reduction 3.

stream is executed in order at each pipeline segment, the last of the resolving instructions to complete execution will always be i_{n-1}, i.e., the closest to i_n of the resolving instructions. Thus, the penalty paid by i_n due to its data dependencies is completely determined by instruction i_{n-1}. ∎

Reduction 2: If there is a nested dependency, i.e., arcs (i_1, i_0) and (j_1, j_0) exist where $j_0 \leq i_0 < i_1 \leq j_1$, then regardless of any other delays that are inherent to the graph, arc (j_1, j_0) can be removed from the graph. (See Fig. 4 for a depiction of this reduction.)

Proof: Since $j_0 \leq i_0$, the dependency (j_1, j_0) will be resolved no later than the time at which the dependency (i_1, i_0) is resolved. In order for instruction i_1 to be executed, the dependency (i_1, i_0) must be resolved. Since (j_1, j_0) is resolved no later than the time at which (i_1, i_0) is resolved, and since the resolution of (i_1, i_0) must occur prior to the time that i_1 begins execution, the dependency (j_1, j_0) will necessarily be resolved prior to the time at which i_1 begins execution. Since $i_1 \leq j_1$, instruction j_1 can begin execution no earlier than instruction i_1. Thus, (j_1, j_0) will have been resolved by the time that j_1 is ready to begin execution. Thus, j_1 will suffer no penalty due to the dependency (j_1, j_0), and hence, the arc (j_1, j_0) can be removed from the dependency graph. ∎

Note that Reduction 2 subsumes Reduction 1, but it is convenient to retain Reduction 1 as a special case.

Reduction 3: If two dependency arcs intersect, i.e., if arcs (i_1, i_0) and (j_1, j_0) exist where $i_0 < j_0 < i_1 < j_1$, and if $D(i_1, i_0) \leq D(j_1, j_0)$, then if no delays (e.g., dependent nodes or branch targets) occur in the interval $[i_0 + 1, j_0]$, then the arc (j_1, j_0) can be removed from the graph. (See Fig. 5 for a depiction of this reduction.)

Proof: The proof is in three parts. First, the reduction is shown to hold when there are no other delays present. Next, the reduction is shown to hold when delays appear in the interval $[j_0 + 1, i_1]$. Finally, the reduction is shown to hold when delays appear in the interval $[i_1 + 1, j_1]$. Note that the interval $[i_0 + 1, j_0]$ is not considered, since no claim is made that Reduction 3 holds when delays are present in this interval.

As outlined above, first consider the simple case where, except for the delays induced by the dependencies (i_1, i_0) and (j_1, j_0), there are no delays of any sort represented in the entire interval $[i_0 + 1, j_1]$. In the absence of other delays, the temporal distance δ_i is equal to the scalar distance D_i plus the delay experienced at node i_1 due to the dependency arc (i_1, i_0), i.e., $\delta_i = D_i + \Delta_{i_1}$ where $\Delta_{i_1} = (N_E - D_i)^+$. Since the node i_1 is spanned by arc (j_1, j_0), the delay experienced at node j_1 is $\Delta_{j_1} = (N_E - D_j - \Delta_{i_1})^+$.

If $D_i \geq N_E$, then $\Delta_{i_1} = 0$, and $\Delta_{j_1} = (N_E - D_j)^+$.

However, in this case, since $D_j \geq D_i$ and $D_i \geq N_E$, it follows that $D_j \geq N_E$, and thus, $\Delta_{j_1} = 0$ also. Therefore, in this case, the arc (j_1, j_0) does not represent a delay, and it can be removed from the graph. On the other hand, if $D_i < N_E$, then $\Delta_{i_1} = N_E - D_i$, and therefore, the delay experienced at node j_1 is $\Delta_{j_1} = (D_i - D_j)^+$. Since $D_j \geq D_i$, $\Delta_{j_1} = 0$, and hence, arc (j_1, j_0) can be removed from the graph.

Now consider the case where other delays exist in the interval $[j_0 + 1, i_1]$, and let the sum of these delays be Δ_α. Since this interval is spanned by both of the arcs (i_1, i_0) and (j_1, j_0), Δ_α appears as a component in both of the temporal distances δ_i and δ_j. Since $D_j \geq D_i$, it follows that $\delta_j \geq \delta_i$, and the same arguments (as used in the previous case) apply. Thus, arc (j_1, j_0) can be removed from the graph.

Finally, consider the case where other delays exist in the interval $[i_1 + 1, j_1]$, and let the sum of these delays be Δ_β. This interval is spanned by the arc (j_1, j_0), but it is not spanned by the arc (i_1, i_0). Thus, Δ_β is a component of the temporal distance δ_j, but it is not a component of the temporal distance δ_i. Since $D_j \geq D_i$, it follows that $\delta_j > \delta_i$, and the arguments used above still apply. Thus, arc (j_1, j_0) can be removed from the graph. ∎

B. Trace Rendering Algorithm

For a new trace tape, the algorithm that is presented in this section makes one pass through the tape to construct an equivalent data-dependency graph for the trace. It then makes three successive passes through the dependency graph to apply Reductions 1, 2, and 3, respectively. After all reductions have been applied, it makes a final pass to collect statistics. The particular algorithm presented here is not the most efficient algorithm that can accomplish this task. It was chosen for this presentation only because it is simple to understand.

On the final statistical pass, the algorithm counts the number of taken branches in the graph, and collects information about the chains formed by the data-dependency arcs. For those chains that are composed of a single arc, no information about N_E or N_S is required, i.e., these chains can be represented by a two-dimensional histogram. The dimensions of the histogram represent the dependency distance associated with the arc, and the number of taken branches spanned by the arc, respectively. For those chains that are composed of multiple arcs, a statistical histogram cannot be constructed without specific knowledge of N_E and N_S. Instead, this algorithm saves information about multiple-arc chains in the form of a list of stacks; a stack is constructed for each such chain, where each element of a stack represents an arc in the chain. This list of stacks can be constructed without specific knowledge of N_E or N_S.

After the statistical pass is made, all of the statistics are written to a save file. These statistics are: the length of the trace, the number of taken branches in the trace, the two-dimensional histogram that represents the single-arc chains, and the list of stacks that represent multiple-arc chains. These statistics characterize the trace tape; once they are collected, this process need not ever be repeated for the same tape, regardless of changes made to N_E or N_S.

Note that if the list of stacks is empty, then the entire trace is characterized by the two-dimensional histogram, and the number of taken branches in the trace. However, if the list of stacks is not empty, then the algorithm prompts the user to input the values of N_E and N_S, and it processes the stacks with these values, and increments the appropriate bins in the two-dimensional histogram. The final histogram characterizes the trace subject to specific values of N_E and N_S. Probabilities are estimated by dividing these final statistics by the length of the trace (in number of instructions).

Thus, the complexity of this particular algorithm is linear in the length of the trace the first time that the trace is processed (but note that five passes are made in this process). However, for subsequent runs, the algorithm merely reads in the intermediate statistics from the save file, and processes the list of stacks subject to new values of N_E and N_S. Thus, for subsequent runs, the complexity of the algorithm is linear in the number of multiple-arc chains that cannot be reduced by Reductions 1, 2, or 3. Brief descriptions of the steps used in the algorithm follow.

Step 1: Construct the data-dependency graph. The graph is implemented as a linear linked list, where each node in the graph represents an instruction on the trace tape. Each node has four attributes: a node name, a flag that indicates whether the node is the target of a taken branch, a list of pointers to resolving nodes, and a list of pointers to dependent nodes.

Scan the execution trace starting with the first instruction on the trace, and for that instruction, create the first node of the graph. Give the first node the name 1. For each new instruction record encountered, create a new node, and append it to the data dependency graph. If the name of the last node in the graph is i, then the next node to be appended is named $i + 1$. The name of the last node in the graph is the number of instructions in the trace. For each instruction record that is the target of a taken branch, mark the corresponding instruction node accordingly.

Meanwhile, maintain a list of all sink-operand locations that are encountered. With each sink-operand location, keep a pointer to the most recent instruction node that set the operand.

For all source operands encountered, find the name of the source operand in the operand list, and use the associated pointer to establish the relevant dependency arcs between the dependent and the resolving instruction nodes. ∎

For example, Fig. 1 is a graphic representation of the set of data dependencies and branches that is obtained by applying Step 1 to the associated trace of ten instructions.

Step 2: Apply Reduction 1. Since Reduction 1 is merely a statement of the fact that the delay experienced at a dependent node depends only on the proximity of the nearest resolving node, application of Reduction 1 is straightforward. Namely, for each node in the graph that has more than one resolving node in its resolving-node list, remove the dependency arcs associated with all but the closest resolving node. The closest resolving node is the node with the largest name. ∎

Fig. 6 is a graphic representation that shows the extent to which Step 2 reduces the graph in Fig. 1.

Step 3: Apply Reduction 2. The purpose of this reduction is to remove nested dependency arcs. This step is performed with a stack since it is straightforward to identify nesting with a stack. Scan the nodes of the dependency graph in order. When a resolving node is found, first perform the analog of Step 2, i.e., if the node has more than one dependent node, then remove all of the associated arcs, except for the one from the nearest (lowest numbered) dependent node. Then push a pointer to the resolving node onto the stack.

When a dependent node is found, locate its respective resolving node on the stack. Remove from the graph all dependency arcs associated with resolving nodes that are older in the stack than this resolving node. (Since these "older" nodes are still stacked, their dependent nodes have not yet been encountered, hence, they represent outer levels of nesting.) Finally, remove from the stack the pointer to this resolving node, i.e., its dependent node (the current node) has been encountered.

After the application of Reductions 1 and 2, no node in the list will point to more than one dependent node, no node in the list will point to more than one resolving node, and there will be no nested arcs in the graph. ∎

Fig. 7 is a graphic representation that shows the extent to which Step 3 further reduces the graph in Fig. 1.

Step 4: Apply Reduction 3. This step is also easily performed with a stack algorithm and a single in-order scan of the trace. As each resolving node is encountered, a pointer to it is stacked along with its associated dependency distance and a tag that is set when its associated dependent node is reached. As each resolving node j_0 is encountered, search the stack to find an "older" resolving node i_0 with the following properties: i) the tag at i_0 is not set (arcs i and j overlap), ii) the dependency distance of i is no longer than that of j, and iii) no other delays (i.e., branch targets or dependent nodes) occur between i_0 and j_0. If such an i_0 is found, then remove arc j from the dependency graph. When the tags for all elements of the stack have been set, then the stack can be purged, since all dependent nodes have been reached; this marks the end of an inseparable chain. ∎

Fig. 8 is a graphic representation that shows the extent to which Step 4 further reduces the graph in Fig. 1.

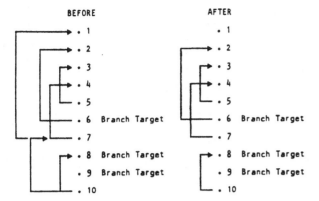

Fig. 6. Application of Reduction 1 to Fig. 1.

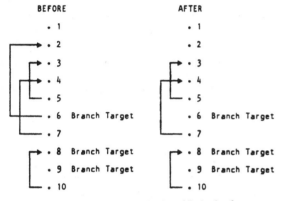

Fig. 7. Subsequent application of Reduction 2.

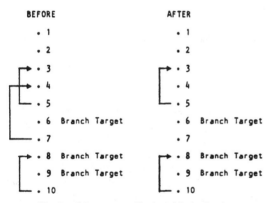

Fig. 8. Subsequent application of Reduction 3.

Step 5: Collect statistics. Define $\omega_{i,j}$ as the number of data-dependency arcs in the trace that span i nodes (excluding the resolving node but including the dependent node) of which j nodes are targets of taken branches. Let $p_{i,j}$ be the probability of such an arc, and estimate $p_{i,j}$ as the ratio of $\omega_{i,j}$ to the number of instructions in the trace. Similarly, define ω_b as the number of taken branches in the trace. Let p_b be the probability of a taken branch, and estimate p_b as the ratio of ω_b to the number of instructions in the trace. Initialize $\omega_{i,j} = 0$ for all reasonable values of i and j, and set $\omega_b = 0$.

Collecting statistics can once again be done with a stack in a two-step process. While scanning through the dependency graph, the steps are to find inseparable chains, and then to collect whatever data are suitable from each chain. As the dependency graph is scanned, the statistic ω_b is incremented whenever a node is found that is marked as the target of a taken branch.

When resolving nodes are encountered, they are stacked as was done in Step 4. When each dependent node is encountered, the corresponding tag in the stack is set. When all of the tags in the stack are set, the stack represents an inseparable chain. Note that the last dependent node of an inseparable chain can also be the first resolving node of the next inseparable chain (i.e., the graph is separable at such a node). In this event, a copy of the node is added to the graph, i.e., the node is split into two nodes: one that only reflects resolving nodes, and one that only reflects dependent nodes.

For each stack, the "oldest" element of the stack is used to increment the statistic $\omega_{i,j}$ according to its associated dependency distance (i), and the number of taken branches that are spanned by the corresponding dependency arc (j). This is only done for the "oldest" element of the stack, since it is only this element whose corresponding delay is unaffected by the dependency arcs represented by other elements of the stack.

If the stack contains exactly one element, then it can be discarded, since the dependency histogram has already been made to reflect the presence of the associated dependency arc. If the stack contains multiple elements, then it is saved on a list of stacks for further processing subject to N_E and N_S. ■

As observed from experiments, the vast majority of inseparable chains contain only a single arc once the trace has been reduced. Thus, the list of stacks that results from a given trace tape is typically small. If the list of stacks is empty, then Step 6 (as follows) is not required.

Step 6: Render statistics from the list of stacks. For this step, the specific values of N_E and N_S must be known. For each stack in the list, proceed as follows.

For each entry in the stack, let D represent the associated dependency distance (in number of instructions), let δ represent the corresponding temporal distance (in cycles), and let Δ represent the delay experienced at the dependent node (in cycles). Initially, assign $\delta = D$ for all entries in the stack.

Starting with the "oldest" entry in the stack, and continuing until all entries have been processed, proceed as follows. Increment the statistic $\omega_{\delta,j}$ on behalf of the entry, unless the entry is the "oldest" entry in the stack (recall that the statistic for the "oldest" entry was collected in Step 5). Next, if j is the number of taken branches spanned by the dependency arc represented by the current entry, then assign $\Delta = (N_E - \delta - j(N_S - 1))^+$ for the entry. For each entry in the stack that spans the dependent node of this entry, increment its temporal distance δ by this value of Δ. Another entry spans the dependent node of the current entry if its resolving node is "older" than the dependent node of the current entry, and the dependent node of the current entry is "older" than the dependent node of the other entry. ■

Within our experience, most traces fully reduce to inseparable chains, each composed of a single arc. For such traces, the statistics $\omega_{i,j}$ are independent of N_E and N_S, i.e., the statistics

111

that characterize such traces are independent of the hardware under study. However, for traces that do not fully reduce, it is only necessary to reprocess the list of stacks obtained in Step 5 when different values of N_E and N_S are being investigated.

For any pipeline that is characterized by N_E and N_S, and for any execution trace that is characterized by $p_{i,j}$ and p_b, the inverse bandwidth of the pipeline running that trace is

$$BW^{-1} = 1 + p_b(N_S - 1) + \sum_{i=0}^{N_E-1} \sum_{j=0}^{i} p_{i,j}(N_E - i - j(N_S - 1))^+.$$

For example, the fully reduced trace-segment in Fig. 7 is characterized by the statistics

$$p_b = 3/10, \ p_{2,0} = 1/10, \ \text{and} \ p_{2,1} = 1/10$$

independently of N_E and N_S. For the values $N_E = N_S = 5$, the inverse bandwidth as computed from the formula above is

$$BW^{-1} = 1 + \frac{3}{10}(5-1) + \frac{1}{10}(5-2)^+ + \frac{1}{10}(5-2-1(5-1))^+$$

$$= 1 + 1.2 + 0.3 + 0.0$$

$$= 2.5.$$

This value agrees with the value obtained via hand simulation (see Fig. 2).

In the next section, the effectiveness of these reductions is demonstrated on two sample execution traces. Statistics are given on the complexity of the dependency chains (i.e., the number of arcs in the chains) after each reduction is applied, and the resulting statistics that characterize the traces are shown.

IV. Examples of Trace Reduction

To demonstrate the effectiveness of trace reduction, two execution traces taken from an IBM System 370 processor were reduced in the manner specified above. One of them is an eigenvalue kernel which was monitored over 54 693 instructions, and the other is a Gaussian elimination kernel which was monitored over 63 612 instructions. In these cases, memory locations, registers, and condition codes are considered to be the data items that give rise to dependencies. The tracer provided the address, the opcode, and the data references made by each instruction during execution.

The first set of statistics, presented in Table I, shows the effectiveness of each reduction. The dependencies in each of the traces initially formed one inseparable chain. Even after applying Reduction 1, neither of the chains was separated. In the case of the eigenvalue kernel, the chain comprised 39 852 dependency arcs. In the case of the Gaussian elimination kernel, the chain comprised 49 174 dependency arcs.

The application of Reduction 2 separated the eigenvalue kernel into 32 253 inseparable chains, only 66 of which comprised more than a single arc. The Gaussian elimination kernel was separated into 41 361 inseparable chains, only 323 of which comprised more than a single arc. For both traces, Reduction 2 left no chains composed of more than three arcs. Reduction 3 completely reduced the eigenvalue kernel into

TABLE I
EFFECTIVENESS OF TRACE REDUCTIONS

	EIGEN		GAUSS	
Trace Length	54693		63612	
Reduction 1	1 chain of 39852		1 chain of 49174	
	# arcs	# chains	# arcs	# chains
Reduction 2	1	32187	1	41038
	2	65	2	322
	3	1	3	1
	# arcs	# chains	# arcs	# chains
Reduction 3	1	32254	1	41346
	2	0	2	16

32 254 chains, each consisting of a single arc. For this kernel, the statistics $\omega_{i,j}$ are independent of N_E and N_S. The Gaussian elimination kernel was separated into 41 346 chains each consisting of a single arc, but 16 chains each consisting of two arcs were left. Thus, in addition to the statistics $\omega_{i,j}$ and ω_b, the Gaussian elimination kernel requires a list of 16 stacks, each with two elements, to characterize it independently of N_E and N_S.

The second set of statistics, presented in Table II, is the set of first-order sufficient statistics for the kernels. The upper part of the table is a histogram of dependency distance versus the number of taken branches spanned, i.e., these are the statistics $\omega_{i,j}$. For example, the reduced eigenvalue dependency graph contains 304 dependency arcs of distance 3 that span a single taken branch. The statistic $p_{i,j}$ is obtained by dividing the entries in this histogram by the trace length.

The "extra delays" shown in the table for the Gaussian elimination kernel correspond to those 16 arcs that are the second arcs of the inseparable chains composed of two arcs. For any specific N_E, these delays could appear in the table of $\omega_{i,j}$ statistics, however, they are kept separate to make the statistics more general. Note that for chains composed of two arcs that cannot be split by Reduction 3, if the dependency distances of the arcs are D_i and D_j, and if no taken branches are spanned, then the delay experienced at the second dependent node is equal to $(N_E - D_j - (N_E - D_i)^+)^+$.

In all 16 such cases that appear in the Gaussian elimination kernel, the first arc is characterized by $D_i = 7$, the second arc is characterized by $D_j = 6$, and no taken branches are spanned. Since the delays associated with these first arcs are independent of the presence of the second arcs, the first arcs appear in Table II in the distance = 7 row, branches = 0 column. The penalties associated with the second arcs appear as "extra delays" in the table. Since for these arcs, $(N_E - 6 - (N_E - 7)^+)^+$ is 0 for $N_E \leq 6$ and is 1 for $N_E \geq 7$ these 16 arcs contribute 16 cycles of delay over-and-above the delays attributable to the $\omega_{i,j}$ statistics in pipelines having $N_E \geq 7$. The net effect of these irreducible chains is thus to add $16/63\ 612$ to the BW^{-1} calculated from the $\omega_{i,j}$ and p_b in the table for cases where $N_E \geq 7$.

The final statistic shown in the table is the number of taken branches that appear in the traces. The statistic p_b is obtained by dividing the total number of branches that appear in the

TABLE II
SUFFICIENT STATISTICS FOR EXAMPLE TRACES

	EIGEN			GAUSS		
Dependency Histogram	Number of Branches			Number of Branches		
	0	1	2	0	1	2
Distance 1	28494	115	0	35989	520	0
2	1020	991	254	3522	916	17
3	333	304	1	26	106	1
4	376	21	0	22	1	0
5	78	0	0	209	0	0
6	13	0	0	0	0	0
7	0	0	0	16	0	0
Extra Delays	0			16 if $N_E \geq 7$		
Taken Branches	4027			7688		

trace by the trace length. This set of statistics fully characterizes the traces.

V. OPTIMAL PIPELINE LENGTH AS A FUNCTION OF TRACE STATISTICS

Thus far, it has been shown that any execution trace can be reduced in a manner that allows a set of first-order statistics to characterize the trace exactly. Given that a processor designer has a set of traces that is believed to characterize a workload, it is possible to use trace statistics to choose the optimal pipeline length for that workload with a given technology in mind.

Since the performance of a pipeline is measured in terms of instructions per second, performance is decomposable into aspects of machine organization (which determine instructions per cycle), and aspects of technology (which determine cycle time). For the purposes of this paper, it is assumed that the machine organization is fixed as specified above, i.e., it is a pipeline comprising a setup section and an execution section.

The one unspecified parameter is the length of the pipeline, or the granularity into which tasks are to be decomposed. As is apparent from the equation for inverse bandwidth pertaining to this machine organization, the cycles per instruction increases monotonically with the length of the pipeline due to data dependencies and branches. However, as the length of the pipeline is increased (or equivalently, the granularity into which tasks are decomposed becomes finer), the cycle time of the pipeline decreases. Thus, as the length of the pipeline increases, extrinsic delays degrade cycles per instruction, while intrinsically, cycles per second is improved. Recent work by Kunkel and Smith reports and analyzes such a tradeoff for vector machines [19]. In the following sections, it is shown how to trade off these two aspects of performance to arrive at a pipeline length that delivers maximum bandwidth for a given set of trace statistics.

In Section V-A, the impact of pipeline granularity on cycles per instruction is analyzed. For any specific pipeline having specific values of N_E and N_S, the pipeline can be characterized by the ratio of these lengths, $E/S = N_E/N_S$, and by the value n where $N_E = nE$ and $N_S = nS$. With this view, it is assumed that changing the pipeline granularity is merely a matter of varying n, i.e., it is assumed that the characteristic length ratio E/S is invariant in n for any base design.

The inverse bandwidth for a pipeline that is characterized by E/S and n is denoted $BW_{E,S}^{-1}(n)$. Inverse bandwidth is the sum of three terms: the constant 1, a term for branch delay, and a term to account for data dependencies in the presence of branch delay. Of these three terms, it is only the data dependency term that is unwieldy; it contains a double summation, and the nonlinear operator $(x)^+$. For convenience, the data-dependency term is denoted $D_{E,S}(n)$. In Section V-A, data from Table II are used to obtain a general estimator for this term subject to the eigenvalue benchmark. This is done by using the difference $D_{E,S}(n) - D_{E,S}(n-1)$ to obtain a recursion in n. This recursion facilitates making an estimate of $BW_{E,S}^{-1}(n)$ from an exact solution to $D_{E,S}(k)$ where $k \ll n$.

In Section V-B, the impact of pipeline granularity on cycle time is analyzed. Cycle time can be obtained as a function of n for any specific technology; however, it is more generally useful to have a function of n that is less dependent on the specific technology used. That is, a function of n is sought that is independent of the specific cycle time that is obtainable with a particular technology.

For a given technology, let C be the longest path (in nanoseconds) through a nonpipelined machine, and let L be the time (in nanoseconds) associated with latching. Let γ be the ratio C/L. The single parameter γ is sufficient for specifying all technologies that are characterized by C/L.

It is shown that the speedup of a pipelined machine, denoted $\Psi(n)$, over a nonpipelined machine is the product of the pipeline bandwidth and a function of the parameters n and γ. That is, speedup is a function that is separable into two components: the function $BW_{E,S}^{-1}(n)$ which can be estimated as shown in Section V-A, and a function that is dependent on the technology parameter γ. Since γ is independent of the specific cycle-time that is offered by a technology, the speedup function provides a convenient means for determining the optimal pipeline granularity.

In Section V-C, the two components of $\Psi(n)$ are reviewed. The first component is a function of only γ and n, and it is monotonically increasing in n. The second component, $BW_{E,S}(n)$, is monotonically decreasing in n. The product of these two components, $\Psi_{E,S}(n)$, forms a bitonic sequence. This is demonstrated by showing that the derivative of $\Psi_{E,S}(n)$ has a double root, and no other roots. The double root is a maximum (optimal design point) determined by $n_{opt}^2 = \gamma \alpha_{E,S}(k)$, where $\alpha_{E,S}(k)$ is a function of the statistics that are gathered via trace reduction evaluated at some pipeline length,

113

$k(E + S)$. The eigenvalue benchmark statistics are applied to this result for illustrative purposes.

Since $\alpha_{E,S}(k)$ is fixed for any specific E/S subject to any specific benchmark and an arbitrarily chosen k, the solution for n_{opt} is only a function of γ. This fact is used to derive the sequence γ_i whose elements define ranges of γ for which particular values of n are optimal. In particular, γ_n is that point at which $\Psi_{E,S}(n) = \Psi_{E,S}(n + 1)$ when $\gamma = \gamma_n$. It is shown that the sequence γ_i as derived yields exact values of γ_n for n greater than a specified threshold value.

A. Cycles Per Instruction as a Function of Pipeline Length

As derived in Section III, the formula for inverse bandwidth is

$$BW^{-1} = 1 + p_b(N_S - 1) + \sum_{i=0}^{N_E-1} \sum_{j=0}^{i} p_{i,j}(N_E - i - j(N_S - 1))^+.$$

This formula is the sum of three components, namely: the constant 1, a term associated with branch delay, and a term to account for data dependency degradation in the presence of branch delay. The constant 1 is inherent to any pipeline that decodes at most 1 instruction per cycle, i.e., the upper bound on pipeline performance is assumed to be 1 cycle per instruction. The branch-delay term is a function only of the branch probability, and the length of setup N_S. The most complex of the terms is the data-dependency degradation. This term involves the two-dimensional statistic, $p_{i,j}$, as well as the lengths of the setup and the execution pipeline sections, N_S and N_E, respectively. It is this last term that is the primary focus of this section.

Let E/S be the length ratio N_E/N_S. Assume that any increases in the length of the pipeline (i.e., any refinements in the pipeline granularity) are distributed in both sections of the pipeline so as to preserve this ratio. Without loss of generality, make the restriction that either $E = 1$ and/or $S = 1$, or that E and S are relatively prime. Thus, when a pipeline length is chosen, n is defined so that the length of setup is $N_S = nS$, the length of execute is $N_E = nE$, and the overall length of the pipeline is $N = N_S + N_E = n(S + E)$. Let the inverse bandwidth for the pipeline be denoted as $BW_{E,S}^{-1}(n)$, so that all pipelines having the characteristic E/S can be described by the single parameter n. Similarly, denote the data-dependency component for the pipeline as $D_{E,S}(n)$. Thus,

$$BW_{E,S}^{-1}(n) = 1 + p_b(nS - 1) + D_{E,S}(n)$$

where

$$D_{E,S}(n) = \sum_{i=0}^{nE-1} \sum_{j=0}^{i} p_{i,j}(nE - i - j(nS - 1))^+.$$

Table III shows the number of penalty cycles associated with data dependencies in the eigenvalue benchmark over a range of values of nS and nE. These data are plotted in Fig. 9. These numbers were computed by using the statistics in Table II; any particular value of $D_{E,S}(n)$ can be obtained by dividing the appropriate table entry by the tracelength 54 693.

TABLE III
DATA DEPENDENCY PENALTY CYCLES FOR EIGENVALUE BENCHMARK

nE	nS 1	2	3	4	5	6	7	8	9
1	0	0	0	0	0	0	0	0	0
2	28609	28494	28494	28494	28494	28494	28494	28494	28494
3	59483	58123	58008	58008	58008	58008	58008	58008	58008
4	90995	89076	87970	87855	87855	87855	87855	87855	87855
5	122904	120963	119299	118193	118078	118078	118078	118078	118078
6	154891	152950	151010	149600	148494	148379	148379	148379	148379
7	186891	184950	183009	181324	179914	178808	178693	178693	178693
8	218891	216950	215009	213069	211638	210228	209122	209007	209007
9	250891	248950	247009	245068	243383	241952	240542	239436	239321

Note that for $E/S \leq 1$, the value $D_{E,S}(n)$ is independent of nS. This property occurs because no data dependency that spans a taken branch has performance implications when $E/S \leq 1$ since all such data dependencies are obviated by branch delays. Thus, $D_{E,S}(n)$ is determined by the statistic $p_{i,0}$ if $S \geq E$. Since a closed form estimator for $BW_{E,S}^{-1}(n)$ is sought, and since it is only the $D_{E,S}(n)$ component that is not trivial, the normalized difference $(D_{E,S}(n) - D_{E,S}(n-1))/D_{E,S}(n)$ was computed for various fixed values of the ratio E/S using the numbers in Table III to obtain the approximations shown in Table IV. These approximations are plotted in Fig. 10. As demonstrated in this table, an approximate estimator for this difference given any E/S is

$$\frac{D_{E,S}(n) - D_{E,S}(n-1)}{D_{E,S}(n)} \simeq \frac{E}{nE - 1}.$$

Thus, an approximation to the data-dependency penalty can be expressed recursively as follows.

$$D_{E,S}(n) \simeq \frac{nE - 1}{(n-1)E - 1} D_{E,S}(n - 1).$$

This approximation is valid over any set of statistics $p_{i,j}$ that tends to be concentrated over small values of i and j. Furthermore, if $p_{i,j} = 0$ for $i \geq nE$ and $j \geq nS$, then the approximation is extremely good, i.e., it becomes more accurate as n increases. Assume that $D_{E,S}(k)$ has been computed exactly for some value k, and that an estimator for $D_{E,S}(n)$ is desired where $n > k$. Using the recursion above,

$$D_{E,S}(n) \simeq \left(\prod_{i=k+1}^{n} \frac{iE - 1}{(i-1)E - 1} \right) D_{E,S}(k) = \frac{nE - 1}{kE - 1} D_{E,S}(k)$$

where $D_{E,S}(k) > 0$, i.e., kE is greater than the smallest i for which $p_{i,j} > 0$. Note that the best estimator is the one for which $k = n - 1$, and that an exact solution is obtained in the case that $k = n$. Thus, a family of estimators in k for inverse bandwidth as a function of n is given by

$$BW_{E,S}^{-1}(n) \simeq 1 + p_b(nS - 1) + \frac{nE - 1}{kE - 1} D_{E,S}(k).$$

B. Speedup as a Function of Pipeline Length

In Section V-A, a class of estimators was built that determines the increase in cycles per instruction as a function of pipeline length for a known workload given the fixed ratio

114

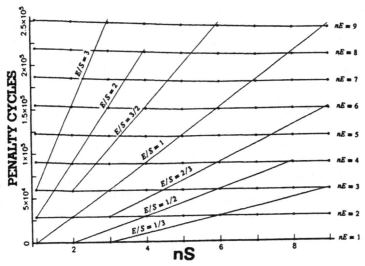

Fig. 9. Data dependency penalty cycles for various nE and nS.

TABLE IV
THE NORMALIZED DIFFERENCE $(D_{E,S}(n) - D_{E,S}(n-1))/D_{E,S}(n)$

ACTUAL

		1/4	1/3	1/2	2/3	3/4	E/S 1	4/3	3/2	2	3	4
n	2	1.000	1.000	1.000	0.676	0.609	1.000	0.582	0.611	0.679	0.611	0.581
	3	–	0.509	0.509	0.408	–	0.509	–	0.382	0.410	0.381	–
	4	–	–	0.340	–	–	0.340	–	–	0.291	–	–
	5	–	–	–	–	–	0.256	–	–	–	–	–

APPROXIMATE

		1/4	1/3	1/2	2/3	3/4	E/S 1	4/3	3/2	2	3	4
n	2	1/1	1/1	1/1	2/3	3/5	1/1	4/7	3/5	2/3	3/5	4/7
	3	–	1/2	1/2	2/5	–	1/2	–	3/8	2/5	3/8	–
	4	–	–	1/3	–	–	1/3	–	–	2/7	–	–
	5	–	–	–	–	–	1/4	–	–	–	–	–

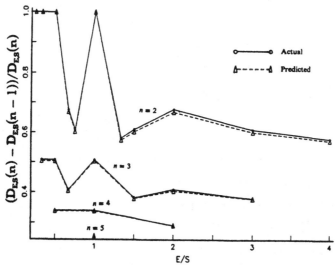

Fig. 10. Approximations to $(D_{E,S}(n) - D_{E,S}(n-1))/D_{E,S}(n)$ for various E/S and n.

115

E/S. In this current section, the fact that increasing the pipeline length decreases the cycle time is taken into account, and an equation for speedup as a function of pipeline length is derived subject to any given function $BW_{E,S}^{-1}(n)$. Since cycle time decreases monotonically as a function of n to an asymptote (i.e., the shortest possible cycle time must include latch delay), and since $BW_{E,S}^{-1}(n)$ increases monotonically as a function of n for any E/S, there exists a specific n that maximizes speedup for any specific workload given a value of E/S. This optimization is pursued in Section V-C.

Let BW_{ser}^{-1} denote the inverse bandwidth for a serial (nonpipelined) machine, and let BW_{pip}^{-1} denote the inverse bandwidth for a pipelined machine. Assume that $BW_{ser}^{-1} = 1$ cycle per instruction, since branches and data dependencies do not degrade the performance of such a machine. From the basic approach used by Larson and Davidson [20], let C denote the longest path (in nanoseconds) through the serial machine, i.e., C represents the longest path that would exist in a machine with all latches removed. Assume that the penalty associated with a single latch is L nanoseconds. L should include all aspects of latching, such as setup and hold time, clock skew, etc.; valuable insight is offered by Kunkel and Smith [19] and by Unger and Tan [21] as to the actual overheads associated with latching in pipelines. The clock period for a serial machine (assuming that the final output is latched on every cycle) is then $\Phi_{ser} = C + L$ nanoseconds, and the throughput of the machine is given by $T_{ser} = BW_{ser}/\Phi_{ser}$ instructions per nanosecond.

Since a pipelined machine having N stages has the same logical pathlength C, and since each stage includes a latch, the

equation for speedup is

$$\Psi = BW_{pip} \cdot \left[\frac{N(\gamma + 1)}{N + \gamma} \right].$$

C. Optimal Pipeline Length as a Function of Job Load

Recall that the pipeline under consideration is specified by the known ratio E/S, and that the length of the pipeline is given by $N = n(E + S)$. In Section V-A, an estimator for inverse bandwidth was developed for an E/S pipeline of length N, namely $BW_{E,S}^{-1}(n)$. The speedup of an E/S pipeline as a function of n can then be estimated by

$$\Psi_{E,S}(n) = BW_{E,S}(n) \cdot \left[\frac{n(S+E)(\gamma+1)}{n(S+E)+\gamma} \right]$$

$$\simeq \left(1 + p_b(nS - 1) + \frac{nE-1}{kE-1} \cdot D_{E,S}(k) \right)^{-1}$$

$$\cdot \left[\frac{n(S+E)(\gamma+1)}{n(S+E)+\gamma} \right]$$

for some computed value of $D_{E,S}(k)$. Since this speedup is relative to instructions per second, the best performing pipeline is that pipeline characterized by the particular n that maximizes $\Psi_{E,S}(n)$.

This estimate is used from here on. For any fixed k, the function $\Psi_{E,S}(n)$ has exactly one critical point (maximum), and thus, it describes a bitonic sequence. This is demonstrated by showing that the derivative of $\Psi_{E,S}(n)$ has one double root, and no other roots, as follows. First, a separation of variables on the equation above yields

$$\Psi_{E,S}(n) = \frac{\gamma+1}{(S+E)\left(1 - p_b - \dfrac{D_{E,S}(k)}{kE-1}\right) - \gamma\left(p_b S + \dfrac{ED_{E,S}(k)}{kE-1}\right)} \cdot \left[\frac{(S+E)\left[\dfrac{(kE-1)(1-p_b) - D_{E,S}(k)}{(kE-1)p_b S + ED_{E,S}(k)}\right]}{n + \dfrac{(kE-1)(1-p_b) - D_{E,S}(k)}{(kE-1)p_b S + ED_{E,S}(k)}} - \frac{\gamma}{n + \dfrac{\gamma}{S+E}} \right].$$

clock period for a pipelined machine is $\Phi_{pip} = (C/N) + L$ nanoseconds. The pipelined throughput is thus $T_{pip} = BW_{pip}/\Phi_{pip}$ instructions per nanosecond. Speedup, denoted Ψ, is defined to be the ratio between the pipelined and the serial throughputs, namely,

$$\Psi = \frac{T_{pip}}{T_{ser}} = \frac{BW_{pip}(C+L)}{BW_{ser}[(C/N)+L]} = BW_{pip} \cdot \left[\frac{N(C+L)}{C+LN} \right].$$

Since the exact values of C and L may not be known at the start of a design, it simplifies matters to define a technology parameter that is the ratio between them. Let $\gamma = C/L$ denote this parameter. Although C and L may not be known, it is reasonable to expect that given a technology, and given an idea of the circuit complexity that is to be designed, a designer should be able to estimate γ. As will be demonstrated later, it is not essential to know an exact value of γ in order to select the optimal pipeline length, since optimal lengths are applicable over ranges of the parameter γ. Defined in terms of γ, the

The derivative with respect to n is

$$\frac{\partial \Psi_{E,S}(n)}{\partial n}$$

$$= \frac{\gamma+1}{(S+E)\left(1 - p_b - \dfrac{D_{E,S}(k)}{kE-1}\right) - \gamma\left(p_b S + \dfrac{ED_{E,S}(k)}{kE-1}\right)}$$

$$\cdot \left[\frac{-(S+E)\left[\dfrac{(1-p_b)(kE-1) - D_{E,S}(k)}{p_b S(kE-1) + ED_{E,S}(k)}\right]}{\left(n + \dfrac{(1-p_b)(kE-1) - D_{E,S}(k)}{p_b S(kE-1) + ED_{E,S}(k)}\right)^2} \right.$$

$$\left. + \frac{\gamma}{\left(n + \dfrac{\gamma}{S+E}\right)^2} \right].$$

116

and the roots of the derivative, denoted n_{opt}, are determined by

$$n_{opt}^2 = \frac{\gamma((1-p_b)(kE-1)-D_{E,S}(k))}{(S+E)(p_b S(kE-1)+ED_{E,S}(k))}.$$

Thus, $\Psi_{E,S}(n)$ increases monotonically to a maximum point (the double root as determined above), and then it decreases monotonically.

Note, however, that $\Psi_{E,S}(n)$ only has a physical interpretation for integer values $n \geq 1$. Therefore, in the region $n \geq 1$, the sequence determined by $\Psi_{E,S}(n)$ is: monotonic if the double root is ≤ 1, bitonic if the double root is ≥ 2, and either monotonic or bitonic if the double root is >1 and <2. If $\Psi_{E,S}(n)$ is monotonic in the range of interest, then the best choice of n is $n = 1$. If $\Psi_{E,S}(n)$ is bitonic in the range of interest, then the best choice of n is either $\lfloor n_{opt} \rfloor$ or $\lceil n_{opt} \rceil$.

Note that n_{opt}^2 is the product of the technology parameter γ, and a function of the trace statistics subject to a given length ratio E/S. In particular, define

$$\alpha_{E,S}(k) = \frac{1}{S+E} \left[\frac{(kE-1)(1-p_b)-D_{E,S}(k)}{(kE-1)p_b S+ED_{E,S}(k)} \right]$$

so that $n_{opt} = \sqrt{\gamma \alpha_{E,S}(k)}$. For any given E/S subject to any specific workload and an arbitrarily chosen k, the value of $\alpha_{E,S}(k)$ is fixed, and hence, the value of n that maximizes speedup is only a function of γ.

For example, suppose that for a particular pipeline, $E/S \simeq 1$, i.e., it is known that the length of setup is approximately equal to the length of execution. Furthermore, suppose that the eigenvalue benchmark is believed to characterize the workload. Then,

$$\alpha_{1,1}(k) = \frac{1}{2} \left[\frac{(k-1)(1-p_b)-D_{1,1}(k)}{(k-1)p_b+D_{1,1}(k)} \right]$$

where $p_b = 4027/54\,693$ as shown in Table II, and $D_{1,1}(k)$ is the estimator obtained by dividing the (k, k) entry in Table III by the tracelength for $k > 1$. Arbitrarily, choose $k = 2$. Then from Table III, $D_{1,1}(2) = 28\,494/54\,693$, and $\alpha_{1,1}(2) = 0.34089$. The optimal value of n is then estimated to be either the floor or the ceiling of $n_{opt} = \sqrt{0.34089 \cdot \gamma}$. Note that the choice $k = 3$ yields a slightly different estimator, $n_{opt} = \sqrt{0.32790 \cdot \gamma}$.

While the methodology above provides a value of n_{opt}, it does not positively identify which of $\lfloor n_{opt} \rfloor$ or $\lceil n_{opt} \rceil$ is truly the optimal choice for n. Furthermore, since $D_{E,S}(n)$ is merely an estimate that is computed from a known $D_{E,S}(k)$, the value of k that is chosen may generate more uncertainty in the optimal choice of n depending on γ. For example, if $\gamma = 75$ in the example above, then the choice $k = 2$ yields $n_{opt} = 5.056$, and the choice $k = 3$ yields $n_{opt} = 4.959$ (i.e., the best choice of n could be 4, 5, or 6).

For small values of n, this does not pose a serious problem, since the exact values of $\Psi_{E,S}(n)$ can be readily computed and compared. However, when γ is very large, the inaccuracy inherent to $\alpha_{E,S}(k)$ may be such as to position n_{opt} far away from the actual best choice of n. Inaccuracy in $\alpha_{E,S}(k)$ arises because the nonlinear operator $(x)^+$ used in the computation

of $D_{E,S}(n)$ causes the difference $D_{E,S}(n) - D_{E,S}(n - 1)$ to vary with n when n is small.

For large values of n, the difference $D_{E,S}(n) - D_{E,S}(n - 1)$ is a constant. This property allows for an exact solution for optimal n when n is large. Let $I = \max \{i\}$ for which $p_{i,j} \neq 0$. Then for $n \geq (I + 1)/E$, the difference $D_{E,S}(n + 1) - D_{E,S}(n)$ can be written as

$$D_{E,S}(n+1) - D_{E,S}(n) = \sum_{i=0}^{I} \sum_{j=0}^{i} p_{i,j}([(n+1)(E-jS) - (i-j)]^+ - [n(E-jS)-(i-j)]^+).$$

Note that since $i \geq j$ is all terms, then for a term to be nonzero, it must be the case that $j < E/S$. The difference in the equation above is nonlinear only if both of the conditions $(n + 1)(E - jS) > (i - j)$ and $n(E - jS) < (i - j)$ hold for some $i \geq j$. However, if $n \geq (i - j)/(E - jS)$ for every $\{(i, j)\}$ for which $i \geq j$, $j < E/S$, and $p_{i,j} \neq 0$, then the difference $D_{E,S}(n + 1) - D_{E,S}(n)$ is a constant. That is, for large values of n,

$$D_{E,S}(n+1) - D_{E,S}(n) = \sum_{i=0}^{I} \sum_{j=0}^{i} p_{i,j}(E-jS) = K, \text{ a constant.}$$

For example, in the $E/S = 1$ pipeline, the constraint $j < E/S$ dictates that only the statistics $p_{i,0}$ are relevant. In the eigenvalue benchmark, $p_{i,0} = 0$ if $i > 6$, and therefore, $I = 6$. The constraint $n \geq (i - j)/(E - jS)$ subject to $j = 0$ and $i \leq 6$ dictates that $D_{E,S}(n + 1) - D_{E,S}(n)$ is a constant for all $n \geq 6$. In particular, for the eigenvalue benchmark running on an $E/S = 1$ pipeline, $K = \Sigma p_{i,0} = 30\,314/54\,693$. In the remainder of this section, K is used to solve for ranges of γ in which particular values of n maximize pipeline performance.

Define the sequence γ_i such that $\Psi_{E,S}(n) = \Psi_{E,S}(n + 1)$ at the point $\gamma = \gamma_n$. That is, each particular γ_n defines the region boundary for which Ψ is maximized at the point n if $\gamma = \gamma_n - \epsilon$, and Ψ is maximized at the point $n + 1$ if $\gamma = \gamma_n + \epsilon$, where ϵ is arbitrarily small. For $n \geq (i - j)/(E - jS)$ subject to the constraints on i and j as stated above, it was shown that $D_{E,S}(n + 1) = D_{E,S}(n) + K$. For a particular n, the boundary γ_n is that value of γ that satisfies $\Psi_{E,S}(n + 1) = \Psi_{E,S}(n)$. Equating these two values of Ψ in terms of K at the point γ_n yields

$$\frac{1+p_b(nS-1)+D_{E,S}(n)+[p_b S+K]}{1+p_b(nS-1)+D_{E,S}(n)}$$

$$= \left[\frac{(n+1)(S+E)(\gamma_n+1)}{(n+1)(S+E)+\gamma_n} \right] \cdot \left[\frac{n(S+E)+\gamma_n}{n(S+E)(\gamma_n+1)} \right].$$

Straightforward manipulation results in

$$\gamma_n = \frac{(S+E)(p_b S+K)}{1-p_b+D_{E,S}(n)-nK} \cdot n(n+1).$$

Note that although the denominator in the equation for γ_n appears to be a function of n, in fact it is a constant. Since $D_{E,S}(n + 1) = D_{E,S}(n) + K$ when n is sufficiently large, the

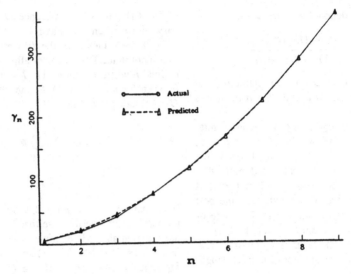

Fig. 11. Predicted and actual values of γ_n for $E/S = 1$.

difference $D_{E,S}(n) - nK$ is invariant for large n. For example, in the $E/S = 1$ pipeline subject to the eigenvalue benchmark, it was shown that $D_{E,S}(n + 1) = D_{E,S}(n) + K$ for $n \geq 6$. Therefore, for $n \geq 6$, the difference $D_{E,S}(n) - nK$ is equal to $D_{1,1}(6) - 6K$. From Table III, $D_{1,1}(6) = 148\,379/54\,693$, and from above, $K = 30\,314/54\,693$. Since $p_b = 4027/54\,693$, the sequence γ_i is given by $\gamma_n = (68\,682/17\,161)n(n + 1)$, or equivalently, $\gamma_n = 4.00221n(n + 1)$ for the $E/S = 1$ pipeline subject to the eigenvalue benchmark.

Note that γ_n is an exact solution for $n \geq 6$. For example, $\gamma_6 = 168.093$ for this pipeline. The significance of this is that if it is known that the actual value of $\gamma = C/L$ is exactly 168, then the best $E/S = 1$ pipeline that can be built has six setup segments and six execute segments. However, if the actual value of γ is exactly 169, then the best pipeline that can be built has seven setup segments and seven execute segments. Fig. 11 is a plot of γ_i as computed above for $E/S = 1$. In Table V, the constants K and the associated sequences γ_n are listed for various E/S subject to the eigenvalue benchmark. These sequences are plotted in Fig. 12.

VI. Machines with Complex Setup and Execution Units

Thus far, it has been assumed that the setup section of a machine consists of N_S pipeline segments each of which has unit service time, and that in the absence of taken branches, setup does not influence the performance of the machine. In many machines (particularly machines having complex architectures), the segments of setup are difficult to identify. In addition, the nature of the interactions between the components of setup and the memory system can be complex. However, setup was assumed to be simple in nature so that the branch penalty could be easily assessed. Thus, the only real consequence that complex setup sections have is that the branch penalty for such machines must be estimated. Fortunately, a fairly good approximation can be made rather easily.

If any suitable analytic model, as in [22]–[28], is applied just to the setup section of a machine, assuming no branching or data dependencies, then a raw bandwidth figure can be

TABLE V
THE SEQUENCES γ_n FOR VARIOUS E/S

E/S	K	γ_n	EXACT
1	30314/54693	$4.00221^* n(n+1)$	$n \geq 6$
2	62059/54693	$12.79166^* n(n+1)$	$n \geq 3$
2/3	60628/54693	$21.18437^* n(n+1)$	$n \geq 3$
3	94059/54693	$25.31578^* n(n+1)$	$n \geq 2$
3/2	92373/54693	$32.39790^* n(n+1)$	$n \geq 3$
4	126059/54693	$41.96864^* n(n+1)$	$n \geq 2$
3/4	90942/54693	$43.66587^* n(n+1)$	$n \geq 2$

obtained, BW_S. The only information that is required to obtain BW_S is the topology of the machine along with the cycle times and effective access times of its associated components. If the memory system is hierarchical, miss ratios must also be assumed. Thus, the first estimate of setup bandwidth might require no workload information other than a rough estimate of cache miss ratio. Note that the inverse bandwidth in this case is calculated for an unflushed system, and it represents the average latency (i.e., the time between two consecutive instructions) in setup if there were no setup flushes due to taken branches.

Whenever there is a taken branch, there can be (at worst) a complete flush of setup. Although the estimate of BW_S gives the average instruction frequency in an unflushed pipeline, the full flush penalty requires knowledge of the average latency in a flushed pipeline (i.e., the average time at the end of setup between a taken branch and its target instruction). Since this flushed latency may be significantly more than the average inverse bandwidth during steady-state operation, an estimate of the average flushed latency L_F is required.

L_F is equal to the time for a branch target instruction to traverse the setup section once the prior branch instruction is resolved at the end of setup. For example, in a machine with no branch target prefetch and no overlap between memory accesses, let T_f be the average number of cycles to fetch the target instruction, T_D be the number of cycles to decode the instruction, T_m be the average access time in cycles to fetch a

118

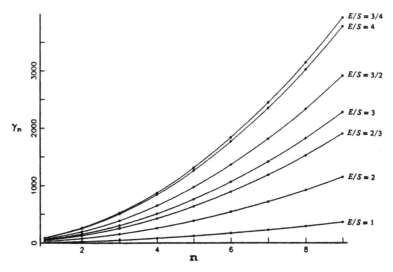

Fig. 12.   The sequences γ_n for various E/S.

memory operand, T_R be the number of cycles to read a register, p_r be the average number of register operands per instruction, and p_m be the average number of memory operands per instruction. Then a good estimator for L_F is

$$L_F = T_f + T_D + p_r T_R + p_m T_m.$$

T_f and T_m would include estimates of hit ratios, access conflict cycles, communication delays, access times, and block-transfer effects for various levels of the memory hierarchy.

T_f would be 0 if branch target prefetching always occurs prior to the actual setup section (i.e., target prefetch is always completed before branch resolution). The $p_r T_R$ and $p_m T_m$ terms may be reduced if operand-access overlap features are included in the machine. A more accurate probabilistic model for estimating L_F would include an actual probability distribution for the various terms, rather than simply the averages (distribution means) of those distributions [27].

This estimate of the instruction-setup latency L_F can be used as the full flush penalty. In the case of short forward branches, a full flush may not be required. Note that, in the absence of taken branches, the average number of instructions in setup at any time is $N_S = L_F B W_S$. N_S thus represents the effective number of pipeline segments in setup. Thus, if the distance (in instructions) d from a forward branch to its target is less than N_S, then the flush penalty is only $(d - 1)/B W_S$. N_E can be evaluated similarly from the effective concurrency in the execution pipeline in the absence of data dependencies.

In machines having multiple execution units of different classes, there can be instruction passing after setup. For example, consider a machine that has a three-segment pipe-lined adder, and a seven-segment pipelined multiplier. An add instruction can begin as much as three cycles after a multiply instruction begins, and still complete its execution before the multiply has completed. This effective passing is not reflected in the way that the trace reductions are performed on an execution trace, i.e., the add is not allowed to resolve any dependencies until at least one cycle after the multiply has completed.

The effect can be effectively handled by the trace reductions by modifying the definition of temporal dependency distance. Let each node i in the dependency graph be tagged with the execution time in cycles e_i associated with its instruction type. Then the generalization of effective dependency-distance must include the amount of time required by the resolving instruction to complete execution. Recall that the temporal distance associated with a dependency arc is the number of cycles between starting the resolving instruction in execution and starting the dependent instruction in execution. Assuming a steady-state instruction flow, the temporal distance associated with the scalar distance D_i can be estimated, in the absence of other overlapping dependencies, as

$$\delta_i = D_i \cdot BW_S^{-1} + (e_{i_0} - D_i \cdot BW_S^{-1})^+$$

where i_0 is the resolving instruction. If the same reductions are applied to any trace using this more general form of temporal distance, the resulting set of first-order statistics will characterize the trace for the corresponding machine architecture. When this assumption does not yield a good approximation, BW_S^{-1} can be replaced with an entire distribution rather than the mean. This will generate a higher instruction frequency due to the nonlinearity of the $(x)^+$ term in the δ_i formula [27].

VII. CONCLUSION

The nature of the interaction between data dependencies and branches in a program can be quite complex. If one tries to model the performance of a machine by examining an execution trace without performing reductions, no set of simple statistics is sufficient. Thus, the alternatives to date have been simulation, and simple models using first-order approximations.

In this paper, a set of reductions was presented that reduces a dependency graph to an equivalent simplified graph for which characterization by first-order statistics is sufficient and straightforward. These trace reductions were derived by assuming that a machine comprises a single pipeline having a setup section followed by an execution section. Several estimation techniques were also presented for use with more complex machines. These techniques hinge on broadening the definition of "dependency distance." Except for the setup–execute assumption, the trace reductions are machine independent, and thus, any workload can be accurately characterized by a set of first-order statistics.

It was shown that data dependencies and branches cause a monotonic increase in cycles per instruction as the pipeline length is increased. However, lengthening the pipeline corresponds to reducing its cycle time if the architecture is fixed. These two opposing effects were used in conjunction to derive a general equation for the pipeline length that achieves maximum performance for executing a particular set of traces, given one technology parameter, namely the relative overhead for latching in the pipeline.

References

[1] L. A. Belady, "A study of replacement algorithms for a virtual storage computer," *IBM Syst. J.*, vol. 5, pp. 78–101, 1966.

[2] O. Babaoglu and D. Ferrari, "Two-level replacement decisions in paging stores," *IEEE Trans. Comput.*, vol. C-32, pp. 1151–1159, 1983.

[3] A. J. Smith, "Cache memories," *Comput. Surv.*, vol. 14, pp. 473–530, 1982.

[4] ——, "Sequentially and prefetching in database systems," *ACM Trans. Database Syst.*, vol. 3, pp. 223–247, 1978.

[5] ——, "Disk cache-miss ratio analysis and design considerations," *ACM Trans. Comput. Syst.*, vol. 3, pp. 161–203, Aug. 1985.

[6] ——, "Long term file migration: Development and evaluation of algorithms," *Commun. ACM*, vol. 24, pp. 521–532, 1981.

[7] J. E. Smith, "A study of branch prediction strategies," in *Proc. 8th Annu. Symp. Comput. Architecture*, vol. 9, 1981, pp. 135–148.

[8] J. Lee and A. J. Smith, "Branch prediction strategies and branch target buffer design," *Computer*, vol. 17, pp. 6–22, Jan. 1984.

[9] D. E. Lang, T. K. Agerwala, and K. M. Chandy, "A modeling approach and design tool for pipelined central processors," in *Proc. 6th Annu. Symp. Comput. Architecture*, vol. 7, Apr. 1979, pp. 122–129.

[10] B. Kumar and E. S. Davidson, "Performance evaluation of highly concurrent computers by deterministic simulation," *Commun. ACM*, vol. 21, pp. 904–913, Nov. 1978.

[11] ——, "Computer system design using a hierarchical approach to performance evaluation," *Commun. ACM*, vol. 23, pp. 511–521, Sept. 1980.

[12] B. L. Peuto and L. J. Shustek, "An instruction timing model of CPU performance," in *Proc. 4th Annu. Symp. Computer Architecture*, 1977, pp. 165–178.

[13] D. W. Clark and H. M. Levy, "Measurement and analysis of instruction use in the VAX 11/780," in *Proc. 9th Int. Symp. Computer Architecture*, Apr. 1982, pp. 9–17.

[14] R. P. Blake, "Exploring a stack architecture," *Computer*, vol. 10, pp. 30–41, May 1977.

[15] M. Kobayashi, "Dynamic profile of instruction sequences for the IBM, System/370," *IEEE Trans. Comput.*, vol. C-32, pp. 859–861, Sept. 1983.

[16] ——, "Dynamic characteristics of loops," *IEEE Trans. Comput.*, vol. C-33, pp. 125–132, Feb. 1984.

[17] M. H. MacDougall, "Program behavior and processor design," in *The Measurement of Computer Software Performance*, Los Almos National Lab., 1983.

[18] R. W. Doran, "The Amdahl 470 V/8 and the IBM 3033: A comparison of processor designs," *Computer*, vol. 15, pp. 27–36, Apr. 1982.

[19] S. R. Kunkel and J. E. Smith, "Optimal pipelining in supercomputers," in *Proc. 13th Annu. Symp. Comput. Architecture*, 1986, pp. 404–411.

[20] A. G. Larson and E. S. Davidson, "Cost-effective design of special-purpose processors: A fast Fourier transform case study," in *Proc. 11th Annu. Allerton Conf. Circuit Syst. Theory*, Oct. 1973, pp. 547–557.

[21] S. H. Unger and C. J. Tan, "Clocking schemes for high-speed digital systems," *IEEE Trans. Comput.*, vol. C-35, pp. 880–895, Oct. 1986.

[22] T. C. Chen, "Parallelism, pipelining, and computer efficiency," *Comput. Design*, pp. 69–74, Jan. 1971.

[23] P. M. Kogge, *The Architecture of Pipelined Computers*. New York: Hemisphere, 1981.

[24] K. Hwang and F. A. Briggs, *Computer Architecture and Parallel Processing*. New York: McGraw-Hill, 1984.

[25] M. J. Flynn, "Some computer organizations and their effectiveness," *IEEE Trans. Comput.*, vol. C-21, pp. 948–960, Sept. 1972.

[26] C. V. Ramamoorthy and H. F. Li, "Pipeline architecture," *Comput. Surv.*, vol. 9, pp. 59–102, Mar. 1977.

[27] P. G. Emma and E. S. Davidson, "A residual-time model for pipeline performance," submitted for publication.

[28] ——, "A class of performance estimators for pipelines with embedded buffers," submitted for publication.

Optimal Pipelining

Pradeep K. Dubey

Purdue University, West Lafayette, Indiana 47907

AND

Michael J. Flynn*

Stanford University, Stanford, California 94305

Pipelining is one of the most attractive and widely used design alternatives in high-speed computer systems as it offers a potential speedup of N when N pipeline stages are used. This study is an attempt to understand the trade-offs and overhead that limit this theoretical speedup. A mathematical model has been developed to provide insight into the effective roles played by different parameters involved. *Optimization of a pipeline* refers to partitioning the pipeline into an optimum number of segments such that overall throughput is maximized. The first section of this paper summarizes previous related work in this area. The next section provides the details of the model. The following section derives certain inferences from the model and illustrates its close agreement with corresponding results obtained via CRAY-1S simulations by Kunkel and Smith [*Proc. 13th Annual Symposium on Computer Architecture*, 1986, pp. 404–411]. The last section discusses some potential improvements in the model. © 1990 Academic Press, Inc.

1. INTRODUCTION

The following are the main practical constraints that limit the performance of pipelined processors:

(i) *Instruction dependencies:* An instruction may be dependent on previous instructions for either data or control. This may cause less than full utilization of the pipeline.

(ii) *Resource conflicts:* An instruction may require the use of a certain pipeline resource during the same period as an earlier instruction, thus necessitating a delay in its start. This can also limit utilization of the pipeline [4].

(iii) *Latch overhead:* This places some constraints on the maximum clock frequency that can be used. There are three main components of this overhead [4]:

* This research was supported in part by NASA under Contract NAG2-248, using facilities provided by NASA under Contract NAGW 419.

(a) propagation delay through the latch,

(b) data skew resulting from the difference between the minimum and the maximum signal propagation times through various logic paths, and

(c) clock skew between the different stages of the pipeline.

(iv) *Partitioning overhead:* A pipeline stage must consist of integer number of gate levels; hence the propagation delay of a pipeline stage is quantized, which may reduce the maximum clock frequency used for the entire pipeline.

(v) *Setup or flush time overhead:* The larger the pipeline the more time required to fill it up and flush it. This time can have significant effect on the overall throughput. Note that apart from the initial setup time, additional flushes result from instruction dependency.

(vi) *Control path limitations:* The time required to generate control signals for the pipeline stages also determines a minimum data path delay within any pipeline segment [4].

Thus, there are *two* kinds of limitations: those that limit the full utilization of the pipeline and those that limit the maximum clock frequency. Besides the constraints mentioned above, insufficient utilization of a pipeline can also result from not having enough data to keep the pipeline full. Such a restriction arises frequently in systems where full utilization of a computational resource is limited by, for example, insufficient I/O bandwidth.

1.1. Previous Research

A significant amount of work has been done on detecting hazards (resulting from instruction dependency or resource conflict) and optimal scheduling [5, 6]; but most of these studies assumed no restriction on clock period. In the area of latch timing, Cotten [1] and Hallin and Flynn [3] developed some basic latch timing constraints. Hallin/Flynn's work was extended by Fawcett [2]. Recently Kunkel and Smith [4] further analyzed Fawcett's constraints and also provided some CRAY-1S simulation results to illustrate the effect of different overheads. Kunkel/Smith's work is the motivating factor for this paper. Simulation results were obtained by them for the specific case of the polarity-hold latch and using a single-phase clock.

The following latch timing constraints [2, 3] form the basis for analyzing and modeling the latch overhead:

(i) Minimum clock high time: Clock pulse has to be wide enough to ensure that valid data are latched.

(ii) Maximum clock high time: Clock pulse must be shorter than the minimum propagation delay from the input of one latch to the input of the next.

(iii) Minimum clock period: Minimum clock period must be longer than the maximum propagation delay from the input of one latch to the input of the next, to ensure that valid data are latched.

Kunkel/Smith's paper starts with performance measurements assuming no latch overhead. In the next step, it includes the *data skew* component of latch overhead. In the final phase, the *clock skew* component is incorporated, first assuming *two-level* fanout and then assuming *four-level* fanout circuitry. In each case scalar, vector, and combined loops are used as the three kinds of inputs. Based on these results they concluded that 8 to 10 levels of gate delay per segment yields optimum, combined (scalar and vector) performance.

Kunkel/Smith's paper does not provide much insight into the factors governing the nature of the performance curves, i.e., the reasons behind certain characteristics displayed by the performance measurements, which leads to the motivation for this paper:

Can one come up with a theoretical model which will include different overheads associated with a generic pipeline and provide insights which will help predict the nature of modulations in the performance curve and the optimal performance?

This is a theoretical model for better understanding of the behavior of a pipelined architecture.

2. A GENERIC MODEL

Let T be the latency of a logic tree without any pipelining. If the tree is divided into s segments, without considering any kinds of overhead, the clock period with pipelining would be given by

$$\Delta t = T/s.$$

Considering full utilization, throughput, G, would be

$$G = 1/\Delta t.$$

Pipeline utilization can be quantified in terms of a utilization parameter, u, defined as

$$u = s_{av}/s,$$

where

s_{av} = average number of segments active at a time
s = total number of available segments in the pipeline.

Thus, $u = 0$ for unutilized pipelines and $u = 1$ for fully utilized pipelines. Therefore actual throughput can be modified to

$$G = u/\Delta t. \qquad (1)$$

Equation (1) represents the effect of the pipeline limitations that result in inefficient utilization of the pipeline.

Similarly, the actual clock period would not simply be inversely proportional to the number of segments, but rather involve certain overhead components. Pipeline overheads can be grouped into the following two categories:

(a) *Static overhead* (c): This kind of overhead is associated with each pipeline stage and is independent of the number of partitions of the pipeline. Propagation delay overhead (through the stage latch) and the clock skew overhead fall under this category.

(b) *Dynamic overhead* ($k(s)$): This kind of overhead is a function of the number of partitions of the pipeline; i.e., it is a function of s. Data skew overhead, setup/flush time overhead, and partitioning overhead belong to this category.

Therefore, with these overheads included clock period, Δt, can be rewritten as

$$\Delta t = k(T/s) + c. \qquad (2)$$

Under ideal conditions, i.e., without any overhead, $k = 1$ and $c = 0$. For example, we take a look at some of the timing constraints developed by Kunkel/Smith [4] on the basis of earlier work in this area by Fawcett [2]. Assuming polarity-hold latches and single-phase clock, after satisfying the constraints mentioned in Section 1.1, the minimum clock period with pipelining can be expressed as

$$\Delta t = (n + 2)t_{max},$$

where

n = number of gate levels between latches (excluding two levels of gate delay in the latch itself)
t_{max} = maximum gate delay.

In our terminology, the above expression can be written as

$$\Delta t = T/s + 2t_{max}$$

after separating the constant overhead term. In order to satisfy the lower bound on clock period (third constraint in Section 1.1), there must be a minimum number of gate levels between latches for proper operation. Thus, if s is large, delay padding may be required. Again, repeating the result derived by Kunkel/Smith [4], assuming wire delay padding, the clock period in this range can be expressed in our terminology as

$$\Delta t = (1 - \mu)T/s + (6 - 4\mu)t_{max},$$

where

μ = ratio of minimum gate delay to maximum gate delay.

This indicates a dynamic overhead, $k = (1 - \mu)$, and a static overhead, $c = (6 - 4\mu)$. Interestingly, k turns out to be less than 1 in this example, which may be confusing at first sight. To help alleviate this source of possible confusion, remember that the above equation is valid only when using delay padding to satisfy the constraint on minimum number of gate levels between latches. Since s is typically large in this range, any apparent reduction in Δt due to reduced k is more than offset by a larger constant overhead term (c), when the above equation is compared with Eq. (2) under ideal conditions.

Combining Eqs. (1) and (2), we obtain

$$G = u/[k(T/s) + c]. \qquad (3)$$

The optimal value of s, i.e., the number of segments which maximizes the throughput, can be obtained by solving $dG/ds = 0$. This results in the following equation to be solved,

$$c(du)s^2 + kT(du)s + ukT = 0, \qquad (4)$$

where

$du = du/ds$, the first-order derivative of u

with respect to s.

The above equation does not presume any specific utilization pattern. Hence, it can be used for any known utilization pattern.

Clearly pipeline utilization u is some function of s, the number of pipeline segments. In only the simplest problem could we expect a linear function $u = b - as$ (where a, b are arbitrary constants). Normally shorter pipelines are easily filled and hence result in higher utilization. As the number of segments starts to go up, utilization starts to drop in a nonlinear manner. There is an upper limit to pipeline utilization independent of the number of segments which can be set, for example, by the maximum memory bandwidth. This maximum utilization is referred to as u_{max} and is independent of s. As loading in a program environment is likely

to cause at least a second-order term, in this paper a second-order utilization pattern is assumed for the purpose of simulation,

$$u = u_{max} - rs^2 - vs. \qquad (5)$$

Therefore,

$$du = du/ds = -2rs - v, \qquad (6)$$

where the coefficients r and v are constants for any given program environment. These can be empirically determined and depend among other things on the amount of vectorization and instruction dependency in a given program. In the above equation, r represents the effect of increasing dependency and issuing delay between instructions. For example, a two-segment pipeline can only have a single-stage dependency but with increasing number of segments; utilization would tend to drop due to increased dependency. v represents the first-order coefficient in our utilization model.

This is one of the simpler possible models for program utilization. The second-order equation has been chosen only so that, as the number of segments changes, the utilization changes at a varying rate. Any equation of order two or more can capture this effect.

Using Eqs. (5) and (6), Eq. (4) can be simplified to

$$es^3 + fs^2 + gs + h = 0, \qquad (7)$$

where

$$e = 2rc$$
$$f = cv + 3kTr$$
$$g = 2kTv$$
$$h = -(u_{max})kT.$$

Equation (7) can be solved to obtain the solution for optimal number of partitions, s_{opt}, under different conditions of utilization and overhead parameters. This equation was used to generate the performance tables (Tables I–V) and corresponding curves (Figs. 1–5) to illustrate the sensitivity with respect to each parameter. Utilization coefficients have been varied in a range such that the utilization given by Eq. (5) is between 0 and 1. A given partitioning of a pipeline can be considered suboptimal or overoptimal depending on whether the number of segments in the pipeline is less than or more than the optimal number of segments, respectively. Performance measurements have been taken at suboptimal, optimal, and overoptimal points. All the throughput measurements are normalized with respect to G_{norm}, which represents the throughput at certain nominal values of *all*

TABLE I

Normalized Throughput vs c

c (ns)	s_{opt}	G_{subop}	G_{opt}	G_{ovrop}
0	6.29	0.36	1.47	0.62
10	5.51	0.33	1.01	0.35
20	5.03	0.31	0.78	0.24
30	4.69	0.29	0.64	0.19
40	4.44	0.28	0.55	0.15
50	4.23	0.26	0.48	0.13
60	4.05	0.25	0.43	0.11
70	3.91	0.23	0.39	0.10
80	3.78	0.22	0.35	0.09
90	3.66	0.21	0.32	0.08
100	3.56	0.20	0.30	0.07

Note. Input parameters other than those indicated in a table are held at their nominal values.

TABLE III

Normalized Throughput vs u_{max}

u_{max}	s_{opt}	G_{subop}	G_{opt}	G_{ovrop}
1.00	7.08	0.56	2.06	1.74
0.95	6.91	0.53	1.92	1.57
0.90	6.73	0.51	1.78	1.39
0.85	6.54	0.48	1.64	1.22
0.80	6.35	0.45	1.51	1.04
0.75	6.15	0.42	1.38	0.87
0.70	5.95	0.39	1.25	0.70
0.65	5.73	0.36	1.13	0.52
0.60	5.51	0.33	1.01	0.35
0.55	5.27	0.31	0.89	0.17
0.50	5.02	0.28	0.78	0.00

parameters. There are clearly other options for normalization. The chosen option is preferred assuming that more often one would be interested in estimating the throughput with respect to an existing (nominal) setup. Under nominal conditions, static overhead is assumed to be about 1/10 of the period without pipelining. Dynamic overhead is assumed to be 1.3, as compared to 1 in the ideal case. The assumed nominal values of the utilization coefficients result in about half-utilization of the pipeline.

Suppose there is an existing pipeline design with a certain number of segments, s_{nom}, and corresponding throughput, G_{nom}. Now, if the number of partitions is changed to s, with corresponding throughput G, then the throughput gain in moving from s_{nom} to s partitions can be defined as the ratio

$$G_{gain} = G/G_{nom}. \qquad (8)$$

Tables VI through X and corresponding graphs (Figs. 6–10) show the sensitivity of this gain as a function of over-

head and utilization coefficients. All the gain calculations are with respect to a reference pipeline having number of segments, $s_{nom} = 5$. Nominal values used for all the parameters can be found in a tabular form in the Appendix.

3. INFERENCES

Let us first analyze the effect of the overhead and the utilization coefficients on the actual (normalized) throughput:

(i) As the static overhead (c) increases, the optimum throughput (G_{opt}) and the optimum number of partitions (s_{opt}) decreases. From Fig. 1, we can see that for small values of c, changes in c have a predominant effect. This indicates the possibility of dramatic change in the optimal throughput (G_{opt}), as well as optimal partitioning (s_{opt}), if a balanced clock (negligible unintended skew) is disturbed.

(ii) As the dynamic overhead (k) increases, G_{opt} goes down whereas, unlike the previous case, s_{opt} goes up. From Fig. 2, it can be seen that similar to the earlier case, a given Δk is more effective when k is small than when it is large. In a typical system where k is closer to 1, whereas c is closer

TABLE II

Normalized Throughput vs k

k	s_{opt}	G_{subop}	G_{opt}	G_{ovrop}
1.00	5.34	0.43	1.20	0.40
1.10	5.40	0.39	1.13	0.38
1.20	5.46	0.36	1.07	0.36
1.30	5.51	0.33	1.01	0.35
1.40	5.55	0.31	0.96	0.33
1.50	5.59	0.29	0.91	0.32
1.60	5.62	0.28	0.87	0.31
1.70	5.65	0.26	0.83	0.30
1.80	5.68	0.25	0.79	0.29
1.90	5.71	0.23	0.76	0.28
2.00	5.73	0.22	0.73	0.27

TABLE IV

Normalized Throughput vs v

v	s_{opt}	G_{subop}	G_{opt}	G_{ovrop}
0.0010	6.09	0.34	1.14	0.66
0.0030	5.96	0.34	1.11	0.59
0.0050	5.82	0.34	1.08	0.52
0.0070	5.69	0.34	1.05	0.45
0.0090	5.57	0.34	1.02	0.38
0.0110	5.45	0.33	1.00	0.31
0.0130	5.33	0.33	0.97	0.24
0.0150	5.21	0.33	0.95	0.17
0.0170	5.09	0.33	0.92	0.10
0.0190	4.98	0.33	0.90	0.03

TABLE V

Normalized Throughput vs r

r	s_{opt}	G_{subop}	G_{opt}	G_{ovrop}
0.0005	11.03	0.34	1.57	1.57
0.0010	9.02	0.34	1.40	1.39
0.0015	7.90	0.34	1.29	1.22
0.0020	7.14	0.34	1.21	1.04
0.0025	6.58	0.34	1.15	0.87
0.0030	6.15	0.34	1.09	0.70
0.0035	5.80	0.34	1.05	0.52
0.0040	5.51	0.33	1.01	0.35
0.0045	5.26	0.33	0.97	0.17
0.0050	5.04	0.33	0.94	0.00

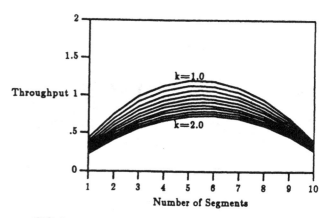

FIG. 2. Normalized throughput vs dynamic overhead (k).

to 0, on comparing Figs. 1 and 2, we conclude that a given Δc would normally have stronger impact on system performance than an equivalent Δk.

(iii) As utilization (u) goes up, G_{opt} as well as s_{opt} goes up. A comparison of Figs. 3–5 would lead us to conclude that higher-order coefficients have stronger effect on optimal partitioning (s_{opt}) and the optimal throughput (G_{opt}), as compared to the lower-order coefficients. In other words, higher-order coefficients would require tighter control for maintaining certain optimal performance. It should also be observed that for large s, the slope of the performance curves (i.e., dG/ds) in Fig. 3 becomes highly insensitive to the variations in u_{max}, which represents the constant term in the utilization model. A mathematical explanation for this, although avoided here, is not very difficult to derive from the expression for dG/ds (Eq. (13)) given in a later section.

The following conclusions can be made from the gain plots:

(i) As the static overhead (c) increases, gain increases for smaller than existing (reference) number of segments. For more than the reference number of segments, gain de-

creases with increasing c (Fig. 6). A gain can be considered an incentive if it is greater than 1. Thus in other words, with increasing c, there is higher incentive to move an existing (reference) pipeline to a lesser number of segments. On the other hand, with increasing c, the incentive for moving to a greater number of segments decreases. This behavior is seen as a result of s_{opt} going down with increasing c.

(ii) As the dynamic overhead (k) increases, gain decreases for fewer than the reference number of segments. For more than the existing number of segments, gain increases with increasing k (Fig. 7). Therefore, with increasing k, there is lower incentive to change an existing pipeline to a smaller number of segments and vice versa.

(iii) As the utilization (u) increases, gain decreases for less than the existing number of segments. For more than the reference number of segments, gain increases with increasing utilization (Figs. 8–10). Again, since s_{opt} goes up with higher utilization, there is increasing incentive to move an existing pipeline to one with a larger number of segments. It should also be observed that a variation in any of the utilization coefficients would have stronger perfor-

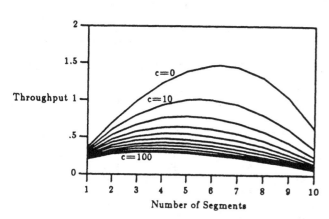

FIG. 1. Normalized throughput vs static overhead (c).

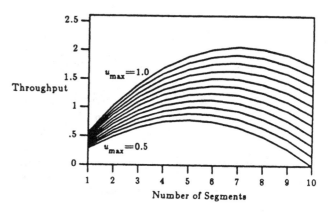

FIG. 3. Normalized throughput vs constant term of the utilization model (u_{max}).

125

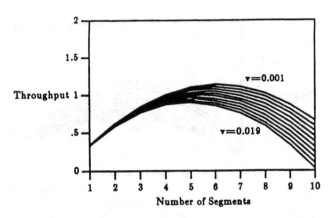

FIG. 4. Normalized throughput vs first-order coefficient of the utilization model (v).

TABLE VI

Throughput Gain vs c

c (ns)	s_{opt}	G_{gsbop}	G_{gopt}	G_{govop}
0	6.29	0.26	1.06	0.44
10	5.51	0.33	1.01	0.35
20	5.03	0.40	1.00	0.31
30	4.69	0.46	1.00	0.29
40	4.44	0.51	1.01	0.28
50	4.23	0.55	1.02	0.27
60	4.05	0.59	1.02	0.26
70	3.91	0.63	1.03	0.26
80	3.78	0.66	1.04	0.25
90	3.66	0.69	1.05	0.25
100	3.56	0.71	1.05	0.25

mance impact on the system with large number of segments than the system with fewer segments.

An interesting but not very obvious property of the gain plots is the nonmonotonicity of the optimal gain. Let us look at the gain plot for the static overhead c (Fig. 6). It can be seen that the optimal gain is at its minimum when c is at 20 ns. Figure 11 shows the effect of utilization change on the optimal gain minima. If the utilization is increased, we would notice a shift of minima when c is at 50 ns.

Therefore, for a certain change in the static overhead c, say from $c = 25$ to 45 ns, scalar code (smaller utilization) can show an increase in optimal gain, whereas vector code (higher utilization) continues to show a drop in the optimal gain. A similar effect is observed in Kunkel/Smith's simulation results, when as a result of moving from two-level fanout clock skew overhead to four-level fanout clock skew overhead (in other words, in moving to higher constant overhead), scalar optimal gain increases, whereas the vector optimal gain continues to drop.

The optimal gain minimum is seen when s_{opt} drops to s_{nom}. Since s_{opt} is higher for a vector environment, with an

increase in c it drops to s_{nom} later than in the case of a scalar environment. As a result, we notice the effect just described.

3.1. Correlation with Kunkel/Smith Experimental Results

Minimum clock period expressions in Kunkel/Smith's paper [4] can be rearranged to obtain the corresponding static and dynamic overhead terms. In the range where s is large, inclusion of data skew overhead decreases the dynamic overhead (k), whereas the static overhead (c) increases, in the range where s is large. As explained above, gain decreases as a result of these changes, and there is dramatic reduction in throughput because of a change in c from zero to a nonzero value. A decrease in the dynamic overhead (k) tends to increase the s_{opt}, but this effect is overridden by the large reduction in s_{opt} caused by the increase in c. Hence, s_{opt} goes down, i.e., moves toward a smaller number of segments and becomes noticeable for the scalar code. For the vector code because of higher utilization, s_{opt} still stays high enough to be unnoticed. Inclusion of clock skew overhead further increases the constant overhead (c) and hence s_{opt} continues to move toward a smaller number

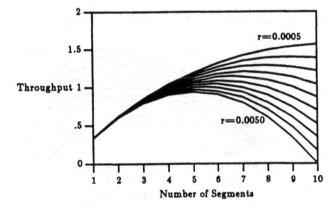

FIG. 5. Normalized throughput vs second-order coefficient of the utilization model (r).

TABLE VII

Throughput Gain vs k

k	s_{opt}	G_{gsbop}	G_{gopt}	G_{govop}
1.00	5.34	0.36	1.00	0.33
1.10	5.40	0.35	1.01	0.34
1.20	5.46	0.34	1.01	0.34
1.30	5.51	0.33	1.01	0.35
1.40	5.55	0.33	1.01	0.35
1.50	5.59	0.33	1.01	0.36
1.60	5.62	0.32	1.01	0.36
1.70	5.65	0.32	1.01	0.36
1.80	5.68	0.32	1.02	0.37
1.90	5.71	0.31	1.02	0.37
2.00	5.73	0.31	1.02	0.37

		TABLE VIII		
		Throughput Gain vs u_{max}		
u_{max}	s_{opt}	G_{gsbop}	G_{gopt}	G_{govop}
1.00	7.08	0.30	1.09	0.92
0.95	6.91	0.30	1.08	0.88
0.90	6.73	0.30	1.07	0.83
0.85	6.54	0.31	1.06	0.78
0.80	6.35	0.31	1.05	0.72
0.75	6.15	0.32	1.04	0.65
0.70	5.95	0.32	1.03	0.57
0.65	5.73	0.33	1.02	0.47
0.60	5.51	0.33	1.01	0.35
0.55	5.27	0.34	1.00	0.20
0.50	5.02	0.36	1.00	0.00

		TABLE X		
		Throughput Gain vs r		
r	s_{opt}	G_{gsbop}	G_{gopt}	G_{govop}
0.0005	11.03	0.28	1.32	1.31
0.0010	9.02	0.29	1.20	1.19
0.0015	7.90	0.30	1.13	1.07
0.0020	7.14	0.30	1.09	0.94
0.0025	6.58	0.31	1.06	0.80
0.0030	6.15	0.32	1.03	0.66
0.0035	5.80	0.33	1.02	0.51
0.0040	5.51	0.33	1.01	0.35
0.0045	5.26	0.34	1.00	0.18
0.0050	5.04	0.35	1.00	0.00

of segments. It can also be noticed that as a result of constant increase in the static overhead (c), gain continuously moves up in the suboptimal region, whereas it moves down in the overoptimal region of all the performance tables obtained in [4].

4. POTENTIAL IMPROVEMENTS IN THE MODEL

The definition of the utilization parameter, u, as given in the previous section in relation to its role in Eq. (1) best fits the case of *constant unit delay* pipelines, i.e., pipelines where each segment always takes only one clock period. Such pipelines are typically at a lower subsystem level, e.g., a floating-point multiplier pipeline. If we include pipelines of *variable delay*, i.e., pipelines where a segment may take more than one clock, then u as defined earlier does not fit our needs. For example, if every stage takes, say, two clocks, then although the utilization as defined may be 1 (or 100%), the throughput would only be one result every two clocks and not one result every clock, as given by Eq. (1). Such pipelines are typically at the system level, e.g., an instruction fetch–decode–execute pipeline.

In Eq. (1), in a more generic sense, pipeline utilization (u) should be thought of as the factor by which the maximum possible throughput ($1/\Delta t$) is modified to yield the actual throughput (G). Actual throughput is strictly determined by the rate at which the outputs are available from the last segment. If any data item takes more than one clock in the last segment, a drop in throughput results. Similarly, if any data item takes more than one clock in any segment, say segment i, the effect of this slowdown of segment i will finally ripple through and result in the same slowdown in the last segment, segment s, after $(s - i)$ clocks. Let us assume there is no *overlap*; i.e., while the effect of slowdown of one stage is rippling to the final stage, there is no other stage that slows down. Under these conditions, the following equation provides a model for u,

$$ u = \frac{1}{1 + (s-1)b + \sum_{i=1}^{s} \sum_{j=2}^{J} (j-1)x_{i,j}}, \qquad (9) $$

where

b = average setup/flush frequency (i.e., average number of setup/flush sequences per data item)

		TABLE IX		
		Throughput Gain vs v		
v	s_{opt}	G_{gsbop}	G_{gopt}	G_{govop}
0.0010	6.09	0.31	1.03	0.60
0.0030	5.96	0.31	1.03	0.55
0.0050	5.82	0.32	1.02	0.49
0.0070	5.69	0.33	1.02	0.44
0.0090	5.57	0.33	1.01	0.38
0.0110	5.45	0.34	1.01	0.32
0.0130	5.33	0.34	1.00	0.25
0.0150	5.21	0.35	1.00	0.18
0.0170	5.09	0.36	1.00	0.11
0.0190	4.98	0.37	1.00	0.04

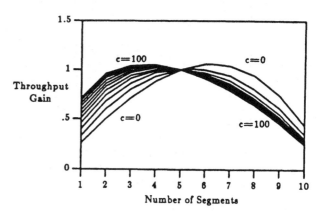

FIG. 6. Throughput gain vs static overhead (c).

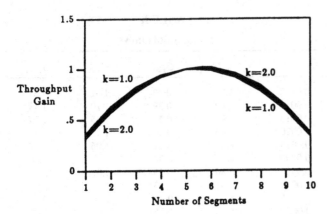

FIG. 7.   Throughput gain vs dynamic overhead (k).

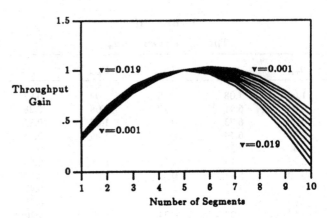

FIG. 9.   Throughput gain vs first-order coefficient of the utilization model (v).

J = maximum number of cycles any data item spends in any segment

$x_{i,j}$ = probability that a data item takes j cycles in the ith segment.

For example, let us consider a 5-stage instruction pipeline in an environment such that an average of 1 out of every 10 instructions takes 2 clocks in the execution stage (last segment) and 1 out of every 10 instructions is a branch instruction. As a result we have $s = 5$, $b = 0.1$, $J = 2$, $x_{5,2}$ = 0.1, and $x_{1,2} = x_{2,2} = x_{3,2} = x_{4,2} = 0$. This results in u = 10/15. Any random sequence of 10 instructions would be expected to lose 4 clocks during a branch and 1 clock due to a 2-clock instruction, and hence take 15 clocks.

For further analysis, we assume a simplified view of an instruction pipeline such that $J = 2$ and for any segment i, $x_{1,2} = x$. As an example, if the ith segment refers to the operand fetch stage, x refers to the fraction of instructions spending an additional clock during operand fetch. Typically each stage would have its own independent fraction of instructions which occupy the stage for more than one

clock; but since this is not critical to our purpose, we choose not to introduce additional variables in our model.

As a result, from Eq. (9)

$$u = \frac{1}{1 + (s - 1)b + sx}. \tag{10}$$

Therefore, throughput can be expressed as

$$G = \frac{1}{1 + (s - 1)b + sx} * \frac{1}{k(T/s) + c}. \tag{11}$$

For maximum throughput,

$$s_{\text{opt}} = \sqrt{\frac{(1 - b)kT}{(x + b)c}}. \tag{12}$$

Tables XI–XII and corresponding curves (Figs. 12–13) show the variation in normalized throughput as a function of the number of pipeline segments. As branch frequency

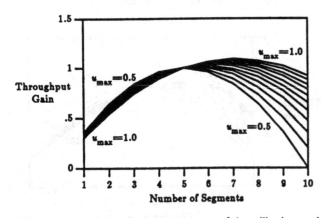

FIG. 8.   Throughput gain vs constant term of the utilization model (u_{max}).

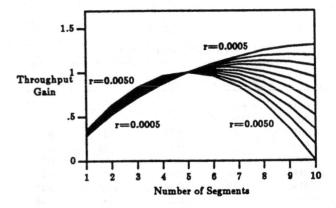

FIG. 10.   Throughput gain vs second-order coefficient of the utilization model (r).

128

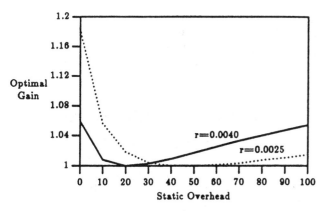

FIG. 11.   Optimal throughput gain vs static overhead (c).

TABLE XII

Normalized Throughput vs x

x	s_{opt}	G_{subop}	G_{opt}	G_{ovrop}
0.02	9.87	0.48	1.42	1.42
0.04	9.14	0.47	1.30	1.29
0.06	8.55	0.46	1.20	1.19
0.08	8.06	0.45	1.11	1.10
0.10	7.65	0.44	1.04	1.03
0.12	7.29	0.44	0.98	0.96
0.14	6.98	0.43	0.93	0.90
0.16	6.71	0.42	0.88	0.85
0.18	6.46	0.41	0.84	0.80
0.20	6.24	0.41	0.80	0.76

(b) decreases, s_{opt} and corresponding optimal throughput both go up. In other words, for a fixed partitioning, we move toward the suboptimal region as b decreases. The same observation holds for x. It should be noted that as static overhead (c) reduces to zero, the optimum number of segments (s_{opt}) shifts to an infinitely high value. Again as observed before, for small values, c has a dominant effect.

Effect of buffering. In the discussion so far we have not assumed additional buffering at a segment output. In the presence of such buffers, unlike the previous case, slowdown of an intermediate segment does not necessarily slow down the final segment. Although it is quite often used in system-level pipelines (e.g., instruction FIFO), its inclusion would considerably complicate our model. The solution to a general model of this type can be derived using queuing theory techniques.

Second-order Effects. The utilization model assumed in Section 2 also hides certain second-order details. Let us, for example, consider the rate of change of throughput with respect to s. From Eqs. (1) and (2),

$$\frac{dG}{ds} = \frac{du}{T} + \frac{ukT}{s^2 \Delta t^2}. \qquad (13)$$

Considering the given utilization model, with increasing s, the first term in the above equation becomes more and more negative, whereas the second term becomes less and less positive. In other words, dG/ds monotonically decreases with increasing s leading to diminishing return (reduced throughput improvement) with increasing s. In an actual environment this may not be the case. Utilization of a pipeline does not necessarily go down with an increasing number of segments. For example, if a larger number of partitions leads to better mapping of the reservation tables (i.e., better resource allocation), utilization might even go up. Also, for the same number of segments, utilization may change in a statistical/periodic fashion. If these possibilities are incorporated into the utilization model, throughput curves could potentially have multiple maxima and minima and there would be points of maximum and minimum return from incremental change in partitioning.

5. CONCLUSION

This paper provides an approximate model of the behavior of a pipeline and the understanding of the factors involved in determining the optimal performance. In spite of

TABLE XI

Normalized Throughput vs b

b	s_{opt}	G_{subop}	G_{opt}	G_{ovrop}
0.02	10.30	0.44	1.36	1.36
0.04	9.44	0.44	1.26	1.26
0.06	8.74	0.44	1.18	1.17
0.08	8.15	0.44	1.10	0.09
0.10	7.65	0.44	1.04	1.03
0.12	7.21	0.44	0.99	0.97
0.14	6.83	0.44	0.94	0.91
0.16	6.48	0.44	0.90	0.86
0.18	6.17	0.44	0.86	0.82
0.20	5.89	0.44	0.83	0.78

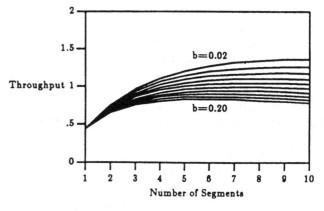

FIG. 12.   Normalized throughput vs branch frequency (b).

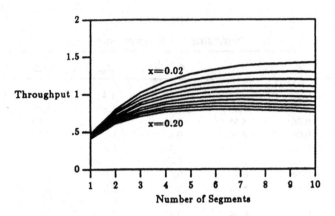

FIG. 13. Normalized throughput vs segment showdown frequency (x).

G_{nom}:   actual throughput at $s = s_{nom}$
G_{gopt}:   throughput gain at $s = s_{opt}$ (with respect to G_{nom})
G_{gsbop}:   throughput gain at $s = s_{subop}$ (with respect to G_{nom})
G_{govop}:   throughput gain at $s = s_{ovrop}$ (with respect to G_{nom})

$$T = 100 \text{ ns} \qquad s_{nom} = 5$$
$$s_{subop} = 1 \; (<s_{opt}) \qquad s_{ovrop} = 10 \; (>s_{opt})$$
$$u_{max(nom)} = 0.6000 \qquad v_{nom} = 0.0100$$
$$r_{nom} = 0.0040 \qquad k_{nom} = 1.3000$$
$$c_{nom} = 10 \text{ ns} \qquad b_{nom} = 0.1000.$$
$$x_{nom} = 0.1000$$

its simplicity, the model can be considered a useful first-order tool for comparative study or sensitivity analysis of the performance of a pipeline in different environments with different overheads. Pipeline utilization models were presented for both subsystem- and system-level pipelines. Effects of branching and segment slowdown were also considered in the case of simple system-level pipelines.

Small changes in the constant overhead term were shown to have a large impact on optimal pipeline behavior. Increasing dynamic overhead increases the optimal number of segments, whereas increasing static overhead requires fewer segments for optimal performance. The results obtained are found to be in very close agreement with CRAY-1 simulation results obtained by Kunkel/Smith, providing an analytical basis for their results as well as additional insight in the *pipeline optimization* problem.

APPENDIX: NOMENCLATURE

T: latency of the logic tree (no pipelining)
δt: clock period
G: throughput of the pipeline
u_{max}:   constant term in the utilization equation
v: first-order coefficient in the utilization equation
r: second-order coefficient in the utilization equation
k: dynamic overhead term
c: constant overhead term
b: branch frequency
x: two-clock instruction frequency
s_{opt}:   optimum number of segments
G_{norm}:   throughput at nominal values of all parameters
G_{opt}:   actual throughput at $s = s_{opt}$ (normalized with respect to G_{norm})
G_{subop}:   actual throughput at $s = s_{subop}$ (normalized with respect to G_{norm})
G_{ovrop}:   actual throughput at $s = s_{ovrop}$ (normalized with respect to G_{norm})

Received April 8, 1988; revised February 13, 1989

ACKNOWLEDGMENT

The authors thank Professor George Adams of Purdue University for his very valuable comments.

REFERENCES

1. Cotten, L. W. Circuit implementations of high-speed pipeline systems. *AFIPS Fall Joint Computer Conference,* 1965, pp. 489–504.
2. Fawcett, B. K. Maximal clocking rates for pipelined digital systems. M.S. thesis, Department of Electrical Engineering, University of Illinois at Urbana–Champaign, 1975.
3. Hallin, T. G., and Flynn, M. J. Pipelining of arithmetic functions. *IEEE Trans. Comput.* C-21, 8 (Aug. 1972), pp. 880–886.
4. Kunkel, S. R., and Smith, J. E. Optimal pipelining in supercomputers. *Proc. 13th Annual Symposium on Computer Architecture,* 1986, pp. 404–411.
5. Shapiro, H. D. A comparison of various methods for detecting and utilizing parallelism in a single instruction stream. *1977 International Conference on Parallel Processing,* Aug. 1977, pp. 67–76.
6. Tjaden, G. S., and Flynn, M. J. Detection and parallel execution of independent instructions. *IEEE Trans. Comput.* C-19, 10 (Oct. 1970), 889–895.

PRADEEP K. DUBEY received the B.S. degree in electronics from Birla Institute of Technology, Mesra, India, in 1982 and the M.S. degree in electrical engineering from University of Massachusetts at Amherst in 1984. He is currently pursuing the Ph.D. degree program in the electrical engineering department of Purdue University. He is also a part-time employee of Intel Corporation, Santa Clara, California, where he has worked full-time since 1984 in the Microprocessor Division and has been part of the 80386 and 80486 design teams. While working for Intel, he was also involved in graduate research at the electrical engineering department of Stanford University.

MICHAEL J. FLYNN is a professor of electrical engineering at Stanford University. His experience includes ten years at IBM Corp. working in computer organization and design. He was also a faculty member at Northwestern and Johns Hopkins University, and the director of Stanford's Computer Systems Laboratory from 1977 to 1983. Flynn has served as vice president of the Computer Society and was founding chairman of CS's Technical Committee on Computer Architecture, as well as ACM's Special Interest Group on Computer Architecture.

Branch Strategies: Modeling and Optimization

Pradeep K. Dubey and Michael J. Flynn

Abstract— Instruction dependency introduced by conditional *branch* instructions, which is resolved only at run-time, can have a severe performance impact on pipelined machines. A variety of strategies are in wide use to minimize this impact. Additional instruction traffic generated by these branch strategies can also have an adverse effect on the system performance. Therefore, in addition to the likely reduction a branch prediction strategy offers in average branch delay, resulting excess i-traffic can be an important parameter in evaluating its overall effectiveness. The objective of this paper is twofold: to develop a model for different approaches to the branch problem and to help select an optimal strategy after taking into account the additional i-traffic generated by branch strategies.

The model presented provides a flexible tool for comparing different branch strategies in terms of the reduction it offers in average branch delay and also in terms of the associated cost of wasted instruction fetches. This additional criterion turns out to be a valuable consideration in choosing between two almost equally performing strategies. More importantly, it provides a better insight into the expected overall system performance. Simple compiler-support-based low implementation-cost strategies can be very effective under certain conditions. An active branch prediction scheme based on loop buffer can be as competitive as a branch-target-buffer based strategy

Index Terms— Branch prediction, conditional branches, degree of dependency, instruction dependency, instruction traffic, pipelining.

Manuscript received December 28, 1987; revised October 5, 1990. M. J. Flynn was supported by NASA under Contract NAG2-248.

P. K. Dubey is with the School of Electrical Engineering, Purdue University, West Lafayette, IN 47907.

M. J. Flynn is with the Department of Electrical Engineering, Stanford University, Stanford, CA 94305.

IEEE Log Number 9143286.

I. INTRODUCTION

This paper provides a common platform for modeling different schemes for reducing the branch-delay penalty in pipelined processors as well as evaluating the associated increased instruction bandwidth. The first section presents the details of the model which also forms the basis of a new classification of the different branch strategies commonly employed. Following sections derive certain inferences from the results obtained and lead us to some hybrid strategies.

Previous Research: Throughput in a pipeline environment is obtained by overlapping different instructions in different stages of execution. This implies an ability to predict and issue successive instructions before the completion of an instruction execution. *Instruction dependency*, i.e., the dependency of an instruction on the result of its predecessor limits this ability. Tjaden and Flynn [8] provide an early framework in the area of formalizing the concept of instruction dependency. Impact of conditional branches on system performance was further substantiated by Riseman and Foster [5]. Interest in different branch strategies for minimizing the performance impact has been renewed with the advent of new RISC machines. Most of the recent work in this area has mainly concentrated on specific branch strategies and on improving prediction accuracy. Smith [6] discusses in detail different strategies for improving prediction accuracy. Lee/Smith [3] and McFarling/Hennessey [4] examine a range of schemes for reducing branch penalty. DeRosa/Levy [13] provide a quantitative comparison for different design alternatives for the *branch* instruction. Hsu/Davidson [11] suggest a scheme whereby on machines such as CRAY-1, where conditional branch resolution may take 14 clocks, a large number of these time-slots may be filled with *guarded* instructions. These instructions are considered "guarded" because in case the branch resolution is not as expected, they are effectively turned into NOP's. Ditzel/McLellan [15] and Grohoski *et al.* [16] discuss branch strategies as implemented on the Clipper and RS6000 processors, respectively.

The model: Consider a pipeline with S segments (Fig. 1) executing an instruction J, which enters the pipeline the very next clock after instruction I. Assume a pipeline segment delay as equivalent to the system clock period. Suppose the instruction J at the start of its p_jth stage of execution requires the result available at the completion of the q_ith stage of execution of instruction I. The *degree of dependency* in such a case is defined as $d_{ij} = (q_i - p_j)$, where we assume $q_i > p_j$. I and J above refer to successive instructions. Instead of entering the pipeline the very next clock after I, suppose J follows after an *additional* delay of x_{ij} clocks. Thus, if instruction I enters the pipeline in clock i and J enters in clock j, then, $x_{ij} = j - i - 1$. The degree of dependency is now reduced to

$$d_{i,j} = q_i - p_j - x_{ij}. \qquad (1)$$

Any segment freeze possibility, i.e., the possibility that a data item may spend more than one clock in a certain pipeline segment is ignored. If $d_{ij} \leq 0$, I and J are considered to have *null pipeline dependency*, which means this dependency has no impact on the pipeline throughput. On the other hand, if $d_{ij} > 0$, I and J are considered to have *positive pipeline dependency*, which suggests this dependency has impact of d_{ij} clocks on the pipeline throughput. In other words, there is no pipeline output for d_{ij} clocks. Degree of dependency is maximum when $p_j = p_{j(\min)} = 1$, $q_i = q_{i(\max)} = S$ and $x_{ij} = x_{ij(\min)} = 0$, i.e., $d_{ij(\max)} = S - 1 = $ *maximum* pipeline dependence.

We next consider instruction dependency due to *branch* instructions. Let I represent a conditional branch instruction. In such a case, the following instruction J (i.e., $x = 0$), cannot be fetched until the execution of I is complete. Assuming instruction fetch (IF) stage as the first stage of the pipeline ($p_j = 1$) and the execution (E) stage,

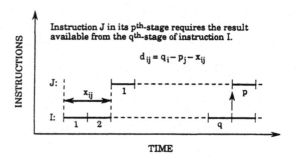

Fig. 1. Instruction dependency in a pipeline.

which tests the condition-code, as the last pipeline-stage ($q_i = S$), this leads to maximum pipeline dependency of $(S - 1)$. Note that, although the condition code testing by the branch instruction I can be typically done in a stage prior to the execution stage, normally it can only be done after the previous instruction $I - 1$ clears the execution stage and sets the condition code. In other words, branch instructions can potentially result in the maximum possible slowdown of $(S - 1)$ clocks. In general, branch instructions need not wait until the last pipeline stage for their resolution, especially the unconditional branches.

We have not considered so far any freeze situations. A pipeline stage is considered *frozen* if it cannot accept a new data item at the end of the current clock period. Such a situation arises when some unexpected condition is encountered, such as, a cache miss or a branch. A freeze implies the addition of wait cycles for the subsequent pipeline stages as they wait for the frozen stage output. A successful *branch* instruction involves the fetch and execution of an *out of sequence* instruction. Fetching the branch target instruction consists of 1) a target address calculation and 2) a target fetch. Each of these steps has freeze-potential. In this note, other possible freeze conditions are deliberately ignored.

A. Classification of Branch Strategies

Branch strategies can be classified based on how they attempt to reduce the branch penalties, as shown in Table I. The names of most of the strategies are self-descriptive. We briefly describe the unobvious ones.

The *Loop Buffer* strategy is based on a high-speed memory in the instruction-fetch stage of the processor. Some CDC machines (6600, 7600, and Star-100) as well as CRAY-1 have used this idea. These buffers (Fig. 3) can detect if the branch target (forward or backward) lies within the environment captured by the buffer and if so, the instruction-fetch delay and the possible freeze delay can be eliminated. Since a hit in the loop-buffers avoids any external memory access, it also reduces extra i-traffic in case of incorrect prediction. Although, loop buffers may appear to be similar to i-caches, they are much smaller in size and hence lower in implementation cost. This strategy further assumes that branches are not likely to be taken.

Usually branch-instruction execution does not require any operand-fetch. Some IBM machines (370 series) use the operand-fetch (OF) slot of the pipeline for fetching from the branch target-path. Branch is still assumed as not likely to be taken. *Fetch Target in OF-slot* strategy is based on this technique.

The *Fetch Both Paths* strategy, also used on some IBM machines (370/168, 3033) uses the brute-force approach of fetching (not decoding) both the sequential and nonsequential instruction streams in case a branch is decoded.

The *Delayed Branch* [4] and *Predict Branch Always Taken with Target Copy* strategies modify the instruction sequence at compile

TABLE I
CLASSIFICATION OF BRANCH STRATEGIES

Strategy	Label	Reduce dependency by			Reduce target-fetch freeze	Reduce address-calc freeze
		increasing p_j	decreasing q_i	increasing x_{ij}		
Predict Never Taken	PBNT	X				
Loop Buffer	LB	X			X	
Pre-calculate Target Address	PTA	X				X
Fetch Target in OF-slot	FTOF	X			X	X
Predict Always Taken	PBAT		X			
Predict Always Taken with Target Copy	PTTC	X	X		X	X
Fetch Both Paths	FBP		X		X	X
Delayed Branch	DB	X	X	X	X	X
Taken/Not-taken Switch in the Decode Stage	TNTD		X			
Branch Target Buffer	BTB	X	X			X

Note: X refers to how the strategy attempts to reduce the branch cost.

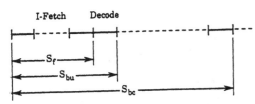

S_f: number of sub-stages in the fetch-stage
S_{bu}: pipeline stage that resolves unconditional branches
S_{bc}: pipeline stage that resolves conditional branches

Fig. 2. An instruction pipeline.

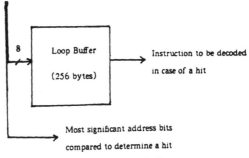

Fig. 3. Loop buffer.

time. The former delays the entry of the dependent branch instruction by inserting instructions that are common to both the sequential and nonsequential paths. In the latter strategy, a portion of target code (as dictated by the effective pipeline length for branch resolution) is copied (Fig. 4) following the branch instruction. This strategy is also assumed to predict branches as *always* taken. Note that the *Delayed Branch* and *Target Copying* strategies also indirectly reduce the address-calculation and target-fetch freezes by delaying reliance on the target code and thereby offering time to calculate the address and fetch the target.

The last two strategies in Table I are based on active branch prediction [3]. This prediction information can be obtained and improved for accuracy in many different ways [6]. *Branch Target buffer (BTB)* refers to a small associative memory in the instruction-fetch stage of the processor. Instruction-fetch addresses are associatively matched with the buffer contents and in case of a *hit* it predicts the most likely branch outcome as well as the most recent target address (Fig. 5). As a result, target-fetch does not need to wait for the branch-decode and target-address calculation. In case of a *miss* in BTB, branch instructions are handled in a manner similar to *Predict Branch Never Taken* strategy.

B. Branch Prediction

Branch strategies do not eliminate branch delay but do so only with a certain probability. They make an implicit assumption about the most likely branch outcome and commit themselves to the sequential or the branch path to varying degrees. This commitment normally reduces the penalty associated with the chosen path but may increase the penalty of taking the discarded path in case of incorrect prediction. As a result, overall performance improvement becomes critically dependent on the probability of correct prediction. Table II defines and explains the terms associated with our model. Note that for $K = 0$ or $b = 0$, performance throughput G is assumed to be at its peak rate of one instruction per cycle. Thus, all other pipeline overheads [1] are ignored.

C. Cost of Branch Prediction

The discussion above has centered around assessing the performance of different branch strategies. Consider the two primary costs involved: 1) implementation cost and 2) operational cost. *Implementation cost* refers to the hardware/software costs involved

TABLE II
TABLE OF DEFINITIONS

Predicted	Actual	Probability	Branch Penalty	i-traffic Penalty
no branch	no branch	$p_{n,n}$	$k_{n,n}$	$t_{n,n}$
no branch	branch	$p_{n,b}$	$k_{n,b}$	$t_{n,b}$
branch	no branch	$p_{b,n}$	$k_{b,n}$	$t_{b,n}$
branch	branch	$p_{b,b}$	$k_{b,b}$	$t_{b,b}$

$$\text{Av. Branch Penalty, } K = p_{n,n} * k_{n,n} + p_{n,b} * k_{n,b} + p_{b,n} * k_{b,n} + p_{b,b} * k_{b,b}$$

$$\text{Average Throughput, } G = \frac{1}{1 + K * b}$$

$$\text{Av. Wasted i-traffic, } T = p_{n,n} * t_{n,n} + p_{n,b} * t_{n,b} + p_{b,n} * t_{b,n} + p_{b,b} * t_{b,b}$$

$$\text{Merit Ratio, } MR = \frac{1}{(1 + K * b) * (1 + T * b)}$$

Notes:

All the four probabilities can be easily expressed in terms of

the probability of *branch−to−be−taken* prediction and the probability of *correct* prediction.

b refers to the branch frequency

```
          CMP     R1, R2        Instructions marked with an asterisk (*) are the
          JZ      xx            instructions copied from the target (xx) at compile-time.
          *ADD    R3, R4        In case of a successful branch, control transfers to the
          *SUB    R3, R5        label xx+4, after executing the marked (*) target
          *INC    R4            instructions through sequential fetch. In case the
          *ADD    R3, R4        branch is not taken, marked instructions are discarded
          MOV     R6, R7        without execution after fetch and decode.
          ADD     R6, R2
          MOV     R1, mem
          ..      ..
          ..      ..

    xx:   ADD     R3, R4
          SUB     R3, R5
          INC     R4
          ADD     R3, R4
    xx+4: MOV     R6, R3
          ..      ..
          ..      ..
```

Fig. 4. Predict Branch Always Taken with Target Copy (PTTC).

in implementing the branch strategy. Since such costs are variable with technology, this cost is ignored. On the other hand, relatively less obvious *operational cost* refers to the added run-time cost, for example, the additional instruction traffic that results on the system bus with every incorrect branch-prediction. Although incorrect predictions are the primary source of extra i-traffic, even delayed correct prediction can cause wasted instruction fetch. For architectures that allow machine-state update by instructions in the predicted path, there is an additional run-time overhead of *shadowing* the original machine-state to be able to recover in case of an incorrect prediction. For the sake of simplicity, this cost is not included in our calculations and we do not expect it to alter our conclusions. Thus, the only operational cost studied is that of the additional i-traffic. Refer to Table II for the terms associated with this cost of wasted i-fetches. An ideal

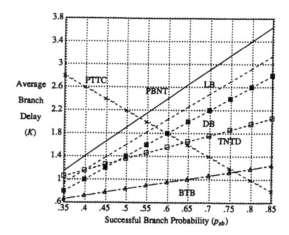

Branch Instruction Address	Branch Prediction	Predicted Target Address
.	.	.
.	.	.

Fig. 5. Branch target buffer.

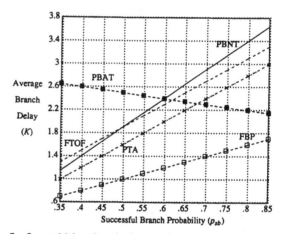

Fig. 6. Successful branch probability (p_{sb}) versus average branch delay (K).

Fig. 7. Successful branch probability (p_{sb}) versus average branch delay (K).

machine, which can always correctly predict the branch outcome and if needed, can start fetching the target path right after the branch-instruction fetch would have, $K = T = 0$ and hence, $G = C = 1$, resulting in unit merit ratio MR irrespective of the branch frequency b. Interestingly, freeze conditions, which tend to increase the branch delay, reduce the average additional i-traffic. When a certain path is predicted, freeze situations reduce the number of instructions that can be fetched, which reduces the number of wasted i-fetches in case of incorrect prediction. This reduction has been taken into account in our calculations [12].

The following simplifying assumptions have been made (Fig. 2).

1) Instruction fetch stage is assumed to consist of S_f slots (each containing a prefetched instruction) followed by the decode stage.

2) Let S_b refer to the pipeline length up to the stage that resolves the pending branch instruction. In case of unconditional branches, we assume branches are resolved as soon as they are decoded, therefore, $S_b = S_{bu} = S_f + 1$. Whereas in case of conditional branches, $S_b = S_{bc}$ is dependent on the pipeline stage that sets the condition-code.

3) Each instruction is assumed to make a common trip through the pipeline stages. For pipelines with functional-level stages, such as fetch and execute stages, this should be considered a reasonable assumption.

4) Additional i-traffic during freeze-handling, e.g., in software page-fault handling is ignored.

5) For the sake of simplicity, handling of multiple pending branches in the pipeline is restricted. If a branch is predicted as likely to be taken, it is assumed that we do not encounter additional branches with *to-be-taken* prediction before resolving the first branch. This assumption can be a source of some significant inaccuracy only for very long pipelines with prediction schemes which allow this possibility.

6) Finally, we have ignored any on-chip i-cache in our discussion as it has no impact on the *relative* nature of the branch delay and additional i-traffic performance curves.

II. Results

The model described above, can be used to obtain the average branch delay (K), average number of wasted i-fetches per branch (T) and the overall merit ratio (MR), once the variables outlining the system-environment are defined. We assume certain nominal values for some of these variables; e.g., branch frequency, $b = 0.25$, where 80% of the branches are conditional. Probability of a freeze during target address calculation is assumed to be 0.5 with a freeze duration of 2 cycles. Probability of freeze during target-fetch is ignored. For delayed-branch approach, an average of one useful common instruction is assumed. One such machine employing delayed branch approach MIPS [4], [10], reported use of a single delay slot about 70% of the time. There may be special cases, such as when using *guarded* instructions [11] where significant number of delayed branch slots may be utilized. Based on Smith [6], we assume a correct prediction probability of 0.85 for conditional branches. In the case of Branch Target Buffer, probability of correct target address prediction is optimistically set at 0.9, assuming stable branch targets [6]. Probability of BTB hit for nonbranch instructions in case of writable code segments is assumed very low at 0.05. We assume nominal loop-buffer hit-ratio, $p_{lh} = 0.6$ and nominal BTB hit ratio, $p_{th} = 0.8$. Peuto/Shustek [9] report a hit ratio of 0.6 for a loop buffer of ±256 entries, whereas Lee/Smith [6] report a hit ratio of around 0.8 for a target buffer with 256 entries and a set size of 4 or 8. *Set size* refers to the degree of associativity in contrast to fully-associative BTB search.

We concentrate initially on the input parameter, p_{sb}, successful branch probability (conditional and unconditional combined). Results are obtained for the three performance parameters, average branch delay (K), average number of wasted i-fetches T, and the cost–performance merit-ratio MR as shown in Figs. 6–11. Ref. [12] provides details of these calculations. While p_{sb} is varied, other parameters are kept at their nominal values.

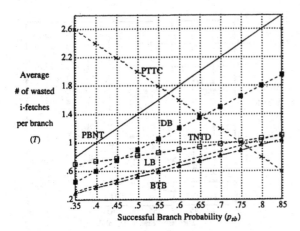

Fig. 8. Successful branch probability (p_{sb}) versus average number of wasted i-fetches per branch (T).

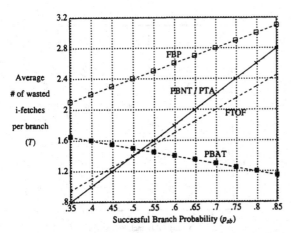

Fig. 9. Successful branch probability (p_{sb}) versus average number of wasted i-fetches per branch (T).

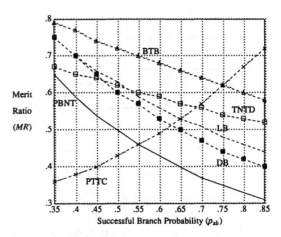

Fig. 10. Successful branch probability (p_{sb}) versus merit ratio (MR).

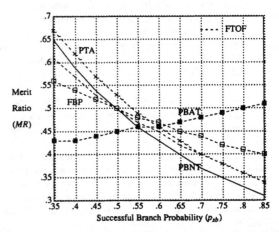

Fig. 11. Successful branch probability (p_{sb}) versus merit ratio (MR).

A. Inferences

The following inferences can be made regarding the three performance parameters as a function of the successful branch probability (p_{sb}).

1) As one might expect, BTB strategy outperforms others for the entire typical operating range ($0.55 < p_{sb} < 0.7$).

2) The Predict-branch-always-taken scheme with target copy (PTTC), emerges as a good second choice around p_{sb} of 0.65 or more. Interestingly, even without any active-branch-prediction support, it exhibits better performance potential than BTB around $p_{sb} \geq 0.75$. This advantage stems primarily from the fact that this scheme does not have to pay the delay penalty of incorrect target address prediction. BTB strategy has a cost of incorrect target address prediction even with correct branch prediction. As a cautionary note, the PTTC scheme also exhibits the steepest slope in terms of all the three performance parameters as opposed to relatively stable performance curves of active-prediction schemes like *Branch Taken/Not-taken Switch in the Decode Stage* and BTB.

3) In terms of excess i-fetches, loop buffer scheme performs almost as well as the BTB strategy. Loop buffers can significantly cut down the cost of excess i-traffic resulting from incorrect

predictions.

4) At nominal p_{sb} (0.6) both strategies *Predict Branch Never Taken* and *Predict Branch Always Taken* have the same branch delay. Which of the two should be the preferred scheme? A look at the additional i-traffic cost can help resolve the issue. *Predict Branch Always Taken* scheme has lower cost of wasted i-fetches and hence has better merit ratio (MR). In the absence of any possible address-calculation-freeze (or target-fetch-freeze), on an average *Predict Branch Never Taken* scheme wastes more instructions during misprediction than *Predict Branch Always Taken*. A similar dilemma between *Predict Always Taken with Target Copy* strategy and *Delayed Branch* strategy can be resolved in favor of *Delayed Branch* scheme, due to its lower added i-traffic cost. In both the scenarios, implementation costs are almost identical for the two strategies in question, hence the excess i-traffic T provides an important decisive input. Interestingly, at $p_{sb} = 0.5$, three different strategies: predict branch never-taken, target-fetch in the OF-slot as well as the scheme to fetch both the paths show almost identical merit-ratio. Here implementation cost can probably be the only decisive input.

5) Not only does excess i-traffic cost T help us choose between two almost equally performing strategies (as shown above), it can also caution us about otherwise very well

performing strategies. FBP strategy (fetch both the paths) provides an interesting study in this regard. In terms of average branch delay (K), it performs almost as well as the BTB strategy. But after considering the cost of wasted i-fetches, in terms of the overall merit ratio (MR), it is not much better than the worst-performing *Predict Branch Never Taken* strategy. Thus, a conclusion based solely on average branch delay K may be elusive one as far as the overall system performance is considered. Garcia/Huynh [2] discuss the efforts made to reduce the resulting high contention on the system bus in an early IBM 370 implementation using this strategy.

Next we looked at the variation in system performance as a function of S_f, i.e., number of buffer stages in the instruction-fetch stage. Again BTB outperforms every other strategy, followed by *Predict Always Taken with Target Copy*, in terms of average branch delay (K) for any amount of buffering in the fetch stage. All the strategies are seen to have almost identical performance slope on the merit-ratio curve and show identical sensitivity with respect to S_f.

Finally, performance curves were analyzed as a function of S_{bc}, i.e., the total number of pipeline stages required for conditional branch resolution. BTB strategy continued to be the first choice for any number of segments in terms of overall merit-ratio. But for long pipelines ($S_{bc} > 6$), it slipped, instead, fetching both the path scheme (FBP) finally won with its constant branch delay with respect to S_{bc}. Note that just a branch taken/not-taken switch in the decode stage (TNTD scheme) significantly reduces the branch delay. The additional reduction in branch delay obtainable through BTB rapidly decreases with larger S_{bc}. Ref. [12] contains additional details.

Therefore, in the typical operating range ($0.6 < p_{sb} < 0.75$), we have three competing strategies: Loop Buffer (LB), Predict Branch Always Taken with Target Copy (PTTC), and Branch Target Buffer (BTB). Our branch-delay numbers for *Predict Branch Never Taken, Delayed Branch,* and *BTB* strategies under nominal conditions come quite close (within 30%) to those reported by McFarling/Hennessey [4], even though our nominal conditions, while close, are not exactly the same as theirs. Assuming, branch frequency $b = 0.2$, our results indicate a throughput (G) of around 10% in the above mentioned operating range of p_{sb}. This is also in close agreement with MIPS simulation results [14] of around 9% and the analysis of DeRosa/Levy [13], suggesting an improvement of around 8%.

In the following section, we discuss some hybrid strategies based primarily on these three strategies. Delayed branch strategy and *Taken/Not-taken Switch in the Decode Stage* strategy also show good performance potential in possible combinations with above strategies.

III. HYBRID STRATEGIES

The following hybrid strategies are considered.

1) *Predict Branch Always taken with target-copy and delayed branch (TTCDB):* This is the only hybrid strategy considered with almost no additional implementation cost and only some software (compiler) cost.
2) *Predict Branch Always taken with target-copy, delayed branch and Loop buffer (TTDLB).*
3) *Taken/Not-taken Switch in the Decode Stage with Loop buffer (TNTLB).*
4) *Taken/Not-taken Switch in the Decode Stage with Branch target buffer (TNBTB):* Finally, we consider a combination of TNTD and BTB strategies above. In case of a miss in the BTB, instead of falling back on the default *Predict Branch Never Taken* (predict-branch-never-taken) case, this strategy assumes a branch taken/not-taken switch in the decode stage similar to TNTD scheme.

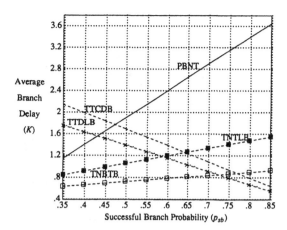

Fig. 12. Successful branch probability (p_{sb}) versus average branch delay (K).

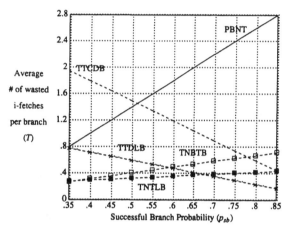

Fig. 13. Successful branch probability (p_{sb}) versus average number of wasted i-fetches per branch (T).

A. Inferences

Sensitivity-plots of the performance parameters, K, T, and MR are obtained with respect to p_{sb} and S_{bc} (Figs. 12–15).

1) Around the nominal values of system parameters, out of the hybrid strategies, the minimum implementation cost TTCDB strategy, performs better than every other nonhybrid strategy of previous section except BTB. For p_{sb} around 0.7, it even outperforms BTB strategy in terms of average branch delay (K) as well as the merit-ratio (MR).
2) Around our nominal conditions, the last three hybrid strategies: TTDLB, TNTLB, and TNBTB are almost equally competitive. For shorter pipelines ($S_{bc} < 5$), TTDLB has a slight edge over the other two, whereas for longer pipelines, active branch prediction becomes more important and TNTLB and TNBTB schemes perform better than the rest and continue to follow each other closely. Therefore, on a system with a branch-taken/not-taken prediction switch in the instruction decode stage, if one were to choose between the addition of either the loop buffer or the branch target buffer, careful consideration should be given to implementation-cost issues which may tilt the balance slightly in favor of the loop-buffer based TNTLB scheme.

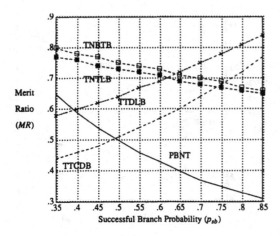

Fig. 14. Successful branch probability (p_{sb}) versus merit ratio (MR).

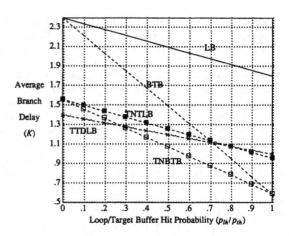

Fig. 16. Loop/target buffer hit probability (p_{lh}/p_{th}) versus average branch delay (K).

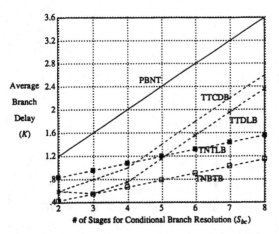

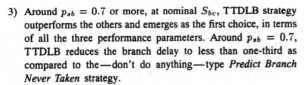

Fig. 15. Number of stages for conditional branch resolution (S_{bc}) versus average branch delay (K).

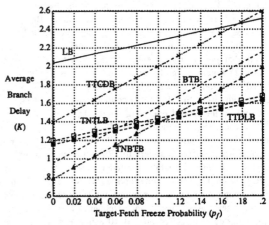

Fig. 17. Target-fetch freeze probability (p_f) versus average branch delay (K).

3) Around $p_{sb} = 0.7$ or more, at nominal S_{bc}, TTDLB strategy outperforms the others and emerges as the first choice, in terms of all the three performance parameters. Around $p_{sb} = 0.7$, TTDLB reduces the branch delay to less than one-third as compared to the—don't do anything—type *Predict Branch Never Taken* strategy.

Effect of Loop/Target-buffer hit probability: Target-buffer based strategies show more sensitivity to the hit-ratio, p_{th} than the loop-buffer based strategies in terms of average branch delay (Fig. 16). As expected, loop-buffer based strategies were found more sensitive than the target-buffer based strategies in terms of the excess i-traffic cost with respect to the corresponding hit-ratio p_{lh}. As a result, both classes of strategies exhibit almost identical slope on the merit-ratio performance curve.

Effect of Target-fetch freeze probability: In our discussion so far we have ignored any potential for a freeze (due to say, cache miss or page fault) while attempting to fetch the branch-target. Assuming a fetch-freeze duration (Y_f) of ten clocks, we take a look at the performance sensitivity with respect to the fetch-freeze probability, p_f. Loop-buffer based strategies are at an advantage in such a case because a hit in the loop buffer also eliminates any page-fault type potential associated with external memory access. As a result, loop-buffer based strategies show more performance stability with respect

to p_f than the BTB-based strategies. For example, if p_f increases from 0 to 0.1 average branch delay for loop-buffer based TNTLB strategy increases by 20%, whereas that in the case of BTB-based TNBTB strategy increases by more than 75% (Fig. 17).

IV. CONCLUSION

A common analytical platform, based on certain system and program parameters, can be developed for classifying and comparing different branch strategies. Such an approach has the advantage of being far less time-consuming and more flexible compared to simulation-based approaches. Excess i-traffic caused by different branch strategies has been overlooked in the past. Additional i-traffic helped to distinguish an overall performance difference between some apparently equally well performing strategies. A branch strategy using a branch-taken/not-taken switch in the decode stage is found to be almost as effective in combination with the loop buffer as with the branch target buffer. In a typical microprocessor environment with less than five segments with a successful branch probability around 0.6, a branch strategy based on default prediction of branch always taken, along with compiler support for target-copy and delayed branch is shown to provide performance potential comparable to a branch strategy based on Branch Target Buffer.

Finally, we have ignored certain components of branch delay, which should be incorporated in future research in this area. For example, some machines [17] have an added delay during branches if the target is misaligned. Also some compilers, such as trace-scheduling [18] compiler have an additional overhead of *patch-up* code if their compile-time prediction of a branch is found incorrect at run-time. These were ignored in our discussion.

APPENDIX

Nominal values:

Average branch frequency: 0.25

Average fraction of conditional branches: 0.8

Overall fraction of successful branches: 0.6 (conditional/unconditional combined)

Number of pipeline stages until unconditional branch resolution: 2

Number of buffer substages in the instruction-fetch stage: 1

Number of pipeline stages until conditional branch resolution: 5

Probability of freeze during target address formation: 0.5

Duration of target-address-calculation freeze: 2 cycles

Probability of freeze during target-fetch: 0

Duration of target-fetch freeze: 10 cycles

Probability of loop-buffer hit: 0.6

Probability of BTB hit: 0.8

Probability of correct address prediction from BTB: 0.9

Probability of BTB-hit for nonbranch instruction: 0.05

Average number of delay-slots filled in delayed branch approach: 1

For cases with active prediction schemes (TNTD, BTB, TNTLB, TNBTB):

Correct prediction probability for unconditional branches: 1.0

Correct prediction probability for conditional branches: 0.85

REFERENCES

[1] P. K. Dubey and M. Flynn, "Optimal pipelining," *J. Parallel Distributed Comput.*, pp. 10–19, Jan. 1990.

[2] L. C. Garcia and T. Huynh, "Storage fetch contention reduction using instruction branch prediction," *IBM Tech. Disclos. Bull.*, vol. 23, no. 6, 1980.

[3] J. K. Lee and A. J. Smith, "Branch prediction strategies and branch target buffer design," *IEEE Comput. Mag.*, vol. 17, no. 1, Jan. 1984.

[4] S. McFarling and J. Hennessey, "Reducing the cost of branches," in *Proc. 13th Annu. Symp. Comput. Architecture*, June 1986, pp. 396–403.

[5] E. Riseman and C. Foster, "The inhibition of potential parallelism by conditional jumps," *IEEE Trans. Comput.*, vol. C-21, Dec. 1972.

[6] J. E. Smith, "A study of branch prediction strategies," in *Proc. 8th Annu. Symp. Comput. Architecture*, May 1981.

[7] G. S. Tjaden and M. Flynn, "Representation of concurrency with ordering matrices," *IEEE Trans. Comput.*, pp. 752–761, Aug. 1973.

[8] ——, "Detection and parallel execution of independent instructions," *IEEE Trans. Comput.*, pp. 889–895, Oct. 1970.

[9] B. L. Peuto and L. J. Shustek, "Current issues in the architecture of microprocessors," *IEEE Comput. Mag.*, pp. 20–25, Feb. 1977.

[10] T. R. Gross and J. Hennessey, "Optimizing delayed branches," in *Proc. 15th Workshop Microprogramming*, 1986.

[11] P. Y. T. Hsu and E. S. Davidson, "Highly concurrent scalar processing," in *Proc. 13th Annu. Symp. Comput. Architecture*, June 1986, pp. 386–395.

[12] P. Dubey and M. Flynn, "Branch strategies: Modelling and optimization," Tech. Rep. CSL TR 90-411, Comput. Syst. Lab., Stanford Univ., Feb. 1990.

[13] J. A. DeRosa and H. M. Levy, "An evaluation of branch architectures," in *Proc. 14th Annu. Symp. Comput. Architecture*, June 1987.

[14] T. Gross, "Code optimizations of pipeline constraints," Tech. Rep. CSL TR 83-255, Comput. Syst. Lab., Stanford Univ., Dec. 1983.

[15] D. R. Ditzel and H. R. McLellan, "Branch folding in CRISP microprocessor," in *Proc. 14th Annu. Symp. Comput. Architecture*, June 1987, pp. 2–9.

[16] G. F. Grohoski, J. A. Kahle, L. E. Thatcher, and C. R. Moore, "Branch and fixed-point instruction execution units," IBM RISC System/6000 Technology, Publication SA 23-2619, IBM Corp., 1990.

[17] M. D. Smith, M. Johnson, and M. A. Horowitz, "Limits on multiple instruction issue," in *Proc. ASPLOS III*, Boston, MA, Apr. 1989, pp. 290–302.

[18] J. A. Fisher, "Trace scheduling: A technique for global microcode compaction," *IEEE Trans. Comput.*, vol. C-30, pp. 478–490, July 1981.

Chapter 3

Cache Memory Models

The growing disparity between processor and memory speeds poses severe problems for computer designers. It is no use having very fast processors if the memory system cannot provide access at the rate required by the processors.

Fortunately, in most applications, there is locality of referencing. That is, a program does not seek access uniformly over the entire address space; rather, it usually concentrates on a small subset of that space. As a result, one can use small but fast memories—caches—to try to mitigate the effects of having slow main memory. If most of what a program wants to access is in the cache, the effects of having a slower main memory are reduced.

If one looks at the address trace of a program, one finds the following phenomenon. The number of *new lines*, that is, lines not accessed before by the program, is very high initially. As time goes on, the new-line access rate drops. Figure 3.1 illustrates this. Every time the program accesses a new line, it generates a cache miss regardless of the cache size. The rate of new line access is therefore a lower bound on the cache miss rate.

There are also *dead lines* in cache. These are lines which have been accessed in the past, but will never be accessed again before they are ejected from the cache. Of course, the operating system has no way of knowing this. The Least Recently Used replacement policy is, however, an effective way of replacing these lines.

There are two factors which determine the miss rate of a cache. The first—and most obvious—is cache size. All other things being equal, the larger the cache, the lower its miss rate tends to be. The second factor is the cache organization. Caches are typically broken

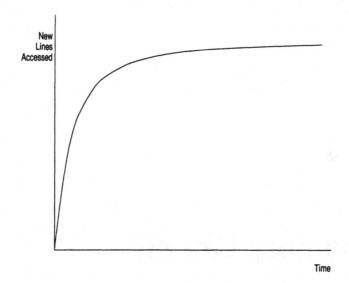

Figure 3.1. New Line Access Pattern

down logically into *sets*, each of which maps onto some distinct, nonoverlapping portion of the address space. Such caches are said to be *associative*. See Figure 3.2. When an address a is accessed, it must be placed in the set which "covers" that address.

The obvious design question is how many sets to have, and what the line size should be. When there is a miss, it is not just the word that caused the miss which is brought into the cache: it is the entire line or block to which that word belongs. The reason for this is locality, namely, that if a program accesses a particular address, it is likely to access other addresses close by. If the line is very small, we do not take sufficient advantage of locality. If the line is very large, the fraction of words that is read into cache but never accessed by the processor becomes large. The designer must choose a happy medium between these extremes.

Choosing the number of sets is also a design problem. If we have a very large number of small sets, then it is possible that one or more of these sets will generate a large number of misses (owing to their small size) while others will go largely unused. On the other hand, if the number of sets is very small, this may mean that each set consists of a lot of lines. This can cause delays in searching the cache directory to find whether a desired word is in cache or not. In general, the search time is the logarithm of the size of the cache set. Once again, the designer's job is to find an appropriate number of sets between these two extremes.

The mean time to satisfy an access request is given by

$$t_{access} = ht_{cache} + (1 - h)t_{offcache} \qquad (3.1)$$

where

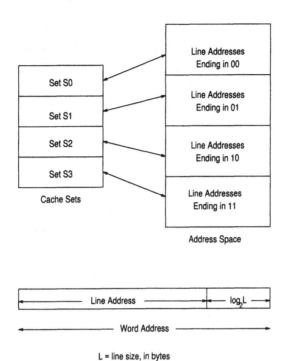

Figure 3.2. Address Mapping onto Cache Sets

- h is the cache hit rate, that is, the fraction of accesses that are found in the cache.

- t_{cache} is the cache access time.

- $t_{offcache}$ is the mean access time when going off-cache (to main memory, disk, tape, etc.).

From Equation 3.1, we have

$$\frac{t_{access}}{t_{cache}} = h + (1 - h)\frac{t_{offcache}}{t_{cache}} \qquad (3.2)$$

This shows clearly that the greater the ratio $(t_{offcache}/t_{cache})$, the greater is the impact of the hit rate. The current trend is toward an increase in this ratio, and so the importance of having a high hit rate is likely to increase with time.

A cache performance model computes the cache hit rate as a function of the cache structure, (that is, its size and its organization, in terms of the set associativity and line (block) size) and of the workload.

The above discussion is as valid for multiprocessors as it is for uniprocessors. However, with multiprocessors, we also have the overhead incurred by *cache coherency*. That is, the system must ensure that if copies of the same datum are held in multiple caches, they must all be the same, or *coherent*. If any of the copies change, the other copies must be invalidated or updated in response. The need to maintain cache coherency can result in considerable message traffic between the various caches, and such traffic can have an impact on the system performance.

This chapter can be divided into two parts, with the first dealing with models of uniprocessor, and the second with models of multiprocessor, systems. These are, for reasons of tractability, approximate models. Their purpose is to provide the architect with a relatively inexpensive way to obtain rough performance estimates. Of course, no model can adequately capture the complexity of a real computing environment: one must turn to detailed simulations or experiments for that.

Thiébaut and Stone show how to model the *reload transient* of a cache. Suppose, for example, that process A is suspended, and process B begins execution. When process A is reinitiated, it may find that some, or all, of its lines in the cache have been discarded to make room for lines referenced by process B. As a result, there will be a period following reinitiation, over which the number of cache misses generated by process A is much greater than the steady-state rate. This is the reload transient. It is a function of the cache size, and of the number of lines in the working set of the various processes.

Agarwal, Horowitz, and Hennessy present a comprehensive model of cache miss rate. The inputs to this model are the cache size, the degree of associativity, the line size, the multiprogramming level, and the duration of the time slice after which a process is swapped out. They compare their analytical results with trace-driven simulations, and show that their model provides accurate results.

Mendelson, Thiébaut, and Pradhan consider the issue of live and dead lines in a cache. Recall that a line in cache is said to be dead if it will never be referenced by the processor before it is swapped out of the cache. As the term implies, a live line is one which is not dead. The larger the cache size and the smaller the rate at which lines are swapped out, the greater the fraction of dead lines in the cache. Dead lines are useless, and so if the cache is large, it might be best to divide the cache into portions and allocate one portion to each (or some) of the processes currently being executed. This can reduce the reload transient.

Stone, Turek, and Wolf provide a model of dividing the cache into portions. They first consider the effects of dividing it up into data and instruction cache regions. This can be advantageous because data and instruction streams tend to have different access characteristics, and instructions are never written into. Next, they focus on a multiprogramming system. As the amount of cache allocated to a process increases, the miss rate tends to decrease. However, because of the dead-line effect referred to earlier, the marginal gain in increasing cache size tends to decline. Stone et al. suggest that an executing process not always be allowed to use the entire cache space. Instead, they suggest increasing the cache space allocated to a process until the marginal gain in miss rate reaches a set threshold value. Beyond this point, the process is not allowed any additional cache space. This tends to reduce the reload transient that occurs when the executing process is swapped out and replaced by another. They carry out similar studies when a two-level cache is used.

The remaining set of papers in this chapter deals with multiprocessor issues. Patel models the utilization of processors in a private-cache multiprocessor, where only unshared variables are cached. The system is not multiprogrammed: a processor is assumed to be idle whenever it is waiting to load something from the main memory. The basic approach is to recognize that as the processor utilization increases, so also does the number of cache misses. An increasing number of misses results in a greater demand on the main memory and the interconnection network carrying these requests. This results in an increase in the time taken to carry out a load or store operation, which in turn tends to reduce the processor utilization. In other words, the system exhibits the characteristics of negative feedback.

Vernon, Lazowska, and Zahorjan model the performance of a number of snoopy-cache protocols. The model can take into account the impact of interference at the bus, main memory, and cache levels. Simulations show that this model is quite accurate over a wide range of parameter values.

Tsai and Agarwal show how to obtain the data access patterns in a multiprocessor system. They assume a write-invalidate cache-coherence policy. The cache miss rate can be calculated once the data access patterns have been obtained. This approach will only work well if the data access patterns are fairly regular and not chaotic. Detailed examples of the Fast Fourier Transform and Parallel Dynamic Quicksort are provided.

Footprints in the Cache

DOMINIQUE THIEBAUT
University of Massachusetts
and
HAROLD S. STONE
IBM Thomas J. Watson Research Center

This paper develops an analytical model for cache-reload transients and compares the model to observations based on several address traces. The cache-reload transient is the set of cache misses that occur when a process is reinitiated after being suspended temporarily. For example, an interrupt program that runs periodically experiences a reload transient at each initiation. The reload transient depends on the cache size and on the sizes of the footprints in the cache of the competing programs, where a program footprint is defined to be the set of lines in the cache in active use by the program. The model shows that the size of the transient is related to the normal distribution function. A simulation based on program-address traces shows excellent agreement between the model and the observations.

Categories and Subject Descriptors: B.3.2 [**Memory Structures**]: Design Styles—*associative memories, cache memories, virtual memory*; B.3.3 [**Memory Structures**]: Performance Analysis and Design Aids—*formal models, simulation*; C.4 [**Computer Systems Organization**]: Performance of Systems—*design studies, modeling techniques, performance attributes*; D.4.1 [**Operating Systems**]: Process Management—*multiprocessing/multiprogramming*; D.4.2 [**Operating Systems**]: Storage Management—*swapping*

General Terms: Design, Experimentation, Performance

Additional Key Words and Phrases: Cache miss-ratio, program footprint, trace-driven simulation

---

1. INTRODUCTION

In this paper we present an analytical model for cache-reload transients. The reload transient phenomenon is typically observed when a process is invoked periodically such as by an interrupt generated by a timer. A program running at the time the interrupt occurs is temporarily halted while the interrupt handler and interrupt service routine are executed. The first instructions of the interrupt processes cause a large number of cache misses as the processes bring their

A shorter version of this paper (without the data reported here) appeared in *Proceedings of Performance '86 and ACM SIGMETRICS 1986 Joint Conference on Computer Performance, Modeling, Measurement and Evaluation* (Raleigh, NC, May 27–30, 1986). ACM, New York, 1986, pp. 4–8.
Authors' Addresses: D. Thiebaut, Electrical and Computer Engineering Department, University of Massachusetts, Amherst, Mass. 01003; H. S. Stone, IBM Thomas J. Watson Research Center, Yorktown Heights, N.Y. 10598.

working sets from main memory into the cache. When the interrupted process resumes after the interrupt service is complete, it also experiences a reload transient as some of its cache environment has been displaced from the cache by the interrupt processes.

We refer to the active portion of a process that is present in the cache as its *footprint* in the cache. In the model presented here, the cache-reload transient experienced by a process, say Process A, when running in a round-robin fashion with another process, say Process B, has four parameters: the size of the footprint of Process A, the size of the footprint of Process B, the number of congruence classes in the cache N, and the number of program lines stored in each congruence class, K. This last parameter is also referred to in the literature as the *degree of associativity*, or *set associativity*, of the cache.

When the size of the cache $(N \times K)$ is very large compared to the size of the footprints of the processes, the collision between the footprints is very small, and, as a consequence, the cache-reload transient experienced by the processes as they resume execution is negligible. The intersection between two small footprints is not necessarily empty since there exists a nonzero probability that both programs will access a common active row, and that the total number of lines assigned to that row will exceed the physical length of the row. In this case, the competition is fierce as each process erases the other process's footprint in that row as it writes its own into the cache. The penalty increases with the number of rows for which the processes compete. The penalty is maximal for very small caches, since each process resumes execution with a cache virtually emptied of that process's environment. For each invocation of Process A during the execution of Process B, performance degradation is caused by two reload transients: the reload transient of Process A when it starts executing, and the reload transient of Process B as it resumes and restores the part of its cache environment erased by A.

Gecsei [5], Fagin [3], Smith [10, 11], Clark [1], and Fenwick [4], among others, have studied the performance of cache memories as a function of their design parameters through the observation of the average miss-ratio or of the average hit-ratio. Their approach contributes to a general understanding of the behavior of cache memories and program execution, but does not address the influence of what we perceive as two intrinsically different phenomena: the reload transient and the steady state phases. Easton [2] studied the influence of the reload-transient phenomenon by running simulations on program traces and by regularly flushing the cache (cold starts) in an attempt to simulate reload transients. This approach provides a clearer picture of the influence of the reload-transient phenomenon, but supplies only a crude approximation of the subtle interference programs exert on each other.

Strecker [13], in a model later enhanced by Fenwick [4], proposes a model for the influence of the reload transient experienced by two interleaved programs based on the continuous flow model. This model assumes a 100 percent filling-factor of program lines in the cache and cannot be easily characterized in terms of the cache-design parameters. The model requires measurements for two cache sizes to establish two points on a curve, and fits a curve through these points that yields the values for a range of other cache sizes. Therefore, the cache-reload effect is predicted by observations that are dependent on the transient data. Moreover, the parameters measured do not have a simple physical interpretation. Our model predicts transient effects from an independent parameter, footprint size, that can be measured or predicted by independent means. It is also very easy to relate the footprint sizes of competing processes to total cache size to obtain a direct intuitive understanding of the reload transient.

The statistical behavior of cache misses has also been studied by Voldman and Hoevel [14] and Voldman et al. [15]. They produce results consistent with our model and show that cache misses appear to occur in bursts between which are relatively long periods virtually free of misses. The results suggest that transients, either from cache reloads or from other sources, account for a significant fraction of cache misses. They offer a fractal model to explain the observed data, but they do not give an underlying model of program behavior that can predict the cache misses without actually running the program. The intent of this paper is to produce such a model for the misses produced from cache reloads.

There are two main results in this paper—the presentation of the footprint model and its validation. The footprint model is a statistical model based on binomial probabilities, and establishes that the cache-reload transient is closely related to the normal distribution. Validation was done by gathering traces of several programs and by simulating cache contention for all possible combinations of two programs scheduled in a round-robin fashion. The simulation was run for several cache sizes and several degrees of set associativity. The reload-transient curves obtained show an excellent match with the model prediction, with a slight divergence for small cache sizes. The observed differences are due to clustering of references in cache lines, and usually produce a lower transient than the transient predicted by the model.

We assume that the reader is familiar with cache memories and their basic principles of operation. When the discussion depends on specific details of a cache memory, this paper summarizes the relevant details to keep it self-contained. Excellent sources of information on caches appear in Smith [11], Puzak [7], and Hwang and Briggs [6].

Section 2 of this paper describes the reload-transient phenomenon. The derivation of the reload-transient model is in Section 3. In Section 4 we present a validation of the analytical model through experimental data. The final section contains a discussion of the extension of this model to computer systems with virtual memory and to other applications.

2. THE RELOAD TRANSIENT AND BASIC CACHE MODEL

Figure 1(a) shows the execution of two programs. The tall rectangle represents the execution of Program A while the low rectangle represents the execution of Program B. In Figure 1(a), we assume that both programs share an infinite cache. Their total execution time is the best possible execution time in this cache environment. In Figure 1(b) we now assume that the cache is of finite size, and that its size is small compared to the amount of information each program brings from main memory to the cache. When Program B starts executing, it creates a footprint in the cache. In general, the footprint that Program A leaves in the cache after its first invocation is partially displaced from the cache by

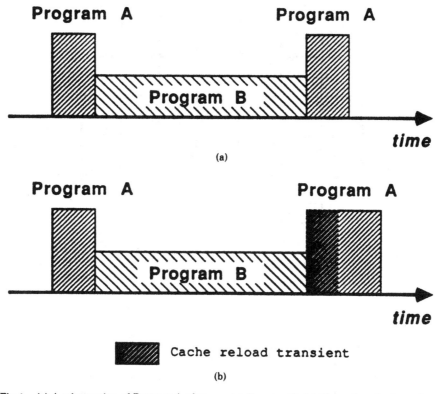

Fig. 1. (a) A reinvocation of Program A after running Program B. (b) The cache-reload transient experienced by Program A.

Program B. When A is invoked a second time (the second tall rectangle in Figure 1(b)), it experiences an initial burst of cache misses. We call this burst the *cache-reload transient* experienced by Program A.

Our goal in this paper is to model the reload transient experienced by a given program as a function of the sizes of the footprints of the competing programs and of the total cache size. The derivation of the model is based on the assumptions that only two programs compete for the cache and that their respective footprints are known, although it can easily be generalized to more complex situations.

To review the basic definitions of the major cache parameters, recall that a cache memory consists of two distinct parts—the directory and the storage array. The directory contains an identification tag for each block of data stored in the storage array. The directory also maintains information on the access history of data to assist in the selection of data to remove from the cache. For this discussion we merge the two functions and treat the cache as a single array. The entities of information stored in the cells of the cache are called *lines* or *blocks*. A line may contain from two to four bytes in small computer systems, and up to 128 bytes

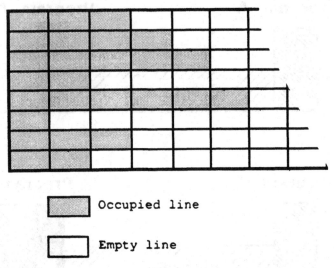

Occupied line

Empty line

Fig. 2. An 8-row infinite cache with grey blocks depicting the footprint of Program A in the cache.

in larger machines. In this paper we do not make any assumptions on the size of the lines, but we assume that it is constant and totally independent of the variation of other cache-design parameters. Consequently, the footprint and cache sizes are implicitly expressed in terms of cache lines and can be directly expressed in terms of bytes by multiplying them by the appropriate factor.

We can represent a cache as a two-dimensional array as shown in Figure 2. This cache has eight rows and an infinite number of columns. Although this cache is purely imaginary, such a concept is useful in understanding the influence of the cache size on the reload transient. The rows of the cache are called the *congruence classes* of the cache. This term stems from the algorithm generally used to assign lines from main memory to specific rows of the cache. The most popular algorithm extracts a bit field from the main memory address of a line. This bit field is the address in the cache of the row in which that line is stored. Because the most significant part of the address bus does not participate in the algorithm, the line-placement algorithm is a modulo operation on the main memory address.

In Figure 2 the cache contains eight congruence classes. Each congruence class is selected by a three-bit field extracted from the address generated by the processor. The 26 shaded boxes represent the active lines that constitute the footprint in the cache of a program in execution. When the processor requests a piece of data from memory, the cache is searched first. Once the congruence class identified by the bit field is located, the whole congruence class is searched in parallel. If the line containing the piece of data requested by the processor is in the cache, a main memory access is avoided (a *cache hit*). If, however, the search fails, the access must be forwarded to main memory (a *cache miss*).

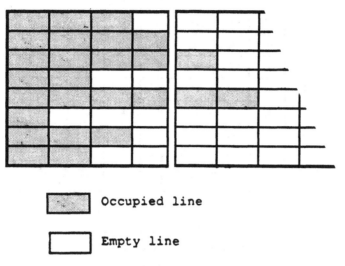

Occupied line

Empty line

Fig. 3. An 8-row, 4-way set-associative cache. Three lines of the program's footprint do not fit in the cache.

In theory, the entire cache can lie in one congruence class, in which case the entire cache is searched for each cache access. In practice, a full search of the entire cache is not economical because almost equal performance at higher speed and less expense can be obtained by searching only a small fraction of the cache. Therefore, a typical cache is organized with only K columns for a K that is a small power of 2. All columns of one congruence class are searched in parallel, thus requiring K simultaneous Read and Compare operations. The integer K is said to be the *set associativity* of the cache, and in most systems the value of K is 1, 2, or 4. A one-way set-associative cache ($K = 1$) is said to be a *direct-mapped* cache. When K is maximum, all lines lie in one congruence class, and the cache is said to be *fully associative*.

In Figure 3 we show how a finite cache affects the behavior of a program. The assumptions are the same as that in Figure 2, except that the cache is only four-way set associative. To illustrate the reload transient, consider an example reference sequence that consists of one cycle of the 26 distinct references of Figure 2, followed by a second cycle consisting of the same 26 references in some other order. We assume that each line is touched exactly once in each cycle. For the infinite cache shown in Figure 2, the program experiences 26 misses in the first cycle followed by 26 hits when the references are repeated in the second cycle because the lines have become resident in the cache. In Figure 3, however, the program's footprint does not fit totally into the four-way set-associative cache. Three lines must be overwritten during the first cycle of 26 references. The number of cache misses is still 26 during the first cycle, but at its completion the full 26-line cycle is not resident in cache. When the program executes the second cycle of 26 references, it experiences at least three cache misses that are

	1	2	3	4	5	6	7	
	X	X	X	O	O			...
	X	X	X	X	O	O	O	...
	X	X	X	X	X	O		...
	X	X	O	O	O	O		...
	X	X	X	X	X	X	O	...
	X	O	O	O				...
	X	X	X	O	O			...
	X	X	O	O	O	O		...

(a)

X = Footprint of Program A
O = Footprint of Program B

	1	2	3	4	5	6	7	
	O	O	X	X	X			...
	O	O	O	X	X	X	X	...
	O	X	X	X	X	X		...
	O	O	O	O	X	X		...
	O	X	X	X	X	X	X	...
	O	O	O	X				...
	O	O	X	X	X			...
	O	O	O	O	X	X		...

(b)

Fig. 4. (a) An infinite cache in the state that exists when Program A finishes running after Program B. (b) The same cache in the state that exists when Program B finishes running after Program A.

not observed when the cache is infinite. In addition to these misses, there are other misses whose number depends on the specific order of the references in the second cycle. We assume throughout the paper that the cache-replacement policy is Least Recently Used (LRU), which displaces the least-recently used line in a congruence class to make room for a new line.

The situation in which two programs compete for cache is illustrated in Figure 4. The lines brought in the cache by Program A are shown as Xs. The lines from Program B are shown as Os. In Figure 4(a), Program B runs first, followed by Program A. The references are arranged in their order of occurrence so that the most recent reference in a row is in Column 1 and the least recent access in a row is the rightmost entry in that row.

The cache shown in Figure 4 has an infinite number of columns. If we assume, however, that the size of the cache is limited to, say, five columns ($K = 5$), then the execution of Program A forces six B-lines to be displaced. When A stops and B resumes, B experiences a reload transient of six lines to reload the lines displaced by A. If B touches all lines in its footprint during its subsequent execution, then its missing six lines are reloaded and the cache state becomes that shown in Figure 4(b). Still assuming a set associativity of five, we see that Program A has seven lines on the right side of the fifth column. These lines are lines that have been displaced by B. As a consequence, A experiences a cache-reload transient of seven lines when it regains control of the processor. For a set associativity of six, the reload transient for both programs is two, since they both have two lines on the right side of the sixth column.

We see that the size of the footprints as well as the size of the cache directly influence the reload transient experienced by the programs. In the next section we define a simple analytic model for the transient that depends on the statistical behavior of the assignment of program lines to the congruence classes of a cache.

3. AN ANALYTICAL MODEL

Our model is based on the assumption that the assignment of lines to the congruence classes of the cache is by a random process in which each congruence class is equally likely to be the destination of a line, and that successive references to cache are independent selections. For this reason we need only study the behavior of the program lines in one row of the cache; then the results obtained for the row can simply be multiplied by the number of rows (N) in the cache to obtain the statistics for the whole cache.

Assuming that we have selected one row of the cache at random, we define three random variables X, Y, and Z associated with the lines present in that row. X is the number of lines belonging to Program A, Y is the number of lines belonging to Program B, and Z is the number of A-lines overwritten by B-lines.

The domain of values taken by the above three random variables is $[0, K]$, where K is the set associativity of the cache. The probability distributions of X and Y are given below:

$$P[X = i] = \text{probability that a row contains } i \text{ A-lines}$$
$$= \binom{F_A}{i} p^i (1 - p)^{F_A - i} \quad \text{for} \quad 0 \leq i \leq K - 1 \tag{3.1}$$

where $p = 1/N$, and F_A is the size of the A-footprint, and

$$P[X = K] = prob[K \text{ lines are assigned to the row}]$$
$$+ prob[K + 1 \text{ lines are assigned to the row}]$$
$$+ \cdots$$
$$+ prob[F_A \text{ lines are assigned to the row}] \tag{3.2}$$

or,

$$P[X = K] = \sum_{j=K}^{F_A} \binom{F_A}{j} p^j (1 - p)^{F_A - j} \tag{3.3}$$

The reasoning behind Eq. (3.2) is that the process is binomial with F_A trials, each with probability of success $p = 1/N$ of selecting 1 of N congruence classes. The formula for $P[X = K]$ sums the probabilities for K or more hits to a single class.

Similarly, we let F_B be the footprint of Program B, and we obtain:

$$P[Y = i] = \binom{F_B}{i} p^i (1 - p)^{F_B - i}, \quad \text{for} \quad 0 \le i \le K - 1 \tag{3.4}$$

and

$$P[Y = K] = \sum_{j=K}^{F_B} \binom{F_B}{j} p^j (1 - p)^{F_B - j} \tag{3.5}$$

The probability density for Z takes two different forms:

$$
\begin{aligned}
P[Z = 0] &= \text{probability that no A-lines are overwritten} \\
&= P[X = 0]P[0 \le Y \le K] \\
&\quad + P[X = 1]P[0 \le Y \le K - 1] \\
&\quad \cdots \\
&\quad + P[X = K]P[Y = 0] \\
&= \sum_{i=0}^{K} P[X = i] \sum_{j=0}^{K-i} P[Y = j]
\end{aligned} \tag{3.6}
$$

and for $0 < i \le K$:

$$
\begin{aligned}
P[Z = i] &= \text{probability that } i \text{ A-lines are overwritten by B-lines} \\
&= P[X = i]P[Y = K] \\
&\quad + P[X = i + 1]P[Y = K - 1] \\
&\quad + \cdots \\
&\quad + P[X = K]P[Y = i] \\
&= \sum_{j=i}^{K} P[X = j]P[Y = K + i - j]
\end{aligned} \tag{3.7}
$$

The expectations of X and Z are given by:

$$\bar{X} = \sum_{i=1}^{K} iP[X = i] \tag{3.8}$$

$$\bar{Z} = \sum_{i=1}^{K} iP[Z = i] \tag{3.9}$$

Hence, the average number of A-lines in the cache when Program B starts executing is $N\bar{X}$ and the average number of A-lines erased by program B when Program A resumes execution is $N\bar{Z}$. The average number of transient misses that Program A experiences when it regains control of the processor is:

$$\text{Average reload transient} = F_A - (N\bar{X} - N\bar{Z}) \tag{3.10}$$

154

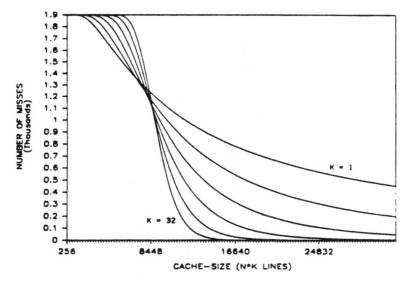

Fig. 5. The cache-reload transient predicted by the model.

which is the total footprint size of Program A less its lines remaining in the cache when Program A resumes control. Figure 5 shows the plot of the reload transient experienced by Program A as a function of the cache size NK, with K varying from 1 to 32. In this example, F_A has size 7900 lines, and F_B has 1900 lines.

The shape of the curve in Figure 5 is related to the normal distribution function. To see why, consider Figure 4. The number of Xs displaced from a K-way cache is the number of Xs to the right of the Kth column. The total number of entries in any row is binomially distributed, and is the number obtained by flipping a coin $F_A + F_B$ times with probability of success equal to $p = 1/N$. This probability is approximately normal, although the approximation is not very good for the small values of p of interest to us for cache designs. Nevertheless, the shape of the function is the general shape of the normal density even though the approximation is not accurate. For each value of K, some of the entries to the right of column K will be Xs and some will be Os, but in every case the Xs in a row are displaced before the Os because they are less recent accesses than the Os. If only Xs are displaced, then the number displaced is approximately the integral of the tail of a normal density. Hence the shape of the curve in Figure 5 looks like the curve obtained by subtracting a normal distribution from a constant. The approximation is not exact because the normal density does not closely approximate the binomial distribution for the parameters of interest, and because both Xs and Os are displaced in Figure 4, not just Xs as assumed for the approximation to hold.

We now proceed to find an envelope for the family of K-curves that model the cache-reload transient. As K increases, for a fixed cache size, N decreases. In the limit, as K becomes very large, the cache becomes fully associative, that is,

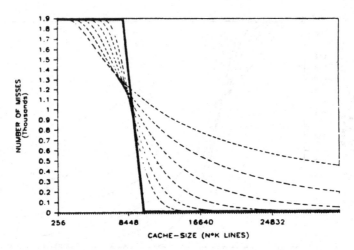

Fig. 6. Reload transient of a fully associative cache.

$N = 1$. The curve for $N = 1$ (for which the total cache size is equal to the set associativity K) is the curve shown as a continuous heavy line in Figure 6. This curve is the asymptote towards which the family of K-curves tends, as K increases.

If we study the asymptote for the reload transient of Program A, the abscissa of the point where the asymptote leaves the 100 percent level is equal to F_B. The abscissa of the point where the curve intersects the 0 percent level is equal to $F_A + F_B$, the sum of the sizes of the footprints of the two programs. For any point on the asymptote, the cache contains one row, and all lines accessed by both programs are assigned to that row. As long as the cache size is less than the size of the B-footprint, the A-footprint is entirely erased during the execution of Program B because it takes over all available cache up to the size of its footprint. As the cache size increases past the value F_B, the reload transient decreases linearly with increasing cache size until the cache is sufficiently large to hold both footprints. At this point, no reload transient occurs because the two programs can reside in cache without mutual interference.

Since Program B occupies as much space in a fully associative cache as it possibly can when it takes control of the processor, Process A is relegated to the space left over. When the roles of Programs A and B are reversed, the asymptote leaves the 100 percent level at a cache size of F_A and reaches the 0 percent level for a cache size of $F_A + F_B$.

The previous curve gives us an asymptote toward which the family of curves converges as K increases. This asymptote together with the curve corresponding to the parameter $K = 1$ provide us with an envelope for the family of K-curves with the possible exception of the small region of points where the curves intersect. The equation of the curve for $K = 1$ is the following:

Cache-reload transient for Program A in a one-way cache =

$$F_A - N[1 - (1 - p)^{F_A} - (1 - (1 - p)^{F_A})(1 - (1 - p)^{F_B})] \qquad (3.11)$$

156

This follows because in the case $K = 1$ the expectations of X and Z take especially simple forms:

$$\bar{X} = P[X = 1] \tag{3.12}$$

$$\bar{Z} = P[Z = 1] \tag{3.13}$$

In the next section we use the envelope formed by the two curves to compare the simulation results to the model.

4. PROGRAM TRACES AND SIMULATION

To validate the model, we simulated the execution of several programs taken two at a time in caches of different sizes and degrees of associativity. The reload transient experienced by the two programs was then plotted for different values of the parameter K. In this simulation the cache size varied from 256 lines to 32,768 lines, and the associativity of the cache from 1 to 32. These curves were then compared to the analytically derived envelope defined above. We used a Least Recently Used (LRU) line-replacement algorithm throughout the simulation.

4.1 Program Traces

The input to the cache simulator were program traces obtained from the execution of four programs on an IBM Personal Computer. Published research presenting results from simulation on program traces is very often based on the use of mini- or mainframe computers (Puzak [7], Clark [1], and Smith [11].) We chose to validate the model on a microprocessor because of the relative ease of obtaining instruction traces on such a system. However, the system used does not directly support multitasking, so that the effects of two or more programs competing for cache were simulated artificially by interleaving traces of two programs. We were unable to capture real data by measuring programs executing in a multitasking environment. We feel, however, that the methodology of interleaving traces of two programs is a reasonable simulation of the task switching that occurs in virtual-memory systems. The agreement between the model and the simulated task switching is very good in general, so we expect it to work as well for multitasking environments on the same machine. Moreover, the model is likely to be accurate for other computer systems since it depends on the structure of the cache and not on the specific architecture of the processor.

The four programs traced were a Pascal Compiler (Turbo Pascal Version 2), the execution of an interpreted BASIC program (Microsoft BASIC Interpreter), a spelling-checker program (Wordproof), and a simulation program written in Turbo Pascal.

The generation of the traces was carried out by special software that logged the address references during program execution. Rather than use a machine simulator (cf., [1]), the tracing in our case was executed while the program was running, using a technique similar to the one described by Satyanarayanan and Bhandarkar [8] for their study of the VAX-11 translation lookaside-buffer. The single-step interrupt vector (interrupt number 1 of the 8088 microprocessor) was mapped to a cache-simulator routine appended to the disk operating system. At

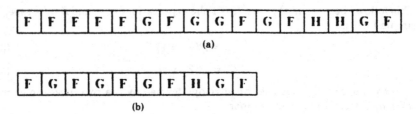

(a)

(b)

Fig. 7. Stripping of a series of line references by Puzak's algorithm. (a) Unstripped trace.
(b) After stripping.

the beginning of the execution of each of the four target programs, the Trace
flag-bit of the 8088 was turned on, forcing the 8088 to execute the cache simulator
routine after each traceable instruction of the program. The state of the microprocessor was then analyzed by the interrupt routine, the current instruction
decoded, and all the memory accesses computed. These memory references were
then passed to a one-way associative, N-class cache simulator ($N = 32$ for our
traces) with a line-size of eight bytes. Only the misses produced by this simulator
were saved in a trace file. Puzak [7] shows that the stripped trace obtained by
this means can be used to simulate with full accuracy any N'-class, K-way set
associative cache for $N' \geq N$ and $K \geq 1$, yet a stripped trace is only about 10
percent of the length of a full trace.

To clarify the usefulness and mechanism of the stripping scheme, imagine that
we have a series of memory references as depicted in Figure 7. In this figure,
different letters represent memory lines that are assigned to a specific congruence
class of the cache. A real trace contains references to the other lines interspersed
with the references shown in the figure. In this example we see that our program
touches Line F several times in a row (possibly while executing a purely sequential
piece of code.) Then the program hits Line F and G successively several times,
with a pair of references to Line H occurring at the end of sequence. By using
Puzak's stripping algorithm and by assuming that the cache is empty when it
receives the series of lines shown in the first line of Figure 7, only the references
shown in the second line of Figure 7 are recorded. For any cache whose line size
is eight with any set associativity and at least $N = 32$ congruence classes, the
simulation of that cache on our stripped traces produces the same number of
misses as would be produced on the full program trace. This holds for any cache
replacement policy that does not discard the most recently used line in a
congruence class. Four stripped traces were generated by this process.

This trace generation process has several disadvantages. The main drawback
of an all-software tracing process is that the execution of the programs traced is
very slow. For each instruction traced, hundreds of instructions of the trace
routine have to be executed in order to (1) save the state of the microprocessor;
(2) decode the instruction pointed to by the instruction pointer; (3) calculate the
effective addresses of the possibly many memory references generated by the
instruction; and (4) pass these effective addresses to the cache simulator. The
second, more serious disadvantage of a tracing process triggered by the 8088
single-step interrupt is that critical sections and interrupt routines cannot be

158

Table I. Trace Characteristics.

Trace	Program	Stripped-tape length (number of references)
1	Pascal compiler	206,276
2	Basic program	206,276
3	Speller checker	206,276
4	Simulation program	206,276

traced. These portions had to be executed with the single-step interrupt disabled. For this reason some of the operating system code, particularly portions that must execute is realtime, were not captured by our trace routine. This scheme, however, captures more information than does a machine simulation of user processes only. Nevertheless, the reader should be aware of Clark's concerns regarding the validity of software generated traces [1], and note that the concerns are less likely to hold for the traces we generated than for traces generated through simulation.

The four traces, whose characteristics are given in Table I, contain the memory addresses of both the instructions and their operand(s). The results shown in this paper thus apply to caches that hold both instructions and data.

Because of time and memory-space limitations, the length of the traces was truncated at 206,276 three-byte addresses (20 bits corresponding to the IBM PC real address and four bits used as pad). Since the stripped trace is roughly 10 percent of the length of a full trace, the data analyzed corresponds to a trace length of more than two million address references, or roughly one million instructions executed.

4.2 Results

To simulate the cache-interaction of two programs, Program A and Program B, executing in a round-robin fashion, we first selected two traces from the four shown in Table I. Each trace is configured in blocks of 6016 line references. This number corresponds to the size of the file buffer used during the tracing process, and is equal to the amount of free memory left available after the trace utilities and target program were loaded in the PC's main memory. When a block of 6016 line references was written to magnetic storage during the tracing process, the cache simulator cleared the cache. This ensured that the references in each block do not depend upon the configuration of the cache at the end of the previous block. As a result, each block of 6016 line references in a trace is independent of its adjacent neighbors, is self-contained, and can be extracted from the trace without any loss of information. This is exactly what is required to simulate the interleaved execution of Program A and Program B. Consecutive blocks from Trace A, $A_1A_2A_3A_4A_5A_6$, and from Trace B, $B_1B_2B_3B_4B_5B_6$, are interwoven as follows to simulate the interleaving of the two programs:

$$A_1B_1A_2B_2A_3B_3A_4B_4A_5B_5A_6B_6.$$

Six blocks from each trace are interleaved in such a way, and the reload transient for each program is calculated at the points between B_3 and A_4, A_4 and B_4, B_4 and A_5, A_5 and B_5, B_5 and A_6, and finally, A_6 and B_6. The first three blocks

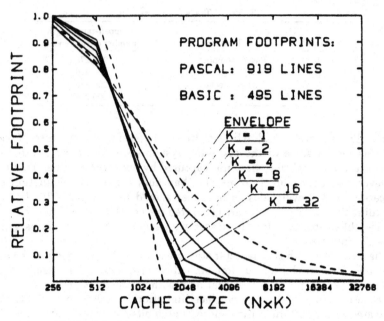

Fig. 8.   Reload transient: Pascal compiler and BASIC progam.

of each trace are used only for cache initialization purposes, allowing the cache under study to reach equilibrium before the reload transients are measured. The average of the three reload transient values obtained for each program is recorded. By repeating the same experiment for different cache sizes NK, ranging from 256 to 32,768 lines, with a degree of associativity K, ranging from 1 to 32, we obtain the reload transient of a Program A running against Program B (and vice versa) as a function of the cache size NK, and parameterized in K.

Thus, for each pair of traces, sequences of 36,096 successive addresses were interlaced to simulate a transient. Because the traces were stripped, the sequences correspond to full traces with roughly 360,000 addresses. The sequences to interlace were selected at random from stripped traces, but in every case the sequences contained six full consecutive blocks of 6016 address references. For each pair of competing programs, the same pair of sequences was used to measure the transient of A due to B and of B due to A.

The stripped trace does not give accurate results for caches whose line sizes are different from the eight-byte line size of the cache used to produce the stripped trace. Hence, our data are not useful for measuring the influence of line size on the reload transient.

The 12 sets of curves resulting from the analysis of the four programs are shown in Figures 8 through 19. For each family of curves we have also plotted, in dashed lines, the envelope given by the analytical model. The dashed line with the steeper slope corresponds to the $K = 32$ curve given by the analytical model, while the other dashed line corresponds to the $K = 1$ curve. To offer a better means of comparison between the different figures, we normalized

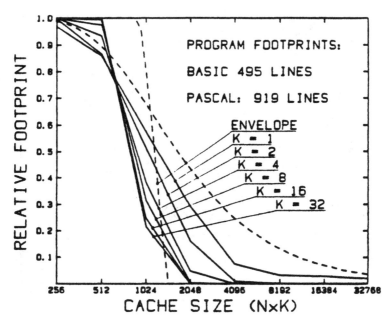

Fig. 9.   Reload transient: BASIC program and Pascal compiler.

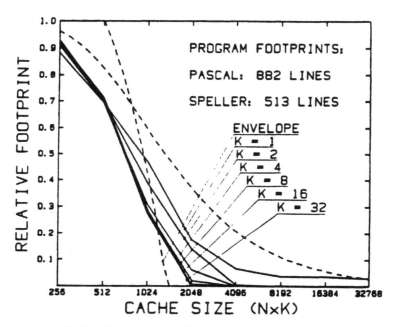

Fig. 10.   Reload transient: Pascal compiler and spell-checker.

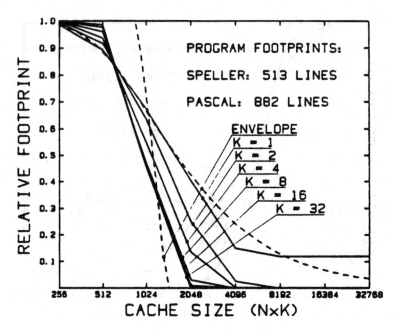

Fig. 11. Reload transient: spell-checker and Pascal compiler.

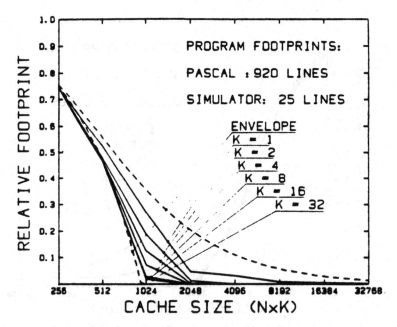

Fig. 12. Reload transient: Pascal compiler and simulation program.

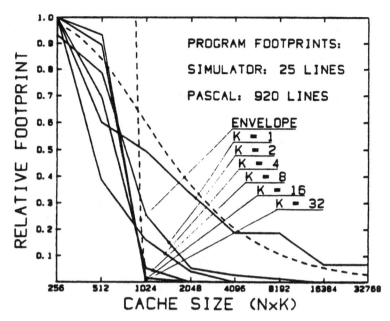

Fig. 13.   Reload transient: simulation program and Pascal compiler.

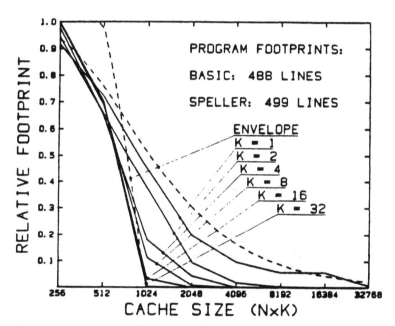

Fig. 14.   Reload transient: BASIC program and spell-checker.

163

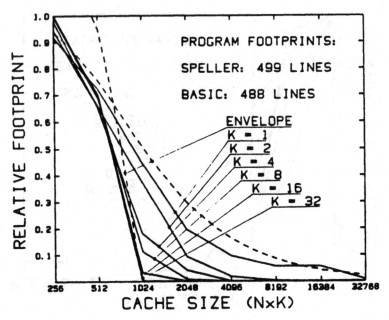

Fig. 15. Reload transient: spell-checker and BASIC program.

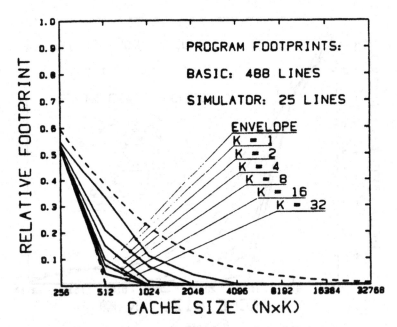

Fig. 16. Reload transient: BASIC program and simulation program.

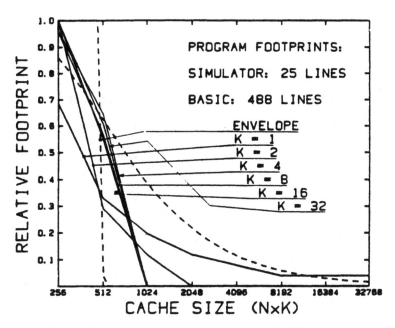

Fig. 17. Reload transient: simulation program and BASIC program.

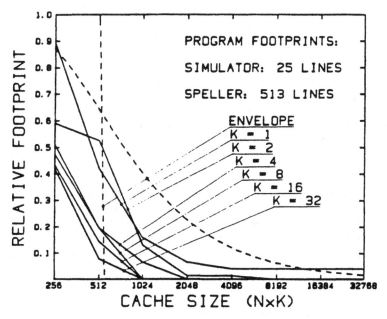

Fig. 18. Reload transient: spell-checker and simulation program.

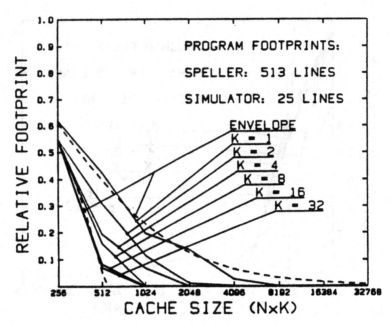

Fig. 19.   Reload transient: simulation program and spell-checker.

the reload-transient axis. This was done by plotting the right-hand side of Eq. (3.10) divided by the footprint size F_A. The total footprint size was estimated by measuring the size of the program footprint in the largest cache simulated, which in each case was sufficiently large relative to the footprint size to be treated as an infinite cache.

The reload transient of the Pascal compiler executing in conjunction with the interpreted BASIC program is shown in Figure 8. The reload transient of the interpreted BASIC program executing in conjunction with the Pascal compiler is shown in Figure 9. The other combinations of pairs of programs are shown accordingly in adjacent figures.

4.3 Analysis

Both the model and the simulation results show that the K-curves intersect and that, for small cache sizes, the reload transient is smaller in caches with low associativity than in caches with high associativity. The reason for such a behavior is best illustrated in Figure 20 where the footprint of a program is shown in an eight-congruence class cache with an infinite degree of associativity. In this example, we see that statistical effects leave some rows empty and other rows with several entries. The reload transient for finite caches depends on the number of rows that contain more entries than the set associativity of the cache. The reload transient for finite caches depends on the number of rows with more entries than the set associativity of a cache.

X	X	X				
X						
X	X					
X	X					
X	X	X				
X						
X	X					

Fig. 20.   Footprint in an 8-congruence class cache.

Compare Figure 21 with Figure 20 to see the effect of reducing N to $N/2$. Each row of Figure 21 is the sum of two rows of Figure 20, and thus, the standard deviation of the number of entries per row in Figure 21 is less than that of Figure 20, so that the entries are more evenly distributed through the rows of a cache. Such rows are less likely to overflow the cache for a variety of values of the product NK.

When the cache size is much larger than the size of the footprint, the opposite behavior is observed. The reload transient in caches with high associativity is smaller than that in caches with low associativity. The reason is that rows that receive several lines because of clusters of high activity are truncated in caches with low associativity. As a result, the footprint of a given program is smaller in a one-way associative cache than in a two- or more-way associative cache with an identical number of lines. This explains why the reload transient increases as the associativity decreases for very large cache sizes (compared to the footprints' sizes.)

Figures 8 and 17 show the best fit between the model and the simulation results. In the other figures, the curves for $K = 1$ from both the model and the simulation are very close, with the curves for $K = 32$ showing the most divergence between model and simulation. The quasi-consistency with which the simulation curve for $K = 1$ remains below the model curve for $K = 1$ shows that the true reload transient is less than that predicted by the model, which can have two possible explanations: (1) the number of lines remaining in the cache before a program starts executing is larger than the number predicted by the model, or (2) the number of lines reloaded in the cache is less than that predicted by the model.

As for the first hypothesis, one possible explanation is that once a line belonging to Program A is in a congruence class, it is not as likely to be erased by a line from Program B as the model predicts, implying that the probability distribution of the lines to the congruence class is not binomial, but instead has some degree of clustering. When a line is assigned to congruence class i, the probability that other lines will be assigned to congruence classes i, $i - 1$, or $i + 1$ is greater than

X	X	X	X	X	X				
X									
X	X	X							
X	X	X	X						

Fig. 21. Footprint in a 4-congruence class cache.

for other congruence classes. This stems from the temporal and spatial locality exhibited by programs. Consequently the actual distribution of program lines in the cache shows clusters of lines rather than a uniform distribution of lines over the whole cache. The actual line distributions provide less damage due to footprint overlays than the model assumes.

It is paradoxical that our assumption of binomial distribution of the lines among the congruence classes that first appears as an optimistic assumption proves to be too pessimistic in light of the simulation curves! Many researchers have tried to transform the distribution of lines among congruence classes and introduce more randomness in order to improve the cache hit-ratio (cf., [10]). Our analysis suggests that, at best, this technique improves the steady-state hit-ratio. But the reload transient is greater because a more even distribution of references through the rows of the cache is likely to cause more transient collisions, not fewer, of one process with another in their references to cache. A heavily clustered distribution of references reduces the collision between the two footprints, and thereby reduces the reload transient, although each individual process may have a higher miss rate in the steady state when the references are clustered than when they are not. This provides a possible explanation for the unexpectedly small increase in performance reported by Smith when a randomization was introduced in the assignment of lines to congruence classes. The increase in performance gained during the steady state was negated in part by a decrease in performance due to reload transients.

As for the second hypothesis about the difference between the simulated and the predicted reload transients, a possible contributing factor is the influence of dead lines in the cache. Our model assumes that each A-line displaced by Program B will have to be reloaded by Program A when it resumes. This is not always true. Because we assume an LRU-replacement algorithm, the first A-lines in a given congruence class that Program B displaces are the least recently used lines, and they may very well be dead lines, i.e., lines that will never be accessed by Program A for the remainder of its execution. So the number of lines that Program A really needs to reload is the number of *live* lines displaced by Program B, while our model counts the number of live lines plus the number of dead lines as the amount of reload transient.

While we do not, at present, possess data about the influence of line-clustering or about the influence of the dead lines on the reload transient, we conjecture that *both* the clustering process and the influence of the dead lines account for the difference between the model and the simulation results.

The validation is given only for eight-byte lines. The question remains open as to whether the model holds for longer lines, especially much longer lines. For short lines, the discussion above indicates that there is likely to be some clustering of references among neighboring cache rows, which is not properly accounted in the statistical model. The affect of the clustering tends to make the estimated reload transient larger than the actual transient. We conjecture that longer lines are likely to lead to less correlation between references in adjacent rows than do short lines, so that as line size increases, the statistical assumptions of the model are likely to become more accurate estimates of the actual transients.

5. CONCLUSIONS

In this paper we present a new, powerful yet simple model for the estimation of the influence of cache size on the reload transients. The reload transient is an important phenomenon to study because it accounts for a substantial fraction of the cache misses, and hence directly influences the performance of the computer. The cache misses have been shown by Voldman et al. [15] to occur in bursts followed by a period with very few misses. The distribution of the gaps between bursts is a fractal distribution. Some of these bursts can be attributed to reload transients occurring when different programs or tasks are swapped. Our model provides a predictive tool for the influence of the cache-design parameters on such reloads.

Our model is likely to be most useful in exploring the effects on cache of changes in the dispatching intervals of a multitasking system. Consider, for example, cache reloads produced by task switches that are initiated on I/O events. Differences in relative timing of I/O devices and processors may cause task switches to occur at different relative rates. We would like to calculate cache-miss ratios as a function of the relative processor and I/O speeds without performing detailed cache simulations. It may be possible to isolate the transient misses caused by task switches from the steady-state miss rate, and then determine how the transient misses change as a function of the interval between task switches. If this is possible, the cache designer will be able to compute the miss ratio across a broad range of processor and I/O performance ratings by calculating the reload transient misses and adding this to the steady-state misses.

The estimates provided by the model agree closely with the results from a simulation based on address traces generated on a personal computer. The only disagreements noted were instances in which the model predicted too high a transient because the references were more clustered than the model assumes. The disagreement diminishes for large caches because statistical effects tend to bring real reference patterns in line with the assumed reference patterns. We conjecture that the model's accuracy improves with increasing line size; but even for the small eight-byte line size, the predictive properties of the model are excellent.

ACKNOWLEDGMENT

The authors wish to thank Bernard Cooperman of Unisys Corporation and members of his staff for posing the problem that led to this model, and for obtaining initial data that confirmed the model. The authors are indebted to

K. S. Natarajan of IBM T. J. Watson Research Center for his careful reading of the manuscript and his helpful comments. The authors also thank the referees for their perceptive comments and suggestions that helped to shape the final manuscript.

REFERENCES

1. CLARK, D. W. Cache performance in the VAX11/780. *ACM Trans. Comput. Syst. 1*, 1 (Feb. 1983), 24–37.
2. EASTON, M. C. Computation of cold-start miss ratios. *IEEE Trans. Comput. C-27*, 5 (May 1978), 404–408.
3. FAGIN, R., AND EASTON, M. C. The independence of miss ratio on page size. *J. ACM 23*, 1 (Jan. 1976), 128–140.
4. FENWICK, P. M. Some aspects of the dynamic behavior of hierarchical memories. *IEEE Trans. Comput. C-34*, 6 (June 1985), 570–573.
5. GECSEI, J. Determining hit ratios for multilevel hierarchies, *IBM J. Res. Dev. 18*, 7 (July 1974), 316–327.
6. HWANG, K., AND BRIGGS, F. A. *Computer Architecture and Parallel Processing.* McGraw-Hill, New York, 1984.
7. PUZAK, T. R. Analysis of cache replacement algorithms. Ph.D. dissertation, Univ. of Massachusetts, Amherst, 1985.
8. SATYANARAYANAN, M., AND BHANDARKAR, D. Design trade-offs in VAX-11 translation buffer organization. *Computer 14*, 12 (Dec. 1981), 103–111.
9. SLUTZ, D. R., AND TRAIGER, I. L. A note on the calculation of average working set size. *Commun. ACM 17*, 10 (Oct. 1974), 563–565.
10. SMITH, A. J. A comparative study of set-associative memory-mapping algorithms and their use for cache and main memory. *IEEE Trans. Softw. Eng. SE-4*, 2 (Mar. 1978), 121–130.
11. SMITH, A. J. Cache memories. *ACM Comput. Surv. 14*, 3 (Sept. 1982), 473–530.
12. STONE, H. S., AND THIEBAUT, D. Footprints in the cache. In *Proceedings of Performance '86 and ACM SIGMETRICS 1986 Joint Conference on Computer Performance, Modeling, Measurement and Evaluation* (Raleigh, NC, May 27–30, 1986). ACM, New York, 1986, pp. 4–8.
13. STRECKER, W. D. Transient behavior of cache memories. *ACM Trans. Comput. Syst. 1*, 4 (Nov. 1983), 281–293.
14. VOLDMAN, J., AND HOEVEL, L. W. The software-cache connection. *IBM J. Res. Dev. 25*, 6 (Nov. 1981), 877–893.
15. VOLDMAN, J., MANDELBROT, B., HOEVEL, L., KNIGHT, J. AND ROSENFELD, P. Fractal nature of software-cache interaction. *IBM J. Res. Dev. 27*, 2 (Mar. 1983) 164–170.

Received October 1986; revised April 1987; accepted June 1987

An Analytical Cache Model

ANANT AGARWAL, MARK HOROWITZ, and JOHN HENNESSY
Computer Systems Laboratory, Stanford University

Trace-driven simulation and hardware measurement are the techniques most often used to obtain accurate performance figures for caches. The former requires a large amount of simulation time to evaluate each cache configuration while the latter is restricted to measurements of existing caches. An analytical cache model that uses parameters extracted from address traces of programs can efficiently provide estimates of cache performance and show the effects of varying cache parameters. By representing the factors that affect cache performance, we develop an analytical model that gives miss rates for a given trace as a function of cache size, degree of associativity, block size, subblock size, multiprogramming level, task switch interval, and observation interval. The predicted values closely approximate the results of trace-driven simulations, while requiring only a small fraction of the computation cost.

Categories and Subject Descriptors: B.3.2 [**Memory Structures**]: Design Styles—*associative memories, cache memories, virtual memory*; B.3.3 [**Memory Structures**]: Performance Analysis and Design Aids—*formal models, simulation*; C.4 [**Computer Systems Organization**]: Performance of Systems—*design studies, modeling techniques, performance attributes*

General Terms: Design, Measurement, Performance, Theory

Additional Key Words and Phrases: Cache miss rate, cache model, cache performance, program behavior, spatial locality, temporal locality, trace-driven simulation, working set

1. INTRODUCTION

1.1 The Case for the Analytical Cache Model

Two methods predominate for cache analysis: trace-driven simulation and hardware measurement. The survey article by Smith [22] uses the former technique extensively, while a comprehensive set of hardware measurements is presented by Clark [8]. Other examples of cache studies using the above methods include [5, 12, 14, 23, 3]. These techniques provide an accurate estimate of cache performance for the measured benchmarks. The problem is that they cannot be used to obtain quick estimates or bounds on cache performance for a wide range of programs and cache configurations. Simulation is costly and must be repeated

This work has been supported by the Defense Advanced Research Project Agency, under contract MDA 903-83-C-0335.

Authors' address: Computer Systems Laboratory, Stanford University, Stanford, CA 94305. A. Agarwal is currently with the Laboratory for Computer Science (NE 43-418), MIT, Cambridge, MA 02139.

"An Analytical Cache Model" by A. Agarwal, M. Horowitz, and J. Hennessy from *ACM Trans. Computer Systems*, Vol. 7, No. 2, May 1989, pp. 184–215. Copyright © ACM, Inc., 1989. Reprinted by permission.

for each possible cache organization.[1] Large caches requiring longer traces for simulation exacerbate the problem. Multiprogramming effects are seldom studied using simulation due to the lack of multitasking traces; the availability of such traces [3] introduces additional dimensions over which simulations must be done. Hardware measurement, which usually involves costly instrumentation, requires an existing cache and gives data for only one cache organization (sometimes with possible size variations [8]). Furthermore, simulation and measurement inherently provide little insight into the nature of programs and the factors that affect cache performance. Analytical models on the other hand, if simple and tractable, can provide useful "first cut" estimates of cache performance. Simple models provide more intuition, but may lack the accuracy of more complex models. Architectural and system-specific effects, such as shared libraries, code sharing, lightweight processes, and physical or virtual addressing, are also hard to capture without complicating the model. Therefore, if more detailed results are needed, simulations can be carried out to fine-tune the cache organization.

There are added advantages to having a simple model for cache behavior. For example, an understanding of the exact dependence of cache miss rate on program and workload parameters can identify those aspects of program behavior where effort would be best justified to improve cache performance. Cheriton et al. [6] suggest that building caches with large blocks (cache pages), in conjunction with program restructuring to exploit the increased block sizes, could yield significant performance benefits. A cache model that incorporates the spatial locality of programs would be useful in analyzing the effects of various program restructuring methods. In addition, this model could be incorporated into optimizing compilers to evaluate trade-offs in decisions, such as procedure merging, that affect cache performance.

1.2 Overview of the Model

Our cache model is hybrid in nature, involving a judicious combination of measurement and analytical techniques. Since the intended application of our model is to obtain fast and reliable estimates of cache performance, the time spent in measurement of parameters from the address trace and, more importantly, in model computations must be significantly less than simulation. To minimize the number of parameters that have to be recorded and stored, average quantities are often used instead of detailed distributions. Using averages also decreases computation time. Besides, the typical value of interest—the miss rate—is an average. Mean Value Analysis (MVA), an example of this approach [16], gives accurate predictions of computer system performance using average measured system parameters to drive analytical models, and has been a key motivating factor in our cache modeling efforts.

Our model derives cache miss rates for various cache organizations and workloads from a few parameters recorded from an address trace. These parameters are meaningful by themselves and provide a good indication of cache performance.

---

[1] Stack processing techniques can sometimes be used to reduce the number of simulations [17].

Cache miss rates can be derived by representing the following factors that cause cache misses:

Start-up effects. When a process begins execution for the first time on a processor, there is usually a flurry of misses corresponding to the process getting its initial working set into the cache. In the early portion of any trace, a significant proportion of the misses in a large cache can be attributed to start-up effects. This effect is also observed when a program abruptly changes phases of execution. Since miss-rate statistics for different phases of the same program are often widely uncorrelated, just as those of different programs are, each phase has to be separately characterized for maximum accuracy. However, for simplicity, or if the phases are short or if phase changes are small, their effects can be smoothed into the nonstationary category, which we discuss in the following paragraphs. Start-up effects are excluded when warm-start (or steady-state) miss rates are needed [10]. Inclusion yields cold-start miss rates.

Nonstationary behavior. This behavior is caused by the slow change of a program's working set over time. The misses that occur when program blocks are fetched for the first time after the start-up phase are included in this category. Any program performing the same sort of operation on each element of a large data set shows this behavior. Subtle changes of phase over small intervals of time, corresponding to change in the cache working set, can also be modeled as a nonstationary effect. Often, all phase behavior within a trace can be conveniently treated as nonstationary.

Start-up and nonstationary behaviors are evident from working-set plots [9] of programs. Working-set plots have a roughly bilinear nature with a sharply rising initial portion corresponding to start-up, and a gradual slope thereafter, denoting nonstationarity. The misses caused by the above two effects are dependent on the block size—assuming that a block is fetched from the main store on a cache miss. Increasing the block size (up to a limit) takes advantage of the spatial locality in programs and reduces cache miss rate. A model of spatial locality is proposed to account for this effect.

Intrinsic interference. Due to finite cache size, multiple program blocks may compete for a cache set and collide with each other. If the number of cache sets is S, then all addresses that have the same index (i.e., a common value for the address modulo S) will have to be in the same cache set. Intrinsic interference misses occur when these blocks have to be fetched after being purged from the cache by a colliding block of the same process. The total number of intrinsic interference misses are computed as the product of two components. The first component is the number of program blocks that can potentially be displaced from the cache due to collisions, and is statically determined from the distribution of addresses over the address space. The derivation of this static component is based on the assumption that any program block has a uniform probability of falling into any cache set. Section 5 discusses the limitations of this assumption. The second component is the actual number of times a block that can potentially be displaced actually suffers a collision. This dynamic effect is related to the sequencing of references, and is represented using a measured parameter from the trace, called the collision rate. Unlike the distribution of blocks in the cache, which is dependent on the cache size, the collision rate is shown to be reasonably stable over a wide range of cache and block sizes (see Section 2.3.2 and Appendix B).

Extrinsic interference. Multiprogramming is an additional source of misses because memory references of a given process can invalidate cache locations that contained valid data of other processes. The impact of multitasking, not widely considered in previous cache studies, is particularly important for large caches. Extrinsic interference will increase with the level of multiprogramming and decrease with the quantum of time that a process executes before being switched out. Other causes of extrinsic interference such as I/O, clock interrupts, and cache consistency invalidations are not included in this study but could be added. Extrinsic interference is modeled in the same manner as intrinsic interference, with only the static characterization being necessary. The dynamic component, characterized by the collision rate in intrinsic interference, is not needed because a block can suffer a multiprogramming-induced collision only once after a process switch.

All the above effects are included in our comprehensive model of cache behavior. Start-up effects and extrinsic interference characterize the transient behavior of programs, and nonstationary effects, intrinsic and extrinsic interference determine steady-state performance. The extent to which each effect contributes to the miss rate is a strong function of the cache organization and workload. In small caches, misses are predominantly caused by intrinsic interference, whereas in caches large enough to hold the working set of the program, nonstationarity and extrinsic interference are the important sources of misses.

1.3 Related Research

Our approach differs from some of the earlier memory hierarchy modeling efforts that tend to focus on some specific aspect of cache performance but did not adequately address the issue of a comprehensive cache model.

Some of the early memory hierarchy studies use empirical models. Chow [7] assumes a power function of the form $m = AC^B$ for the miss ratio, where C is the size of that level in the memory hierarchy and A and B are constants. They do not give a basis for this model and do not validate this model against experimental results. Smith [22] shows that the above function approximates the miss ratio for a given set of results within certain ranges for appropriate choices of the constants. However, no claims are made for the validity of the power function for other workloads, architectures, or cache sizes.

The Independent Reference Model [4] is used by Rao to analyze cache performance [18]. This model was chosen primarily because it was analytically tractable. Miss rate estimates are provided for direct-mapped, fully-associative, and set-associative caches using the arithmetic and geometric distributions for page reference probabilities. A problem with this technique is that it assumes fixed page sizes and the number of parameters needed to describe the program is very large. Furthermore, validations against real program traces are not provided.

Smith focused on the effect of mapping algorithm and set-associativity [21] using two models, a mixed exponential and the inverse of Saltzer's linear paging model [20], for the miss-ratio curve of a fully-associative cache. The miss-rate formulas compared well with trace-driven simulation results. However, separate characterization is necessary for each block size, and time-dependent effects and multiprogramming issues are not addressed.

Haikala [13] assessed the impact of the task switch interval on cache performance. He uses a simple Markov chain model to estimate the effect of cache flushes. The LRU stack model of program behavior [24] and geometrically distributed lengths of task switch intervals are assumed. The model is reasonably accurate for small caches where task switching flushes the cache completely and pessimistic for large caches where significant data retention occurs across task switches as shown in [3].

Easton and Fagin [10] stressed the need for accurately determining the cold-start effect of finite trace lengths, particularly for large caches. They used cold-start miss ratios to analyze the impact of task switching on cache performance and proposed models to accurately obtain cold-start miss rates from steady-state miss rates for fully-associative caches. Easton [11] further showed how the miss rates of caches of different sizes for several task-switching intervals could be efficiently computed.

Strecker [26] analyzes transient behavior of cache memories for programs in an interrupted execution environment using the linear paging model for the miss-ratio function. The analysis accounts for data retention in the cache across interruptions. The form of the miss-ratio function used is $(a + bn)/(a + n)$, where n is the number of cache locations filled; a and b are constants obtained by measuring the program miss rates at two cache sizes. Predicted miss rates of several real programs run individually and interleaved for various execution intervals compare reasonably well with trace-driven simulation results.

The transient behavior of caches is also studied by Stone and Thiebaut [25]. They calculate the minimum number of transient cache refills necessary at process switch points as a function of the number of distinct cache entries touched by the program, also called the program footprint, for two processes executing in a round robin fashion. They have also shown that the predictions of the reload transients agree well with simulation results. However, they do not give a method of obtaining the footprint[2] and limit their discussion to a multi-tasking level of two.

The effect of block size was not included in the above studies and program behavior had to be separately characterized for each block size. Kumar [15] investigates spatial locality in programs and proposes an empirical technique to estimate the working set of a program for different block sizes. The miss rate calculated as a function of block size is shown to correlate well with the results of trace-driven simulation. Besides being specific to block-size effects, the study has certain drawbacks. Validation is carried out only for very large caches to exclude the effect of program blocks colliding with each other in the cache. Hence, only start-up effects can be considered to be adequately modeled in this study.

The above papers have been valuable milestones in analytical cache modeling and have characterized various aspects of cache behavior. However, the program

---

[2] Our working set parameter u could yield a measure of the footprint.

models used and the assumptions made in most studies tailored the analysis to some specific cache parameters limiting the scope of their application.

In the following section we first describe a basic cache model, taking into account start-up, nonstationary, and interference effects for a set-associative cache with a fixed block size. Sections 3 and 4 extend the model by including the effects of block size and multitasking respectively. A discussion of the results of our experiments and model validations against several address traces are provided in Section 5. Section 6 summarizes the model and our results.

2. A BASIC CACHE MODEL

This section describes a model for set-associative caches with a fixed block size. The total number of misses is calculated as the sum of the misses due to start-up, nonstationary, and intrinsic interference effects. Only one process, i, is assumed to be active. In general, all parameters associated with this process will be subscripted with the letter i. However, for simplicity, we will bring in this subscript only when necessary to distinguish between processes.

A notion of time in the context of a reference stream is necessary to study the transient behavior of caches. We assume that each reference represents a time step. We also define a larger time unit, called a *time granule* (*tg*), for use in the model. A time granule is sequence of τ references. Average parameter values are calculated over a time granule, processes are assumed to execute on the processor for an integral multiple of time granules, and process switches occur on a *time granule* boundary. This may not be the case in real life, but, as we shall see, this approximation is still useful in predicting average cache performance and has little effect on the actual results. In the model, all sizes are specified in words, where a word is four bytes.

A cache organization, C, is denoted as a triple (S, D, B), where S is the number of sets, D is the set size or degree of associativity, and B is the block size or line size. The cache size in blocks is the product of the number of sets and the set size. It is assumed that a block of data is transferred between the main store and the cache on a cache miss.

In the derivation of the model, we will use an address trace of Interconnect Verify (IVEX) as an example to illustrate various ideas and principles. Detailed validation of the model components against several address traces are provided in Section 5. Interconnect Verify is a program used at DEC, Hudson, to compare two VLSI connection net lists; IVEX is a trace of Interconnect Verify operating on a processor chip. Trace details for this and other traces used in this paper are in Section 5.

First we need some definitions:

τ: The number of references per time granule. A typical value is 10,000. As we shall see in the discussion on sensitivity analysis in Appendix A, the choice of τ is not critical to the analysis. Ideally, τ should be bounded below by the average time spent in start-up activity (as defined in Appendix A) and above by the average context switch interval.

T: Total number of time granules of a process i, or the trace length in number of references divided by τ.

t: Represents a particular time granule. t varies from 1 to T.

$u(B)$: The average number of unique memory blocks accessed in a time granule by the process, termed the working set of the process. Clearly, u is a function of block size.

$U(B)$: The total number of unique memory blocks used in the entire trace. In the basic cache model, we drop the use of B and use the notation U and u, since the block size is kept constant. In practice, U is less than $T * u$ because many blocks are common across time granules.

$m(C, t)$: The miss rate for process i up to and including its tth time granule for cache C: (S, D, B). This is the total number of misses divided by the total number of references in the first t time granules.

As an example, for the IVEX trace, with a block size of one word (four bytes) and τ chosen to be 10,000, $u(1)$ is 1624, $U(1)$ is 7234, and T is 40.

2.1 Start-Up Effects

The initial filling of the cache with the working set of the process causes start-up misses. If we choose the time granule size τ to be greater than the start-up period, these misses will happen in the first time granule. Then, for the first time granule, the miss ratio due to start-up effects is the ratio of the number of unique blocks accessed in that time granule to the total number of references:

$$m(C, 1)_{\text{startup}} = \frac{u}{\tau}.$$

We use the average number of unique blocks per time granule in the trace as an estimate of the unique blocks in the first time granule. This estimate is reasonable within a given phase of program execution, and more so for trace samples (such as ours) from the middle of program execution. (When entire program traces are available, a separate measurement of the initial working set might be considered for more accuracy.)

The start-up component decreases monotonically with time because the number of start-up misses is constant:

$$m(C, t)_{\text{startup}} = \frac{u}{\tau t}. \tag{1}$$

The case where start-up related activity continues past the first time granule is discussed in [2].

2.2 Nonstationary Effects

Nonstationary misses occur due to changes in the working set of a process. For example, this behavior is seen when a program is operating at any instant on a small segment of a large array of data. As the program moves to new portions of the array, these references to new blocks will give rise to an added component of misses.

In our model, during the first time granule, a large number of blocks (u) referenced for the first time are fetched into the cache. In subsequent periods, some of these blocks will not be rereferenced and will be replaced by new blocks. The first reference to such a new block will cause a nonstationary miss. In keeping with our assumption of the average being a good predictor of the actual value, we can estimate the average number of nonstationary misses in a time granule as the number of unique blocks in the entire trace minus the initial start-up misses divided by T, the total number of time granules. Therefore,

$$\text{Average number of nonstationary misses per time granule} = \frac{U - u}{T},$$

where U is the number of unique blocks in the entire trace and T is the total number of time granules represented by the trace. The corresponding miss rate is obtained by dividing the number of nonstationary misses by the number of references per time granule τ,

$$m(C, t)_{\text{nonstationary}} = \frac{U - u}{T\tau}. \tag{2}$$

The nonstationary component is independent of time t. The sum of the start-up and nonstationary components of the miss rate for the entire trace ($t = T$) is $U/T\tau$, which is simply the cost of fetching all the blocks into the cache for the first time.

2.3 Intrinsic Interference

Some cache misses are caused by multiple program blocks competing for the same cache block. Referencing a program block that has been purged from the cache by another block causes an interference miss or a collision miss. This effect lessens as cache size grows because fewer program blocks, on the average, compete for any given cache block. To include this effect in the model, we need to estimate the number of collision-induced misses that will occur as a function of the cache size and the set size.

Interference misses are estimated as the product of two factors, one static and one dynamic. The static component gives the number of program blocks that can potentially be displaced from the cache, while the dynamic component is the average number of times each such block is actually displaced.

As an illustration, Figure 1 shows a direct-mapped cache with eight sets, $S0$ through $S7$. A program block is denoted by a shaded rectangle. Let us concentrate on the set $S6$ that contains block $B5$. Block $B6$, which is not cache-resident, potentially collides with $B5$. A reference pattern that accesses these blocks in the sequence $B6$, $B5$, $B6$, $B5$, $B6$, $B5$ will result in six interference misses, while the pattern $B5$, $B5$, $B5$, $B6$, $B6$, $B6$ results in just one miss. The number of blocks that potentially collide in this set—the static component—is two, and the average number of times each block is actually displaced—the dynamic component—is three for the former sequence and one-half for the latter. The product of the two components yields the right number of misses for both sequences.

2.3.1 *Static Characterization.* The static characterization estimates the number of program blocks that can suffer collisions in the cache, and is based on how blocks are distributed into the cache sets.

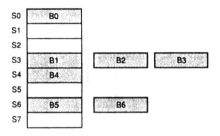
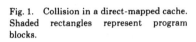

Collision sets: S3, S6
Colliding blocks: B1, B2, B3, B5, B6

Fig. 1. Collision in a direct-mapped cache. Shaded rectangles represent program blocks.

A *collision* occurs when a block that will be referenced in the future is purged from the cache by another block. We define a *potential collision set* as a set that has more than D blocks mapped to it, where D is the degree of associativity. A *potential colliding block* is defined as any block that maps into a potential collision set. In other words, a potential colliding block is one that could be displaced from the cache by another block. By this definition, the number of potential collision sets in the cache in Figure 1 is two ($S3$ and $S6$), and the number of potential colliding blocks in five ($B1$, $B2$, $B3$, $B5$, and $B6$).

The key assumption we make in our derivations is that a program block has a uniform probability of being in any cache set. Many factors contribute to the validity of this assumption. The hashing operation that maps the large process address space to the smaller number of sets in the cache randomizes the selection of any given set. In physical caches, virtual pages can be mapped to an arbitrary physical page. Also, since code and data for user and system tend to reside in different segments of the address space, they are mutually independent with respect to the cache sets they occupy. This assumption is less likely to hold in large virtual-address caches, and is a source of error in estimating the interference component (see Section 5).

Assuming random placement in the cache, the probability $P(d)$ that d blocks fall into any given cache set (depth of overlap d) has a binomial form. The probability that a block maps into a given cache set is $1/S$, and that d blocks map into this cache set is $(1/S)^d$. The probability that a block does not map into the given set is $(1 - 1/S)$. As usual, we leave out the dependence of this probability on B for notational brevity. Thus,

$$P(d) = \binom{u}{d}\left(\frac{1}{S}\right)^d\left(1 - \frac{1}{S}\right)^{u-d}. \tag{3}$$

The number of potential colliding blocks can now be calculated from Eq. 3. Collisions will not occur in a cache set that has at most D program blocks. Hence, in a cache with set size D, the probability that a cache set is a noncollision set is $P(0) + P(1) + \cdots + P(D)$, and the number of noncolliding blocks is $S[0P(0) + 1P(1) + \cdots + DP(D)]$. We can then compute the number of potential colliding

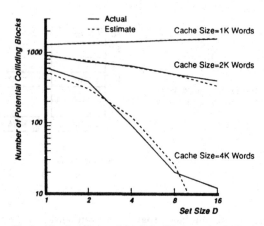

Fig. 2. Number of potential colliding blocks versus D. Block size is one word.

blocks to be the difference between the number of unique memory blocks u and the number of noncolliding blocks, or,

$$\text{Average number of potential colliding blocks} = u - \sum_{d=0}^{d=D} S \, d \, P(d). \quad (4)$$

Figure 2 shows potential colliding blocks in IVEX for several cache sizes, with set sizes ranging from 1 through 16. For small caches, all the blocks can collide, yielding a maximum of u potential colliding blocks, while for large caches this number approaches zero for large set sizes.

2.3.2 *Dynamic Characterization*. The dynamic characterization yields the number of times a potential colliding block actually induces a miss. This number depends on the dynamic sequencing of references.

We define a *dead block* to be one that is not going to be referenced in the future, and a *live block* as one that is still active. As stated before, a *collision* occurs when a block that will be referenced in the future is purged from the cache by another block. A collision induces a cache miss. The minimum number of misses occur if every block that is brought into the cache lands on top of a *dead* one. For example, if two blocks that compete for a cache block are live only in alternate halves of a time granule, the number of collision induced misses due to these two blocks will be zero. However, as demonstrated in our earlier example, if the references to these blocks are finely interleaved, then these will cause thrashing in that cache block.

Let the *collision rate* c be the average number of times a potential colliding block suffers a collision in a time granule. In other words:

$$c = \frac{\text{Average number of collisions in a tg}}{\text{Average number of potential colliding blocks}}, \quad (5)$$

and the actual miss rate due to intrinsic interference is given by

$$m(C, t)_{\text{intrinsic}} = \frac{c * \text{Average number of potential colliding blocks}}{\tau}$$

$$= \frac{c[u - \sum_{d=0}^{d=D} S \, d \, P(d)]}{\tau}. \tag{6}$$

We now need a characterization for the collision rate c. Consider a cache in which all the blocks collide and where every reference is a miss. Then, the intrinsic miss ratio is 1 and c is τ/u. Conversely, when no misses occur c is 0. Therefore, c is bounded as

$$0 \leq c \leq \frac{\tau}{u}.$$

The collision rate c will depend on a number of factors, including the number of times loops are executed in the given program, the time interval between the live periods of potentially colliding blocks, and the cache organization. Let us first consider a direct-mapped cache. Intuition leads us to believe that, for any given trace, c will be approximately the same for caches in which not all sets are collision sets. Appendix B presents an intuitive basis and empirical measurements to support this. Once the cache becomes so small that all cache sets are collision sets, then c will monotonically increase as cache size is reduced, until c reaches its maximum, τ/u, for $S = 1$. Thus, we can measure a value for c from the given trace for a representative direct-mapped cache with a block size of one and number of sets S_0 and use this value of c in miss-rate projections for other cache sizes as well.[3] Hence, we derive c as follows:

$$c = \frac{\text{Average number of collisions in a tg when } S = S_0}{\text{Average number of potential colliding blocks}}.$$

Intertime-granule carryover effects in the above measurement of c are assumed insignificant because collisions in a given time granule caused by blocks displaced in a previous time granule are expected to be compensated by collisions in a later time granule due to blocks displaced in the given time granule. (Recall that a collision is a miss on a previously displaced block.)

As an illustration, consider c for the IVEX trace, choosing $S_0 = 1024$ sets, $B = 1$, and $D = 1$. Table I shows that c is reasonably stable for other cache sizes as well, and the variations do not seem to show any pattern. The percent error in the estimated value of c for the caches is also shown. The 37 percent error in c for a 64K-set cache has negligible effect on the miss-rate accuracy because the number of collision sets is very small.

For set-associative caches, the *replacement algorithm* has to be considered in determining the average number of times a block collides. Since we do not have use information, modeling LRU replacement is hard. Appendix B shows how the collision rate can be obtained for set sizes greater than one from the value of c measured from a direct-mapped cache using random replacement. The results can be used as a good estimate for the miss rates given by other nonusage-based

---

[3] Derivation of c for other set sizes and block sizes is discussed in Appendix B.

Table I. Measured collision rates for various cache sizes. Percentage differences are also shown.

Sets	1K	2K	4K	8K	16K	32K	64K
c	1.9 (0%)	2.0 (-5%)	2.1 (-11%)	1.6 (16%)	1.9 (0%)	2.2 (-16%)	1.2 (37%)

replacement schemes such as FIFO [22]. Smith also shows that random replacement has about 10 percent worse cache miss rate than LRU replacement on average. Thus, our predicted miss rates can be used as a loose estimate on those with LRU replacement also.

Summarizing, the basic cache model for unit block size gives the miss rate as a sum of start-up (Eq. 1), nonstationary (Eq. 2), and intrinsic interference effects (Eq. 6):

$$m(C, t) = \frac{u}{\tau t} + \frac{U - u}{\tau T} + \frac{c}{\tau}\left[u - \sum_{d=0}^{d=D} S\, d\, P(d)\right]. \qquad (7)$$

In the steady state (as t tends to ∞) the first term drops out and the miss rate becomes independent of start-up effects. This simple cache model predicts uniprogramming miss rates as a function of time, cache size, and set size, keeping the block size constant. Detailed validations against several address traces are provided in Section 5. (The model's accuracy in predicting the miss rate as a function of time is discussed in [2].)

3. MODELING SPATIAL LOCALITY AND THE EFFECT OF BLOCK SIZE

In the previous section we derived miss-rate estimates using a cache with a fixed block size. We now extend the model to include block size. By increasing the block size, we can take advantage of the spatial locality in address streams because both u and U are decreasing functions of the block size. The dependence of u and U on the block size is determined by two factors: the distribution of run lengths and the distribution of space interval between runs.

The *distribution of run lengths* is needed to estimate the effect of changing block size, where a *run* is defined as a maximum stream of sequential references. As an example, if some data objects are isolated words, then we will need one block for each of these data items for most reasonable block sizes. Runs of length B aligned on block boundaries will be contained in blocks of size B. Further, if blocks cannot be aligned on arbitrary word boundaries, then the alignment of the given run within a block will also matter.

The second factor accounts for the capture of multiple runs by a single block. While run lengths usually range from one to ten words, empirical cache studies have shown that much larger block sizes can still capture additional localities. The reason is that a large enough block can capture more than a single run. Thus, we need *the distribution of space intervals between runs* to predict the usefulness of increasing block sizes beyond average run lengths.

The ensuing discussion uses only the distribution of run lengths to characterize spatial locality in programs and determines the dependence of the miss rate on the block size. The spatial locality model is extended to include the capture of multiple runs in a single block in [2].

3.1 Run-Length Distribution

Direct measurement of run-length distributions from an address trace is difficult for two reasons. First, typical address traces contain interleaved streams of instruction and data addresses. Even after separating these streams, the data addresses from the stack and the heap could be interleaved. For example, a VAX trace can contain a sequence starting with an instruction address, followed by addresses of the first, second, and third operands. Sequentiality of this nature has to be detected in the address traces to derive run-length statistics. (Rau [19] presents an interesting discussion on this issue.) An efficient method (albeit approximate) of separating these streams is to sort the references to blocks in successive segments of the trace based on the address values. After this sorting, the addresses that belong to a run will appear consecutively.

The second problem is that an accurate characterization of run lengths mandates the use of a large number of parameters—one for every possible run length. To minimize computation and the number of parameters, we propose a simple Markov model to depict the spatial locality in programs and approximate the distribution of run lengths using two average parameters measured from the trace.

In general, an n-stage Markov model is required (see Figure 3) to characterize run lengths, where n is the largest run length in the trace. In the figure, state $R1$ corresponds to the beginning of a run; state Rk is reached if the first k addresses are sequential. f_{lk} is the probability that the next address will be sequential given that the first k addresses are. Since the longest run is of length n, the probability of a sequential reference in state Rn is zero, and a new run is begun with probability one.

In practice, the complication of a n-stage model is not actually necessary; we can make a good approximation using a two-stage model. The reason is quite simple. Addresses typically fall into two categories: those that form part of a run of unit length and those that do not. The former are called singular addresses. Addresses (in particular those that correspond to data references such as global variables) have a reasonably high probability $(1 - f_{l1})$ of being singular.[4] Furthermore, given that an address is nonsingular, it has a high probability of having a sequential successor $(f_{li}, i = 1, 2, 3, \ldots, n)$. Instruction streams and clustered accesses in data structures display this behavior. We have observed that nonsingular addresses show a memoryless property to some extent: the probability that a nonsingular address has a sequential successor does not depend strongly on the number of preceding addresses in the run.

The values of f_{lk} for IVEX are: $f_{l1} = 0.56$, $f_{l2} = 0.72$, $f_{l3} = 0.70$, $f_{l4} = 0.84$, $f_{l5} = 0.86$, $f_{l6} = 0.90$, and $f_{l7} = 0.88$. The values of f_{lk} for $k > 1$ are quite close. For a two-stage Markov model, f_{l1} remains the same, while f_{l2} is chosen to be the weighted average of the other f_{lk}'s. For IVEX, $f_{l1} = 0.56$ and $f_{l2} = 0.88$.

From the model, the probability of any run being of length l is given by

$$R(l) = 1 - f_{l1}, \qquad l = 1,$$
$$R(l) = f_{l1} \, f_{l2}^{l-2} \, (1 - f_{l2}), \quad l > 1.$$

---

[4] This is the reason why a two-stage model is chosen; a one-stage model would fail to capture the dichotomous nature of reference patterns.

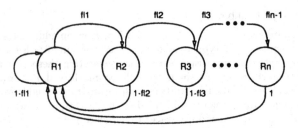

Fig. 3. An *n*-stage Markov model depicting spatial locality in programs

Furthermore, the probability of being in state R_1 in the steady state is the fraction of references that begin a new run, the reciprocal of which gives the average run length:

$$l_{av} = \frac{1 + f_{l1} - f_{l2}}{1 - f_{l2}}.$$

(8)

We measure f_{l1} as the fraction of singular addresses in the trace, and we derive f_{l2} from the measured average run length and Eq. 8. We also need an estimate of the average number of unique runs in a time granule. This is the mean of the ratios of the number of unique references in each time granule to the average run length in that time granule. As we verified in our traces, this ratio is similar for all the time granules in any phase of program execution, which allows us to estimate the expected number of unique runs as the average number of unique references divided by the average run length, which is $u(1)/l_{av}$.

The next step is to calculate $u(B)$, the number of unique blocks in a time granule. We define the *cover* for a run to be the set of blocks that have to be fetched on average to bring the entire run into the cache, and the *coversize* to be the number of blocks in the cover. Note that a reference to any word in a block causes the entire block to be fetched. For the present, we assume that a cover for a run can contain at most one run. For a run of length l with ideal alignment (the run starts on a block boundary), at least $\lceil l/B \rceil$ blocks are needed. In general, the alignment is random, and the average number of blocks needed to contain a run of length l, or the cover size, is given by the following equation:

$$\text{Cover size} = 1 + \frac{l - 1}{B}.$$

(9)

For example, assuming a block size of four words, exactly one block is needed for a run of length one. For a run of length two, we need at least one block; two blocks are used up if the run is aligned such that it crosses block boundaries. This happens with probability $\frac{1}{4}$, giving a cover size of 1.25 for the run.

Hence, given a block size B, the total number of unique program blocks corresponding to $u(1)$ unique words is equal to the cover size for a run of length

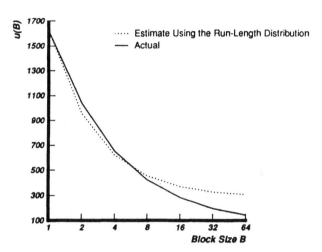

Fig. 4. $u(B)$ versus the block size B in 4-byte words.

l times the number of runs of length l, summed over all l:

$$u(B) = \frac{u(1)}{l_{av}} \sum_{l=1}^{l=\infty} R(l)\left(1 + \frac{l-1}{B}\right)$$

$$= u(1) \frac{(1 + (f_{l1}/B) - f_{l2})}{(1 + f_{l1} - f_{l2})}. \tag{10}$$

Figure 4 compares predicted and actual values of $u(B)$ as a function of block size for IVEX. From our experience, the above simple model is sufficient for block sizes less than about 16 words. For larger block sizes, the model incorrectly predicts that $u(B)$ is insensitive to block size. The cause of this error is our assumption that a block can capture only a single run. Because average run lengths are of the order of four to eight, larger blocks will be mostly empty, having little impact on $u(B)$ in the model.

Actually, the probability of a block capturing more than a single run is nonnegligible if the distance between the runs (interrun interval) is small, and it becomes necessary to include interrun intervals in the models [2]. Basically, the cover size for a given run, as calculated in Eq. 9, includes a fraction of a block that could presumably cover neighboring runs. The portion of the block utilized for other runs, determined from a measured average interrun interval and the run-length distribution, is subtracted from the cover size to yield the actual number of words allocated to the run. $u(B)$ is then computed as in Eq. 10.

The miss rate can now be estimated using $u(B)$ and $U(B)$ calculated as shown above. Appendix B provides a discussion on the impact of block size on the collision rate c. Basically, we show that block size does not significantly impact c. The miss-rate formulation from Eq. 7 is repeated here including the dependence on B. For subblock placement with block size B and subblock size B_s, the miss rate is approximately $u(B_s)/u(B)$ times the miss rate shown below.

$$m(C, t) = \frac{u(B)}{\tau t} + \frac{U(B) - u(B)}{\tau T} + \frac{c}{\tau}\left[u(B) - \sum_{d=0}^{d=D} S\, d\, P(B, d) \right].\quad (11)$$

4. EXTRINSIC INTERFERENCE

The discussion thus far assumed single process execution. Because workloads of real systems usually consist of multiple processes, multiprogrammed cache models are necessary to estimate cache performance accurately. Large caches can often hold the entire working set of a single process, and most misses occur immediately following a process switch when a process needs to refill its data purged by intervening processes.

The following discussion assumes round-robin scheduling with constant duration time slices; time-slice lengths can be measured or picked from an appropriate distribution. Let mpl represent the multiprogramming level and t_x represent the number of time granules in a time slice. Our derivation assumes that the cache is physically addressed, or in the case of a virtually addressed cache, assumes that each process has a unique process identifier (PID) that is appended to the cache tags to distinguish between the virtual addresses of different processes. These schemes do not require flushing the cache on a context switch. Flushing can also be modeled in an even simpler manner.

We concentrate on the miss rate for a process i. Let $m_i(C, t_i)$ be the aggregate miss rate for process i after its t_ith time granule and, as before, let the average number of unique blocks of process i used in a time granule be u_i. We introduce the notion of a *carry-over set* to denote the set of blocks that a process leaves behind in a cache on being switched out and *reuses* on its return (or the live blocks), and let $v_i(B)$ be the average number of blocks in the carry-over set. It is easy to see that the maximum number of multiprogramming-induced misses due to a context switch that can occur after a process resumes execution after being switched out is $v_i(B)$. The number of blocks in the carry-over set is bounded above by the cache size.

We first estimate the size of the carry-over set and then derive the multiprogramming-induced miss rate. We approximate the number of blocks in the carry-over set in a cache $C: (S, D, B)$ by the sum of all the blocks in noncolliding cache sets:

$$v_i(B) = S \sum_{d=0}^{d=D} P_i(d)\, d.\quad (12)$$

The assumption is that all noncolliding blocks will be rereferenced, which may lead to pessimistic extrinsic interference miss rates if some fraction of these are dead blocks. (Although for more accuracy, the average fraction of dead blocks can be estimated from the nonstationary component of misses.) Furthermore, we assume that potential colliding blocks that could also be cache resident do not induce extrinsic interference misses, as they are more likely to be purged due to intrinsic interference.

Using this carry-over set estimate, we now compute the effect of multiprogramming on cache performance. Suppose that a process i has been scheduled to run on the processor after being switched out. Since there would have been $mpl - 1$ processes between instances of process i, its carry-over set gets partially purged. The resulting misses can be estimated by applying binomial statistics to the carry-over set of process i and the set of blocks of all intervening processes. Denoting the number of unique blocks of all intervening processes as $u_{i'}(B)$,

$$u_{i'}(B) = \sum_{j=1, j \neq i}^{j=mpl} u_j(B),$$

and the probability that d blocks fall into any given cache set,

$$P_{i'}(d) = \binom{u_{i'}}{d} \left(\frac{1}{S}\right)^d \left(1 - \frac{1}{S}\right)^{u_{i'}-d}.$$

Before proceeding with the derivation, we must address the replacement issue in a multiprogramming context. The intrinsic interference model uses random replacement because the order of use of blocks required to model LRU replacement is not available. However, LRU replacement is the natural choice for multiprogramming because the order of execution of processes determines the reference order. Consider the case where process i, having just relinquished the processor, is followed by $mpl - 1$ intervening processes. With LRU replacement the blocks of process i will be purged before those referenced by the intervening processes. In the ensuing derivation, LRU replacement is first used for simplicity, followed by random replacement.

Continuing with the model of process i followed by $mpl - 1$ processes, a block of process i can get purged from a given cache set only if the sum of blocks of process i (say d) and all intervening processes i' (say e) that map to that set exceeds the set size D (the residual cache-resident blocks of a process i unreferenced in the last execution interval of i are assumed dead in our model). The number of blocks of process i purged in any cache set is the minimum of (1) the number of blocks of process i in that set, d; (2) the set size D; and (3) the difference between the sum of the number of blocks of process i and i', and the set size D, or $(e + d - D)$. Cases (1) and (2) are trivial, while (3) (corresponding to $d \leq D$) deserves comment. Of the e blocks of intervening processes, $D - d$ can coreside in the set, while the remaining $e - (D - d) = e + d - D$ will collide with the blocks of process i. The number of blocks of process i purged in any set is, therefore,

$$\sum_{d=0}^{d=D} P_i(d) \sum_{e=0}^{e=u_{i'}(B)} \mathrm{MIN}(d, D, e + d - D) P_{i'}(e). [5] \tag{13}$$

The number of blocks of process i purged in the entire cache is the number purged per set times the number of sets S. Therefore, simplifying Eq. 13 and assuming each of the blocks purged is rereferenced, the number of extrinsic

---

[5] A similar equation for two processes was derived simultaneously and independently by Stone and Thiebaut [25].

interference misses that occur when process i resumes is given by

$$S \sum_{d=0}^{d=D} P_i(d) \sum_{e=D+1}^{e=u_{i'}(B)} \text{MIN}(d, e + d - D)P_{i'}(e). \tag{14}$$

Since these misses do not happen in the first time slice of process i, and subsequently happen only once every time slice, the multiprogramming induced miss rate is

$$m_i(C, t_i)_{\text{extrinsic}}$$
$$= \frac{1}{t_i \tau} \left\lfloor \frac{(t_i - 1)}{t_x} \right\rfloor S \sum_{d=0}^{d=D} P_i(d) \sum_{e=D+1}^{e=u_{i'}(B)} \text{MIN}(d, e + d - D)P_{i'}(e). \tag{15}$$

Random replacement, modeled in a slightly different fashion, assumes that all blocks in a fully occupied cache set are equally likely to be purged, irrespective of which process they belong to. For random replacement, the term $\text{MIN}(d, e + d - D)$ in the inner summation of Eq. 14 is replaced by the term

$$\sum_{n=0}^{n=\text{MIN}(d,c)} \binom{e}{n} \left(\frac{d}{D}\right)^n \left(1 - \frac{d}{D}\right)^{c-n},$$

which approximates the average number of blocks of process i purged due to random collisions in any cache set, given that d blocks of process i and e blocks of the intervening processes i' map into that set.

This concludes the derivation of the cache model in the multiprogramming environment. The overall miss rate is the sum of the four components calculated in Eqs. 1, 2, 6, and 15.

5. APPLICATIONS OF THE MODEL

Our cache model has been applied to study a number of cache organizations for both uniprogramming and multiprogramming workloads. The workloads chosen represent realistic environments that include operating system activity. Both overall miss rates and miss-rate components are first computed from the model for several cache organizations. These are then compared to simulation results using random replacement.

5.1 Program Traces

Traces are obtained using the ATUM (Address Tracing Using Microcode) tracing method described in [3]. In this scheme, the microcode of a processor writes out to a reserved portion of memory all the addresses of memory references made by a processor. ATUM yields realistic traces by capturing complete information of the workload including operating system kernel and multiprogramming activity. The uniprocessor traces are roughly 400,000 references each, corresponding to a half-second snapshot execution on a VAX 8200—a machine the speed of a VAX-11/780.

Eight benchmark traces of large programs running under VMS, having between 5 and 50 percent system references (with an average of about 20 percent), are used in the uniprogramming cache model study:

PASC0   PASCAL compile of a microcode parser program;

LISP0   LISP runs of BOYER (a theorem prover);

SPIC0   SPICE simulating a 2-input tristate NAND buffer;

FORL0   FORTRAN compile of LINPACK;

DEC0   a behavioral simulator at DEC, DECSIM,
simulating some cache hardware;

IVEX   a DEC program, Interconnect Verify,
checking net lists in a VLSI chip;

AL1   a trace sample of a microcode address allocator;

TMIL1   MIPS instruction-level simulator
running TLB, a TLB simulator.[6]

We also used three VMS traces of multiprogramming workloads: MUL6 with multiprogramming level six, MUL9 with nine, and MUL12 with twelve to analyze the multiprogramming cache model. Among the processes active in MUL6 are a FORTRAN compile of LINPACK, the microcode address allocator, and a directory search; those in MUL9 are two FORTRAN compiles of LINPACK and a numerical analysis program, the microcode address allocator, a SPICE run, a PASCAL compile of a microcode parser, and LINPACK; and those in MUL12 include the six programs in MUL6, a numerical benchmark JACOBI, a string search in a file, MACRO—an assembly-level compile, an octal dump, and a linker. The number of *user* references in MUL6, MUL9 and MUL12 are 1.3 million, 1.3 million, and 0.9 million, respectively. Trace characteristics are summarized in Tables II and III.

5.2 Uniprogramming Results and Analysis

The miss rates from the cache model for the eight uniprogram traces are averaged and displayed in Figure 5. The figures show plots of miss rates versus cache size for two block sizes and set sizes. Corresponding cache performance figures obtained through trace-driven simulation for both LRU and random replacement are also shown to assess the accuracy of the model. Analytical model results are shown in solid lines, LRU replacement results in dashed lines, and random (or FIFO) replacement in dotted lines. The model uses $\tau = 10,000$ and $S_0 = 1K$. All cache sizes are in bytes. Mean and maximum relative errors in miss-rate estimates over all cache sizes for random replacement are shown in Table IV. These errors are the difference between the simulation miss rates and the analytical model miss rates divided by the simulation miss rates.

Figure 6 shows the individual components (start-up, nonstationary, and intrinsic interference) of the miss rate, calculated using the model and simulation with random replacement for a cache with set-size two, and block sizes of four and 16 bytes. (Results for the other cache types are similar and are not shown due to space limitations.) The start-up component in simulation is measured as the number of first-time misses in the first τ references, the nonstationary component

---

[6] TMIL1 was obtained by tracing a user process on a VAX-11/780 using the T-bit technique.

Table II. Summary of uniprogramming benchmark statistics.
Word sizes are 4 bytes and the number of references are in
thousands.

Bench- mark	Total Refs.	Instr. Refs.	Data Refs.	User Refs.	System Refs.	Words Used
PASC0	555	174	381	535	20	2646
LISP0	262	147	115	248	14	5454
SPIC0	317	131	186	277	40	7174
FORL0	297	147	150	190	107	15629
DEC0	319	158	162	206	113	14209
IVEX	394	169	225	361	33	7234
AL1	305	194	111	288	17	4445
TMIL1	400	211	189	400	0	5739

Table III. Summary of multiprogram benchmark statistics.
Word sizes are 4 bytes and the number of references are in
thousands. Average context switch intervals (C. S. Intvl.)
are in thousands of references.

Process (Benchmark)	Total Refs.	Instr. Refs.	Data Refs.	C.S. Intvl.	Words Used
A081E (MUL12)	130	60	70	27	1881
1B429E (MUL12)	132	92	40	24	772
DDA9E (MUL12)	172	56	116	30	241
C5B9E (MUL12)	115	44	71	25	1488
1B061E (MUL9)	209	78	131	28	3935
1A141E (MUL9)	300	114	186	26	1813
18461E (MUL9)	325	105	220	38	376
1C6E9E (MUL6)	425	172	253	27	5946
1EC99E (MUL6)	448	308	140	26	1019
EE11E (MUL6)	441	168	273	24	2097

as the first-time misses in the remainder of the trace, and intrinsic interference as the rest of the misses. For direct-mapped caches in our uniprogramming traces, the intrinsic interference component dominates the miss rate for caches less than 64K bytes, while the nonstationary and start-up components are important in larger caches. The start-up component is fairly small, indicating a low likelihood of introducing cold-start errors in simulations of small caches using our traces.

Besides seeking absolute cache miss-rate numbers, the computer architect is often interested in the relative performance of two cache organizations. The usefulness of a model is thus predicated on how closely it can distinguish between the performance of caches with a small variation in the cache parameters. We first compare the performance of direct-mapped caches with block sizes 4 and 16 bytes in Figure 5(a). While increasing block size is beneficial to all caches, the proportional improvement is greater in large caches, and can be explained using Figure 6, which shows the components of the miss rate for these two block sizes in direct-mapped caches.

In large caches the start-up and nonstationary components dominate the miss rate in our traces because the entire working set of the process can often be

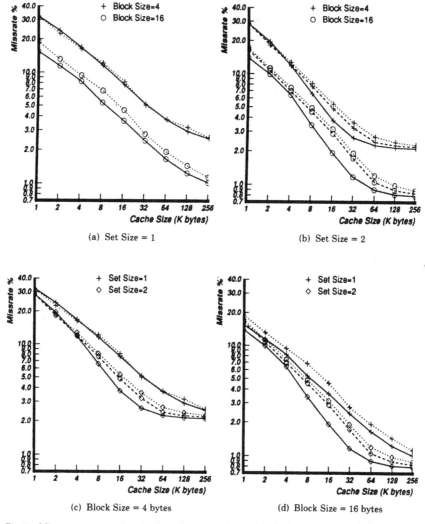

Fig. 5.   Miss rate versus cache size for uniprogramming workloads. In (a), (b), set size is constant, in (c), (d), block size is constant.

comfortably retained in the cache, making intrinsic interference negligible. The former components are always positively affected by a larger block size. However, increasing block size impacts intrinsic interference in two ways. A larger block size fetches more data into the cache per miss, but also increases interference because, for a given cache size, the number of program blocks competing for any cache block increases. This phenomenon occurs because a greater fraction of

Table IV. Percentage error in estimated miss
rates over all cache sizes

Set Size	Block Size (Bytes)	% Error in Miss Rate	
		Mean	Max
1	4	4.0	7.9
1	16	15.3	22.3
2	4	13.5	29.1
2	16	22.8	39.0

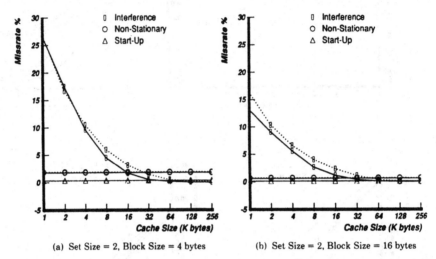

(a) Set Size = 2, Block Size = 4 bytes   (b) Set Size = 2, Block Size = 16 bytes

Fig. 6. Components of the miss rate versus cache size for uniprogramming workloads for $D = 2$, $B = 4$, and $B = 16$ bytes. Solid lines represent model calculations and dotted lines represent simulation results for random replacement.

larger blocks tend to be unused. Thus a larger block size has a reduced impact on small caches where the intrinsic interference component dominates.

Overall miss-rate prediction is quite good for all the benchmarks and block sizes for a direct-mapped cache. The mean error in miss-rate estimates is about 4 percent for 4-byte blocks and 15 percent for 16-byte blocks, as seen from Table IV. The miss-rate components are also in good agreement.

The miss rates for caches with a set size of two are shown in Figure 5(b). Interestingly, the miss-rate curves bottom out after a cache size of 32K bytes in two-way set-associative caches, but not in direct-mapped caches. The reason is that intrinsic interference, the only cache-size related component in the miss rate for uniprogramming workloads, becomes negligible in large set-associative caches. For example, referring to Figure 6, the intrinsic interference component crosses the nonstationary component at a 16K-byte cache of set size two, but only at a 64K-byte cache of set size one.

Simulation results show that random replacement is only slightly worse than LRU replacement on average, and hence the model can be used to approximate the performance of LRU replacement also. The miss-rate predictions by the model were consistently lower than simulated miss rates for caches in the size range 8K through 32K bytes and set size two. These underestimations are consistent over all benchmarks; we analyze their cause in detail later.

Next we compare the performance of caches with a fixed block size. Figure 5(c) shows the variation of miss rate with cache size for a block size of 4 bytes and set sizes of one and two. In Figure 5(d), the block size is 16 bytes and set sizes are one and two. Both the model and simulations show that associativity has a reduced impact on either very small or very large caches. In small caches, increasing associativity does not decrease the number of potential colliding blocks (see Figure 2 for an example plot of potential colliding blocks versus cache size and associativity), and in large caches the only component impacted by associativity—intrinsic interference—is small compared to start-up and nonstationary effects. Figure 5(d) shows that large caches with a block size of 16 bytes are affected more favorably by associativity than caches with a block size of 4 bytes. This phenomenon occurs because larger block sizes tend to make interference in large caches more important, which is reduced by associativity.

The correspondence between simulation and the model results is generally good, both for the miss rate and its components, except when the caches are between 8K and 32K bytes and the set size is two. For example, the mean relative error in the miss rates of a cache with set size two and block size of 4 bytes is quite significant at 14 percent and for a block size of 16 bytes is 23 percent. Figure 6(b) shows that this error is due to a much higher intrinsic interference component in simulation than that computed by the model.

Our first hypothesis as to why simulations showed higher miss rates was that program blocks were distributed nonuniformly across the cache. Even in our uniprogramming workloads, a multiprogramming situation exists between the user program and the operating system. If frequently used regions from the user and system spaces preferentially mapped to the same cache sets, *hot spots* would arise in the cache. To test if these systematic collisions inflated miss rates, we hashed the user/system and the instruction/data bits in with the address bits that select the cache set to randomize the relative placement of these blocks in the cache. This change marginally reduced the simulation miss rate for all cache organizations. The relative error in the mean miss rate for caches with set size two and block size 4 bytes dropped to 12 percent and for block size 16 to 22 percent.

The above hypothesis still does not explain why the miss-rate predictions for set-associative caches are particularly worse. Our second hypothesis is that the derivation for potential colliding blocks assumed that interference misses were constrained to potential collision sets. However, when random replacement is used, collision misses can occur in any set that has more than one program block mapped to it. By not counting these extra misses the model can potentially give optimistic results. To test this hypothesis we inflated the number of potential colliding blocks to account for sets that have more than one program block. The model miss rate increases significantly for the 8K through 32K caches and gives a better match with simulated results. As expected, there is no change in the direct-mapped cache results. The relative error in the miss rate for a cache with set size two and a block size of 4 bytes is reduced to 6 percent and for block size 16 to 9 percent.

The miss rates predicted by the model for large block sizes were generally lower than simulation. The term that causes this error is the collision rate. Error in the estimates of $u_i(B)$ and $U_i(B)$ are ruled out because the start-up and nonstationary components show a good match with simulation. The fact that the model miss rate was off by a constant amount for all cache sizes led us to believe that the collision rate was underestimated. Appendix B discusses the impact of the block size on the collision rate. The analysis shows that c will tend to be underestimated with increasing block size if references to potential colliding blocks are finely interleaved.

5.3 Multiprogramming Results and Analysis

The multiprogramming analysis was carried out using traces MUL6, MUL9, and MUL12. The multiprogramming cache model basically yields the miss rate of a *given* process in a task-switching environment from the parameters of that process and those of the other active processes in the trace. We designed our simulation experiments to also yield the individual miss rates of the constituent processes in the multitasking traces. The results that we present are the averages obtained over ten processes selected at random from the three traces. The model parameters r and S_0 have the same values as in the uniprogramming study, while t_s is chosen as the average of the process' execution intervals measured from the ATUM traces. We used only user references in the multiprogramming study because the sharing of system code and data among the processes can complicate the analysis. Details of these process traces are in Table III.

Figure 7(a) summarizes the cache performance of multiprogramming workloads. Cache sizes smaller than 4K bytes are not shown because the curves are very similar to each other. Curves with the triangle symbol depict the uniprogramming miss rate, which is obtained by simulating each process in the cache individually, without interruptions. The diamond symbol corresponds to the multiprogramming miss rate, assuming that each process is assigned a unique process identifier (PID) appended to the tag portion of the address. The PID scheme allows blocks of multiple processes to coreside in a virtual address cache. The PID scheme also approximates the miss rate of a physical address cache. The circle symbol depicts the miss rate of a cache flushed on every context switch.

A virtual cache that is flushed on every process switch performs poorly relative to the PID scheme for cache sizes greater than 32K bytes because in our traces a significant fraction of the blocks of a process are reused across process switches. All of the schemes perform in the same way for small caches, as the number of blocks that can be reused across task switches (the carry-over set) is bounded by the cache size. Because very large caches can simultaneously hold the working sets of several processes, the uniprogramming miss rates of large caches are similar to the multiprogramming miss rates with the PID scheme.

The form of the multiprogramming-induced component of the miss rate for the PID scheme is made evident by Figure 7(b). The extrinsic interference component is low in both small and large caches. The reason for the low value

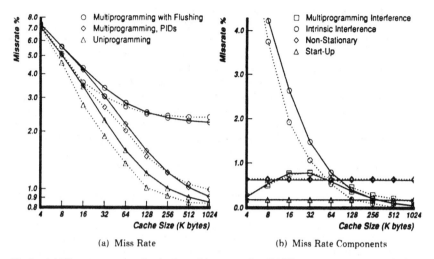

| | (a) Miss Rate | (b) Miss Rate Components |

Fig. 7. (a) Miss rate versus cache size for multiprogramming. (b) Miss rate components for the PID scheme. Block size is 16 bytes and caches are direct-mapped. Solid lines are model estimates and dotted lines denote simulation results.

in small caches, despite the high probability of the process blocks being purged, is that the size of the carry-over set is small. Conversely, in large caches, the carry-over set is large, but the probability of blocks being purged is small.

The model curves in Figure 7(a) have the same form as the simulation curves but are generally shifted upwards. The multiprogramming curves for large caches, however, are lower than simulation curves. Figure 7(b) helps explain this dual behavior. The intrinsic interference component is always overestimated by the model, while in large caches the extrinsic interference component is underestimated. We analyze each of these two inaccuracies in turn.

We hypothesized that the lower intrinsic interference component in simulation is due to a high temporal and spatial correlation in the user-only traces. Our multiprogramming user workloads included programs such as string search, directory search, octal dump, and LINPACK, which are expected to show a high degree of spatial correlation in their accesses. Simple run-length estimates in the multiprogram traces were over four times those in our uniprogram traces. We also simulated caches using both random selection of cache sets and conventional bit-selection placement, and compared their intrinsic interference components with the model estimates. Random placement increased intrinsic interference considerably, and the model estimate fell in between the two placement schemes. This experiment also reaffirms our faith in bit selection for the placement of program blocks in the cache.

We believed that the higher extrinsic interference in simulations was due to the systematic collisions induced when blocks from different processes clustered in the same cache sets. For example, the heavily used low address space and the user stack-top of all processes map into the same cache regions. To randomize the mapping of a process's blocks with respect to the blocks of other processes, the PID is hashed with the set selection bits. Hashing does reduce the extrinsic interference component in large caches (256K to 1M bytes) and provides a better match with model results. For example, the extrinsic interference component obtained through simulation with and without hashing and the estimated component in a 256K-byte cache are 0.25, 0.29, and 0.21 percent, respectively.

In summary, the spatial and temporal correlation between references in uni-programming workloads tends to reduce interference, while the correlation between the references of different processes tends to increase interference. This fact also explains why, in caches where both the intrinsic and extrinsic interference components are of the same order of magnitude, the model and simulation results are very similar. We also conclude that modeling multiprogramming in a physical cache by purging the cache every Q references is a viable method for small caches.

In general, parameter extraction is reasonably straightforward, but may require analyzing the entire trace if maximum accuracy is desired; parameters can otherwise be extracted from sample segments of the trace. For example, the start-up component estimated by the model is very close to the start-up component in the trace, implying that u can be accurately estimated using the number of unique blocks in the first time granule. While u and U—the average number of unique references in a time granule and in the entire trace, respectively—are easily measured, some of the other parameters deserve more comment. The collision constant, c, is obtained by simulating a typical cache. If the cache is small enough, the entire trace need not be used because, once steady state is reached, only a few more references need be simulated to give a good indication of c. The spatial locality parameter, f_{l1}, is simply the fraction of singular addresses in the trace; f_{l2} can be derived using Eq. 8 and the measured average run-length. Depending on the desired accuracy in multiprogramming results, either an average time slice parameter or a distribution (measured or assumed) can be used. The estimated results are most accurate if the trace parameters are measured from a cache in close vicinity to the cache types of interest, and provides a useful strategy to obtain fine-tuned results. For example, parameters could be measured by keeping the block size fixed throughout the analysis.

We concentrated on the effects of various cache parameters on the miss rate. Analyzing the sensitivity of the miss rate on various program and workload parameters and multiprocessor caching are the subjects of ongoing research.

6. CONCLUSIONS

An analytical model for caches driven by a few parameters measured from program traces has been presented. A judicious combination of measurement and analytical techniques reduce computation time without significantly sacrificing accuracy. Cache performance due to start-up effects, gradual locality changes in program execution, contention for a cache block, and multiprogramming can be quickly estimated for most cache parameters of interest, including cache size, block size, subblock size, degree of associativity, trace size, and multiprogramming level. A more important result is that the model parameters are meaningful in themselves and give an early indication of cache performance. Conversely, explicitly displaying the sensitivity of the miss rate on various program and workload parameters helps identify areas in which further research in improving cache performance would be fruitful.

APPENDIX A. Sensitivity of the Miss Rate on Time Granule Size τ

The choice of τ in the cache model thus far has been rather ad hoc; we now examine the sensitivity of the miss rate for uniprogramming to this choice. We will concentrate on the intrinsic interference component only, because the sum of the start-up and nonstationary components of the miss rate is simply the ratio of the total number of unique blocks to the total length of the trace, and hence does not depend on the choice of the time granule τ. The choice of τ directly affects u, the average number of unique blocks in a time granule.

The following equation gives the intrinsic miss-rate component for direct-mapped caches:

$$m(C, t)_{\text{intrinsic}} = \frac{c[u(B) - SP(1)]}{\tau}.$$

Replacing the collision rate and $P(1)$ by their respective formulas and gathering the factors that are independent of u (and τ) into the constant K shows the complete dependence of the intrinsic miss rate component on u:

$$m(C, t)_{\text{intrinsic}} = K \frac{u(B)}{u(1)} \frac{1 - (1 - (1/S))^{u(B)}}{1 - (1 - (1/S_0))^{u(1)}}.$$

If τ is chosen to be greater than the start-up portion of the trace, variations in τ will not affect the miss rate significantly because u changes gradually after the start-up region, and the ratio of $u(B)$ and $u(1)$ changes even more slowly.

Since the discussion hinges on the definition of a *start-up* period, we digress a little to analyze some of the common notions of start-up time. Recall that for the purpose of our model the start-up period in a trace is the time (or number of references) required to bring the initial working set of the program into the cache for the first time. This definition is solely a function of the program and independent of the cache organization. Because the initial working set of a program is hard to quantize precisely, estimating the start-up period in a trace is nontrivial.

A pertinent definition for the start-up period that is not a function of cache size, but solely dependent on the address trace in question, is based on the working-set model [9] of program behavior. The number of unique blocks used by a process in a time granule increases rapidly as the time granule is increased from zero to some value, and increases only gradually thereafter, causing working-set curves to have a bilinear nature [24]. We define the *start-up portion* to be the region of the working-set curve before its knee point. The latter part will then represent the *nonstationary region*. Figure 8 shows $u(1)$ as a function of time granule size τ for the trace IVEX. The knee occurs between ten and fifteen thousand references. The dotted line, which is the derivative of the working-set curve, is the number of additional blocks accessed for a given increase in granule size. After about 10,000 references the increase in u is small and steady. For phased programs the working-set curve might show slightly different behavior; this issue is addressed in [2].

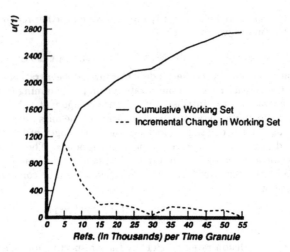

Fig. 8. Number of unique blocks $u(1)$ per time granule versus granule size τ.

Returning to our earlier discussion on the stability of the intrinsic interference component, once τ is greater than 10,000 references, increasing it further will cause little change in $u(1)$ and still less in the ratio of $u(B)$ to $u(1)$. Thus we have shown that choosing τ greater than the start-up period will cause the intrinsic miss rate to be insensitive to changes in τ. For smaller values of τ, u varies enormously and potential for large errors exists. However, since changes proportional to $u(B)$ and $u(1)$ are expected in the numerator and denominator of the intrinsic miss-rate equation, the differences should cancel out to first order, and the miss rate should be reasonably stable.

APPENDIX B. Characterization of the Collision Rate c

The intrinsic interference model uses the collision rate c—the ratio of the total number of dynamic collisions to the number of potential colliding blocks—to quantize the dynamic interference component among program blocks. The product of the number of potential colliding blocks and the average number of times a block actually collides, c, gives the average number of misses in the cache due to intrinsic interference in a time granule. The thesis is that c is reasonably stable for caches of different numbers of sets and block sizes. The collision rate, however, varies with set size (associativity or number of columns) and is not stable when the cache becomes much smaller than the size of the program working set. This section addresses these issues as follows: Section B.1 provides an intuitive basis and some measured data for the assumption that c is stable for different cache sizes. Section B.2 extends c to all cache organizations.

B.1 On the Stability of the Collision Rate

We present the following brief argument as an intuitive substantiation of the claim that c is constant for most cache sizes and organizations. This is also verified by our measurement data. More details and some measurement data are presented in [2]. A direct-mapped cache with a block size of 4 bytes is assumed in the ensuing discussion unless otherwise stated.

Recall that a *potential collision set* is a set with multiple blocks mapped to it, and a *potential colliding block* is a block that maps into a potential colliding set. The average number of collisions per block in a collision set will be an increasing function of the number of program blocks present in that set. Clearly, the more the number of blocks in a collision set, the greater the probability that a block will be purged by intervening references, and hence the greater the collision rate. Therefore, the variation in c with the number of sets will be similar to the variation in the static parameter c', which we define to be the number of potential colliding blocks in an average collision set. Note that c' is not used to estimate c. In the cache shown in Figure 1, $c' = 2.5$.

As derived earlier (see Eq. 4), the number of potential colliding blocks is $u - SP(1)$ and the number of colliding sets is $S(1 - P(0) - P(1))$. Making the approximation that the binomial distribution tends to the Poisson for large u and small $(1/S)$, we get

$$c' = \frac{u}{S} \frac{(1 - e^{-u/S})}{(1 - e^{-u/S} - (u/S)e^{-u/S})}. \tag{16}$$

We plotted c' and the collision rate c to check their correspondence [2] and found that c' (and hence a corresponding c) is stable for $u/S < 1$. Intuitively, for cache sizes greater than or equal to 1,024 words, both the number of collision sets and colliding blocks decrease in the same proportion with cache size. Below 1,024 words ($u/S > 1$), c' increases (c shows a similar anomalous upward trend) because the denominator starts to decrease in proportion to S and the numerator stays constant at u. Thus, c can be expected to remain stable if the cache size is greater than half the working-set size u.

B.2 The Collision Rate and Block Size

Changing the block size does not significantly affect c as long as the cache is bigger than u. The rationale is that the dynamic behavior of program blocks in the cache is statistically similar to that of their component words when bit-selection placement is used. We present an informal two-part proof to demonstrate this. Part I shows that the statistical properties of words within spatial localities are similar. Part II argues that when the block size is increased, the properties of a block (in particular its collision rate) will be similar to that of any of its component words. Part II makes the assumption that if two spatial localities in the virtual address space map into the same cache sets, then references to these two localities are not finely interleaved. For example, let w_i represent a word and r_i a reference to it. If words $w_1 w_2 \ldots w_n$ in a run collide with corresponding words in another run $w_1' w_2' \ldots w_n'$, we assume that an access pattern of the type $repeat(r_1 r_2 \ldots r_n r_1' r_2' \ldots r_n')$ is the common case, while the pattern $repeat(r_1 r_1' r_2 r_2' \ldots r_n r_n')$ is rare, where $repeat(x)$ denotes $xxxxx. \ldots$

In the first part we show that words in the same spatial locality have similar miss rates. Given the nature of programs, words in a run have a high temporal locality besides their obvious spatial locality. In a cache with bit-selection mapping, these adjacent words map to adjacent cache sets, too. Thus one can imagine different program localities interfering with each other in the cache, making adjacent words have similar miss rates. Although sometimes this is not true, for example, the program word following a backward branch is spatially local but may not be temporally local. We did the following experiment to demonstrate that words in a spatial locality have similar miss rates. We measured the miss rate for every unique word in our traces. The word miss rate is the number of misses suffered by a reference to that word divided by its reference frequency. The measured correlation between the miss rates of words that belonged to a spatial neighborhood was very high. In fact, a difference of zero is by far the most frequent case. Detailed results are reported in [1].

The second part uses the fact that these adjacent words fall into the same or adjacent blocks in the cache with bit selection; and if two words collided in the cache, then the blocks that contain these words also collide. To prove this, consider words W_i and W_j with word addresses w_i and w_j that map to the same set S_u with index s_u in a cache with S sets. That is, in a cache with a block size of one word, their set-selection addresses w_i modulo S and w_j modulo S are both s_u. In a cache with a block size of B words and number of sets S_B, let the words W_i and W_j be contained in blocks B_i and B_j with block addresses $b_i = w_i/B$ and $b_j = w_j/B$. The set-selection addresses of these two blocks are b_i modulo S_B and b_j modulo S_B. If the cache size remains the same, $S_B = S/B$, which implies that the two set-selection addresses are still the same.

There are two cases to consider in the rest of the second phase of our proof: (1) the colliding localities start and end on block boundaries and are also aligned with respect to each other, and (2) the localities are randomly aligned.

Case 1. When block size B is increased, u/S does not change, given perfect alignment. (*Note*: S decreases in inverse proportion to B when cache size is constant.) Then c' computed in Eq. 16, and hence c, remains constant.

Case 2. In this case, as block size is increased, the decrease in u is slower than the decrease in S, or u/S increases with B. As discussed earlier, c' is still constant when $u/S < 1$, but increases when $u/S > 1$, as is the case in small caches.

There are two caveats to this analysis. We assume that references to words in colliding runs are not finely interleaved. If this is untrue, c will increase with block size because the number of misses will stay the same while the number of potential colliding blocks decreases. The probability of such interleaving is high in (small) caches with few sets. The second problem occurs when increasing the block size increases the number of potential colliding blocks that are not active at the same time. In this case, c decreases because the actual number of misses still stays the same. This can occur in large caches where blocks remain for long periods of time in the cache. The former problem is more likely in direct-mapped caches and the latter in set-associative caches. Note that a set size of two can break up collisions between finely interleaved references to two localities, and finely interleaved references to more than two colliding localities is extremely unlikely.

B.3 The Collision Rate and Set Size

The collision rate depends on the set size, and this dependence is discussed next. Let $c(D)$ denote the value of c for a cache with set size D. In a direct-mapped cache, a reference to a block that is not the most recently referenced one in the set will cause a miss. For a larger set size, however, reference to as many as $D - 1$ blocks, besides the most recently referenced one, may not cause a miss. Assuming random behavior, the probability of a hit to any one of the d blocks mapped into the set is $(D - 1)/(d - 1)$. The most recently referenced block is excluded because its effect has already been included in c. The corresponding probability of a miss is one minus the above quantity. Therefore, $c(D, d)$, the collision rate for a set of size D with d overlapping blocks is $c(1)$ weighted by this fraction, where, as before, $c(1)$ is the collision rate for a direct-mapped cache with the same number of sets.

$$c(D, d) = c(1)\left(1 - \frac{D - 1}{d - 1}\right).$$

We can then obtain an average of $c(D, d)$ over all d's as

$$c(D) = \frac{\sum_{d=D+1}^{d=\infty} c(D, d)dP(d)}{\sum_{d=D+1}^{d=\infty} dP(d)}.$$

We compared the estimated values of c with the measured values of c, using LRU and FIFO replacement for IVEX in a variety of cache sizes and organizations (see data in [2]). In general, we observed that c is relatively stable when cache size is greater than half $u(1)$. Potential for a large error in c exists if the number of colliding blocks is small (for example, in large caches). Fortunately, this error does not affect the overall miss rate because the intrinsic interference component of the miss rate becomes very small compared to the other components. A method for estimating c for very small caches is also provided in [2], but is excluded from this paper, as this region of the cache organization spectrum is only of marginal interest.

ACKNOWLEDGMENTS

We are grateful to Ed Lazowska for some stimulating discussions at the start of this research, and to Alan Smith, Mark Hill, Susan Eggers, and the referees for providing useful feedback on the paper.

REFERENCES

1. AGARWAL, A. Trace compaction using cache filtering with blocking. Computer Systems Lab. Rep. TR 88-347, Stanford Univ., Stanford, Calif., Jan. 1988.
2. AGARWAL, A., HOROWITZ, M., AND HENNESSY, J. An analytical cache model. Computer Systems Lab. Rep. TR 86-304, Stanford Univ. Stanford, Calif., Sept. 1986.
3. AGARWAL, A., SITES, R. L., AND HOROWITZ, M. ATUM: A new technique for capturing address traces using microcode. In *Proceedings of the 13th Annual Symposium on Computer Architecture* (June 1986). IEEE, New York. 1986, 119–127.
4. AHO, A. V., DENNING, P. J., AND ULLMAN, J. D. Principles of optimal page replacement. *J. ACM 18*, 1 (Jan. 1971), 80–93.
5. ALPERT, D. Performance tradeoffs for microprocessor cache memories. Computer Systems Lab. Rep. TR 83-239, Stanford Univ., Stanford, Calif., Dec. 1983.

6. CHERITON, D. R., SLAVENBERG, G. A., AND BOYLE, P. D.   Software-controlled caches in the VMP multiprocessor. In *Proceedings of the 13th Annual Symposium on Computer Architecture* (June 1986). IEEE, New York, 1986, 367–374.

7. CHOW, C. K.   Determining the optimum capacity of a cache memory. *IBM Tech. Disclosure Bull. 17*, 10 (Mar. 1975), 3163–3166.

8. CLARK, D. W.   Cache performance in the VAX-11/780. *ACM Trans. Comput. Syst. 1*, 1 (Feb. 1983), 24–37.

9. DENNING, P. J.   The working set model for program behavior. *Commun. ACM 11*, 5 (May 1968), 323–333.

10. EASTON, M. C., AND FAGIN, R.   Cold-start vs. warm-start miss ratios. *Commun. ACM 21*, 10 (Oct. 1978), 866–872.

11. EASTON, M. C.   Computation of cold-start miss ratios. *IEEE Trans. Comput. C-27*, 5 (May 1978).

12. GOODMAN, J. R.   Using cache memory to reduce processor-memory traffic. In *Proceedings of the 10th Annual Symposium on Computer Architecture* (June 1983). IEEE, New York, 1983, 124–131.

13. HAIKALA, I. J.   Cache hit ratios with geometric task switch intervals. In *Proceedings of the 11th Annual Symposium on Computer Architecture* (June 1984). IEEE, New York, 1984, 364–371.

14. HILL, M., AND SMITH, A. J.   Experimental evaluation of on-chip microprocessor cache memories. In *Proceedings of the 11th Annual Symposium on Computer Architecture* (June 1984). IEEE, New York, 1984, 158–166.

15. KUMAR, B.   A model of spatial locality and its application to cache design. Unpublished Report, Computer Systems Lab., Stanford Univ., Stanford, Calif., 1979.

16. LAZOWSKA, E. D., ZAHORJAN, J., GRAHAM, G. S., AND SEVICK, K. C. *Quantitative System Performance*. Prentice-Hall, Englewood Cliffs, N.J., 1984.

17. MATTSON, R. L., GECSEI, J., SLUTZ, D. R., AND TRAIGER, I. L.   Evaluation techniques for storage hierarchies. *IBM Syst. J. 9*, 2 (1970), 78–117.

18. RAO, G. S.   Performance analysis of cache memories. *J. ACM 25*, 3 (July 1978), 378–395.

19. RAU, B. R.   Sequential prefetch strategies for instructions and data. Tech. Rep. 131, Digital Systems Lab., Stanford Univ., Stanford, Calif., Jan. 1977.

20. SALTZER, J. H.   A simple linear model of demand paging performance. *Commun. ACM 17*, 4 (Apr. 1974), 181–186.

21. SMITH, A. J.   A comparative study of set associative memory mapping algorithms and their use for cache and main memory. *IEEE Trans. Softw. Eng. SE-4*, 2 (Mar. 1978), 121–130.

22. SMITH, A. J.   Cache memories. *ACM Comput. Surv. 14*, 3 (Sept. 1982), 473–530.

23. SMITH, J. E., AND GOODMAN, J. R.   A study of instruction cache organization and replacement policies. In *Proceedings of the 10th Annual Symposium on Computer Architecture* (June 1983). IEEE, New York, 1983, 132–137.

24. SPIRN, J. R.   *Program Behavior: Models and Measurements. Operating and Programming Systems Series*, Elsevier, New York, 1977.

25. STONE, H. S., AND THIEBAUT, D.   Footprints in the cache. In *Proceedings of ACM SIG-METRICS 1986* (May 1986). ACM, New York, 1986, 4–8.

26. STRECKER, W. D.   Transient behavior of cache memories. *ACM Trans. Comput. Sys. 1*, 4 (Nov. 1983), 281–293.

Received September 1987; revised May 1988, October 1988; accepted December 1988

Modeling Live and Dead Lines
in Cache Memory Systems

Abraham Mendelson, *Member, IEEE*, Dominique Thiébaut, *Member, IEEE*, and Dhiraj K. Pradhan, *Fellow, IEEE*

Abstract—This paper presents a new analytical model which predicts the fraction of live and dead lines present in a cache memory, in a multitasking environment. The model is two-fold; The first portion evaluates the number of live lines created in a fully associative cache during the execution of a process. The second portion models the interaction of two processes which share a cache and run in an interleaved fashion. The model admits direct-mapped, set-associative, and fully associative cache architectures. The complete model assumes a hyperbolic (or fractal) model of program behavior. Also it predicts the variations of the total number of lines (footprint) as well as the number of live lines held by a process in the various caches as a function of the number of cache accesses. The accuracy of the model is validated through trace driven simulations.

Index Terms— Cache memory, dead lines, fractal model, hyperbolic model, live lines, memory hierarchy, multiprogramming, multitasking, performance, program behavior, program locality.

I. INTRODUCTION

THE performance of a cache-based computer system is affected by the cache architecture (hardware), by the behavior of the software environment, and by the system's use of the memory hierarchy. Well understood is the quantitative influence of the cache design parameters on the system performance, a good survey of which can be found in [13]. The impact of the software environment is not so well established. Several different models have been suggested [1], [2], [4], [12], most of which are geared toward predicting the expected *miss ratio* of the system under different environment constraints.

A fundamental work on program behavior [2] suggests using a "working set" to model the locality of memory accesses exhibited by programs. Two forms of locality are defined here: *temporal locality* and *spatial locality*. More specialized approaches, [4] and [3], model the effect of the initial burst (or *cold start*) that programs experience when the cache is first utilized and initialized.

[1] considers the many execution states associated with the execution of a program. This model was successfully used to approximate the miss ratio of a cache-based system under different software environments such as a multiuser

environment, and to evaluate the impact of operating system activities on the performance of the system.

The influence of multitasking in a cache was analyzed in [17] where the concept of a program's *footprint* (total number of unique lines brought into the cache during execution) was introduced to predict the number of transient misses that interleaved programs create for each other. Prompted by the work of [18] on the application of fractal geometry, a model of hyperbolic program locality was proposed in [15] which can be used to predict the miss ratio of a program in fully associative caches.

This paper presents a novel approach for modeling the relationship between key parameters of program behavior and of cache design so as to predict the performance of a cache memory. Central to this model is that the *lines* a program holds in a cache during execution are not all of equal importance. Some will be referenced again while they are in the cache, resulting in cache access hits, while others will never be accessed again. The first group is often referred to as *live* lines, the second as *dead* lines [11]. It is important for the cache to try to keep the live lines in, as replacing a live line causes a future miss. Dead lines are of no value in the cache. An important quantity to measure is, therefore, the fraction of the live lines a program holds in a cache at any time, and in particular, how this fraction behaves when several programs run in an interleaved fashion.

The model presented here predicts the contents of a cache memory (live versus dead lines) when the locality characteristics of the program which is accessing the cache are known. The variation of the live and dead lines is modeled as a function of the execution time. This information is then used to predict the contents of the cache when external events such as context switches occur.

The contents of the cache memory are predicted for different cache organizations: infinite size, fully associative, set associative and direct mapped. In this paper, the fully-associative architecture plays a key role in analyzing the prediction of live lines, and in particular in the analysis of the interaction of interleaved processes. Throughout the paper the terms *program* and *process* refer to the same entity.

While this paper focuses on multiprogramming on a single-processor cache-based system, the model can also help analyze the performance of multiprocessor systems. In a related work [10] the behavior of live and dead cache lines in uniprocessor system are correlated to the concept of *true* and *false* sharing of lines in multicache/multiprocessor system. The pattern of line sharing across the caches of a multicache system may

Manuscript received February 20, 1990; revised July 20, 1992. This work was supported in part by grant from AFOSR under Grant 88-0205.

A. Mendelson is with the Department of Electrical Engineering, Technion, Haifa 32000, Israel.

D. Thiébaut is with the Department of Computer Science, Smith College, Northampton, MA 01063.

D. K. Pradhan is with the Department of Computer Science, Texas A&M University, College Station, TX 77843.

IEEE Log Number 9204956.

Reprinted from *IEEE Trans. Computers*, Vol. 42, No. 1, Jan. 1993, pp. 1–14. Copyright © 1993 by The Institute of Electrical and Electronics Engineers, Inc. All rights reserved.

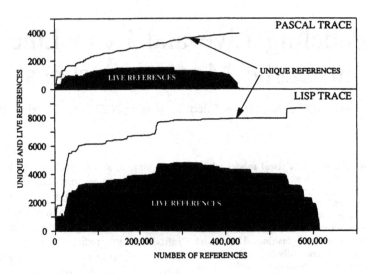

Fig. 1. Unique and live lines. Two examples.

have a significant impact on the performance of the system, as well as a direct influence on the overhead incurred by coherence protocols [19], [9]. Understanding the behavior of live and dead lines in a cache augments the understanding of the parameters which govern sharing patterns and coherence protocol overhead.

This paper's contribution is two-fold. The first portion addresses the case where one process executes in a cache-based uniprocessor system. The model suggests that for practical purposes, the number of live lines in finite-sized caches can be considered constant. The second portion of the model extends to the case when two processes are sharing a cache, and when their execution is interleaved. This second model supports direct-mapped, set-associative, and fully-associative caches.

The live-line model is presented in Section II. The second model is presented in Section III, where the previous model is refined to include the interleaved execution of two processes sharing a fully-associative cache memory. Sections IV and V focus on the fully-associative cache to derive the behavior of interleaved processes in direct-mapped and set-associative caches. Section VI concludes the paper by presenting areas of computer design where the model can be applied.

II. MODELING LIVE LINES IN AN INFINITE CACHE

In this section, we introduce a new model that estimates the number of *live lines* residing in an infinite cache memory during the execution of a given program. First, we define the concept of live and dead cache lines.

Definition 1: A *live cache line* is a line that is present in the cache memory, and that will be referenced again in the future.

Definition 2: A *dead cache line,* on the other hand, will never be referenced again by the processor before being purged out of the cache.

Live lines are important for cache performance since any reference to a live cache line results in a *cache hit.* Dead lines, on the other hand, cannot improve the performance of a cache.

Measurements of the number of live lines and *unique* lines (footprint) are presented in Fig. 1. Two address traces are

used, one of a Pascal compiler, the other of a Lisp program solving a 5-queen problem. Both plots exhibit the same basic characteristics: 1) there is a strong vertical symmetry property around the reference located at the middle of the address trace, 2) the number of live lines is maximum for that mid-trace reference, and, 3) there are no live lines at the beginning or at the end of the trace.

To model the behavior of the live lines, we use an analytical model of program behavior proposed in [16] and [18], where the successive accesses to memory are modeled as the result of a *fractal random walk* through the memory, where the jumps have a hyperbolic probability distribution

$$\Pr[X > u] = \left(\frac{u}{u_0}\right)^{-\theta}. \tag{1}$$

Here $u > 0$, and u_0 and θ are constants. The parameter θ describes the spatial locality of the random walk. As θ increases, the probability of visiting a new line diminishes. So, large values of θ correspond to high levels of locality of the random walk. For random walks with a symmetric hyperbolic distribution (i.e., the positive jumps and the negative jumps are governed by the same distribution $\Pr[X = u] = \Pr[X = -u]$, both of which satisfy (1)). It is shown [5] that for $2 < \theta < 3$, the number of unique cells visited, as a function of the number of the total number of cells visited, grows asymptotically toward a hyperbolic curve given by

$$\text{Number of unique cells} = u(n) \sim K n^{1/(\theta)} \tag{2}$$

where n represents the number of references to the memory. Throughout this paper, we refer to the curve describing the growth of the number of unique lines in the trace as the *footprint* curve.

The main hypothesis of the above model is that the random walk through memory is time invariant. Fig. 2 shows the two ideal footprint curves, one computed by analyzing the address trace from its beginning (going in the direction of positive virtual times); the other, computed by analyzing the address trace backward (going in the direction of negative

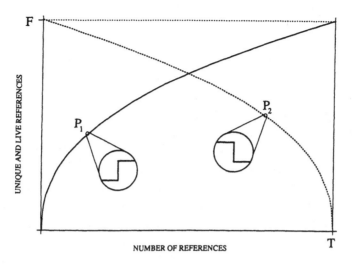

Fig. 2. Positive time and negative time footprint curves.

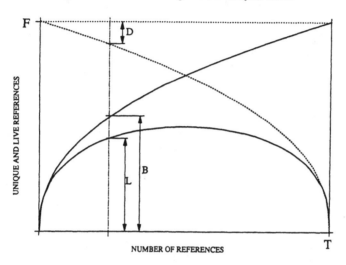

Fig. 3. Computation of live lines in infinite cache.

virtual times). We will refer to the first curve as the *positive-time footprint curve,* and to the second as the *negative-time footprint curve.*

Of interest here is the meaning of the steps taken by both footprint curves. Every time the positive-time footprint increases by one, a new line that had not been accessed before has just been referenced. On the other hand, the negative-time footprint curve decreases by one for every line not yet encountered when the processing starts at the end of the trace. Following the positive time axis, this implies that the line just accessed will never be referenced again before the end of the trace is reached.

This leads directly to our first model, describing the number of live lines present in an infinite cache, as a function of the number of lines accessed n (which also represents the discrete ticks of a virtual time). Referring to Fig. 3, if we assume that L represents the number of live lines at time n, B the number of unique lines encountered since time 0 (Births), and D the number of unique lines that will never be seen again (Deaths,)

then,

$$L = B - D \qquad (3)$$

or

$$L = Kn^{1/\theta} - (F - K(T - n)^{1/\theta})$$
$$= Kn^{1/\theta} + K(T - n)^{1/\theta} - F \qquad (4)$$

where T is the trace length, expressed in lines, and F is the total number of unique lines in the address trace, or footprint $(F = KT^{1/\theta})$. We should emphasize here that (4) holds because we assumed that the positive time footprint mirrors exactly its negative time counterpart.

The model was checked by generating a synthetic trace produced by the fractal model of program behavior [15] with parameters $K = 10$ and $\theta = 1.9$ (Fig. 4). The measured footprint and live-line curves exactly match the model defined by (4). The model was also validated with the Pascal and Lisp traces. The footprint and live-line curves for both the Pascal and Lisp traces are shown in Figs. 5 and 6, along with the

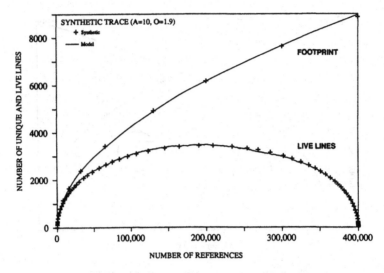

Fig. 4. Footprint and live-line curves of a synthetic trace.

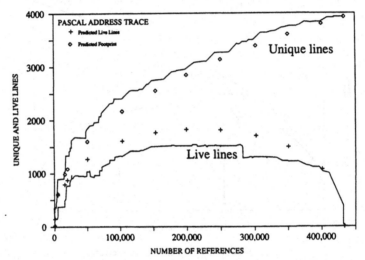

Fig. 5. Footprint and live lines of the Pascal trace.

analytical curves given by the model. The values of K and θ for the Pascal trace are 17.402 and 2.3944, respectively, and 67.022 and 2.7300 for the Lisp trace.

A. Modeling Live Lines in a Finite Cache

In this section the previous model is enhanced by including the effect of limited storage (finite-size fully-associative caches) on the number of live lines residing in the cache. A key result here is that the number of lines contained in the cache becomes approximately constant as soon as the fully associative cache fills up.

Fig. 7 shows the results of feeding the Pascal trace to three finite-size caches (256, 512, and 1024 lines), and to an infinite size cache. The infinite cache is used as a base line, i.e., to generate the footprint curve along with its associative live-line curve. The shaded areas depicts the number of live lines in the caches. Mostly, the lower three curves (associated with the finite caches) remain at a somewhat constant level. (The drops

that do occur are likely accountable to locality changes in the program behavior.) Interestingly, while the level of live lines in the fully associative case is constant, the level is nonetheless lower than the cache size.

The inset in Fig. 7 clearly depicts the growth of the number of misses experienced by the finite caches; the main portion of Fig. 7 corresponds to the shaded region of the inset. Note that the curves are highly liner. It is conjectured in [15] that the derivative of the footprint curve, at the point where the ordinate is equal to the size of a fully associative cache C, is the miss rate in that cache, and that the miss rate remains constant until the end of the trace. This behavior has been independently observed and reported in many works, particularly in [8] and [7].

The curves which portray the number of misses are, to the finite caches, what the footprint curve is for the infinite cache. In the case of a finite cache, B_c and D_c (the birth and death rates in the finite-size cache, respectively) grow and decrease

206

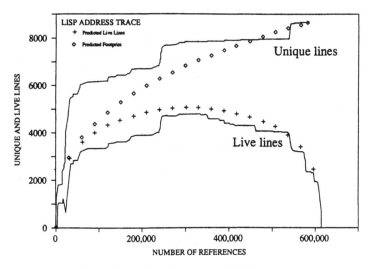

Fig. 6. Footprint and live lines of the Lisp trace.

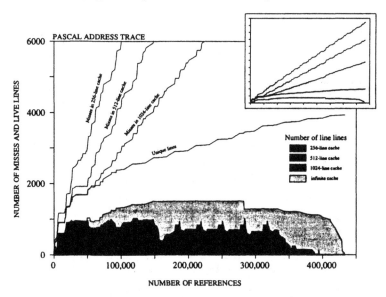

Fig. 7. Misses and live lines in finite size caches.

linearly with slopes of identical magnitude over an interval centered on the middle of the trace. Over the length of that interval, L_c remains constant. This concept is illustrated in Fig. 8.

The value of L_c is found when the linear portion of the live-line curve is reached, which happens when the finite, fully associative cache becomes full. If n_c is the number of references necessary to fill up a cache of size C, then

$$C = K n_c^{1/\theta} \qquad (5)$$

or

$$n_c = (C/K)^\theta. \qquad (6)$$

At that time, we can approximate L_c by

$$L_c = K n_c^{1/\theta} + K(T - n_c)^{1/\theta} - F_c$$
$$= (F_c^\theta - C^\theta)^{1/\theta} - (F_c - C) \qquad (7)$$

where F_c is the total number of misses experienced in the cache of size C:

$$F_c = K T^{1/\theta}. \qquad (8)$$

Using the values of K and θ of Fig. 5, we plotted the measured and predicted number of live lines present in the 256-line, 512-line, and 1024-line fully associative caches when fed the Pascal address-trace. The result is shown in Fig. 9. Of note is the fact that the prediction of the number of live lines between phase transitions is quite accurate. Interestingly, because the model is based on the *asymptotic behavior* of the walk, it predicts the steady state, or average variation of the number of live lines, not its transient behavior.

III. FOOTPRINT AND LIVE LINES OF TWO INTERLEAVED PROCESSES

This section considers two interleaved processes which are competing for the cache. A model that estimates the total

207

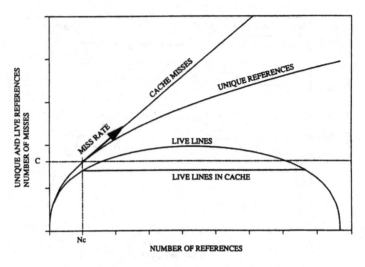

Fig. 8.   Computation of the number of live lines in finite size caches.

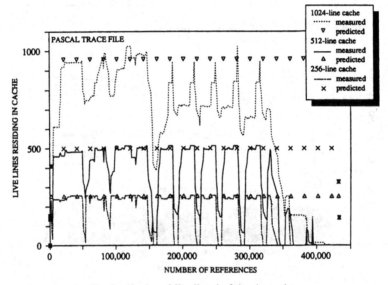

Fig. 9.   Number of live lines in finite size caches.

number of cache lines acquired by a process as a function of its execution time will be formulated. The *incoming* process is the process currently holding the CPU and the cache, while the *switched-out* process refers to the process in the idle state. The model predicts the resident set of lines of both the incoming and switched-out processes. The model provides additional information about the fraction of live and dead lines relating to both processes, and indicates the influence of the cache associativity on the resident sets. A trace-driven simulation is used for validation.

A. Modeling Live and Dead Lines in a Multitasking Environment

Consider two interleaved processes A and B, and the point in time where A is switched out and B takes over. We analyze the variation of the number of A lines as a function of time and as a function of the number of lines the incoming process

B acquires. First, certain new definitions are introduced.

Definition 3: Let the *mirror footprint* of Process B be the number of cache lines *not* belonging to Process B.

Definition 4: A live line is defined as a line that will be referenced again before the process terminates. Therefore, when a process is idle (switched off) then a live line is defined as a line that was live at the time that process got switched off.

Fig. 10 illustrates the live lines of two processes sharing a fully-associative cache managed by an LRU algorithm after A is switched off. In a fully associative cache, the number of A lines remains constant until the replacement point is reached. Indeed, the number of A lines will not change until Process B has accumulated enough lines so that the sum of the A and B lines is equal to the size of the cache. (In set-associative caches, the B Process may potentially replace an A line when the first B lines are brought in, if the B line is mapped to a set already filled with A lines.)

208

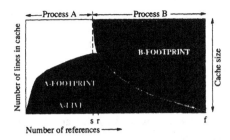

Fig. 10. Interaction of the A and B processes in a finite size cache.

We now model the behavior of the A lines in a fully associative cache. The case of set-associativity will be developed in a later section.

B. Behavior of Live Lines in Fully-Associative Caches

From the point of view of Process A, the loss of dead cache lines to Process B does not result in a penalty. The loss of a live line, on the other hand, will result in a (transient) miss later on, when process A is reactivated. Thus, an important consideration is a measure of the loss of *live A-lines* as a function of the activity of Process B.

From the study of the simulated execution of two interleaved processes, the following important observations can be made: i) the number of live lines of the switched-out process decreases at a slower rate than that process's number of dead lines. ii) Under the LRU replacement policy, the *smaller* the degree of associativity of the cache, the *greater* the probability that a process finds live lines in the cache when it resumes execution. Our first model can be used to explain these and related behaviors in cache systems of varying architectures.

We first introduce the following notations:

F_x^y the number of lines Process y has accumulated after x memory references (virtual time).

L_x^y represents the number of live y-lines in the cache at time x.

C the size of the fully associative cache shared by the two processes.

s the switching point when Process A becomes idle and Process B starts running.

n number of memory references made by Process B since it was last switched on (point s).

r the *replacement point*, i.e., the virtual time at which Process B replaces an A-line for the first time.

f the instant when Process B acquires the entire cache. (If the process terminates before reaching that point, this point represents the point obtained by extrapolating the curve using the hyperbolic model.)

Using the above notation, the followig quantities are derived.

1) The number of lines the incoming process (B) holds in the cache at a given time is estimated by using the hyperbolic model from the previous section, with parameters K_B and θ_B:

$$F_n^B = K_B n^{1/\theta_B}. \qquad (9)$$

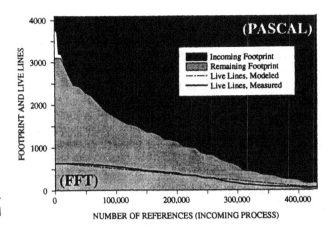

Fig. 11. Measured footprints, and modeled live-line curves.

2) The number of A-lines remaining in the cache is given by

$$F_n^A = \begin{cases} F_s^A & \text{if } n \le r \\ C - K_B n^{1/(\theta_B)} & \text{if } r \le n \le f. \\ 0 & n \ge f \end{cases} \qquad (10)$$

3) We approximate the number of live A-lines held in the system by using a linear fit between time r and f:

$$L_n^A = \begin{cases} L_s^A & \text{if } n \le r \\ MIN(L_s^A \dfrac{n - n_f}{n_r - n_f}, F_n^A) & \text{if } r \le n \le f. \\ 0 & n \ge f \end{cases} \qquad (11)$$

This basic model estimates quite accurately the number of lines belonging to different processes sharing a fully-associative cache in an interleaved fashion, as supported by the measurements presented below.

1) Validation of the Basic Model for Fully Associative-Caches: To validate our first model, we ran a trace-driven experiment where the execution of Process A is simulated by memory accesses taken from the trace of a program computing a Fast Fourier Transform (FFT) on 256 integer points, while Process B is simulated by taking addresses from the Pascal trace. Both traces were captured on an Intel 80 × 86-based computer. Process A is allowed to access 200 000 lines before Process B starts. The size of the cache is 4096 lines of 1 byte each, or 4096 bytes. Fig. 11 shows both the measured and predicted number of lines (footprint and live lines) for Process A after the switching point. The point of abscissa 0 represents the instant in time when Process B commences. Because A has accumulated approximately 3000 lines in the cache, 650 of them live, the B-footprint (not shown) very quickly erodes the A footprint, along with its live lines. Note that the number of dead lines diminishes faster than the number of live lines. The fit given by the model is exemplary of the fit obtained on other traces in similar experiments, not reported here for the sake of simplicity.

IV. Effect of the Cache Associativity on the Footprints and Live Lines. The Raw Model

This section studies the influence of the cache associativity on the footprint, and on the variation of the number of live lines belonging the process that has just been switched out. Because their behavior is a function of i) the parameters governing the execution of the incoming process (quantum of execution time, locality) and ii) the cache architecture, then an accurate estimate of the state that is regained by the switched-out process can be obtained. Such information can be used, in turn, to yield important performance measures, in terms of hit ratio, bus traffic, or data sharing properties in multiprocessor systems [10].

A. Modeling the Variation of the Footprint

First, we focus on the footprint curves of the incoming (Fig. 12) and switched out processes (Fig. 13). In both cases, the cache size is 4K bytes, but the set-associativity varies. Observe that the footprints in the 16-way and 8-way set-associative cache memories are nearly the same as the one associated with the fully-associative cache organization. As the degree of associativity decreases, so does the footprint of the incoming process.

By the same effect, the footprint of the switched-out process is smaller for lower levels of associativity. The rate at which this footprint curve decreases, though, is directly proportional to the level of associativity, to the extent that the remaining footprint of the switched-out process in a direct mapped cache can be higher than that in a fully associative cache, provided the incoming process runs for a sufficiently long time (in this case, long enough to generate more than 250 000 references).

To model the effect of the finite set associativity on the program footprint, a uniform distribution of lines in the sets is assumed, where the statistics governing the number of lines present in each set are well understood and belong to the class of Bernoulli trials. The balls thrown in the urns are the lines assigned to cache sets. Assuming that F balls (lines) are thrown into N urns (sets) with uniform probabilities, the probability that an urn holds exactly t balls is given by

$$\binom{F}{t}\left(\frac{1}{N}\right)^t * \left(1 - \frac{1}{N}\right)^{F-t}, \tag{12}$$

hence, the number of urns holding exactly r balls is

$$U(F, t, N) = N * \binom{F}{t}\left(\frac{1}{N}\right)^t * \left(1 - \frac{1}{N}\right)^{F-t}. \tag{13}$$

When an infinite set-associative cache is used, each set has an infinite capacity, and can hold as many lines as the Bernouilli trials assign to it. When the set-associative cache is of a finite size, then K lines (the degree of associativity) at most can fit in a given set. As a result, the footprint of a process in a finite size set-associative cache is the sum of two components: the contents of sets containing K or fewer lines, plus the contents of sets having received K or more lines, of which the last K

have been kept.

$$F_{\text{set associative}} = \sum_{i=1}^{K} i * U(F, i, N)$$
$$+ \sum_{i=K+1}^{\infty} K * U(F, i, N) \tag{14}$$

where N represents the number of sets, and F, the footprint in an infinite cache.

Direct mapped caches are 1-way set associative caches, and the footprint of a process in this cache organization is simply

$$F_{\text{direct mapped}} = \text{cache\_size} - U(F, 0, N). \tag{15}$$

To estimate the temporal variation of the footprints of the two processes sharing a set-associative cache, the rate at which each process individually fills an empty cache of infinite size is measured. This footprint is affected only by the program behavior and gives the instantaneous number of lines that have been distributed in the cache. This is *the only information required* about Process B to predict the variation of the A-footprint in any cache organization, i.e., fully associative, direct mapped or set associative. We will refer to this quantity as the *Infinite, Fully Associative Cache* footprint, or *IFAC* footprint.

B. The Impact of the Set Associativity on the Switched-Out Process

This section first looks at the direct-mapped cache organization. Then the model is extended for different set-associative cache organizations.

1) Direct-Mapped Caches: Given that n of the A-lines have been distributed into a direct-mapped cache of m sets, from (15), the average number of A-lines in the cache is derived. Similarly, when Process A is switched out, the number of B-lines brought into the cache is controlled by the same equation. Of interest is the number of A-lines remaining when B terminates its quantum, at which point, Process A resumes execution.

Because we assume a uniform distribution of lines in the sets, the B process is just as likely to store its lines in empty sets, as it is to store them in sets already filled with A-lines. As a result, if we call F^B the set of B lines in the cache, then the filling ratio of B is F^B/N, where N is the number of sets. Since the A-lines are equally distributed in the cache, $F^A(F^B/N)$ of them will be erased by B-lines. At any point in time, if the current number of B-lines brought into the cache is F^B, then the number of A-lines is given by

$$\text{Number of } A\text{-lines} = F^A - F^A\left(\frac{F^B}{N}\right)$$
$$= F^A\left(1 - \frac{F^B}{N}\right). \tag{16}$$

Note here that F^A represents the total number of A lines present in the cache *at the end of the A quantum*, while F^B represents the current number of B-lines in the cache, and that *this number is increasing with time*, as the B quantum progresses.

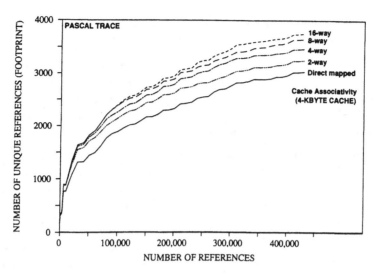

Fig. 12. Variation of Pascal footprints as a function of cache associativity.

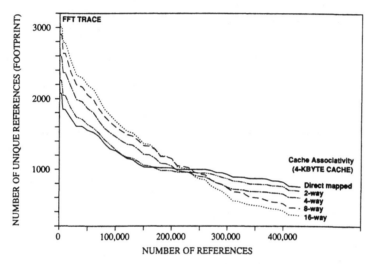

Fig. 13. Variation of FFT footprints as a function of cache associativity.

2) Footprints in Set-Associative Caches: Computing the footprints of both processes in a finite-size, set-associative cache which is managed by an LRU policy is an extension of the direct-mapped case. The direct-mapped cache can be considered as one flat row of sets, or urns. Using the same imagery, the set-associative cache is now decomposed into several similar longitudinal rows that are perpendicular to the cache sets. The lower row contains all the MRU (Most Recently Used) lines of all the sets, and is a direct mapped cache in its own right. The next higher row contains all the next-to-MRU lines, etc. A four-way set associative cache would contain four of these rows.

Using (13), we can compute the number of A lines present in the ith row, where i ranges from 1 to the degree of associativity K. Summed over all values of i, this quantity yields the remaining footprint of Process A in a finite size, set-associative cache.

The number of lines in row i can be derived as

$$R^i = \sum_{j=i}^{\infty} U(F, j, N). \qquad (17)$$

This model allows us to compute, in a simple way, the number of A-lines left in each row at the end of the A-quantum. Knowing that the number of A-lines present in the cache when the B-process starts is F^A, we can compute the variation of the A-footprint as the B-process starts filling the cache, by applying the same model to *each row independently*. In effect, each row is treated similarly to a direct-mapped cache, in which the interaction between the two is governed by the equations of the previous section. The resulting algorithm follows.

1) Compute the number R^i_A of lines Process A holds in each row, independently of the other rows, at the switching time.

211

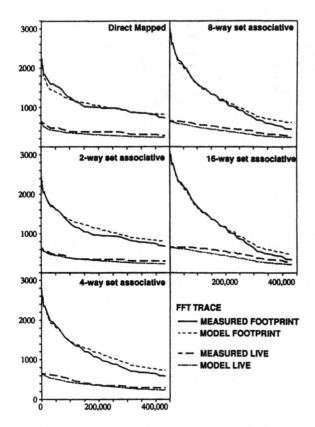

Fig. 14. Footprint of FFT in 5 set associative caches (1).

2) At time n, compute the number of lines $R_B^{i(n)}$ that the incoming Process B stores in each row, independently of the other rows.

3) Assuming a degree of the associativity is K, and summing up, we get

$$\text{Number of } A\text{-lines} = \sum_{j=1}^{K} R_A^j * \left(1 - \frac{R_B^{(K-j+1)(n)}}{N} \right). \tag{18}$$

We verify that by setting $K = 1$ in (18), the formula for direct-mapped caches is derived.

3) Simulation Results: The interleaving of two processes was simulated by feeding addresses from two different traces to a fixed-size cache containing 4096 lines of 1 byte, arranged as a direct-mapped, 2-way, 4-way, 8-way, and 16-way set associative cache. The A and B processes are simulated by taking addresses from the Pascal and FFT traces, respectively. The B process is executed first, and 200 000 of its references are fed to the cache. B is then switched off, and A is started.

Fig. 14 shows the footprint and live lines of the FFT process in the 5 cache architectures. The footprint curves are the top curves in each graph. Note that the curve associated with the model (dashed line) is not smooth. This is due to the fact that it is computed from the IFAC footprint of the Pascal trace, which is not smooth by nature.

The model accurately predicts the behavior of the true footprint in all five cases. The most noticeable divergence between measured and predicted curves occurs at the very end of the graph, when roughly half a million accesses to the cache have been generated.

C. Modeling the Variation of the Number of Live Lines

Modeling the live lines of the switched-out process is similar to modeling the footprint. The main difference is in the assumptions made on the distribution of the lines at switching time.

1) The Model: This section investigates the behavior of the population of the live A-lines in the cache when Process B starts filling it with its own lines. Here again, we assume that we know the exact number of live A-lines in the cache when A is switched off and when B starts.

The distribution of the live A-lines in the cache is unknown, but, because of the principle of temporal locality that is inherent to program behavior, the conjecture is that in caches other than direct-mapped caches, the live A-lines will have a tendency to cluster on the MRU side of the sets. In other words, the probability of finding a live A-line should be greater in the MRU position than in the LRU position of a set.

When generating our model, the extreme assumption is made that live-lines will be distributed first. This approach is oversimplifying, but because of our simulation results, it is an acceptable one to make.

For the case when the number of live cache lines at the switching point is known, we cannot use the above methods to estimate their distribution, so a more sophisticated model is required, called the *restricted urn model*, discussed in [6]. Listed below are the results of significance for our model.

- The number of ways that F balls can be distributed among N different urns, if any urn is restricted to hold at most K balls is given by

$$D1(F,N,K) = \sum_{j=0}^{N} (-1)^j \binom{N}{j} \binom{F + N - j(K+1) - 1}{N - 1}. \tag{19}$$

- The number of ways F balls can be distributed among N different urns, given that the urns can hold, at most, K balls each, and that exactly u urns are holding t balls is given by

$$D2(F,N,K,t,u) = \binom{N}{u} \sum_{j=0}^{N-u} (-1)^j \binom{N-u}{j} \cdot D1(F - (u+j)t, N - (u+j), K). \tag{20}$$

These two results can be used to compute the number of lines contained in a K-way set asociative cache, with N sets. Assuming that a total of F lines have been distributed, then the probability that any given set contains exactly r lines is given by

$$\Pr[\text{set holds } r \text{ lines}] = \frac{\sum_{i=1}^{K} i * D2(F,N,K,r,j)}{D1(F,N,K)}.$$

With this assumption, the live lines in the cache can be modeled in *exactly* the same way as was done for the footprint in the previous section. This time the variation of the footprint of live A-lines is modeled rather than the footprint of live and dead A-lines.

2) Simulation Results: Referring to Fig. 14, the lower of the two curves shown in each graph is now the focus. The measured variation of the live lines is represented by the heavier dashed line, the model represented by the thinner line. Observed is an accurate modeling of the variation of the live lines, with a bias in all cases for predicting *fewer* live lines than actually measured. It should be noted that the assumption that live lines always occupy most-recently-used locations should create the opposite bias. That is, that it is possible that some live lines are interleaved with dead ones, so that as the B-lines are introduced in the cache, live A-lines may be evicted before dead ones. This would indicate a thrashing of live lines faster than predicted by the model, but the model is pessimistic here. It is suggested in [17] that both processes do not uniformly distribute their lines in the cache, instead clustering them in different cache places, creating less interaction than the uniform distribution would.

It should be noted here that in all cases the footprint curve diminishes *proportionately* faster than the live line curve, supporting the original assumption that dead lines are thrown out of the cache faster than live lines. The plausible explanation is that the live lines occupy the most recently used positions in the sets.

V. EFFECT OF THE CACHE ASSOCIATIVITY ON THE FOOTPRINTS AND LIVE LINES. THE HYPERBOLIC MODEL

Thus far, the model presented is accurate in its prediction of the influence of the set-associativity on the behavior of the switched-out process. It does, though, rely on the exact knowledge of the variation of the footprint and of the number of live lines of both processes. A more analytical model will now be demonstrated that an accurate prediction of the variation of both processes' footprints and live lines can be achieved if the footprint and live lines of each process are represented by the hyperbolic equations generated in Section II.

A. The Model

The equations governing the variation of the footprint and live lines in the cache are exactly the same as shown before, with the exception that the instantaneous variation of the IFAC B-footprint is given directly from the hyperbolic model of parameters K_B and θ_B. Identically, the measure of the footprint and number of live lines of the A-process at the end of its quantum is now provided by the same hyperbolic equations, this time with parameters K_A and θ_A.

B. Simulation Results

First we analyze the effect of using the hyperbolic IFAC footprint of B instead of its true IFAC footprint. Using the FFT and Pascal traces to simulate the A and B processes, the same experiment is run as the one shown in Fig. 14. Fig.

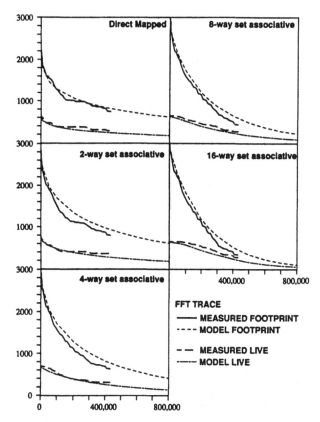

Fig. 15.   Footprint of FFT in 5 set associative caches (2).

15 depicts the new curves. The variation of the Pascal IFAC footprint is now generated by (9).

The new model still captures the general behavior of the remaining lines of the FFT trace. The match between the two, though, is not as accurate as in the previous model since the hyperbolic model is already an approximation of the true IFAC footprint. Interestingly, the two model curves (the one for the footprint and the one for the live lines) provide, in all five cases, an *envelope* for the variation of the true quantities studied. Such an envelope could provide important information for the cache designer faced with many different application-related issues, and this discussion is provided in the conclusion.

The results, though, are encouraging enough to consider replacing the true footprint and live line curves by their hyperbolic models, for *both* the A and B process, and to compare prediction against measurements.

When all measures relating to the A and B process are generated analytically, the behavior shown in Fig. 16 appears. In this new experiment, we used for Process A a trace of a Lisp program solving the 5-queen problem on an Intel 80×86 computer, and for Process B a trace of the Pascal compiler. The Lisp trace was chosen for its longer length, which allowed us to simulate a process switch after 50 000, 100 000, 200 000, 300 000, and 400 000 references. The cache chosen still holds 4096 lines, arranged in 4-way associative sets. This number was chosen as a "mid-point" in the range of associativity considered. The same qualitative

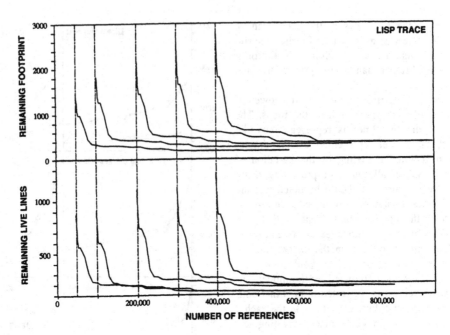

Fig. 16. Five cut points in Pascal program.

results can be obtained on lower and higher-associativity caches, with one representative example given.

Five different switch-points were selected for simulation because the number of live lines in infinite size caches may vary because of phase changes in the execution of the program. As a result, Fig. 17 represents the point-to-point *average* over all five switch points, of the modeled and measured curves. Fig. 16 shows the superimposed individual footprint and live-line curves of the Pascal program when the switch points vary between 50 000 and 400 000. The pair of curves starting at switch point 100 000, for example, are obtained by feeding 100 000 lines from the Lisp trace to the 4-way set associative, 4096-line cache, and by continuing with 430 000 lines from the Pascal program. (For clarity, Fig. 17 depicts the average of the curves generated by the model, and not the individual curves.)

Again, the model measures up well against the true curves, indicating that the prediction of the behavior of a program's live lines in a set-associative cache shared by another process can be predicted with good accuracy, from the sole knowledge of both program's locality measures, K, and θ.

VI. CONCLUSION AND DISCUSSION

This paper introduces a general model for predicting the behavior of the live and dead cache lines of a process, as a function of the process's execution time and the behavior of other interleaved processes competing for the same cache.

This general model is a collection of three new models. The first relates the fractal nature of a program's memory-access pattern to the growth of its footprint and the number of live lines in a cache memory. The second model predicts the diminishing rate at which the dead and live cache lines of a process shrink when new processes take over the processor and the cache. The third model uses results from the theory of

the urn model to extend the second model to set-associative caches, and direct-mapped caches.

The chief advantage of the global model presented here is that it relies on only a few parameters: Two for each process (K and θ), the size of the cache (C), and its degree of associativty (K).

The trace-driven simulations indicate that the model is accurate in predicting the speed at which footprint and live-line curves decay in different cache architectures. The analysis of the influence of set-associativity on the variation of the footprints and live line curves shows that the model provides an envelope for the measured curves. The lower envelope matches the live-line curve accurately over all associativity studied, while the footprint envelope is tighter at lower levels of associativity. The conjecture is that this difference is due to the nonuniformity with which the lines accumulate in the sets, since any skewness in the distribution will be accentuated as the associativity levels increase.

Accurate prediction of the variation of the number of live lines of interleaved process in cache-based systems has important applications, some of which are listed below.

1) In terms of the execution time of a process, the shape of its footprint curve has important consequences on the number of live lines held in a cache. The first implication is that after the process has had time to bring a significant part of its footprint into the cache, the number of live lines of the process remains relatively stable and increases very slowly. Moreover, past the mid-point of the program, i.e., once the program has accessed half the total number of lines it needs for its complete computation, the number of live lines decreases gradually, while the ratio of dead to live lines present in the cache increases significantly until the end of the program.

In set-associative caches, when the size of the footprint is large compared to the size of the cache, it is seen that the

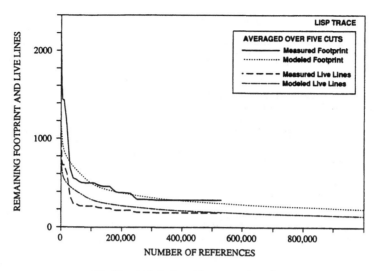

Fig. 17. Analytical model—averaged results.

number of live lines remains bounded. Although the hyperbolic model predicts a constant number of live lines, observation determines that phase transition experienced by the program creates sharp breaks in the number of live lines, with important local minimum values.

These phenomena lead to several conclusions.

- Using very large cache memories is mainly beneficial in improving the probability that a switched-out process find some of its live lines still present when it resumes execution. A direct consequence of the results presented here is that a preferred way to use a very large cache memory is to partition it into segments so that the dead lines will not dominate the content of the cache. The analytical model presented here may be used to provide an efficient way of maintaining the partition size.
- The frequency of task switching can be used to reduce the level of dead lines. By dynamic measurement of the footprint of both competing processes (through hardware recording of the number of unique access to memory [14], for example), it may be feasible to quickly compute the K and θ parameters of each process, deriving the optimum switch point between the two. In such a case, the incoming process would be used to "flush" out the dead lines of the switched out process, until the number of live lines of both have reached some threshold.

2) The lower the degree of cache associativity (for a given cache size), the sooner the flushing of the lines belonging to the switched-out process begins. Conversely, a low degree of associativity causes the live lines of the switched out process to remain in the cache much longer than they would in a fully associative cache of the same size.

- In a multiprogramming environment, when the number of processes competing for the CPU is modest, the use of large cache memories with high degrees of associativity is recommended. This improves the probability that a process will recover most of its live lines when it resumes.
- In a time-sharing environment (or thread-based operating

system) where the number of processes (threads) competing for the CPU is large, the use of caches with low degrees of associativity (direct mapped or 2-way set-associativity) may be preferable. Such caches improve the probability that a live line belonging to a switched-out process remains in the cache, despite the interaction created by the incoming process.

3) Finally, the work in [10] suggests an important extension of the model presented here toward evaluating data sharing in multicache systems. Sharing of data causes a significant design problem, as the cache systems must insure coherence of the data shared. Distinguishing shared live cached data (true sharing) from dead data may have significant implications on the amount of overhead incurred by the protocol which maintains data coherence. The models in [10] provide powerful tools for both understanding sharing patterns in multicache systems, and for improving the performance of these systems.

REFERENCES

[1] A. Agarwal, M. Horowitz, and J. Hennessy, "An analytical cache model," *ACM Trans. Comput. Syst.*, vol. 7, no. 2, May 1989.
[2] P. Denning, "The working set model for program behavior," *Commun. ACM*, vol. 11, no. 5, pp. 323–333, May 1968.
[3] M. C. Easton, "Computation of cold-start miss ratio," *IEEE Trans. Comput.*, vol. C-27, pp. 404–408, May 1978.
[4] M. C. Easton and R. Fagin, "Cold-start versus warm-start miss ratio," *Commun. ACM*, vol. 21, pp. 866–872, Oct. 1978.
[5] J. E. Gillis and G. Weiss, "Expected number of distinct sites visited by a random walk with an infinite variance," *J. Math Phys.*, vol. 11, pp. 1307–1312, Apr. 1970.
[6] N. L. Johnson and S. Kotz, *Urn Model and their Application*. New York: Wiley, 1977.
[7] M. Kobayashi and M. H. MacDonald, "The stack growth function cache line reference model," *IEEE Trans. Comput.*, vol. 38, pp. 798–805, June 1989.
[8] S. Laha, J. H. Patel, and R. K. Iyer, "Accurate low-cost methods for performance evaluation of cache memory systems," Tech. Rep., Coordinated Sci. Lab., Univ. of Illinois at Urbana–Champaign, 1986.
[9] Y.-C. Maa, D. Pradhan, and D. Thiébaut, "Two economical directory schemes for large-scale cache coherent multiprocessors," *Comput. Architecture News*, vol. 19, pp. 10–18, Sept. 1991.
[10] A. Mendelson, D. Thiébaut, and D. K. Pradhan, "Modeling of live lines and true sharing in multi-cache memory systems," in *Proc. Int. Conf. Parallel Processing*, Aug. 1990, pp. 326–330.

[11] T. R. Puzak, "Analysis of cache replacement algorithms," Ph.D. dissertation, Univ. Massachusetts, Amherst, 1985.

[12] A. J. Smith, "Cache evaluation and the impact of workload choice," in *Proc. 12th Int. Symp. Comput. Architecture,* 1985, pp. 64–73.

[13] _____, "Cache memories," *ACM Comput. Surveys,* vol. 14, pp. 473–530, Sept. 1982.

[14] H. S. Stone, private communication.

[15] D. Thiébaut, J. Wolf, and H. Stone, "Synthetic traces for trace-driven simulation of cache memories," *IEEE Trans. Comput.,* vol. 41, pp. 388–410, Apr. 1992.

[16] D. Thiébaut, "On the fractal dimension of computer programs and its application to the prediction of cache miss-ratio," *IEEE Trans. Comput.,* vol. 38, pp. 1012–1026, July 1989.

[17] D. Thiébaut and H. S. Stone, "Footprints in the cache," *ACM Trans. Comput. Syst.,* vol. 5, pp. 305–329, Nov. 1987.

[18] J. Voldman, B. Mandelbrot, L. W. Hoevel, J. Knight, and P. Rosenfeld, "Fractal nature of software-cache interaction," *IBM J. Res. Develop.,* vol. 27, pp. 164–170, Mar. 1983.

[19] W. Wolf-Dietrich and A. Gupta, "Analysis of cache invalidation patters in multiprocessors," in *Proc. 3rd Int. Conf. Architectural Support for Programming Languages and Oper. Syst.,* Boston, MA, ACM, Apr. 3–6, 1989, pp. 243–256.

Optimal Partitioning of Cache Memory

Harold S. Stone, *Fellow, IEEE*, John Turek, *Member, IEEE*, and Joel L. Wolf

Abstract—This paper develops a model for studying the optimal allocation of cache memory among two or more competing processes. It uses this model to show that, for the examples studied, the least recently used (LRU) replacement strategy produces cache allocations that are very close to optimal. The optimal fixed allocation of cache among two or more processes is an allocation for which the miss-rate derivative with respect to cache size is equal for all processes.

The paper also investigates the transient in cache allocation that occurs when program behavior changes, and shows that LRU replacement moves quickly toward the steady-state allocation if it is far from optimal, but converges slowly as the allocation approaches the steady-state allocation. It describes an efficient combinatorial algorithm for determining the optimal steady-state allocation, which, in theory, could be used to reduce the length of the transient. The algorithm generalizes to multilevel cache memories.

For multiprogrammed systems, the paper describes a cache-replacement policy better than LRU replacement. The policy increases the memory available to the running process until the allocation reaches a threshold time that depends both on remaining quantum time and the marginal reduction in miss rate due to an increase in cache allocation. Beyond the threshold time, the replacement policy does not increase the cache memory allocated to the running process.

For all of the questions studied in this paper, the examples shown here illustrate near-optimal performance of LRU replacement, but in the absence of a bound on near optimality the question remains open whether or not LRU replacement is near-optimal in all situations likely to arise in practice.

Index Terms—Cache footprint, cache memory, LRU replacement, memory allocation, memory hierarchy, miss rate, miss ratio, multilevel cache memory, power-law model.

I. INTRODUCTION

THIS paper studies the optimal allocation of cache memory among competing processes. Cache memories are high-speed buffer memories whose contents tend to be the most frequently used items accessed by a program. The contents are normally determined by bringing in new items on demand and by using a replacement policy that discards items that are unlikely to be accessed in the near future. When the replacement policy removes the least recently used (LRU) item, caches tend to be very effective, provided that they are large enough to hold the majority of the items that are likely to be active concurrently.

Practical implementations of LRU replacement algorithms do not usually search all entries in a cache, but instead search a small region of the cache that depends on the address

Manuscript received March 29, 1989; revised January 12, 1990 and May 8, 1991.

The authors are with IBM T. J. Watson Research Center, Yorktown Heights, NY 10598.

IEEE Log Number 9200307.

reference. The region searched is a called a *set*, and the search is said to be *set associative*. When the region searched contains only a single item, the cache is said to be *direct mapped*. When a new item is brought into the set, some item in the same set is discarded. If the replacement algorithm discards the least recently used item in the set, we designate the replacement algorithm to be an LRU algorithm, and thus both set associative and fully associative caches can be managed by LRU replacement algorithms according to this terminology. Additional information on set-associative and fully associative caches can be found in Smith [13] and Hill [9].

The question of interest is to determine just how well caches behave. We introduce two cache-allocation problems in which processes that have different miss-rate behaviors compete for cache allocation. We find that for neither problem does LRU replacement produce optimal allocations, but the examples in this paper exhibit LRU allocations that are very close to optimal. The data in this paper endorses the almost universal practice of managing cache with LRU replacement. All of the results stated here hold both for set-associative caches and fully associative caches.

The first of the problems studied is the allocation of inter-laced data and instruction processes to cache memory. This formulation of the problem was described in Thiebaut, Stone, and Wolf [22]. The paper derives a mathematical model that describes optimal and LRU allocations and gives a validation of the model by means of a trace-driven simulation. Although we are not able to bound the suboptimality of LRU allocations, the evidence presented indicates that they are very good. Our approach is to develop the model of a simpler modified-LRU replacement strategy first, and then embellish this model to obtain a model of pure LRU replacement. The modified-LRU strategy can produce better allocations than those produced by pure LRU for some reference strings.

The measure of optimality used here is the overall miss rate of a cache memory, and an optimal partition is a partition of cache memory among competing processes that achieves a minimum miss rate. Belady [2] introduced an algorithm that is optimal among demand-replacement algorithms. Among all possible ways to choose which cache line to replace on a miss, Belady's algorithm produces the lowest miss rate. Belady's algorithm does not indicate how to partition cache among competing processes, so it cannot be applied directly to the problem addressed in this paper.

For the first allocation problem, the paper also develops a model for the transient behavior of a cache as it moves from one allocation to another in response to a change in the characteristics of data and instruction processes. The differential equation obtained generally cannot be solved neatly in closed form, but can be solved numerically. The model is validated by a trace-driven simulation and by a statistical simulation of the competing processes. Both simulations produce data that fit the mathematical characterization of dynamic behavior. Of related interest in the literature is the paper by Strecker [18], which describes a differential equation to model the dynamics of cache occupancy in the absence of competition.

As a potential means for reducing the allocation transient, we describe an algorithm that first appeared in Thiebaut, Stone, and Wolf [22] for computing the optimal cache allocation. The algorithm allocates lines of cache sequentially among N processes in a way that maintains the miss-rate derivatives as equal as possible, and terminates when the cache memory is fully allocated. We also show how this algorithm generalizes to multilevel cache memory systems.

The second allocation problem treated in this paper is the allocation of cache memory among processes in a multiprogrammed environment. This problem differs from the first because the first scheme deals with interlaced streams, whereas in the second problem, one address-reference stream has exclusive access to cache for a quantum of time, and then yields to a new address-reference stream that has exclusive access for another quantum of time. For the second problem, there tends to be a cache-reload transient each time a new process takes over the processor. The miss rate tends to be high during the early part of the transient, and then drops as the working set of the process becomes resident in cache. A statistical model of the transient that gives an accurate measure of the number of lines reloaded appears in Thiebaut and Stone [21].

For large caches a better replacement policy than LRU replacement is to increase the cache allocation of a running process until the marginal improvement in miss rate multiplied by the time remaining in the quantum is less than some threshold. From this point until the end of the quantum, no additional cache memory should be allocated to the running process. The modified policy tends to retain in cache some items that belong to the next process to run on the machine. When cache is too small to be likely to retain pages of the next process to run, the modified policy is the same as LRU replacement. Thus, the modified policy only makes sense to use when caches are large enough to retain lines of a process in cache through periods when other processes have exclusive use of the processor.

We briefly note some related work. Specifically, Ghanem [7] has studied dynamic partitioning of main memory among competing programs, and his work is the precursor of this work. Replacement strategies for cache have been studied by many people, with notable work by Smith and Goodman [15] and by So and Rechtschaffen [16] among others. Kirk [11] has analyzed the partitioning of an instruction cache into a static partition and an LRU partition. Multilevel caches and the inclusion principle were studied by Baer and Wang [1]. Vernon, Jog, and Sohi [23] have studied performance of hierarchical caches, and proposed optimal multilevel topologies. Przybylski, Horowitz, and Hennessy [12] have also studied optimal multilevel cache hierarchies.

Section II poses the allocation problem for interlaced data and instruction streams, and shows that the miss-rate derivatives are equal when the allocation is optimal. Section III discusses the characteristics of LRU replacement, and shows that it does not converge to the optimal allocation. It also describes a modified-LRU replacement policy and compares its allocations to the LRU allocations. In Section IV, we derive the dynamics for the allocation of memory as it converges to its equilibrium allocation. The efficient algorithm for finding the optimum allocation of cache also appears in Section IV. The results of Sections II through IV rely on several assumptions that are validated in Section V by a trace-driven simulation based on actual data. Section VI treats the allocation of memory to processes in a multiprogrammed system. The generalization of the allocation algorithm to multilevel caches appears in Section VII. An example in Section VII shows that LRU replacement for multilevel cache can come very close to optimal. The last section poses several related research questions that remain open at this time.

II. ALLOCATION OF CACHE MEMORY BETWEEN DATA AND INSTRUCTION STREAMS

The model of cache allocation in this section deals with interlaced instruction and data streams that exhibit different cache behaviors. For this idealized form of the model, we show the optimal allocation occurs at a point where the miss-rate derivatives of the competing processes are equal.

For practical reasons, cache implementations at the fastest level of a memory hierarchy do not use fully associative search when seeking a match or an item to replace. Instead they search a small set of items, and replace the least recently used item in the set searched if replacement is necessary. If the set has four or more lines, typical replacement algorithms are further simplified and they only approximate LRU replacement because the complexity of maintaining LRU information for four or more items becomes excessive. At slower levels of a memory hierarchy, such as cache memories associated with large disks, the caches tend to be searched in a fully associative manner. In such caches, true LRU replacement is used for most references, with exceptions made for sequentially accessed data and other reference patterns that are highly predictable.

The focus of this paper is miss rate as a function of cache allocation of individual competing processes. Central to this paper is the assumption that competing processes can be characterized as having a miss rate as a function of allocation size. For fully associative caches, the miss rate for a given reference stream as a function of allocation is indeed a one-parameter function and depends only on the number of lines allocated to a process, since the entire cache is searched for a match during a cache lookup. For set-associative caches, the miss rate depends not only on how many lines are allocated to a process, but where they are in the cache, since only a set of a few lines is actually searched during a lookup.

Because a model that accounts for the physical locations of lines allocated in cache is extremely complicated, this paper uses a simplified model of set-associative caches in which the miss rate is a one-parameter function, and that parameter is the number of lines allocated, regardless of the physical distribution of lines per set. We ignore the effect of the actual distribution of cache lines on miss rate. Thus, set-associative caches are treated in the same way as fully associative caches, and the model is applicable to both types of caches. Section V validates this assumption by demonstrating the agreement between the model and a trace-driven cache simulation. Hence, we use the notation $M_A(x)$ to denote the miss rate of a process, process A, in a cache for which process A has a current allocation of x lines. The miss rate is also a function of the cache structure parameters, which include the number of sets, the set associativity, and the line size. For the purposes of this paper, we fix the structure of a cache, and vary the allocation of a process within that structure. Hence, we do not explicitly identify the cache-structure parameters on which $M_A(x)$ depends when we use this notation.

Now we examine the processes that generate the cache references. Assume that an address-reference stream is composed of two interlaced streams of addresses. One stream consists of instruction fetches, and the second stream consists of data fetches. The composite stream is an interleaving of the two streams so that its address references alternate between data and instructions. That is, the stream has the form $I, D, I, D, \ldots$, where I and D are instruction and data references, respectively. Each component stream has a known cache behavior given by a miss rate for that stream as a function of the cache memory allocated to the process. Let $M_I(x)$ be the miss rate for the I stream as a function of cache size x, and, similarly, let $M_D(x)$ be the miss rate for the data stream. We assume that both the instruction and data processes are stationary in time, so that the miss rates are not time varying functions.

Although this is a highly idealized model of the I and D processes, the results are not sensitive to the precise way in which the processes are interleaved, provided that the frequencies of the process accesses are equal and long strings of consecutive accesses of one type occur only rarely. The trace-driven validation has approximately equal frequencies of I and D references, but some strings of consecutive D references are hundreds of references long because of the execution of block-move instructions. We also assume that the miss-rate functions are convex functions of cache size. Later in the paper, we examine the case in which the frequencies of the two types of accesses are unequal.

To illustrate the use of the model on representative data, we use the published data from Smith [14] as the source of a running example. Smith's data are design target miss ratios for caches of varying total size and line size, and the data used appear in Figs. 1 and 2. The plots are the miss-rate functions for I and D streams averaged over many different workloads and instruction repertoires. The line sizes in those figures are measured in bytes per line. The log/log plots do not show the convexity of the curves, but the corresponding linear/linear plots demonstrate that these functions are convex except for data caches with 4-byte line sizes in the region between 1K and 4K bytes. We do not claim that Smith's data represent any specific cache design and workload. Therefore, the running example in this section based on Smith's data does not validate the model. The validation appears later.

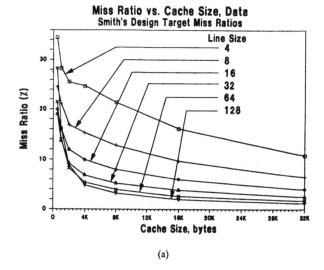

(a)

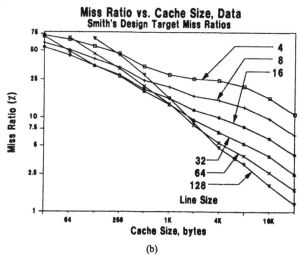

(b)

Fig. 1. Smith's design target miss ratios for data cache. (a) Lin/lin scaling. Line size in bytes. (b) Log/log scaling.

To determine the optimal fixed allocation of cache for the I and D streams, we find an expression for the misses in a period of time that has exactly T references, and find an allocation at which the derivative of the miss rate function goes to zero. Because we take derivatives, we assume that miss-rate functions $M_I(x)$ and $M_D(x)$ are continuous and differentiable, although, in reality, they are measurable only at discrete points on the x-axis. For this derivation we approximate the actual functions by continuous functions.

Assume that we must allocate C bytes of memory between D and I references so that the I stream uses x bytes of memory, and the D stream uses the remaining $C - x$ bytes of memory. Each cache partition is used exclusively by the process that owns it. What value of x achieves the overall minimum miss-rate?

The total number of misses in a time period with T references is the composite miss rate times the length of the period. Since we assume that I and D references occur with equal frequency in the interval T, the total number of misses

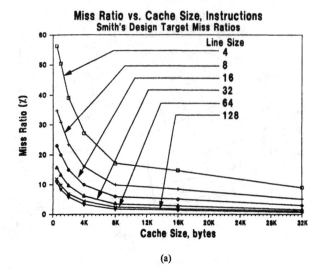

Miss Ratio vs. Cache Size, Instructions
Smith's Design Target Miss Ratios

(a)

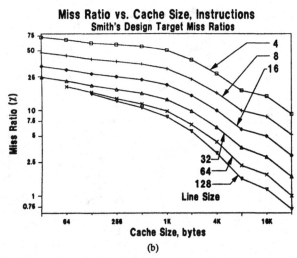

Miss Ratio vs. Cache Size, Instructions
Smith's Design Target Miss Ratios

(b)

Fig. 2. Smith's design target miss ratios for instruction cache. (a) Lin/lin scaling. (b) Log/log scaling.

is given by

$$\text{Total misses} = (M_I(x) + M_D(C - x))T/2. \quad (1)$$

To minimize the overall miss rate, we minimize the total misses given in (1) by setting the derivative of the right-hand side of (1) to 0, which occurs at a value of x that satisfies

$$\frac{dM_I(x)}{dx} = -\frac{dM_D(C - x)}{dx} = \frac{dM_D(y)}{dy}\bigg|_{y=C-x}. \quad (2)$$

By convexity of the miss-rate functions, such a point is indeed a minimum. If either of the miss-rate functions is strictly convex, the point is unique. If the D process occurs r times as frequently in the composite reference stream as the I process, then at the minimum miss-rate the derivative of M_D is weighted by a factor of r. To simplify the discussion, in the remainder of the paper we assume that the factor r is unity, but if not, it should appear as a multiplier of M_D or its derivative wherever they appear. The fact that the optimum allocation appears at a point where the miss-rate derivatives are equal

was observed by Ghanem [7] in the context of page faults in a system in which multiple processes compete for main memory. The report by Thiebaut, Stone, and Wolf [22] derived (2) for I and D processes competing for cache memory.

The notion of "optimal" is with respect to the ensemble of possible address-reference streams as represented by the miss-rate functions. Among the possible address-reference streams described by the miss-rate functions are some streams whose optimal allocations can be different from the optimal allocation of the ensemble.

As an example of the application of this theory, we use the miss-rate functions shown in Figs. 1 and 2. Note that the curves in Figs. 1 and 2 have a strong linear structure when plotted on a log/log graph. When using linear regression to fit a straight line to the data points, the quality of the fit as indicated by the correlation coefficient ρ varies between 0.942 and 0.982 for the instruction caches and between 0.987 and 0.999 for data caches. These measures show that the straight line fit captures the majority of the behavior of the miss ratio with respect to cache size for Smith's data. The second derivative of the fitted function is positive, and the fitted function itself is a strictly convex function of the cache allocation x.

For the running example in this section, we use Smith's data for a 32 K-byte cache and a line size of 32 bytes. The ρ measures for the curve fitted to line sizes of 32 bytes are 0.999 and 0.959, respectively, for data and instruction caches. A straight line fitted to the log/log data produces the following expressions for $M_I(x)$ and $M_D(x)$:

$$\log_{10} M_I(x) = 0.1177 - 0.11484 \log_2(x), \quad (3)$$

$$\log_{10} M_D(x) = 0.5570 - 0.14223 \log_2(x). \quad (4)$$

The logs of miss rates are base 10 and the logs of cache sizes are base 2 to simplify the interpretation of the display of the data. The precision required for the exponents in the model is greater than the precision of Smith's data because the curve fit is very sensitive to small variations of the exponent of the cache size. For the running example, we assume that this precision is available to us. Taking exponents in (3) and (4) produces

$$M_I(x) = 1.311 x^{-0.11484 \log_2 10}$$
$$= 1.311 x^{-0.38151}, \quad (5)$$

$$M_D(x) = 3.606 x^{-0.47249}. \quad (6)$$

Taking the derivatives of (5) and (6) yields

$$\frac{dM_I(x)}{dx} = 0.500 x^{1.38151}, \quad (7)$$

$$\frac{dM_D(x)}{dx} = -1.704 x^{-1.47249}. \quad (8)$$

The miss-rate derivatives in (7) and (8) are plotted in Fig. 3. Also, the argument of (8) in Fig. 3 is $C - x$ rather than x where C is 32K bytes. The crossing point of the curves is the point at which the miss-rate derivatives are equal. The optimal allocation occurs at the point where the I allocation $\hat{x}$ is approximately equal to 14 432 (to the nearest multiple

220

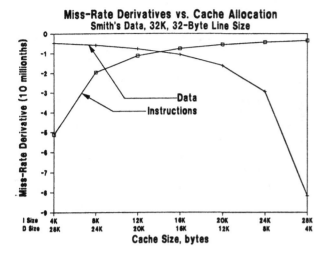

Fig. 3. Miss-rate derivatives as a function of cache allocation.

of 32). At this point the composite miss-rate is equal to the average of (5) and (6), which is

$$
\begin{aligned}
\text{Maximum Miss-Rate} &= (M_I(\hat{x}) + M_D(C - \hat{x}))/2 \\
&= (0.0340 + 0.0349)/2 \\
&\simeq 0.0344.
\end{aligned} \tag{9}
$$

This completes the discussion of the derivation of the optimal allocation of cache memory. In the next section we show that a conventional LRU-replacement policy has a most probable state that is not the optimal allocation of memory between the I and D references streams, but for the example data it produces very good allocations. It does extremely well for the trace-derived data in Section V.

III. THE MOST PROBABLE STATE FOR LRU REPLACEMENT POLICIES

Consider a cache managed by a normal LRU replacement policy. What is the most probable allocation of cache memory between the I and D processes and what is the average allocation between these processes? Are these distinct? Is either allocation equal to the optimal allocation? The development of this section begins with a simplified version of LRU replacement that we call *modified-LRU replacement*. Subsequently, the model is embellished to approximate LRU replacement more closely. For the running example, the modified policy produces better allocations than LRU allocations in some cases, and poorer allocations in many more. In all cases among these examples, LRU allocations are very close to optimal, but are always suboptimal.

To obtain the results of interest, consider the behavior of a program in execution over a long time. We assume that the allocation of memory between data and instructions varies randomly, and is controlled by the statistics of the miss rates $M_I(x)$ and $M_D(x)$, where x is the amount of memory allocated to the I and D processes, respectively. We define the state of the cache to be the number of bytes allocated to the I process. That is, a cache of size C is in state x if x bytes are allocated to instructions and $C - x$ bytes are allocated to data.

The state x of cache is a time varying random variable. To characterize the state of a cache we need to be able to quantify state probabilities, a most-probable allocation, and an average allocation. If the random process is stationary, then we assume that it has been running long enough for transients to have died out. If the random process is nonstationary but varying slowly, as is the most likely case for cache allocations, we assume that measurements of averages and probabilities have significance if they are done during periods when the processes are locally stationary. This permits us to define for each state x, the probability of being in state x, which is denoted as $S(x)$. Given that the state probabilities are well-defined, a cache is in statistical equilibrium during a period of time if at each state x the rate of entering state x from state $x + 1$ by decreasing the cache allocation is equal to the rate of leaving state x by increasing the allocation and causing the cache to enter state $x + 1$. Fig. 4 illustrates this model.

Consider a replacement policy in which an instruction miss increases the number of instructions in the cache unless there are no data lines to replace, and similarly a data miss increases the number of data lines in the cache unless there are no instruction lines to replace. The item replaced is the least recently used item from among the items eligible for replacement. We call this policy the *modified-LRU* policy. An LRU-replacement policy does not distinguish between data and instructions. For fully associative caches, modified-LRU and LRU replacement choose to replace the same item if the globally least recently used item happens to belong to the other process. For set-associative caches, they also choose to replace the same item when all of the items of a set belong to one process. For this reason, the two policies are less distinguishable as associativity diminishes from full associativity to direct mapped. The two policies are identical for direct-mapped caches.

For the modified-LRU policy, the rate at which a cache of size C in state x increases the allocation of of instructions is $S(x)M_I(x)$, and the rate at which state $x + 1$ decreases its allocation of instructions is $S(x + 1)M_D(C - (x + 1))$. Because the rates are in balance at equilibrium, we have for each x in the interval $0 \le x < C$,

$$
S(x)M_I(x) = S(x + 1)M_D(C - (x + 1)). \tag{10}
$$

The boundary conditions are $S(x) = 0$ for $x < 0$ and for $x > C$. The probability ratio of $S(x+1)/S(x)$ at equilibrium is given by

$$
\frac{S(x+1)}{S(x)} = \frac{M_I(x)}{M(C - (x+1))} \tag{11}
$$

for $0 \le x < C$. Equations (10) and (11) are quite accurate for fully associative caches, and become less accurate as associativity diminishes. For direct mapped caches, these equations should not be used, because the modified-LRU policy becomes identical to LRU as described later in this section.

Since both $M_I(x)$ and $M_D(x)$ are nonincreasing functions of x, $M_D(C - x)$ is a nondecreasing function of x. Therefore (11) is a nonincreasing function of x. This and the fact that $S(x)$ is greater than unity at $x = 0$ together imply that $S(x)$ is

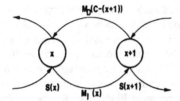

Fig. 4.   State diagram and state transitions for cache allocations.

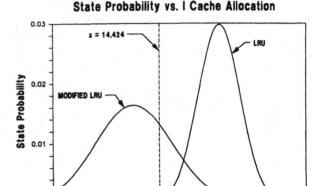

State Probability vs. I Cache Allocation

Fig. 5.   State probabilities for two replacement policies.

a unimodal function. That is, $S(x)$ grows monotonically with x to some peak value, and then diminishes monotonically with x for larger x. The peak occurs where the probability ratio in (11) falls below unity. The probability ratio might actually attain the value of unity at some state x, and it might be equal to unity over a contiguous interval of states. In this case, the peak value of $S(x)$ is attained at several contiguous values of x. Let $\hat{x}$ denote the largest value of x for which the following inequality holds:

$$M_I(x) \geq M_D(C - (x + 1)). \tag{12}$$

Then $S(\hat{x})$ is the maximum state probability over all x.

For the example of the prior section, Fig. 5 plots the probability of state x as a function of x for the two different replacement policies. The curve that describes the state probabilities for (11) is labeled "modified-LRU replacement." The calculation that produced the curves in Fig. 5 is a standard calculation in which the probability of each state is expressed as a multiple of $S(0)$ and the value of $S(0)$ is set to a value that forces the sum of the probability coefficients over all states to be equal to unity.

Although the modified-LRU probability function in Fig. 5 shows a distinct peak, in the region of the peak the probability function is almost constant from state to state. Thus, at the peak, the following approximation holds because $S(\hat{x}) \approx S(\hat{x} + 1)$:

$$M_I(\hat{x}) \simeq M_D(C - (\hat{x} + 1)). \tag{13}$$

Equation (13) indicates that $M_I(x) \approx M_D(C - (x + 1))$ at the most probable state, which is a statement regarding the equality of the miss-rate functions rather than a statement regarding the equality of the derivatives of the miss-rate functions. We can conclude that a replacement policy that produces an allocation that satisfies (13) is not optimal, in general, because this is not the equation satisfied by an optimal policy. Since an optimal allocation occurs when miss-rate derivatives are equal, a policy that produces an optimal allocation must somehow perform replacement as a function of observations of miss-rate derivatives. How this can be implemented efficiently is a subject of a separate paper by Stone, Thiebaut, and Wolf [17].

For the example problem, using the assumption that cache allocations are multiples of 32 bytes, we find that the most probable allocation state for modified-LRU replacement is cache state 13 916 whereas the optimal allocation state is cache state 14 432. The miss rate for state 13 916 is 0.03443. The miss rate for the optimal state, 14 432, is 0.03442. The probability of being in state x changes from 0.01632 to 0.01635 to 0.01637 to 0.01635 as x changes from 13 856 to

13 952 in steps of 32. Consequently, the probability is very nearly flat at this point, and the approximation in (13) is valid for the example. From the probability of being in state x as expressed in Fig. 5, we find the average allocation for that probability density to be 13 921. Since allocations have to be multiples of 32 bytes when the line size is 32 bytes, the most probable state is the state closest to the average allocation for this particular example. If the probability density is narrowly concentrated as is the case in Fig. 5, the average allocation tends to be the same as the most probable allocation.

Because we are interested in LRU replacement, we embellish the model slightly to reflect the behavior of LRU replacement. For LRU replacement, the probability that an instruction replaces a datum by an instruction is equal to the probability that an instruction reference is a miss times the probability that the LRU item is a datum. Regardless of whether a cache is fully associative, set associative, or direct mapped, we assume that the probability that the item to be replaced is a datum is equal to the proportion of data lines in the cache. This same assumption was made by Strecker [18] for characterizing the cache-fill rate. (The assumption is validated in Section V.) Thus, the probability that x increases to $x + 1$ is given by

$$\text{Prob}[x \text{ increases to } x + 1] = (1 - \frac{x}{C})S(x)M_I(x), \tag{14}$$

and, conversely, in state $x + 1$, the probability that the allocation decreases to x is

$$\text{Prob}[x + 1 \text{ decreases to } x]$$
$$= \left(\frac{x + 1}{C}\right)S(x + 1)M_D(C - (x + 1)). \tag{15}$$

When we equate these probabilities, which is the equilibrium condition, we find

$$\frac{S(x + 1)}{S(x)} = \frac{\left(1 - \frac{x}{C}\right)M_I(x)}{\left(\frac{x + 1}{C}\right)M_D(c - (x + 1))}. \tag{16}$$

The monotonicity discussion that follows (11) holds as well for (16). Thus the ratio in (16) is a nonincreasing function of

222

r Value	Optimal Policy		Model or Simulation	Modified-LRU Policy			LRU Policy		
	I-Cache Size	Miss Rate		I-Cache Size	Miss Rate	Standard Deviation	I-Cache Size	Miss Rate	Standard Deviation
0.2500	22,080	0.0321	Model	30,815	0.0404	350.3	23,127	0.0322	388.0
			Simulation	30,820	0.0403	305.8	23,045	0.0324	368.0
0.333	20,608	0.0328	Model	29,355	0.0387	456.5	21,719	0.0329	403.1
			Simulation	29,293	0.0384	324.0	21,529	0.0331	351.1
0.500	18,368	0.0337	Model	25,613	0.0363	626.9	19,571	0.0337	419.0
			Simulation	25,942	0.0364	494.1	19,379	0.0340	260.0
0.750	16,064	0.0342	Model	19,358	0.0347	761.8	17,294	0.0343	427.5
			Simulation	19,704	0.0344	321.7	17,169	0.0346	264.8
1.000	14,432	0.0344	Model	13,919	0.0344	779.6	15,645	0.0345	428.4
			Simulation	14,619	0.0344	373.0	15,530	0.0347	358.6
2.000	10,656	0.0340	Model	3,884	0.0374	525.0	11,773	0.0340	413.1
			Simulation	4,009	0.0372	320.2	11,679	0.0343	376.0
3.000	8,704	0.0333	Model	1,515	0.0404	340.0	9,704	0.0334	393.9
			Simulation	1,575	0.0402	319.0	9,487	0.0335	378.6
4.000	7,456	0.0327	Model	764	0.0423	240.1	8,368	0.0327	376.7
			Simulation	769	0.0425	238.7	8,186	0.0329	364.9

x, and the most probable allocation for the LRU policy occurs at the value $\tilde{x}$, which is the greatest value of x for which the following inequality holds:

$$\left(1 - \frac{x}{C}\right)M_I(x) > \left(\frac{x+1}{C}\right)M_D(C - (x+1)). \quad (17)$$

Because (17) is different from (12), the most probable allocation for LRU replacement is not the same as the most probable allocation for the modified-LRU replacement. We have no basis to judge which replacement strategies produce better allocations in general, but for the running example, the modified-LRU replacement policy produces a slightly better allocation.

For the running example, the most probable state for LRU replacement is 15 648, and the average allocation is 15 645. The miss rate for the most probable allocation is 0.03448 as compared to 0.03442 for the optimal allocation. These results together with simulation results are summarized in Table I. The table shows, respectively, the optimal allocation, the average modified-LRU allocation, and the average LRU allocation for various values of the ratio r. The most probable allocations are very nearly equal to the average allocations in all cases, and have been omitted from the table. With each allocation is the miss ratio at that allocation. The average miss ratios are very nearly equal to the tabulated miss ratios in every case, and have also been omitted from the table. The standard deviation shown in the table gives some idea of the width of the peak of the probability density function for the allocation.

The simulation data in Table I are drawn from simulations of the Markov process model of the cache allocation. The simulations are based on the statistics collected for 125 000 time steps after the system reached the expected steady-state allocation. They controlled the miss-rate function as a function

of allocation, and they also rigidly alternated between I and D processes. Thus the simulations confirm the analytical model, but do not necessarily model actual cache behavior.

The simulation results show what happens when two processes compete for cache and those processes have miss rates expressed by the functions $M_I(x)$ and $M_D(x)$. The LRU simulation used the weights x/C and $(1 - x/C)$ to control the probability of increasing or decreasing the cache allocation. The modified-LRU simulation forced the instruction allocation to increase on an instruction miss and forced the data allocation to increase on a data miss, and thus models the behavior of a fully associative cache, and approximates the behavior of set-associative caches. The observed most probable and average allocations for both LRU and modified-LRU simulations are within a standard deviation of the corresponding model allocations for the two policies obtained from the derivations above.

For the running example, because the optimal allocation occurs very close to the point of equal allocation of storage between D and I processes, the weights x/C and $(1 - x/C)$ are very nearly equal, and thus the weights do not shift the position of $\tilde{x}$ far from the position of $\hat{x}$. Fig. 6 gives a plot of relative miss rate as a function of allocation for the running example, and we see that miss rate is not very sensitive to the exact allocation. The instruction allocation can be anywhere between 8K and 20K, and still produce a miss rate that is not greater than 10% above the minimum. Since the absolute miss-rate is less than 5% in this range, a difference of less than 10% in miss-rate contributes to a performance difference no more than 0.5% across this range of allocations.

Recall that r is the ratio of data references to instruction references. The running example assumes $r = 1$. LRU produces better allocations for most values of r in Table I with the exception being $r = 1$.

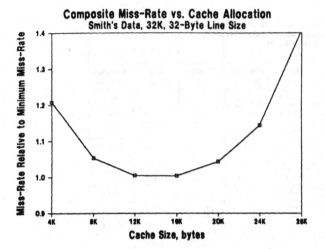

Composite Miss-Rate vs. Cache Allocation
Smith's Data, 32K, 32-Byte Line Size

Fig. 6. Relative miss-rate versus cache allocation.

The LRU policy introduces a weighting factor that tends to force allocations to be more nearly equal than does the modified-LRU policy. In our example, for $r = 1$ the correction factor moves the LRU allocation too close to an equal allocation, and leaves the modified LRU allocation closer to the optimal allocation. For the other values of r, the allocations produced by the modified-LRU policy tend to be fairly extreme, and the LRU policy introduces a correction factor that produces a more nearly balanced allocation that happens to be closer to the optimal allocation.

In general, we find that LRU replacement produces near-optimal allocations provided that:

1) $\tilde{x}$ is close to $C/2$ to reduce the effects of weights x/C and $(1 - x/C)$ in (17), and

2) the miss rate is not very sensitive to the cache allocation in the vicinity of the optimum allocation.

Both of these characteristics hold for the running example, and it is quite possible that they hold for most workloads. However, the near-optimality of the LRU allocation has not been thoroughly investigated for real workloads and real cache designs, so the question is still a matter of future research.

It is rather curious that a small change in the LRU replacement policy can produce a cache allocation that is markedly different than that produced by LRU replacement. Although we have shown that LRU replacement is not optimal, the point of this study is to determine why LRU replacement appears to be so close to optimal.

Occasionally, system designers consider an alternative of allocating a fixed amount of cache to instructions and a fixed amount to data, instead of letting data and instructions compete for cache. If the sole criterion for the allocation is to minimize the long-term miss rate, then the results above indicate that a fixed partition is probably not a good idea because, in practice, cache memory automatically becomes partitioned in a near-optimal way. However, other considerations may force cache to be partitioned, such as to support simultaneous access to data and instructions. The fact that an optimum allocation of memory occurs when the weighted miss-rate derivatives are equal should be helpful to designers of such caches.

IV. CACHE ALLOCATION DYNAMICS

Thus far, we have shown that that LRU replacement can produce near-optimal allocations. This suggests that the LRU policy is a good one to use in general for managing a cache. But LRU is not optimal, and there may some advantages in using a non-LRU policy. What are those advantages?

One possible reason for managing cache with a policy other than LRU replacement is to avoid the transient in cache allocation when the components of a composite address-reference stream change their characteristics. For example, the data process may change from low locality to high locality. As locality characteristics change, the optimum partition of cache between data and instructions changes, and the allocation of an LRU-managed cache moves to a new, hopefully, near-optimum allocation. If by some external means the cache-management algorithm is given the new steady-state allocation, it may be able to impose that allocation on cache immediately, and avoid the transient that a cache would normally experience.

This section shows that during the initial phase of a transient, cache allocation changes rapidly if the new allocation is quite different from the present allocation. The rate of change slows considerably as the current allocation comes close to the steady-state allocation, and in this region it may be possible to improve performance by using another strategy to hasten convergence. We outline a combinatorial approach for finding the steady-state allocation directly, which, if possible to implement in practice, can eliminate the transient.

The question at hand, then, is what is the dynamic behavior of memory allocation of an LRU-managed cache? We start by modeling the dynamics of modified-LRU replacement because it is somewhat simpler, and then embellish the model to deal with LRU replacement.

If we treat x, the amount of memory allocated to the I process, as a state variable of the cache then the rate at which the state of the cache changes is given by

$$\frac{dx}{dt} = \text{Rate of increasing } x - \text{Rate of decreasing } x. \quad (18)$$

For a cache managed by the modified-LRU replacement policy, we have the following differential equation that describes the dynamics of the cache allocation:

$$\frac{dx}{dt} = M_I(x) - M_D(C - x). \quad (19)$$

Strecker's model of cache dynamics captures the fill rate of a process in the absence of competition. Thus, his differential equation uses only the first term of (19), and his characterization of a cache transient is very different from the dynamics of cache allocation in the presence of competition.

For the running example, we substitute (5) and (6) into (19) and we find

$$\frac{dx}{dt} = 1.311x^{-0.38151} - 3.606(C - x)^{-0.47249} \quad (20)$$

There is no neat closed-form solution for this differential equation. But it can be solved numerically, and its solution is plotted in Fig. 7. To find the dynamics for LRU replacement, we have to include the weights x/C and $1 - x/C$. Equation (19) becomes

$$\frac{dx}{dt} = \left(1 - \frac{x}{C}\right)M_I(x) - \left(\frac{x}{C}\right)M_D(C - x). \quad (21)$$

After substituting (5) and (6) in (21), we obtain

$$\frac{dx}{dt} = 1.311\left(1 - \frac{x}{C}\right)x^{-0.38151} - 3.606\left(\frac{x}{C}\right)(C - x)^{-0.47249} \quad (22)$$

The solution to this equation is also plotted in Fig. 7. For comparison purposes, the dynamics produced from the simulations are also plotted, and they track the numerical predictions reasonably well. The simulations, of course, are subject to statistical variations that are not captured by the dynamic model. For this simulation, as time increases beyond the right edge of the graph, the allocation varies over a range centered on the long-term asymptote.

Note that both replacement policies produce rapid convergence when the current value of x is far from steady state but the convergence becomes much slower as x nears the steady-state region. The maximum convergence rate is $rM_D(x)/(1 + r)$ and $M_I(x)/(1 + r)$ when D and I, respectively, are the minority and majority cache owners, and D references occur r times as frequently as I references. This follows because the minority owner increases cache occupancy with every miss and the majority owner does not alter occupancy on its misses.

If the current steady-state allocation is not optimal, can a cache manager move quickly to an optimal allocation to avoid the transient in allocation? We assume that a cache manager is given the parameters of the competing processes, and the goal is to find the optimal allocation without solving (16) numerically. The following discussion presents an efficient solution to this problem. It treats the more general situation in which there are N processes competing for cache, not just two processes. It relies on the fact that at an optimal allocation, all of the miss-rate derivatives are equal. This is a generalization of the result given in (2), and it is proved in Thiebaut, Stone, and Wolf [22], but it follows directly from the arguments used to derive (2) for two competing processes.

To introduce the allocation problem for N competing processes, suppose they are to use a cache of size C. Let M_i denote the miss rate for process i as a function of allocated cache. Suppose that each process i generates P_i references, giving a total of

$$T = \sum_{i=1}^{N} P_i \quad (24)$$

references in all. If each process i is allocated a portion of the cache of size C_i, then the overall miss rate is then given by

$$\sum_{i=1}^{N} P_i M_i(C_i)/T. \quad (25)$$

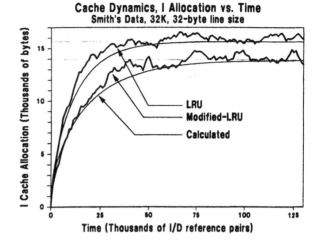

Fig. 7. Dynamic behavior of computed and simulated cache allocations.

We wish to minimize this function subject to the constraint that

$$\sum_{i=1}^{N} C_i = C \quad (26)$$

by giving or taking cache away from a competing process. The least possible overall miss rate occurs when miss-rate derivatives with respect to cache size are equal.

We assume that the cache miss-rate for each process is a (decreasing) strictly convex function of cache size. Thus the functions $F_i(C) = P_i M_i(C)/T$, the fraction of the total miss rate attributed to process i, are also (decreasing) strictly convex functions of cache size C allocated to a process. We wish to minimize the sum of N such functions. The values of the functions $F_i(x)$ are computed for discrete integer values of x in the range $0 \leq x \leq C$.

This problem fits into the category of separable convex resource allocation problems. A greedy algorithm due to Fox [4] solves such problems in time $O(N + C \log N)$. While we base our discussion on this work, we note that the subsequent results due to Galil and Megiddo [1979] and Frederickson and Johnson [6] are more efficient, the latter having complexity $O(\max(N, N \log(C/N)))$. This bound was shown by Frederickson and Johnson to be optimal to within a constant multiplicative factor. We would therefore recommend that an implementation of this approach actually be based on the Frederickson and Johnson algorithm.

Ibaraki and Katoh [10] treat resource allocation problems of this type in depth, and provide excellent background for the optimization problem treated here. Also note that generalizations of the optimization algorithm described above have been solved and employed by Tantawi, Towsley, and Wolf [19], by Wolf, Dias, and Yu [24], and by Wolf, Iyer, Pattipati, and Turek [25] to solve other optimization problems in computer science.

Define for each $1 \leq i \leq N$ and each $1 \leq j \leq C$ the "marginal return" $g_{i,j} = F_i(j - 1) - F_i(j)$. This function is essentially the first-difference discrete analog of the negative of the miss-rate derivative for process i with cache allocation j. Note that for each i, the values $g_{i,1}, \cdots, g_{i,C}$ are positive

225

and nonincreasing because the miss rate of the process is a decreasing convex function of allocated cache. The trick is to allocate cache, chunk by chunk, to the collection of processes to maintain the miss-rate derivatives as equal as possible as cache is added. Fox's algorithm can be defined inductively as follows:

1. *Initialization*: Set $C_1 = \cdots = C_N = 0$.
2. *Induction Step*: Given the kth assignment of values to the C_i, and noting that it satisfies

$$\sum_{i=1}^{N} C_i = k, \tag{27}$$

the induction step produces a new assignment satisfying

$$\sum_{i=1}^{N} C_i = k + 1 \tag{28}$$

by increasing C_i to $C_i + 1$ for some index i. The step selects the first value of i such that

  a. $C_i < C$, and
  b. g_{i,C_i+1} is maximum.

3. That is, the step finds the value of the marginal return function g_{i,C_i} as each C_i is incremented in turn, and then retains the value of C_i for which the marginal return is greatest. All other C_i values remain unchanged.

After C steps through the algorithm, the values $C_1, \cdots, C_N$ form an optimal assignment of cache to the competing processes such that process i receives C_i units of cache, and the total amount of cache allocated is C units.

The algorithm amounts to computing a Cth smallest number in an $N \times C$ matrix whose rows are nondecreasing. This is a special case of the so-called "selection problem," and is solved, as noted above, with considerably greater speed using the algorithm proposed by Frederickson and Johnson [5]. Details may be found there or in Ibaraki and Katoh [10].

This completes the discussion of allocation strategies for interlaced processes. The next section presents the validation of the several assumptions in the model as obtained from actual trace data.

V. Experimental Validation

The model presented in Sections II through IV relies on a number of assumptions that need to be validated. This section shows that a trace-driven simulation behaves almost precisely as predicted by the model. While Smith's data are useful in examples, the published data were created by taking a composite of many workloads and cache structures. The trace-driven validation in this section demonstrates that the predictions of the model hold true for the cache behavior for a specific workload and cache structure.

The trace used comes from a single processor in a two-processor IBM System/370 architecture complex executing a multiprogrammed workload. The workload is commercial, and contains a mixture of user code and operating-systems code. The trace contains over 18 000 000 references in total. It was created with the intention of being representative of

MISS RATIO VS. CACHE SIZE

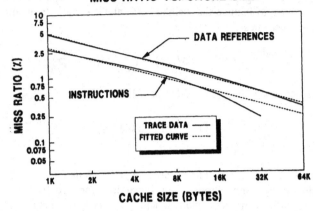

Fig. 8. Miss-ratios as a function of cache size for trace data.

workloads encountered in typical environments and has been used internally in IBM as a representative of such workloads.

The model requires functions $M_I(x)$ and $M_D(x)$. To make the validation as similar as possible to the running example, the cache structure was chosen to be 32 K-bytes, 4-way set-associative, with a line size of 32 bytes. The variation of miss rate with cache size was obtained by varying the number of sets while fixing the line size to 32 bytes and the associativity to 4-way.

The data that characterizes these functions appears in Fig. 8. The analysis of miss rates was performed by simulating the I or the D process in isolation. During the period when the cache was not fully initialized, the trace simulation filled the cache without recording miss-rate statistics. The simulation was continued without recording statistics until the reference count reached the next multiple of 100 000, and at that point the recording of miss-rate statistics began. This eliminated the bias caused from initialization misses in the simulation. Because the I process did not touch all of the lines in a cache of size 32 K-bytes, this cache was declared to be filled when all but 10 lines (out of 1024) were initialized. In this case, 6.4 million references were traced after the initialization point, and in all other cases the number of references traced after initialization exceeded 8 million.

Note that the miss-rate curve for data misses is well approximated by a straight line on a log/log scale. The miss-rate curve for instruction misses is straight for most of its length, but the data point for 32K lies below the straight-line trend. To fit the curves to the data shown, we used all of the points for data caches and dropped the point for the instruction cache of size 32K. The instruction occupancy does not reach 32K in normal operation, and, hence, the region of interest for instruction occupancy is the region of the curve through which the straight-line trend is drawn. The equations for the fitted curves in Fig. 8 are $M_I(x) = 1.996x^{-0.60147}$ and $M_D(x) = 4.072x^{-0.63165}$. The respective ρ's are 0.994 and 0.984, which indicate that the fits are excellent.

The total number of references observed was approximately 16 million, and the ratio r was 0.9606. The model for LRU replacement embodied in (16) predicts an average allocation

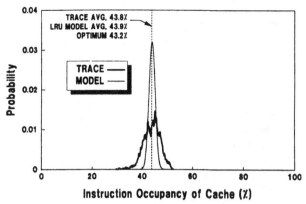

Fig. 9. Cache occupancy probability for trace and model data.

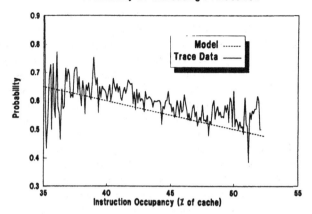

Fig. 10. The probability of increasing instruction occupancy as a function of I cache allocation.

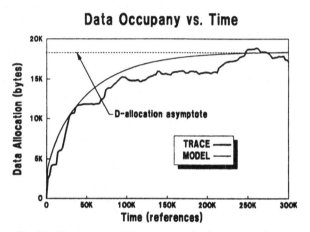

Fig. 11. The dynamics of data occupancy for the trace experiment.

of 14 392 bytes and standard deviation of 400 bytes as plotted in Fig. 9. This compares with an observed average allocation of 14 365 bytes and a standard deviation of 1100 bytes for the trace data. The optimum allocation for these parameters is 14 150 bytes. The model for modified-LRU replacement produces an average allocation of 11 364 with a standard deviation of 564 bytes.

Note that the model for LRU replacement and the observed behavior of the cache give excellent agreement in their average values. The model variance is somewhat less than the observed variance of cache occupancy. Also note that LRU replacement produces an allocation that is essentially optimal.

The wider variance of the trace-driven process is attributed in part to long sequences of references of one type, particularly to long sequences of data references. Nevertheless, the predicted average allocation for LRU replacement lies almost directly where the actual average allocation appears, because the trace-driven allocations lie in a narrow range, even though that range is somewhat larger than the allocation range of the model.

The respective miss rates for the data depicted in Fig. 9 are 0.0074 observed for the trace, 0.0072 for the LRU model, 0.0072 for the optimal allocation, and 0.0073 for the modified LRU-replacement policy.

Equation (16) reflects the assumption that the probability of increasing an allocation is proportional to the fraction of cache currently occupied by the competing process. The trace-driven experiment gathered data that confirmed this hypothesis as well. This is shown in Fig. 10. The data plotted shows the actual probability of increasing allocation as a function of current allocation, and the straight line shows the model. For occupancies less than 36%, there were fewer than 10 misses observed in each state, and thus the data are very noisy and not statistically significant. Above 36%, the data plotted in the graph follow the model closely except that they fall slightly above the model. However, the error in modeling is similar for data and instructions, and these errors tend to cancel in (16) because one error is a factor in the numerator and the other is a factor in the denominator. Hence, the model is an accurate predictor of cache allocation for LRU replacement in

spite of the small inaccuracy. At this writing, it is not known what phenomenon causes the discrepancy between the model predictions and the observations shown in Fig. 10.

Fig. 11 shows the dynamics of data cache occupancy starting with a minimum allocation of data (10 lines). The dotted curve is the numerical solution of the dynamic model, and the horizontal line is the asymptote, which is the average allocation for LRU replacement. Note the good agreement between the mathematical model and actual trace behavior. The data were gathered by simulating a cache on a trace, using just the instruction references from the trace and ignoring the data references until 1014 out of 1024 lines were in the cache. Then the simulation treated both instruction and data references, and recorded the data occupancy in cache as a function of time measured in references.

The validation in this section demonstrates that cache occupancy of instructions and data can be predicted accurately from parameters for the individual processes, and that for this particular experiment, LRU replacement produced an allocation that was essentially optimal. The next section treats the case in which references by competing processes are not tightly interlaced.

VI. Multiprogramming Replacement Strategies

In this section we revisit the allocation problem, but this time consider what happens when processes compete sequentially for cache instead of being tightly intertwined. An example of the problem occurs in multiprogrammed computers in which each process obtains exclusive access of the processor for a time quantum of length Q. For our purposes, we assume that there are two processes with miss rates $M_1(x)$ and $M_2(x)$, respectively. Each process makes precisely Q memory accesses in its time quantum.

How good is an LRU replacement policy in this situation? Because one process runs after the other under an LRU replacement policy, while process 2 is running each cache miss discards items older than any items touched by process 2 in its current quantum. This would usually be items that belong to process 1. Conversely, each miss during the execution of process 1 discards an item belonging to process 2 whenever this is possible.

While this strategy is basically good, let us examine the quality of the decision to replace an item belonging to process 1 when process 2 suffers a cache miss. The miss rate of process 2 improves by an amount $dM_2(x)$, but, if we assume that process 1 will reload the item displaced with probability p, then for each item belonging to process 1 that is discarded, a fraction p of a miss will be recorded when process 1 resumes control.

If a cache is small compared to the working set of process 2, the gain in adding a new item belonging to process 2 outweighs the cost of the miss that will be incurred when process 1 regains control of the machine. Since LRU replacement continually adds to the allocation for process 2, for small caches LRU replacement is the algorithm of choice.

But suppose that the cache is very large, and is large enough to hold the full working set of process 2 as well as lines belonging to process 1. The marginal reduction in misses obtained by increasing the cache allocation of process 2 is the product of the incremental change in miss rate due to the increased allocation times the number of references remaining in the time quantum. That is, if q references remain in the time quantum, then we expect to save $q\,dM_2(x)/dx$ misses by increasing the allocation of memory to process 2. But we must also account for the p additional misses when changing back to process 1, because process 1 will reload the cache line displaced by increasing the allocation of process 2 with probability p. Thus the net reduction in misses is equal to $q\,dM_2(x)/dx - p$. The threshold $q(x)$ is defined to be the remaining time at which the marginal gain is 0, and this is given by

$$q(x) = \frac{p}{dM_2(x)/dx}. \tag{23}$$

If the remaining time in a quantum is less than $q(x)$ for a cache allocation of x, then the replacement policy should not increase the cache allocation of process 2. The replacement policy should replace the least recently used eligible line of process 2, and retain the lines of process 1 currently in cache. If the remaining time exceeds $q(x)$, then the replacement policy

should replace the least recently used lines of process 1, and thereby increase the allocation of process 2.

Clearly, if the marginal gain is very small or the time quantum is nearly over, then it is better to leave items of process 1 in cache because they will be likely to be referenced again in the near future. Small processor caches, typical of those in computers available through the end of the 1980's, rarely hold much more than the working set of a process. In such caches very little of the last run process is left in cache as the currently running process nears the end of its quantum. A non-LRU policy cannot easily benefit by retaining items belonging to process 1 as the time quantum for process 2 runs out. This situation changes when caches become much larger than the working sets of typical processes. With caches in the early 1990's approaching 1 megabyte in size, the possibility of improved performance makes the non-LRU policy an attractive candidate for closer study.

As an example of the use of $q(x)$ in a replacement policy, consider Fig. 10, which plots $q(x)$, the inverse of the miss-rate derivative, for the I-cache miss-rate derivatives plotted in Fig. 3. Fig. 12 shows what the threshold would be for a hypothetical workload and cache structure whose miss rates fit Smith's data for a line size of 32 and for $p = 1$. This is the threshold below which additional cache should not be allocated to the running process. In the middle range of the allocation, the remaining references in the time quantum should be on the order of 1 million for a process to continue to receive additional cache memory. Assume that a process governed by the miss-rate function of Fig. 2 initiates execution and quickly builds a cache allocation of 4K bytes. If the remaining quantum has 100 000 references or more, the allocation should increase, and in fact, under an LRU replacement policy it increases quickly. At some point depending on the time remaining, the miss-rate derivative is sufficiently small that no additional cache should be allocated to the running process. In Fig. 12, the additional allocation should stop when the current allocation is roughly half the cache if less than 1 million references remain. When the allocation is roughly 28K, additional cache allocation should cease if less than 2 million references remain in the quantum. If the initial time quantum is 1 million references, a non-LRU replacement policy will limit the cache allocation to roughly half of cache.

If an interrupt process takes over the cache for a brief period, a non-LRU replacement policy will grant the process only a small initial allocation, and sharply curtail its acquisition of cache beyond this amount because its quantum is so short. This tends to give the interrupt process a small region of cache to hold its working set, and to retain the working set of the interrupted process in anticipation of the future use of that portion of cache memory.

VII. Multilevel Caches

Next, let us consider a common multilevel cache design, in which caches are arranged in hierarchical fashion. The fastest and smallest cache is at level one, the next fastest and smallest is at the level two, and so on. An example of a study of this type of hierarchy appears in Baer and Wang

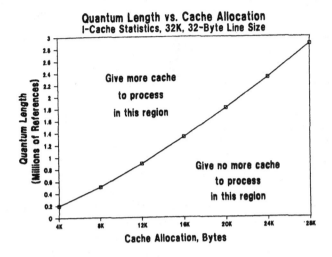

Fig. 12. The quantum-length threshold as a function of allocation.

[1]. In this section we shall extend our solution of the optimal cache-allocation problem to handle competing processes in multilevel hierarchies. An early formulation of a different cache-allocation problem for a cache-memory hierarchy is due to Chow [3].

For simplicity of exposition, we shall again assume that we are given the address streams of two competing processes, one corresponding to instructions and one to data, and that these occur with equal frequency. Furthermore, we shall attempt to allocate memory optimally for the two processes in each level of a two-level cache hierarchy. The extension to arbitrary numbers of competing processes, arbitrary relative frequencies, and arbitrary numbers of cache levels is straightforward. We shall also assume that the line sizes of the caches at each level are equal.

An illustration of a two-level cache hierarchy is given in Fig. 13. The first-level cache sees the full address stream produced by the processor, and passes only its misses to the second-level cache. The second-level cache responds to the residual stream, and sends to main memory only the references of its input stream that produce misses in this cache. Assume that the first-level cache has size c and the second-level cache has size C. In each level of the cache, we would like to use the results of the previous sections to allocate memory optimally. However, in order to deal with the second-level cache, we need to understand how the size of the first-level cache affects the miss rate in the second-level cache. Fortunately, this is quite easy, and we proceed as follows.

Suppose that a fraction $\alpha = \alpha(c, C)$ of the lines appearing in the first-level cache also appear in the second-level cache. Then the total number of distinct lines in the cache is given by $C + (1 - \alpha)c$. The global miss-rate of the combined cache on the full input stream is thus $M(C + (1 - \alpha)c)$, while the local miss-rate of the first-level cache alone is $M(c)$. (The terms *local* and *global* miss rates are due to Hennessy and Patterson [8].) A miss in the combined cache occurs when the reference misses in both levels. In other words, if $M(c, C)$ denotes the miss rate of the second-level cache with respect to the input stream that it receives, then $M(c)M(c, C) = M(C + (1 - \alpha)c)$,

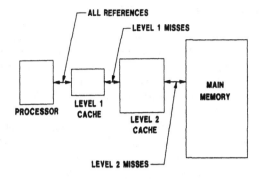

Fig. 13. A memory system with two levels of caches.

or, equivalently,

$$M(c, C) = M(C + (1 - \alpha)c)/M(c). \tag{29}$$

In general, the lines of the first-level cache are nearly completely contained in the much larger second-level cache, so that $\alpha \simeq 1$, or $1 - \alpha \simeq 0$. (In fact, we could force α to be 1 by imposing a cache inclusion condition.) Thus, the approximation

$$M(c, C) \simeq M(C)/M(c) \tag{30}$$

is very good.

Now let t denote the access time for a hit in the first-level cache of size c, T denote the total access time for a hit in the second-level cache of size C, and τ denote the total access time for main memory. By definition we have $t < T < \tau$, and in practice we can assume that $t \ll T \ll \tau$. We can also assume that $c \ll C$. For any partition $c = c_1 + c_2$ of the first-level cache, we can compute local miss rates $M_1(c_1)$ and $M_2(c_2)$. Given this first-level partition and any partition $C = C_1 + C_2$ of the second-level cache, we can compute global miss rates $M_1(c_1, C_1)$ and $M_2(c_2, C_2)$. Thus, the overall access time is given by

$$
\begin{aligned}
&T(c_1, c_2, C_1, C_2) \\
&= \frac{1}{2}\Bigg[\sum_{i=1}^{2} (1 - M_i(c_i))t + \sum_{i=1}^{2} M_i(c_i)(1 - M_i(c_i, C_i))T \\
&\quad + \sum_{=i1}^{2} M_i(c_i)M_i(c_i, C_i)\tau \Bigg].
\end{aligned}
\tag{31}
$$

We want to minimize this function subject to the constraints $c_1 + c_2 = c$ and $C_1 + C_2 = C$. This can be done by repeated application of the algorithm given in Section IV, but there is a simplification that greatly limits the search effort. The simplification relies on the presence of good lower and upper bounds.

To derive a tight upper bound, note that in the region where $\alpha_i(c_i, C_i) \simeq 1$, (26) reduces to

$$T_1 = t + \frac{1}{2}(T - t)\sum_{i=1}^{2} M_i(c_i) + \frac{1}{2}(\tau - T)\sum_{i=1}^{2} M_i(C_i). \tag{32}$$

In fact, T_1 provides an upper bound for T over the entire feasible region, since $\tau > T$. Minimizing (27) is easy, since the first summand is a constant, and $t < T < \tau$ implies that the second and third summands are positive. The problem simply decouples into two disjoint separable convex resource-allocation problems, one for the second summand and one for the third. Both problems are solved by the technique given in Section IV. Since, in practice, α will almost surely be close to 1 in this region, the optimal solution for (27) derived in this manner will be an excellent approximation to the optimal solution for (26).

The lower bound is obtained by investigating the behavior of (26) under the assumption $\alpha = 0$. Equation (26) reduces to

$$T_2 = t + \frac{1}{2}(T - t)\sum_{i=1}^{2} M_i(c_i) + \frac{1}{2}(\tau - T)\sum_{i=1}^{2} M_i(C_i + c_i). \quad (33)$$

T_2 differs from T only in its third summand. We claim that T_2 provides a lower bound for T over the entire feasible region, since $\tau > T$. (This optimization problem does not quite decouple, but given any solution to the problem associated with the second summand, optimal or not, one can solve the problem with respect to the third summand, which is again a separable convex resource-allocation problem.) The corresponding exact reduction associated with T in (26), namely,

$$T = t + \frac{1}{2}(T - t)\sum_{i=1}^{2} M_i(c_i) + \frac{1}{2}(\tau - T)\sum_{i=1}^{2} M_i(C_i + (1 - \alpha_i(c_i, C_i)), c_i), \quad (34)$$

differs from T_1 and from T_2 only in its third summand. This summand does not give rise to a convex optimization problem, but is tightly bound by two problems that are. By utilizing these bounds one can restrict the search for the overall optimal solution to (26) to a neighborhood very close to the optimal solution of (27).

As an example of the application of this theory, we again use the miss-rate functions shown in Figs. 1 and 2. Specifically, we use an instruction stream whose miss rate is described by (5) and a data stream whose miss rate is described by (6). Assume a line size of 32 bytes, with $t = 1, T = 10$, and $\tau = 20$. Assume that the first-level cache is of size 8K bytes, so that $c = 256$ lines, and the second-level cache is of size 64K bytes, so that $C = 2048$ lines. The optimal partitioning occurs at $c_1 = 104$ lines, $c_2 = 152$ lines, $C_1 = 924$ lines, and $C_2 = 1124$ lines, and yields $T = 1.8171$. Fig. 14 shows a contour plot of the various partitioning choices. By contrast, a cache simulation shows that LRU yields a time of $T = 1.8189$, so that, once again, LRU is proven to be quite robust. The contour line for the LRU average access-time is shown as the innermost contour line in Fig. 14.

VIII. SUMMARY AND CONCLUSIONS

The major finding of this study is that the LRU replacement policy is good, but not optimal. We have shown that a modified-LRU replacement produces different allocations of data and instructions, and in some cases the modified policy produces marginally better performance than the LRU

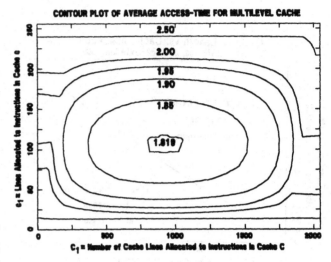

Fig. 14. A contour plot of average access-time as a function of cache allocations in a multilevel cache.

policy. For tightly interlaced address streams generated by two competing processes, the examples in the paper indicate that the miss rates produced by LRU replacement are only negligibly different from the miss rates produced by an optimal cache partition. Because all of the evidence for the quality of LRU is based on examples rather than on firm bounds, we cannot be sure that LRU replacement is as near-optimal in practice as it has turned out to be for the examples used in the paper. Until bounds on the near-optimality of LRU replacement are available, it is an open question whether there is a realizable alternate policy that produces better allocations. While we cannot justify the implementation of non-LRU replacement policies for the examples given in the paper, it may be necessary to partition cache for other reasons. If so, the techniques of the paper are useful in determining the relative sizes of the partitions by showing how to achieve the least miss rate for partitions within a fixed chip area, a fixed board area, or for a fixed total cost.

Research questions that remain open include the following:

1) Is there a simple bound on the near optimality of LRU replacement with regard to its ability to allocate cache between data and instruction processes?

2) Is there a simple replacement policy that actually achieves the optimum allocation between data and instructions?

3) How can the transient associated with cache allocation be reduced without using detailed knowledge about the miss-rate functions?

4) For multiprogrammed systems, what is a practical means for implementing a limit on cache allocation? Does such a scheme produce sufficient benefit to justify its implementation?

5) For cache in a multiprogramming environment, it is clear that there is no justification for using a strategy other than LRU when there is little possibility for retaining lines belonging to other processes in the cache. As caches become large, this is no longer true. But how

large do caches have to be for non-LRU replacement to be worthwhile?

Although LRU replacement is the cache-management algorithm of choice today, the paper has pointed out potential opportunities for improving performance by implementing a non-LRU strategy. On the other hand, the paper has shown that an LRU strategy is robust, near-optimal, and difficult to outperform in practice. Before adopting a non-LRU strategy, it is essential to explore the questions above to determine what strategies are most useful and what their benefits might be.

ACKNOWLEDGMENT

The authors are indebted to the referees for their perceptive comments and suggestions which led to material improvements in this paper. The authors would also like to thank Dr. T. Puzak of the IBM T. J. Watson Research Laboratory for access to the traces used in the simulation.

REFERENCES

[1] J. L. Baer and W.-H. Wang, "On the inclusion properties of multilevel-cache hierarchies," in *Proc. 15th Annu. Int. Symp. Comput. Architecture*, IEEE Cat. 88CH2545-2, June 1988, pp. 73–80.
[2] L. Belady, "A study of replacement algorithms for a virtual-store computer," *IBM Syst. J.*, vol. 5, no. 2, pp. 78–101, 1966.
[3] C. K. Chow, "On optimization of storage hierarchy," *IBM J. Res. Develop.*, vol. 18, pp. 194–203, May 1974.
[4] B. Fox, "Discrete optimization via marginal analysis," *Management Sci.*, vol. 13, pp. 909–918, 1966.
[5] G. N. Frederickson and D. B. Johnson, "The complexity of selection and ranking in $X + Y$ and matrices with sorted columns," *J. Comput. Syst. Sci.*, vol. 24, pp. 197–208, 1982.
[6] Z. Galil and N. Megiddo, "A fast selection algorithm and the problem of optimum distribution of effort," *J. ACM*, vol. 26, pp. 58–64, 1979.
[7] M. Z. Ghanem, "Dynamic partitioning of the main memory using the working set concept," *IBM J. Res. Develop.*, pp. 445–450, Sept. 1975.
[8] J. Hennessy and D. A. Patterson, *Computer Architecture: A Quantitative Approach.* San Mateo, CA: Morgan Kaufman, 1990.
[9] M. D. Hill, "A case for direct-mapped caches," *IEEE Comput. Mag.*, vol. 21, no. 12, pp. 25–40, Dec. 1988.
[10] T. Ibaraki and N. Katoh, *Resource Allocation Problems: Algorithmic Approaches.* Cambridge MA: M.I.T. Press, 1988.
[11] D. B. Kirk, "Process dependent static cache partitioning for real time systems," in *Proc. Real Time Syst. Symp.*, 1988, pp. 181–190.
[12] S. Przybylski, M. Horowitz, and J. Hennessy, "Characteristics of performance optimal multilevel cache hierarchies," in *Proc. 16th Annu. Int. Symp. Comput. Architecture*, 1989, pp. 114–121.
[13] A. Smith, "Cache memories," *ACM Comput. Surveys*, vol. 14, no. 3, pp. 473–530, Sept. 1982.
[14] A. J. Smith, "Line (block) size choice for CPU cache memories," *IEEE Trans. Comput.*, vol. C-36, no. 9, pp. 1063–1075, Sept. 1987.
[15] J. E. Smith and J. R. Goodman, "Instruction cache replacement policies and organizations," *IEEE Trans. Comput.*, vol. C-34, no. 3, pp. 234–241, Mar. 1985.
[16] K. So and R. N. Rechtschaffen, "Cache operations by MRU change," *IEEE Trans. Comput.*, vol. 37, no. 6, pp. 700–709, June 1988.
[17] H. S. Stone, D. F. Thiebaut, and J. L. Wolf, "Improving disk cache hit-ratios through cache partitioning," *IEEE Trans. Comput.*, vol. 41, no. 6, pp. 665–676, 1992. The paper originally appeared as IBM Research Report RC 15072, Oct. 26, 1989.
[18] W. Strecker, "Transient behavior of cache memories," *ACM Trans. Comput. Syst.*, vol. 1, no. 4, pp. 281–293, Nov. 1983.
[19] A. N. Tantawi, D. Towsley, and J. L. Wolf, "An algorithm for a class-constrained resource allocation problem," in *Proc. 1988 ACM Sigmetrics Conf.*, May 1988, pp. 253–260.
[20] D. F. Thiebaut, "On the fractal dimension of computer programs and its application to the prediction of the cache miss ratio," *IEEE Trans. Comput.*, vol. 38, no. 7, pp. 1012–1026, July 1989.
[21] D. F. Thiebaut and H. S. Stone, "Footprints in the cache," *ACM Trans. Comput.*, vol. 5, no. 4, pp. 305–329, Nov. 1987.
[22] D. F. Thiebaut, H. S. Stone, and J. L. Wolf, "A theory of cache behavior," IBM Res. Rep. RC 13309, Nov. 10, 1987.
[23] M. K. Vernon, R. Jog, and G. S. Sohi, "Performance analysis of hierarchical cache consistent multiprocessors," in *Perform. Distributed and Parallel Systems*, Proc. IFIP TC 7/WG 7.3, 1989, pp. 111–126.
[24] J. L. Wolf, D. M. Dias, and P. S. Yu, "An effective algorithm for parallelizing sort merge joins in the presence of data skew," in *Proc. 2nd Int. Symp. Databases in Parallel Distributed Syst.*, pp. 103–115, 1990.
[25] J. L. Wolf, B. R. Iyer, K. R. Pattipati, and J. Turek, "Optimal buffer partitioning for the nested block join algorithm," in *Proc. 7th Int. Data Eng. Conf.*, 1991, pp. 510–519.

An Accurate and Efficient Performance Analysis Technique
for Multiprocessor Snooping Cache-Consistency Protocols

Mary K. Vernon

Edward D. Lazowska
John Zahorjan

Department of Computer Science
University of Wisconsin-Madison
Madison, WI 53706

Department of Computer Science
University of Washington
Seattle, WA 98195

Abstract

A number of dynamic cache consistency protocols have been developed for multiprocessors having a shared bus interconnect between processors and shared memory. The relative performance of these protocols has been studied extensively using simulation and detailed analytical models based on Markov chain techniques. Both of these approaches use relatively detailed models, which capture cache and bus interference rather precisely, but which are highly expensive to evaluate. In this paper, we investigate the use of a more abstract and significantly more efficient analytical model for evaluating the relative performance of cache consistency protocols. The model includes bus interference, cache interference, and main memory interference, but represents the interactions between the caches by steady-state mean collision rates which are computed by iterative solution of the model equations.

We show that the speedup estimates obtained from the mean-value model are highly accurate. The results agree with the speedup estimates of the detailed analytical models to within 3%, over all modifications studied and over a wide range of parameter values. This result is surprising, given that the distinctions among the protocols are quite subtle. The validation experiments include sets of reasonable values of the workload parameters, as well as sets of unrealistic values for which one might expect the mean-value equations to break down. The conclusion we can draw is that this modeling technique shows promise for evaluating architectural tradeoffs at a much more detailed level than was previously thought possible. We also discuss the relationship between results of the analytical models and the results of independent evaluations of the protocols using simulation.

1. Introduction

High-speed local memory that operates as a cache for a larger or more distant main memory can significantly increase the effective execution rate of a processor. When this technique is used in a general-purpose shared-memory MIMD multiprocessor, the problem of maintaining consistency among the data stored in multiple caches arises.

A number of dynamic cache consistency protocols have been developed for the case where the multiprocessor interconnection

network is a shared bus. In this case, each cache controller monitors the traffic on the bus, and takes appropriate actions to maintain data consistency. The simplest protocol is a write-through protocol, in which all writes to a cache are written through to main memory, causing other caches that have the data to update or invalidate their copies [Smit82]. In 1983, Goodman proposed a copy-back multi-cache consistency protocol that has since become known as the Write-Once protocol [Good83]. Since that time, a number of more sophisticated protocols have been proposed. These include the Synapse protocol [Fran84], the Illinois protocol [PaPa84], the RWB protocol [RuSe84], the Dragon protocol [MCCr84], and the Berkeley protocol [KEWP85].

The relative performance of the above protocols has been studied extensively using simulation [ArBa86]. In another approach, the key modifications to the Write-Once protocol that have been included in each of the five successor protocols were identified, and the contribution of each to overall performance was evaluated [VeHo86]. This second study used an analytic technique called Generalized Timed Petri Nets (GTPNs) [HoVe85]. (Results of the GTPN model agreed very well with results of independent evaluations in the various protocol proposals.)

Both of the above studies used relatively detailed models, which capture cache and bus interference rather precisely, but which are highly expensive to evaluate. In this paper, we investigate the use of a more abstract and significantly more efficient analytical model for evaluating the relative performance of the cache consistency protocols. We use the abstract model to reproduce and extend the results in [VeHo86]. The model includes bus interference, cache interference, and main memory interference, but represents the interactions between the caches by steady-state mean collision rates which are computed by iterative solution of the model equations.

One might expect the more abstract mean-value model to be less accurate than the detailed GTPN model. However, we show that the speedup estimates obtained from the mean-value model are surprisingly accurate. The results agree with the speedup estimates of the GTPN model to within 3%, over all modifications studied and over a wide range of parameter values. The validation experiments include sets of reasonable values of the workload parameters, as well as sets of unrealistic parameter values for which one might expect the mean-value equations to break down. The conclusion we can draw is that this modeling technique shows promise for evaluating architectural tradeoffs at a much more detailed level than was previously thought possible.

Greenberg and Mitrani have also recently developed an analytical model of the Write-Through, Write-Once, and Dragon protocols [GrMi87]. Our mean-value model of cache, main memory, and bus interference is more comprehensive and more firmly grounded in queueing network theory than their model. Furthermore, we are able to consider deterministic bus access times for cache block transfers, rather than the exponential access times required in their model.

Our program of research in computer system performance analysis is supported by the National Science Foundation (Grants No. DCR-8352098, DCR-8451405, CCR-8619663, and CCR-8703049), the Naval Ocean Systems Center, U S WEST Advanced Technologies, the Washington Technology Center, Digital Equipment Corporation (the Systems Research Center and the External Research Program), CRAY Research, the AT&T Foundation, Bell Communications Research, Boeing Computer Services, Tektronix, Inc., the Xerox Corporation, and the Weyerhauser Company.

However, our workload model is less sophisticated than their workload model and the workload model in [ArBa86]. We comment on this further in Section 2.3.

The remainder of this paper is organized as follows. Section 2 contains a brief review of the Write-Once protocol, the four modifications to Write-Once that have been proposed, and the workload model in [VeHo86], which is also used in this paper. Section 3 presents our mean-value analytical model of Write-Once and the protocol modifications. Section 4 compares the estimates obtained using the mean-value model with estimates obtained using the GTPN model, and with estimates published in independent studies, for a variety of parameter settings. This section also contains some new results, including the asymptotic performance of the modifications. Section 5 contains the conclusions of this work.

2. Background

The multiprocessor configuration assumed for the snooping cache consistency protocols is illustrated in Figure 2.1. Each processor is connected directly to its local cache. Each cache is connected through the shared bus to main memory and to all other caches.

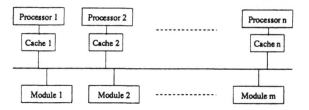

Figure 2.1: Multiprocessor Configuration

2.1. System Assumptions

The system assumptions made in the model developed in this paper are those in [VeHo86]. These assumptions are very similar to the assumptions in [ArBa86], and include the following.

A processor executes for a variable number of cycles, assumed to be exponentially distributed with mean τ, between memory requests. Useful execution is not overlapped with fetching data from memory. Thus, once the request is made, the processor is idle until the request is satisfied. The cache takes one unit of time to satisfy the processor request, either immediately, or following a required bus transaction.

Bus transactions may be one of five types: *read*, *read-mod* (i.e., read-with-the-intent-to-modify), *invalidate*, *write-word*, or *write-block*. The first and second request types are issued when processor read and write requests miss in the cache, respectively. The third or fourth request type is used by the consistency protocol when a processor write request hits in the cache, and the cache block is clean (i.e., unmodified). The fifth request type is used to write a modified data block back to main memory.

Bus requests are served in random order in the GTPN model [VeHo86], but are assumed to be scheduled in first-come first-served order in the mean-value model developed in this paper. Both scheduling disciplines have the same mean waiting time, and thus yield the same predicted speedup measures. Bus requests have priority over processor requests for service in a cache. Dual directories are assumed, so processor requests are only delayed by bus requests that require some action on the part of the cache.

The main memory is divided into m modules, where m is the cache block size, assumed to be four in this paper. Main memory latency is assumed to be three cycles.

Cache block states are assumed to be defined by three bits of state information. (Not all bits are used in exactly the same way by each protocol.) The first bit denotes whether the block is *valid* or *invalid*. The second bit indicates whether the cache knows that it has the only copy of a block, i.e., state *exclusive*, or does not know that it has an exclusive copy, i.e., state *non-exclusive*. The third bit (*wback/no-wback*) denotes whether or not the processor must write back the block when it is purged from the cache. Note that this third bit indicates whether or not the block is modified relative to main memory.

2.2. Review of Snooping Cache Protocols

Below we review briefly the Write-Once protocol, and each of the key modifications that have been proposed to improve performance. In some cases we comment on the potential advantages and disadvantages of the proposed modifications. The reader is referred to [ArBa86], [VeHo86], and the original papers for further detail.

Write-Once

A bus read request loads the cache block in state *non-exclusive* and *no-wback*. A bus read-mod request invalidates all other copies of the block, and loads the block in state *exclusive* and *wback*.

The key idea in the Write-Once cache consistency algorithm is that the *first* time a processor writes a word to a *non-exclusive* block in its cache, the word is written through to main memory. When the word is broadcast on the bus, any cache containing the block invalidates its copy. The write operation changes the state of the block to *exclusive* and *no-wback*.

Writes to a block in state *exclusive* in the cache are written only locally, changing the state to *wback*. If another cache requests the block, indicated by a read or read-mod operation on the bus, a cache containing the block in state *wback* interrupts the bus transaction and writes the block to main memory, thereby updating the contents of main memory before main memory supplies the requested data. The state of the block changes to *no-wback* if the bus request is of type read.

In this protocol, if a cache contains a block in state *wback*, it is the only cache containing the block.

Modification 1

In the first of the proposed modifications, a cache containing a copy of a block requested by a read or read-mod bus operation must raise a *shared* line on the bus. If this line is not raised, the cache block can be loaded in state *exclusive* in the requesting cache. Writes to this block by the requesting cache will not require bus operations to notify other caches. (However, note that writing the block to main memory will be required when the block is purged from the cache.)

This modification reduces the total number of bus operations required by an amount that depends on 1) the workload characteristics and 2) which, if any, of the other three modifications are also implemented. If this is the only modification to the Write-Once protocol, the number of operations required is reduced in the following case: 1) a requested block is not resident in another cache, and 2) the block is written more than once during its tenure in the cache. Modification 1 is included in the Illinois, Dragon, and RWD protocols.

Modification 2

In the second of the proposed modifications, a cache that has a requested block in state *wback*, supplies the copy directly to the requesting cache and does not update main memory. This saves memory traffic and bus operations in the case that the requesting cache modifies the block before purging it.

If the bus operation is a read request, the supplying cache takes responsibility (sometimes called *ownership*) for writing back the block when it is purged. In other words, the supplying cache sets the state to *non-exclusive* and *wback*, and the requesting cache sets the state to *non-exclusive* and *no-wback*, if the bus request is a read

233

operation. Modification 2 is included in the Berkeley and Dragon protocols. The Illinois protocol assumes the data is written to memory and supplied to the requesting cache in the same bus operation, which is another optimization similar to this modification.

Modification 3

In the third modification to Write-Once, a bus *invalidate* operation is performed, instead of the write-word operation, on the first write to a non-exclusive data block. This potentially reduces memory traffic, and eliminates the need for "partial write" operations on the bus. There is potentially a reduction in bus traffic in the case that *write-word* requires two bus cycles and *invalidate* requires one cycle. On the other hand, there is the potential for increased bus traffic with this modification, since the write-word operation sometimes takes the place of writing the entire block to main memory when the block is purged. Modification 3 is included in all five protocols proposed as improvements to Write-Once.

Modification 4

The final modification allows multiple copies of a cache block to remain valid even in the presence of write operations. In this case, all writes to a block in state *non-exclusive*, are broadcast on the bus. All caches update their copies, and main memory is updated by the broadcast write. Cache blocks remain in state *no-wback*.

Note that this modification alone reduces the Write-Once protocol to a write-through protocol. Thus, this modification is only practical when implemented together with modification 1. Modification 4 is included in the RWB and Dragon protocols. Furthermore, the RWB protocol includes the capability to switch between invalidation and broadcast write operations.

Summary

We have presented the above modifications, except as noted, as independent modifications to the Write-Once protocol. The modifications can be implemented in any combination, if the following observation is noted. If modifications 3 and 4 are implemented together, the effect is to broadcast all write operations to non-exclusive blocks, but not to update main memory. In this case, as in modification 2, some cache has to take responsibility for writing back the block when it is purged. We assume the cache performing the broadcast takes this responsibility.

2.3. Our Workload Model

The workload model we use to evaluate the above protocols is the same as the workload model in [VeHo86]. This model was based on the model in [DuBr82], which views the memory reference stream as the merging of two streams, one for private and shared read-only blocks, and one for shared-writable blocks. The first stream was decomposed into two substreams in [VeHo86]. All three streams are treated probabilistically in our model. The probabilistic treatment is very similar to the treatment of the private stream in [ArBa86]. However, less locality is assumed in the shared-writable stream.

The following basic parameters are specified for our workload model:

- $p_{private}$, p_{sro}, and p_{sw}, are the probabilities that a memory reference is to a private, shared read-only (sro), and shared-writable (sw) block, respectively.

- $h_{private}$, h_{sro}, and h_{sw}, are the hit rates for private, sro, and sw streams, respectively.

- $r_{private}$ (r_{sw}) is the probability that the processor request is a read request, given that the reference is of type private (sw).

- $amod_{private}$ ($amod_{sw}$) is the probability that a reference to a private (sw) block that hits in the cache finds the block already modified.

- $csupply_{sro}$ ($csupply_{sw}$) is the probability that a copy of a requested sro (sw) block exists in at least one other cache.

- $wb_{csupply}$ is the probability that the cache supplier contains the data in state *wback*.

- rep_p (rep_{sw}) is the probability that a private (sw) block must be written back to memory when it is purged.

From these parameters, the following model inputs can be computed [VeHo86]:

- p_{local}, the probability that a memory request can be satisfied locally in the cache,

- p_{bc}, the probability that the memory request requires a broadcast write or invalidation,

- p_{rr}, the probability that the memory request requires a remote read or read-mod operation,

- t_{read}, the mean bus access time for a remote read or read-mod operation, which includes main memory write-back by another cache and/or by the requesting cache, if necessary,

- $p_{cswpwb|rr}$, the probability that another cache must write the block to main memory in response to a remote read request, and

- $p_{reqwb|rr}$, the probability that the requesting cache must write back a replaced block on a remote read operation.

We note that our probabilistic treatment of the shared data reference stream treats the relationship between system size and *actual* sharing of data more approximately than the workload models in [ArBa86] and [GrMi87]. The workload submodel of both the mean value model in this paper and the GTPN model should be improved to treat the shared references more similarly to the model in [GrMi87]. However, this should not change the conclusions of this paper with regard to the relative accuracy of the mean value model. Furthermore, we show in Section 4 that results of the model agree well with independent evaluations of the protocols, in spite of the approximate workload representation.

3. Mean Value Models of the Cache Consistency Protocols

In this section, we develop a mean-value model of cache, memory, and bus interference for the Write-Once protocol. We then briefly discuss the iterative model solution technique, and the required model modifications for each of the four potential improvements outlined in the previous section. The results of the mean value models are compared with the results of the corresponding GTPN models in Section 4.

The idea in Mean Value Analysis, which has been used with great success to solve queueing network models of computer system performance, is to construct a set of equations that compute the mean values of various performance quantities in terms of the mean values of various model inputs — frequently resorting to iteration when a direct calculation is not possible. What is important to bear in mind (and will be discussed in Section 3.2) is that our mean value approach to analyzing multi-cache consistency protocols yields a dramatic improvement in the time required to obtain performance measures from the model — a reduction from hours of computing to seconds of computing for large numbers of processors — with a negligible loss in accuracy, as will be shown in Section 4.

The notation used in this section is defined in the development of the equations.

3.1. The Write-Once Protocol

We first consider response times for memory requests, then mean bus waiting time, memory interference, and cache interference.

Response Time Equations

The mean total time between memory requests issued by a processor, R, is the sum of the processor execution time between requests, τ, the weighted mean delays for each of the three ways in which memory requests are handled by the cache (locally, broadcast write-word, or remote read), and the cache supply time ($T_{supply} = 1.0$):

$$R = \tau + R_{local} + R_{broadcast} + R_{RemoteRead} + T_{supply}. \tag{1}$$

The weighted mean response time for a memory request that can be handled locally in the cache, R_{local}, is the product of the probability that the request can be handled locally, the mean number of consecutive bus requests that delay the cache response to the processor request ($n_{interference}$), and the mean number of cycles that each interfering bus request requires in the cache ($t_{interference}$):

$$R_{local} = p_{local} \times n_{interference} \times t_{interference}. \tag{2}$$

The calculation of $n_{interference}$ and $t_{interference}$ is discussed in the subsection on cache interference below.

The mean response time for broadcast write operations is estimated as the sum of the mean waiting time for the bus (w_{bus}), the mean waiting time for the main memory module (w_{mem}), and the fixed bus access time for the write-word operation ($T_{write} = 1.0$). Thus, the weighted mean response time is given by:

$$R_{broadcast} = p_{bc} (w_{bus} + w_{mem} + T_{write}). \tag{3}$$

Equations for w_{bus} and w_{mem} are developed in the following subsections on mean bus waiting time and memory interference, respectively.

Finally, the mean response time for a remote read (or read-mod) operation, is approximately the sum of the mean bus waiting time, and the mean bus access time for the read operation (t_{read}):

$$R_{RemoteRead} = p_{rr} (w_{bus} + t_{read}). \tag{4}$$

Memory interference is not an important factor in the response time for remote reads. This is due to the fact that main memory latency is assumed to be fixed and small (i.e., 3.0 cycles). Thus, the mean wait for memory after the request is served by the bus, is negligible. Note that t_{read} includes the mean time for one and possibly a second and third cache block transfer on the bus, as defined in Section 2.3.

Mean Bus Waiting Time

To complete the response time calculations in equations (1)-(4), we need to compute w_{bus}, w_{mem}, $n_{interference}$, and $t_{interference}$. The equations for w_{bus} are developed next.

An arriving request will wait for the mean remaining bus access time (i.e., the mean *residual life*, $t_{res,bus}$) of the request in service, plus one mean bus access time (t_{bus}) for every other request in the queue when it arrives. Let $\overline{Q}_{bus}$ represent the mean number requests found in the queue by the arrival, and $p_{busy,bus}$ represent the probability an arriving request finds the bus busy. The equation for w_{bus} is thus:

$$w_{bus} = (\overline{Q}_{bus} - p_{busy,bus}) t_{bus} + p_{busy,bus} \, t_{res,bus}. \tag{5}$$

Applying techniques from Product Form queueing networks [LZGS84] in an approximate way, the mean queue length seen by an arriving request is estimated by the steady state mean queue length in the system if the requesting cache were removed. This is approximately the product of the average fraction of time each cache spends in the bus queue, and the number of other caches ($N-1$):

$$\overline{Q}_{bus} = (N-1) \frac{R_{bc} + R_{rr}}{R}. \tag{6}$$

Bus utilization is estimated by the product of the number of caches in the system, and the fraction of time each cache uses the bus:

$$U_{bus} = N \times \frac{p_{bc} (w_{mem} + T_{write}) + p_{rr} \times t_{read}}{R}, \tag{7}$$

from which we can estimate the probability that an arriving request finds the bus busy:

$$p_{busy,bus} = \frac{U_{bus} - \dfrac{U_{bus}}{N}}{1 - \dfrac{U_{bus}}{N}}. \tag{8}$$

Finally, the mean bus access time, and mean residual life of the request in service, are given by the following weighted sums:

$$t_{bus} = \frac{p_{bc}}{p_{bc} + p_{rr}} (T_{write} + w_{mem}) + \frac{p_{rr}}{p_{bc} + p_{rr}} t_{read}, \tag{9}$$

and

$$t_{res,bus} = \frac{p_{bc} (T_{write} + w_{mem})}{p_{bc} (T_{write} + w_{mem}) + p_{rr} \, t_{read}} \times \frac{T_{write} + w_{mem}}{2}$$
$$+ \frac{p_{rr} \, t_{read}}{p_{bc} (T_{write} + w_{mem}) + p_{rr} \, t_{read}} \times \frac{t_{read}}{2}. \tag{10}$$

Memory Interference

The mean time that a broadcast write operation waits for the main memory module (w_{mem}) is the product of the probability that the request finds the module busy ($p_{busy,mem}$) and the mean remaining memory latency. Letting d_{mem} represent the mean total memory latency, assumed to be 3.0 in this paper, the mean memory waiting time is given by:

$$w_{mem} = p_{busy,mem} \times \frac{d_{mem}}{2}. \tag{11}$$

The probability the request finds the module busy is computed from the utilization of the memory module, in the same way that $p_{busy,bus}$ was estimated from the bus utilization. The utilization of the memory module is estimated as the fraction of time each cache uses the memory module, times the number of caches in the system:

$$U_{mem} = N \times \frac{1}{4} \times \frac{[p_{bc} + p_{rr} (p_{csupwb|rr} + p_{repwb|rr})] \times d_{mem}}{R}. \tag{12}$$

Note that the above equation assumes four memory modules, but can easily be modified for some other number of modules.

Cache Interference

The cache interference submodel involves computing $n_{interference}$ and $t_{interference}$.

The mean number of consecutive bus requests that interfere with a processor request, $n_{interference}$ is computed assuming, approximately, that the maximum number of requests that can interfere with the processor request is equal to the number of requests in the bus queue when the processor request is issued (i.e., $\overline{Q}_{bus}$).

Using the model input parameters, and assuming that a block supplied by a cache is equally likely to be supplied by any of the other caches, it is straightforward to compute the following probabilities (see Appendix B): 1) the probability, p, that a cache must service a bus request, and 2) the probability, $p' < p$, that the cache must service the bus request for the entire duration of the bus transaction. An example of an event of the second type is a broadcast write operation on a block contained in the cache. An example of an event of the first type, but not of the second type, is a read-mod operation where the cache has the block in state *no-wback*. The cache must respond by invalidating the block, which is of shorter duration that the bus transaction.

$n_{interference}$ is easily computed from p and p', as follows:

$$n_{interference} = \bar{Q}_{bus}\, p^{\bar{Q}_{bus}-1}\, p + \sum_{k=1}^{\bar{Q}-1} k\, p'^{k-1}[\,(p-p') + p'\,(1-p)\,]$$

$$= p\left[\frac{1-p'^{\bar{Q}}}{1-p'}\right]. \tag{13}$$

$t_{interference}$, the mean cache interference time per request that blocks a processor request, is computed from model inputs in the same way that p and p' are computed (see Appendix B).

3.2. Solution of the Model Equations

The above equations contain cyclic interdependencies, in which R depends on the mean bus and memory waiting times, which in turn depend on R. Thus, the equations must be solved iteratively. We do so, starting with all waiting times set to zero. Solution of the equations converged within 15 iterations in all experiments reported in this paper, yielding results in under one second of cpu time, independent of the size of the system analyzed. In contrast, the time to solve the GTPN model increases exponentially with the number of processors analyzed. With ten processors, the GTPN model requires on the order of one hour of CPU time on a DEC MicroVAX-II with eight megabytes of memory. We note that simulation is equivalently expensive.

3.3. Models of the Four Protocol Modifications

The changes required in the mean-value model for each of the protocol modifications in Section 2.2, are a subset of the required changes in the GTPN model [VeHo86], and mostly involve changes in computing the model inputs.

For modification 1, the calculation of $p_{broadcast}$ no longer includes a term for write hits to private blocks. This term is instead added to p_{local}. The equation for p, the probability of cache interference, must be modified, since write hits to private blocks are no longer broadcast (i.e., p increases slightly). Furthermore, the input parameter rep_p must be increased (from 0.2 to 0.3 in the workload of [VeHo86]), which causes a small increase in t_{read}. For modification 2, the calculations of $t_{contention}$ no longer includes the term for cache supply write-back, and the input parameter rep_{sw} increases (from 0.5 to 0.6 in the workload of [VeHo86]), causing a slight increases in t_{read} and a slight decrease in p'. For modification 3, the term for broadcast writes is removed from equation (12), and the probability rep_{sw} increases, by an amount assumed to be comparable to the effect of modification 2. Finally, for modification 4, changes are required in the calculation of p_{bc}, p_{local}, and p.

4. Results and Accuracy of the Mean Value Models

Speedup is computed from the mean-value models using the formula: $N \times \dfrac{\tau + T_{supply}}{R}$. The input parameter values specified in [VeHo86] are reproduced in Appendix A. The mean value analysis speedup estimates for these parameter values are plotted in Figure 4.1 and tabulated in Table 4.1 for three protocols: 1) the Write-Once protocol, 2) a protocol that includes modification 1 only, and 3) a protocol that includes modifications 1 and 4. Speedups for modifications 2 and 3 are nearly indistinguishable from the results for the protocols without these modifications, and are thus not shown. Results for each of the three levels of sharing considered in the GTPN study (1%, 5%, and 20%), are given for the first two protocols. For the third protocol, only the 5% sharing curve is drawn, since the other two curves are nearly identical (see Table 4.1(c).)

Below we discuss the results of our analysis, the accuracy of the mean value analysis estimates as compared with the GTPN results, and the relationship between the results in this study and results of independent evaluations of the protocols.

4.1. Model Results

As discussed in the next section, the mean-value analysis results are nearly identical to the results of the GTPN model. Furthermore, we are able to analyze the speedup for arbitrarily large systems using the MVA equations. (Solution of the GTPN model is impractical for more than ten or twelve processors.) Table 4.1c includes the MVA results for 100 processors, to verify that the performance does not change appreciably beyond twenty processors, for each curve shown in the figure. The asymptotic results indicate a greater potential gain for modification 4 than was evident from previous results for ten processors.

The conclusions we draw from figure 4.1 are as follows. Modification 1 is clearly advantageous for the workloads we have studied. Modification 4 is more advantageous as system size and the level of sharing increase, assuming this modification substantially increases the value of h_{nw}, as we have assumed in our input parameter values. Modifications 2 and 3 have little effect for the workload we investigated. We comment on this further in Section 4.4.

4.2. Agreement Between the Mean Value Analysis and GTPN Results

In this section we compare the performance estimates obtained from the mean-value equations with estimates obtained from the (expensive) solution of the detailed steady-state equations of the GTPN model.

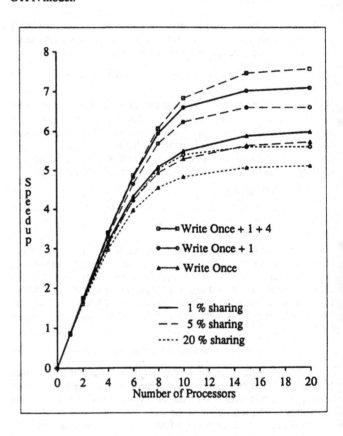

Figure 4.1: The Mean Value Analysis Performance Results

Table 4.1(a) contains the numerical speedup estimates for the Write-Once protocol derived from the two models. Results for each of the three levels of sharing considered in the GTPN study are shown in the table. We find the speedup estimates of the mean value analysis are in excellent agreement with the speedup estimates of the GTPN for each sharing level. Nearly all MVA estimates are within 1% of the GTPN estimates, and the maximum relative error is 2.6%.

We also find very good agreement between the models (i.e., typically less than 5% relative error) for other performance measures, such as bus utilization and mean bus waiting time, which are not shown in the table. For example, in the 6-processor case, the GTPN and MVA estimates of bus utilization are approximately 81% and 77%, respectively. We note, however, that the approximate MVA equations generally underestimate bus utilization and overestimate memory and cache interference relative to the GTPN model.

Table 4.1(b) compares the speedup results from the MVA and GTPN models for the Write-Once protocol plus modification 1 of Section 2.2. Here again we find excellent agreement between the estimates, with most MVA results within 1% of the GTPN values, and a maximum relative error of 4.25%.

We investigated the accuracy of the MVA model further by validating it against the GTPN for each of the other three enhancements. In every case, the MVA model estimates agreed nearly exactly with the GTPN results. We thus conclude that, for the workload parameters in this set of experiments, the MVA model is as accurate as the more detailed GTPN model for assessing the relative merits of all of the proposed modifications to Write-Once. Table 4.1(c) further illustrates the point by giving the estimates from both models for the Write-Once protocol with modifications 1 and 4.

These preliminary results indicate not only that the MVA model is quite accurate, but also that it is *as suitable as the GTPN for evaluating the potential performance gains of the various protocol modifications*. This result is surprising, given that the distinctions among the protocols are quite subtle. This is the first result known to the authors that indicates mean-value queueing analysis techniques may be applied to the evaluation of rather detailed architectural trade-offs. The computational efficiency of the MVA approach allows a wide range of design alternatives to be interactively investigated.

4.3. Accuracy of the Model Under Stress Tests

In the next set of experiments, we modified the workload parameters, in some cases assigning unrealistic values, in an attempt to find cases where the MVA equations are inaccurate. In particular, we experimented with cases that have a large amount of cache

Table 4.1: Comparison Between MVA and GTPN Estimates

(a) Speedups for the Write Once Protocol

Sharing Level	Solution Method	Number of processors								
		1	2	4	6	8	10	15	20	100
1%	MVA	0.86	1.68	3.17	4.33	5.08	5.49	5.88	5.98	6.07
	GTPN	0.86	1.69	3.20	4.41	5.21	5.60			
5%	MVA	0.855	1.67	3.12	4.23	4.93	5.30	5.63	5.72	5.79
	GTPN	0.855	1.67	3.14	4.30	5.04	5.37			
20%	MVA	0.84	1.61	2.97	3.97	4.55	4.83	5.07	5.12	5.16
	GTPN	0.84	1.62	3.02	4.07	4.67	4.87			

(b) Speedups for Enhancement 1

Sharing Level	Solution Method	Number of processors								
		1	2	4	6	8	10	15	20	100
1%	MVA	0.875	1.73	3.37	4.82	5.94	6.59	7.02	7.09	7.04
	GTPN	0.875	1.73	3.37	4.84	6.00	6.72			
5%	MVA	0.87	1.71	3.30	4.65	5.68	6.23	6.59	6.64	6.60
	GTPN	0.86	1.71	3.31	4.71	5.76	6.31			
20%	MVA	0.85	1.63	3.08	4.22	5.03	5.40	5.63	5.66	5.62
	GTPN	0.85	1.65	3.15	4.39	5.19	5.58			

(c) Speedups for Enhancements 1 and 4

Sharing Level	Solution Method	Number of processors								
		1	2	4	6	8	10	15	20	100
1%	MVA	0.88	1.75	3.40	4.90	6.06	6.83	7.49	7.58	7.56
	GTPN	0.88	1.75	3.41	4.91	6.13	6.91			
5%	MVA	0.88	1.75	3.40	4.87	6.06	6.83	7.46	7.57	7.57
	GTPN	0.88	1.75	3.41	4.92	6.16	6.98			
20%	MVA	0.88	1.74	3.35	4.75	5.90	6.70	7.47	7.64	7.70
	GTPN	0.88	1.75	3.39	4.87	6.09	6.93			

interference, since cache interference is represented much less precisely in the MVA model than in the GTPN.

In one experiment, we set the values of rep_p, rep_{sw}, and $amod_{sw}$ to 0.0, $csupply_{sro}$ and $csupply_{sw}$ to 1.0, p_{sw} to 0.2, and hit_{sw} to 0.1. The speedup estimates of the MVA model agreed, within 5% relative error, with the speedup estimates in the GTPN. This was the case in all of the experiments we performed in attempting to stress-test the MVA model. It appears that the MVA model is quite robust.

4.4. Agreement Between the Mean Value Model and Independent Evaluation Studies

It is generally difficult to compare results of the MVA and GTPN models with results of independent protocol evaluation studies, for two reasons. First, the parameter values used in experiments reported in the literature are not always fully specified. Second, if a different workload model is used, the mapping between parameters in the different workload models is generally not straightforward. In spite of these difficulties, we are able to compare our results with the results of independent studies in three cases.

The first comparison we are able to make is in the estimate of *processing power* for the protocol with modifications 1,2, and 3. Processing power is defined as the sum of the processor utilizations, over all processors in the system. Processing power can be computed from the MVA results by taking $\frac{\tau}{R} \times N$. Alternatively, processing power can be computed from the product of speedup and $\frac{\tau}{\tau + T_{supply}}$, which is $\frac{2.5}{3.5}$ or approximately 0.7143 for the workload assumptions in this paper. In either case, we compute a processing power of 4.32 for the protocol with modifications 1, 2, and 3, nine processors, 5% sharing, and parameter values equal to those in the appendix. The GTPN predicts a processing power of 4.1 for this case. Both results agree reasonably well with results of the simple analytical model in [PaPa84], for cache block size equal to four.

The second comparison we are able to make is in the estimate of relative bus utilization for Write-Once and a protocol with modifications 2 and 3. In this case, if the probability that a block is unmodified on a write hit decreases significantly in the protocol with modification 2, the MVA models predict a 10% increase in bus utilization for the Write-Once protocol, 99% sharing, and total loads which do not saturate the bus. This result agrees well with the trace-driven simulation results of Katz et. al. [KEWP85].

The final comparison we make is to the simulation results of Archibald and Baer's study [ArBa86]. An important discrepancy between the results of that study and the results in Figure 4.1 is in the performance estimates for modification 1 relative to modification 2. The simulation study shows a nearly equal performance benefit for each of these modifications. (For example, the Berkeley and Illinois protocols have nearly equal performance in most of their experiments.) Careful examination of their parameter values reveals that the value they use for $amod_p$ in most of their experiments is substantially higher than the value we assumed. If we set $amod_p$ to 0.95, as in many of their experiments, we also find the performance of modification 2 to be roughly equal to the performance of modification 1 for the 1% sharing case in Figure 4.1.

The agreement between the mean-value estimates and estimates from independent studies further increases our confidence in the accuracy of the MVA model.

5. Conclusion

Efficient, accurate tools for studying the performance implications of architectural design decisions are critically important.

In this paper we consider a family of dynamic cache consistency protocols for shared bus multiprocessor systems. The performance of these protocols has been studied extensively using detailed simulation models and Generalized Timed Petri Net models. These modeling techniques, while accurate, have running times measured in hours on 1 MIPS processors, for models of systems of only modest size.

We have devised a new modeling approach, based upon the specification and the iterative solution of sets of equations that express the mean values of interesting performance measures in terms of the mean values of certain model inputs. The equations are intuitive, in the sense that each can be explained simply in terms of the mechanics of the architecture being modeled. The solution technique is extremely efficient, requiring on the order of one second of CPU time for systems of arbitrary size. This makes it possible to explore a large design space quickly and interactively. The results are essentially as accurate as those of the previously existing techniques, which are dramatically more expensive.

We believe that we have convincingly demonstrated the surprising result that simple and efficient models can be used to study the performance of architectural alternatives that differ from one another in only quite subtle ways. The model can be put to good use for evaluating the protocols more thoroughly – all that is needed are workload measurement studies to aid in the assignment of parameter values.

The demonstration of the accuracy of our model is the principal thrust of our paper. Along the way, we have used the model to reproduce and extend the results in [VeHo86], in one case showing a greater benefit of protocol enhancement 4, which could not be anticipated from the existing results due to the inability to solve the more expensive models for large systems.

We believe that computer architects should seriously consider our "customized mean value equation" approach conducting future architectural performance studies. The approach is certainly applicable to the performance analysis of larger and more complex cache-coherent multiprocessors [Wils87, GoWo87]. It is most likely also applicable to realms other than cache consistency protocols.

We also wish to emphasize the utility of the more detailed GTPN and simulation tools for validating the results of the mean-value analysis for small systems. The authors are aware that there are cases where mean value analysis is inaccurate. Thus, validation against more detailed models is critically important when applying the technique to new problem domains.

References

[ArBa86] Archibald, J., and J.-L. Baer, "An Evaluation of Cache Coherence Solutions in Shared-Bus Multiprocessors," *ACM Transactions on Computer Sysytems*, Vol. 4, No. 4, November 1986.

[DuBr82] Dubois, M., and F. A. Briggs, "Effects of Cache Coherency in Multiprocessors", *IEEE Trans. on Computers*, Vol. C-31, November 1982, pp. 1083-1099.

[Fran84] S.J. Frank, "Tightly Coupled Multiprocessor System Speeds Memory Access Times," *Electronics*, Vol. 57, no. 1, January 1984, pp. 164-169.

[Good83] Goodman, J.R., "Using Cache Memory to Reduce Processor-Memory Traffic," *Proc. of 10th Int. Symp. on Computer Architecture*, June 1983, pp. 124-131.

[GoWo87] Goodman, J.R., and P. Woest, "The Wisconsin Multicube: A New Large-Scale Cache-Coherent Multiprocessor," to appear in *Proc. 15th Ann. Int'l. Symp. on Computer Architecture*, Honolulu, Hawaii, May 30 - June 2, 1988.

[GrMi87] Greenberg, A. G., and I. Mitrani, "Analysis of Snooping Caches," to appear in *Proc. of Performance 87, 12th Int'l. Symp. on Computer Performance*, Brussels, December 1987.

[HoVe85] Holliday, M. A., and M. K. Vernon, "A Generalized Timed Petri Net Model for Performance Analysis," *Proc. Int'l. Workshop on Timed Petri Nets*, Torino, Italy, July 1985.

[KEWP85] Katz, R., S. Eggers, D.A. Wood, C. Perkins, and R.G. Sheldon, "Implementing a Cache Consistency Protocol," *Proc. of 12th Int. Symp. on Computer Architecture*, June 1985, pp. 276-283.

[LZGS84] Lazowska, E. D., J. Zahorjan, G. S. Graham, and K. C. Sevcik, *Quantitative System Performance, Computer System Analysis Using Queueing Network Models*, Prentice-Hall, Inc., Englewood Cliffs, N.J., 1984.

[MCCr84] McCreight, E., "The DRAGON Computer System: An Early Overview," *NATO Advanced Study Institute on Microarchitecture of VLSI Computers*, Urbino, Italy, July 1984.

[PaPa84] Papamarcos, M., and J. Patel, "A Low Overhead Coherence Solution for Multiprocessors with Private Cache Memories," *Proc. of 11th Int. Symp. on Computer Architecture*, June 1984, pp. 348-354.

[RuSe84] Rudolph, L., and Z. Segall, "Dynamic Decentralized Cache Schemes for MIMD Parallel Processors," *Proc. of 11th Int. Symp. on Computer Architecture*, June 1984, pp. 340-347.

[Smit82] Smith, A.J., "Cache Memories," *Computing Surveys*, Vol. 14, no. 3, pp. 473-530, September 1982.

[Smit85a] Smith, A. J., "Cache Evaluation and the Impact of Workload Choice," *Proc. of 12th Int. Symp. on Computer Architecture,*, June 1985.

[Smit85b] Smith, A. J., "Line (Block) Size Choice for CPU Cache Memories," Technical Report CSD 85/239, Computer Science Division, Univ. of Calif. at Berkeley, 1985.

[VeHo86] Vernon, M. K., and M. A. Holliday, "Performance Analysis of Multiprocessor Cache Consistency Protocols Using Generalized Timed Petri Nets," *Proc. of Performance 86 and ACM SIGMETRICS 1986 Joint Conf. on Computer Performance Modeling, Measurement, and Evaluation*, Raleigh, N.C., May 1986, pp. 9-17.

[Wils87] Wilson, A. W., "Hierarchical Cache/Bus Architecture for Shared Memory Multiprocessors," *Proc. 14th Annual Int'l. Symp. on Computer Architecture*, Pittsburgh, PA, June 2-5, 1987, pp. 244-252.

Appendix A

The following workload parameter values are used in the experiments in Section 4:

Parameter	Value		
τ	2.5		
$p_{private}$	0.99	0.95	0.80
p_{sro}	0.01	0.03	0.15
p_{sw}	0.00	0.02	0.05
$h_{private}$	0.95		
h_{sro}	0.95		
h_{sw}	0.5		
$r_{private}$	0.7		
r_{sw}	0.5		
$amod_{private}$	0.7		
$amod_{sw}$	0.3		
$csupply_{sro}$	0.95		
$csupply_{sw}$	0.5		
$wb_{csupply}$	0.3		
rep_p	0.2		
rep_{sw}	0.5		

Note that the value of rep_p is increased to 0.3 for Modification 1; rep_{sw} is increased to 0.6 for Modifications 2 or 3, and to 0.7 for a protocol with both modifications; and, finally, hit_{sw} is set to 0.95 for the protocol with modifications 1 and 4.

Appendix B

In this appendix we give the formulas for p, p', and $t_{interference}$, used in Section 3.1. We assume PSRWM, PSWHumod, SRMiss, SWMiss, SWHumod, SRMiss, SWMiss, and SWCSup, are defined as in [VeHo86]. The equations are as follows:

$$p = p_a + p_b,$$

where:

$$p_a = \frac{PSRWM}{PSRWM + PSWHumod} \times (SRMiss + SWMiss) \times 0.5$$

and

$$p_b = \frac{SWHumod}{PSRWM + PSWHumod} \times 0.5.$$

$$p' = p_b + p_a \times \frac{1}{\frac{n-1}{2}} \times (csupply_{sro} \times SRMiss + csupply_{sw} \times SWMiss)$$

$$\times [1-(rep_p \times p_{private} + rep_{sw} \times p_{sw})]$$

$$t_{interference} =$$

$$1.0 + \frac{p_a}{p_a + p_b} \left\{ \frac{1}{\frac{n-1}{2}} \times (csupply_{sro} \times SRMiss + csupply_{sw} \times SWMiss) \right.$$

$$\left. \times [4.0 + (wb_{csupply} + SWCSup) \times 4.0] \right\}$$

Analyzing Multiprocessor Cache Behavior Through Data Reference Modeling

Jory Tsai and Anant Agarwal
Laboratory for Computer Science
Massachusetts Institute of Technology
Cambridge, MA 02139

Abstract

This paper develops a *data reference modeling* technique to estimate with high accuracy the cache miss ratio in cache-coherent multiprocessors. The technique involves analyzing the dynamic data referencing behavior of parallel algorithms. Data reference modeling first identifies different types of shared data blocks accessed during the execution of a parallel algorithm, then captures in a few parameters the cache behavior of each shared block as a function of the problem size, number of processors, and cache line size, and finally constructs an analytical expression for each algorithm to estimate the cache miss ratio. Because the number of processors, problem size, and cache line size are included as parameters, the expression for the cache miss ratio can be used to predict the performance of systems with different configurations. Six parallel algorithms are studied, and the analytical results compared against previously published simulation results, to establish the confidence level of the data reference modeling technique. It is found that the average prediction error for four out of six algorithms is within five percent and within ten percent for the other two. The paper also derives from the model several results on how cache miss rates scale with system size.

1 Introduction

An early phase in the design of multiprocessor systems is the definition of target applications to be run on the system along with potential hardware configurations. Of the various possible hardware configurations, the configuration that yields the best performance for a given cost is typically selected for the final system design specification. Because the cache is a critical determinant of multiprocessor performance, a simple analytical model of cache behavior that can rapidly yield cache miss rates for various parallel algorithms as a function of system and problem parameters, such as the number of processors and problem size, is extremely desirable during the early definition stage of the design process.

This paper develops a data reference modeling methodology to analyze parallel algorithms and obtain information that can be used to estimate the cache miss ratio in multiprocessor systems. Because the model captures the problem size, the system size, and the cache line size as parameters, it can be used to predict cache miss ratios for different system configurations. However, because the method is based on an analysis of parallel algorithms, it is not suitable for the analysis of complex or irregular applications, where the data reference patterns are hard to discern.

The data reference modeling technique consists of the following steps:

1. Identifying different types of shared data blocks accessed during the execution of a parallel algorithm by each processor. This technique is most convenient when the types of shared blocks accessed by each processor is the same for all processors – a behavior commonly exhibited by data parallel applications (i.e., applications in which each processor executes the same code but operates on different data sets).

2. Capturing in a few parameters the cache behavior of each shared block as a function of the problem size, number of processors, and cache line size. We assume that the partitioning strategy is an algorithm-specific property. The parameters essentially characterize a type of *processor locality* inherent in each type of sharing. Processor locality was described in [2] as the tendency of a processor to repeatedly access a given block of data before an access by a remote processor. A similar form of locality was also measured by Eggers [6] using the notion of write runs, and by Dubois and Wang [5] using

the notion of an access burst.

The three parameters used to capture the processor locality are the number of accesses, a, of a specific type of shared block by a given processor, the number of remote writes, w, to that block that result in cache misses suffered by the given processor, and the number of first-time fetches, f, of that block of data that are not preceded by a remote write. The parameter f contributes to the startup miss cost, and only affects the cache miss ratio in the first iteration of typical iterative algorithms. Therefore, f may be ignored when the algorithm executes many iterations. Notice that the ratio a/w yields a measure of the average number of uninterrupted accesses (i.e., a series of local accesses without any remote write) to a block of data following an eviction from a given processor's cache due to a remote write.

3. Constructing an analytical expression for each algorithm to estimate the cache miss ratio. Because the processor locality parameters w and a are expressed as a function of the number of processors, problem size, and cache line size, the expression for the cache miss ratio can be used to predict the performance of systems with different configurations.

This paper validates the model using six parallel algorithms. We find that the average prediction error for four out of six algorithms is within five percent and within ten percent for the other two. The paper also derives from the model several results on how cache miss rates scale with block size, number of processors and problem size.

This paper first discusses related work in Section 2. Section 3 develops the data reference modeling methodology to estimate a multiprocessor's cache miss ratio, and validates it using previously published simulation data for six parallel applications in Section 4. Results for two out of the six applications are discussed in detail. Section 5 uses the model to study the effects of problem size, cache line size, and number of processors on the cache miss ratio. The problem size is the size of the shared data structures indicated in the parallel algorithm. Section 6 concludes the paper.

2 Previous Work

Several previous studies directly relate to our current research: the independent reference model of Dubois and Briggs [4], the processor locality based model of Agarwal [1], the access burst model of Dubois and Wang [5], the write-run model of Eggers [6], and the directory model of Simoni and Horowitz [9].

To our knowledge, the model by Dubois and Briggs [4] was the earliest effort on analytically obtaining cache miss

rates due to invalidation. They estimated miss ratios from a markov model assuming that every shared block was equally likely to be accessed by any processor in the system. Because references to shared memory typically display temporal locality in much the same manner as private references do, the predicted miss rates turn out to be very pessimistic [1].

More recently, researchers have begun using some measure of processor locality in their models. The locality based model of Agarwal used a measure of the processor locality derived from an address trace. Processor locality is derived from a measurement of the interval between references to a given block of shared data by a given processor and the interval between write references to that block of data by other processors. Cache miss rates for systems with other configurations are derived using a simple Markov model. The drawback with this approach is that while the cache miss rate predictions are accurate for the system size from which measurements were made, attempts to extrapolate cache behavior for other system sizes are unsuccessful. The reason for this difficulty lies in our inability to predict data reference patterns arising from algorithmic behavior from a single address trace. An examination of algorithmic behavior, on the other hand, directly reveals this information.

The access burst model is based upon the observation that global shared writable blocks are accessed largely in critical sections. Within a critical section, a block can be assumed to be accessed by a single processor without interruption from other processors. A burst is defined to be a duration of accesses by a processor to a global shared block in an uninterrupted manner. The access burst size is a measure of the processor locality of the shared block. The model also measures the probability that a block is modified during an access burst. The measurements are made for each block size and the problem size is fixed. The model assumes that after a burst, all processors sharing the block are equally likely to access it again, and that the access bursts are independent from one another. Using these assumptions and measurements, a Markov model representing the global state of a shared block is constructed to estimate the likelihood of occurrence of each type of cache event such as an invalidation. The states represent the number of processors sharing the block.

Simoni and Horowitz focused on modeling the performance of limited pointer directory schemes. Their analysis models processor locality by assuming that a *primary* processor is more likely to access a block of data than one of several *secondary* processors. The analysis assumes that the number of processors actively accessing a block of data is fixed. They chose 64 for this number.

Our approach is different from that of Simoni and Horowitz, and Dubois and Wang, in that we analyze the algorithms and derive expressions for a few parameters, as a function of problem size, number of processors and block size, and then compute the miss rate. Thus our analysis does not make assumptions regarding the access probabilities, rather derives it exactly from the algorithm. Our model does not involve measurements of parameters from an actual simulation. Interestingly, our analysis of the algorithm involves a *mental simulation* for generic cases.

Eggers' model characterizes the miss rate by measuring the frequency of switching to write runs involving different processors. Different measurements were made for different block sizes, and the problem size and machine were fixed. The major goal of this work was to determine the relative importance of various factors, such as cache size and cache line size, in predicting coherence miss rates. No attempt was made to predict the miss rates for systems other than those from which the measurements were made. The results of Eggers' study indicate that the cache size is not critical to predicting cache coherence miss rates, but the sharing patterns inherent to different block sizes is important. Accordingly, our analysis assumes sufficient cache size to avoid capacity cache misses and includes the effect of the block size in estimating miss rates.

3   The Data Reference Modeling Approach

The data reference modeling approach analyzes a parallel algorithm and expresses the sources of cache-coherence related misses for each type of shared cache block. The "type" is defined as a set of shared blocks with the same access pattern. Accordingly, the inputs to the modeling process is the parallel algorithm, the number of processors (P), the problem size (N), and the cache block size or cache line size (B).

We consider cache misses caused on a given processor due to write invalidations from other processors and due to first-time references of data. The first-time references of each type of shared block is derived from an analysis of the algorithm. For write-invalidation related misses, we derive parameters from the algorithm that represent the processor locality as defined by Agarwal and Gupta [2] inherent in the access patterns of each processor executing the algorithm. Sequences of references to a shared block can be represented using the notation in [2] as "$r_i^* w_i^* w_o r_i^* w_i^* w_o r_i^* w_i^*$," where, $r_i^* w_i^*$ denotes multiple read or write references to a given block by processor i uninterrupted by writes to the block by other processors, and w_o denotes a write to the block by some *other* processor. The average length of the $r_i^* w_i^*$ sequences measures the processor locality of a given block of data with respect to processor i.

In this paper, we derive for each processor i and for each type of shared block accessed by that processor the following parameters: (1) the number of accesses by processor i (i.e., the total number of events of the type r_i and w_i), (2) the number of remote writes by other processors that are followed by reads/writes from processor i (i.e., the number of w_o events followed by r_i or w_i), and (3) the number of first-time references – which can, of course, only be zero or one – of the block by processor i that are not preceded by a w_o event. These parameters, expressed as a function of P, N, and B, are collectively called the Data Reference Model (DRM) for that type of block. The ratio of the first parameter and the second parameter is an estimate of the processor locality [1] of the shared block with respect to processor i.

While conceptually our modeling process constructs a distinct data reference model (DRM) for each block and each processor, in practice, each DRM can include a plurality of processor-block pairs that exhibit the same access sequences. Thus the total number of DRMs that need to be constructed is the total number of distinct access sequences. For data parallel programs, for example, it usually suffices to construct DRMs for each type of shared block on only one representative processor.

3.1   Assumptions

We make the following assumptions:

1. The cache is of infinite size. Several studies have shown that the cache size has a negligible effect on the coherence-related miss rate, and clearly, no effect on the number of first-time misses. In practice, this assumption is valid when the cache is large enough to hold the working set of the program. For more accurate results, the miss rate component due to conflict misses in finite-sized caches can be computed as described in [3], and added to the miss rate obtained from the analysis in this paper.

2. The cache coherence protocol is write-invalidate. Write-update protocols suffer only first-time misses in caches, and, in the steady state, each shared write results in a network transaction.

3. Although the general data reference modeling method does not require it, we make the following assumption in our experiments to simplify obtaining the parameters required to drive the model. The parallel application is iterative; synchronization is present only at the end of each iteration, and the misses on synchronization variables are ignored. Of course, as systems scale, synchronization-variable misses become more important and the proposed mental simulation technique can be applied to those variables as well.

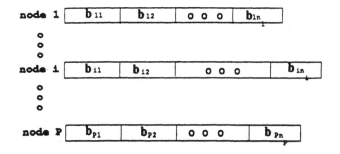

Figure 1: Typical distribution of shared blocks in the caches in a multiprocessor system.

3.2 Notation

On a P-node shared-memory multiprocessor system, shared data blocks are distributed among the caches in the nodes. Figure 1 shows a distribution of various types of shared blocks in the system. Let there be n_i different types of shared blocks in the cache in node i. Blocks with identical access patterns are said to have the same *type*. Miss rates of blocks with the same type can be captured using a single DRM, that is, using a single function of system and problem parameters. Let b_{ij} denote the j-th type of shared block on node i. The types of shared blocks on node i are named b_{i1}, $b_{i2}, \cdots, b_{in_i}$. A DRM is used to present the state of each b_{ij}.

We first introduce the notation for parameters derived from an algorithm. The number of remote-writes on b_{ij} that induce cache misses is denoted w_{ij}, and the number of first references of b_{ij} by processor i that are not preceded by a remote write (i.e., w_o) event is denoted f_{ij}. Let the number of accesses of b_{ij} be captured by a_{ij}. Finally, we will use the variable s_{ij} to denote the probability of accessing b_{ij} on node i; note that s_{ij} is simply $a_{ij} / \sum_j a_{ij}$.

The following are the computed quantities. Let the miss ratio of b_{ij} be called m_{ij}. The miss ratio of a type of shared block is simply the fraction of references of that type of block that results in a miss. Misses are caused both by remote writes followed by local accesses and due to first-time fetches.

Table 1 summarizes the notation used in this paper.

3.3 Processor Cache Miss Ratio

A processor's cache miss ratio is derived from all DRMs on that processor. After all the types of DRMs are identified on the processor, we can determine the n_i, b_{ij}, and w_{ij} from the data partition of an algorithm and the accesses sequence of shared data during the execution. Then, the miss ratios for each b_{ij} is the ratio of the sum of the number of first time misses and the write-invalidate induced misses and the number of accesses of the block.

P	number of processors
N	problem size
B	cache block size
i	index of the node count, $i = 1, 2, \dots, P$
j	index of the types of shared blocks on node i
n_i	number of types of shared blocks on node i
b_{ij}	jth type of shared block on node i
s_{ij}	probability of accessing b_{ij} on node i
f_{ij}	number of first-time fetches of b_{ij}
a_{ij}	number of accesses of b_{ij}
w_{ij}	number of remote writes that cause cache misses on b_{ij}
m_{ij}	miss ratio of b_{ij}
M_i	cache miss ratio of node i
M	cache miss ratio of system

Table 1: Notation

$$m_{ij} = \frac{f_{ij} + w_{ij}}{a_{ij}}$$

The parameters a_{ij}, w_{ij}, and f_{ij}, are algorithm dependent functions of P, N, and the block size B. A processor's miss ratio (M_i) can be derived from the sum of each b_{ij}'s cache miss ratio times the probability of accessing b_{ij}. That is,

$$M_i = \sum_{j=1}^{n_i} (s_{ij} \times m_{ij})$$

To calculate the average cache miss ratio M of all processors in the system, we use M_i and the processor utilization (U_i) of each node i. The average processor cache miss ratio is then:

$$M = \frac{\sum_{i=1}^{P} (M_i \times U_i)}{\sum_{i=1}^{P} U_i},$$

If all processors have the same utilization U, we can write,

$$M = \frac{\sum_{i=1}^{P} (M_i \times U)}{\sum_{i=1}^{P} U} = \frac{1}{P} \times \sum_{i=1}^{P} M_i$$

In our experimental analysis, we will assume that all processors have the same utilization, so that we can make the above simplification.

4 Applications and Validation

In this paper, we demonstrate the accuracy and relative ease of using the data reference modeling approach by comparing results from simulations and modeling. We will use the applications studied by Dubois and Wang [5, 7] both because of the availability of simulation results on these applications and due to the simplicity of the implementations of the parallel algorithms. While Dubois and Wang used nine algorithms, we studied six due to the lack of detailed published information on the others. The six algorithms we study are: Jacobi iteration, successive over relaxation, dynamic parallel quicksort, non-shuffling FFT, shuffling FFT, shortest path, and image component labeling.

The above six algorithms can be further divided into two categories:

- Data independent algorithms: Jacobi, S.O.R., Shuffling FFT, and Non-shuffling FFT. Data independent algorithms are those in which the input data set does not affect the shared-data access patterns.

- Data dependent algorithms: Dynamic quicksort and Image component labeling. Data dependent algorithms are those in which the input data sets may affect the access patterns to shared blocks.

This paper presents a detailed analysis of one algorithm from each category: dynamic parallel quicksort and shuffling FFT. For details on the others see [8]. We hope to use these two types of algorithms to demonstrate different DRM analysis approaches.

The examples show that the number of types of shared blocks for many algorithms, especially for those that are iterative, are very few, so the analysis process of constructing the DRMs for each type of shared block is not onerous. Parallel iterative algorithms in which the iterations are distributed among the processors not only allow extracting the DRMs for shared data types on one processor, but also allow us to focus on one iteration of the algorithm.

By analyzing the application code, we identify all data blocks, both shared and private, accessed within each iteration. The number of references can also be determined from the application code for each iteration. Once the DRMs for an algorithm are identified, the cache miss ratio can be formulated as a function of the cache line size, the problem size, and the system size.

After demonstrating that the model has acceptable accuracy for two algorithms, we will focus on analyzing the effects of cache line size, problem size and system size on multiprocessor cache miss rates. Our validation experiments compare the miss ratios obtained through analysis with the simulation results reported by Dubois and Wang [5, 7].

4.1 Shuffling FFT Algorithm

The shuffling FFT algorithm evaluates the discrete fourier transform. Let $s(k)$, $k = 0, 1, 2, ..., N - 1$ be N samples of a time function. The discrete fourier transform of $s(K)$ is defined to be the discrete function $x(j)$, $j = 0, 1, 2, ...N-1$, where

$$x(j) = \sum_{k=0}^{N-1} s(k)e^{\frac{2\pi ijk}{N}}$$

where $i = \sqrt{-1}$.

The *problem size* of the shuffling FFT algorithm is the N-item array $s(k)$; this array is usually divided into P equal sized chunks where P is the number of processors in the system. The implementation uses a single copy of an N-item array, called the *valid* array; the implementation also uses two copies of the data array for temporaries. A one-dimensional shuffling FFT algorithm for N data items is represented by a butterfly graph with $\log_2 N$ stages. These N data items are stored sequentially in the global memory. Each processor is responsible for computing the FFT on its chunk, which contains $\frac{N}{P}$ data items. In this algorithm, computations of partial FFTs alternate with shuffling phases where data are passed among processors. At most two processors can share a block at any time. Coherence activity is significantly reduced since data locality exists.

Figure 2 presents the shuffling FFT algorithm for $N = 16$ and $P = 4$. During the computation phase, each local processor owns $\frac{N}{P}$ data elements and computes in a butterfly fashion. Write operations always occur within the butterfly computation phase and never occur in the shuffling phase, and each shared block can be written by one processor only. Each block is shared by *at most* two processors when the cache line size $B << N/P$ precondition is held. If the cache line size is too large then data elements stored in a block may be accessed by more than two processors, this may cause additional write invalidations than when the precondition is held.

The algorithm requires a total of $2 \times \lceil \frac{\log_2 N}{\log_2 \frac{N}{P}} \rceil$ iterations; each iteration consists of a computation stage and a shuffling stage. Figure 2 shows data partitioning, synchronization, butterfly computation data flow, and shuffling directions. Each shared block is generally shared by only two processors, except the first $\frac{N}{2P}$ data elements on the first processor and the last $\frac{N}{2P}$ data elements on the last processor. The first and last processors processors are different because they have one neighboring processor, unlike others, which have two neighboring processors.

At the beginning of execution, all processors load their N/P data items into their respective local caches. During the computation phase of the algorithm, each data element has to be read and updated locally. Updated data elements are stored into the *valid* array, and synchronization takes place.

During the shuffling phase, the data elements in the *valid* array are copied into a local temporary array, then restored into relative locations of the *valid* array. The relative locations to which a data element must shuffle is dependent

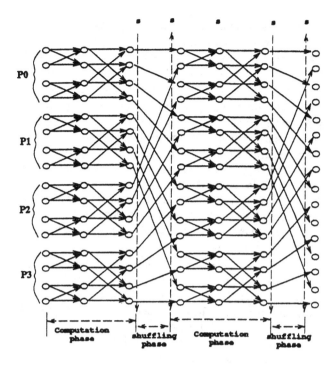

Figure 2: Shuffling FFT algorithm for P=4 and N=16.

on its processor's location. All data elements are virtually divided into two halves: the first half of data elements are shuffled towards the other half, and visa versa. Synchronization is denoted by the dotted line in the figure, and is required before each computation and shuffling phase.

All reads and writes happen locally and no cache misses occur during the computation phase. In the shuffling phase, the order of shuffling operations is remote read, local write, local read, and remote write. Cache misses only occur during the remote read of the shuffling phase. This indicates there is at most one cache miss per cache block, and $w_{ij} = 1$. The only exception is the $N/2P$ data elements mentioned in the first and the last processor, whose $w_{ij} = 0$.

4.1.1 Cache Miss Ratio Validation for Shuffling FFT

In order to calculate the cache miss ratio for the shuffling FFT algorithm one has only to focus on each iteration of both the computation and the shuffling stages. The behavior of each iteration is independent throughout the whole course of execution, which comprises $\lceil \frac{\log_2 N}{\log_2 \frac{N}{P}} \rceil$ stages.

We will first compute the miss ratio of the non-boundary processors, and then adjust the miss rate to account for the first and last processor's access patterns. Within the computation phase, $\log_2(N/P)$ butterfly stages are needed to compute $\frac{N}{P}$ data elements. Each processor performs only two reads and one write on each data element in the computation phase, and two reads and two writes in the shuffling phase.

Therefore, the total number of accesses on b_{ij}, namely a_{ij}, during each stage is $(3 \cdot \log_2 \frac{N}{P} + 4) \cdot B$.

Cache misses happen only in the shuffling phase, where $w_{ij} = 1$. Therefore, for the non-boundary processors,

$$n_i = 1, \ \forall i = 2, 3, ..., P - 1$$

$$w_{ij} = 1$$

and

$$s_{ij} = 1$$

Therefore,

$$m_{ij} = \frac{w_{ij}}{a_{ij}} = \frac{1}{B \cdot (3 \cdot \log_2 \frac{N}{P} + 4)}$$

And, the cache miss ratio for each processor is

$$M_i = \frac{1}{B} \cdot \frac{1}{(3 \cdot \log_2 \frac{N}{P} + 4)} \tag{1}$$

The effect of the first and the last processor can be included as follows. Recall that processor 1 and processor P have two distinct types of blocks: those that have $w_{ij} = 1$ and those that have $w_{ij} = 0$. Each processor has $N/2P$ blocks of each type. Therefore, the miss ratio of the first processor and the last processor is:

$$M_{1,P} = \frac{1}{2} \frac{1}{B} \cdot \frac{1}{(3 \cdot \log_2 \frac{N}{P} + 4)}$$

The average miss ratio for the whole system is given by,

$$M = \frac{P-2}{P} M_i + \frac{2}{P} M_{1,P}$$

Simplifying, we get,

$$M = \frac{P-1}{PB} \cdot \frac{1}{(3 \cdot \log_2 \frac{N}{P} + 4)}$$

Table 2 compares the cache miss ratios derived from this function and those obtained from simulation results published in [5, 7]. The cache miss ratios are collected based on cache line sizes of one, two, four, eight, and 16 words, number of processors varying from two through eight, and a problem size $N = 65536$. The comparisons are also shown in Figure 3. A constant percentage difference is found between simulated results and modeled results for each number of processors. The observed mean difference is 4.3 percent.

4.2 Parallel Dynamic Quicksort

Dynamic quicksort is a *divide-and-conquer* algorithm, which sorts an array A[1], A[2], ..., A[N] by rearranging it to make the condition that A[1],...,A[j-1] $\leq$ A[j] $\leq$

P	B	DRM Results	Simulation Results	Percent Difference
2	1	0.010204	0.010639	-4.08
2	2	0.005102	0.005319	-4.08
2	4	0.002551	0.002659	-4.06
2	8	0.001275	0.001330	-4.09
2	16	0.000638	0.000665	-4.09
4	1	0.016304	0.017045	-4.34
4	2	0.008152	0.008523	-4.35
4	4	0.004076	0.004262	-4.36
4	8	0.002038	0.002131	-4.36
4	16	0.001019	0.001065	-4.32
8	1	0.020349	0.021341	-4.65
8	2	0.010174	0.010671	-4.65
8	4	0.005087	0.005336	-4.66
8	8	0.002544	0.002668	-4.66
8	16	0.001272	0.001334	-4.66

Table 2: DRM versus simulation for shuffling FFT

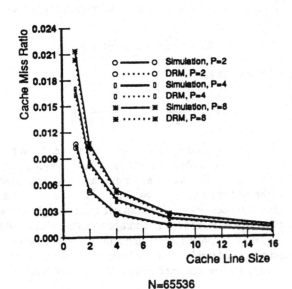

N=65536

Figure 3: DRM versus simulation for shuffling FFT.

A[j+1],...,A[N] holds for some j, and a splitting process to place the two subarrays into a global job queue. By recursively applying the same procedure to the subarrays A[1],...,A[j-1] and A[j+1],...,A[N], the entire array is sorted.

In its parallel implementation, at the end of each splitting phase, the larger subarray is processed by the same processor and a descriptor of the smaller subarray is stored into a global job queue for potential distribution to other processors. The larger subarray is retained to maximize data locality. When a processor is idle it checks the global job queue and picks up a subarray's descriptor if the global job queue is not empty. If the size of the subarray is one then the processor writes the subarray back to shared array and change its state to idle. The algorithm is completed when all processors are idle and the job queue is empty.

The *problem size* of the dynamic quicksort algorithm is the N item array A. In this algorithm, every data item in this array may be accessed by all processors during the course of execution. The implementation of this algorithm uses a single copy of the array. There is no system wide synchronization required for this algorithm during run time. The only restriction on data sharing is that shared data are accessed mutually exclusively while a processor splits the array or the subarray.

Figure 4 shows how shared data elements are accessed during the execution of the algorithm, for $N = 32$ and $P = 4$. Each square represents a data element in the array. Squares grouped by a rectangle in the graph shows those data elements are allocated and sorted by a processor within that stage. The dotted line shows data locality after the initial loading. For simplicity, we assume that the subarrays are of equal size.

During run time, the first processor (say, P1) allocates all data elements initially, and releases less than half of those elements at the end of stage 1. The second processor (say, P2) then picks a subarray from the job queue and sorts the subarray, and other processors follow the same task. After stage 1, there are $(N - 1)/2$ unsorted elements on each processor on average, and the N element array has been divided into 2 subarrays. After stage x, there are $(N - 2^{x-1} + 1)/(2^{x-1})$ unsorted elements on each processor, and the array has been divided into 2^{x-1} subarrays. When the number of unsorted elements on each processor reaches one, the execution is completed. The average run time of the algorithm is $\log_2 N$ stages ($\lceil \log_2(N - 1) \rceil$ iterations).

4.2.1 Cache Miss Ratio and Model Validation

Cache misses in the quicksort algorithm have a high degree of data dependency. That is, it is impossible to figure out exactly the number of cache misses without complete knowledge of the data being sorted. However, we can proceed to formulate a DRM for this type of algorithm by making suit-

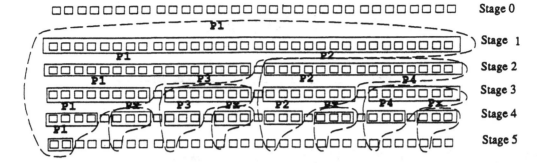

Figure 4: Shared data handling in dynamic quicksort, $P = 4$ and $N = 32$

able assumptions about the data distribution. For simplicity, we make the assumption that the array at each stage is evenly divided into subarrays, since we do not know the exact size of the two sorted subarrays. The assumption of even division represents the worst-case scenario; a 65-35 split is more likely if the numbers in the array are generated randomly. Under this assumption, we can derive DRM parameters and then estimate the cache miss ratio for the algorithm.

At stage x, the N element array has $2^{x-1} - 1$ sorted data elements, an average queue size of $2^{x-1} - P$, and 2^{x-1} subarrays. The average size of a unsorted subarray is therefore $\frac{N - 2^{x-1} + 1}{2^{x-1}}$ elements. To derive the cache miss ratio for a processor in this algorithm, since only one type of shared block exists, it is convenient to consider the whole course of the execution and derive expressions for f, a, and w for this type of shared block. Clearly, the value of n_i is one for all i, and the value of s is also one, since only one type of shared block exists.

Here, we can ignore the work queue's data blocks, since it has the same access pattern as the shared data blocks, and hence will not change the cache miss ratio. However, we need to taking the work queue into account if we are estimating the cache miss count,

There are three types of cache misses that occur during the execution of this algorithm:

- initial loading misses

- loading misses from the job queue, which correspond to cache misses that occur when a subarray is stored in the unsorted job queue and requested by a processor

- invalidation and false-sharing misses within a cache block on account of accesses by different processors.

The sum of the first two comprise the f component of misses, and the third type constitutes the w component.

Given a cache line size B, the number of initial loading misses is simply $\lceil N/B \rceil$.

The loading misses from the job queue as computed as follows. After $\log_2 P$ stages, all processors on the system

become active and the job queue size remains empty, because an idle processor grabs a sorted subarray from the job queue as soon as a sorted subarray is inserted by an active processor. At stage x, there are a total of $2^{x-1} - P$ subarrays in the queue, with an average size of $(N - 2^{x-1} + 1)/(B \cdot 2^{x-1})$ blocks. The probability that a subarray is inserted and taken again from the queue is $1/P$. Consequently, the probability that reloading a subarray misses in the cache is $(P - 1)/P$. Overall, from stage $\log_2 P + 2$ to stage $\log_2 N$, the number of such reloading misses is:

$$(\frac{P-1}{P}) \cdot (\frac{N - 2^{x-1} + 1}{B \cdot 2^{x-1}}) \cdot (2^{x-1} - P).$$

The sum of the above two components is f.

As the algorithm completes, if the size of a subarray is smaller than the cache line size, then write operations to a subarray may cause write invalidations on other subarrays within the same cache block. These misses caused by false sharing within a cache block usually occur when the size of subarrays is very small. A total of

$$(\frac{N}{B}) \cdot \sum_{y=1}^{\log_2 B + 1} [(\frac{P-1}{P}) \cdot (2^{y-1} - 1)]$$

misses occur from stage $\log_2 N - (\log_2 B + 1)$ to stage $\log_2 N$. These comprise the w component of misses.

An approximate total cache access count in stage x is $11 \cdot (N + 2^{x-1} - 1)/(2^x)$, which involves 7 shared data accesses and 4 local variable accesses for each data element in the subarray. The constant access of 11 may be vary depends on the implementation of algorithm. The sum of these values over all the stages, namely, $\sum_{x=1}^{\log_2 N} [11 \cdot \frac{N + 2^{x-1} - 1}{2^x}]$, is the value of a.

Since there is only one type of shared blocks in the system, $m_{ij} = M_i = M$. Thus M is simply $(f + w)$ divided by the total cache access count a. Therefore,

$$M_i = \frac{f + w}{a}$$

$$M_i = \frac{\frac{N}{B} + \sum_{z=\log_2 P+2}^{\log_2 N} [\frac{P-1}{P} \cdot \frac{N-2^{z-1}+1}{B \cdot 2^{z-1}} \cdot (2^{z-1}-P)] + \sum_{y=1}^{\log_2 B+1} [\frac{N}{B} \cdot \frac{P-1}{P} \cdot (2^{y-1}-1)]}{\sum_{z=1}^{\log_2 N} [11 \cdot \frac{N+2^{z-1}-1}{2^z}]}$$

which is simplified to yield,

$$M_i = \frac{\frac{N}{B} + \frac{P-1}{B \cdot P} \cdot [(N+P-1) \cdot \log_2 \frac{N}{P} + 4P-1 + \frac{(N-1) \cdot 2P}{N}] + \frac{N \cdot (P-1)}{B \cdot P} \cdot (2B - \log_2 B - 2)}{11 \cdot [\frac{\log_2 N}{2} + \frac{(N-1)^2}{N}]}$$

Table 3: Expression for the miss rate in quicksort.

P	B	Simulation Results	DRM Results	Percent Difference
2	1	0.076779	0.090916	18.41
2	2	0.043321	0.048300	11.49
2	4	0.025626	0.028412	10.87
2	8	0.018372	0.019179	4.39
2	16	0.018343	0.014917	-18.67
4	1	0.115593	0.122175	5.69
4	2	0.063170	0.065350	3.45
4	4	0.036758	0.039069	6.28
4	8	0.025725	0.026993	4.93
4	16	0.024854	0.021489	-13.53
8	1	0.138924	0.130718	-5.90
8	2	0.074812	0.070332	-5.98
8	4	0.043398	0.042625	-1.77
8	8	0.030225	0.030015	-0.69
8	16	0.028873	0.024332	-15.72

Table 4: Simulation versus DRM result listing for quicksort

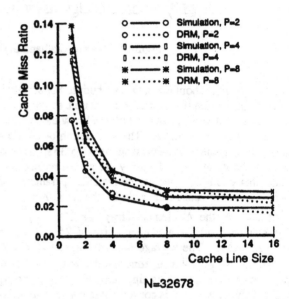

N=32678

Figure 5: DRM versus simulation for quicksort.

and, substituting for f, w, and a, we obtain the miss rate as depicted in Table 3.

Table 4 compares the cache miss ratios derived from this function and the miss rates from simulations. Simulations use cache line sizes of one, two, four, eight, and 16 words, processor numbers of two, four, and eight, and a problem size of 32678. The comparisons are also shown in Figure 5. An average difference of 8.5 percent was found between simulated results and modeled results. We believe the difference is primarily due to the unpredictability of the input data set, as discussed in Section 4.2.1. Nevertheless, we find that the analysis is still reasonable for this type of algorithm with suitable assumptions about data distributions.

4.3 Summary of Results for Six Algorithms

Table 5 lists the differences between the analytically obtained miss ratios and the miss ratios obtained through simulations for the six algorithms studied. We observe that the data reference modeling approach is fairly accurate in estimating the cache miss ratios for all studied cases, and is generally significantly more accurate than the Access Burst Model [5] for the same set of benchmarks. For example, the data reference modeling approach yields average and maximum

errors of 0.63 and 1.30 percent respectively for Jacobi, while the Access Burst Model yields average and maximum errors of 10.03 and 17.82 percent respectively.

The average is the absolute difference divided by the simulation data, abs(model-sim)/sim. Maximum is the absolute maximum difference.

Since our approach essentially does a mental simulation of algorithms, why are the differences not zero? There are several reasons for the mismatch between simulations and analysis. In algorithms where the cache miss ratios is data dependent (quicksort and image labeling), the errors are relatively larger than the others because of the lack of fealty in the assumptions about data distributions. In the other algorithms, the differences are much smaller; we believe these can be attributed to our incomplete knowledge of the specific implementations of the algorithms.

5 Predicting The Cache Miss Ratio

Armed with the knowledge that the data reference modeling method is acceptably accurate in predicting cache miss ratios for several system configurations, we can now apply the

Algorithm	Average Difference (percent)	Maximum Difference (percent)
Jacobi	0.63	1.30
S.O.R.	0.39	0.76
Shuffling FFT	4.30	4.66
Non-shuffling FFT	0.00	0.00
Quicksort	8.50	18.67
Image labeling	5.75	13.77

Table 5: Summary of simulation versus DRM results for six algorithms. The first four algorithms are data independent, while the last two are data dependent.

method to understand the behavior of systems for different problem sizes, different numbers of processors and various cache line sizes. Because algorithm analysis correctly accounts for boundary effects at small problem sizes, an extrapolation to a large number of processors is reasonable. However, we note that for better accuracy at large numbers of processors synchronization variables should also be analyzed. In this paper we pick two sets of experiments, one each for shuffling FFT and dynamic quicksort. For more sensitivity results see [8].

In the ensuing study, we use the cache miss ratio as a metric of performance. However, we note that in practice one might want to couple the cache miss ratio model with an interconnection network model to account for the effects of latency and derive overall system performance, for example, using processor utilization as a metric. More importantly, when the number of processors is also varied, an increase in the miss rate can often be tolerated if the speedup in application execution makes up for the loss in performance of each individual processor. However, for a given number of processors, the system configuration with the lowest cache miss ratio is often a good choice. Our goal here is to demonstrate the types of questions we can answer with the model.

5.1 Shuffling FFT

From equation 1, we know that the cache miss ratio for a processor running the shuffling FFT application is:

$$M_i = \frac{P-1}{P \cdot B} \cdot \frac{1}{(3 \cdot \log_2 \frac{N}{P} + 4)}.$$

Figure 3 (in Section 4.1.1) plots this miss ratio as a function of the cache line size. Figure 6 plots this miss ratio as a function of the number of processors. This figure uses a cache line size of four, and a variety of problem sizes. We find that the processor miss ratio is close to a log function of N/P and inversely proportional to B. (Recall from Figure 3

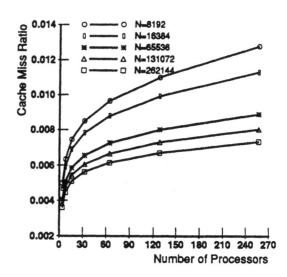

Figure 6: Cache miss ratios for shuffling FFT, B=4.

that the cache miss ratios level off for cache line sizes greater than four).

Figure 7 shows the cache miss ratios when we fixed the system size at 16 processors and the cache line size at four, and varied the problem size from 8192 to 262144. We find that, in this case, the cache miss ratio is a log function of the problem size.

Based on the observations above, a cache line size greater than or equal to four is preferable for the given partitioning of the problem. Furthermore, because for a given problem size the miss rate increases with the number of processors, using more processors should be traded off against their decreased effectiveness due to the higher cache miss rate.

5.2 Parallel Dynamic Quicksort

The cache miss ratio for dynamic quicksort can be calculated from the equation in Table 3. For a given a problem size, the best cache line size should be suggested by the lowest cache miss ratio configuration. Figure 8(a) shows the cache miss ratios for different cache line sizes for a fixed problem size. We see that the cache miss ratio is only lightly affected by the cache line size when the size is greater than or equal to four.

For a given cache block size, the most suitable system configuration to run the quicksort algorithm can be suggested by analyzing the results in Figures 8(b), 8(c), and 8(d). Note that the vertical axis scales are different for each of 4 graphs in Figure 8. These figures display the miss ratios when we vary the problem size from 1024 to 131072, vary the number of processors from two through 128, and vary cache block size from one through 16.

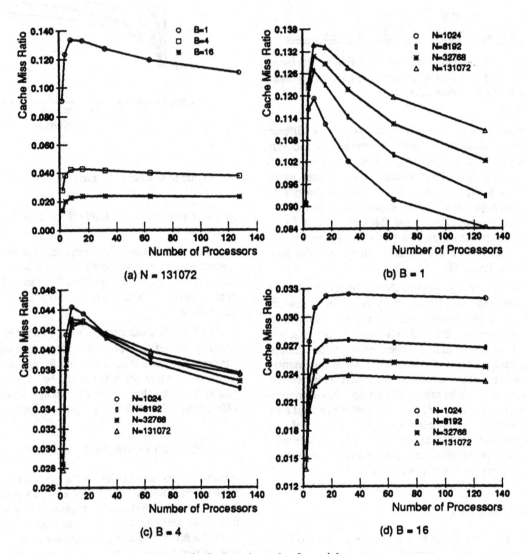

Figure 8: Cache miss ratios for quicksort.

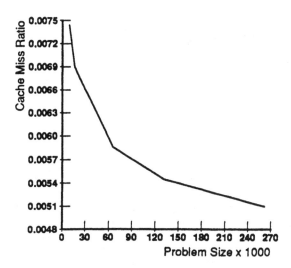

Figure 7: Cache miss ratio for shuffling FFT, B=4 and P=16.

One of the most interesting features of these graphs is the relationship between cache miss ratio and the problem size for a given cache line sizes. Figure 8(b), corresponding to B = 1, shows that when the problem size increases the cache miss ratio also increases. Figure 8(c), corresponding to B = 4, shows that the cache miss ratio is largely insensitive to the problem size. Figure 8(d), corresponding to B = 16, shows that when the problem size increases the cache miss ratio decreases.

The reason for this behavior is that a larger cache line size (greater than four) reduces the cache miss ratio significantly during the early stages of algorithm execution, when the first-time miss cost is most significant. On the other hand, a larger cache line size pays a higher cache miss penalty toward the end of the execution, when coherence related invalidations abound. Notice that for the B=16 case, the flat miss ratio curves indicate that the cache miss ratio is less sensitive to the number of processors than when the cache line size is large. These results suggests that a cache line size greater than or equal to four is preferable to smaller line sizes.

6 Conclusions

This paper presented a data reference modeling approach to computing the cache miss ratios of multiprocessors for different algorithms. The method involves a mental simulation of the algorithm. The approach is validated by comparing analytically obtained results with those from simulations.

The modeling approach analyzes algorithms to derive a few parameters that capture the processor locality in applications. These parameters are expressed as a function of the problem size, the number of processors, and the cache line size. By analyzing the algorithm, we can accurately capture the impact of the system configuration and problem size on the cache miss ratio. This approach is different from methods developed by others in that it does not analyze an address trace. We found that using parameters measured from address traces alone allows us to study applications behavior under a similar system environment where the trace are derived. Furthermore, even when the application behavior is similar, we have found it to be virtually impossible to predict the miss rate as various system parameters are changed without considering algorithm characteristics.

After showing that the data reference modeling approach is accurate and is not too onerous to use, we used the model to predict the cache miss ratios for different system configurations.

7 Acknowledgments

The research reported in this paper is funded by NSF grant # MIP-9012773 and DARPA contract # N00014-87-K-0825. Jory Tsai was supported by Digital Equipment Corporation.

References

[1] Anant Agarwal A Locality-Based Multiprocessor Cache Interference Model. *MIT VLSI memo 89-565*, October 1989.

[2] Anant Agarwal and Anoop Gupta. Memory-Reference Characteristics of Multiprocessor Applications under MACH, In Proceedings of ACM SIGMETRICS, May 1988.

[3] Anant Agarwal, Mark Horowitz, and John Hennessy. *An Analytical Cache Model. ACM Transactions on Computer Systems, Vol. 7, No. 2*, Pages 184-215, May 1989.

[4] Michel Dubois and Faye A. Briggs. Effects of Cache Coherence in Multiprocessors. In *Proceedings of the 9th International Symposium on Computer Architecture*, pages 299–308, IEEE, New York, May 1982.

[5] Michel Dubois and Jin-Chin Wang. *Shared Block Contention in a Cache Coherence Protocol. IEEE Transactions on Computers, Vol. 40, No. 5*, May 1991.

[6] Susan J. Eggers. *Simplicity Versus Accuracy in a Model of Cache Coherency Overhead. IEEE Transactions on Computers, Vol. 40, No. 8*, August 1991.

[7] Jin-Chin Wang. Analytical modeling of shared block contention in cache coherence protocol. *Ph.D. Dissertation*, University of Southern California, Dec. 1990.

[8] Jory Tsai. *Cache Modeling for Very Large Multiprocessor System*. Master thesis, 1992, LCS, Massachusetts Institute of Technology.

[9] Richard Simoni and Mark Horowitz. Modeling the Performance of Limited Pointers Directories for Cache Coherence. In *Proceedings 18th Annual International Symposium on Computer Architecture*, IEEE, 1991.

Analysis of Multiprocessors with Private Cache Memories

JANAK H. PATEL, MEMBER, IEEE

Abstract—This paper presents an approximate analytical model for the performance of multiprocessors with private cache memories and a single shared main memory. The accuracy of the model is compared with simulation results and is found to be very good over a broad range of parameters. The parameters of the model are the size of the multiprocessor, the size and type of the interconnection network, the cache miss-ratio, and the cache block transfer time. The analysis is extended to include several different read/write policies such as write-through, load-through, and buffered write-back. The analytical technique presented is also applicable to the performance of interconnection networks under block transfer mode.

Index Terms—Cache memories, crossbar, delta networks, interconnection networks, multiprocessors, parallel memories, performance analysis.

I. INTRODUCTION

WITH the emergence of VLSI technology and low cost processors, multiprocessors are becoming increasingly attractive. Current VLSI designs suffer from a mismatch between internal and external data transfer rates. The data transfer rates on the chip can be made much higher than the transfer rates across chip boundaries, that is, on the pins. This mismatch can be alleviated by placing a private cache on the chip with the processor, and then implementing a multiprocessor organization like that of Fig. 1. In such a design, the traffic across the cache-main memory interface is lower than the traffic across the processor-cache interface. This paper presents analytic and simulation results for the performance of multiprocessors with a two-level memory hierarchy of the type shown in Fig. 1. The first level of memory is a private cache and the second level of the memory is the main memory shared by all processors. The two levels are connected through a switch. In this paper we shall restrict ourselves to switches which are full crossbars or delta networks.

The multiprocessor organization with private cache memories is somewhat restrictive compared to an organization in which all memories are fully shared by each processor. The principal drawback of private cache is that of data consistency, that is, the possibility of creation of several copies of a single variable, where a copy is manipulated in private memory independent of other copies, thus producing inconsistent values among the copies of the same variable. Such problems can be

Manuscript received January 1, 1981; revised May 1, 1981 and December 1, 1981. This work was supported in part by the Joint Services Electronics Program under Contract N00016-79-C-0424.

The author is with the Department of Electrical Engineering and the Coordinated Science Laboratory, University of Illinois, Urbana, IL 61801.

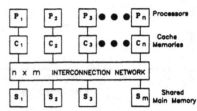

Fig. 1. Multiprocessor organization with private cache memories.

solved through hardware or software interlocks, but only with a substantial penalty in performance [3], [15]. However, there are many applications where the problem of data inconsistency does not arise, for example, in the sharing of reentrant procedures or in the use of read only data. For this paper we shall assume an environment in which data consistency is not a problem.

Design of a cache-based multiprocessor system involves many parameters. These include the cache capacity, the block size and the set size, read and write policies (e.g., write-through and load-through), the size and the type of interconnection network, and the transfer rate between the cache and the main memory. In the absence of an analytical method of performance evaluation, simulation is the only alternative. However, simulation involving so many parameters is truly a formidable task. To reduce the range of parameter values, over which to simulate, even the most rudimentary analysis is of some value. Therefore, an approximate but fairly accurate analysis is of definite help to a designer. The analysis presented in this paper serves such a purpose. In addition, the technique presented is potentially useful for obtaining approximate solutions to many similar problems.

In the next section we present the physical description of the system under study. Following this we develop the analysis of a particularly simple cache organization. This simple cache organization is especially helpful in explaining the development of the approximate analysis. This analysis is evaluated by comparing the results with simulation results. The agreement between the two is within 2 percent in the region of interest. Finally, the analytical method developed for the simple cache organization is applied to more complex cache organizations of practical interest. In particular three organizations, namely, write-through, load-through, and buffered write-back are discussed. As an example, the write-through is evaluated for several different values of the parameters and compared with the simulation results, showing the applicability of the analytical technique to very complex problems.

II. THE PHYSICAL MODEL

A. The Cache

The memory organization assumed here is a two-level memory hierarchy. As the memory speeds and costs continue to change, two-level memory hierarchies may be designed which cannot be classified as a cache/main memory or as a main/secondary memory with their traditional meaning. We shall distinguish these two by several attributes. This is not an attempt to define the two memory systems. However, the distinction is necessary for our analytical model. The model is only discussed in relation to a cache-main memory hierarchy, where a cache-main is assumed to have the following description.

For the purposes of this paper, a cache-main memory hierarchy will be assumed to have a miss ratio less than 0.1 and a block size small enough and/or memories fast enough so that a block transfer time is no greater than about 64 cache cycles. In contrast, a main-secondary memory hierarchy may have fault rates much less than 0.005 and page transfer times far greater than cache block transfer times. In addition, a cache memory is much smaller than the primary memory of a paging hierarchy.

An implication of the above attributes is that in a cache-main memory system it is not profitable to switch processes on a cache miss. This is because a process switching time is comparable to a block transfer time and also because cache is not large enough to hold more than one working set for an acceptable miss ratio. Therefore, we can assume that on a cache miss, the processor is idle while the desired block is being transferred. Thus, the system throughput of a multiprocessor with cache-main memory can be computed directly from the total time spent in doing block transfers, if the processor execution is not overlapped with a block transfer. Note that such an assumption cannot be justified in a main-secondary paging system because the processor execution and the page transfers are almost always overlapped.

B. Cache-Main Interconnection

Two interconnection networks that will be studied here are full crossbars and delta networks [7]. Both networks will be used here in the circuit switching mode. Once a fault occurs in a cache, the fault handling hardware requests a block transfer from a particular main memory module and the network establishes a path between the cache and the main memory module. This path is held until the memory transaction is complete. The path cannot be preempted by any other requests coming from other cache modules. In this description it is assumed that a block resides in a single memory module. However, a memory module itself may be interleaved to increase its bandwidth. The advantage of using circuit switching and storing the block in one memory module is the reduction in block transfer time. Both in the crossbar and delta network there is an initial delay in establishing a path due to arbitration, decoding, and setting of appropriate switches. Once the path is established the data can be transferred at a high rate.

Another advantage of circuit switching is the ease of performing one or more indivisible read/write operations in the main memory. This in turn simplifies the implementation of synchronization and mutual exclusion primitives which are required in most multiprocessing environments.

III. ANALYSIS

A. Simple Cache Model

In this section we develop an analytical model for a very simple cache organization. This will be extended later to include more complex cache organizations. The following assumptions define the simple cache model.

1) Each cache fault involves one block-write to a main memory module followed by one block-read from the same memory module. As a consequence of this, we further assume that once a path is established between the faulting cache and the requested memory module, the transaction (read and write of a block) takes a constant time.

2) Cache requests to main memory are random and uniformly distributed over all main memory modules.

The first assumption is satisfied in a set-associative cache with no write-through or load-through capability by requiring that all blocks that map to a single set be stored in the same memory module. This assumption will be modified later in our treatment of more complex cache organizations.

Thus, in the simple cache model a cache fault generates a request to a main memory module, which is accepted after some wait due to network conflicts. After the request is granted the cache-main memory transaction takes a constant time. Let this time be t time units, where the time unit can be thought of as the processor minor cycle or the unit of the smallest activity in the processor. Thus, all cache and memory cycles are some integral multiples of the CPU minor cycle. Furthermore, we assume that requests from the CPU to the cache are generated at the integral boundaries of the time unit.

The second assumption about the cache-fault behavior is justified for our multiprocessor system. If the processors are not interacting heavily with each other, then very little correlation exists between the address streams of different processors. The uniform distribution assumption is further aided by interleaving the blocks in the main memory, that is, assigning block i to memory module $i \bmod M$, where M is the number of main memory modules. (Note that this does not contradict the earlier assumption of blocks of the same set in a single memory module.) Two successive cache faults of a single processor may be less independent. However, in the time interval between these two faults other cache modules are also faulting. Thus, the requests that a main memory module sees are fairly independent and random.

The miss ratio of a program as a function of cache size, block size, and set size have been measured by several researchers [4], [6], [8], [14], [16]. Also, some analytical models for estimating cache miss ratios exist [5], [9]. From such data it is possible to determine the request rate from a cache to the main memory. Let m be the probability that a cache makes a request to main memory in a given time unit, that is, m is the probability that the processor makes a request to the cache and that it is a fault. m typically would be less than the miss ratio because not every CPU cycle is a memory reference.

To summarize the simple cache model, at each time unit a cache makes a request to the main memory with probability m, after some wait time a transaction between a main memory module and the faulting cache takes place, which lasts for t time units. Throughout this period the processor remains idle.

B. Approximate Analysis of Simple Cache Model

A processor in our multiprocessor is in one of two states. It is either busy doing useful work or it is idle waiting for a cache-fault service to be completed. The throughput of the system is directly proportional to the processor utilization. Therefore, we shall use the processor utilization as a measure of the system performance. This can be computed as follows.

Consider Fig. 2, which shows the effect of cache faults and wait times on the processor activity. Since each processor cycle generates a cache fault with probability m, there are on the average mk faults for k units of useful computation. Let w be the average wait encountered at each request. Since a block transfer takes t time units, the k units of useful processor activity take $k + mk(w + t)$ time units. Assuming N processors and M main memory modules, the following can be computed directly from Fig. 2(c). The processor utilization

$$U = k/[k + mk(w + t)] = 1/[1 + m(w + t)]. \quad (1)$$

The average number of busy main memory modules

$$B = Nmkt/[k + mk(w + t)]$$
$$= Nmt/[1 + m(w + t)]. \quad (2)$$

In terms of utilization U

$$B = NmtU. \quad (3)$$

In the above expressions the only unknown is the average wait time w. It is clear that the wait time depends on several factors, such as request rate m, number of processors N, number of memory modules M, block transfer time t, and the type of the interconnection network. Let us see what are the difficulties involved in computing the average wait time w.

Consider a specific case with $m = 1$ and $t = 1$ and the crossbar as the memory switch. In other words, a request is generated at each time unit. Furthermore, assume that the memory transfer is overlapped with the CPU execution. While this is not a realistic case for our system, it illustrates a point here about the analysis of such problems. This case is identical to the parallel memory model studied by several researchers for the evaluation of memory bandwidth. No exact closed form solution exists to this date for this problem. Given specific numeric values for N and M, exact Markov analysis is possible but involves a large amount of computation. Bhandarkar [2] gave a procedure to carry out such a computation. Others have given approximate analyses for closed form solutions [1], [11]–[13], of which Rau's result [10] comes closest to the exact value.

Now consider our more general case where m and t are not necessarily 1 and the memory transfers are not overlapped with the CPU execution. Exact Markov analysis is always possible for specific numeric values of m, t, N, and M because of the

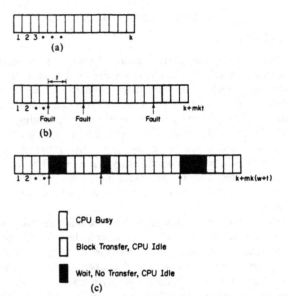

Fig. 2. Effect of cache faults and wait time on CPU utilization. (a) CPU activity with no faults. (b) mk faults with no wait for block transfer. (c) mk faults with average w wait per fault.

finite number of states. However, the state space is much larger than for the often studied case of $m = 1$ and $t = 1$, and therefore computationally far more complex. In the absence of a reasonable analysis, simulation is the only other viable alternative. We have done extensive simulation of the simple cache model. One important outcome of the simulation was an observation that the processor utilization of a given sized multiprocessor system with a specific network (crossbar or delta) can be approximated as a function of the product mt, where m is the probability of a cache to main request and t is the block transfer time. In the terminology of the queueing theory, mt may be described as the offered traffic intensity. Mathematically, the processor utilization most surely will not be a function of the product mt. As a matter of fact, the Markov analysis of a very simple case $N = M = 2$ showed that it is not purely a function of mt. However, the simulation showed that the individual influences of m or t are small compared to the effect of product mt. In other words, the processor utilization depends primarily on the traffic intensity and to a lesser extent on the nature of the traffic. This is the clue we use in obtaining an approximate analysis of the simple cache model. The principle idea behind the analysis is to transform the given simple cache model into an "equivalent" model in which the offered traffic intensity is maintained and for which we also have an approximate solution.

Consider Fig. 2(c) once again which shows the activity of a single processor. While the processor is waiting, the cache is resubmitting the block transfer request again and again until it is accepted by the network; on the average this happens for w time units. After the request is granted, the network holds a path to a memory module for t time units. One can view this as t consecutive requests to the same module, each request requiring one time unit of service. Thus, on each cache fault the network sees an average of $w + t$ consecutive requests for unit service time. Referring to Fig. 2(c), in $k + mk(w + t)$ time units a total of $mk(w + t)$ requests for unit service are made to the network. Therefore, the request rate (for unit service) from a cache module as seen by the network is

$$m' = m(w + t)/[1 + m(w + t)]. \qquad (4)$$

In terms of processor utilization U of (1) we have

$$m' = 1 - U. \qquad (5)$$

The approximation that we introduce here is that $w + t$ consecutive requests to a single memory module can be decomposed into $w + t$ separate requests which are random, independent, and uniformly distributed over all memory modules, without essentially changing the system behavior. Clearly, the transformation is not equivalent to the original system. However, the offered traffic between the cache and the main is maintained as before. Moreover, we do have an approximate analytical solution to the transformed model.

The model that we will analyze is a system of N sources and M destinations; each source generates a request with probability m' in each time unit. The request is independent, random, and uniformly distributed over all destinations. Each request is for one unit service time. Rejected requests are resubmitted as new independent requests and are made part of the new request m'. First, we analyze the system with a crossbar and then with a delta network.

The Crossbar: We already know the average number of busy main memory modules. This from (3) is

$$B = NmtU. \qquad (3)$$

Another way to compute the same quantity assuming the crossbar is as follows. A similar derivation for parallel memory bandwidth was used by Strecker [13].

Each main memory module is addressed with probability m'/M from a cache. The probability that none of the N cache modules make a request to a particular main memory module is $(1 - m'/M)^N$. Therefore, on the average $M[(1 - m'/M)^N]$ modules are not doing any memory transfers, or to put it another way, $M[1 - (1 - m'/M)^N]$ main memory modules are making a memory transfer. Therefore, the average number of busy memory modules is

$$B = M[1 - (1 - m'/M)^N] \qquad (6)$$

substituting for $B = NmtU$ from (3) and $m' = 1 - U$ from (5) we have

$$NmtU - M[1 - (1 - (1 - U)/M)^N] = 0. \qquad (7)$$

The above equation in U can be solved by standard numerical algorithms using iterative techniques. Most of these algorithms require a good initial value for the unknown U. A good initial value for U is obtained by setting wait time $w = 0$ in (1), that is, setting $U = 1/(1 + mt)$, which incidently corresponds to the maximum possible processor utilization.

Note that U in (7) is a function of N, M, and mt. This should be no surprise since our approximation is based on the assumption that the utilization is a function of mt, and not m or t independently.

The Delta Network: A delta network is an n stage network constructed from $a \times b$ crossbar switches with a resulting size

of $a^n \times b^n$. Thus, in our model it is required that $N = a^n$ and $M = b^n$. For a more complete description, see [7]. Functionally, a delta network is an interconnection network which allows any of the N cache modules to communicate with any one of the M main memory modules. However, unlike in a crossbar two requests may collide in the delta network even if the requests were to two different memory modules. Following the analysis in [7], we apply the result of the $a \times b$ crossbar recursively, to each stage of delta network to obtain the average number of busy main memory modules B. It is computed using the following system of equations.

$$B = Mm_n \qquad (8)$$

where

$$m_{i+1} = 1 - (1 - m_i/b)^a \qquad 0 \le i < n$$

and

$$m_0 = m'.$$

Equating this with B of (3) we have

$$NmtU = Mm_n$$

substituting for $m' = 1 - U$ from (5) we have a system of equations for evaluating the utilization U.

$$NmtU - Mm_n = 0 \qquad (9)$$

where

$$m_{i+1} = 1 - (1 - m_i/b)^a \qquad 0 \le i < n$$

and

$$m_0 = 1 - U.$$

Note that in these equations, as in the crossbar, the utilization is a function of the network size $N \times M$ and the product mt. These equations can also be solved numerically. Here too a starting value for $U = 1/(1 + mt)$ is appropriate for iterative solutions.

IV. COMPARISON OF ANALYTICAL AND SIMULATION RESULTS

In this section we present several results obtained using the above approximate analysis and compare these with the simulation results. The results were compared over a wide range of parameters. The parameter ranges were: request rate m from 1/128 to 1, block transfer time t from 1 to 64 units, and the number of processors and memories from 1 to 128. As an example, Table I shows the CPU utilization obtained through simulation of a 32×32 multiprocessor with a crossbar. The simulation was run for 40 000 time units for each different value of m and t. Table I also lists the confidence intervals for 99 percent confidence level. Each interval was computed using Student's t-distribution, with sample points taken every 1000 time units for a total of 40 points over the simulation run.

The first noticeable thing in the table is the nearly identical values of CPU utilization for a constant mt. The values corresponding to a constant mt can be seen in any forward diagonal of the table. For example, the main diagonal corresponds to the product $mt = 1$. Notice also the small values of the

TABLE I
Mean CPU Utilization for a 32 × 32 Multiprocessor ± (99 Percent Confidence Interval)

	Block Transfer Time t						
Request rate m	1	2	4	8	16	32	64
2^0	42.65±.05	25.24±.06	13.69±.05	7.14±.04	3.65±.03	1.82±.03	.91±.02
2^{-1}	62.21±.09	42.57±.09	25.27±.10	13.71±.11	7.17±.09	3.64±.05	1.85±.04
2^{-2}	78.23±.09	62.23±.17	42.58±.23	25.15±.19	13.78±.20	7.07±.16	3.61±.08
2^{-3}	88.28±.08	78.18±.16	62.13±.26	42.43±.32	25.01±.27	13.62±.25	7.22±.18
2^{-4}	93.97±.06	88.27±.12	78.21±.26	62.28±.37	42.55±.44	25.39±.41	13.85±.36
2^{-5}	96.90±.04	93.91±.09	88.34±.14	78.33±.32	62.16±.51	42.48±.61	25.24±.63
2^{-6}	98.45±.03	96.91±.05	93.91±.10	88.21±.24	78.59±.41	62.19±.66	41.82±.85
2^{-7}	99.20±.02	98.45±.04	96.97±.08	93.99±.15	88.36±.36	78.01±.57	62.60±1.09

confidence intervals, indicating that the simulation values are very close to the steady-state values of the system under consideration.

Now let us see the difference between the analytical and simulation results. Table II shows the difference (analytical–simulation) in CPU utilization for the above example of 32 × 32 multiprocessor. The table shows that the analysis overestimates the CPU utilization in most cases, although by a very small amount, an amount comparable to 99 percent confidence interval. If we compute the percentage difference relative to the simulation result, then it is evident that the highest relative differences are 8 to 10 percent, which occur at values of mt near 64. The relative differences are about 2 percent for $mt = 1$. For $mt < 1$ the differences are less than 1 percent and all differences for $mt < 1/2$ are well within the confidence intervals of Table I. In other words, the approximate analysis of the multiprocessor cache organization is quite accurate in the region where $mt < 1$. As we shall see in the following discussion, it is this region which is of practical interest.

Consider Fig. 3, which is a graph of processor utilization over a broad range of parameters. The utilization plotted may be interpreted as simulation results or analytical results, since the differences are so small that they are not visible on the graph with the scale used. Since in the analysis the processor utilization is a function of mt, the parameters m and t are not separated in this and other graphs. The graph shows three different systems: the first is $N = 64$, and $M = 64$ using 64 × 64 crossbar, the second is $N = 64$, $M = 64$ using $2^6 \times 2^6$ delta network, and the third is the single processor system $N = M = 1$. Since the wait time is zero in the case of $N = M = 1$ system, the processor utilization from (1) is $1/(1 + mt)$, which serves as the upper bound on the processor utilization. It is clear from the graph that for $mt > 1$ the processor utilization is less than 50 percent. Therefore, in a practical system one must have the product mt much smaller than 1 for an acceptable level of performance. Therefore, the region of interest is $mt < 1$. As pointed out earlier, it is in this region of interest that our approximate analysis is most accurate. Comparing the analytical results with a large number of simulation results, we observed that the differences between analytical and simulation results

TABLE II
The Difference in CPU Utilization (Analytical–Simulation) for a 32 × 32 Multiprocessor

	Block Transfer Time t						
Request rate m	1	2	4	8	16	32	64
2^0	.82	1.04	.75	.47	.24	.15	.08
2^{-1}	.43	.90	1.01	.73	.44	.25	.12
2^{-2}	.06	.41	.89	1.13	.66	.54	.28
2^{-3}	.04	.11	.51	1.04	1.27	.82	.39
2^{-4}	-.02	.05	.08	.36	.92	.89	.59
2^{-5}	.03	.04	-.02	-.04	.48	.99	1.04
2^{-6}	.00	.02	.04	.11	-.30	.45	1.65
2^{-7}	.02	.00	-.04	-.04	-.04	.28	.04

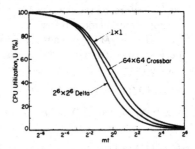

Fig. 3. CPU utilization as a function of mt.

are far less sensitive to the network type (crossbar or delta) and its size, compared to the product mt. This probably is due to the sensitivity of the processor utilization itself, which is much more sensitive to the product mt than the network type or size. Figs. 4 and 5 show the processor utilization in the region of interest. Fig. 4 shows a graph for a 32 × 32 crossbar network and a graph for $2^5 \times 2^5$ delta network. Fig. 5 shows the processor utilization as a function of the network size $N \times N$ using a crossbar. Both figures are obtained from the analytical model of the previous section.

Other measures of performance may also be evaluated from

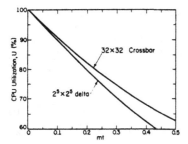

Fig. 4. CPU utilization as a function of *mt*.

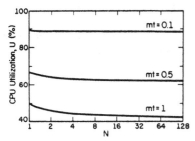

Fig. 5. CPU utilization as a function of the crossbar size $N \times N$.

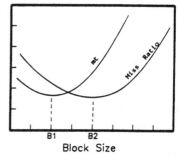

Fig. 6. A typical curve of miss ratio and a hypothetical curve of *mt* as a function of block size.

the analysis. For example, the average number of busy main memory modules is *NUmt* from (3). The average wait time *w* of a request can also be computed in terms of *U*, *mt*, and *m* from (1).

From a designer's perspective the above analysis shows that for optimum performance one must choose *mt* as small as possible. Recall that *m* is not the miss-ratio itself but it is directly proportional to the miss ratio, and *t* is some function of the block size. For example, in an interleaved main memory with access time *a* and transfer rate *c* words/time unit, one can express the block transfer time as $t = a + bc$, where *b* is the block size in words. A typical curve of miss ratio versus block size for a fixed cache size is shown in Fig. 6. The miss-ratio drops when the block size is increased from 1 due to locality in the address stream. However, beyond a certain block size the miss ratio worsens because the additional words fetched in the block are no longer a part of the working set, and furthermore these words occupy valuable cache space by displacing words which are part of the working set. From the graph of miss ratio, one can compute the graph of *mt* as a function of block size, where *m* is the probability that the CPU cycle is a memory reference and that it is a miss, and *t* is the block transfer time. A hypothetical graph of *mt* versus block size is superimposed on the graph of miss ratio in Fig. 6. From the graph one can choose the optimum block size corresponding to the minimum *mt*. For a given cache size, the optimum block size for the maximum throughput may or may not correspond to the minimum miss ratio. For the hypothetical example of Fig. 6, block size *B*1 yields the maximum throughput, not the block size *B*2. A similar argument to use *mt* as a measure of performance rather than *m* in a uniprocessor system was put forward by Meade [6]. To reduce *mt* below this value, one can either decrease the miss ratio by choosing a larger cache or reduce the block transfer time by using a faster main memory. Another alternative is to change

the simple cache organization so that some of the block transfer time can be overlapped with the processor execution. This alternative is discussed in the next section.

V. EXTENSIONS OF THE SIMPLE CACHE MODEL

The three most common extensions of a simple cache organization are: 1) write-through, 2) buffered write-back, and 3) load-through. All of these achieve the same objective, namely, overlap of the CPU execution with the data transfers between the cache and the main memory. In this section we apply the analytical technique that we used for the simple cache model in the evaluation of processor utilization. The approximation in each case is to treat the memory traffic as consisting of single cycle requests rather than block requests. Thus, the analysis treats the request rate as unit service requests distributed uniformly over all memory modules. Once the unit request rate is computed, it can be substituted in (6) or (8) to evaluate the cache-main memory traffic, which is also evaluated in another way similar to (2) or (3).

In the following, the write-through cache is discussed in detail with some numeric examples and compared with simulation results. The other two organizations are presented with only the method of analysis. These two organizations are similar in complexity as write-through, and therefore no further numerical evaluation is presented. The following discussion does not concern itself with the evaluation of relative merits of different cache organizations, since our major objective here is to present the technique of analysis, and not an optimum cache design.

Let us describe some notations to be used in the following analyses. Subscript *r* is used to indicate a read request from cache to main memory for a block transfer, subscript *s* is used for store (write) of a block into the main memory, subscripts *r*1 and *s*1 represent single word requests for read and store, respectively. The parameters *m*, *t*, and *w* are, as before, the request rate, transfer time, and the wait time, respectively. Thus, some of the variables used have the following meaning; other variables will be defined in the course of the discussion as they are needed.

m_r = probability that there is a read request from the cache to the main memory for a block transfer.

m_{s1} = probability that there is a store request from the cache to the main memory for a single word transfer.

t_r = time to read a block from the main memory into the cache.

257

t_{s1} = time to store a single word into the main memory from the cache.

w_r = average wait time at the network for a block read request.

w_{s1} = average wait time at the network for a one word store request.

For the following analysis, let us assume that the interconnection network gives equal priority to all requests. Thus, the network is unbiased towards the read or write requests and towards the block or single word requests. This is reasonable since to a network a request is for establishing a path between a cache and a main memory module. Once the path is established it can be used for any type of transfers. This implies that average wait time at the network is the same for any request. Let this wait time be w. That is

$$w = w_r = w_{r1} = w_s = w_{s1}. \qquad (10)$$

Write-Through (Store-Through): In this cache organization whenever the processor attempts to write a word in the cache, the word is stored in the main memory, regardless of whether the corresponding block is present in the cache or not. If the block is present in the cache then the word will also be written in the cache. As a consequence, on a read miss the desired block is loaded in the cache and the block being replaced is not required to be written back. If write-through operations are sufficiently buffered, then essentially no penalty exists for successive write-through operations. In practice, this can be satisfied with a small size buffer since the write operations are far less frequent than read operations. For this analysis we shall assume that the write operations are buffered in a buffer of unlimited size.

Since each processor is assumed to have only one communication port to the interconnection network, a read and a write request from the same cache cannot be serviced simultaneously. We shall assume that a read miss from a processor has a higher priority over its own pending write requests. However, once a write request has successfully established a path through the network, it cannot be preempted. Thus, during a write operation to the main memory if a cache miss occurs then the read must wait until the write operation is finished. Let the wait time a read request incurs on a write operation from its own cache be w_r'. After w_r', the read request can be issued to the network. Due to the network conflicts resulting from requests of other processors, the read request will wait on average w_r more time units. Thus, a read miss waits on average $w_r' + w_r$ time units, of which w_r' can be determined as follows.

Recall the definitions of m_r and m_{s1} given earlier in this section. Rephrasing these definitions in the current context of write-through cache, we have m_r as the probability that a processor cycle is a read cycle and that it is a miss; and m_{s1} is the probability that a processor cycle is a write cycle. Thus, in k cycles of processor activity, there are $m_r k$ read requests and $m_{s1} k$ write requests from the cache to the main memory. Given that a write request is in progress between a cache and a main memory, if a read miss occurs in the same cache immediately after the first unit of service of the write request, then the read waits for $(t_{s1} - 1)$ time units before it can be issued to the network, where t_{s1} is the write service time. This event occurs

with a probability m_r. If the read occurred not after the first but after the second time unit, then it waits for $(t_{s1} - 2)$ time units. This happens with a probability $(1 - m_r)m_r$. On the average, each write request will contribute to the wait time of read requests given by the following expression:

$$m_r(t_{s1} - 1) + m_r(1 - m_r)(t_{s1} - 2) + \cdots$$
$$+ m_r(1 - m_r)^{i-1}(t_{s1} - i) + \cdots.$$

Thus, over a run of k useful CPU cycles, $m_{s1}k$ write requests contribute

$$m_{s1}k \sum_{1 \le i \le t_{s1}} m_r(1 - m_r)^{i-1}(t_{s1} - i)$$

time units of wait to $m_r k$ read requests. Thus, the average wait suffered by a read request over a write from the same cache is

$$w_r' = m_{s1} \sum_{1 \le i \le t_{s1}} (1 - m_r)^{i-1}(t_{s1} - i). \qquad (11)$$

Now we derive the equations involving the other unknowns. Following the method of Fig. 2, we can express the processor utilization U, the average memory bandwidth B, and the unit request rate m' as seen by the network as follows.

$$U = \frac{1}{1 + m_r(w_r' + w_r + t_r)} \qquad (12)$$

$$B = \frac{m_r t_r + m_{s1} t_{s1}}{1 + m_r(w_r' + w_r + t_r)} \qquad (13)$$

$$m' = \frac{m_r(w_r + t_r) + m_{s1}(w_{s1} + t_{s1})}{1 + m_r(w_r' + w_r + t_r)}. \qquad (14)$$

By (10) we have $w_r = w_{s1} = w$, therefore the expression for m' in (14) involves only one unknown w. Substituting this expression for m' in the bandwidth of (6) for crossbar (or (8) for delta network) and then equating it with the bandwidth of (13) above, we have an equation in one unknown, w. The equation in w can be solved iteratively and then used in (12) to obtain the CPU utilization. A suitable starting value for iterative method of solutions is $w = 0$.

The above method of analysis was used in computing the processor utilization for a 4×4 and a 32×32 multiprocessor system with crossbar. Several different values of the parameters m_r, m_{s1}, t_r, and t_{s1} were used for the above analysis and also for the simulation of the write-through cache model. To get a reasonable range of values of these parameters for a typical system, the following reasoning can be used.

Let us say that in a typical processor about 80 percent of all memory references are read operations and 20 percent are write operations. Let us further assume that of the processor cycles available about 75 percent generate memory references. Therefore, the probability that a processor cycle generates a read reference is 0.6. Assuming a cache miss ratio of 10 percent, the probability that a processor cycle results in a read request from the cache to the main memory is $m_r = 0.06$. In the write-through organization every write request generated by the processor also results in a write request from the cache to the main memory. Thus, $m_{s1} = 0.15$. This argument simply establishes what m_r and m_{s1} might look like in a typical system. The range of values we chose for computation is wide enough to cover large variations in the parameter values of the above "typical" system. The analysis and simulation were carried out for all combinations of the following parameters:

m_r = 0.01, 0.05 and 0.1 m_{s1} = 0.1 and 0.2,

the read block transfer time t_r = 2, 4, 8, and 16,

the write word time t_{s1} = 1, 2, and 4 with the restriction that t_{s1} is less than t_r.

Table III compares the analytical and simulation results. To keep the table size small not all combinations of the parameters are shown. Each simulation was run for 40 000 time units. The confidence intervals for 99 percent certainty were computed for simulations. No interval was greater than 2 percent, while most were less than 1 percent. Table III again points out the close agreement between our approximate analysis and the simulation results. Considering the complexity of the system, the analysis is remarkably accurate and provides a valuable aid in the design phase of a multiprocessor system.

In the above discussion, the analysis and the simulation both assumed an infinite write buffer. To see the effect of a finite buffer, we also ran simulations with a buffer size of 5 words. Whenever the buffer became full, the processor was made idle until the buffer was no longer full. For the entries in the Table III there was no noticeable change in the performance due to a finite buffer. However, for certain combinations of parameter values which imply a high traffic intensity, the performance was much worse than the infinite buffer case. For example, m_{s1} = 0.2 and t_{s1} = 4 implies a traffic intensity of 0.8 for the write requests. In addition, there are read requests and the network interference. For such cases the system sometimes approached an unstable state with monotonically increasing queue size; and limiting the buffer size resulted in the reduced processor utilization. However, if such cases are indeed frequent in a practical system, then it can be surmised that the system is poorly designed.

Buffered Write Back: On a cache miss the block to be replaced, i.e., written back, is first stored in a high speed buffer. The desired block is then read into the cache module. Following this, the buffer is written back to the main memory module. Assume that the buffer is large enough to handle successive cache faults. For the analysis we shall assume a buffer of unlimited size. The activities of the system can be described quantitatively as follows.

On a cache fault the cache transfers the block to be replaced to the buffer in time t_b, after which the cache issues a read request to the network. The read request is granted after an average wait of w_r time units after which the block is read in time t_r. Thus, the processor is idle during $t_b + w_r + t_r$ time units; after this the buffer issues a store request, which after an average wait of w_s time units is granted and completed in t_s units. During the write back operation the processor is busy. Again let us assume as in the write-through case that once the write operation to the main memory begins, it cannot be preempted and if another cache miss occurs during this operation, then the read request from the cache must wait on average w_r' time units before it can be issued to the network. This wait time can

TABLE III
ANALYTICAL AND SIMULATION RESULTS FOR A WRITE-THROUGH CACHE

m_r	t_r	m_{s1}	t_{s1}	CPU Utilization U% 4 x 4		32 x 32	
				analy.	sim.	analy.	sim.
.01	2	.1	1	97.99	97.92	97.97	97.92
.01	4	.1	2	95.86	95.80	95.79	95.57
.01	8	.1	2	92.25	91.95	92.17	92.01
.01	16	.1	1	86.03	85.27	85.98	85.09
.01	16	.1	2	85.78	85.61	85.67	84.68
.01	2	.2	1	97.94	97.88	97.91	97.89
.01	16	.2	2	85.55	85.06	85.38	83.27
.05	2	.1	1	90.49	90.60	90.36	90.17
.05	8	.1	2	69.11	67.81	68.47	66.32
.05	16	.1	1	53.27	51.00	52.56	48.45
.05	16	.1	2	52.54	50.87	51.66	47.87
.05	4	.2	1	82.48	82.07	82.20	81.22
.05	16	.2	1	53.73	50.80	53.13	48.21
.10	2	.1	1	82.21	81.95	81.87	81.45
.10	4	.1	2	67.97	67.39	67.07	65.66
.10	8	.1	4	48.45	46.01	46.99	44.86
.10	16	.1	4	32.50	30.13	31.23	28.83
.10	2	.2	1	81.93	81.79	81.49	80.58
.10	16	.2	1	35.20	32.29	34.25	29.88

be computed as in the case of write-through and like (10) it is

$$w_r' = m_s \sum_{1 \le i \le t_s} (1 - m_r)^{i-1}(t_s - i). \tag{15}$$

In the current context, the definitions of parameters m_r and m_s can be rephrased as follows. Since every cache miss results in a read request to the main memory, m_r is the probability that the processor cycle generates a memory reference (read or write) and that it is a miss. Since for every cache miss a block must be replaced, the probability m_s of making a write request to the main is the same as m_r. Now following the method of Fig. 2, we can express the processor utilization U, memory bandwidth B, and unit service request rate m' as seen by the network as follows.

$$U = \frac{1}{1 + m_r(t_b + w_r' + w_r + t_r)} \tag{16}$$

$$B = NU(m_r t_r + m_s t_s) \tag{17}$$

$$m' = U[m_r(w_r + t_r) + m_s(w_s + t_s)]. \tag{18}$$

Substituting this m' in the appropriate bandwidth equations for crossbar (6) or delta network (8) and then equating it with the bandwidth of (17), we have an equation in U and w, where $w = w_r = w_s$ from (10). This equation along with the (16) of U and w can be solved iteratively. An appropriate starting value for w is 0.

Two improvements are possible in the basic write-back strategy. One is to overlap the time t_b to write the block in the high speed intermediate buffer with the time $w_r + t_r$ of a block read. This can be done by issuing the read request to the network at the same time when the block to be replaced is being written into the buffer. It is safe to assume that the first word from the memory will not arrive before time t_b. This in essence reduces the time t_b to zero in the above set of equations.

Another improvement in the basic write-back organization is to write back only those blocks which are modified. If the probability of a block being modified is known then it can be reflected in the parameter m_s. This reduces the traffic and therefore the wait time of a request, which in turn improves the processor utilization.

Load-Through: On a cache-miss for a read reference, the desired word is directly loaded into a CPU register from the main memory; after which the whole block containing that word is read into the cache module. This strategy tries to overlap the CPU execution with a block read. Load-through can be combined with either of the two previous strategies of write-back and write-through. As an illustration let us take load-through with write-through. In this analysis we assume that the successive reads to the same block which is not yet fully loaded will not be treated as faults. In practice this assumption does not hold. However, the analysis under this assumption gives a tight upper bound on the system throughput.

Let t_{r1} be the time to load-through a single word and let the other variables be same as in the write-through case. Then

$$U = 1/[1 + m_r(w_{r1} + w'_r + t_{r1})] \tag{19}$$

where w'_r is the same as in (10).

$$B = NU[m_r(t_{r1} + t_r) + m_{s1}t_{s1}] \tag{20}$$

$$m' = U[m_r(w_r + t_{r1} + t_r) + m_{s1}(w_{s1} + t_{s1})]. \tag{21}$$

The above equations can be solved in the same manner as for the other cases. In all of the above analyses the crucial simplifying step was the approximation we proposed earlier in the simple-cache model, namely, breaking up any requests to the main memory into unit requests and then treating them as random, independent, and uniformly distributed requests. If a cache organization does not exactly fit one of the above descriptions, then it can still be analyzed by obtaining the appropriate equations for U, B, and m' along the same lines as one of the above organizations. Although we have not given a theoretical argument to show that our approximation will always give fairly accurate results in similar cases, the experimental data do strongly point in that direction.

VI. Concluding Remarks

In this paper we have presented an approximate analytical model for multiprocessors with private cache memories. The accuracy of the model is remarkably good considering the complexity of the problem. In the region of practical interest the error of the analytical model is less than 1 percent. The same model is useful in computing several different measures of performance, such as the processor utilization, the average wait time of request, and the memory traffic.

The central idea introduced in this paper is that of breaking up a request for a block transfer into several unit requests as well as treating waiting requests as several unit requests for the purpose of the analysis. This idea made the analysis of more complex cache organizations like write-back, write-through, and load-through as easy as the simple cache organization. As a side benefit we now also have a way to evaluate the bandwidths of crossbar and delta networks under asynchronous block transfer mode.

References

[1] F. Baskett and A. J. Smith, "Interference in multiprocessor computer systems and interleaved memory," *Commun. Ass. Comput. Mach.*, vol. 19, pp. 327–334, June 1976.

[2] D. P. Bhandarkar, "Analysis of memory interference in multiprocessors," *IEEE Trans. Comput.*, vol. C-24, pp. 897–908, Sept. 1975.

[3] L. M. Censier and P. Feautrier, "A new solution to coherent problems in multicache systems," *IEEE Trans. Comput.*, vol. C-27, pp. 1112–1118, Dec. 1978.

[4] K. R. Kaplan and R. O. Winder, "Cache based computer systems," *Computer*, pp. 30–36, Mar. 1973.

[5] A. Lehmann, "Performance evaluation and prediction of storage hierarchies," *ACM Sigmetrics, Performance '80*, vol. 9, pp. 43–54, May 1980

[6] R. M. Meade, "On memory system design," in *Proc. Fall Joint Comput. Conf.*, 1970, pp. 33–43.

[7] J. H. Patel, "Performance of processor-memory interconnections for multiprocessors," *IEEE Trans. Comput.*, vol. C-30, pp. 771–780, Oct. 1981.

[8] B. L. Peuto and L. J. Shustek, "An instruction timing model of CPU performance," in *Proc. 4th Symp. Comput. Architecture*, 1977, pp. 165–178.

[9] G. S. Rao, "Performance analysis of cache memories," *J. Ass. Comput. Mach.*, vol. 25, pp. 378–395, July 1978.

[10] B. R. Rau, "Interleaved memory bandwidth in a model of a multiprocessor computer system," *IEEE Trans. Comput.*, vol. C-28, pp. 678–681, Sept. 1979.

[11] C. V. Ravi, "On the bandwidth and interference in interleaved memory systems," *IEEE Trans. Comput.*, vol. C-21, pp. 899–901, Aug. 1972.

[12] C. Skinner and J. Asher, "Effect of storage contention on system performance," *IBM Syst. J.*, vol. 8, no. 4, pp. 319–333, 1969.

[13] W. D. Strecker, "Analysis of the instruction execution rate in certain computer structures," Ph.D. dissertation, Carnegie-Mellon Univ., Pittsburgh, PA, 1970.

[14] ——, "Cache memories for PDP-11 family computers," in *Proc. 3rd Symp. Comput. Architecture*, Jan. 1976, pp. 155–158.

[15] C. K. Tang, "Cache system design in the tightly coupled multiprocessor system," in *Proc. Nat. Comput. Conf.*, 1976, pp. 749–753.

[16] C-C. Yeh, "Shared cache organization for multiple-stream computer systems," Coordinated Sci. Lab., Univ. of Illinois, Urbana, Tech. Rep. R-904, Jan. 1981.

Chapter 4

Main Memory Models

In this chapter, we consider the modeling of memory bandwidth. We mentioned in the chapter on cache memory that a major performance bottleneck is induced by the growing disparity between the speed of the processing units and that of memory units. One way of mitigating the effects of such a disparity is to use multiple memory banks.

Figure 4.1 illustrates the structure of the systems that are considered in this chapter. There is one or more processors which originates memory-access requests. The main memory consists of multiple *banks*. Improvements in net memory bandwidth result from the way that the data are stored in the memory modules. Suppose, for example, that we interleave the data in the four memory modules by their last two address bits. That is, the addresses are mapped as shown in the following table.

Bank	Addresses
M0	0, 4, 8, 12, 16, 20, $\cdots$
M1	1, 5, 9, 13, 17, 21, $\cdots$
M2	2, 6, 10, 14, 18, 22, $\cdots$
M3	3, 7, 11, 15, 19, 23, $\cdots$

Suppose now that the memories are accessed in sequence, starting at, say, module M0. This will result in the following cycle of memory accesses: M0, M1, M2, M3, M0, M1, M2, M3, $\cdots$. If the memory access time is t cycles, then it is possible for the processor to obtain up to

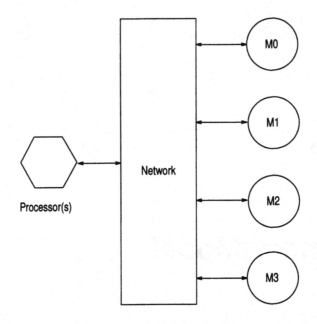

Figure 4.1. Illustration of Multiple Memory Banks

4 accesses every t cycles. The maximum memory bandwidth, then, is $4/t$ accesses per cycle. This system thus has a bandwidth of up to four times a single memory module.

Unfortunately, accesses are not always in sequence. Suppose, for example, that we wished to access addresses separated by 4. That is, the access sequence would be $i, i+4, i+8, \cdots$. All the accesses will then map onto the same memory module, and the bandwidth of the system will drop to that of a single memory module. This problem is not as rare as one might think. Consider a 4×4 array, which is stored in the four modules thus:

Bank	Array Elements Stored
M0	(0,0), (0,1), (0,2), (0,3)
M1	(1,0), (1,1), (1,2), (1,3)
M2	(2,0), (2,1), (2,2), (2,3)
M3	(3,0), (3,1), (3,2), (3,3)

If the accesses take place in column-major order, then this is an optimal storage configuration. If, on the other hand, we want to access them in row-major order, this is the worst possible configuration. The problem is that the same array in memory can be expected to be accessed both in row-major, and in column-major order. To handle both types of accesses, one can stagger the contents thus:

Bank	Array Elements Stored
M0	(0,0), (1,1), (2,2), (3,3)
M1	(1,0), (2,1), (3,2), (0,3)
M2	(2,0), (3,1), (0,2), (1,3)
M3	(3,0), (0,1), (1,2), (2,3)

The problem of finding a good storage configuration in general is nontrivial, and depends on the expected access pattern.

The question of how to model the expected bandwidth of interleaved memory systems is of great importance to architects, since it strongly influences the effective speed of the computer.

Typically, a Markov model is used to analyze multibank memories. Accurate models are impractical since they lead very quickly to models whose number of states is unacceptably large. Therefore, the challenge is to find approximations which, while being numerically tractable, are still sufficiently accurate to be useful. If we have a multiprocessor, then the interconnection network that connects the processors to the memories plays a large role in determining the effective memory bandwidth: the bandwidth can be limited as much by the ability of the network to handle the required traffic as by the memory throughput.

In this chapter, we reprint several papers dealing with the modeling of main memory systems. All deal with multiprocessors or vector machines, since the problem of memory bandwidth is most acute in such systems. The expressions that are derived in many of these papers can, however, also be used, with minor modifications, in a uniprocessor context.

Harper and Jump consider the impact of skewed storage in memory-interleaved vector machines. A skewed storage function maps the components of a vector onto the set of memory modules. In other words, it specifies which memory module contains the i'th element of a vector. The authors provide a model for memory throughput under the skewing function which allocates the i'th element of a vector in an N-memory-module system to the $(i+\lfloor i/N \rfloor) \bmod N'$th memory.

Patel analyzes the impact of the interconnection network that is used to connect the processors to the memory modules. His model can analyze the performance of crossbars and multistage networks to find the memory bandwidth.

The papers by Šmilauer, Fukuda, and Ganesan and Weiss deal with issues of memory interference. Memory interference results whenever two or more processors attempt to access the same memory module. The extent of memory interference depends on the memory access rate, the number of processors and memory modules, the interconnection network connecting the processors to the memory modules, and the access pattern. The papers contain models to compute memory bandwidth.

Zhang provides a model to study the effects of virtual memory paging, synchronization barriers, sequential code, and cache coherence on the performance of a shared-memory multiprocessor. Regression on experimental results is used for the most part.

Geist and Trivedi study multilevel storage hierarchies. The storage hierarchy consists of the cache, main memory, and auxiliary memory (such as disks). The problem is how to assign a set of files across the memory hierarchy to maximize system throughput. The paper contains an algorithm to do this, based on the access time of each level, the size of the program and data segments, and the access rate. This algorithm can also be embedded in a search algorithm to size the hierarchy optimally, that is, to determine the optimal capacity of each level based on the workload.

Vector Access Performance in Parallel Memories Using a Skewed Storage Scheme

DAVID T. HARPER III AND J. ROBERT JUMP, SENIOR MEMBER, IEEE

Abstract—The degree to which high-speed vector processors approach their peak performance levels is closely tied to the amount of interference they encounter while accessing vectors in memory. In this paper we present an evaluation of a storage scheme that reduces the average memory access time in a vector-oriented architecture. A skewing scheme is used to map vector components into parallel memory modules such that, for most vector access patterns, the number of memory conflicts is reduced over that observed in interleaved parallel memory systems. Address and data buffers are used locally in each module so that transient nonuniformities which occur in some access patterns do not degrade performance.

Previous investigations into skewing techniques have attempted to provide conflict-free access for a limited subset of access patterns. The goal of this investigation is different. The skewing scheme evaluated here does not eliminate all memory conflicts but it does improve the average performance of vector access over interleaved systems for a wide range of strides.

It is shown that little extra hardware is required to implement the skewing scheme. Also, far fewer restrictions are placed on the number of memory modules in the system than are present in other proposed schemes.

Index Terms—Address distributions, conflict-free access, memory performance, parallel memories, skewing schemes, vector access.

INTRODUCTION

THE difference between processor cycle times and memory cycle times causes interference in parallel memories to have profound effects on system performance. This is particularly true in vector processing environments where high data rates must be sustained to keep pipelines occupied. When collisions occur in the memory unit, valuable processor performance is wasted.

This paper evaluates the use of a skewed memory architecture to reduce the performance degradation caused by memory collisions. This reduction is achieved by lowering the number of collisions which occur during a given vector access.

Skewing vector data is not a new idea. Several skewing techniques have been proposed by previous authors [1]–[5] to obtain conflict-free vector accesses for a subset of access patterns. While the memory organization presented here does

Manuscript received January 26, 1987; revised May 27, 1987. This work was supported by National Science Foundation Grants MCS 80-01661-01 and MCS 81-21884.

D. T. Harper III is with the School of Engineering and Computer Sciences, University of Texas at Dallas, Richardson, TX 75083.

J. R. Jump is with the Department of Electrical and Computer Engineering, Rice University, Houston, TX 77251-1892.

IEEE Log Number 8717031.

not eliminate all conflicts, it does improve the average memory access time over that exhibited by nonskewed systems. Additionally, the proposed organization is useful over a wider range of access strides and a more flexible number of memory modules than previous schemes.

CONFLICTS IN PARALLEL MEMORY SYSTEMS

Memory conflicts occur when the rate at which service is requested from a single module exceeds the rate at which the module can respond. One solution to this problem is to use parallel memory modules. Historically, interleaving has been the most common organization found in parallel memory systems. Interleaving assigns the ith element of a vector to memory module $M_i = i \mod N$, where N is the number of modules in the memory system. Fig. 1(a) shows the distribution of elements for $N = 6$. Interleaving works quite well when most reference sequences address successively numbered modules. If the ratio between the time required to issue a request and the time required to service a request is N then a factor of N increase in performance is obtained by allowing all N modules to operate in parallel. However, when the sequence of addresses does not access successive modules, the gain in performance can be significantly less than N. Locations marked in Fig. 1(b) are referenced when a vector is accessed with a stride S of 2. Strides other than one are quite common in a multiprocessor vector processing environment where each processor will generate highly correlated sequences of addresses. It is seen [6] that if the gcd $(S, N) > 1$ then the performance of the interleaved system will suffer because references will not be distributed over all modules. Oed and Lange [7] present further analysis of vector accesses in conventional interleaved memories.

Skewing schemes have been used to eliminate the conflicts that arise from strides greater than one [1]–[3]. However, it has been shown that there is no single skewing scheme which allows conflict-free access to a vector using all strides [1]. Therefore, the goal of this paper is to use skewing to improve the average performance of the memory system. That is, the elements of a vector are distributed among the memory modules in such a way that the average vector access time for most strides will be less than in nonskewed systems. While memory conflicts do occur for some strides, this happens less frequently than it does in nonskewed systems.

A skewing scheme is a method for assigning the elements of a vector to the memory modules. It can be specified by a function which maps the indexes of a vector to the set of memory modules. Several general classes of skewing schemes

M_0	M_1	M_2	M_3	M_4	M_5
0	1	2	3	4	5
6	7	8	9	10	11
12	13	14	15	16	17
18	19	20	21	22	23
24	25	26	27	28	29
30	31	32	33	34	35

(a)

M_0	M_1	M_2	M_3	M_4	M_5
0	1	2	3	4	5
6	7	8	9	10	11
12	13	14	15	16	17
18	19	20	21	22	23
24	25	26	27	28	29
30	31	32	33	34	35

(b)

Fig. 1. (a) Six-way interleaved memory. (b) Stride = 6, interleaved memory.

M_0	M_1	M_2	M_3	M_4	M_5
0	1	2	3	4	5
11	6	7	8	9	10
16	17	12	13	14	15
21	22	23	18	19	20
26	27	28	29	24	25
31	32	33	34	35	30

(a)

M_0	M_1	M_2	M_3	M_4	M_5
0	1	2	3	4	5
11	6	7	8	9	10
16	17	12	13	14	15
21	22	23	18	19	20
26	27	28	29	24	25
31	32	33	34	35	30

(b)

Fig. 2. (a) Six-way skewed storage scheme. (b) Stride = 6, skewed storage scheme.

have been investigated and characterized by previous researchers [5], [4]. The skewing scheme used in this paper is defined by a function m that maps the ith element of a vector into memory module

$$m(i) = \left(i + \left\lfloor \frac{i}{N} \right\rfloor \right) \bmod N,$$

where N is the number of memory modules and $\lfloor i/N \rfloor$ denotes the greatest integer less than or equal to i/N. It will be seen that this skewing pattern works well for most values of N. In contrast, the skewing schemes used to obtain conflict-free access have severe restrictions on the values of N that can be used [1]-[3]. Fig. 2(a) illustrates the skewing scheme in a six-module memory system, while Fig. 2(b) shows the locations referenced when the vector is accessed with a stride of 2. Note that the skewing scheme has the effect of skipping one module after every N vector elements have been assigned. That is, the first N elements are stored in modules $0, 1, 2, \cdots, (N-1)$, the next N elements are stored in modules $1, 2, \cdots, (N-1)$, 0, the next N in modules $2, \cdots, (N-1), 0, 1$, and so on. In this example, the conflicts that were experienced by accessing a nonskewed vector with a stride of two have been eliminated.

It is possible to use other techniques such as array reshaping to avoid memory conflict. Array reshaping is performed by embedding an $a \times b$ matrix within an $\alpha \times \beta$ matrix where $a < \alpha$ and $b < \beta$. This can cause problematic strides to occur less frequently. For example, using the $N = 6$ interleaved memory system described earlier, referencing a column of a 6 $\times$ 6 matrix stored in row major form causes all references to fall in the same module, thus causing disastrous performance. If the 6 $\times$ 6 matrix is embedded within a 7 $\times$ 7 matrix where element (i, j) of the original matrix is placed in the (i, j) element of the new matrix and elements $(k, 6)$ and $(6, k)$, $0 \leq k < 6$, of the new matrix are unused then a row major format leads to a column access pattern which distributes references evenly over all modules. This technique can be effective for simple accessing patterns which are known at compile time. However, if accessing patterns are complex or if several access patterns are used on a single data structure, then it may

be difficult or impossible to find a reshaping scheme which gives good performance in all cases. Additionally, if an access is data dependent, then array reshaping may require a significant overhead to rearrange large amounts of data within memory. This rearrangement can also have unforseen side effects such as introducing errors into pointer variables.

Maintaining multiple copies of a single data structure is another technique which can be used to improve vector access performance. This technique also suffers if the access patterns are data dependent and has the added disadvantage of requiring extra memory space. The data skewing scheme presented above and analyzed in the remainder of this paper avoids many of the drawbacks inherent in these other schemes.

A BUFFERED PARALLEL MEMORY MODEL

The proposed memory system is shown in Fig. 3. Parameters affecting the performance of this system include the number of modules, the ratio of the memory cycle time to the bus cycle time, and the depth of buffering on each module.

For a read cycle, the system operates as follows. A cycle begins when the address source places a request on the address bus. This request references one of the N modules in the system. If the input buffer of the referenced module is not full, then the request is removed from the bus and placed in the buffer; if the buffer is full, then the bus blocks and waits until the buffer can accept the request. When the request is accepted by a buffer, the address source may place another request on the address bus.

A memory module is idle until a request arrives in its input buffer. The request is removed from the input buffer, tagged with an identifier, and the memory becomes busy for the memory cycle time t_m. After that time, if the module's output buffer is not full, the data accessed during the memory cycle is placed in the output buffer; if the output buffer is full, then the memory blocks until the buffer becomes available.

Once the data have been placed in the output buffer they are sequenced onto the data bus in the same order that the requests were presented on the address bus. This is done by comparing identifier tags which were attached to the address when the request arrived at the module. The data sink removes data

266

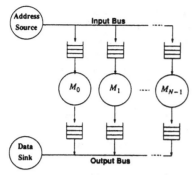

Fig. 3. System model.

from the data bus. Both the data bus and the address bus are assumed to operate with a minimum delay equal to the bus cycle time t_b. The system is said to be matched when $t_b = t_m/N$.

ADDRESS CALCULATION

Before proceeding with a discussion of the performance of the proposed architecture, it is desirable to comment on the obvious deficiency of a skewed system, the increased cost of generating addresses. If the cost of addressing elements of a vector is high, then performance gained by skewing the vector across the modules will be lost. This section describes a method for generating addresses at a rate sufficient to saturate an input bus, while at the same time avoiding expensive and complex hardware.

For a vector access with stride S, beginning at location I, (1) can be used to calculate the module address of the kth access directly

$$m_S(k) = \left(kS + I + \left\lfloor \frac{kS+I}{N} \right\rfloor \right) \bmod N. \qquad (1)$$

When vectors are accessed with a regular pattern, it is possible to form a recursive expression to generate the module address. To this end, the recursive equation (2) was developed by Harper [6].

$$m_S(0) = \left(I + \left\lfloor \frac{I}{N} \right\rfloor \right) \bmod N,$$

$$m_S(k+1) = \left(m_S(k) + S + \left\lfloor \frac{S}{N} \right\rfloor + \left\lfloor \frac{X_S(k)}{N} \right\rfloor \right) \bmod N. \qquad (2)$$

The parameter $X_S(k)$ is generated as a recursion in parallel with $m_s(k)$ and is calculated by (3).

$$X_S(0) = I \bmod N + S \bmod N,$$

$$X_S(k+1) = X_S(k) \bmod N + S \bmod N. \qquad (3)$$

It may not be obvious that a hardware implementation of these recursions is less expensive than an implementation of the original expression (1). To see that it is, consider the recursion for $X_S(k)$.

The initial value for X_S is determined as soon as the stride of the access is known, often this is as early as compile time and

can be calculated by the compiler. The iteration step appears to require two divisions and an addition but the parameter $S \bmod N$ is constant over the access and again can often be determined by the compiler. Noticing that $X_S(k)$ is always less than $2N$, the mod N operation can be performed by a simple ROM lookup. Thus, the entire recursive definition for $X_S(k)$ can be implemented by a ROM and an adder.

The implementation of $m_S(k)$ is no more complex. Using a similar argument, the initial value of $m_S(k)$ can be determined prior to the actual vector access. Two terms, S and $\lfloor S/N \rfloor$, are independent of k and can be combined into one term S'. The mod operator is then applied to S' to yield $S*$, $0 \le S* < N$. The expression for $m_S(k + 1)$ is now (4).

$$m_S(k+1) = \left(m_S(k) + S* + \left\lfloor \frac{X_S(k)}{N} \right\rfloor \right) \bmod N. \qquad (4)$$

Since $X_S(k)$ is always less than $2N$, the third term in (4) can only take on the values of 0 or 1. The ROM table used to calculate $X_S(k) \bmod N$ can easily be augmented to also generate the bit required here. Because the first and second terms are integers constrained to lie on the interval $[0, N)$, the sum of the three terms is always less than $2N$. Again the mod operation can be implemented as a ROM table with the sum of the terms serving as the index. Computing the sum itself requires a two input adder with the carry-in of the adder being driven by the ROM table used to calculate $\lfloor X_S(k)/N \rfloor$. A block diagram of the address calculating hardware is shown in the Appendix. The rate at which memory requests can be issued is limited by the rate at which addition can be performed.

ANALYSIS

Prior to discussing the simulation results, two analytical results that help to characterize the behavior of this accessing technique will be presented. The first is a closed form expression for the periodicity of the sequence of module numbers generated during a vector access.

Theorem 1: $m_S(k)$ is periodic with a fundamental period given by $P = N^2/\gcd(S, N^2)$.

Proof: The proof consists of two parts. First, it will be shown that $m_S(k) = m_S(k + nP)$ for any integer n. Second, it will be shown that if, for all integers k, $m_S(k) = m_S(k + nP')$ for any P', then $P|P'$. Show that $m_S(k) = m_S(k + nP)$.

$$m_S(k+nP) = \left((k+nP)S + I + \left\lfloor \frac{(k+nP)S+I}{N} \right\rfloor \right) \bmod N$$

$$= \left(\left(k + \frac{nN^2}{\gcd(S, N^2)} \right) S + I \right.$$

$$\left. + \left\lfloor \frac{\left(k + \frac{nN^2}{\gcd(S, N^2)} \right) S + I}{N} \right\rfloor \right) \bmod N. \qquad (5)$$

267

Now let $s = \dfrac{S}{\gcd(S, N^2)}$.

$$= \left((k + nN^2 s)S + I + \left\lfloor \frac{(k + nN^2 s)S + I}{N} \right\rfloor \right) \bmod N$$

$$= \left(kS + nN^2 sS + I + nNsS + \left\lfloor \frac{kS + I}{N} \right\rfloor \right) \bmod N$$

$$= \left(kS + I + \left\lfloor \frac{kS + I}{N} \right\rfloor \right) \bmod N$$

$$= m_S(k).$$

This establishes that $m_S(k)$ has a period of length P. Now it is necessary to show that P represents the fundamental period of $m_S(k)$. Show that if for all integers k, $m_S(k) = m_S(k + nP')$ then $P \mid P'$.

$$m_S(k) = m_S(k + nP') \tag{6}$$

$$kS + I + \left\lfloor \frac{kS + I}{N} \right\rfloor \underset{N}{\equiv} (k + P')S + I + \left\lfloor \frac{(k + P')S + I}{N} \right\rfloor \tag{7}$$

$$\left\lfloor \frac{kS + I}{N} \right\rfloor \underset{N}{\equiv} P'S + \left\lfloor \frac{(k + P')S + I}{N} \right\rfloor. \tag{8}$$

Rewrite P' as $P' = qP + r$ and show that $r = 0$.

$$\left\lfloor \frac{kS + I}{N} \right\rfloor \underset{N}{\equiv} (qP + r)S + \left\lfloor \frac{kS + (qP + r)S + I}{N} \right\rfloor$$

$$\underset{N}{\equiv} \frac{qN^2 S}{\gcd(S, N^2)} + rS$$

$$+ \left\lfloor \frac{kS + \dfrac{qN^2 S}{\gcd(S, N^2)} + rS + I}{N} \right\rfloor$$

$$\underset{N}{\equiv} qN^2 s + rS + \left\lfloor \frac{kS + rS + I}{N} + qNs \right\rfloor$$

$$\underset{N}{\equiv} rS + \left\lfloor \frac{kS + I + rS}{N} \right\rfloor$$

$$\underset{N}{\equiv} rS + \left\lfloor \frac{kS + I}{N} \right\rfloor + \left\lfloor \frac{rS}{N} \right\rfloor - c_1. \tag{9}$$

Noting that the value of I merely indicates the initial address of a vector and therefore can be set to zero, a rearrangement of terms generates $m_S(r) = c_1$. By the definition of r and the periodicity of $m_S(k)$:

$$c_1 = m_S(r)$$

$$= m_S(P' - qP)$$

$$= m_S(P' - qP + P')$$

$$= m_S(P' - qP + P' - qP)$$

$$= m_S(2r). \tag{10}$$

By induction it can be shown that $m_S(nr) = c_1$ for all integer n. If $n = 0$ is chosen then it follows that $c_1 = 0$. Substituting for c_1 indicates that r also is zero. Therefore, $P \mid P'$ and P is in fact the fundamental period of $m_S(k)$.

The periodicity of the sequence of module addresses is used to show the second result. The following theorem generates an expression for the number of modules referenced during a vector access. This result in turn gives a rough prediction of the system's performance under specific access patterns and helps to explain the simulation results which are presented later.

Theorem 2: Let $P = N^2/\gcd(S, N^2)$. Then A, the number of modules referenced by (1) is $A = \min(P, N)$.

Proof: The proof will be in two parts. First it will be shown that $P < N \Rightarrow A = P$. Second, it will be shown that $P \geq N \Rightarrow A = N$.

Assume that $P < N$, then from the definition of P stated earlier,

$$\frac{N^2}{\gcd(S, N^2)} < N. \tag{11}$$

It is clearly true no more than P modules can be referenced in one period. Thus, $A \leq P$. To show that A is exactly equal to P it will be assumed that $A < P$ and a contradiction will be shown. At least two of the references within a single period must be to the same module. That is, at least two of the integers generated in a period by $m_S(i)$ must be equal to each other. Let these two integers be generated by the ith and the jth accesses, where $0 \leq j < i < N^2/\gcd(S, N^2)$.

$$m_S(i) = m_S(j) \tag{12}$$

$$iS + \left\lfloor \frac{iS}{N} \right\rfloor \underset{N}{\equiv} jS + \left\lfloor \frac{jS}{N} \right\rfloor \tag{13}$$

Let $k = i - j$; $k > 0$.

$$iS + \left\lfloor \frac{iS}{N} \right\rfloor \underset{N}{\equiv} (i - k)S + \left\lfloor \frac{(i - k)S}{N} \right\rfloor \tag{14}$$

$$kS \underset{N}{\equiv} \left\lfloor \frac{(i - k)S}{N} \right\rfloor - \left\lfloor \frac{iS}{N} \right\rfloor$$

$$\underset{N}{\equiv} \frac{(i - k)S}{N} - \frac{iS}{N} - \frac{(i - k)S \bmod N}{N} + \frac{iS \bmod N}{N}$$

$$\underset{N}{\equiv} -\frac{kS}{N} + \frac{kS \bmod N}{N}$$

$$\underset{N}{\equiv} -\left\lfloor \frac{kS}{N} \right\rfloor \tag{15}$$

$$kS = -\left\lfloor \frac{kS}{N} \right\rfloor + cN \tag{17}$$

$$kSN = -kS + kS \bmod N + cN^2. \tag{18}$$

Let $kS = qN + r$ where $0 \leq r < N$.

$$kSN = -qN + cN^2. \tag{19}$$

Now divide (19) by the greatest common factor of S and N^2.

$$\frac{kSN}{\gcd(S, N^2)} = \frac{-qN}{\gcd(S, N^2)} + \frac{cN^2}{\gcd(S, N^2)} . \quad (20)$$

Let $\alpha = S/\gcd(S, N^2)$ and $\beta = N^2/\gcd(S, N^2)$. Equation (20) can then be rewritten as

$$\alpha kN = \frac{-qN}{\gcd(S, N^2)} + \beta c. \quad (21)$$

Equation (21) implies that $\gcd(S, N^2) | qN$. Let $qN = \gcd(S, N^2) \cdot \gamma$.

$$kS = \gcd(S, N^2) \cdot \gamma + r \quad (22)$$

$$\frac{kS}{\gcd(S, N^2)} = \gamma + \frac{r}{\gcd(S, N^2)} \quad (23)$$

$$\alpha k = \gamma + \frac{r}{\gcd(S, N^2)} . \quad (24)$$

Both sides of (24) must be integers and because γ is an integer $r/\gcd(S, N^2)$ must also be an integer. Noting that $r < N$ and $\gcd(S, N^2) > N$ it is seen that r must be zero. Using this fact, kS can be written as $kS = qN$. Additionally, by substituting for kS in (20) and rearranging terms, it is true that $q \equiv_N -r$ and thus $q \equiv_N 0$. It is obvious that $S | kS$ and because $q \equiv_N 0$, $N^2 | kS$ as well. These facts allow kS to be written as the product of an integer and the least common multiple of S and N^2.

$$kS = \text{lcm}(S, N^2) \cdot \delta. \quad (25)$$

An elementary result of number theory [8] states that the least common multiple of a pair of integers can be expressed as the quotient of their product and their greatest common factor.

$$kS = \delta \frac{SN^2}{\gcd(S, N^2)} \quad (26)$$

$$k = \delta \frac{N^2}{\gcd(S, N^2)} . \quad (27)$$

Equation (27) states that k is equal to an integral multiple of the period. Due to the restrictions placed on the range of k, the only value δ can have is zero. This forces k to be zero as well and the assumption that $i \neq j$ is contradicted. The first part of the proof is complete. If the period P is less than the number of modules in the system, then exactly P distinct modules will be referenced.

The second part of the proof will show that $P \geq N \Rightarrow A = N$. This part of the proof is preceded by an argument that shows for all strides S, $P \geq N$ and $S > N$, there is an equivalent stride g, $g \leq N$ such that the equations describing the accessing patterns for each stride will reference equivalent sets of modules. This statement will allow the remainder of the proof to consider only those strides which are less than N.

The following argument shows that for all S and P, such that $P \geq N$ and $S > N$, there exist integers g and ρ such that 0

$< g \leq N$ and $m_S(\rho i) = m_g(i)$. The argument is as follows:

$$P \geq N \quad (28)$$

$$\frac{N^2}{\gcd(S, N^2)} \geq N \quad (29)$$

$$N \geq \gcd(S, N^2). \quad (30)$$

Let $g = \gcd(S, N^2)$, this implies $g \leq N$. By Euclid's Theorem, g can also be written as $g = \rho S + \sigma N^2$ where ρ and σ are integers.

$$m_S(i) = \left(iS + I + \left\lfloor \frac{iS}{N} \right\rfloor\right) \bmod N \quad (31)$$

$$m_S(i\rho) = \left(i\rho S + I + \left\lfloor \frac{i\rho S}{N} \right\rfloor\right) \bmod N$$

$$= \left(ig - i\sigma N^2 + I + \left\lfloor \frac{ig}{N} - \frac{i\sigma N^2}{N} \right\rfloor\right) \bmod N$$

$$= \left(ig + \left\lfloor \frac{ig}{N} \right\rfloor\right) \bmod N$$

$$= m_g(i). \quad (32)$$

We now proceed, considering only those values of S such that $S \leq N$. It now will be shown that for all strides S, $0 < S \leq N$, $m_S(i)$ references all modules. This is equivalent to showing that $m_S(i)$ generates a complete residue system over N. There exists some i, $0 \leq i < P : m_S(i) = n$, for all n and $S : 0 \leq n < N$, $0 \leq S < N$.

Let $u = \gcd(S, N)$. Again using Euclid's Theorem, u can be expressed as $u = \alpha S + \beta N$ where α and β are integers.

$$m_S\left(\frac{N}{u}i + k\right) \equiv_N \left(\frac{N}{u}i + k\right)S + \left\lfloor \frac{\left(\frac{N}{u}i + k\right)S}{N} \right\rfloor$$

$$\equiv_N \frac{S}{u}iN + kS + \left\lfloor \frac{iS}{u} + \frac{kS}{N} \right\rfloor$$

$$\equiv_N kS + \frac{iS}{u} + \left\lfloor \frac{kS}{N} \right\rfloor. \quad (33)$$

If $m_S((N/u)i + k)$ generates a complete residue system, then $m_S(i)$ will generate one as well. The problem is further reduced to showing that $m_S((N/u)i + k)$ generates a complete residue system. Next it will be shown that there exist some i, k, such that for all $n : 0 \leq n < N$, $m_S((N/u)i + k) \equiv_N n$. Since $0 < (S/N) \leq 1$, there exists some k such that $\lfloor kS/N \rfloor = n$. Choose this value of k and show that

$$kS + \frac{iS}{u} + n \equiv_N n; \qquad kS + \frac{iS}{u} \equiv_N 0. \quad (34)$$

Equation (34) is true if there exists some c such that $kS = -iS/u + cN$. We now demonstrate that such a c does exist.

269

$$kS = \frac{kS}{u} u$$

$$= \frac{kS}{u}(\alpha S + \beta N)$$

$$= \alpha kS \frac{S}{u} + \frac{\beta kS}{u} N. \qquad (35)$$

One solution for c is $c = \beta kS/u$ and i is given by $-i = \alpha kS$. Therefore, it is shown that for all S such that $0 < S \leq N$, there exists an integer i such that for all values of n, $0 \leq n < N$, $m_S(i) = n$.

This result combined with the preliminary argument showing stride equivalence stated earlier in this section shows that $P \geq N \Rightarrow A = N$ with no additional restrictions on S. Both halves of the theorem have now been proven and thus it is shown that $A = \min(P, N)$.

It should be noted that A does not give a complete picture of the addressing sequence. While the number of modules referenced is a good measure of performance when long vectors are accessed, A may be misleading when short vectors are accessed. For example, consider the $N = 6$ system when a vector is accessed with $S = 5$. In this case the first access is to module 0, but then six consecutive references are made to module 5; these are followed by six references to module 3, etc. Despite the fact that the accesses are equally distributed over all modules, the transient behavior of the system is far from optimal. For this reason the use of buffers at the modules is critical. The effects of buffer depth are considered in a later section.

Transient system behavior has proved to be difficult to capture analytically. One method of doing this considered in a previous investigation of interleaved memory [7] is to calculate *return numbers* for the memory access. Return numbers are defined as the number of accesses made between accesses to a given module. This works very nicely for nonskewed memories; however, as was seen in the example presented above, in skewed memories the return numbers are not constant over the sequence of references. It is possible to speak of a mean return number defined over a single period of the reference stream but this measure does not seem to yield any additional insight into transient reference distributions.

Fig. 4 shows TP as a function of vector length for an $S = 5$ access in the $N = 6$ system. Worst case transient performance is observed when $S = N - 1$. In this case a sequence of N consecutive accesses are directed to a single module. Fig. 4 was obtained by performing simulations. The details of the simulations are described in the next section.

It was stated in the Introduction that the proposed scheme does not eliminate all memory collisions. Inspection of the expressions for the number of modules referenced during a vector access and for the periodicity of the module number sequence gives some insight to the efficiency of particular accesses.

If the access is to perform well, gcd (S, N^2) must be less than N. If this is true the access proceeds at peak speed and there are no problems. Most parallel memory systems have $N = 2^n$ modules. In this case the periodicity of module

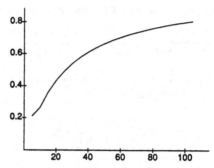

Fig. 4. *TP* versus vector length, $S = N - 1$.

sequences is given by

$$P = \frac{2^{2n}}{\gcd(S, 2^{2n})}$$

and problems arise when strides are of the form $S = 2^s$, where $n < s \leq 2n$. Unfortunately, many algorithms, particularly those used in signal processing applications, process vectors using strides of this form. There are two solutions to this problem.

First, the value of N used to compute addresses is not constrained to be the number of physical modules present in the system. It is quite legitimate to use some $N' = N - c$, where c is a positive integer, to *both store and retrieve* vectors known to be accessed with problematic strides. An efficient compiler can detect these cases if they are known at compile time. The compiler can also place scalar data in unused modules. The disadvantage to this scheme is that potential parallelism in the memory system is unused. If there are more modules in the system than are required to match the bus, then this may not degrade performance at all.

The other solution to the problem is to use a less composite number of physical modules in the system. Since physical memory rarely occupies the entire address space in 32-bit address machines, no penalty need be paid for this departure from tradition. A prime number of modules is obviously the optimal architecture from this viewpoint. When a prime number of modules are used then unless the stride of the access is congruent to N^2 all accesses proceed smoothly. We do not propose the use of a prime number of modules for two reasons. First, the choice of system configurations becomes less flexible as the distance between primes increases. Second, we feel that the first solution accomplishes the same goal without introducing a dependence on the number of modules into the system. An additional benefit of using the first solution is that scalar address calculation, which normally performs multiplication and division with shifting and masking operations, can be performed efficiently. If an N is not of the form $N = 2^n$ the actual multiplication and division operations must be performed when doing address arithmetic. This is prohibitively expensive.

Simulation

As stated in the previous paragraph the number of modules referenced during a vector access provides only a rough estimate of the system's performance; this estimate has been augmented using simulation techniques. The use of a discrete event simulator allows parameters of the system such as request buffering and stride distribution to be examined. The simulation package used to perform this analysis was the CSIM package [9] developed at Rice University.

The primary performance measure obtained from this model is the throughput of the memory system *TP*. *TP* is defined here as the number of accesses per bus cycle and is calculated by the expression

$$TP = \frac{nt_b}{t_T},$$

where *n* is the number of accesses made to the memory system, t_b is the bus cycle time, and t_T is the time required to complete all accesses. Note that this is a normalized measure where the maximum possible throughput is 1; it is reduced by memory conflicts that cause idle bus cycles.

Simulations were performed by developing a discrete event model of Fig. 3 and driving the model with a stream of module addresses. The operation of the architectural model was described in an earlier section. The load model is described at this point.

An assumption is made that the memory system is initially idle. At some later point in time a stream of addresses is sent to the memory at the maximum possible rate allowed by the bus and the buffers in the memory modules. This is intended to represent vector accesses which are separated in time so that one completes before the next begins. The vector being accessed is assumed to be of sufficient length so that steady-state behavior is measured. Generally, this means that the vectors are several hundred elements long. The module addresses are dependent upon the stride of the access and are precomputed for each simulation run. Each address is offered sequentially to the bus. When all accesses are complete, the elapsed time is measured and the *TP* is calculated. The simulations are strictly deterministic, no probabilistic arguments are used except when considering the scatter/gather operations described in a later section. It is possible, although quite tedious, to calculate the vector access performance data using a simple timing diagram.

EFFECT OF STRIDE ON THROUGHPUT

This section discusses two facets of the stride's effect on throughput. The first question is one which is related to individual accesses: how does the memory perform on a single access with a particular stride? The second question is related to the load presented to the system: how does the distribution of single vector access strides, over a large number of accesses, affect the throughput of the system?

The stride of an access is a critical factor in determining the throughput of the memory. By inspecting (4), it can be seen that the module numbers generated for a given stride *S*, are equivalent to those generated by the stride *S'*, where *S'* = *S* mod N^2. This fact eliminates the need to consider the access patterns for strides greater than N^2. Fig. 5 shows *TP* plotted against stride for a single vector access.

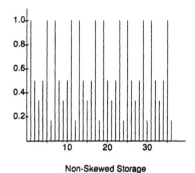

Non-Skewed Storage

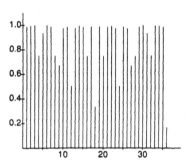

Skewed Storage

Fig. 5. *TP* versus stride; $N = 6$, $t_m/t_b = 6$.

The lower values for *TP* are found when the stride of the access prevents *P*, as given by Theorem 1, from being a multiple of *N*. These lower performance values are caused by the fact that either

1) not all modules are accessed, which occurs if $P < N$ or
2) the references are not uniformly distributed over all modules.

Both of these situations lead to collisions in the system that cannot be eliminated if the vector is long.

The skewed system has an obvious performance advantage. The reason for this may be seen in the expression for the period. The period of reference sequences in the nonskewed system is

$$P_I = \frac{N}{\gcd(S, N)},$$

this period is less than *N* whenever *S* and *N* are not relatively prime. Comparing this to the period in a skewed system, given in Theorem 1, it is seen that, on the average, the skewed vectors are distributed over more modules than the nonskewed vectors.

It is expected that accesses with a stride of one would be the most common. To evaluate memory performance in this case, a weighted average over several strides is plotted in Fig. 6.

These graphs were obtained by accessing a vector with strides ranging from 1 to N^2 and recording the values of the *TP* in each case. The points plotted represent a weighted average of the *TP* values. The weighting function assigns a given weight *p*, $0 \le p \le 1$, to the $S = 1$ case and then assigns the remaining weight $1 - p$ equally to the other cases. The

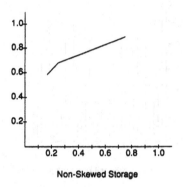

Non-Skewed Storage

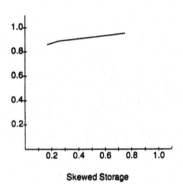

Skewed Storage

Fig. 6. *TP* versus percentage of $S = 1$ accesses; $N = 6$, $t_m/t_b = 6$.

values of p range from $1/N$ to 0.75. The increase in performance observed in the skewed memory is gained by performing accesses with $S \neq 1$. When $S = 1$ the two systems show equivalent throughputs.

Another type of memory operation encountered in vector processing environments is the *scatter/gather* operation. The following discussion is presented in terms of the gather operation but applies equally to scattering. The gather operation involves the collection, or gathering, of a set of vector elements which may be arbitrarily distributed in the vector. Because there is no fixed stride associated with the access pattern, the sequence of modules referenced will not be as highly structured as the constant stride sequences.

Scatter/gather operations can be modeled simply by a random access uniformly distributed over all modules. In this model it is clear that the performance of the skewed storage scheme will be equivalent to the nonskewed scheme in terms of memory throughput. This has been verified using simulation.

Another issue which must be considered when evaluating scatter/gather operations is address generation. Recall that addresses for the skewed storage scheme are generated recursively to avoid computational overhead. This technique cannot be used in scatter/gather operations because in general there is no constant stride between required vector elements. This means that significant overhead may be involved in computing addresses. The worst situation occurs when the value of N is not of the form $N = 2^n$; in this case several integer divisions are required to calculate an address. This is not only true of skewed storage schemes; even if a nonskewed

scheme is used when $N \neq 2^n$ division operations are required to compute module addresses. If $N = 2^n$ then the skewed scheme requires only an additional shift operation to compute an individual element address as compared to the nonskewed scheme.

BUFFERS

The buffers on the inputs and outputs of the memory modules play an important role in the memory architecture. Buffering allows transient nonuniformities in the distribution of references over the set of modules to be processed without blocking the bus. To a large degree it is this technique which allows the skewed system to perform well for general access strides. This section investigates the relationship between buffer depth and the performance of the memory systems.

Fig. 7 shows the performance of skewed and nonskewed storage using the depth of the buffers as the independent variable. In these simulations six modules are present in a system with the bus cycle time matched to the memory.

The plots show a large increase in *TP* when the buffer depth is increased from 1 to 2. In the nonskewed case, no further improvement is observed as the buffer depth is increased. In the skewed system, increased performance is obtained as the buffer depth increases until the depth is equal to the number of modules.

The nonskewed system is inherently unable to utilize buffering techniques to improve performance. This can be understood by considering the expression for the period of m_s in a nonskewed system. The number of modules referenced is given in Theorem 2 as $A = \min(P, N)$ where $P = N^2/\gcd(S, N^2)$, N is the number of memory modules, and S is the stride of the access. Since P, in a nonskewed system, cannot exceed N there will never be more than one reference to a given module within one period. If the period is N then each module will be referenced once during each N bus cycles and always in identical order. The memory is thus always finished with an access as the next request arrives. If P is less than N then not all modules are referenced, but those which are referenced experience a request rate in excess of their response rate. This is an unstable situation and no buffer depth will be sufficient to prevent the input bus from blocking.

In a skewed system the value of P can exceed N. If the bus and memory speeds are matched and if, over P bus cycles, each module is not referenced an equal number of times, then buffering is of no use except in the trivial case where the number of elements accessed is insufficient to fill the buffers. The advantage of the buffers appears when each module is referenced equally over P accesses. In this case, unlike in the nonskewed system, a module may not be referenced exactly once during every N cycles. While the number of accesses to each module is equal, the accesses to a given module may not occur at equal intervals. These transient reference distributions can be buffered. The buffering allows the system to function as if the modules were accessed exactly once during the N bus cycle period. The cutoff in improvement at a buffer depth of N is caused by the fact that there are never more than $N - 1$ consecutive references to the same module within a single period.

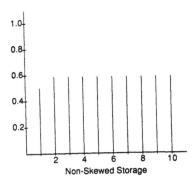

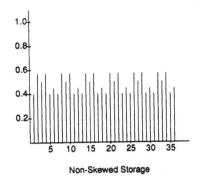

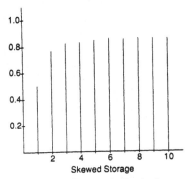

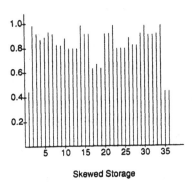

Fig. 7. *TP* versus buffer depth.

Fig. 8. *TP* versus row size; multiple vector access.

MULTIPLE VECTOR ACCESS

The previous sections of this paper have considered only single vector accesses. In this section the concurrent access of several vectors is discussed. The model used to investigate multiple vector accesses remains unchanged except that the sequence of module addresses is composed of addresses for several vectors. The addresses are interleaved in a round-robin fashion. The first address on the bus is the address of the first element of the first vector. It is followed by the first element of the second vector, etc. Only when the first elements of all vectors have been sent to the memory is the second element of the first vector accessed. The other alternative, accessing all elements of the first vector followed by all elements of the second vector is equivalent to the single vector accesses considered earlier.

One problem encountered when evaluating the two storage schemes is to define realistic loads. An area in which vector accesses frequently occur is linear algebra. Solutions of many linear algebra problems involve the accessing of matrix cross sections. The two most commonly used cross sections are rows and columns. Other special sections include diagonals and reverse diagonals. The performance of the two storage schemes will be compared when the cross sections listed above are extracted from a matrix. Without a loss of generality it is assumed that the matrix is stored in row major order.

Fig. 8 compares the performance of the two vector storage schemes for concurrent access of the four matrix cross sections. Because the matrix is stored in row major order the strides of the vectors are equal to 1, r, $r + 1$, and $r - 1$, where r is the number of elements in a matrix row (all strides

are modulo the square of the number of memory modules). Clearly, different sized matrices will generate different sets of strides so the performance data are parameterized by r.

SUMMARY

We have shown that for vector accesses the use of a simple data skewing scheme increases memory throughput over the throughput that can be obtained by the use of conventional interleaving without skewing. This increase in performance occurs regardless of the number of modules in the system or the degree of buffering on the modules themselves. The degree of performance improvement is related to the types of accessing patterns. Analysis of several access patterns which occur in linear algebra applications has shown an increase of more than 50 percent in memory throughput when data skewing is used [10]. It was seen that strides which cause gcd $(S, N^2) > N$ result in many memory collisions in this skewing scheme. Often, collisions can be avoided by storing the elements of the vector over a subset of the modules such that N is changed and gcd (S, N^2) is no longer greater than N.

The inherent disadvantage of the skewed system is the increased complexity of address generation. We have shown how this disadvantage can be reduced for regular vector accesses by using a recursive expression to calculate the module address.

APPENDIX

The hardware shown in Fig. 9 calculates the addresses of vector elements according to the skewing scheme described in the body of the paper. Only hardware implementing data paths is shown, control circuitry would unnecessarily obscure

273

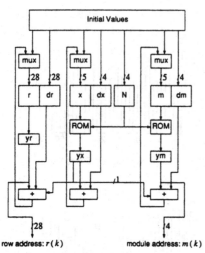

Fig. 9. 32-bit address generation hardware.

the circuit. Diagrams of the control logic are available from the authors. In the schematic, mux refers to a 2-1 multiplexer of the appropriate width, ROM are read-only memories used to store tables so that modulo operations may be computed directly from lookup tables. The r, dr, x, dx, m, dm, and N blocks are register files used to store the corresponding values. Register files are used rather than simple registers so that several vector accesses can be multiplexed on a single hardware unit. There are three pipeline registers, yr, yx, and ym which are used to allow the register files to be both read and written in consecutive cycles without violating timing constraints; three adders are also required.

Vector accesses begin by loading the initial set of parameters through the multiplexers into the register files. These parameters are: the number of modules used to store the elements of the vector, N; the module containing the first element to be accessed from the vector, $m = (I + \lfloor I/N \rfloor) \bmod N$; a constant added to m to form the next value of m, $dm = (S + \lfloor S/N \rfloor) \bmod N$; the address within the module of the first element to be accessed from the vector, $r = \lfloor I/N \rfloor$; a constant added to r to form the next value of r, $dr = \lfloor S/N \rfloor$; the initial value of the function X_S, $x = I \bmod N + S \bmod N$; and a constant added to x to form the next value of x, $dx = S \bmod N$. One set of these parameters is loaded into the register file for each vector to be accessed.

After the parameters are loaded the generation of addresses begins. The parameters for the first vector are read from the register files. r is latched into the yr pipeline register. At the same time, m and N are used as addresses to a 512×4 bit ROM which looks up the result of $m \bmod N$. This result is then latched into the ym pipeline register. Concurrent to these operations, x and N are used as addresses to the other ROM, 512×5 bits, which produces 4 bits, $x \bmod N$ and a single bit equal to $\lfloor x/N \rfloor$. These 5 bits are latched into yx. At this time the address of the first element of the vector is ready and can be sent to the memories.

The second phase of operation computes the address of the next element to be accessed and is much simpler. To determine the next value of m, the old value is added to the value of dm with $\lfloor x/N \rfloor$ being used as the carry-in of the adder. Note that the modulo operation is performed at the beginning of the subsequent cycle so all 5 result bits (4 plus the carry-out) must be saved. The next value of r is calculated in the same way. The new value of x is computed by adding the current value of x to the value of dx. No part of this operation requires the intervention of an external processor which allows vector accesses to proceed concurrently with the operation of the remainder of the system.

REFERENCES

[1] P. Budnik and D. J. Kuck, "The organization and use of parallel memories," *IEEE Trans. Comput.*, vol. C-20, pp. 1566–1569, Dec. 1971.

[2] D. H. Lawrie, "Access and alignment of data in an array processor," *IEEE Trans. Comput.*, vol. C-24, pp. 1145–1155, Dec. 1975.

[3] D. H. Lawrie and C. R. Vora, "The prime memory system for array access," *IEEE Trans. Comput.*, vol. C-31, pp. 435–442, May 1982.

[4] H. A. G. Wijshoff and J. van Leeuwen, "The structure of periodic storage schemes for parallel memories," *IEEE Trans. Comput.*, vol. C-34, pp. 501–505, June 1985.

[5] H. D. Shapiro, "Theoretical limitations on the efficient use of parallel memories," *IEEE Trans. Comput.*, vol. C-27, pp. 421–428, May 1978.

[6] D. T. Harper III, "Performance analysis of data skewing in parallel memories," M.S. Thesis, Rice Univ., Houston, TX, Feb. 1985.

[7] W. Oed and O. Lange, "On the effective bandwidth of interleaved memories in vector processing systems," *IEEE Trans. Comput.*, vol. C-34, pp. 949–957, Oct. 1985.

[8] I. Niven and H. S. Zuckerman, *An Introduction to the Theory of Numbers.* New York: Wiley, Dec. 1979.

[9] R. G. Covington, "CSIM user's guide," TR 8501, Dep. Elec. Comput. Eng., Rice Univ., Houston, TX, Jan. 1985.

[10] D. T. Harper III and J. R. Jump, "Performance evaluation of vector accesses in parallel memories using a skewed storage scheme," in *Proc. 13th Annu. Int. Symp. Comput. Architecture*, June 1986.

Performance of Processor-Memory Interconnections for Multiprocessors

JANAK H. PATEL, MEMBER, IEEE

Abstract—A class of interconnection networks based on some existing permutation networks is described with applications to processor to memory communication in multiprocessing systems. These networks, termed delta networks, allow a direct link between any processor to any memory module. The delta networks and full crossbars are analyzed with respect to their effective bandwidth and cost. The analysis shows that delta networks have a far better performance per cost than crossbars in large multiprocessing systems.

Index Terms—Crossbar, interconnection networks, memory bandwidth, multiprocessor memories.

Manuscript received March 24, 1980; revised February 17, 1981. This work was supported in part by the Joint Services Electronics Program under Contract N00016-79-C-0424.

The author is with the Coordinated Science Laboratory and the Department of Electrical Engineering, University of Illinois, Urbana, IL 61801.

I. INTRODUCTION

WITH the advent of low cost microprocessors, the architectures involving multiple processors are becoming very attractive. Several organizations have been implemented or proposed. Principally among these are parallel (SIMD) type processors [1], computer networking, and multiprocessor organizations. In this paper we focus our attention on multiprocessors.

The principal characteristics of a multiprocessor system is the ability of each processor to share a single main memory. This sharing capability is provided through an interconnection network between the processor and the memory modules, which logically looks like Fig. 1. The function of the switch is to provide a logical link between any processor and any

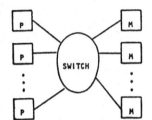

Fig. 1. Logical organization of a multiprocessor.

memory module. There are several different physical forms available for the processor-memory switch; the least expensive of which is the time-shared bus. However, a time-shared bus has a very limited transfer rate, which is inadequate for even a small number of processors. At the other end of the bandwidth spectrum is the full crossbar switch, which is also the most expensive switch. In fact, considering the current low costs of microprocessors and memories, a crossbar would probably cost more than the rest of the system components combined. Therefore, it is very difficult to justify the use of a crossbar for large multiprocessing systems. It is the absence of a switch with reasonable cost and performance which has prevented the growth of large multimicroprocessor systems. To circumvent the high cost of switch, some "loosely coupled" systems can be defined. In these systems sharing of main memory is somewhat restricted, for example, some memory accesses may be fast and direct while many other references may be slow, indirect, and may even involve operating system intervention. There is considerable research on the permutation networks for parallel (SIMD) processors but very little research on processor-memory interconnections requiring random access capabilities.

In this paper we study a specific class of interconnection networks, termed delta networks, which are far less expensive than full crossbars. Moreover, delta networks are modular and easy to control. The delta networks form a subset of a very broad class of networks called banyan networks, initially defined in graph theoretic terms by Goke and Lipovski [2]. Informally, in terms of Fig. 1 the switch is a banyan network if and only if there exists a unique path from every processor to every memory module. The control of delta networks resembles the control of permutation networks of Lawrie [3] and Pease [4]. However, these networks were not applied or analyzed for random access of memories which invariably involves path conflicts in the network, as well as memory conflicts.

In Section II we present the basic principle involved in the design and control of delta networks. Then we describe the generalized delta networks with some examples. Following this we give the detailed logic of a 2×2 delta module which is the basic building block of $2^n \times 2^n$ delta networks. In Section V we analyze full crossbar networks for effective bandwidth and probability of conflicts, given the rate of memory requests from processors. The results of crossbar are used in turn to analyze arbitrary delta networks. Finally, we present quantitative comparison of crossbars and delta networks.

II. PRINCIPLE OF OPERATION

Before we define delta networks, let us study the basic principle involved in the construction and control of delta networks. Consider a 2×2 crossbar switch (Fig. 2). This 2×2 switch has the capability of connecting the input A to either the output labeled 0 or output labeled 1, depending on the value of some control bit of the input A. If the control bit is 0, then the input is connected to the upper output and if 1, then it is connected to the lower output. The same description applies to terminal B, but for the time being ignore the existence of B. It is straightforward to construct a 1×2^n demultiplexer using the above described 2×2 module. This is done by making a binary tree of this module. For example, Fig. 3 shows a 1×8 demultiplexer tree. The destinations are marked in binary. If the source A requires to connect to destination $(d_2 d_1 d_0)_2$, then the root node is controlled by bit d_2, the second stage modules are controlled by bit d_1, and the last stage modules are controlled by bit d_0. It is clear that A can be connected to any one of the eight output terminals. It is also obvious that the lower input terminal of the root-node also can be switched to any one of the 8 outputs.

At this point we add another capability to the basic 2×2 module, the capability to arbitrate between conflicting requests. If both inputs require the same output terminal, then only one of them will be connected and the other will be blocked or rejected. The probability of blocking and the logic for arbitration is treated later on.

Now consider constructing an 8×8 network using 2×2 switches; the principle used is the same as that of Fig. 3. Every additional input must also have its own demultiplexer tree to connect to any one of the eight outputs. Basically, the construction works as follows. Start with a demultiplexer tree, then for each additional input superimpose a demultiplexer tree on the partially constructed network. One may use the already existing links as part of the new tree or add extra links and modules if needed. We have redrawn the tree of Fig. 3 as Fig. 4(a). The addition of next tree is shown with heavy lines in Fig. 4(b). This procedure is continued until the final 8×8 network of Fig. 4(d) results. The only restriction which must be strictly followed during this construction is that if a 2×2 module has its inputs coming from other modules, then both inputs must come from upper terminals of other modules or both must be lower terminals of other modules. (All upper output terminals are understood to have label 0 and the lower terminals, label 1.) Other than this there is considerable freedom in establishing links between the stages of the network. In the construction of the above 8×8 network we had the benefit of some hindsight that 12 modules are necessary and sufficient to build this network. If more modules are used then some inputs of some modules will remain unconnected. We could have stopped in the middle of the construction to obtain a 4×8 or a 6×8 network, such as Fig. 4(b) and (c), however in each case some inputs of the 2×2 modules will remain unutilized.

We term the networks constructed in the above manner *digit* controlled or simply *delta* networks, since each module is

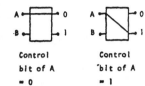

Fig. 2. A 2 × 2 crossbar.

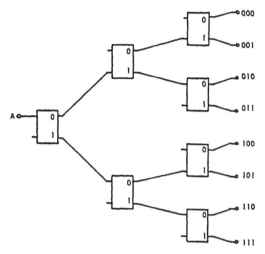

Fig. 3. 1 × 8 demultiplexer.

controlled by a single digit from the destination address. Furthermore, no external or global control is required. Digit controlled networks are not new; Lawrie's omega networks [3] and Pease's indirect binary n-cube [4] are subsets of delta networks.

Under the formal definition of delta networks presented in the next section, Fig. 4(d) is a delta network, but not Fig. 4(a), (b), or (c). Note that the network of Fig. 4(d) does not allow an identity permutation, that is, the connection 0 to 0, 1 to 1, $\cdots$, 7 to 7 at the same time. An identity permutation is useful if say memory module 0 is a "favorite" module of processor 0, and module 1 that of processor 1, and so on. Thus, identity permutation allows most of the memory references to be made without conflict. A simple renaming of the inputs of Fig. 4(d) will allow an identity permutation. This is shown in Fig. 5; in here if all 2 × 2 switches were in the straight (=) position, then an identity permutation is generated. As a matter of fact, since one and only one path is available from any source to any destination, every different setting of the form × and = generates a different permutation. Thus, the network of Fig. 5 generates 2^{12} distinct permutations. This brings us to another somewhat unrelated topic of permutation networks. The procedure to construct a delta network can be used to generate different permutation networks. For example, we could have started with a tree in which the first stage was controlled by bit d_1, the second by d_0, and third by d_2. This would of course require relabeling the outputs. But does this really produce a "different" network? Siegel [5] has shown that by a simple address transformation the networks of Lawrie [3] and that of Pease [4] can be made equivalent, i.e., they produce the

same set of permutations. As far as we know, the network of Fig. 5 cannot be made equivalent to either Lawrie's or Pease's network by a simple address transformation. It is quite possible that there are only two nonequivalent 8 × 8 delta networks, namely Lawrie's omega network and the network of Fig. 5. We shall not pursue this subject any further, as our primary interest lies in the random access capabilities of these networks and not permutations.

III. Design and Description of Delta Networks

So far we have not defined the delta networks in a formal and rigorous manner. For the purpose of this paper we define them as follows.

Let an $a \times b$ crossbar module have the capability to connect any one of its a inputs to any one of the b outputs. Let the outputs be labeled $0, 1, \cdots, b - 1$. An input terminal is connected to the output labeled d if the control digit supplied by the input is d, where d is a base-b digit. Moreover, an $a \times b$ module also arbitrates between conflicting requests by accepting some and rejecting others.

A *delta network* is an $a^n \times b^n$ switching network with n stages, consisting of $a \times b$ crossbar modules. The link pattern between stages is such that there exists a *unique* path of constant length from any source to any destination. Moreover, the path is digit controlled such that a crossbar module connects an input to one of its b outputs depending on a single base-b digit taken from the destination address. Also, in a delta network no input or output terminal of any crossbar module is left unconnected.

One can determine the number of crossbar modules in each stage from the above definition. Specifically, the conditions of constant length paths and no unconnected terminals require that all the output terminals of one stage be connected to all the input terminals of the next stage in one-to-one fashion. The inputs of the first stage are connected to the source and the outputs of the final stage are connected to the destination. Thus, $a^n \times b^n$ delta network has a^n sources and b^n destinations. Numbering the stages of the network as $1, 2, \cdots$ starting at the source side of the network requires that there be a^{n-1} crossbar modules in the first stage. The first stage then has $a^{n-1}b$ output terminals. This implies that the stage two must have $a^{n-1}b$ input terminals, which requires $a^{n-2}b$ crossbar modules in the second stage. In general, ith stage has $a^{n-i}b^{i-1}$ crossbar modules of size $a \times b$. Thus, the total number of $a \times b$ crossbar modules required in an $a^n \times b^n$ delta network is

$$\sum_{1 \le i \le n} a^{n-i}b^{i-1} = \frac{a^n - b^n}{a - b} \qquad a \ne b$$
$$= nb^{n-1} \qquad a = b.$$

The construction of an $a^n \times b^n$ delta network follows the principle presented in the previous section. Informally, the procedure can be stated as follows.

Construct a b-ary demultiplexer tree using $a \times b$ crossbar switches. A b-ary tree has b branches for every node. For a 1 × b^n demultiplexer, the tree has n levels. Each level is con-

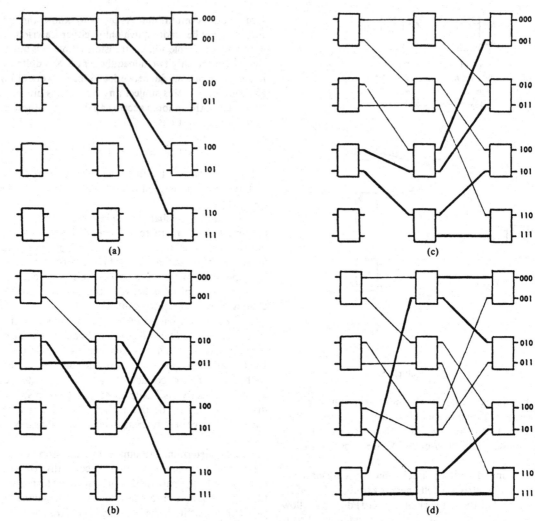

Fig. 4.   Construction of an 8 × 8 delta network.

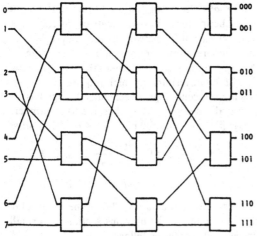

Fig. 5.   An 8 × 8 delta network to allow identity permutation.

trolled by a distinct base-b digit taken from the destination address. For every additional input source, superimpose a new tree on the partially completed network. Each superimposition must satisfy the condition that an $a \times b$ module which receives inputs from other $a \times b$ modules must have all its inputs connected to identically labeled outputs, where the outputs of each $a \times b$ module are labeled $0, 1, \cdots, b - 1$, as was described earlier.

As one can see from the above construction procedure, there is a large number of link patterns available for an $a^n \times b^n$ delta network. It is natural to wonder if one topology is better than the others. We shall see later that, as far as probability of acceptance or blocking for random access is concerned, all delta networks are identical. However, different topologies may have different permutation capabilities in $b^n \times b^n$ delta networks.

Since the link pattern between stages of a delta network is of no particular concern to us, we may ask if there is some regular link pattern, which can be used between all stages and thus avoid the cumbersome construction procedure for every different delta network. There is indeed such a pattern which we describe below.

Let a q-shuffle of qr objects, denoted S_{q*r}, where q and r are some positive integers, be a permutation of qr indices $\langle 0, 1, 2, \cdots, (qr - 1) \rangle$, defined as

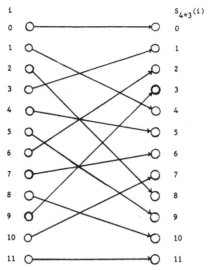

Fig. 6. 4-shuffle of 12 objects.

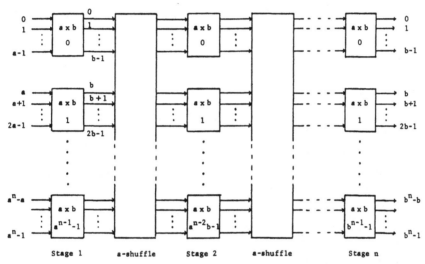

Fig. 7. An $a^n \times b^n$ delta network.

$$S_{q*r}(i) = \left(qi + \left\lfloor \frac{i}{r} \right\rfloor\right) \bmod qr \qquad 0 \le i \le qr - 1.$$

Alternately, the same function can be expressed as

$$S_{q*r}(i) = qi \bmod (qr - 1) \qquad 0 \le i < qr - 1$$
$$= i \qquad\qquad\qquad i = qr - 1.$$

A q-shuffle of qr playing cards can be viewed as follows. Divide the deck of qr cards into q piles of r cards each; top r cards in the first pile, next r cards in the second pile, and so on. Now pick the cards, one at a time from the top of each pile; the first card from top of pile one, second card from the top of pile two, and so on in a circular fashion until all cards are picked up. This new order of cards represents a S_{q*r} permutation of the previous order. Fig. 6 shows an example of 4-shuffle of 12 indices, namely the function S_{4*3}. From the above description it is clear that a 2-shuffle is the well-known perfect shuffle [6]. One can also show that q-shuffle is an inverse permutation of r-shuffle of qr objects. That is, S_{q*r} is an inverse of S_{r*q}. Thus,

$$S_{q*r}(S_{r*q}(i)) = i \qquad 0 \le i \le qr - 1.$$

We show below that an $a^n \times b^n$ delta network can be constructed by using the a-shuffle as the link pattern between every two stages. If the destination D is expressed in base-b system as $(d_{n-1}d_{n-2}\cdots d_1d_0)_b$, where $D = \sum_{0 \le i < n} d_i b^i$ and $0 \le d_i < b$, then the base-b digit d_i controls the crossbar modules of stage $(n - i)$. The a-shuffle function is used to connect the outputs of a stage to the inputs of the next stage where the inputs and outputs are numbered $0, 1, 2, \cdots$ starting at the top. Fig. 7 shows a general $a^n \times b^n$ delta network. Note that the shuffle networks between stages are passive, i.e., simply wires, and not active like the stages themselves. Two delta networks, one $4^2 \times 3^2$ and $2^3 \times 2^3$, derived from Fig. 7 are shown in Figs. 8 and 9; the interstage patterns are, respectively, 4-shuffle and 2-shuffle. The destinations are labeled in base 3 in Fig. 8 and in base 2 in Fig. 9. Now we prove that the a-shuffle link pattern indeed allows a source to connect to any destination using the destination-digit control of each $a \times b$ crossbar module.

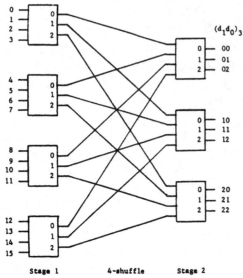

Fig. 8. A $4^2 \times 3^2$ delta network.

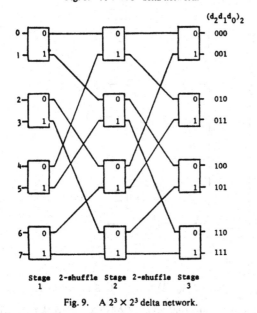

Fig. 9. A $2^3 \times 2^3$ delta network.

Theorem: An $a^n \times b^n$ delta network which uses a-shuffles as interstage link pattern, can connect any source to any destination $D = (d_{n-1}d_{n-2}\cdots d_1 d_0)_b$ by switching the source to the output terminal d_{n-i} at each stage i, where the outputs of each $a \times b$ crossbar are assumed to have labels $0, 1, \cdots, (b-1)$ from top to bottom.

Proof: Let the source S need a connection to destination D, where

$$S = (s_{n-1}s_{n-2}\cdots s_1 s_0)_a \text{ in base-}a \text{ system}$$

and

$$D = (d_{n-1}d_{n-2}\cdots d_1 d_0)_b \text{ in base-}b \text{ system.}$$

In other words

$$S = s_{n-1}a^{n-1} + s_{n-2}a^{n-2} + \cdots + s_1 a + s_0$$
$$\text{and } 0 \le s_i \le a - 1$$

$$D = d_{n-1}b^{n-1} + d_{n-2}b^{n-2} + \cdots + d_1 b + d_0$$
$$\text{and } 0 \le d_i \le b - 1.$$

If the $a \times b$ modules are numbered $0, 1, 2, \cdots$ from top to bottom (see Fig. 7), then S is connected to module number $\lfloor S/a \rfloor = s_{n-1}a^{n-2} + \cdots + s_2 a + s_1$. By the destination-digit control algorithm, the source S is switched to the output terminal d_{n-1} of the module number $\lfloor S/a \rfloor$. Assuming all output lines of stage 1 are numbered $0, 1, 2, \cdots$ from top, the source S is switched by stage 1 to its output line number $L_1 = \lfloor S/a \rfloor b + d_{n-1}$, that is

$$L_1 = (s_{n-1}a^{n-2} + \cdots + s_2 a + s_1)b + d_{n-1}.$$

This line, when the a-shuffle of $a^{n-1}b$ output lines of stage 1 is done, becomes

$$L_1' = \left(L_1 a + \left\lfloor \frac{L_1}{a^{n-2}b} \right\rfloor\right) \bmod a^{n-1}b.$$

Let us first evaluate the floor function.

$$\frac{L_1}{a^{n-2}b} = s_{n-1} + \frac{s_{n-2}a^{n-3} + \cdots + s_1 + d_{n-1}/b}{a^{n-2}}.$$

Since $d_{n-1}/b < 1$ the numerator of the second term is less than a^{n-2}. Therefore

$$\left\lfloor \frac{L_1}{a^{n-2}b} \right\rfloor = \lfloor s_{n-1} + \text{fraction} \rfloor = s_{n-1}.$$

Therefore

$$L_1' = (L_1 a + s_{n-1}) \bmod a^{n-1}b$$
$$= s_{n-1}a^{n-1}b + (s_{n-2}a^{n-2} + \cdots + s_1 a)b$$
$$\quad + d_{n-1}a + s_{n-1} \bmod a^{n-1}b$$
$$= \left(s_{n-2}a^{n-2} + \cdots + s_1 a + \frac{d_{n-1}a + s_{n-1}}{b}\right)b \bmod a^{n-1}b$$

since $d_{n-1} < b$ and $s_{n-1} < a$ the quantity $(d_{n-1}a + s_{n-1})/b$ is less than a. Thus, the expression in the parentheses is less than a^{n-1}. Therefore

$$L_1' = (s_{n-2}a^{n-2} + \cdots + s_1 a)b + d_{n-1}a + s_{n-1}$$

which is the input to stage 2 of the network. This line is connected to module $\lfloor L_1'/a \rfloor$ of stage 2 and is switched according to digit d_{n-2} and becomes the output line number L_2 of stage 2, where

$$L_2 = \left\lfloor \frac{L_1'}{a} \right\rfloor b + d_{n-2}$$
$$= (s_{n-2}a^{n-3} + \cdots + s_2 a + s_1)b^2 + d_{n-1}b + d_{n-2}.$$

After the a-shuffle of $a^{n-2}b^2$ lines, the line number L_2 becomes

$$L_2' = \left(L_2 a + \left\lfloor \frac{L_2}{a^{n-3}b^2} \right\rfloor\right) \bmod a^{n-2}b^2.$$

After simplifying the right-hand side as before, the input to stage 3 is line number

$$L_2' = (s_{n-3}a^{n-3} + \cdots + s_1 a)b^2$$
$$\quad + (d_{n-1}b + d_{n-2})a + s_{n-2}.$$

This line when switched by stage 3 becomes the output of stage 3 at line number

$$L_3 = \left\lfloor \frac{L_2'}{a} \right\rfloor b + d_{n-3}$$

280

$$= (s_{n-3}a^{n-4} + \cdots + s_2 a + s_1)b^3$$
$$+ (d_{n-1}b^2 + d_{n-2}b + d_{n-3}).$$

By finite induction it can be shown that the source is connected to an output terminal of stage i at line number

$$L_i = (s_{n-i}a^{n-i-1} + \cdots + s_2 a + s_1)b^i$$
$$+ (d_{n-1}b^{i-1} + d_{n-2}b^{i-2} + \cdots + d_{n-i})$$

which after the a-shuffle of $a^{n-i}b^i$ lines becomes the input of stage $i + 1$ at line number

$$L_i' = (s_{n-i-1}a^{n-i-1} + \cdots + s_2 a^2 + s_1 a)b^i$$
$$+ (d_{n-1}b^{i-1} + \cdots + d_{n-i})a + s_{n-i}.$$

And after the final stage n, the source is connected to the output line number

$$L_n = d_{n-1}b^{n-1} + \cdots + d_1 b + d_0$$

which is the desired destination D.   □

When $a = b$, the above proof can be simplified because the b-shuffle of b^n lines has a simple form. Take, for example, any integer i, $0 \le i < b^n$ in its base-b representation. Let $i = (c_{n-1}c_{n-2} \cdots c_1 c_0)_b$, then the b-shuffle changes it to $(c_{n-2}c_{n-3} \cdots c_1 c_0 c_{n-1})_b$, which is simply a left rotation of the digits of i. This property was used by Lawrie [3] in proving a statement similar to the theorem above, when $a = b = 2$.

IV. IMPLEMENTATION OF DELTA NETWORKS

Within the current technological limitations it is uneconomical to encode base b digits, where b is not a power of 2. Thus, in practice an $a \times b$ crossbar module for a delta network is more cost-effective if b is a power of 2, since our modules require base b digits for control. Again, due to the cost and technological limitations modules of size 8×8 or greater are not very practical at this time. This leaves $a \times 2$ and $a \times 4$ modules, where a is 1-4, as the most likely candidates for implementation of delta networks. Here we give the functional and logical description of 2×2 modules. This in turn will be used to estimate the cost and delay factors of delta networks.

The functional block diagram of a 2×2 crossbar module of a delta network appears in Fig. 10. All single lines in the figure are one bit lines. The double lines on INFO box represent address lines, incoming and outgoing data lines, and a Read/Write control line. The data lines may or may not be bidirectional. The function of the INFO box is that of a simple 2×2 crossbar; if the input X is 1, then a cross connection exists and if X is 0, then a straight connection exists.

The function of the CONTROL box is to generate the signal X and provide arbitration. A request exists at an input port if the corresponding request line is 1. The destination digit provides the nature of the request; a 0 for the connection to upper output port and a 1 for the lower port. In case of conflict the request r_0 is given the priority and a busy signal $b_1 = 1$ is supplied to the lower input port. A busy signal is eventually transmitted to the source which originated the blocked request.

The priority among processors can be randomized by connecting the two outputs of each 2×2 module to two different priority input ports at the next stage. For example, output port 0 can be connected to a high priority input port and the port

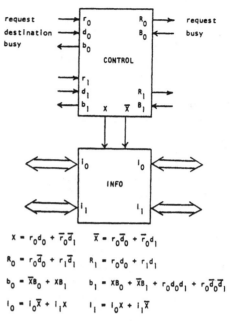

$$X = r_0 d_0 + \bar{r}_0 d_1 \qquad \bar{X} = r_0 \bar{d}_0 + \bar{r}_0 d_1$$
$$R_0 = r_0 \bar{d}_0 + r_1 \bar{d}_1 \qquad R_1 = r_0 d_0 + r_1 d_1$$
$$b_0 = \bar{X}B_0 + XB_1 \qquad b_1 = XB_0 + \bar{X}B_1 + r_0 d_0 d_1 + r_0 \bar{d}_0 \bar{d}_1$$
$$I_0 = I_0 \bar{X} + I_1 X \qquad I_1 = I_0 X + I_1 \bar{X}$$

Fig. 10.   Implementation details of a 2×2 module.

1 to a low priority input of the next stage. The logic equations for all the labeled signals are given with the block diagram. For INFO box the equations are given for left to right direction. The parallel generation of X and $\bar{X}$ reduces one gate level. Signal X and $\bar{X}$ are valid after 3 gate delays. Assuming that one level of buffer gates for X and $\bar{X}$ in the INFO box exists due to fan-out limitations of X and $\bar{X}$, the total delay to establish the connections of INFO box is 6 gate delays, of which 4 gate delays are due to X and $\bar{X}$. Thus, after the initial setup time, the data transfer requires only 2 gate delays per stage of the network.

The operation of a $2^n \times 2^n$ delta network using the above described 2×2 modules is as follows; recall that there are n stages in this network.

All processors requiring memory access must submit their requests at the same time by placing a 1 on the respective request lines. After $8n$ gate delays the busy signals are valid. If the busy line is 1, then the processor must resubmit its request. This can be accomplished simply by doing nothing, i.e., continue to hold the request line high. The Read data is valid after $8n$ gate delays plus the memory access time if the busy signal is 0. Thus, the operation of the implementation described here is synchronous, that is, the requests are issued at fixed intervals at the same time. An asynchronous implementation is preferable if the network has many stages. However, such an implementation would require storage buffers for addresses, data, and control in every module and also a complex control module. Thus, the cost of such an implementation might well be excessive. We have analyzed only the synchronous networks in this paper.

V. ANALYSIS OF CROSSBARS AND DELTA NETWORKS

In this section first we analyze $M \times N$ crossbar networks and then delta networks. Both networks are analyzed under identical assumptions for the purpose of comparison. We analyze the networks for finding the expected bandwidth given the rate of memory requests. Bandwidth is expressed in number of memory requests accepted per cycle. A cycle is defined to be the time for a request to propagate through the logic of the network plus the time to access a memory word plus the time to return through the network to the source. We shall not distinguish the read or write cycles in this analysis. The analysis is based on the following assumptions.

1) Each processor generates random and independent requests; the requests are uniformly distributed over all memory modules.

2) At the beginning of every cycle each processor generates a new request with a probability m. Thus, m is also the average number of requests generated per cycle by each processor.

3) The requests which are blocked (not accepted) are ignored; that is, the requests issued at the next cycle are independent of the requests blocked.

The last assumption is there to simplify the analysis. In practice, of course, the rejected requests must be resubmitted during the next cycle; thus the independent request assumption will not hold. However, to assume otherwise would make the analysis if not impossible, certainly very difficult. Moreover, simulation studies done by us and by others and more complex analyses reported [7]-[10] for similar problems have shown that the probability of acceptance is only slightly different if the third assumption above is omitted. Thus, the results of the analysis are fairly reliable and they provide a good measure for comparing different networks.

Analysis of Crossbars: Assume a crossbar of size $M \times N$, that is, M processors (sources) and N memory modules (destinations). In a full crossbar two requests are in conflict if and only if the requests are to the same memory module. Therefore, in essence we are analyzing memory conflicts rather than network conflicts. Recall that m is the probability that a processor generates a request during a cycle. Let $q(i)$ be the probability that i requests arrive during one cycle. Then

$$q(i) = \binom{M}{i} m^i (1-m)^{M-i} \qquad (1)$$

where $\binom{M}{i}$ is the binomial coefficient.

Let $E(i)$ be the expected number of requests accepted by the $M \times N$ crossbar during a cycle; given that i requests arrived in the cycle. To evaluate $E(i)$, consider the number of ways that i random requests can map to N distinct memory modules, which is N^i. Suppose now that a particular memory module is not requested. Then the number of ways to map i requests to the remaining $(N-1)$ modules is $(N-1)^i$. Thus, $N^i - (N-1)^i$ is the number of maps in which a particular module is always requested. Thus, the probability that a particular module is requested is $[N^i - (N-1)^i]/N^i$. For every memory module, if it is requested, it means one request is accepted by the network for that module. Therefore, the expected number of acceptances, given i requests, is

$$E(i) = \frac{N^i - (N-1)^i}{N^i} \cdot N$$

$$= \left[1 - \left(\frac{N-1}{N} \right)^i \right] N. \qquad (2)$$

Thus, the expected bandwidth BW, that is, requests accepted per cycle is

$$BW = \sum_{0 \le i \le M} E(i) \cdot q(i)$$

which simplifies to

$$BW = N - N \left(1 - \frac{m}{N} \right)^M. \qquad (3)$$

Let us define the ratio of expected bandwidth to the expected number of requests generated per cycle as the probability of acceptance P_A, that is, the probability that an arbitrary request will be accepted. Thus, P_A is a measure of the wait time of blocked requests. A higher P_A indicates a lower wait time and a lower P_A indicates higher wait time. The expected wait time of a request is $(1/P_A - 1)$.

$$P_A = \frac{BW}{mM} = \frac{N}{mM} - \frac{N}{mM} \left(1 - \frac{m}{N} \right)^M. \qquad (4)$$

It is interesting to note the limiting values of BW and P_A as M and N grow very large. Let $k = M/N$, then

$$\lim_{N \to \infty} \left(1 - \frac{m}{N} \right)^{kN} = e^{-mk}.$$

Thus, for very large values of M and N

$$BW \simeq N(1 - e^{-mM/N}) \qquad (5)$$

$$P_A \simeq \frac{N}{mM} (1 - e^{-mM/N}). \qquad (6)$$

The above approximations are good within 1 percent of actual value when M and N are greater than 30 and within 5 percent when $M, N \ge 8$. Note that for a fixed ratio M/N the bandwidth of (5) increases linearly with N.

Analysis of Delta Networks: Assume a delta network of size $a^n \times b^n$ constructed from $a \times b$ crossbar modules. Thus, there are a^n processors connected to b^n memory modules. We apply the result of (3) for an $M \times N$ crossbar to an $a \times b$ crossbar and then extend the analysis for the complete delta network. However, to apply (3) to any $a \times b$ crossbar module we must first satisfy the assumptions of the analysis. We show below that the independent request assumption holds for every $a \times b$ module in a delta network.

Each stage of the delta network is controlled by a distinct destination digit (in base b) for setting of individual $a \times b$ switches. Since the destinations are independent and uniformly distributed, so are the destination digits. Thus, for example, in some arbitrary stage i an $a \times b$ crossbar uses digit d_{n-i} of each request; this digit is not used by any other stage in the network. Moreover, no digit other than d_{n-i} is used by stage i. Thus, the requests at any $a \times b$ module are independent and uniformly distributed over b different destinations. Thus, we can apply the result of (3) to any $a \times b$ module in the delta network.

Given the request rate m at each of the a inputs of an $a \times$

b crossbar module, the expected number of requests that it passes per time unit is obtained by setting $M = a$ and $N = b$ in (3), which is

$$b - b\left(1 - \frac{m}{b}\right)^a.$$

Dividing the above expression by the number of output lines of the $a \times b$ module gives us the rate of requests on any one of b output lines

$$1 - \left(1 - \frac{m}{b}\right)^a.$$

Thus, for any stage of a delta network the output rate of requests m_{out} is a function of its input rate and is given by

$$m_{out} = 1 - \left(1 - \frac{m_{in}}{b}\right)^a.$$

Since the output rate of a stage is the input rate of the next stage, one can recursively evaluate the output rate of any stage starting at stage 1. In particular, the output rate of the final stage n determines the bandwidth of a delta network, that is, the number of requests accepted per cycle.

Let us define m_i to be the rate of requests on an output line of stage i. Then the following equations determine the bandwidth, BW of an $a^n \times b^n$ delta network, given m, the rate of requests generated by each processor.

$$\text{BW} = b^n m_n \tag{7}$$

where

$$m_i = 1 - \left(1 - \frac{m_{i-1}}{b}\right)^a \text{ and } m_0 = m$$

and the probability that a request will be accepted is

$$P_A = \frac{b^n m_n}{a^n m}. \tag{8}$$

VI. Effectiveness of Delta and Crossbar Networks

Since we do not have a closed form solution for the bandwidth of delta networks (7), we cannot directly compare the bandwidths of crossbar (3) and delta networks. We have computed the values of the expected bandwidth and the probability of acceptance for several networks. These results are plotted in Figs. 11, 12, and 13.

Fig. 11 shows the probability of acceptance P_A, for $2^n \times 2^n$ and $4^n \times 4^n$ delta networks and $N \times N$ crossbar, when the request generation rate of each processor is $m = 1$. The curve marked delta-2 is for delta networks using 2×2 switches and delta-4 for delta networks using 4×4 switches. The graphs are drawn as smooth curves in this and other figures only for visual convenience, in actuality the values are valid only at specific discrete points. In particular, an $N \times N$ crossbar is defined for all integers $N \geq 1$, a delta-2 is defined only for $N = 2^n$, $n \geq 1$, and delta-4 is defined only for $N = 4^n$, $n \geq 1$.

Notice in Fig. 11 that P_A for crossbar approaches a constant

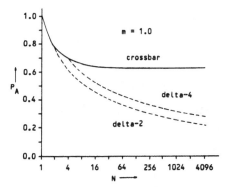

Fig. 11.   Probability of acceptance of $N \times N$ networks.

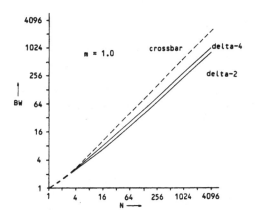

Fig. 12.   Expected bandwidth of $N \times N$ networks.

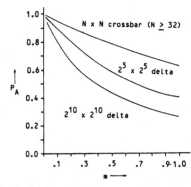

Fig. 13.   Probability of acceptance versus mean request rate.

value as was predicted by (6) of the previous section. P_A for delta networks continues to fall as N grows. Fig. 12 shows the expected bandwidth BW as a function of N. The bandwidth is measured in number of requests accepted per cycle. In all fairness we must point out that a cycle for a crossbar could be smaller than a cycle for a large delta network. Taking into account fan-in and fan-out constraints, the decoder and arbiter for a $N \times N$ crossbar has a delay of $0(\log_2 N)$ gate delays. A $2^n \times 2^n$ delta network also has $0(\log_2 N)$ gate delays, from the analysis of Section IV. However, the delay of a delta network is approximately twice the delay of a crossbar. If the delay is small compared to the memory access time, then the cycle time (the sum of network delay and memory access time) of a

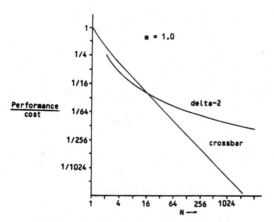

Fig. 14. Cost-effectiveness of $N \times N$ networks.

crossbar is not too different from that of a delta network. Thus, the curves for bandwidth provide a good comparison between networks.

Fig. 13 shows P_A as a function of the request generation rate m. The curve for the crossbar is the limiting value of P_A as N grows to infinity. Curves for $N \geq 32$ are not distinguishable with the scale used in that graph.

Finally, the graph of Fig. 14 is an indication of cost-effectiveness of delta networks. The cost of a $N \times N$ crossbar or delta network is assumed to be proportional to the number of gates required. The constant of proportionality should be the same in both cases because the degree of integration, modularity, and wiring complexity in both cases is more or less the same. For the $N \times N$ crossbar the minimum number of gates required is one per crosspoint per data line. Depending on the assumptions used on fan-in, fan-out, the complexity of the decoder and the arbiter, one can estimate the gate complexity of a crossbar anywhere from one gate to six gates per crosspoint. Let us assume the lowest cost figure of one gate per crosspoint.

The cost of $2^n \times 2^n$ delta network is estimated from the Boolean equations of the 2×2 module of Fig. 10. The number of gates in a 2×2 module is 23 gates for the control plus 6 gates per information line. Assuming the number of information lines to be large, the gates for control can be ignored. Thus, the gate count of a $2^n \times 2^n$ delta network is $6n2^{n-1}$ per information line because the network has $n2^{n-1}$ modules.

Thus, the cost of $N \times N$ networks are kN^2 for crossbar and $3kN\log_2 N$ for delta ($N = 2^n$), where k is the constant of proportionality. We have used these cost expressions in the computation of performance-cost ratio for Fig. 14; the ratio is that of expected bandwidth over cost. Taking this ratio for a 1×1 crossbar as unity, the Y-axis of Fig. 14 represents the performance over cost relative to a 1×1 crossbar. The Y-axis may

also be interpreted as bandwidth per gate per information line. Notice that delta network is more cost-effective for network size N greater than 16. If the cost of the crossbar was assumed as 2 or more gates per crosspoint, then the curve for the crossbar would shift downward and the effectiveness of delta becomes even more pronounced. However, if one assumed the cycle time of a crossbar half as much as that of a delta network, then the curve for crossbar would shift upwards relative to the curve for delta, thus shifting the crossover point of the two curves towards right. Thus, depending on the assumptions, the crossover point may move slightly left or right; but in any case the curves clearly show the effectiveness of delta networks for medium and large scale multiprocessors.

VIII. Concluding Remarks

We have presented in this paper a class of processor-memory interconnection networks, called delta networks, which are easy to control and design, and are very cost-effective. We also presented the combinatorial analysis of delta networks and full crossbars. It is seen that delta networks bridge the gap between a single time-shared bus and a full crossbar. The cost of an $N \times N$ delta network varies as $N\log_2 N$, while that of crossbar varies as N^2. Thus, delta networks are very suitable for relatively low cost multimicroprocessor systems.

References

[1] M. J. Flynn, "Very high speed computing systems," *Proc. IEEE*, vol. 54, pp. 1901–1909, Dec. 1966.
[2] L. R. Goke and G. J. Lipovski, "Banyan networks for partitioning multiprocessor systems," in *Proc. 1st Annu. Symp. Comput. Arch.*, Dec. 1973, pp. 21–28.
[3] D. H. Lawrie, "Access and alignment of data in an array processor," *IEEE Trans. Comput.*, vol. C-24, pp. 1145–1155, Dec. 1975.
[4] M. C. Pease, "The indirect binary *n*-cube microprocessor array," *IEEE Trans. Comput.*, vol. C-26, pp. 458–473, May 1977.
[5] H. J. Siegel, "Study of multistage SIMD interconnection networks," in *Proc. 5th Annu. Symp. Comput. Arch.*, Apr. 1978, pp. 223–229.
[6] H. S. Stone, "Parallel processing with the perfect shuffle," *IEEE Trans. Comput.*, vol. C-20, pp. 153–161, Feb. 1971.
[7] D. Y. Chang, D. J. Kuck, and D. H. Lawrie, "On the effective bandwidth of parallel memories," *IEEE Trans. Comput.*, vol. C-26, pp. 480–490, May 1977.
[8] W. D. Strecker, "Analysis of the instruction execution rate in certain computer structures," Ph.D. dissertation, Carnegie-Mellon Univ., Pittsburgh, PA, 1970.
[9] F. Baskett and A. J. Smith, "Interference in multiprocessor computer systems with interleaved memory," *Commun. Ass. Comput. Mach.*, vol. 19, pp. 327–334, June 1976.
[10] D. P. Bhandarkar, "Analysis of memory interference in multiprocessors," *IEEE Trans. Comput.*, vol. C-24, pp. 897–908, Sept. 1975.

General Model for Memory Interference in Multiprocessors and Mean Value Analysis

BOHDAN ŠMILAUER

Abstract —This correspondence seeks to generalize and clarify the general model for memory interference (GMI) in multiprocessors as proposed by Hoogendoorn. The interference model creates a queueing network where some service centers are FCFS with constant service times; therefore, we also apply the mean value analysis (MVA) approximation suggested by Reiser to solve this model. Furthermore, we reduce the computations in this approximation by applying the iterative scheme suggested by Schweitzer. Although many authors have studied the memory interference problem, nobody has used the above-mentioned MVA approximations. We study these MVA approximations in the context of the memory interference problem and show that they produce better results with much less computation.

Manuscript received March 12, 1984; revised January 29, 1985.

The author is with the Research Institute for Mathematical Machines, P.O. Box 65, Parlerova, 169 00 Prague 612, Czechoslovakia.

Index Terms — Analytic models, closed queueing networks, constant service time, mean value analysis, memory interference, multiprocessors, performance evaluation.

I. Introduction

In this correspondence we assume n processors interconnected with m memories via a crossbar switch causing no delay in memory access, FCFS queues at the memory modules, and constant service time ts.

The problem of interference in such a multiprocessor system has been treated by a number of authors.

Skinner and Asher [10] present a closed-form analytic solution for a system with two processors and m memories allowing arbitrary distribution of memory reference between the memory modules. Their analysis is exact, using a discrete Markov chain model. McCredie [11] assumes exponentially distributed cycle time for processors and memories. One of the processors has different access probability to the memory modules. Jackson's formula is used for closed queueing networks under these assumptions. Strecker [7] presents an approximate formula for a system of m identical memories and n identical processors with uniformly distributed memory access probabilities. Bhandarkar [4] presents some discrete Markov chain models for the memory interference problem. He offers an exact solution for the problem of m memory modules and n identical processors with uniformly distributed memory access probabilities under the assumption that the processor processing time tp is zero. This solution cannot be expressed in analytic form, but can be given as a solution of a set of equations. Bhandarkar also presents an approximate solution of systems with arbitrary memory access probability and processing time $tp = 0$ and/or with uniformly distributed memory access probability for processing time $tp > 0$. Hoogendoorn [1] presents his GMI model, which is approximate but more general than all the previously mentioned ones. He assumes arbitrary memory access probabilities and nonzero processing time. He further assumes that queued processors are selected randomly, so that when i processors are waiting, each has the same probability $1/i$ of being served. Baskett and Smith [5] assume the uniform request distribution, n identical processors, m memory modules, and $tp = 0$. They used the $M/D/1$ queueing model for memory modules and also the more accurate binomial distribution of request arrivals. They have derived an asymptotically exact formula. Rau [12] obtained the same formula using a different method. Sethi and Deo [6] have derived an empirical formula for the uniform reference model.

Hoogendoorn's approximate method GMI is the most general one; it is analyzed and slightly generalized in our correspondence, and a close relation to mean value analysis (MVA) [2] is shown. It is demonstrated in this correspondence that the GMI is an approximate solution of a closed queueing network with many customer classes, provided the harmonic mean queue length is considered instead of the arithmetic mean queue length, and the problem is solved numerically by the iterative approximation suggested by Schweitzer [8].

In the Section IV of this correspondence, the MVA method is adapted to examine multiprocessor systems. This adaptation to constant service times is done by an approximation suggested by Reiser [3] in the formula for mean queue length; an approximation for zero queue length probability and Schweitzer's iterations are also used. This new method (called MVAIC) usually yields more accurate results than the GMI method, as is illustrated by examples; moreover, the MVAIC method is significantly simpler numerically than the GMI method. The MVAIC method yields a new analytic formula for an average number of busy memories in uniformly distributed request models with identical processors, memories, and zero processing time.

II. The General Memory Interference (GMI) Model

In this section we shall explain Hoogendoorn's generalized model; all assumptions will be explained in the text.

The processors issue requests for memory accesses in a multi-

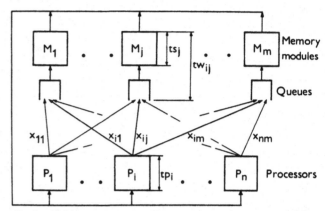

Fig. 1. Multiprocessor system with n processors and m memory modules.

processor system containing $i = 1, 2, \cdots, n$ processors and $j = 1, 2, \cdots, m$ memory modules. The proportion of processor i requests directed to memory module j is given by x_{ij} with

$$\sum_{j=1}^{m} x_{ij} = 1, \qquad i = 1, 2, \cdots, n. \tag{1}$$

The values x_{ij} depend only on the characteristics of the job executed by processor i and are not affected by the behavior of the surrounding system.

Memory modules are linked to the processors by means of a crossbar switch, which does not cause any delay in access to the memory modules. If the memory module is busy, the processor memory requests line up in front of the memory modules. After serving one processor request for service (access) time ts_j, memory module j is ready to service the next request. Mean processing (operating) time of the served processor i after completing access to memory module j and before request for a new access is given by tp_{ij}.

We define a new value tw_{ij}, which is the average waiting time of processor i request for memory j access in one cycle, i.e., the sum of the time for which processor i is waiting in the queue and time ts_j for which it is accessing memory j.

The average cycle rate λ_i of processor i is the inversion of average processor i cycle time

$$\lambda_i = \frac{1}{\sum_j x_{ij}(tw_{ij} + tp_{ij})}, \qquad \text{for all } i. \tag{2}$$

Let y_{ij} be the proportion of time that processor i spends referencing memory j, that is, either successfully accessing it or waiting to do so. Little's formula yields

$$y_{ij} = \frac{x_{ij} tw_{ij}}{\sum_j x_{ij}(tw_{ij} + tp_{ij})}, \qquad \text{for all } i, j. \tag{3}$$

Let p_{ij} be the proportion of time for which processor i is successfully accessing memory j (it is not waiting). Analogously, we have

$$p_{ij} = \frac{x_{ij} ts_j}{\sum_j x_{ij}(tw_{ij} + tp_{ij})}, \qquad \text{for all } i, j. \tag{4}$$

From (3) and (4) we obtain

$$tw_{ij} = ts_j \frac{y_{ij}}{p_{ij}}. \tag{5}$$

Until now, the characteristics x_{ij}, y_{ij}, p_{ij} have had an operational nature, and (1)–(5) have held without further assumptions. Hereinafter, we assume that values y_{ij} are probabilities; then the value y_{ij} is the probability that processor i is referencing memory module j.

The values x_{ij} then represent the routing probabilities of processor i. In a real sequence of accesses to the memory by a processor, there usually exists serial correlation between successive addresses. This dependence is not considered in the GMI and other models discussed in this correspondence; the same assumption has been made by various authors in [1], [4], [5], [7], [10]–[12]. The effect of this assumption has been assessed, e.g., by Hoogendoorn in [1]. He compared the GMI results to trace driven simulation results; the simulations have shown that serial correlation between successive memory accesses does not appear to have a marked effect on memory interference in the treated examples.

The probability p_{ij} of processor i just accessing memory j is then

$$p_{ij} = \text{Prob(processor } i \text{ alone is referencing memory } j)$$

$$+ \frac{1}{2} \text{Prob(processor } i \text{ and another processor}$$
$$\text{referencing memory } j)$$

$$+ \frac{1}{3} \text{Prob(processor } i \text{ and another two processors}$$
$$\text{referencing memory } j)$$

$$\vdots$$

$$+ \frac{1}{n} \text{Prob(all processors referencing memory } j).$$

Mathematically, we approximate p_{ij} as if y_{ij} were probabilities of mutually independent events

$$p_{ij} \approx y_{ij}(1 - y_{1j})(1 - y_{2j}) \cdots (1 - y_{i-1j})(1 - y_{i+1j}) \cdots (1 - y_{nj})$$
$$+ \frac{1}{2} y_{ij} y_{1j}(1 - y_{2j})(1 - y_{3j}) \cdots$$
$$\vdots$$
$$+ \frac{1}{2} y_{ij}(1 - y_{1j})(1 - y_{2j}) \cdots \cdots \cdots (1 - y_{n-1j})y_{nj}$$
$$+ \frac{1}{3} y_{ij} y_{1j} y_{2j}(1 - y_{3j})(1 - y_{4j}) \cdots \cdots (1 - y_{nj})$$
$$+ \frac{1}{3} y_{ij} y_{1j}(1 - y_{2j})y_{3j}(1 - y_{4j}) \cdots \cdots (1 - y_{nj})$$
$$\vdots$$
$$+ \frac{1}{n} y_{ij} y_{1j} y_{2j} y_{3j} \cdots y_{nj}, \qquad \text{for all } i, j. \qquad (6)$$

Due to this approximation, the GMI algorithm is not exact even if the successive routing probabilities x_{ij} are independent.

We can formally express p_{ij} as

$$p_{ij} \approx y_{ij} \cdot f_{ij}^*(y_{1j}, y_{2j}, \cdots, y_{k \neq ij}, \cdot, y_{nj}) \qquad (7)$$

where function f_{ij}^* follows from expression (6).

From (5) and (7) we obtain

$$tw_{ij} \approx \frac{ts_j}{f_{ij}^*}, \qquad \text{for all } i, j. \qquad (8)$$

The $n \cdot m$ equations (3) and $n \cdot m$ equations (8) together give $2 \cdot n \cdot m$ equations for $2 \cdot n \cdot m$ unknown values y_{ij}, tw_{ij}; this set of equations can be solved by iterations. A generalized GMI algorithm is thus obtained:
1) Initialize $y_{ij} = x_{ij}$ for all i, j
2) Compute

$$tw_{ij} = \frac{ts_j}{f_{ij}^*} \qquad \text{for all } i, j \qquad (9)$$

3) Compute

$$y_{ij}' = \frac{x_{ij} tw_{ij}}{\sum_j x_{ij}(tw_{ij} + tp_{ij})} \qquad \text{for all } i, j \qquad (10)$$

4) If $y_{ij}'/y_{ij} = 1 \pm \varepsilon$ for all i, j, then y_{ij} is the solution; otherwise, substitute y_{ij}' for y_{ij} and go back to step 2).

This GMI algorithm is more general than the original algorithm by Hoogendoorn because it considers various access times ts_j for various memories j and various processing times tp_{ij} of processor i after access to various memory modules j. Note that only mean values ts_j, tp_{ij} are considered in the GMI model, and no assumption regarding their distribution is required. The random selection queueing discipline was used for deriving the GMI model, but according to Kleinrock's conservation law, the queueing discipline has no influence upon mean waiting time in work conserving systems. Therefore, if we use the GMI model for such systems, the queueing discipline is irrelevant.

III. The Approximate Iterative Algorithm Using Mean Value Analysis (MVAIE) and its Relation to the GMI Algorithm

The multiprocessor system represents a special case of a closed queueing network. In this section we introduce an approximate method for solving such queueing networks by means of MVA, and we show its close relation to the GMI.

Each processor i request is a customer of class i routing the network where the memory modules are service centers. Only one customer is in every class, i.e., one processor issues only one request, and thus the mean number of processor i requests in service center j is the probability y_{ij} of a processor i request being in service center j. Now we compute mean waiting time tw_{ij} (queueing plus service) by means of the MVA.

Reiser and Lavenberg [2] proved that for queueing networks whose state probabilities can be expressed in a product form (e.g., FCFS queues and exponentially distributed service times with mean ts_j) the following expression holds:

$$tw_{ij} = f_{ij}^{\text{MVARE}}(y_{1j}^{(i)}, y_{2j}^{(i)}, \cdots) = ts_j\left(1 + \sum_k y_{kj}^{(i)}\right) \qquad \text{for all } i, j. \qquad (11)$$

Here ts_j denotes the service time in center j without waiting time, and $y_{kj}^{(i)}$ is computed as the mean number of class k customers in center j in a system with one customer less in class i. The set of equations (3) and (11) can be solved recursively. We shall call this recursive algorithm MVARE (MVA, recursive and exponential).

Schweitzer [8] proposed an approximation

$$y_{kj}^{(i)} = y_{kj} \qquad \text{for } i \neq k, \qquad (12)$$

which means that the mean number of class k customers in service center j does not depend on removing a customer of another class i. In a multiprocessor system with just one customer in each class i, we obtain

$$y_{ij}^{(i)} = 0 \qquad \text{for all } i, j. \qquad (13)$$

This means that no request from processor i can be waiting in memory j queue while a request from processor i is arriving. Equation (11) then becomes

$$tw_{ij} \approx f_{ij}^{\text{MVAIE}}(y_{1j}, y_{2j}, \cdots) = ts_j\left(1 + \sum_{k \neq i} y_{kj}\right). \qquad (14)$$

Equations (3) and (14) form a set with unknown values tw_{ij} and y_{ij}, which can be solved by the iterative method. This approximate method MVAIE (MVA, iterative and exponential), suggested in a general form by Schweitzer [8] and Bard [13], reduces the computing complexity of systems with large numbers of customers and classes.

By replacing (9) in the GMI algorithm with (14), we obtain the MVAIE algorithm. Hence, the function f_{ij}^{MVAIE} is used in the computation of tw_{ij} instead of $f_{ij}^{\text{GMI}} = ts_j/f_{ij}^*$. In the Appendix it is shown that the function f_{ij}^{MVAIE} uses the arithmetic mean of the queue length, while the function f_{ij}^{GMI} uses the harmonic mean of the queue length. It is further shown that for queues where at least two requests can meet, the following relation holds:

$$f_{ij}^{\text{GMI}} < f_{ij}^{\text{MVAIE}} \quad \text{(with the same arguments)}. \quad (15)$$

The GMI algorithm considers shorter delays in queues than the MVAIE one.

IV. Generalization of MVAIE for Constant Service Times, MVAIC

A constant service time ts_j and FCFS queues are typical for a memory system forming a service center. For this reason we shall try to adapt (11), which is valid precisely for exponential distribution of service times, for constant service times.

A system with exponential service time is memoryless, and therefore, the arriving customer sees the queue as if the service for the first customer has just started. This fact is expressed in (11). If the service times are constant, and assuming the incoming customer arrives at random time, the first customer can naturally be expected to be in the middle of his service interval when the next customer arrives. Therefore, if l customers are in the queue, the mean waiting time of the incoming customer is approximated by

$$tw_{ij} \begin{cases} \approx ts_j\left(l - \dfrac{1}{2} + 1\right) = ts_j\left(l + \dfrac{1}{2}\right), & \text{for } l = 1, 2, \cdots \\ = ts_j, & \text{for } l = 0. \end{cases} \quad (16)$$

This approximation was introduced by Reiser [3]. After expansion we obtain (see also the Appendix)

$$
\begin{aligned}
tw_{ij} &\approx ts_j\left(P_{0j}^{(i)} + P_{1j}^{(i)}\left(1 + \frac{1}{2}\right) + P_{2j}^{(i)}\left(2 + \frac{1}{2}\right) + \cdots\right) \\
&= ts_j\left(P_{0j}^{(i)} + \sum_{l=0}^{n} P_{ij}^{(i)} \cdot l + \frac{1}{2}\sum_{l=1}^{n} P_{ij}^{(i)}\right) \\
&= ts_j\left(P_{0j}^{(i)} + \sum_{k} y_{kj}^{(i)} + \frac{1}{2}(1 - P_{0j}^{(i)})\right) \\
&= ts_j\left(\sum_{k} y_{kj}^{(i)} + \frac{1}{2} + \frac{1}{2}P_{0j}^{(i)}\right)
\end{aligned} \quad (17)
$$

where $P_{ij}^{(i)}$ is the probability of the queue length in service center j being l at the moment of a class i customer arrival. We approximate the probability $P_{0j}^{(i)}$ by

$$P_{0j}^{(i)} \approx \prod_{k=1}^{n} (1 - y_{kj}^{(i)}) \quad (18)$$

while $y_{ij}^{(i)} = 0$ for all j. This is an approximation since we assume the probability of empty queue j is a product of probabilities that no customer of any class is present in this queue.

Equations (17) and (18) together with (3) yield a recursive scheme MVARC (MVA, recursive and constant) for constant service times.

If we use the same approximation as in (12), we obtain

$$tw_{ij} \approx ts_j\left(\sum_{k \neq i} y_{kj} + \frac{1}{2} + \frac{1}{2}\prod_{k \neq i}(1 - y_{kj})\right). \quad (19)$$

This equation together with (3) provides an iterative scheme for constant service time—MVAIC (MVA, iterative and constant). The use of the MVAIC algorithm is justified only if the used approximations are valid.

In the following will be demonstrated that the values obtained in such cases by the MVAIC method (as well as GMI results) agree well with results obtained by simulation. Numerically, the MVAIC method is significantly simpler than the GMI one. The GMI method needs $n \cdot 2^{n-1}$ multiplications for the computation of a single tw_{ij} in one iteration step, while the MVAIC method needs n multiplications only.

V. Evaluation

The GMI, MVAIC, MVAIE, MVARC, and MVARE methods will be compared in this section. Simulation will be used to determine the errors of approximate methods for those systems where no exact analysis is available.

A. Multiprocessor Systems with n Identical Processors and m Memories with Uniformly Distributed Requests and Zero Processing Times

In this model, a memory module is characterized by its access time $ts_j = ts$, and the distribution of processor requests for memory accesses is uniform:

$$x_{ij} = \frac{1}{m}; \quad tp_{ij} = 0; \quad i = 1, 2, \cdots, n; \quad j = 1, 2, \cdot, m.$$

Utilization of the system is characterized by the value of the average number of busy memories (ANBM). Utilization of memory j by one processor i is given by

$$p_{ij} = \lambda_i \cdot x_{ij} \cdot ts_j = \frac{1}{tw_{ij}} \cdot \frac{1}{m} \cdot ts.$$

A total utilization of all memories by all processors, i.e., the ANBM, is given by

$$\text{ANBM} = m \cdot n \cdot p_{ij} = \frac{n \cdot ts}{tw_{ij}}. \quad (20)$$

In our case, tw_{ij} are the same value tw for all i, j.

ANBM for the treated multiprocessor system derived by various methods is tabulated in Table I.

Bhandarkar [4] computed exact results using a Markov chain model for the discussed system; his results are not expressible in analytic form. Baskett and Smith [5] derived an analytic formula for ANBM, and they proved that their formula is asymptotically exact for $n, m \to \infty$. Bhandarkar [4] further showed that the ANBM is symmetrical for systems with n processors and m memories and for systems with m processors and n memories, and therefore, he changed the formula of Strecker [7] into a symmetrical one. The same was done by Sethi and Deo [6] with their empirical formula. The symmetry is achieved by setting $i = \max(n, m)$, $j = \min(n, m)$. The formula derived by MVAIC or MVARC algorithms is nonsymmetrical, but we can change it into a symmetrical formula analogously:

$$\text{ANBM}/m = \frac{j}{\frac{1}{2}\left[1 + \left(1 - \frac{1}{i}\right)^{j-1}\right] + \frac{j-1}{i}}$$

$$i = \max(n, m), \quad j = \min(n, m). \quad (21)$$

This symmetrization has eliminated the errors which arise for systems with relatively many processors and few memory modules due

288

TABLE I
Average Number of Busy Memories (ANBM) Derived by Methods MVAIC, MVAIE, MVARC, MVARE

$ANBM^{MVAIC}$	$ANBM^{MVAIE}$	$ANBM^{MVARC}$	$ANBM^{MVARE}$
$\dfrac{n}{\frac{1}{2}\left[1+\left(1-\frac{1}{m}\right)^{n-1}\right]+\frac{n-1}{m}}$	$\dfrac{n\cdot m}{n+m-1}$	$\dfrac{n}{\frac{1}{2}\left[1+\left(1-\frac{1}{m}\right)^{n-1}\right]+\frac{n-1}{m}}$	$\dfrac{n\cdot m}{n+m-1}$

TABLE II
Various Formulas for ANBM/m (i.e., Utilization of One Memory Module) and their Asymptotic Values

Method	General n, m	$n=m\to\infty$
MVARE, MVAIE	$\dfrac{n}{n+m-1}$	$\dfrac{1}{2}=0.500$
MVARC, MVAIC symmetrical	$\dfrac{j}{\frac{1}{2}\left[1+\left(1-\frac{1}{i}\right)^{j-1}\right]+\frac{j-1}{i}}$ $i=\max(n,m)$ $j=\min(n,m)$	$\dfrac{2}{3-\frac{1}{e}}\approx0.593$
Markov chain, Bhandarkar's exact result	——	$2-\sqrt{2}\approx0.589$
Bhandarkar's formula, GMI, Strecker	$\dfrac{i}{m}\left[1-\left(1-\frac{1}{i}\right)^{j}\right]$ $i=\max(n,m)$ $j=\min(n,m)$	$1-\dfrac{1}{e}\approx0.632$
Baskett-Smith, R. Rau	$\dfrac{1}{m}\left[n+m-\frac{1}{2}-\sqrt{\left(n+m-\frac{1}{2}\right)^2-2mn}\right]$	$2-\sqrt{2}\approx0.589$
Sethi-Deo	$\dfrac{1}{m}\left[j-\frac{j(j-1)}{2i}\right]$ $i=\max(n,m)$ $j=\min(n,m)$	$\dfrac{1}{2}=0.500$

TABLE III
Approximations of ANBM Based on MVAIC Formula (21) Tabulated and Compared to Other Formulas

	M=1	M=2	M=3	M=4	M=5	M=6	M=7	M=8	M=9	M=10	M=11	M=12	M=16
N=1	1.0000	1.0000	1.0000	1.0000	1.0000	1.0000	1.0000	1.0000	1.0000	1.0000	1.0000	1.0000	1.0000
N=2	1.0000	1.6000	1.7143	1.7778	1.8182	1.8462	1.8667	1.8824	1.8947	1.9048	1.9130	1.9200	1.9394
N=3	1.0000	1.7143	2.1600	2.3415	2.4590	2.5412	2.6018	2.6483	2.6851	2.7149	2.7396	2.7606	2.8184
N=4	1.0000	1.7778	2.3415	2.7380	2.9499	3.1023	3.2169	3.3059	3.3770	3.4350	3.4832	3.5238	3.6381
N=5	1.0000	1.8182	2.4590	2.9499	3.3227	3.5517	3.7277	3.8667	3.9790	4.0715	4.1489	4.2146	4.4005
N=6	1.0000	1.8462	2.5412	3.1023	3.5517	3.9107	4.1505	4.3432	4.5011	4.6323	4.7431	4.8376	5.1081
N=7	1.0000	1.8667	2.6018	3.2169	3.7277	4.1505	4.5004	4.7477	4.9529	5.1255	5.2723	5.3985	5.7638
N=8	1.0000	1.8824	2.6483	3.3059	3.8667	4.3432	4.7477	5.0912	5.3440	5.5588	5.7432	5.9029	6.3707
N=9	1.0000	1.8947	2.6851	3.3770	3.9790	4.5011	4.9529	5.3440	5.6827	5.9397	6.1622	6.3562	6.9318
N=10	1.0000	1.9048	2.7149	3.4350	4.0715	4.6323	5.1255	5.5588	5.9397	6.2747	6.5350	6.7636	7.4504
N=11	1.0000	1.9130	2.7396	3.4832	4.1489	4.7431	5.2723	5.7432	6.1622	6.5350	6.8670	7.1300	7.9295
N=12	1.0000	1.9200	2.7604	3.5238	4.2146	4.8376	5.3985	5.9029	6.3562	6.7636	7.1300	7.4596	8.3721
N=16	1.0000	1.9394	2.8184	3.6381	4.4005	5.1081	5.7638	6.3707	6.9318	7.4504	7.9295	8.3721	9.8316

The area of more accurate approximations for ANBM than

Strecker's Formula   Bhandarkar's Formula   Sethi-Deo's Formula

to the bottleneck on memory modules. These systems do not satisfy the used approximations in the MVAIC or MVARC algorithm.

Various formulas for ANBM are compared and their asymptotic values for a system with $n=m\to\infty$ are presented in Table II. It is obvious that the MVAIC algorithm yields asymptotically a very good approximation for ANBM.

Estimation of ANBM based on (21) is compared to estimations based on other formulas, for values $n=1,\cdots,12,16$ and $m=1$, $2,\cdots,12,16$ in Table III, and the area where the MVAIC symmetric formula yields more accurate results than some other methods (Strecker, Bhandarkar, Sethi–Deo) is marked by a (dashed, full, dotted, respectively) line.

The Baskett–Smith formula was found to be a very good approximation. It yields the best approximations in the entire examined area. The data of Bhandarkar [4] and simulation results of Sethi and Deo [6] were used as the exact values for comparison in Table III.

TABLE IV

AVERAGE NUMBER OF BUSY MEMORIES (ANBM) AND THE DIFFERENCE
BETWEEN ANBM AND THE CENTER OF 90 PERCENT CONFIDENCE INTERVAL OF
SIMULATION. MULTIPROCESSOR SYSTEM IS OF THE ORDER 8 × 8, $ts_j = 1$ FOR
ALL j, $tp_{ij} = 0$ FOR ALL i, j. THE MOST ACCURATE RESULTS ARE FRAMED.

Method of bias	α	Simulation 90% Interval		Centre of Int.	GMI	MVAIC	MVAIE	MVARC	MVARE
Diag.	0.25	4.9315	5.0492	4.9904	5.2796 +5.8%	5.1359 +2.9%	4.3036 -13.8%	5.1541 +3.3%	4.3260 -13.3%
Diag.	0.5	5.3112	5.4034	5.3573	5.5209 +3.0%	5.4836 +2.4%	4.6060 -14.0%	5.5842 +4.2%	4.7459 -11.4%
Diag.	0.75	6.1044	6.1967	6.1506	6.1376 -0.2%	6.2824 +2.1%	5.3882 -12.5%	6.4503 +4.9%	5.6841 -7.6%
Col. 1	0.2	4.5210	4.6733	4.5971	4.8103 +4.6%	4.6794 +1.8%	4.0003 -13.0%	4.8128 +4.7%	4.0560 -11.8%
Col. 1	0.3	3.2407	3.3948	3.3177	3.3326 +0.5%	3.4259 +3.3%	3.1029 -6.5%	3.6888 +11.2%	3.2412 -2.3%
Col. 1	0.4	2.4291	2.5285	2.4788	2.5000 +0.9%	2.6173 +5.6%	2.4141 -2.6%	2.7406 +10.6%	2.4936 +0.6%

TABLE V

AVERAGE NUMBER OF BUSY MEMORIES (ANBM) AND THE DIFFERENCE
BETWEEN ANBM AND THE CENTER OF 90 PERCENT CONFIDENCE INTERVAL OF
SIMULATION. MULTIPROCESSOR SYSTEM WITH UNIFORM ACCESS DISTRIBUTION
$x_{ij} = 1/m$, $ts_j = 1$, $tp_{ij} = 1$ FOR ALL i, j. THE MOST ACCURATE RESULTS
ARE FRAMED.

n	m	Simulation 90% Interval		Centre of Int.	GMI	MVAIC	MVAIE	MVARC	MVARE
4	2	1.5647	1.5843	1.5745	1.5400 -2.8%	1.5464 -1.8%	1.3336 -15.4%	1.5792 +0.3%	1.3772 -12.8%
4	4	1.8194	1.8276	1.8235	1.7917 -1.8%	1.7904 -1.8%	1.6368 -10.1%	1.7984 -1.7%	1.6536 -9.3%
8	4	2.8460	2.9206	2.8833	2.9789 +1.6%	2.8932 +0.4%	2.4971 -13.4%	2.9331 +1.8%	2.5330 -12.2%
8	8	3.4858	3.5346	3.5102	3.5221 +0.4%	3.4887 -0.6%	3.1633 -9.9%	3.4988 -0.3%	3.1809 -9.4%

B. Multiprocessor Systems with Arbitrary Access Probabilities x_{ij} and Zero Processing Times

For general systems of this kind (studied in this and the following sections) we can use only approximate methods GMI, MVAIC, MVAIE, MVARC, and MVARE. No exact method exists. The results obtained by these methods and those gained by simulation are compared by numerical examples which were studied by Hoogendoorn [1].

Each processor access pattern can be biased towards a specific memory module. The proportion of accesses directed to the specific memory will be denoted as α where $\alpha > 1/m$, and the proportion of accesses directed to each of the other memories will be denoted as β where $\beta = (1 - \alpha)/m - 1$. Two systems with different kinds of biases are studied: 1) all processors are biased to memory module 1, i.e., to column 1 in the matrix x_{ij}; and 2) each processor is biased to its "own" memory module (diagonal) so that $x_{ij} = \alpha$ for $i = j$ and $x_{ij} = \beta$ for $i \neq j$.

The results are compared in Table IV. The center of a 90 percent confidence interval obtained from simulation was used as an exact value for comparison.

C. Multiprocessor Systems with Uniformly Distributed Access Probabilities and Nonzero Processing Times

The results for systems of this kind are presented in Table V.

D. Multiprocessor Systems with Generally Distributed Access Probabilities and Nonzero Processing Times

In Table VI we present results for the systems with access probability x_{ij} biased to one memory module (to column 1) or biased diagonally. Processing times are uniformly distributed between tp_{min} and tp_{max} in the simulation runs.

In Table VII we present results for the systems with biased access probability x_{ij} and with different processing times. Processing time

tp_{ij} is zero for the odd-numbered processors, and tp_{ij} has integer values between 0 and $2 \cdot tp_{avg}$ for the even-numbered processors.

VI. CONCLUSIONS

The studied algorithms MVAIC, MVAIE, MVARC, and MVARE are based on the idea of studying a multiprocessor system as a closed queueing network by means of MVA with some approximations. The development of the algorithms and the approximations used with them are illustrated in Fig. 2.

The derivation of the MVAIC algorithm assumes certain approximations; their validity must be verified before their use for a specific system.

1) $$y_{kj}^{(i)} \approx y_{kj}, \qquad \text{for } i \neq k, \qquad \text{see (12)}.$$

This approximation may be used if removing processor i from the system does not significantly affect the average number of the processors waiting for access to memory j. This condition is satisfied in large systems with long processing times tp_{ij}.

2) $$tw_{ij} \begin{cases} \approx ts_j\left(l + \dfrac{1}{2}\right), & \text{for } = 1, 2, \cdots \\ = ts_j, & \text{for } l = 0, \quad \text{see (16)}. \end{cases}$$

This approximation can be used when the flow of arriving requests is random (Poisson) or when the probability that the queue is empty is large. It is valid for systems with great dispersion of individual tp_{ij}, without bottleneck and with long processing times tp_{ij}.

3) $$P_{0j}^{(i)} \approx \prod_{k=1}^{n} (1 - y_{kj}^{(i)}) \qquad \text{see (18)}.$$

This approximation can be used when individual processors do not interact much and the flow of requests is nearly independent. It is valid for systems with a low degree of congestion.

TABLE VI
Average Number of Busy Memories (ANBM) and the Difference Between ANBM and the Center of 90 Percent Confidence Interval of Simulation. Multiprocessor System has $ts_j = 1$ for all j, $tp_{min} \leq tp_{avg} \leq tp_{max}$ for All Processors and Biased Access Probability. The Most Accurate Results are Framed.

n m and Method of bias	α	tp_{min} / tp_{max}	tp_{avg}	Simulation 90% Interval	Centre of Int.	GMI	MVAIC	MVAIE	MVARC	MVARE
2 2 Diag.	0.7	0 / 2	1	0.9281 0.9518	0.9400	0.9384 −0.2%	0.9468 +0.7%	0.8932 −5.0%	0.9500 +1.0%	0.9048 −3.7%
2 2 Col. 1	0.7	0 / 2	1	0.9074 0.9275	0.9174	0.9101 −0.8%	0.9268 +1.0%	0.8578 −6.5%	0.9324 +1.6%	0.8734 −4.8%
8 8 Diag.	0.25	0 / 2	1	3.4437 3.5178	3.4807	3.5303 +1.4%	3.5006 +0.6%	3.1778 −8.7%	3.5126 +0.9%	3.2001 −8.1%
8 8 Diag.	0.25	1 / 1	1	3.4927 3.5549	3.5238	3.5303 +0.2%	3.5006 −0.6%	3.1778 −9.8%	3.5126 −0.3%	3.2001 −9.2%
8 8 Col. 1	0.25	0 / 2	1	3.2363 3.3409	3.2886	3.3491 +1.8%	3.2840 −0.1%	2.9298 −11.0%	3.3490 +1.8%	2.9987 −8.2%
8 8 Diag.	0.5	0 / 2	1	3.5649 3.6040	3.5844	3.5981 +0.4%	3.5886 +0.1%	3.2919 −8.2%	3.6079 +0.7%	3.3360 −7.0%
8 8 Col. 1	0.5	0 / 4	2	1.8945 1.9685	1.9315	1.9565 +1.3%	1.9230 −0.4%	1.7309 −10.4%	2.0756 +7.5%	1.8434 −4.6%
8 8 Diag.	0.75	0 / 2	1	3.7278 3.7775	3.7526	3.7436 −0.2%	3.7557 +0.1%	3.5392 −5.7%	3.7746 +0.6%	3.5936 −4.2%

TABLE VII
Average Number of Busy Memories (ANBM) and the Difference Between ANBM and the Center of 90 Percent Confidence Interval of Simulation. Multiprocessor System has $ts_j = 1$ for all j, $tp_{ij} = 0$ for Odd-Numbered Processors and $0 \leq tp_{ij} \leq 2tp_{ijavg}$ for Even-Numbered Processors and for all j. Access Probability is Biased. The Most Accurate Results are Framed.

n m and Method of bias	α	tp_{ijavg}	Simulation 90% Interval	Centre of Int.	GMI	MVAIC	MVAIE	MVARC	MVARE
4 4 Diag.	0.5	odd 0 / even 1	2.3417 2.3755	2.3586	2.4014 +1.8%	2.4214 +2.7%	2.0984 −11.0%	2.4460 +3.7%	2.1404 −9.3%
4 4 Col. 1	0.5	odd 0 / even 1	1.8740 1.9374	1.9057	1.9244 +1.0%	2.0024 +5.1%	1.6960 −11.0%	2.1114 +10.8%	1.7824 −6.5%
8 8 Diag.	0.5	odd 0 / even 1	4.5634 4.6465	4.6049	4.7080 +2.2%	4.6932 +1.9%	4.0631 −11.8%	4.7578 +3.3%	4.1669 −9.5%
8 8 Col. 1	0.25	odd 0 / even 1	3.5775 3.6676	3.6225	3.7563 +3.7%	3.6811 +1.6%	3.1982 −11.7%	3.8323 +5.8%	3.3000 −8.9%

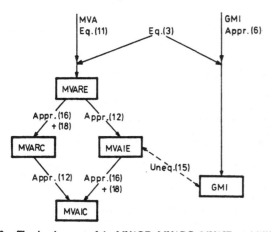

Fig. 2. The development of the MVARE, MVARC, MVAIE, and MVAIC algorithms, the used approximations, and the relation of the MVAIE algorithm to the GMI one.

Observing the results treated in Section V, we see that the MVAIC method gives excellent results on the condition that the three above-mentioned approximations provide near-true values. The GMI method also gives good results for such systems, but compared with the MVAIC method, it is more suitable for systems with some degree of congestion on some memory module (bottle-neck), e.g., see the last row in Table IV or the second row in Table VII.

The MVAIE method has close relation to the GMI method given by (15). Hence, that is the reason why the GMI method yields more accurate results than the MVAIE method for multiprocessor systems. The memory access times are constant and not exponentially distributed, as is assumed in the MVAIE and the MVARE algorithms. It is known from the theory of queues that the mean waiting time for the $M/D/1$ queue is shorter than for the $M/M/1$ queue (assumed by the MVAIE and MVARE models). The assumption of Poisson arrival does not exactly hold in our case, but closed queueing networks with deterministic service times exhibit, in general, shorter delays in queues than networks with exponentially distributed service times. We can see from Tables IV–VII that the MVAIE and MVARE algorithms really underestimate the ANBM and thus overestimate the interferences in the multiprocessor system.

Contrary to the MVAIC or GMI methods, the MVARC method does not use approximation (12), which converts recursion to iteration. Despite that, the results obtained by the MVARC method are less satisfactory than those obtained by the MVAIC or GMI methods. The difference can probably be explained by the fact that some approximations made in the MVAIC or GMI methods have cancellation effects which are not quite clear at this time, or by the recursive nature of the MVARC algorithm; the number of recursive steps is of the order 2^n, and the deviations caused by approximations (16) and (18) in each separate step of the recursive algorithm can accumulate.

We conclude that the most suitable analytical method for determining interference in the studied multiprocessor systems is the MVAIC; it gives very good results for systems with low interferences and is numerically simple. The GMI method gives better results than the MVAIC for systems with a slight degree of congestion, but it is more complex numerically. The value of the MVAIE, MVARC, and MVARE methods for multiprocessor systems is rather theoretical; they help to reveal the substance of the MVAIC and GMI approximations.

Appendix

Lemma: Let $N_1, N_2, \cdots, N_n$ be arbitrary numbers, and let numbers P_l be defined by the following equations:

$$P_0 = (1 - N_1)(1 - N_2)(1 - N_3) \cdots \cdots (1 - N_n)$$

$$\begin{aligned} P_1 = {} & N_1(1 - N_2)(1 - N_3) \cdots \cdots (1 - N_n) \\ & + (1 - N_1)N_2(1 - N_3) \cdots \cdots (1 - N_n) \\ & \vdots \\ & + (1 - N_1)(1 - N_2)(1 - N_3) \cdots \cdots (1 - N_{n-1})N_n \end{aligned}$$

$$\begin{aligned} P_2 = {} & N_1 N_2(1 - N_3)(1 - N_4) \cdots \cdots (1 - N_n) \\ & + N_1(1 - N_2)N_3(1 - N_4) \cdots \cdots (1 - N_n) \\ & \vdots \\ & + (1 - N_1)(1 - N_2)(1 - N_3) \cdots \cdots (1 - N_{n-2})N_{n-1}N_n \end{aligned}$$

$$\dot{P}_n = N_1 N_2 N_3 N_4 \cdots \cdots \cdots N_n. \tag{22}$$

Then the following holds:

$$\sum_{l=0}^{n} P_l \cdot l = \sum_{k=1}^{n} N_k \quad \text{and} \quad \sum_{l=0}^{n} P_l = 1. \tag{23}$$

The proof is entirely algebraic and will be omitted.

We can make the following substitution in (14)

$$\sum_{k \neq i} y_{kj} = \sum_{l=0}^{n} P_{ij}^{(l)} \cdot l \quad \text{for all } i, j \tag{24}$$

where $P_{ij}^{(l)}$ are computed in the same way as in (22) for all i and j. The fact that (24) does not include y_{kj} for $k = i$ must be considered when we compute $P_{ij}^{(l)}$ using (22) by setting $y_{ij} = 0$ ($N_{ij} = 0$).

The sum $\sum_{k \neq i} y_{kj}$ is an approximation of the mean queue length encountered by the arriving customer i, and thus $P_{kj}^{(l)}$ is an approximation of the probability that this queue has exactly k customers at the instant of customer i arrival.

Hence,

$$tw_{ij} \approx f_{ij}^{\text{MVAIE}} = ts_j \left(\sum_{k \neq i} y_{kj} + 1 \right) = ts_j \sum_{l=0}^{n} P_{ij}^{(l)} (l + 1). \tag{25}$$

In the GMI model we replace N_{ij} by y_{ij}. Comparing formulas (22), (6), and (7), we obtain

$$f_{ij}^* = \sum_{l=0}^{n} P_{ij}^{(l)} \cdot \frac{1}{l + 1}.$$

It follows from this equation and from (8) that the function f_{ij}^{GMI} used in the GMI model is

$$tw_{ij} \approx f_{ij}^{\text{GMI}} = ts_j \frac{1}{\sum_{l=0}^{n} P_{ij}^{(l)} \cdot \dfrac{1}{l + 1}}. \tag{26}$$

Comparing (25) and (26) we see that function f_{ij}^{MVAIE} uses the arithmetic mean of the queue length, and the function f_{ij}^{GMI} uses the harmonic mean of the queue length.

Lemma: Let P_l be nonnegative numbers of which at least two are positive, $l = 0, 1, \cdots, n$, and suppose $\sum_{l=0}^{n} P_l = 1$. Then the following inequality holds:

$$\sum_{l=0}^{n} P_l(l + 1) > \frac{1}{\sum_{l=0}^{n} P_l \cdot \dfrac{1}{l + 1}}. \tag{27}$$

Proof: The assertion (27) is equivalent to

$$\sum_{l=0}^{n} \sum_{j=0}^{n} P_l P_j \frac{l + 1}{j + 1} > \left(\sum_{l=0}^{n} P_l \right)^2 \quad \text{because } \sum_{l=0}^{n} P_l = 1.$$

Hence,

$$\sum_{l=0}^{n} \sum_{j>l} P_l P_j \left(\frac{l + 1}{j + 1} + \frac{j + 1}{l + 1} \right) > 2 \sum_{l=0}^{n} \sum_{j>l} P_l P_j. \tag{28}$$

Further,

$$(l + 1)^2 + (j + 1)^2 > 2(l + 1)(j + 1) \quad \text{for } l \neq j,$$

i.e.,

$$\frac{l + 1}{j + 1} + \frac{j + 1}{l + 1} > 2 \quad \text{for } l \neq j.$$

Since at least one $P_l \cdot P_j$ is positive, the inequality (28) holds, and the proof is completed.

From the preceding lemma and (25), (26) we arrive at conclusion (15).

References

[1] C. H. Hoogendoorn, "A general model for memory interference in multiprocessors," *IEEE Trans. Comput.*, vol. C-26, pp. 998–1005, Oct. 1977.

[2] M. Reiser and S. S. Lavenberg, "Mean value analysis of closed multichain queueing networks," *J. ACM*, vol. 27, pp. 313–332, Apr. 1980.

[3] M. Reiser, "A queueing network analysis of computer communication networks with window flow control," *IEEE Trans. Commun.*, vol. COM-27, pp. 1199–1209, Aug. 1979.

[4] D. P. Bhandarkar, "Analytic models for memory interference in multiprocessor computer systems," Ph.D. dissertation, Carnegie-Mellon Univ., Pittsburgh, PA, Sept. 1973.

[5] F. Baskett and A. J. Smith, "Interference in multiprocessor systems with interleaved memory," *Commun. ACM*, vol. 19, pp. 327–334, June 1976.

[6] A. S. Sethi and N. Deo, "Interference in multiprocessor systems with localized memory access probabilities," *IEEE Trans. Comput.*, vol. C-28, pp. 157–163, Feb. 1979.

[7] W. D. Strecker, "Analysis of the instruction execution rate in certain computer structures," Ph.D. dissertation, Carnegie-Mellon Univ., Pittsburgh, PA, 1970.

[8] P. Schweitzer, "Approximate analysis of multiclass closed networks of queues," in *Proc. Int. Conf. Stochastic Contr. Optimization*, Amsterdam, The Netherlands, 1979.

[9] M. Reiser, "Mean value analysis of queueing networks, A new look at an old problem," in *Performance of Computer Systems*, M. Arato, A. Butrimenko, and E. Gelenbe, Eds. Amsterdam, The Netherlands: North-Holland, 1979, pp. 63–77.

[10] C. Skinner and J. Asher, "Effect on storage contention on system performance," *IBM Syst. J.*, vol. 8, pp. 319–333, 1969.

[11] J. W. McCredie, "Analytic models as aids for multiprocessor design," in *Proc. 7th Annu. Princeton Conf. Inform. Sci. Syst.*, Princeton, NJ, Mar. 1973, pp. 186–191.

[12] R. Rau, "Interleaved memory bandwith in a model of a multiprocessor system," *IEEE Trans. Comput.*, vol. C-28, pp. 678–681, Sept. 1979.

[13] Y. Bard, "Some extentions to multiclass queueing network analysis," in *Performance of Computer Systems*, M. Arato, A. Butrimenko, and E. Gelenbe, Eds. Amsterdam, The Netherlands: North-Holland, 1979, pp. 51–61.

Equilibrium Point Analysis of Memory Interference in Multiprocessor Systems

AKIRA FUKUDA, MEMBER, IEEE

Abstract—An approximate analytic tool called the equilibrium point analysis is applied to the problem of memory interference in multiprocessor systems. This is a simple and powerful analytic tool based on the fluid approximation. It has been widely used in the area of packet broadcast systems. It is shown that we can study quite general multiprocessor systems by this technique with amazing simplicity. For example, we deal with systems made up of many classes of processors and memory modules with arbitrary static memory reference patterns, systems with dynamic memory reference patterns, and systems with bus connections between processors and memories. In most cases, the approximation of the analysis is shown to be sufficiently good. One of the nice properties of this technique is that the error is smaller for larger systems for which we have had no appropriate analytic tools thus far.

Index Terms—Bus connection, crossbar connection, dynamic reference pattern, equilibrium point analysis, memory interefence, multiprocessors, performance evaluation, queueing system, static reference pattern.

I. INTRODUCTION

A memory conflict occurs whenever two or more processors attempt to access the same memory module simultaneously in a multiprocessor system with a main memory made up of several memory modules. The effect of these conflicts is a decrease in the execution rate of processors. The performance of such multiprocessor systems has been widely studied in recent years, since the decrease in the execution rate may be quite severe in some situations [1]. Many researchers have studied the performance of crossbar-connected systems [2]–[10], and others have tried to analyze bus-connected ones [11], [12]. There are some papers in which systems with so called localized or dynamic memory access patterns are dealt with [7]. Some researchers also studied systems with private cache memories [8].

Various kinds of analytic techniques have been utilized in these studies. However, most of them are applicable only to systems with a small number of processors and memory modules [2]–[7], [11], [12]. A few techniques applicable to larger systems can treat only systems with homogeneous processors and memory modules [8], [9]. Thus, we can say that there has been no simple and general analytic tool in this area so far.

In this paper, we propose to apply the equilibrium point analysis (EPA) to this problem. It is an approximate analytic

tool for complicated stochastic flow systems which was proposed by the author in 1978 to study the dynamic behavior of various kinds of packet broadcast systems [13]–[15]. Since then, it has been widely used in that area by some researchers.

We shall see that we can analyze quite general multiprocessor systems by this technique with amazing simplicity. The approximation is well enough in most cases. The error is smaller when the system has a larger number of processors and memory modules. This is an extremely nice property of the EPA since there have been accurate analytic tools only for small scale systems thus far.

Although many kinds of multiprocessor systems have been studied so far, we treat here only some representative ones since the main purpose of this paper is to show the possibility that we can study various problems in this and related areas by the EPA.

In Section II, we apply the EPA to the simplest system, that is, to a system with P homogeneous processors and M homogeneous memory modules where each processor has probability $1/M$ to access each module. We explain the basic idea of the EPA applied to multiprocessor systems and examine the error of the analysis in detail.

In Section III, nonhomogeneous systems are studied where processors and memory modules are divided into groups according to their memory request rate, memory access pattern, service time at memories, etc. We assume a general reference pattern p_{ij} where p_{ij} is the probability that a processor in the ith group accesses a memory module in the jth group. In this section, however, we assume that p_{ij} does not depend on the memory module which the processor in the ith group visited in the past.

On the other hand, Section IV considers the case of the so called localized or dynamic reference pattern system where each processor memorizes which memory module it visited in the past.

In Sections II–IV, we assume that the system has a crossbar connection between processors and memories, that is, we assume that any processor can access any memory module as long as the memory module is not being accessed by some other processor. In Section V, systems with bus connections are briefly covered, where each system has B buses ($B < $ min $[P, M]$).

Throughout the paper, we assume that the time axes are discrete. It is almost no concern of the EPA whether the time axis is discrete or continuous because the EPA is essentially a fluid approximation.

The accuracy of the EPA is studied by comparing the results to analytic ones in other papers and simulation results.

Manuscript received December 28, 1984; revised June 29, 1987.

The author is with the Department of Electrical Engineering, Shizuoka University, Hamamatsu, 432 Japan.

IEEE Log Number 87177726.

In this section, we apply the EPA to the simplest multiprocessor system. The system has P processors and M memory modules as is shown in Fig. 1. A $P \times M$ full crossbar interconnection between processors and memories is assumed. The entire system is supposed to be synchronous with the slotted time axis. The slot length is the unit of time throughout the paper. The statistical properties of all processors and memory modules are identical.

One cycle of the behavior of a processor consists of a period of computation followed by a request to a specific memory module to read or write a datum. We consider two cases for the computing time t_p; I) each processor which is executing its job without requesting a memory is said to be in the P mode and has a memory request probability λ in each slot. That is, the time t_p ($t_p = 1, 2, \cdots$) during which the processor works without a memory request is geometrically distributed with average $1/\lambda$. II) zero computing time, that is, $t_p = 0$. In this section, we focus our attention on Case I). Case II) is considered in a more general context in the next section. Case I) corresponds, for example, to a system with private cache memories [8].

We assume in this section that the memory reference pattern is completely random, that is, we suppose that each memory request is to the memory module i ($1 \leq i \leq M$) with probability $1/M$. There is a queue of processors waiting for their turn to be served by the memory module. A processor waits a random time t_w. The queueing discipline at each queue is assumed to be of the first-in-first-out type. Requests which arrived simultaneously to the same queue are served in a random order. These assumptions are valid throughout the paper.

Here we study two cases for the service time (memory transfer time) t_a at memories; 1) t_a is a constant. 2) t_a is a geometrically distributed random variable with average $1/\mu$. A processor is said to be in the M mode when it is either waiting for a memory or being served by it.

The most important performance measure in this study will be the utilization η of processors which is defined as follows.

$$\eta = \frac{t_p}{t_p + t_w + t_a} = \frac{N_P}{P} \qquad (1)$$

where N_p is the average number of processors in the P mode. Another important performance measure which we consider in this paper is the utilization ρ of memories.

A. Systems with Constant Service Time

Now we apply the EPA to the above system. We study first the case of constant service time. This is the same system as that studied by Patel [8].

The EPA is fundamentally the fluid approximation of stochastic processes. However, it only deals with the steady-state behavior of the process. Suppose that there are K processors in the M mode (Fig. 2). It is apparent that K fluctuates randomly slot by slot. But we assume for the moment that K is a constant. Thus, we can say that, for each memory module, there are $(P - K)$ processors each of them

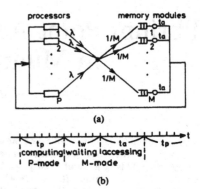

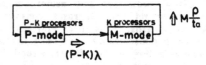

Fig. 1. Queueing model for a $P \times M$ homogeneous system. (a) The system. (b) Behavior of the processors.

Fig. 2. EPA of the system in Fig. 1.

has probability λ/M to access it. So we roughly suppose that each memory module behaves like a discrete time M/D/1 queueing system with a Poisson arrival rate $(P - K)\lambda/M$. Formally applying the Pollazeck–Khinchine formula [16] for the continuous time M/D/1 system to this discrete time system, we have

$$\rho = n + 1 - \sqrt{n^2 + 1} \qquad (2)$$

where ρ is the busy probability of the memory module and n is the average number of processors waiting for or receiving service from it. Thus, we observe that, when there are K processors in the M mode, $(P - K)\lambda$ processors move from the P mode to the M mode in the next slot on the average. On the other hand, $M\rho/t_a$ processors move from the M mode to the P mode on the average. This is because there are M homogeneous memory modules and each of them has busy probability ρ and service rate $1/t_a$.

We define an equilibrium point of the system to be a specific state K where the average increase (or decrease) of the number of processors in each mode is zero. We denote it by K_e. We treat K_e as a real number, even though it is an integer. Hereafter we will suppose that $K_e = Mn_e$ when the system is at an equilibrium point. n_e will be called an equilibrium point, too.

In this system, the average increment δ_p in the number of processors in the P mode is given by

$$\delta_p = \frac{M}{t_a}(n + 1 - \sqrt{n^2 + 1}) - (P - Mn)\lambda \qquad (3)$$

where the approximation $K = Mn$ was used. Obviously $\delta_M = -\delta_P$, where δ_M is the average increment in the number of processors in the M mode. Thus, the equilibrium point n_e is the root of the following equilibrium point equation for n.

$$\frac{M}{t_a}(n + 1 - \sqrt{n^2 + 1}) = (P - Mn)\lambda. \qquad (4)$$

In the EPA, we assume that the system is always at the equilibrium point. As we have discussed above, we know that in reality the state of the system fluctuates around the equilibrium point. We expect, however, that the positive and negative deviations from the equilibrium point will be compensated when we study the average properties of the system. We find detailed studies on these aspects of the EPA in [13]–[15] and many other papers on the application of the EPA to packet broadcast systems. Even though some systems may have stable and unstable equilibrium points, the latter need not be considered in the EPA. When a system has two or more stable equilibrium points, we assume that the system is always at the worst equilibrium point, i.e., the one with the largest K_e, to evaluate the worst case performance.

It is quite easy to solve the quadratic equation (4) for n. It always has a root

$$n_e = \frac{\sqrt{\alpha(\alpha+2) + (1-\alpha\beta)^2} - (1+\alpha)(1-\alpha\beta)}{\alpha(\alpha+2)} \quad (5)$$

in the range $0 \le K_e \le P$, that is, in the range $0 \le n_e \le P/M$, where $\alpha = t_a\lambda$ and $\beta = P/M$. The utilization η of processors is given by

$$\eta = \frac{P - K_e}{P} = 1 - \frac{n_e}{\beta} . \quad (6)$$

The utilization of memories is given by ρ of (2), where n is replaced by n_e. Thus, we know that η and ρ do not depend on t_a, λ, P, and M individually but depend only on α and β.

In the above procedure of the application of the EPA, we rely on the fact that the number of processors in the M mode is about K_e most of the time. Thus, from the law of large numbers, we can imagine that the error of the approximate analysis will be larger when P and M are smaller.

Next, we study the error of the analysis comparing the numerical results to those in [8] and some simulation results. One of the previous conclusions that t_a and λ have influence on η and ρ only through the product $\alpha = t_a\lambda$ has been completely verified as a result of many simulations. We do not show the detailed data here since Table I in [8] also shows the fact clearly. In this paper, we sometimes show simulation results and analytic ones referring only to α. In such cases, we implicitly assume that $\lambda = 1$ and $t_a \ge 1$ when $\alpha \ge 1$, and $t_a = 1$ and $\lambda \le 1$ when $\alpha \le 1$.

Table I shows η amd ρ for $P \times M = 32 \times 32$ systems. All the simulation results in this paper are the average value for 5000 unit time run for each entry. We see that the error of the EPA is comparable to that of the technique in [8] except for the region $\alpha \ge 2^{-1}$ where the EPA gives fairly better approximation. The maximum percentage error ($|\eta_E - \eta_S|/\eta_S \times 100$) of the EPA is 1.38 percent at $\alpha = 2$. The last column of Table I shows the difference between η's given by the analysis and simulation both in [8].

Now we consider the effect of the scale of the system. The EPA says that P and M have influence on the performance of the system only through their ratio $\beta = P/M$. Table II shows that this conclusion is not exactly correct. The error of the EPA is larger when the system is smaller. Obviously the

TABLE I
AVERAGE PROCESSOR AND MEMORY UTILIZATION FOR 32 × 32 CONSTANT SERVICE TIME HOMOGENEOUS SYSTEMS (PERCENT)—SIMULATION VERSUS EPA COMPARISON

α	EPA		simulation		$n_E - n_S$	*
	n_E	ρ_E	n_S	ρ_S		
2^{-7}	99.22	.7770	99.22	.7781	0.00	0.02
2^{-6}	98.45	1.538	98.42	1.569	0.03	0.00
2^{-5}	96.92	3.033	96.91	3.049	0.01	0.03
2^{-4}	93.95	5.877	93.88	5.936	0.07	-0.02
2^{-3}	88.28	11.04	88.30	11.06	-0.02	0.04
2^{-2}	78.10	19.53	78.22	19.50	-0.12	0.06
2^{-1}	62.02	31.01	62.22	31.08	-0.20	0.43
2^{0}	42.27	42.27	42.63	42.61	-0.36	0.82
2^{1}	25.00	50.00	25.35	50.68	-0.35	1.04
2^{2}	13.56	54.26	13.73	54.87	-0.17	0.75
2^{3}	7.050	56.42	7.076	56.48	-0.03	0.47

* The difference between η's given by the analysis and simulation in [8].

TABLE II
AVERAGE PROCESSOR UTILIZATION η FOR CONSTANT SERVICE TIME HOMOGENEOUS SYSTEMS (PERCENT)—EFFECT OF SYSTEM SIZE

α	simulation					EPA
	4x4	8x8	16x16	32x32	64x64	
2^{-6}	98.45	98.38	98.47	98.42	98.43	98.45
2^{-5}	96.83	97.01	96.86	96.91	96.96	96.92
2^{-4}	93.91	93.86	93.85	93.88	94.01	93.95
2^{-3}	88.64	88.26	88.25	88.30	88.33	88.28
2^{-2}	78.57	78.00	78.37	78.22	78.16	78.10
2^{-1}	63.34	62.87	62.26	62.22	62.27	62.02
2^{0}	45.71	43.81	43.00	42.63	42.46	42.27
2^{1}	27.31	26.20	25.47	25.35	25.17	25.00
2^{2}	15.12	14.32	14.00	13.73	13.57	13.56

Entries within dotted and solid lines have percentage error larger than 0.5 percent and 1 percent, respectively.

meaning of this observation is that the performance of the system depends on its scale. The simple approximate technique EPA fails in explaining this point. However, the influence of the scale on the performance of the system is only slight if P and M are not extremely small. Fortunately, we have more accurate analytic tools applicable to such small systems. Moreover, it is easy to study such systems by simulations.

In this paper, we show numerical examples only for systems with $P = M$. We have no definite reason for this. Many simulations showed that systems with $P \ne M$ have no special properties worth our particular attention.

B. Systems with Geometric Service Time

It is apparent that we can study the behavior of a system with geometrically distributed service time at memories in just the same manner. We only need to replace t_a by $1/\mu$, and ρ of

(2) by $\rho = n/(n+1)$ in the analysis in Section II-A, where $1/\mu$ is the average service time.

We have a unique equilibrium point n_e,

$$n_e = \frac{\sqrt{\{1 + \alpha(1-\beta)\}^2 + 4\alpha^2\beta} - \{1 + \alpha(1-\beta)\}}{2\alpha} \quad (7)$$

where $\alpha = \lambda/\mu$ and $\beta = P/M$. The utilization η and ρ of processors and memories are given by

$$\eta = 1 - \frac{n_e}{\beta}, \quad \rho = \frac{n_e}{n_e + 1}, \quad (8)$$

respectively.

The EPA says again that the performance of the system depends only on α and β. In this case, however, it is also not exactly true that the performance depends on λ and μ only through their ratio $\alpha = \lambda/\mu$. We show Table III to examine this point. In the table, entries in dotted line have percentage error larger than 2 percent. The performance has almost no relation to μ, when α is small. When α is large, however, the EPA gives a poorer approximation for the system with smaller $1/\mu$. Also, we can see that the approximation of the analysis is generally poorer here compared to that in the last section. We can easily imagine that to approximate a discrete time arrival process by a continuous one has only slight influence on the analytical result in a constant service time system where the service time is an integer multiple of the unit time. This is also the reason why the conclusion from the EPA that η and ρ do not depend on λ and t_a individually is correct in the case of constant service time systems. On the other hand, the effect of the replacement of discrete service time by continuous one is not so small, especially when $1/\mu$ is small.

III. General Systems with Static Memory Reference Pattern

In this section, we generalize the mathematical model of multiprocessor systems studied in the previous section. The processors are classified into I groups as is shown in Fig. 3. Each group consists of P_i processors where $P = \Sigma_{i=1}^{I} P_i$. The system has J groups of memory modules each of them consists of M_j modules where $M = \Sigma_{j=1}^{J} M_j$.

We consider two processor models corresponding to Cases I) and II) of Section II. In Case I), the memory request probability and the processing mode for processors in the ith group are denoted by λ_i and the P_i mode, respectively. A processor in the ith group waiting for or accessing a memory module in the jth group is said to be in the M_{ij} mode. A processor in the ith group accesses one of the M_j memory modules in the jth group with probability p_{ij}/M_j.

In this section, we assume a deterministic service time t_j for each memory module in the jth group. It is apparent from the following discussions that we can also easily study a system with geometrically distributed service time in the same manner.

A. Systems with Geometrically Distributed Computing Time

It is easy to show that the behavior of a memory module in the jth group can be approximated by an M/D/1 system with a

TABLE III
AVERAGE PROCESSOR UTILIZATION η FOR 32×32 GEOMETRIC SERVICE TIME HOMOGENEOUS SYSTEMS (PERCENT)—SIMULATION VERSUS EPA

	simulation				EPA
α	$1/\mu = 2$	2^2	2^3	2^4	
2^{-6}	98.46	98.52	98.50	98.33	98.44
2^{-5}	96.91	96.97	96.67	97.13	96.88
2^{-4}	93.94	93.88	94.03	93.73	93.77
2^{-3}	88.03	88.15	88.03	88.11	87.69
2^{-2}	77.13	76.55	76.79	75.42	76.39
2^{-1}	60.56	59.78	58.51	59.31	58.58
2^0	40.44	39.68	38.86	37.64	38.20
2^1	23.57	22.85	22.82	21.96	21.92
2^2	–	12.15	12.09	12.21	11.72

Entries within the dotted line have percentage error larger than 2 percent

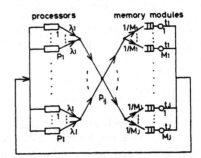

Fig. 3. Queueing model for a general system with static memory reference pattern.

Poisson arrival rate

$$\sum_{i=1}^{I} \left\{ P_i - \sum_{l=1}^{J} K_{il} \right\} \lambda_i \frac{p_{ij}}{M_j} \text{ requests/slot}, \quad (1 \le j \le J) \quad (9)$$

when K_{il} processors are in the M_{il} mode (Fig. 4). From the Pollazeck–Khinchine formula, we have

$$\rho_j = \sum_{l=1}^{I} n_{lj} + 1 - \sqrt{\left(\sum_{l=1}^{I} n_{lj}\right)^2 + 1}, \quad (1 \le j \le J) \quad (10)$$

where n_{lj} is the average number of processors in the lth group waiting for or accessing a memory module in the jth group and ρ_j is the busy probability of a module in the jth group. Here, let $K_{il} = M_l n_{il}$ again. We have the following equilibrium point equation.

$$\left\{ P_i - \sum_{l=1}^{I} M_l n_{il} \right\} \lambda_i p_{ij} = \frac{M_j}{t_j} \frac{n_{ij}}{\sum_{l=1}^{I} n_{lj}}$$

$$\cdot \left\{ \sum_{l=1}^{I} n_{lj} + 1 - \sqrt{\left(\sum_{l=1}^{I} n_{lj}\right)^2 + 1} \right\}, \quad \left(\begin{array}{c} 1 \le i \le I \\ 1 \le j \le J \end{array}\right). \quad (11)$$

This is a system of IJ simultaneous nonlinear equations for n_{ij} $(1 \le i \le I, 1 \le j \le J)$.

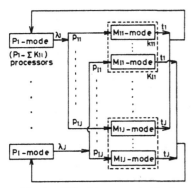

Fig. 4. EPA of the system in Fig. 3.

Let $n_e = \{n_{eij}\}$ be a solution of (11). We call it an equilibrium point. It is rather difficult to discuss the number of equilibrium points of this quite general system. However, we intuitively imagine that such a system always has only one equilibrium point. So, we proceed assuming that (11) always has only one solution.

Multiplying both sides of (11) by t_j/M_j, you will see that the EPA says that the performance of the system depends only on $\alpha_{ij} = \lambda_i t_j$ and $\beta_{ij} = P_i/M_j$.

The average utilization of processors in the ith group is given by

$$\eta_i = \frac{P_i - \sum_{l=1}^{J} M_l n_{eil}}{P_i} = 1 - \sum_{l=1}^{J} \frac{n_{eil}}{\beta_{il}}, \qquad (1 \le i \le I). \quad (12)$$

The average utilization of memory modules in the jth group is given by ρ_j of (10) where n_{ij} is replaced by n_{eij}.

In Table IV, the performance of systems with two processor groups and two memory groups is shown. The equilibrium point n_e is easily obtained from (11) using some numerical method. The approximation of the EPA is again quite satisfying. More complicated systems can also be studied easily.

When either $I = 1$ or $J = 1$, we can easily have a nonlinear equation for only one unknown variable. Let us consider the case of $I = 1$ for instance.

In this case, (11) reduces to

$$\left\{ P_1 - \sum_{l=1}^{J} M_l n_{1l} \right\} \lambda_1 p_{1j} = \frac{M_j}{t_j} \left\{ n_{1j} + 1 - \sqrt{n_{1j}^2 + 1} \right\},$$

$$(1 \le j \le J). \quad (13)$$

Let $\alpha_j = \lambda_1 t_j$, $\beta_j = P_1/M_j$, and replace n_{1j}, P_1, and p_{1j} by n_j, P, and p_j, respectively. Let also

$$K = \sum_{j=1}^{J} M_j n_j. \quad (14)$$

From (13) we have the following relation.

$$n_j = \frac{\alpha_j \beta_j (P-K)\{2 - \alpha_j \beta_j (P-K)\}}{2\{1 - \alpha_j \beta_j (P-K)\}}, \qquad (1 \le j \le J). \quad (15)$$

TABLE IV
AVERAGE PROCESSOR AND MEMORY UTILIZATION FOR 32×32 GENERAL SYSTEMS (I) (PERCENT) $I = J = 2$, $P_1 = P_2 = M_1 = M_2 = 16$, $\lambda_2 = 2\lambda_1$, $t_2 = 2t_1$, $p_{11} = p_{22} = 3/4$, $p_{12} = p_{21} = 1/4$

	EPA				simulation			
α	η_1	η_2	ρ_1	ρ_2	η_1	η_2	ρ_1	ρ_2
2^{-6}	98.05	94.70	1.889	5.205	98.10	94.84	1.854	5.064
2^{-5}	96.12	89.70	3.654	9.911	96.18	89.80	3.581	9.876
2^{-4}	92.31	80.61	6.846	18.00	92.29	80.55	6.835	18.11
2^{-3}	85.03	65.70	12.08	29.95	84.83	65.86	12.08	30.20
2^{-2}	72.31	45.91	19.30	43.47	72.45	46.32	19.34	43.70
2^{-1}	54.26	27.13	27.13	54.26	54.35	27.51	27.32	54.94
2^0	35.35	14.38	33.70	60.81	35.48	14.46	33.63	61.64
2^1	20.56	7.292	38.14	64.31	20.17	7.489	38.06	65.49
2^2	11.14	3.652	40.71	66.10	11.22	3.770	41.93	66.39

Substituting these n_j's into (14), we get an equilibrium point equation for K. Then we have n_{ej}'s substituting the solution K_e back into (15). Obviously, the worst equilibrium point corresponds to the largest K_e. Table V shows the performance of systems with four groups of memory modules.

B. Systems with Zero Processing Time

In this section, we consider a system with zero processing time. Although it is not difficult to treat the problem as generally as in the previous section, we only study here the following system.

In the system, we assume homogeneous processors. Each processor has the next memory request immediately after it has been served by a memory. Let the probability that the request is for the jth memory module be p_j ($1 \le j \le M$, $\sum_{j=1}^{M} p_j = 1$). Let the constant service time of the jth memory module be t_j. We then have the following relation when the system is at an equilibrium point.

$$\left\{ \sum_{l=1}^{M} \frac{\rho_l}{t_l} \right\} p_j = \frac{\rho_j}{t_j}, \qquad (1 \le j \le M) \quad (16)$$

where ρ_j is the utilization of the jth memory module. This equation means that

$$\rho_j = \frac{p_j t_j}{p_1 t_1} \rho_1, \qquad (1 \le j \le M). \quad (17)$$

We have an equilibrium point equation for ρ_1 substituting (17) into the relation

$$n_j = \frac{\rho_j(1 - \rho_j/2)}{1 - \rho_j}, \qquad (1 \le j \le M) \quad (18)$$

and then substituting the resultant n_j's into the relation

$$\sum_{j=1}^{M} n_j = P. \quad (19)$$

We use the average number of busy memory modules

$$\text{ANBM} = \sum_{j=1}^{M} \rho_j \quad (20)$$

297

TABLE V
AVERAGE PROCESSOR AND MEMORY UTILIZATION FOR 32 × 32
GENERAL SYSTEMS (II) (PERCENT) $I = 1, J = 4, M_1 = \cdots = M_4 = 8,$
$p_1 = p_2 = 0.3, p_3 = p_4 = 0.2, t_1 = t_3, t_2 = t_4 = 2t_1$

	EPA			simulation				
α	η	ρ_1	ρ_2,ρ_3,ρ_4	η	ρ_1	ρ_2	ρ_3	ρ_4
2^{-6}	97.68	1.831		97.70	1.830	3.710	1.105	2.440
2^{-5}	95.41	3.578		95.52	3.600	7.010	2.330	4.495
2^{-4}	90.99	6.825		91.01	6.713	13.76	4.493	9.025
2^{-3}	82.74	12.41	$\rho_2=2\rho_1$	82.64	12.34	24.89	8.320	16.71
2^{-2}	68.50	20.55	$\rho_3=2\rho_1/3$	68.29	20.55	41.00	13.84	27.37
2^{-1}	48.44	29.07	$\rho_4=4\rho_1/3$	48.36	29.36	57.70	19.37	39.08
2^{0}	28.90	34.68		28.71	34.38	68.98	22.90	46.06
2^{1}	15.58	37.38		15.54	37.27	74.75	24.26	50.05
2^{2}	8.044	38.61		7.939	38.25	75.44	25.80	50.56

to discuss the performance of the system. Here, we only show one numerical example. Equation (29) gives ANBM = 15.89 for a system with $P = M = 32, t_1 = \cdots = t_{16}, t_{17} = \cdots = t_{32} = 2t_1, p_1 = \cdots = p_8 = p_{17} = \cdots = p_{24} = 0.025,$ and $p_9 = \cdots = p_{16} = p_{25} = \cdots = p_{32} = 0.0375.$ On the other hand, the simulation shows that ANBM = 16.11. The percentage error is 1.38 percent. The theoretical values of memory utilization are 0.2649, 0.3973, 0.5297, and 0.7946 for memory modules 1–8, 9–16, 17–24, and 25–32, respectively. Corresponding simulation results are 0.2688, 0.4056, 0.5317, and 0.8082.

IV. SYSTEMS WITH DYNAMIC MEMORY REFERENCE PATTERN

In this section, we study systems in which the memory access pattern of each processor is dependent on which memory module it visited in the past. We call it a localized or dynamic memory reference pattern.

Let the system have P homogeneous processors. We only study Case I) for the processor model. M memory modules are classified into J groups with M_j $(1 \leq j \leq J)$ modules, respectively. A memory module in the jth group has a deterministic service time t_j.

We can easily imagine that to study a system with some groups of processors will not be difficult. Here, however, we restrict ourselves to the above relatively simple system to study the effect of locality in the memory reference pattern.

We suppose that a processor which has accessed a memory module in the ith group has probability r_{ij}/M_j to access one of the M_j memory modules in the jth group, at the next time it requests a memory.

We have the following equilibrium point equation for this system.

$$\lambda \left(P - \sum_{l=1}^{J} M_l n_l \right) \frac{\sum_{l=1}^{J} M_l \rho_l r_{lj}/t_l}{\sum_{l=1}^{J} M_l \rho_l/t_l} = \frac{M_j}{t_j} \rho_j, \qquad (1 \leq j \leq J) \tag{21}$$

where n_l is the average number of processors waiting for or accessing a memory module in the lth group and $p_l = n_l + 1 - \sqrt{n_l^2 + 1}$. In (21), the term $\{\Sigma_{l=1}^{J} M_l \rho_l r_{lj}/t_l\}/\{\Sigma_{l=1}^{J} M_l \rho_l/t_l\}$ represents the ratio of the number of memory requests for a memory module in the jth group to the whole requests. Modifying (21), we have

$$\sum_{l=1}^{J} \left(\frac{M_l}{M_j} \right) \left(\frac{\rho_l}{\rho_j} \right) \left(\frac{t_j}{t_l} \right) r_{lj} = \sum_{l=1}^{J} \left(\frac{M_l}{M_1} \right) \left(\frac{\rho_l}{\rho_1} \right) \left(\frac{t_1}{t_l} \right),$$
$$(2 \leq j \leq J). \tag{22}$$

It is convenient to use one of the relations contained in (21) and $J - 1$ relations in (22) as the equilibrium point equation. Again, it is difficult to discuss the number of solutions of these J simultaneous nonlinear equations on $\rho_1, \rho_2, \cdots, \rho_j$. Here, we proceed intuitively assuming that the system has only one equilibrium point. In Table VI, we show an example of the behavior of system with $J = 3$.

Next we study the special case of a completely symmetric system. In the system, $t_j = t, M_j = M/J,$ and

$$r_{ij} = \begin{cases} q & (i=j) \\ \dfrac{1-q}{J-1} & (i \neq j) \end{cases}, \qquad (1 \leq i, j \leq J). \tag{23}$$

We easily have

$$\rho_1 = \rho_2 = \cdots = \rho_J, \tag{24}$$

substituting (23) into (22). Thus, substituting (24) into (21), we can show that the equilibrium point equation for this system is nothing but that for the homogeneous one studied in Section II.

It has been shown in [7], however, that this kind of localization in memory reference pattern has some influence on the performance of the system. This fact can also be deduced intuitively as follows. It is true that in such a

299

TABLE VI

AVERAGE PROCESSOR AND MEMORY UTILIZATION FOR 30 × 30 DYNAMIC MEMORY REFERENCE PATTERN SYSTEMS (PERCENT) $J = 3$, $M_j = 10 \ (1 \le j \le 3)$, $t_j = t$,

$$(p_{ij}) = \begin{pmatrix} 0.8 & 0.1 & 0.1 \\ 0.5 & 0.1 & 0.4 \\ 0.3 & 0.2 & 0.5 \end{pmatrix}$$

	EPA				simulation			
α	η	ρ_1	ρ_2	ρ_3	η	ρ_1	ρ_2	ρ_3
2^{-6}	98.44	2.995	.5674	1.052	98.45	3.050	.5820	.9633
2^{-5}	96.90	5.897	1.116	2.072	96.96	5.807	1.109	2.029
2^{-4}	93.85	11.42	2.161	4.013	93.85	11.59	2.152	3.918
2^{-3}	87.91	21.40	4.048	7.519	87.88	21.49	4.066	7.572
2^{-2}	76.70	37.34	7.064	13.12	76.99	37.47	6.933	12.96
2^{-1}	57.89	56.37	10.66	19.81	58.59	56.42	10.88	20.22
2^{0}	35.80	69.71	13.19	24.48	36.47	70.98	13.36	25.05
2^{1}	19.46	75.81	14.34	26.64	19.76	77.15	14.24	27.13
2^{2}	10.07	78.42	14.84	27.55	10.21	79.62	14.97	27.79

symmetric system, a long time observation of the system shows that the ratio of the number of visits of a processor to a memory module to the number of its whole memory requests is $1/M$ without any relation to q. However, the state of the system changes more slowly when q is larger. Thus, when q is large, occasional accidental congestion in a module will last longer and the system may have lower processor utilization.

This effect is usually negligible, however, see Table VII, for instance. Although this is an example of a nonsymmetric system ($t_2 = 2t_1$), we can easily imagine that, in such a weakly localized system, there is almost no influence of the locality of memory reference on the performance.

Next, refer to Table VIII where $J = M$. In this case, larger q implies very strong locality in memory reference. The system with $q = 1/32$ corresponds to the one with static reference pattern. From the table we can conclude that, in some systems with strong locality in memory reference pattern, the effect of the locality is fairly large. In such systems, the error of the EPA is also fairly large. Thus, we cannot use the EPA to estimate the influence of the locality.

We show Table IX to check some details of this issue. It shows the percentage difference between simulation results for systems with a dynamic memory reference pattern and that for systems with a static one. We conclude that the influence of the locality in memory reference is fairly large when $\alpha \ge 2^0$ and $q \ge 0.3$ in this example.

V. SYSTEMS WITH BUS CONNECTIONS

Finally we study systems with bus connections between processors and memories. As is shown in Fig. 5, the system has P processors and M memory modules. However, there are only B ($B < \min [P, M]$) buses through which processors can access memories. Here we only study the simplest case. In the system, each processor has memory request probability λ in each slot. The memory reference pattern is completely random. The memory request at the top of a queue for a memory module can access it, if and only if, there is a bus available to it.

TABLE VII

AVERAGE PROCESSOR UTILIZATION FOR 32 × 32 SYMMETRIC DYNAMIC MEMORY REFERENCE PATTERN SYSTEMS (I) (PERCENT) $J = 2$, $t_2 = 2t_1$, $p_{ij} = q \ (i = j)$, $p_{ij} = 1 - q \ (i \ne j)$

	simulation			EPA
α	$q = 0.8$	0.1	0.5	
2^{-6}	97.62	97.63	97.75	97.66
2^{-5}	95.46	95.46	95.56	95.42
2^{-4}	90.98	91.10	91.08	91.02
2^{-3}	82.83	82.96	82.77	82.82
2^{-2}	68.80	69.01	68.69	68.80
2^{-1}	49.43	49.67	49.60	49.19
2^{0}	30.15	30.28	30.40	29.87
2^{1}	16.35	16.67	16.59	16.33
2^{2}	8.571	8.652	8.702	8.500

TABLE VIII

AVERAGE PROCESSOR UTILIZATION FOR 32 × 32 SYMMETRIC DYNAMIC MEMORY REFERENCE PATTERN SYSTEMS (II) (PERCENT) $J (= M) = 32$, $p_{ij} = q \ (i = j)$, $p_{ij} = (1 - q)/31 \ (i \ne j)$

	simulation					EPA
α	$q = 1/32$	0.05	0.1	0.5	0.9	
2^{-3}	88.30	88.26	88.27	88.13	88.38	88.28
2^{-2}	78.22	78.15	78.19	78.04	78.07	78.10
2^{-1}	62.22	62.18	62.22	61.80	61.64	62.02
2^{0}	42.63	42.66	42.50	42.01	41.75	42.27
2^{1}	25.35	25.23	25.07	23.80	23.31	25.00
2^{2}	13.73	13.67	13.57	12.69	12.34	13.56

TABLE IX

PERCENTAGE DIFFERENCE IN SIMULATION RESULTS OF AVERAGE PROCESSOR UTILIZATION BETWEEN DYNAMIC AND STATIC MEMORY REFERENCE 32 × 32 SYSTEMS

α	$q = .05$	0.1	0.3	0.5	0.7	0.9
2^{-3}	0.05	0.03	0.00	0.19	0.03	-0.08
2^{-2}	0.10	0.05	0.00	0.24	0.13	0.20
2^{-1}	0.07	0.00	0.31	0.69	0.52	0.94
2^{0}	-0.08	0.30	1.4	1.4	1.6	2.1
2^{1}	0.49	1.1	4.1	6.1	8.4	8.1
2^{2}	0.42	1.2	4.1	7.6	9.5	10.2

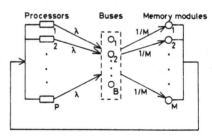

Fig. 5. Queueing model for a $P \times M \times B$ homogeneous system with bus connection.

Here we only show a simple possible application of the EPA to the problem since it is more complicated than those studied in the previous sections. More sophisticated treatment may be needed to discuss the behavior of such systems in more detail.

Let t_a be the average service time of each memory module. The average number of processors waiting for and accessing memory modules are denoted by n and m, respectively. We analyze the behavior of the system studying the following three cases separately. Here, it should be noted that the words heavy, medium, and light loads defined below are arbitrarily chosen by the author and rather vaguely defined.

1) *Heavy Load:* In this case, the number of busy buses may be always close to B. Let us assume that a memory request has been completed in a slot. In the next slot, none of the n waiting requests can access a memory module if all of them are distributed among the L queues with busy memories. We suppose here that $L = B - 1$. Thus, we have the following equilibrium point equation for n.

$$(P - n - B)\lambda = \left\{1 - \left(\frac{B-1}{M}\right)^n\right\}\frac{B}{t_a}. \qquad (25)$$

Here, the term $\{(B - 1)/M\}^n$ is the probability that $M - B + 1$ predetermined urns are empty when n balls are randomly distributed into M urns. We use (25) when it has a solution n_e in the region $0 \le n_e \le P - B$. The utilization factors of processors and memories are given by the following η and ρ, respectively.

$$\eta = \frac{P - B - n_e}{P}, \quad \rho = \frac{B}{M}. \qquad (26)$$

2) *Medium Load:* In this case, we assume that m buses are busy. Note that, even when $m < B$, there may be some memory requests waiting for memory modules. When one of the m requests has been completed, none of the waiting n requests can access the memory module if all of them are distributed among the $m - 1$ queues with busy memories. Referring to Fig. 6, we have the equilibrium point equation for n and m.

$$(P - n - m)\lambda = \frac{m}{t_a},$$

$$(P - n - m)\lambda\frac{m}{M} = \frac{m}{t_a}\left\{1 - \left(\frac{m-1}{m}\right)^n\right\}. \qquad (27)$$

In the figure, the W mode is the mode of processors waiting for a bus or a memory module and the A mode accessing a memory module. We use the above equation when it has a root n_e, m_e in the region $1 \le m_e \le \min\left[\alpha P/(1 + \alpha), B\right]$ where $\alpha = \lambda t_a$. The utilization factors of processors and memories are

$$\eta = \frac{P - n_e - m_e}{P} = \frac{m_e}{\alpha}, \quad \rho = \frac{m_e}{M}. \qquad (28)$$

3) *Light Load:* Next, we consider the case of a very light load since the method in 2) cannot be used when $m < 1$. In this case, we can neglect the possibility of memory requests to

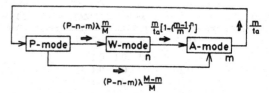

Fig. 6. EPA of the system in Fig. 5.

wait for the memories or buses. Thus, we have

$$(P - M)\lambda = \frac{m}{t_a} \qquad (29)$$

as the equilibrium point equation for m. We use this equation when the solution

$$m_e = \frac{\alpha P}{1 + \alpha} \qquad (30)$$

satisfies $m_e \le 1$. We have

$$\eta = \frac{P - m_e}{P} = \frac{P}{1 + \alpha}, \quad \rho = \frac{m_e}{M} = \frac{\alpha P}{(1 + \alpha)M}. \qquad (31)$$

We can see from (25), (27), and (29) that the behavior of the system depends on λ and t_a only through the product α.

In Table X, we show a numerical example. We adopt the arithmetic mean of the results when we can apply two or more methods shown above. Some examples are the fourth and fifth rows of the table which are the arithmetic means of the results given by (26) and (28).

All the simulation results in the table are for $t_a = 5$. In this rather rough analysis, we only used the average service time of the memory. In the table, however, simulation results for systems with deterministic and geometric service times at memories are shown. The simulation results for the case of deterministic service time show closer coincidence with the analytical ones than those for systems with geometric service times.

In the columns of simulations for η's, entries in the dotted line have percentage errors larger than 1 percent. The maximum percentage errors are 1.8 and 4.6 percent for systems with deterministic and geometric service times, respectively. The approximation of this simple analysis is satisfactory except for the case of medium to high load in the system with a geometric service time distribution.

VI. Conclusions

It has been shown that the EPA is a powerful analytic tool for the performance evaluation of quite general multiprocessor systems. It has been applied, for instance, to systems with general static memory reference pattern, systems with dynamic reference pattern, and systems with insufficient buses between processors and memories.

The error of this simple approximate technique is usually small enough. In some cases, however, the error is rather large. It may be large when the scale of the system is small, the service time at memories is not deterministic but distributed probabilistically, and the system has strong locality in its

TABLE X

AVERAGE PROCESSOR AND MEMORY UTILIZATION FOR $P \times M \times B = 32 \times 32 \times 8$ BUS-CONNECTED SYSTEMS (PERCENT) $t_a = 5$

	EPA			simulation			
				deterministic		geometric	
α	η	ρ	*	η	ρ	η	ρ
0.01	.9901	.0099	L	.9906	.0094	.9902	.0095
0.05	.9509	.0476	M	.9499	.0486	.9487	.0485
0.1	.9028	.0903	M	.9040	.0917	.9019	.0907
0.3	.7206	.2346	M,H	.7254	.2186	.7059	.2146
1/3	.7009	.2427	M,H	.6884	.2309	.6700	.2250
0.5	.5000	.2500	H	.4932	.2493	.4987	.2474
1	.2500	.2500	H	.2505	.2499	.2487	.2499
5	.0500	.2500	H	.0501	.2500	.0503	.2500

* H, M, and L in this column mean that methods 1), 2), and 3) are applicable, respectively.

memory reference pattern. We have to improve the technique shown in this paper to study such problems in more detail. We also have to refine it to study systems with bus connections.

Another rather mathematical problem which needs further study is a rigorous discussion on the presence and number of equilibrium points in some complex systems such as ones in Sections III and IV.

However, it can be said that the main purpose of this paper, that is, to show the possible usefulness of the EPA for many problems in this and related areas, has been fulfilled.

Here, we did not concern ourselves in depth with real multiprocessor systems themselves. We can easily imagine that their behavior can be studied by the EPA in the same manner. We can also imagine that there will be many other problems in the area of computer performance evaluation to which the EPA is successfully applicable.

ACKNOWLEDGMENT

The author wishes to thank Prof. J. Wolf and Prof. D. Towsley of the University of Massachusetts for their valuable discussions during the course of the study.

REFERENCES

[1] Y. Nunotani, S. Sumita, and O. Hashida, "Performance evaluation for multiprocessor systems," *J. Instit. Electron. Commun. Eng. Japan.* (in Japanese), vol. 66, pp. 1261-1266, Dec. 1983.

[2] F. Baskett and A. J. Smith, "Interference in multiprocessor computer systems with interleaved memory," *Commun. ACM*, vol. 19, June 1976.

[3] D. P. Bhandarkar, "Analysis of memory interference in multiprocessors," *IEEE Trans. Comput.*, vol. C-24, pp. 897-908, Sept. 1975.

[4] C. E. Skinner and J. R. Asher, "Effects of storage contention on system performance," *IBM Syst. J.*, vol. 8, no. 4, pp. 319-333, 1969.

[5] B. R. Rau, "Interleaved memory bandwidth in a model of a multiprocessor computer system," *IEEE Trans. Comput.*, vol. C-28, pp. 678-681, Sept. 1979.

[6] C. H. Hoogendoorn, "A general model for memory interference in multiprocessors," *IEEE Trans. Comput.*, vol. C-26, pp. 998-1005, Oct. 1977.

[7] A. S. Sethi and N. Deo, "Interference in multiprocessor systems with localized memory access probabilities," *IEEE Trans. Comput.*, vol. C-28, pp. 157-163, Feb. 1979.

[8] J. H. Patel, "Analysis of multiprocessors with private cache memories," *IEEE Trans. Comput.*, vol. C-31, pp. 296-304, Apr. 1982.

[9] D. W. L. Yen, J. H. Patel, and E. S. Davidson, "Memory interference in synchronous multiprocessor systems," *IEEE Trans. Comput.*, vol. C-31, pp. 1116-1121, Nov. 1982.

[10] S. Ikehara, "Analysis of memory contention in multiprocessors," *Trans. Instit. Electron. Commun. Eng. Japan.* (in Japanese), vol. 63-D, pp. 334-341, Apr. 1980.

[11] M. A. Marsan and M. Gerla, "Markov models for multiple bus multiprocessor systems," *IEEE Trans. Comput.*, vol. C-31, pp. 239-248, Mar. 1982.

[12] M. A. Marsan, G. Balbo, and G. Conte, "Modeling bus connection and memory interference in a multiprocessor system," *IEEE Trans. Comput.*, vol. C-32, pp. 60-72, Jan. 1983.

[13] A. Fukuda, "Equilibrium point analysis of ALOHA-type systems," *Trans. Instit. Electron. Commun. Eng. Japan.* (in Japanese), vol. 61-B, pp. 959-966, Nov. 1978.

[14] A. Fukuda and S. Tasaka, "The equilibrium point analysis—A unified analytic tool for packet broadcast networks," in *Proc. GLOBECOM'83*, San Diego, CA, 1983.

[15] A. Fukuda and S. Tasaka, "Stochastic flow systems and the equilibrium point analysis," *J. Instit. Electron Commun. Eng. Japan.* (in Japanese), vol. 66, pp. 1228-1233, Dec. 1983.

[16] L. Kleinrock, *Queueing Systems, Vol. I : Theory*. New York: Wiley, 1975.

Scalar Memory References in Pipelined Multiprocessors: A Performance Study

Ravi Ganesan and Shlomo Weiss, *Member, IEEE*

Abstract—Interleaved memories are essential in pipelined computers to attain high memory bandwidth. As a memory bank is accessed, a reservation is placed on the bank for the duration of the memory cycle, which is often considerably longer than the processor cycle time. This additional parameter, namely, the bank reservation time or the bank busy time, adds to the complexity of the memory model. For Markov models, exact solutions are not feasible even without this additional parameter due to the very large state space of the Markov chain. In this paper we develop a Markov model which explicitly tracks the bank reservation time. Because we only model one processor and the requested bank, the transition probabilities are not known and have to be approximated. The performance predicted by the model is in close agreement with simulation results.

Index Terms— Pipelined computers, supercomputers, interleaved memory, Markov chains, memory conflicts.

I. INTRODUCTION

INTERLEAVED memories are commonly used in pipelined processors to increase the memory bandwidth beyond the bandwidth of a single memory module (or bank). The performance of interleaved memory systems depends on the number of banks, the bank cycle time, the number of processors, and the pattern of requests generated. The design of such systems involves a number of trade-offs which are dominated by the nature of the interrelationships between these factors. Performance analysis of interleaved memory systems yields insights into these interrelationships, thus enabling the designer to study cost/performance trade-offs and determine system parameters.

A large amount of useful work has been done in this area, and we briefly survey the various approaches and their implications. Of special interest is Bailey's work [1] on memory contention in vector computers. While in [1] the focus is on vector memory references, Bailey also introduced a Markov model, which is the starting point of our research. Our primary thrust is to develop a more accurate Markov model by relaxing the restrictive condition that at most one processor can be blocked on a busy bank.

Stochastic models are commonly used to study the performance of parallel memories. A basic assumption in these models is that memory references are randomly distributed.

Manuscript received June 21, 1991; revised August 29, 1991. Recommended by E. Gelenbe.

R. Ganesan is with Bell Atlantic, Beltsville, MD 20705.

S. Weiss is with the Department of Computer Science, University of Maryland, Baltimore, and the Institute for Advanced Computer Studies, University of Maryland, College Park, MD 20742.

IEEE Log Number 9104758.

This is clearly not the case in vector processing, where each reference is at a constant distance from the previous reference. Hence the model developed in this paper is not intended for vector processors. One reasonable area of application for the model is a transaction processing environment, which is characterized by a large number of independent transactions executing concurrently. The model developed in this paper can be also applied to pseudorandomly interleaved memories [2]–[8]. In a pseudorandomly interleaved memory the address sequence presented to the memory system is a pseudorandom sequence which is generated by "scrambling" the address pattern produced by the processor. Randomizing memory schemes have been implemented in the IBM RP3 [3] and Cydrome Cydra 5 [7] memory systems.

The remainder of this paper is organized as follows. In Section II we look at prior work on memory performance modeling. We point out that assumptions commonly made in many multiprocessor memory analyses are not applicable in the context of pipelined computers. We summarize Bailey's model in Section III. Comparing it with simulation results (Section IV), we conclude that Bailey's model often overestimates performance, primarily because of the restriction that at most one processor can be blocked on a busy bank. We develop a Markov model in Sections V and VI and present results predicted by it in Section VIII. Finally, in Section IX we discuss the accuracy of our model.

II. SURVEY OF MEMORY PERFORMANCE MODELING TECHNIQUES

The contention problem in memory systems is a well-known problem that has received considerable attention in the literature. Cheung and Smith [9] analyze the memory system of the CRAY X-MP by considering the various ways in which memory references interact with other references from the same vector stream or from other vector streams. This deterministic approach, taken also by Oed and Lange [10], is most appropriate for the memory system of a vector multiprocessor, since vector references are clearly not random. Cheung and Smith point out, however, that when several vector streams are active simultaneously, and each may have a different stride, the number of different stride combinations is too large to analyze each case separately.

The more common approach to analyze contention in parallel memories is the use of probabilistic models. In an early work, Hellerman [11] proposed a model in which he assumes that in each cycle a sequence of b requests is presented to a parallel memory system with b banks. In this model, Hellerman assumes that memory requests are independent and randomly distributed. If multiple requests arrive at the same bank, one is serviced and the others are rejected. Rejected requests are dropped and b new independent requests are submitted in the next cycle to randomly selected banks. The stream of b requests is inspected in the arrival order in one cycle. Requests arriving prior to a conflict are forwarded to memory within the same cycle. The rest of the b requests are rejected.

Based on this model, Hellerman derived a formula for the average number of busy banks and showed that $b^{0.56}$ is an approximation of this formula to within 4%, for $b \leq 45$. Knuth and Rao [12] showed that Hellerman's expression is a well-studied function with known asymptotic behavior. Ravi [13] changed Hellerman's model to allow all requests that arrive to distinct banks, within the same cycle, to be forwarded to memory. That is, in a stream of m requests arriving in a given cycle (where $m \leq b$, the number of banks), a conflict does not block other requests that are directed to different banks. Ravi showed that removing this constraint in Hellerman's model significantly enhances the predicted memory bandwidth.

Ravi's memory model with m processors and b banks is equivalent to a combinatorial problem with m balls and b partitions, in which m balls are randomly distributed among the b partitions in each cycle. Also, in each cycle, one ball is removed from each partition, which corresponds to forwarding a request to a memory bank. In Ravi's model, unserviced requests are simply dropped at the end of the cycle. Chang, *et al.* [14] point out that this assumption makes Ravi's model somewhat optimistic, because unserviced requests can cause additional conflicts in later cycles.

A memory model similar to Ravi's was analyzed by Bhandarkar [15] using Markov chain techniques. The state of this Markov chain is defined by a b-tuple $(k_1, k_2, \cdots, k_b)$, where b is the number of banks, and k_i, $1 \leq i \leq b$ is the number of memory requests issued to bank i in a given cycle. With m processors, $0 \leq k_i \leq m$ and $\sum_{i=1}^{b} k_i = m$. Even for modest size systems (i.e., $b = 16$ and $m = 16$), this Markov chain leads to a very large number of states. By making the assumption that the processors are identical, Bhandarkar was able to obtain and solve a system with fewer states.

Following are the assumptions in Ravi's and Bhandarkar's model:

A) The processors are statistically identical.
B) The memory requests are independent and randomly distributed in the range $1 \ldots b$.
C) Each of the m processors generates one memory reference per cycle with probability 1; that is, m requests are submitted to the memory system in every cycle.
D) There are not conflicts in the processor–memory interconnect (i.e., a crossbar switch).
E) The memory cycle time is constant.
F) A processor blocks while its request is being serviced. This assumption implies that either the processor is bound by the speed of the memory, or the processor cycle time is equal to the memory cycle time.
G) Rejected requests are dropped and a new set of inde-

pendent requests is submitted in the next cycle.

While assumption F may be realistic in SIMD parallel processors (e.g., the Burroughs Scientific Processor—BSP) or in some MIMD machines, it is clearly incorrect in the context of pipelined supercomputers (e.g., CRAY computers). A common characteristic of pipelined processors is the short clock period, which leads to efficient pipeline operation. The memory system cannot match the speed of the processor, and one memory cycle corresponds to multiple processor cycles. Furthermore, a processor does not block while its request is being serviced by a memory bank; rather, one processor can have multiple requests simultaneously in service.

Assumption G is also problematic. If a processor is waiting for a bank whose remaining reservation is 10 cycles, for example, then in the next 10 cycles that processor will gain access to memory with probability 0. The processor has a much higher chance to succeed in accessing memory if it is permitted to select a bank, at random, in each of the following 10 cycles. Clearly, this assumption leads to a model that overestimates memory bandwidth, particularly in pipelined vector multiprocessors (e.g., the CRAY-2), where the memory is characterized by long bank busy times.

Both assumptions F and G are common in most of the multiprocessor memory analyses reported in the literature [16]–[26]. Notable exceptions are [27], [28], and [1]. Mudge and Al-Sadoun [27] make assumption G, but not F. Their Markov chain model is primarily targeted to applications where the connection times between processors and memories is variable (e.g., variable size data blocks transferred over a bus).

Queueing models represent an alternative approach to the models discussed above. Bucher and Calahan [29] derived a scaling relation, which indicates that memory access delays depend quadratically on the bank reservation time for light memory load. For heavy load, delays scale linearly with the ratio of processors to the number of memory banks. Bucher and Calahan also developed an open and closed queueing model of memory conflicts, and validated the model by simulation. A heuristic extension of the open model provides results chose to simulation for scalar and long vector references.

III. Bailey's Model

In a recent paper [1], Bailey introduced a simple Markov chain model for memory bank contention in vector computers. The important characteristic of this model, and the reason for choosing it as the starting point of our analysis, is that it does not make assumption F. That is, the memory cycle time is an integer multiple of the processor cycle time, and, if the requested bank is free, the processor does *not* block while its request is being serviced. We briefly summarize Bailey's model below.

The system consists of m processors and a shared interleaved memory with b banks. The bank cycle time is c. In any cycle, a processor may make a request with probability r (request rate). To keep track of the state of a bank, a reservation of c cycles is placed on a bank when it is accessed. In each

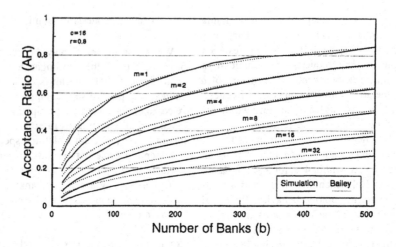

Fig. 1. Bailey's model normally overestimates the memory acceptance ratio. The acceptance ration (AR) is the ratio of accepted requests to total requests.

subsequent cycle the remaining reservation on the bank is decremented by one until it reaches 0, at which time the bank becomes free.

Assuming that processors are statistically identical, it is sufficient to model a single processor. A processor is in state 0 (the free state) if it is not blocked. Otherwise, the processor is in state i, where $1 \leq i \leq c$, in which case the processor is blocked on a bank that has i cycles remaining to process a previous request. In each cycle, a blocked processor performs a transition with probability 1 from state i to state $i - 1$ until the requested bank becomes free.

Let x be the probability that a bank is busy. Then rx is the probability that a free processor makes a request to a busy bank. Assuming that the reservation on a busy bank is uniformly distributed in the range $1 \ldots c$, the transition probability from state 0 to state i is given by

$$p_{0,i} = \frac{rx}{c}, \qquad 1 \leq i \leq c.$$

Based on this approximation, Bailey solved the Markov chain in terms of x. He obtained a second equation from the following consideration. The mp_0 free processors request rmp_0 banks. In the steady state the number of requested banks equals the number of banks that are freed in that cycle, which is bx/c. Hence

$$rmp_0 = \frac{bx}{c}. \qquad (1)$$

Substituting the value of x from this equation, Bailey solved the Markov chain in terms of the system parameters m, r, c, and b.

IV. ANALYSIS OF BAILEY'S MODEL

In this section we compare figures obtained using Bailey's model with simulation results, and comment on the accuracy of the model. The following two basic assumptions in Bailey's model have a significant impact on its accuracy:

Assumption 1

At most one processor may be blocked on a busy bank.

Assumption 2

The remaining reservation on a busy bank is uniformly distributed in the range $1 \ldots c$.

Assumption 1 considerably simplifies the Markov chain and limits the number of states to c. As this assumption ignores memory conflicts caused by multiple processors contending for the same bank, we expect Bailey's model to overestimate the memory performance. This effect is indeed confirmed by simulation (see Fig. 1), and becomes especially prominent as the number of processors is increased.

Assumption 2 allows the approximation of transition probabilities. There are, however, situations in which this assumption does not hold, as demonstrated by the following pathological case with $m = 1$, $b = 1$, $c = 4$, and $r = 1.0$ (i.e., one processor, one bank, and the processor makes a request on every cycle it is not blocked). On the first cycle the processor will make a request that is accepted, and on the next the processor's request will hit the bank when it has 3 cycles left. This leaves the processor blocked. The processor will get unblocked after three cycles when its initial request is complete and its second request is accepted. Since the request rate r is 1.0, the processor will immediately make a request which will hit the bank when it has 3 cycles left. From then on every request the processor makes will go to the bank when it has 3 cycles left.

Hence the transition probabilities are $p_{0,1} = p_{0,2} = 0$, and $p_{0,3} = 1$. Interestingly enough, $p_{0,4}$ is also 0, since the only way the processor may request a bank with four reservations remaining is that another processor has requested, and obtained access to, the same bank in the same cycle. This is not possible in the above example, however, since $m = 1$.

Modeling a single processor drastically reduces the size of the Markov state space, but results in loss of information, which manifests itself in the inability to determine exact transition probabilities. Hence the need to approximate transition probabilities, which leads to inaccuracies in the model, as indicated above. Markov chains that explicitly model each memory bank permit the calculation of exact transition probabilities. However, as noted earlier, such chains suffer from an explosion in the size of their state space.

V. MARKOV CHAIN MODEL

We have seen in the previous section that Bailey's model tends to overestimate the memory performance, because of the assumption that at most one processor can be blocked on a busy bank. This may be also regarded as a model in which a queue is attached to each bank to hold incoming requests, but the size of the queue is restricted to one request. Even in this relatively simple model the transition probabilities are not known and have to be approximated.

Attaching unbounded[1] queues to each bank greatly complicates attempts to obtain reasonable approximations for the transition probabilities. Further, the state space of the chain also grows. Hence our approach was to incrementally increase the size of the queue (i.e., allow for a queue size of 2, 3, ...), approximate the transition probabilities, and solve the corresponding Markov chain until the performance results predicted by the Markov model were within a few percentage points of the simulation figures. A somewhat surprising result was that at the queue size of 2, our model was predicting accurate figures for a large range of system parameter values. Hence we restrict our attention to the case where the maximum length of the queue attached to a bank is 2.

The model must be able to keep track of two quantities: (a) the number of reservation cycles remaining on the requested bank if it is busy, and (b) the number of pending requests in the queue of a busy bank. We define a Markov chain as follows. Let the random variable X_t be 0 if the processor is free, of i if the processor is blocked on a busy bank that is reserved for i additional cycles. Let the random variable Y_t be 0 if the requested bank is free, or j if the bank is busy and there are j processors blocked on this bank. The processor currently serviced by the bank is not blocked and therefore is not included in the count of the j blocked processors. Then $\{X_t, Y_t, t \geq 1\}$ is a Markov chain with the transition probabilities:

$$P_{ij,kl} = \text{Prob}[X_{t+1} = k, Y_{t+1} = l | X_t = i, Y_t = j].$$

As before, we assume that there are m processors, b banks, and when a bank accepts a request it becomes reserved (busy) for c cycles. In each cycle a processor issues a request with probability r, and x is the probability that a bank is busy. Hence the probability that a free processor makes a request to a busy bank is rx. We make the following two assumptions regarding the status of the busy bank requested by the processor.

1. There are no processors blocked on the busy bank (again, the processor whose request is being processed by the busy bank is *not* blocked).
2. The remaining reservation on the busy bank is uniformly distributed in the range, $1 \ldots c$.

These assumptions are needed to approximate the transition probabilities from the free state (00) to a blocked state $(i1)$. Using the notation,

$$\alpha = \frac{rx}{c} \qquad (2)$$

we get:

$$P_{00,i1} = \alpha, \qquad 1 \leq i \leq c.$$

When the system is in a blocked state $(i1)$, $1 \leq i \leq c$, a new request from a different processor may arrive at the same bank. To determine the probability of such a request arriving, we need to know the number of free processors. This number depends on P_{00}, the probability that a processor is free. Therefore the transition probabilities from states $(i1)$, $1 \leq i \leq c$, depend on the probability that the system is in state (00). But in a Markov chain the history of the process does not go beyond the last state. Hence the need to make a third approximating assumption. We assume that approximately half of the processors $(m/2)$ are free to generate requests, and therefore the request rate in the entire system is $mr/2$. Since these requests are uniformly distributed across b banks, the probability of a new request arriving at the bank is

$$\beta = \frac{mr}{2b} \qquad (3)$$

and the transition probabilities are approximately given by

$$P_{i1,(i-1)2} = \beta, \qquad 2 \leq i \leq c.$$

The Markov chain is shown in Fig. 2. The remaining transition probabilities are derived as follows. When the system is in state (12), the bank is reserved for one more cycle, and is about to become free in the next cycle. With two requests pending in the queue, the request accepted by the bank is chosen at random. If the accepted request belongs to the processor being modeled, the transition is to state (00), indicating that the processor became free. Otherwise, the transition is to state $(c1)$, indicating that the processor is now waiting for a bank that has just accepted a request and is reserved for c more cycles. Hence

$$P_{12,00} = \frac{1}{2}$$

$$P_{12,c1} = \frac{1}{2}.$$

If the system is in state (11) just one cycle before the bank becomes free and a new request arrives (with probability β), there are again two requests, and one is accepted at random. If the new incoming request is accepted (with probability $1/2$), the transition is to state $(c1)$, since a reservation of c cycles has just been placed on the bank. Therefore,

$$P_{11,c1} = \frac{\beta}{2}.$$

[1]If we assume that a processor blocks until its request is accepted for service, than the maximum number of requests in a bank's queue will be bounded by m, the number of processors.

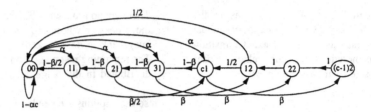

Fig. 2. Markov model. An accepted request places a reservation of c cycles on the bank, and the reservation is decremented by one in each subsequent cycle. Up to two requests may be blocked on the bank.

Otherwise, the processor becomes free and the transition probability is

$$P_{11,00} = 1 - \frac{\beta}{2}.$$

VI. DERIVATION OF STATE PROBABILITIES

The balance equations for the Markov chain are given by:

$$P_{00} = (1 - \alpha c)P_{00} + \left(1 - \frac{\beta}{2}\right)P_{11} + \frac{1}{2}P_{12}$$

$$P_{i1} = \alpha P_{00} + (1 - \beta)P_{(i+1)1}, \qquad 1 \leq i \leq c - 1$$

$$P_{c1} = \alpha P_{00} + \frac{\beta}{2}P_{11} + \frac{1}{2}P_{12}$$

$$P_{i2} = \beta P_{(i+1)1} + P_{(i+1)2}, \qquad 1 \leq i \leq c - 2$$

$$P_{(c-1)2} = \beta P_{c1}.$$

The state probabilities can be obtained in terms of P_{00}:

$$P_{i1} = \alpha P_{00}\left[\frac{k}{(1-\beta)^{i-1}} - \sum_{j=1}^{i-1}\frac{1}{(1-\beta)^j}\right], \qquad 1 \leq i \leq c$$

where

$$k = \frac{\left(\sum_{j=1}^{c-1}\frac{1}{(1-\beta)^j}\right) + c + 1}{\frac{1}{(1-\beta)^{c-1}} - \beta + 1}$$

and

$$P_{i2} = \alpha P_{00}\left[k' - \beta k\sum_{j=1}^{i-1}\frac{1}{(1-\beta)^j} + \beta\sum_{j=1}^{i-1}\frac{(i-j)}{(1-\beta)^j}\right],$$
$$1 \leq i \leq c - 1$$

where

$$k' = 2\left[c - k\left(1 - \frac{\beta}{2}\right)\right].$$

Define:

$$S = \sum_{i=1}^{c}\left[\frac{k}{(1-\beta)^{i-1}} - \sum_{j=1}^{i-1}\frac{1}{(1-\beta)^j}\right]$$
$$+ \sum_{i=1}^{i=c-1}\left[k' - \beta k\sum_{j=1}^{i-1}\frac{1}{(1-\beta)^j} + \beta\sum_{j=1}^{i-1}\frac{(i-j)}{(1-\beta)^j}\right].$$
$$(4)$$

Since the state probabilities sum to one, we obtain:

$$P_{00} + \sum_{i=1}^{i=c}P_{i1} + \sum_{i=1}^{i=c-1}P_{i2} = 1.$$

But since,

$$\sum_{i=1}^{i=c}P_{i1} + \sum_{i=1}^{i=c-1}P_{i2} = \alpha P_{00}S$$

we get:

$$P_{00} = \frac{1}{1 + \alpha S}. \qquad (5)$$

Equation (1) can be rewritten in the context of the Markov chain as:

$$rmP_{00} = \frac{bx}{c}$$

which combined with (2) yields:

$$\alpha = \frac{mr^2 P_{00}}{b}.$$

Substituting this expression of α into (5), we obtain:

$$P_{00} = \frac{\sqrt{1 + 4mr^2 S/b} - 1}{2mr^2 S/b} \qquad (6)$$

where S is given in (4).

VII. PERFORMANCE MEASURES

Several measures have been used in the literature to quantify the performance of the memory system. The most common one is the effective bandwidth (BW), defined to be the expected number of requests accepted by the memory in one cycle (see [26], for example). Bailey [1] introduced a different measure, called *memory efficiency*, which is similar to Cheung and Smith's *acceptance ratio* (AR) [9]. Let A be the number of accepted requests in a period of k cycles, and R be the number of rejected requests in the same time interval. A request rejected by the memory on the first attempt will be resubmitted in each subsequent cycle until accepted. The AR is the ratio of accepted requests to total number of requests:

$$AR = \frac{A}{A + R}. \qquad (7)$$

P_{00} is the probability that a processor is free, and r the probability that a free processor makes a memory request. In k

306

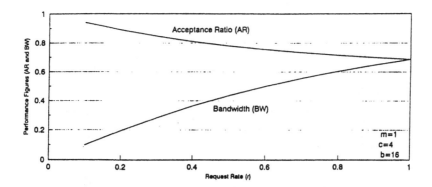

Fig. 3. Acceptance ratio and bandwidth for $m = 1$, $b = 16$, $c = 4$, and variable request rate r.

cycles, a processor issues $rP_{00}k$ requests. Of these, j requests are rejected. Assume that a rejected request is resubmitted an average of π times until accepted. Hence πj attempts lead to $(\pi - 1)j$ rejected requests and j accepted requests. We have:

A = requests accepted on the first attempt

+ the last (and successful) attempt of requests

submitted multiple times

$= [rP_{00}k - j] + j$

$= rP_{00}k$

R = the first atempt of rejected requests

+ subsequent attempts, with the exception of the

last one

$= j + (\pi - 1)j$

$= \pi j.$

We get:

$$AR = \frac{rP_{00}k}{rP_{00}k + \pi j}.$$

In a time interval of k cycles, the processor is blocked for $(1 - P_{00})k$ cycles. πj is the number of resubmissions, but since in a blocked state the processor resubmits a pending request on every cycle, this is also the total cycles in which the processor is blocked. Hence $\pi j = (1 - P_{00})k$, and we obtain:

$$AR = \frac{rP_{00}}{rP_{00} + (1 - P_{00})}. \tag{8}$$

The bandwidth is the total accepted requests for the m processors:

$$BW = mrP_{00}. \tag{9}$$

To compare these two measures, namely, BW and AR, consider a system with $m = 1$, $b = 16$, and $c = 4$. We chose these parameters as an example to correspond to the CRAY-1 memory system. Fig. 3 shows the AR and BW predicted by our model as a function of r, the probability that a processor makes a request on a given cycle (request rate). A higher request rate corresponds to a higher load on the memory

system, and, as we would expect, a higher load leads to more conflicts and lower performance. This is clearly indicated by the acceptance ratio, which changes from 0.94 to 0.69 as r is varied in the range of 0.10 to 1.00. In the same range, however, the bandwidth increases from 0.10 to 0.69 accepted requests per cycle, because the extra bank conflicts are masked by the higher request rate. In the remainder of this paper we use the acceptance ratio to measure the memory performance.

Another performance measure that arises naturally in queueing models is the *delay* D. This is the measure used by Bucher and Calahan [29]. The delay D can be related to P_{00} by the following observation. In k cycles, a processor is free for $P_{00}k$ cycles and issues $rP_{00}k$ requests. Each request is delayed by D cycles. Hence the total delay is $rP_{00}kD$, during which the processor is busy waiting for requests to be serviced. Hence:

$$P_{00} = \text{(free cycles)}/\text{(free cycles} + \text{busy cycles)}$$
$$= P_{00}k/(P_{00}k + rP_{00}kD)$$
$$= 1/(1 + rD).$$

VIII. PERORMANCE RESULTS

The memory performance predicted by the Markov model, as measured by the acceptance ratio, can be calculated by substituting the value P_{00} from (6) into (8). Figs. 4–6 show performance results for the Markov model. In Fig. 4 we illustrate the relationship between the AR and the number of banks for a different number of processors. We fixed the request rate and bank cycle time to $r = 0.8$ and $c = 16$, respectively. As the graph shows for a given processor size, there is an increase in the AR until a point where further increase does not yield increases in the same proportion. For a given m, c, and r, choosing a value of b at the knee of the graph would provide a good cost–benefit ratio. This is, however, not true when the number of processors is high, since then the relationship appears to be fairly linear in the range shown, without an observable knee.

Fig. 5 illustrates the variations in AR caused by changes in the number of processors m. Again, we present the data for the case where $r = 0.8$ and $c = 16$. This graph contains information similar to Fig. 4, although from a different perspective. It is instructive to note that even for a relatively small number

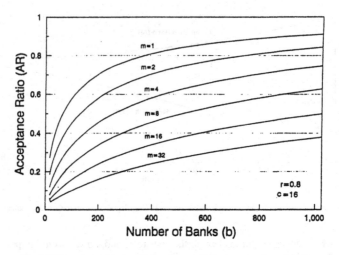

Fig. 4. Memory performance (acceptance ratio) versus number of banks.

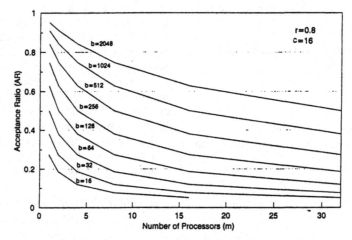

Fig. 5. Memory performance (acceptance ratio) versus number of processors.

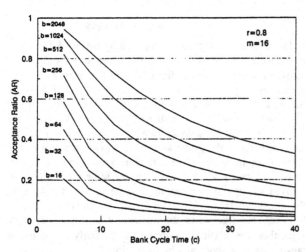

Fig. 6. Memory performance (acceptance ratio) versus bank cycle time.

of processors (e.g., 4), the number of banks required to obtain a reasonable acceptance ratio (e.g., 0.8) is very high.

In Fig. 6 we consider the relationship between the AR and changes in the bank cycle time c. Here, $r = 0.8$ and $m = 16$. The sharp drop shown in the acceptance ratio for increases in the bank cycle time are at the crux of a growing practical problem. Since the clock speeds of processors have been falling at sharper rates than the speeds of memories (especially high capacity–low cost dynamic memories), there is a steady increase in the bank cycle times. The increased efficiency of processors will not transfer into a corresponding improvement in system performance if memory becomes the bottleneck.

IX. DISCUSSION AND CONCLUSIONS

Most of the memory performance models studied in the literature assume that: (a) the memory cycle time is identical to the processor cycle time, or (b) the memory cycle time may be longer than the processor cycle time, and then a processor whose request has been accepted blocks for the duration of the memory cycle. Neither of these two assumptions hold in pipelined computers. In a pipelined machine, the operation of the memory itself is pipelined and a processor is free to perform computations or submit other memory requests while

308

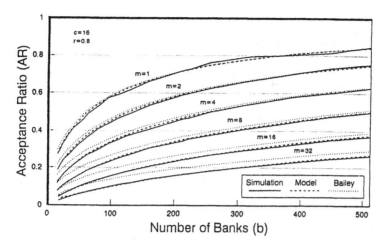

Fig. 7. Comparison with Bailey's model.

one or more of its previous requests are still in the "memory pipeline." Hence a processor does not block for the duration of the memory cycle if its request has been accepted. A reservation, though, is placed on the requested bank for the length of the memory cycle. A processor can have multiple requests simultaneously pending in the memory system as long as different banks are involved.

To capture this behavior a performance model has to keep track of the status of each memory bank (free or busy: if busy, the length of the remaining reservation). Even without this additional information, Markov memory models with a practical number of banks have a very large state space and direct solutions are not feasible. Bailey's approach to this problem is to assume that all processors are statistically identical and to model a single processor and the requested memory bank if the bank is reserved by a previous request. The model explicitly keeps track of the remaining reservation on the busy bank.

To approximate the transition probabilities, which are unfortunately unknown in this model, Bailey made a number of simplifying assumptions. These include the restriction that at most one processor may be blocked on a busy bank. By ignoring contention between processors for the same bank, Bailey's model overestimates memory performance unless the memory system is lightly loaded.

The primary objective of this research was to improve Bailey's model by allowing multiple requests to be blocked on the same memory bank. The resulting Markov chain still has a reasonably small state space, but again, the transition probabilities are not known. Faced with the task of approximating transition probabilities, we proceeded in a step-wise fashion, by first allowing at most two processors to be blocked on a busy bank (this corresponds to a queue length of two). Even with this restriction, the model is close to the simulation, as shown in Fig. 7. This conclusion, namely, that a queue length of two is sufficient in most circumstances, is in close agreement with Bucher and Calahan's work [29]. They point out that, for the range of b, m, and c common in today's computers, the average queue lengths are always quite short.

In summary, the Markov model developed in this paper approximates the behavior of interleaved memories by modeling one processor and the requested memory bank. The model explicitly maintains the remaining length of the reservation placed on a busy bank. Inaccuracies are introduced in the model by the restriction that at most two processors may be blocked on the same bank, and by the approximation of transition probabilities. For large m, the absolute difference in the acceptance ratio between the model and simulation is within 3%. This deviation increases for $m \leq 4$; the largest difference that we have observed being 10% for $m = 1$. Since the model is intended for multiprocessors, we feel that this is a reasonable limitation.

ACKNOWLEDGMENT

The authors would like to thank D. Bailey and I. Bucher for their comments and suggestions.

REFERENCES

[1] D. H. Bailey, "Vector computer memory bank contention," *IEEE Trans. Computers*, vol. C-36, pp. 293–298, Mar. 1987.
[2] J. M. Frailong, W. Jalby, and J. Lenfant, "XOR-schemes: a flexible data organization in parallel memories," in *Proc. 1985 Int. Conf. Parallel Process.*, Aug. 1985, pp. 276–283.
[3] A. Norton and E. Melton, "A class of boolean linear transformations for conflict-free power-of-two access," in *Proc. 1987 Int. Conf. Parallel Process.*, Aug. 1987, pp. 247–254.
[4] M. Balakrishnan, R. Jain, and C. S. Raghavendra, "On array storage for conflict-free memory access for parallel processors," in *Proc. 1988 Int. Conf. Parallel Process.*, Aug. 1988, pp. 103–107.
[5] D. Lee, "Scrambled storage for parallel memory systems," in *Proc. 15th Ann. Int. Symp. Computer Arch.*, May 1988.
[6] G. S. Sohi, "High-bandwidth interleaved memories for vector processors—a simulation study," Computer Sci. Dept., Univ. Wisconsin-Madison, Tech. Rep. 790, Sept. 1988.
[7] B. R. Rau, M. S. Schlansker, and D. W. L. Yen, "The Cydra 5 stride-insensitive memory system," in *Proc. 1989 Int. Conf. Parallel Process.*, Aug. 1989, pp. 242–246.
[8] R. Raghavan and J. P. Hayes, "On randomly interleaved memories," in *Proc. Supercomputing '90 Conf.* (New York), Nov. 1990.
[9] T. Cheung and J. E. Smith, "A simulation study of the CRAY X-MP memory system," *IEEE Trans. Computers*, vol. C-35, pp. 613–622, July 1986.
[10] W. Oed and O. Lange, "On the effective bandwidth of interleaved memories in vector processor systems," *IEEE Trans. Computers*, vol. C-34 pp. 949–957, Oct. 1985.

[11] H. Hellerman, *Digital Computer Systems,* 2nd ed. New York: McGraw-Hill, 1973.

[12] D. E. Knuth and G. S. Rao, "Activity in interleaved memory," *IEEE Trans. Computers,* vol. C-24, pp. 943–944, Sept. 1975.

[13] C. V. Ravi, "On the bandwidth and interference in interleaved memory systems," *IEEE Trans. Computers,* vol. C-21, pp. 899–901, Aug. 1972.

[14] D. Y. Chang, D. J. Kuck, and D. H. Lawrie, "On the effective bandwidth of parallel memories," *IEEE Trans. Computers,* vol. C-26, pp. 480–489, May 1977.

[15] D. P. Bhandarkar, "Analysis of memory interference in multiprocessors," *IEEE Trans. Computers,* vol. C-24, pp. 897–908, Sept. 1975.

[16] F. Baskett and A. J. Smith, "Interference in multiprocessor computer systems with interleaved memory," *Commun. ACM,* vol. 19, pp. 327–334, June 1976.

[17] G. Chiola, M. A. Marsan, and G. Balbo, "Product-form solutions techniques for the performance analysis of multiple-bus multiprocessor systems with nonuniform memory references," *IEEE Trans. Computers,* vol. C-37, pp. 532–540, May 1988.

[18] M. A. Holliday and M. K. Vernon, "Exact performance estimates for multiprocessor memory and bus interferences," *IEEE Trans. Computers,* vol. C-36, pp. 76–85, Jan. 1987.

[19] C. H. Hoogendoorn, "A general model for memory interferences in multiprocessors," *IEEE Trans. Computers,* vol. C-26, pp. 998–1005, Oct. 1977.

[20] K. B. Irani and I. H. Onyuksel, "A closed-form solution for the performance analysis of multiple-bus multiprocessor systems," *IEEE Trans. Computers,* vol. C-33, pp. 1004–1012, Nov. 1984.

[21] J. H. Patel, "Processor–memory interconnections for multiprocessors," *IEEE Trans. Computers,* vol. C-30, pp. 771–780, Oct. 1981.

[22] B. R. Rau, "Interleaved memory bandwidth in a model of multiprocessors," *IEEE Trans. Computers,* vol. C-28, pp. 678–681, Sept. 1979.

[23] A. S. Sethi and N. Deo, "Interference in multiprocessor memory systems with localized memory access probabilities," *IEEE Trans. Computers,* vol. C-28, pp. 157–163, Feb. 1979.

[24] C. E. Skinner and J. R. Asher, "Effects of storage contention on system performance," *IBM Syst. J.,* vol. 8, pp. 319–333, 1969.

[25] D. Towsley, "Approximate models of multiple bus multiprocessor systems," *IEEE Trans. Computers,* vol. C-35, pp. 220–228, Mar. 1986.

[26] D. W. L. Yen, J. H. Patel, and E. S. Davidson, "Memory interference in synchronous multiprocessor systems," *IEEE Trans. Computers,* vol. C-31, pp. 1116–1121, Nov. 1982.

[27] T. N. Mudge and H. B. Al-Sadoun, "Memory interference models with variable connection time," *IEEE Trans. Computers,* vol. C-33, pp. 1033–1038, Nov. 1984.

[28] F. A. Briggs and E. S. Davidson, "Organization of semiconductor memories for parallel-pipelined processors," *IEEE Trans. Computers,* vol. C-26, pp. 162–169, Feb. 1977.

[29] I. Y. Bucher and D. A. Calahan, "Access conflicts in multiprocessor memories queueing models and simulation studies," in *Proc. 1990 Int. Conf. Supercomput.* (Amsterdam, The Netherlands), June 1990, pp. 428–438.

Performance Measurement and Modeling to Evaluate Various Effects on a Shared Memory Multiprocessor

Xiaodong Zhang

Abstract— Shared memory multiprocessor performance is strongly affected by factors such as sequential code, barriers, cache coherence, virtual memory paging, and the multiprocessor system itself with resource scheduling and multiprogramming. This paper presents several timing models and analyses for these effects. A modified Ware model based on these timing models is given to evaluate comprehensive performance of a shared memory multiprocessor. Performance measurement has been done on the Encore Multimax, a shared memory multiprocessor. Our evaluation models are the analyses based on a general shared memory multiprocessor system and architecture, and can be applied to other types of shared memory multiprocessors. Both analytical and experimental results give a clear understanding of the various effects and a correct measuring of the performance, which are important for the effective use of a shared memory multiprocessor.

Index Terms— Barrier, cache coherence, performance measurement and modeling, shared memory multiprocessors, virtual memory paging.

I. INTRODUCTION

ALL multiprocessors apply the simple idea: a task can be divided into several subtasks which may be executed in parallel. Theoretical analyses of many parallel algorithms predict that speedup increases with the number of processors when the algorithms are implemented on a multiprocessor. However, actual experience shows that reasonably large numbers of processors invariably slow the speedup (e.g., see [19] and [20]). One reason is that some runtime interactions and variations present in a multisystem that affect performance are difficult to capture in theoretical analyses. In addition, this discrepancy is connected to the effects of the parallel programs and systems in which the algorithms are implemented.

An important performance factor in parallel processing is the estimation of the speedup as a function of the number of processors used. The well-known *Amdahl's Law* [2] gives a fundamental concept to this issue,

$$\text{Speedup} = \frac{t_s + t_p}{t_s + t_p/p}, \tag{1}$$

where t_s is the amount of time spent on serial parts of a program, t_p is the amount of time spent on parts of the program that can be executed in parallel, and p is the number of processors used. Ware [18] gives an identical timing model of parallel processing which is also a function of the number of processors used, and is formulated exactly as the denominator of (1). Since both models were given before real parallel architectures were developed,

they only provide a conceptual guideline to parallel processing. There have been some analytical and experimental works on the topic of classifying, measuring and analyzing speedup performance recently. Gustafson [13] uses some timing results for a 1024-processor system to demonstrate that the assumptions underlying Amdahl's Law in (1) are inappropriate for the current approach to ensemble parallelism. Amdahl's Law is reevaluated based on the experiments and some new assumptions. The limitation of the work is that the reevaluated Amdahl's law is still unable to interpret different system effects in parallel processing. Gelenbe [7]–[9] gives a set of formulas which can provide insight into the effective speedup taking into account the capacity of a program to use effectively its parallel structure. However, these performance models need support from experimental results from performance measurements. Based on the simple Ware model, we investigate overall parallel performance on a shared memory multiprocessor both analytically and experimentally. In this paper, we discuss several timing models in order to clearly interpret various effects such as sequential code, cache, virtual memory paging, and others, and to correctly measure and model the system performance on a shared memory multiprocessor.

In Section II, we review the simple timing model given by Ware [18] considering the effects of sequential code only. Since the parallel efficiency is not only affected by the sequential code but by other system effects as well, the Ware model is too simple to use to evaluate dynamically the complicated parallel system performance. We develop several timing models to estimate various effects on a shared memory multiprocessor by experiments and analyses. The Ware model is then modified based on these individual timing models so that it is able to estimate the comprehensive performance of a shared memory multiprocessor. All our experiments have been done on the Encore Multimax, a bus-based shared memory multiprocessor. In Section III, we introduce this parallel computer system and briefly discuss some performance characteristics of the system. In Section IV, we discuss the issues of barriers. The issues of cache coherence are addressed in Section V. In Section VI, we discuss the issues of virtual memory paging and develop a timing model for interpreting and measuring the effects. Finally, we give a summary and conclusions in Section VII.

II. THE WARE MODEL AND EFFECTS OF SEQUENTIAL CODE

The timing model for a perfectly parallelized program is simply defined as a function of the number of processors used

$$T(p) = \frac{t_p}{p}, \tag{2}$$

where t_p is the perfectly parallelized time section, and p is the number of processors involved in the computation. The speedup

Manuscript received February 15, 1990; revised August 22, 1990. Recommended by E. Gelenbe. This work was supported in part by the U.S. Air Force under Grant AFOSR-85-0251 and by the University of Texas at San Antonio under a Faculty Research Award, and currently is being supported in part by the National Science Foundation under Grants CCR-9008991 and CCR-9047481. The experiments were performed on the Encore Multimax at the University of Colorado at Boulder.

The author is with the Division of Mathematics and Computer Science, University of Texas, San Antonio, TX 78285.

IEEE Log Number 9040271.

is given by

$$S(p) = \frac{T(1)}{T(p)} = p, \tag{3}$$

which is linearly proportional to the number of processors p in this ideal case. In real applications, the timing and speedup performance is affected by many other influences, the simplest of which is the sequential code.

Ware [18] gives a simple timing model showing the general shape of the execution time versus the number of processes for an imperfectly parallelized program. This model can be viewed as separating a program into a perfectly parallelized time section t_p, and a strictly sequential time section t_s. It postulates that parallel programs exhibit a behavior of execution time versus p of the form

$$T(p) = t_s + \frac{t_p}{p}. \tag{4}$$

A simple least squares fit to determine t_s and t_p can be applied to a suitable portion of the execution time versus number of processors curve to estimate the degree of parallelization. For example, if data is available for 1 through p processors, then t_s and t_p are

$$t_s = \frac{\left(\sum_{i=1}^{p} \frac{1}{i^2}\right)\left(\sum_{i=1}^{p} T(i)\right) - \left(\sum_{i=1}^{p} \frac{T(i)}{i}\right)\left(\sum_{i=1}^{p} \frac{1}{i}\right)}{p\left(\sum_{i=1}^{p} \frac{1}{i^2}\right) - \left(\sum_{i=1}^{p} \frac{1}{i}\right)^2} \tag{5}$$

and

$$t_p = \frac{p\left(\sum_{i=1}^{p} \frac{T(i)}{i}\right) - \left(\sum_{i=1}^{p} \frac{1}{i}\right)\left(\sum_{i=1}^{p} T(i)\right)}{p\left(\sum_{i=1}^{p} \frac{1}{i^2}\right) - \left(\sum_{i=1}^{p} \frac{1}{i}\right)^2} \tag{6}$$

Clearly, the effects of the sequential code make the speedup curve nonlinear, and no matter how many processors are used, the speedup will be no more than α, where

$$\alpha = \lim_{p \to \infty} S(p) = \frac{t_s + t_p}{t_s}. \tag{7}$$

Obviously, the lower bound for the execution time is t_s. Fig. 1 gives the curves of the models considering the effects of the sequential code.

For instance, we have run a program on the 20-processor Multimax to compute complex expressions on an 80×40 array 16 times. The computation is perfectly parallelized, but two sections of sequential code are used for measuring the timing results: getting the starting time before the computation, and getting the finishing time and computing the time difference after the computation. By applying the least square fit to the experimental results, we obtain the timing function

$$T(p) = 4.1244 \times 10^{-2} + \frac{10.0347}{p}.$$

The upper bound of the speedup is

$$\alpha = \frac{t_s + t_p}{t_s} = 244.3.$$

The experimental results are consistent with the timing models which interpret the effects of the sequential code. The experiment is designed for measuring the sequential code effects. However, other influences, such as barrier, paging, cache coherence also make contributions to t_s. But they are trivial and almost not

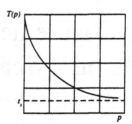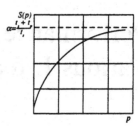

Fig. 1. Sequential code effects to parallel timing and speedup.

measurable in this experiment. The ratio of the sequential code in the whole computation is given by

$$r = \frac{t_s}{t_s + t_p} = \frac{1}{\alpha} \tag{8}$$

which we call the *overhead factor*; $r = 0.4\%$ in the present example. However, when the number of sequential sections in the parallel program becomes larger, the overall computing time increases, as shown in Fig. 2.

III. OVERVIEW OF THE SYSTEM EFFECTS ON THE ENCORE MULTIMAX

The Encore Multimax system [5] incorporates from 2 to 20 32-bit processors. System features include fast shared memory (4 to 32 Mbytes) and configurable I/O capacity (1–10 intelligent network and mass storage channels). In the tightly-coupled architecture, the microprocessors, memory, and I/O interface are coupled across a wide, high-speed main system bus.

The operating system for the Multimax, UMAX 4.2, is a full implementation of Berkeley Unix 4.2 with multiprocessing and memory sharing extensions. Programs running on different processors can get simultaneous access to operating system services from a single shared copy of UMAX. The system allows all processors running programs to perform operating system calls on their own, simultaneously. On the Multimax, all processors are equal; they can service interrupts, run the operating system, and run any user's process. Such symmetry of operation between processors is critical to system performance. A technique called *multithreading* is used in the Multimax system to implement symmetrical multiprocessing, that is, allowing simultaneous streams of control for all processes through the operating system kernel. Thus, the Multimax provides maximal concurrency of operation between the user's job and available processors with minimal delay. In fact, the effect of sharing the operating system is not measurable in our experiments.

The Multimax decreases memory access time and bus loading by storing frequently referenced instructions and data in a 32K-byte high speed buffer memory, or *cache*. Each group of two processors accesses storage through their own cache. Since one must prevent the accessing of outdated copies of data in one cache that have been updated in shared memory or in another cache, *cache coherence* is implemented on Multimax. Executing a program in multiple processors tends to affect the degree of memory reference locality compared to its execution in a single processor. In addition, if the program memory utilization exceeds the effective cache size, parts of the required data such as the arrays and programs must be loaded into the cache more than once, each time incurring the cost of storage-to-cache transfer. We will study these effects and possible ways to ensure the efficient utilization of the cache, in Section V.

The Multimax system is a virtual memory system. Sequences of bytes are grouped into fixed-sized (512 bytes) pages that

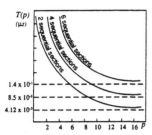

Fig. 2. Increasing number of sequential code sections will decrease parallel performance.

can be treated as units. In conventional demand-paging systems, pages are moved from secondary storage to main memory and back. In the Multimax system a similar approach is used, except that pages are shared among more than one processor that are used to run the same program. Demand paging greatly reduces the work necessary to manage task address spaces since only those pages actually referenced ever get moved or copied. However, a large amount of memory utilizations and the frequent demand for memory may increase the possibility of page faults which is an important effect of the multiprocessor performance. We will discuss the virtual memory paging effects in detail in Section VI.

The Multimax is also a multiuser system. Multiprogramming effects in each processor will influence the multiprocessor performance since the distributed programs may have to wait for the system service while other users' jobs are running. In order to avoid the multiprogramming effects, we have run all the experiments under a special environment which allows a user to "politely" kick off all other users and background jobs and take over the Multimax system in "single user" mode for running timing experiments.

IV. EFFECTS OF BARRIERS

On a shared memory multiprocessor, a synchronization barrier defines a logical point in the control flow of an algorithm at which all processes must arrive before any are allowed to proceed further. A barrier is clearly one of the most important forms of synchronization for parallel computation, since, in effect, it requires that every process communicate with every other process. Additionally, since all processes must wait at the barrier until the slowest finishes, the consequences of fluctuations in execution time or imperfect load balancing are maximized. By choosing the barrier timing data from a normal probability distribution, we derive an analytical timing model which predicts the effect of the synchronization barrier on a shared memory multiprocessor. The model assumes that there are p processors that begin the work section simultaneously; the time each takes has mean μ and standard deviation σ. Assuming mutual independence, it can be shown that the instant at which the last processor completes the work section, has average value t_w, given by

$$t_w = \mu + \sigma\sqrt{2\log p}. \qquad (9)$$

Thus, keeping the load balanced among the independent processes (reducing σ), and reducing the number of barriers will decrease the potentially large performance penalties caused by the synchronization barrier because the ratio $\frac{\sigma}{\mu}$ will decrease. From (9), a simple barrier effect timing function is given by

$$t_b = \sigma\sqrt{2\log p}. \qquad (10)$$

There are several different influences on the standard deviation σ in (10). The major ones (e.g., see in [6] and [14]) are as follows.

Delays in process ends. The purpose of the barrier is to synchronize processes arriving at different times, so the ideal performance is to wait for the slowest process. The fluctuations of different ending times determine the standard deviation σ:

$$\sigma = \sqrt{\frac{\sum_{i=1}^{p}(t_i - \mu)^2}{p}}$$

where p is the total number of processes, t_i is the arrival time for each individual process, and μ is the mean of arrival time for p processes.

Efficiency of the waiting mechanism. Once processes start arriving at the barrier, the early arrivals must wait for the later ones. The waiting mechanism may be busy waiting, virtualization of processes (swapping them out), or something intermediate between the two. Busy waiting wastes processor cycles during long delays, while virtualization is associated with an irreducible minimum overhead, which is often quite large. Which waiting mechanism is more efficient for the barrier is application dependent.

Implementation of the barrier. The actual code executed by processes in a specific barrier implementation depends on the structure of the barrier implementation chosen. It also depends on the system primitives used to implement it, such as critical sections, interrupt software, and hardware and others.

V. EFFECTS OF CACHE-RELATED COMPUTING

The Multimax system is implemented using a memory hierarchy. Each of two processors in the system shares a 32K cache which can provide memory accesses without substantial delay. Information needed to execute programs (instructions and data) is transferred to and from the cache through lower levels of the storage hierarchy. The second level in the storage hierarchy is the central memory. Larger virtual address spaces can be supported through functions provided by the hardware and the operating system that move data from the third level in the storage hierarchy, the secondary storage. These levels have a larger capacity but slower data delivery rates. A direct-mapped cache implemented on Encore Multimax has only one cache block (or cache line) to which a given location in memory can be assigned. There are no instructions that a programmer can invoke to explicitly retain data in the cache.

As long as a processor accesses data that is not shared with any other processor, the cache works like a uniprocessor's cache, keeping a copy of recently-used data or locations. However, when a memory location is shared among processors, the multiprocessing complicates caches and poses the familiar and complex problem of *cache coherence,* namely, the problem of how to maintain data coherence among various copies which reside in multiple caches and main memory. This mechanism is called *cache-coherence protocol,* or the CCP (e.g., see [4], [16], [17]). In order to simplify the cache-coherency strategy, Encore Multimax uses *write through cache* technique which means that all writes are done directly to the memory banks. There are two flavors of such caches: write-allocate and no-write-allocate. A no-write-allocate cache merely writes the given value to the memory location, updating the cache if that value is also there. A write-allocate cache does the same, but insists that the given memory location also be placed into the cache, even if it is not already there. Thus any writes to write-through cache automatically go directly to memory. Besides Encore Multimax, many commercial multiprocessors, such as Sequent Symmetry and Alliant FX/8 are cache-coherent shared memory multisystems. In this section, we first examine the effects of the new locality introduced by the cache-coherence, and present the experimental performance on the Multimax. Then, we discuss the effects of the limited size of the cache.

Recall that in a conventional computer system, efficient operation of a virtual memory system is dependent upon the degree of *locality of reference* in programs, or the *neighborhood of a program* (e.g., see [15]) which states that over an interval of time a program will concentrate its references in a particular area. Locality can be divided into two classes: temporal locality and spatial locality. *Temporal locality* refers to an observed property of most programs, i.e., once a location (data or instruction) is referenced, it is often referenced again very soon. This behavior can be rationalized by program constructs such as loops, frequently used variables, and subroutines. *Spatial locality* refers to the probability that once a location is referenced, a nearby location will be referenced soon. This behavior can be rationalized by program constructs such as sequential instruction sequencing, linear data structures, and the tendency of programmers to put commonly used variables near one another.

Parallel computing makes a new type of locality, called *processor locality* [1], desirable; this requires that data references to memory come from a single processor. To keep high processor locality, unnecessary interleaving of references by more than one processor to the same memory data should be avoided. Indeed, nonlocal operations will transfer the modified location between the processor's caches. If writes are frequent enough and the processor locality low, the traffic generated by these operations heavily loads the memory system, and can penalize to the system's performance.

We construct an experiment to measure the effects of processor locality to system performance. Given a large two-dimensional matrix, we compute an expression for each element row by row for m times ($m > 1$). This is a straightforward parallel operation, in which the matrix is partitioned into p sets of rows, each of which is processed by a processor independently for m times. The first experiment is to perform all operations on the same partitioned set of rows in the same processor, which keeps the high degree of processor locality by minimizing the interference of other processors. The second experiment is to schedule different processors to perform operations on different partitioned set of rows in each of m times. Both experiments yield equivalent operations mathematically, but have different processor locality on a shared memory multiprocessor. Therefore, different performance results. We choose $m = 10$, and run the two experiments from 1 to 16 processors on the Encore Multimax. Both experiments are conducted five times, and the average timing results are plotted in Fig. 3 showing the effects of different processor localities. There is no extra overhead to generate traffic among the processors in the first experiment since all the operations on a subset of rows execute on the same processor. In contrast with the first experiment, the second experiment ignores the processor locality and generates unnecessary interleaving of references by more than one processor to the same subset of rows in the matrix, which decreases the performance (increases the whole computational time).

In the case of computation on a shared memory multiprocessor, the general principle to adhere to is: if each process is to access the some subset of a data pool repeatedly, have each process always access the same subset. Once the cache of a processor is loaded, that processor will be able to work within it. In this way,

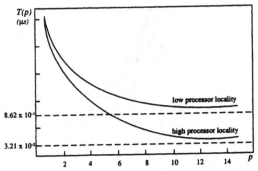

Fig. 3. The effects of the processor locality on the Encore Multimax.

the data is not constantly being transferred between the caches of different processors via main memory.

Although we know that cache size is 32K, this is not the effective cache size for data utilization of a program since the operating system and program object code use the cache at the same time, the sizes of which are hardly predictable. We measured the execution rate of a $n \times n$ square matrix multiplication $A \times B = C$ on the 20 processor Multimax in millions of floating-point operations per second (Mflops) for all processors. The system distributes the rows of matrix A evenly among the 20 processors, each processor keeps a copy of matrix B. Since the multiplication is organized in row operations, the rows of the result matrix C are written by the same processors.

Performance monotonically increases from $n = 10$ to the peak of $n = 40$, and then decreases. When $n = 40$, approximately 20K bytes are used for the arrays of A, B, and C, which is the optimal data size of this multiplication problem, since it makes the maximum utilization of the cache. The parallel granularity of the program is not large enough for $n < 40$ so that it makes the execution rate lower. The effects of the limited size of the cache for $n > 40$ is a reflection of the cost of the extra storage-to-cache data transfer since the memory utilization of the program exceeds the effective cache size. The optimal data size of each individual problem may be determined by computational experiments. Fig. 4 gives curves of the execution rates versus the data size of the multiplication on the 20 processor Multimax. Since it is hard to get a timing model to measure the effects of the limited size of the cache, we evaluate a related effect, virtual memory demand-paging in the next section.

VI. Effects of Virtual Memory Demand-Paging

The demand-paging virtual memory effects are closely related to the cache effects since the efficient use of the paging system reduces the storage-to-cache data transfers and increases the parallel performance. Demand-paging is a well discussed subject in terms of performance (e.g., see [11]). The Multimax uses demand-paging virtual memory techniques.

The effects of the demand-paging to the performance of the multiprocessors are quite measurable as the memory utilization of a program gets larger. The reason for this is simple. When a large memory space is required, the needed pages are swapped into memory. At the same time, a page or several pages may be moved from the memory since the physical memory may be already full. Removing and then immediately needing one of them again due to a page fault referencing of that page would be very unfortunate. Frequently moving pages back and forth between

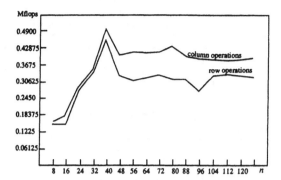

Fig. 4. The execution rate with different cache utilizations.

TABLE I
PARALLEL TIMING PERFORMANCE OF ROW OPERATIONS
VERSUS DIFFERENT SIZES OF MEMORY UTILIZATIONS

Array Size	T_s	T_p	α	r
80×40	0.0412	10.03	244.3	0.4%
160×40	0.155	9.90	65.1	1.5%
320×40	0.233	9.85	43.3	2.3%
640×40	0.287	9.84	35.3	2.8%
1280×40	0.466	9.75	21.9	4.6%

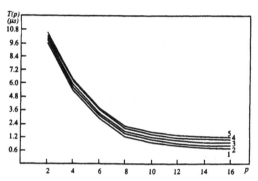

Fig. 5. Timing of demand-paging effects caused by different memory requirements. The array sizes are 1) 80×40, 2) 160×40, 3) 320×40, 4) 640×40, and 5) 1280×40, respectively.

physical memory and secondary storage may cause unreasonably large overhead. In order to measure the consequences of the demand-paging caused by different memory utilizations, we have run several experiments by keeping the computation the same but memory utilization requirements different.

Recall that the last test problem is to compute the 80×40 array 16 times, and the performance results and the timing function fit by model (4) in Section II. To keep the same amount of computation as the problem mentioned above, we compute a 160×40 array, which is double the size of the 80×40 array, 8 times. Based on the experimental results, the timing function becomes

$$T(p) = 0.1545 + \frac{9.9027}{p}.$$

The upper bound of the speedup is

$$\alpha = \frac{t_s + t_p}{t_s} = 65.1$$

and the overhead factor is

$$r = \frac{1}{\alpha} = 1.5\%.$$

By the same strategy, we compute a 320×40 array four times, and a 640×40 two times, and a 1280×40 array 1 time, respectively. The timing functions, upper bound speedups and overhead factors of all experiments are listed in Table I. Fig. 5 gives the group of timing curves to compare the demand-paging effects caused by different program memory utilizations.

A visual examination of our experimental results show that the paging effects caused by the larger memory appear to show t_s of the timing model (4) exponentially increasing with the increase of the logarithm of the array size, but with very little change to t_p. Thus, a new timing model is proposed for purely measuring and interpreting the paging effects for a given parallel algorithm

$$T(p, m) = t(m) + \frac{t_p}{p} \tag{11}$$

where $t(m)$ has the form of

$$t(m) = c_1 + c_2 e^{c_3 \log(m)}. \tag{12}$$

Then (12) may be further simplified to

$$t(m) = c_1 + c_2 m^{c_3} \tag{13}$$

where m is the size of the memory allocation. A simple least square fit to determine c_1, c_2, and c_3 can be applied to a suitable

portion of the overhead time versus the size of the memory utilization to estimate the effects of the demand-paging. The $t(m)$ model is useful when a large number of processors are used, since the demand-paging effects can not be easily measured for a small number of processors.

For a conventional computer, Belady and Kuehner [3] proposed the *lifetime function* as an analytic approximation to empirical observations made on a number of real programs. Under a fixed allocation strategy and a given paging replacement algorithm, the mean CPU time interval between consecutive page faults $\bar{e}$ was found to be related to m, the size of the memory allocation

$$\bar{e} = \frac{a}{\bar{v}_{\text{cpu}}} m^k, \tag{14}$$

where a and k depend on the properties of the program, and $\bar{v}_{\text{cpu}}$ is the processor speed in instructions/second. The timing function (13) derived from the experiments applies the same approximation method as the one that the lifetime function uses on a sequential machine. However, the parameters c_1, c_2, and c_3 in function $t(m)$ depend on the properties of the parallel processing on a shared memory multiprocessor, including the effects of cache coherence, the bus contention and others.

Data partitioning and column operations for Fortran programs can help minimize paging by effectively using data in a page between the replacements. *Data partitioning* is to partition the memory utilization into several pieces to use in order to reduce the effects of the demand-paging caused by a single contiguous memory allocation, such as a large array. The large memory utilization may cause data in the cache to be displaced since there is likely not enough space in the cache for all the memory requests. In addition, the main memory may not be large enough for the large number of memory requests, thus, fragmentation can be a significant problem. Data partitioning simply divides the memory requests into different parts, for example, declaring several submatrices which are equivalent to a large matrix, rather than declaring the large matrix so that the size of the single contiguous memory allocation is reduced.

The efficiency of this simple method is quite measurable. The following timing functions based on the experimental results of computing a set of partitioned arrays from 1 to p processors on the Multimax show the advantage of the data partitioning. As the size of the submatrices is decreased, the overhead time section t_s is decreased, overhead factor r is also decreased.

Partitioning 1280×40 array into 2:

$$T(p) = 0.4376 + \frac{9.7770}{p}, \quad \alpha = 23.3, \quad r = 4.2.$$

Partitioning 1280×40 array into 4:

$$T(p) = 0.4021 + \frac{9.8170}{p}, \quad \alpha = 25.41, \quad r = 3.9.$$

Partitioning 1280×40 array into 8:

$$T(p) = 0.3109 + \frac{9.9445}{p}, \quad \alpha = 33.0, \quad r = 3.0.$$

Partitioning 1280×40 array into 16:

$$T(p) = 0.2287 + \frac{9.9533}{p}, \quad \alpha = 44.5, \quad r = 2.2.$$

A phenomenon, called *page breakage* or *internal fragmentation* does occur in the demand-paging system, especially when the one-time memory utilization is small but the total memory utilization is large. The page size and fragmentation on a conventional computer have been studied considerably (e.g., see [10] and [12]). Jobs are assigned whole blocks of memory. For example, if a job requires 5K bytes and the block size is 4K, two blocks must be allocated (i.e., 8K is allocated but only 5K are needed). A tradeoff must be made between cutting wastage due to page breakage, which favors small pages, and reducing the number of entries in the Page Map Tables, which favor large pages. Thus the process of partitioning the one-time memory utilization cannot be continued forever, since this process in fact increases the effects of the page breakage in the demand-paging system. Our experiment shows that when the 1280×40 array is partitioned further into 32 pieces, the performance is no better than partitioning into 16 pieces:

$$T(p) = 0.2295 + \frac{9.8042}{p}, \quad \alpha = 44.47, \quad r = 2.2.$$

Recall that we measured the execution rate of an $n \times n$ square matrix multiplication $A \times B = C$ in row operations on the 20 processor Multimax by increasing the size of the matrix gradually. The overhead time section t_s is increased quite fast as the size of the matrix is increased. When we simply exchanged the indexes of row and column in the same program, the multiplication became column operations, and the Multimax gave improved results. Fig. 4 shows the two execution rate curves for row and column operations, respectively.

Column operations for Fortran programs consider the special storage format of Fortran, storing the data in column order. Sequences of bytes are also grouped in column order in one page for Fortran programs. An operation for one row may access several pages, but several column operations may only access one page. Thus, column operations for the Fortran programs ensure the maximum utilization of the pages although the scientific programming algorithms often used by Fortran are row-oriented.

TABLE II
PARALLEL TIMING PERFORMANCE OF COLUMN OPERATIONS
VERSUS DIFFERENT SIZES OF MEMORY UTILIZATIONS

Array Size	T_s	T_p	α	r
80×40	0.0157	9.97	637.08	0.156%
160×40	0.083	9.87	119.52	0.836%
320×40	0.0939	9.90	106.48	0.939%
640×40	0.0963	9.95	105.96	0.945%
1280×40	0.0970	10.08	104.87	0.953%

The timing functions, upper bound speedups, and overhead factors of the column operations to compute different sizes of the array in different times are given in Table II. Compare these parameters to the same computation of row operations in Table I.

All the timing factors are very stable although the memory utilizations have changed dramatically. The overhead time section t_s increases more slowly with the increase of the memory utilization compared to the same computation by row operations. Thus the paging effects are minimized by using column operations in Fortran programming in the Multimax.

VII. CONCLUSIONS

We have studied various effects on shared memory multiprocessor performance by experiments and by analyses. The experimental results are consistent with the analysis models. Based on the simple model proposed by Ware

$$T(p) = t_s + \frac{t_p}{p}$$

our studies show that t_s is a complicated variable resulting from various influences. Besides the effects of sequential code and barriers, t_s may be a function of the memory utilization size as a result of demand-paging. System effects, such as resource scheduling and multiprogramming also influence t_s. Based on our analyses and experiments, the timing model of a shared memory multiprocessor may be linearly related to all the effects we have studied in the paper. Regression analysis can be used to approximate the functional dependence of one or more functions. The approximate functional relationship can then be used to predict values of the dependent function, including the timing model from values of independent functions, such as the timing functions for various effects in our study. Thus, a modified Ware model for evaluating the effects on a shared memory multiprocessor by linear regression approximation may be given as

$$T(p) = \hat{t}_s + t_b + t(m) + \frac{t_p}{p} \tag{15}$$

where $\hat{t}_s$ is the sequential code time section, t_b is the barrier overhead time section, $t(m)$ is the paging effect time section, and t_p is the perfectly parallelized time section.

Understanding and avoiding all these effects in a parallel computation on a shared memory multiprocessor is more important than determining the complicated overhead variable t_s. The goal of this paper is to address the effective use of a shared memory multiprocessors. Our conclusion is that a good performance may be achieved on a shared memory multiprocessor if a parallel program runs with a small amount of sequential code, with a small number of barriers, with balanced subtask distributions to different processors, with cache utilization (including effective

316

use of the pages, such as column operations, if necessary). More research is needed to develop and implement techniques to reduce these effects automatically in parallel compilers.

ACKNOWLEDGMENT

The author is grateful to C. Schauble from the University of Colorado at Boulder for reading the paper several times with valuable comments and helpful discussions. The author also wishes to thank K. Robbins from the University of Texas at San Antonio for her important suggestions. Finally, many thanks go to E. Gelenbe from the EHEI, France, for providing important references and comments to improve the technical quality, the clarity, and the readability of the paper.

REFERENCES

[1] A. Agarwal and A. Gupta, "Memory-reference characteristics of multiprocessor applications under MACH," in *Proc. ACM SIG-METRICS Conf. Measurement and Modeling of Computer Systems*, 1988, pp. 215–226.

[2] G. A. Amdahl, "Validity of the single-processor approach to achieving large scale computing capabilities," in *AFIPS Conf. Proc.*, vol. 30. Reston, VA: AFIPS Press, 1967, pp. 483–485.

[3] L. A. Belady and C. J. Kuehner, "Dynamic space sharing in computer system," *Commun. ACM*, vol. 12, pp. 282–288, May 1969.

[4] L. M. Censier and P. Feautrier, "A new solution to coherence problems in multicache systems," *IEEE Trans. Comput.*, vol. C-27, no. 12, pp. 1112–1118, 1978.

[5] Encore Computer Corp., *Multimax Technical Summary*, Marlboro, MA, 1985.

[6] H. F. Jordan, "Problems in characterizing barrier performance," in *Instrumentation for Future Parallel Computing Systems*, M. Simmons, R. Koskela, and I. Bucher, Eds. New York: ACM Press, 1989, pp. 185–200.

[7] E. Gelenbe, *Multiprocessor Performance*. New York: Wiley, 1989.

[8] ——, "Multiprocessor performance and the activity set model of program behavior," in *High Performance Computing*, J.-L. Delhaye and E. Gelenbe, Eds. Amsterdam, The Netherlands: North-Holland, 1989, pp. 121–132.

[9] E. Gelenbe *et al.*, "Asymptotic processing time of a model of parallel computation," in *Proc. Nat. Comput. Conf.*, Las Vegas, NV, Nov. 1986.

[10] E. Gelenbe, J. Boekhorst, and J. Kessels, "Minimizing wasted space in partitioned segmentation," *Commun. ACM*, vol. 16, no. 6, pp. 343–349, 1973.

[11] E. Gelenbe and I. Mitrani, *Analysis and Synthesis of Computer Systems*. New York: Academic, 1980.

[12] E. Gelenbe, P. Tiberio, and J. Boekhorst, "Page size in demand paging systems," *Acta Inform.*, vol. 3, pp. 1–23, 1973.

[13] J. L. Gustafson, "Re-evaluating Amdahl's Law," *Commun. ACM*, vol. 31, no. 5, pp. 532–533, 1988.

[14] C. P. Kruskal and A. Weiss, "Allocating independent subtasks on parallel processors," in *Proc. 1984 Int. Conf. Parallel Processing*, 1984, pp. 236–240.

[15] H. Lorin and H. Deitel, *Operating Systems*. Reading, MA: Addison-Wesley, 1981.

[16] L. Rudolph and Z. Segall, "Dynamic decentralized cache schemes for MIMD parallel processors," in *Proc. 11th Int. Symp. Computer Architecture*, 1984, pp. 340–347.

[17] A. J. Smith, "Cache memories," *Comput. Surveys*, vol. 14, no. 3, pp. 473–530, 1982.

[18] W. H. Ware, "The ultimate computer," *IEEE Spectrum*, pp. 84–91, Mar. 1972.

[19] X. Zhang, "Parallel block SOR methods and various effects on shared and local memory multiprocessors," *Supercomputer*, vol. VI, no. 3, pp. 24–35, 1989.

[20] ——, "Experiments and analysis concerning the various effects on shared memory multiprocessor performance," in *Proc. Fourth Int. Conf. Supercomputing*, vol. 1, 1989, pp. 194–201.

Optimal Design of Multilevel Storage Hierarchies

ROBERT M. GEIST AND KISHOR S. TRIVEDI

Abstract—An optimization model is developed for assigning a fixed set of files across an assemblage of storage devices so as to maximize system throughput. Multiple levels of executable memories and distinct record sizes for separate files are allowed. Through the use of this model, a general class of file assignment problems is reduced to the optimization of a convex function over a convex feasible region. A high-speed search procedure specifically tailored to solve this optimization problem is then presented, along with numerical examples from real systems which demonstrate orders of magnitude improvement in execution time over existing routines for solving the file-assignment problem. The optimal device capacity selection problem is then solved by simply calling the file assignment routine for each candidate set of device capacities.

Index Terms—Capacity selection, file-assignment problem, optimization, performance evaluation, performance-oriented design, queueing networks.

I. INTRODUCTION

THE problem of assigning a set of program and data modules across a set of storage levels has been studied by many authors [1], [9]–[11], [18], [25], [29]. This paper develops a comprehensive file assignment model, consolidating and extending the previous efforts. An efficient procedure for solving this important problem is also developed.

In [1] Arora and Gallo develop a two-stage model for this problem in which they iterate, over a range of device capacities, between a file-assignment model and a central-server queueing model. Their file-assignment model can be shown to provide an optimal assignment when restricted to a uniprogramming environment, but it is known to produce suboptimal assignments in a multiprogramming environment [9].

It is the purpose of this paper to extend their results by removing this restriction. Specifically, in Section II we reformulate the file-assignment problem as the optimization of a convex function over a convex feasible space. This formulation of the file-assignment (FA) problem extends the FA problem in [25] by allowing multiple levels of executable memories and a distinct record size for each file. Given this formulation, and given that the size of the problem (in terms of number of files and number of memory levels) is not too large, any of a number of nonlinear optimization routines, such as IMSL's ZXMIN [14], can then be applied to obtain an optimal loading for the given device capacities and degree of multiprogramming.

Nevertheless, real-world problems such as the airline reservation system in [1], with 42 files to be allocated across five

memory levels, quickly push the computation time required by these classical optimization routines beyond acceptable limits. Therefore, in Section III we develop the linear loading routine (LLR), a high-speed search procedure which is specifically tailored to the general FA problem. Using this routine to solve the file-assignment problem, we can then iterate over the range of capacity choices which lie within a fixed budget to solve the general design problem.

This approach to determine optimal device capacities and file-assignments should be contrasted with our earlier approach [25], where we considered the overall design problem as a continuous nonlinear optimization problem (much like the development in Section II of this paper). We then derived a variable reduction technique resulting in an efficient solution procedure. Recognizing that capacity choices are discrete in practice, we proposed several methods to discretize the continuous optimum and studied the errors incurred as a result [30]. Due to our current assumption of a distinct record size per file, the variable reduction technique of [25] does not apply. Nevertheless, since we have found an efficient file-assignment procedure (which is applicable to our earlier model of [25]) we can now directly deal with discrete capacity choices.

Several useful extensions of the basic model of Section II are developed in Section IV.

In Section V we discuss applications of our model to several real-world problems. Experimental results indicate that, in general, dramatic improvements in system throughput (over that which results from using the so-called "Vogel loading" of Arora and Gallo) can be obtained by using the LLR for file allocation in a multiprogramming environment, but only slight improvement in system throughput is possible in the special case that component capacities are chosen optimally. Thus, as a system hardware selection tool the algorithm [1] seems very close to the mark, but as a system tuning tool our approach yields significantly better throughput. In addition, in comparing LLR with other existing approaches to the problem we have consistently observed a reduction in required execution time by a factor exceeding 100.

Kleinrock [16] and Chandy *et al.* [3] have developed optimization models for open queueing networks suitable for the design of computer-communication networks. Other authors have used decision models of closed queueing networks for computer hardware configuration selection [5], [8], [15], [26]–[29].

The software configuration design problem of optimally allocating a set of files over a set of storage devices has been discussed by several authors. Ramamoorthy and Chandy [20] studied this problem, but they assumed no queueing delays and hence their approch is not applicable to a multiprogramming

Manuscript received January 26, 1981; revised July 7, 1981. This work was supported in part by the National Science Foundation under Grant 78-22327 and the National Library of Medicine Project under Grant LM-03373.

The authors are with the Department of Computer Science, Duke University, Durham, NC 27706.

environment. The model by Arora and Gallo [1] includes optimal device capacity selection in addition to optimal file assignment. Recognizing the complexity of the problem, they solve it by a two-stage process. The file assignment is performed in the first stage by a simple loading rule based on Vogel's method. This stage ignores queueing delays. Next, a cyclic queueing model is used to select optimal device capacities. We have improved upon the Vogel loading by including queueing delays in the file assignment stage.

Foster and Browne incorporated queueing delays in their consideration of the file assignment problem [9]. However, they used a hybrid model consisting of simulation and analytic submodels, while our approach to the problem is purely analytical. Other authors [10], [18] have decomposed the file assignment problem by first removing device-capacity constraints and then solving for the optimal branching probabilities. A separate model is then used in an attempt to assign files to devices so as to match the optimal branching probabilities subject to capacity constraints. Since the parameters of the queueing model vary with the file assignment, the optimal branching probabilities also vary with the file assignment. Therefore, an iteration is required between the two models in order to achieve convergence [10]. Our version of the file assignment problem is more general since it determines the optimal file assignment subject only to device-capacity constraints, and requires no such iteration to achieve convergence.

One contribution of this paper is the formulation of a comprehensive file assignment problem as a convex programming problem. The main contribution, however, is the development of a highly efficient search technique for solving this important problem. The general design problem can then be solved by simply calling the file assignment routine for each candidate set of device-capacities.

The need for optimization of the I/O subsystem stems from the large speed differential between the CPU and the I/O devices [19], [21]. Besides an improved file assignment, techniques such as blocking (or use of larger page size in a paged system), prefetching, and caching of I/O streams can be used to improve performance [21], [23]. Several extensions to the file assignment technique developed here are desired in order to make its use practical. Both sequentiality and randomness in the file access pattern need to be modeled [29], and extensions to allow multiple job types, as well as extensive validations of such techniques, are needed.

II. THE BASIC MODEL

We assume a memory system with two types of devices. Executable memories are relatively fast so that the CPU will wait while accessing information resident in them. (While our model assumes multiple levels of executable memories, the more common case of a single executable memory is certainly a special case.) On the other hand, while accessing information from relatively slow nonexecutable memories, the CPU is switched to another ready process. Thus, in order to access a record resident in a nonexecutable memory, it must first be fetched into an executable level. We assume that each auxiliary memory is permanently matched with a specified executable memory.

The input parameters to the model are the same as those used by several authors (see [1], [25], [9], and [11]) and deemed sufficiently important to warrant the cost of measurement. Specifically, the parameters for the various memory levels are as follows:

b_i = average instruction execution time for the ith executable memory level,

a_i = average access time (latency plus seek time) for the ith auxiliary memory level,

c_i = average transfer time per word from the ith auxiliary memory to its matched executable memory.

The workload will consist of program and data segments for which we have the following fixed parameters:

S_j = size of the jth segment in words,

I_j = average number of instruction-words executed per reference to the jth segment,

r_j = average record size of the jth segment in words,

f_j = average number of references (requests directed) to the jth segment per job.

At the most basic level then we wish to determine the values for each X_{ji}, the number of words of segment j loaded into memory level i, which will maximize system throughput subject to either capacity constraints (the file-assignment problem) or a global cost constraint (the device capacity selection problem). We assume a static loading of file segments, while a model allowing file migration is treated elsewhere [10], [27], [28]. The first task, however, is to derive an expression for system throughput as a function of the system parameters, the workload parameters, and our decision variables, the X_{ji}'s.

Consider the central server network [7] of Fig. 1. The "CPU" time in this network is assumed to model the time between two requests to auxiliary memories, and hence it consists of time to access the executable levels between two auxiliary memory requests. Upon completion of a CPU burst, a job will request service from the ith auxiliary device with probability p_i and terminate with probability $p_0 = 1 - \sum_{i=1}^{m} p_i$, whereupon a new job will enter the system via the new program path. We will assume that the queueing network belongs to the product form class [2], [24] with the further restriction of a single class of jobs and single server at each node.

If we here let t_i denote the average number of trips (requests) per job to the ith auxiliary device, then clearly

$$t_i = \sum_j f_j(X_{ji}/S_j), \qquad i = 1, 2, \cdots, m$$

and hence the average number of trips to the CPU

$$t_0 = \sum_{i=1}^{m} t_i + 1.,$$

Note that these terms are related to the branching probabilities by: $t_0 = 1/p_0$ and $t_i/t_0 = p_i, i = 1, \cdots, m$. Now we can easily express the average record size demanded for segments residing on auxiliary device i by

$$\left(\sum_j f_j(X_{ji}/S_j)r_j \right) \Big/ t_i$$

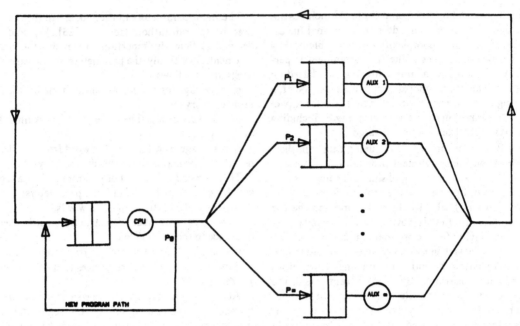

Fig. 1. Central server network.

and thus the average service time of a request to the ith auxiliary device, denoted $1/\mu_i$, is given by

$$1/\mu_i = a_i + c_i \left(\sum_j f_j(X_{ji}/S_j) r_j \right) \Big/ t_i \qquad (1)$$

whence the average total I/O time per job for the ith auxiliary device is

$$t_i/\mu_i = \sum_j (a_i + c_i r_j) f_j(X_{ji}/S_j). \qquad (2)$$

Similarly, the total CPU time per job can be easily expressed; corresponding to each level i (executable or auxiliary) the average number of instructions executed per job is

$$\sum_j f_j(X_{ji}/S_j) I_j .$$

Thus, the total CPU time per job can be expressed as

$$\sum_{\text{executable} i} b_i \left(\sum_j f_j(X_{ji}/S_j) I_j \right)$$
$$+ \sum_{\text{auxiliary} i} b_{m_i} \left(\sum_j f_j(X_{ji}/S_j) I_j \right) \qquad (3)$$

where m_i = executable level matched to auxiliary level i. Since no confusion results, we can simplify notation by writing b_i for b_{m_i}; now total CPU time per job is given by

$$\sum_i \sum_j b_i f_j(X_{ji}/S_j) I_j \qquad (4)$$

and hence the average service time per trip to the CPU

$$1/\mu_0 = \left(\sum_i \sum_j b_i f_j(X_{ji}/S_j) I_j \right) \Big/ t_0 . \qquad (5)$$

Note that the operating system overhead time can be added to (4) above by increasing I_j by an appropriate factor.

Observe that if we regard t_i as the relative throughput of device i, $(i = 0, 1, \cdots, m)$, then $y_i = t_i/\mu_i$ is its relative utilization. Note that for any constant c, ct_i/μ_i can also be defined as the relative utilization; however, the choice of constant $c = 1$ is crucial in obtaining y_i as a linear function of the decision variables. Our choice of c here avoids some of the difficulties encountered by other authors [9], [10]. Now the system throughput as a function of $y = (y_0, y_1, \cdots y_m)$ is given by [7], [13]

$$T(y) = \mu_0 p_0 y_0 \frac{G_{n-1}(y)}{G_n(y)} \qquad (6)$$

$$= \frac{G_{n-1}(y)}{G_n(y)}$$

where

$$G_n(y) = \sum_{\substack{(k_0, k_1, \ldots, k_m) \\ \sum k_i = n}} \prod_{i=0}^{m} y_i^{k_i}$$

and n is the degree of multiprogramming.

Since reciprocal throughput $G_n(y)/G_{n-1}(y)$ is convex in y [18] and each y_i is linear in the X_{ji}'s, we can now formulate our problems succinctly as follows.

File Assignment (FA) Problem:
Minimize $G_n(y)/G_{n-1}(y)$ subject to the constraints

$$X_{ji} \geq 0 \text{ all } j, i \qquad (7a)$$

$$\sum_i X_{ji} = S_j \text{ all } j \qquad (7b)$$

$$\sum_j X_{ji} \leq K_i, \text{ capacity of level } i, \text{ all } i \qquad (7c)$$

320

$$y_i = \sum_j (a_i + c_i r_j) f_j(X_{ji}/S_j), \qquad i = 1, 2, \cdots, m \quad (7d)$$

$$y_0 = \sum_i \sum_j b_i f_j(X_{ji}/S_j) I_j . \qquad (7e)$$

Device Capacity Selection and File Assignment (DCFA) Problem:

Minimize $G_n(y)/G_{n-1}(y)$ subject to the constraints

$$X_{ji} \geq 0 \text{ all } j, i \qquad (8a)$$

$$\sum_i X_{ji} = S_j \text{ all } j \qquad (8b)$$

$$\sum_i g_i(K_i) \leq \text{BUDGET} \qquad (8c)$$

$$y_i = \sum_j (a_i + c_i r_j) f_j(X_{ji}/S_j), \qquad i = 1, 2, \cdots, m \quad (8d)$$

$$y_0 = \sum_i \sum_j b_i f_j(X_{ji}/S_j) I_j \qquad (8e)$$

where $K_i = \sum_j X_{ji}$, $g_i(K_i)$ is the cost of memory level i as a function of its capacity K_i, and g_i is assumed to be convex in K_i.

In either case we wish to minimize a convex function over a convex feasible region, and hence we have the following result.

Theorem 1: Both the FA problem and the DCFA problem have the property that any local minimum is also the global minimum.

Thus, any of a number of nonlinear optimization routines should have little trouble in arriving at a solution, *if* the number of segments and the number of memory levels (and hence constraints (7b) + (7c) above) are not too numerous. Experiments with 10 segments to be allocated over 5 levels showed this was indeed the case. Nevertheless, as mentioned earlier, increasing the number of segments or levels rapidly pushes computation time beyond acceptable limits. As an example, for the airline reservation system of [1] (detailed in Section V) in which there are 42 segments to allocate over 5 levels, we are faced with 210 decision variables and 257 constraints. Of course, we can eliminate positivity constraints by using decision variables z_{ji}, where $z_{ji}^2 = X_{ji}$, and we can use the effective nature of the constraint in (b) to reduce the number of decision variables to 168; yet, even with these modifications a solution to the FA problem for degree of multiprogramming (DMP) = 1 using IMSL subroutine ZXMIN required one-half hour of CPU time on an Amdahl 470 V/8.

Now one might argue that second-order gradient methods such as ZXMIN, in which projected movement is approximated by $-$ (Hessian)$^{-1}*$ (gradient) cannot be expected to be effective for reciprocal throughput functions, which are notoriously flat. Nevertheless, the classical pattern search methods fare no better, if so for another reason: too many constraints. Specifically, it seems that unilateral adjustment of variables in a local exploration cannot properly account for

an excessive number of diagonally placed constraints, and bilateral adjustment again requires excessive computation time.

These considerations led us to the new search procedure to be discussed next.

III. THE LINEAR LOADING ROUTINE

We now develop an efficient search routine specifically tuned to the FA problem (device capacities are fixed until further notice). This routine can be categorized as a directed pattern search over a certain affine subspace (vector subspace, offset from origin by a fixed translation vector) of the space of assignment vectors $\{(\cdots X_{ji}, \cdots) \mid X_{ji} \in R\}$ of file segments to memory levels. The direction of search at each stage will be determined by making use of special characteristics of the reciprocal throughput function $z_n(y) = G_n(y)/G_{n-1}(y)$, which is, after all, our objective function.

The translation vector which brings us into the affine space over which we shall search, our starting point, is the Vogel loading given by Arora and Gallo in [1] which we now describe.

For all segments j and levels i define

$$d_{ji} = (I_j f_j b_i + (a_i + r_j c_i) f_j)/S_j$$

where $a_i = c_i = 0$ if i is executable, and b_i = instruction execution time of the matched executable level, if i is auxiliary. Observe that for DMP = 1, the FA problem is simply to minimize $\Sigma d_{ji} X_{ji}$ subject to capacity and segment size constraints, and hence d_{ji} can be regarded as the "cost" of loading a word of segment j into level i. Two very reasonable assumptions are made in [1] in order to rank the levels according to these "loading costs" d_{ji}: for any levels $i1$ and $i2$:

1) if $a_{i1} < a_{i2}$, then $c_{i1} \leq c_{i2}$, i.e., faster access implies faster transfer,

2) if $a_{i1} \leq a_{i2}$, then $b_{i1} \leq b_{i2}$, where here again b_i = reciprocal speed of matched executable level, if i is auxiliary.

We can thus rank the levels, executable in order of execution speeds followed by auxiliary in order of access times, so that d_{ji} is monotone nondecreasing in i for all j.

Finally, calculate the row differences $\Delta_{ji} = d_{j,i+1} - d_{ji}$, and load segments in descending order of Δ_{ji}'s, starting with $i = 1$ and moving to the next level when this level is filled.

Then we have [1, page 310] the following.

Theorem 2: For DMP = 1, the Vogel loading rule gives the optimal solution to the FA problem.

(Note: Should assumptions 1) and 2) above not hold, Vogel loading still provides a good initial point for our search routine.)

Next, we must consider those special properties of the objective function $z_n(y) = G_n(y)/G_{n-1}(y)$, which will direct our search. If we begin with a Vogel loading, then in terms of the relative utilizations y_i we are (by virtue of Theorem 2) at that point in the feasible region where $\Sigma y_i = z_1(y)$ reaches a minimum value; denote the value of Σy_i here by W_0. At that point y in the feasible region where $z_n(y)$ reaches a minimum (our goal), Σy_i will, of course, take on some value $W_1 \geq W_0$.

Let us define a function h, for fixed n, by

$$h(W) = \min\{z_n(y) \mid y \in \text{feasible region}; \Sigma y_i = W\}.$$

Lemma: The function h is monotone nonincreasing on $[W_0, W_1]$.

A proof of the lemma is given in the Appendix.

Next, we note that the minimum value of h, $h(W_1)$, is the minimum value of $z_n(y)$, our goal; thus we merely need to find the minimum of the single-variable function h and record the loadings giving rise to this minimum.

At this stage the careful reader might well remark: this is merely a reparameterization of the original model; what has *really* been gained? The answer is the key point of the linear loading routine (LLR): each evaluation of h requires at most 1 evaluation of z_n!

Thus, although we have yet to specify *how* we will evaluate h and record loadings, our top-level algorithm for the FA problem can be described as follows.

```
choose initial increment Δ_I;
choose final increment Δ_F; 0 < Δ_F < Δ_I
W = W_0; /* Vogel loading*/
Δ = Δ_I;
min = h(W);
while (Δ > Δ_F) {
    while (h(W + Δ) < min) {
                        W = W + Δ;
                        min = h(W);
                                        }
    Δ = Δ/2;
    min = MIN(h(W − Δ), h(W), h(W + Δ));
    if (min = h(W − Δ)) W = W − Δ;
    else if (min = h(W + Δ)) W = W + Δ;
                                        }
```

Now evaluation of h, by its very definition, requires optimization of $z_n(y)$ restricted to a plane of the form $\Sigma y_i = K$. Thus, it should not be surprising that we will make use of the following result.

Theorem 3: For $n \geq 2$, $z_n(y)$ restricted to the plane $\Sigma y_i = K$ is a convex function with minimum at $y_0 = y_1 = \cdots = y_m = K/m + 1$, and is symmetric about this minimum.

A proof is supplied in the Appendix. It should be noted that the point of equal relative utilizations need not lie in the feasible region of the FA problem.

Having characterized the important properties of z_n and presented the top-level search-directing algorithm, we can now describe the details of LLR.

Start with a Vogel loading, so that $W = \Sigma y_i$ is at the minimum W_0; we assume that any excess device capacity is filled with the "null" segment, for which $f_j = I_j = r_j = 0$. Any move from this point is now restricted to the affine space spanned by the set of all exchange vectors

$$\{(0, \cdots 0, -1, 0, \cdots 0, 1, 0, \cdots 0, 1, 0, \cdots 0, -1, 0, \cdots 0)\}$$
$$\quad\quad X_{JL} \quad\quad X_{JK} \quad\quad X_{ML} \quad\quad X_{MK}$$

that is, we permit only *exchanges* of words between segment J level L and segment M level K, where, of course, $J, M \in$

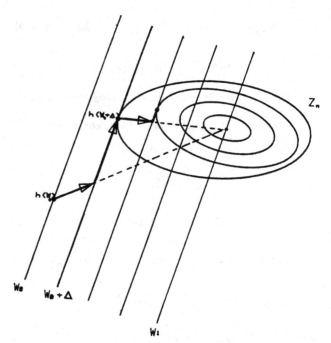

Fig. 2.   The LLR search function h.

$\{\text{segments}\}$ and $L, K \in \{\text{levels}\}$. Since all devices are always fully loaded (perhaps with "null" words) and all segments completely assigned, the capacity and segment size constraints are built into the search space and we need only worry about the positivity constraints on the X_{ji}'s.

Now in the move from plane W to plane $W \pm \Delta$ required by the top-level algorithm, we would (by virtue of Theorem 3) like to move as close as possible to an assignment point giving relative utilizations $y_0 = y_1 = \cdots = y_m = (W \pm \Delta)/(m + 1)$. We detail below a highly efficient technique for selecting the bilateral exchange (J, K, L, M) which would move us closest to this point. Our evaluation of $h(W \pm \Delta)$ then amounts to carrying out this exchange and computing z_n. The resulting value is, admittedly, an approximation to h. Although no other bilateral exchange will bring us closer to the point of equal relative utilizations, it is conceivable *a priori* that a multilateral exchange would have a more beneficial effect in reducing z_n on this plane. Nonetheless, we should observe that this evaluation of h amounts to the local exploration phase of the classical pattern search. The fact that we have found the minimum value of z_n over a finite collection $\{(\cdots, X_{ji}, \cdots)\}$ of spanning vectors determined (as seen below) by the top-level routine, rather than the minimum over a local continuum in the y_i's, does not detract from the fact that we have found a "new low" value of z_n which can serve as a basis for the next local exploration. Thus, we should regard the top-level routine as a guidance system which serves to speed up convergence of a pattern search over the X_{ji}'s by directing us toward a succession of restricted minima, $h(W_0), h(W_0 + \Delta), \cdots h(W_1)$; of course, we need not actually pass through each point in the succession in order to arrive at the goal.

Yet remaining are the details of the procedure by which we select that exchange which most nearly equalizes relative utilizations. Obviously, we would like to have an exchange of

322

words between a relatively active segment on an over-utilized (y_i > aver.) level and a relatively inactive segment on an under-utilized (y_i < aver.) one. To effect this, we first decompose each d_{ji} into two summands

$$d1_{ji} = I_j f_j b_i / S_j$$

$$d2_{ji} = (a_i + r_j c_i) f_j / S_j$$

then for each pair of levels K and L and each pair of segments J and M (including the null segment), an exchange of 1 word between segment J level L and segment M level K would have the following effects:

change in relative utilization of device L,
change$U$dev$L$ = $d2_{ML} - d2_{JL}$,
change in relative utilization of device K,
change$U$dev$K$ = $d2_{JK} - d2_{MK}$,
change in relative utilization of the CPU,
change$U$CPU = $(d1_{ML} - d1_{JL}) + (d1_{JK} - d1_{MK})$,
effect upon the sum of the relative utilizations,
EOW = change$U$dev$L$ + change$U$dev$K$ + change$U$CPU.

Note: Device i = device 0 = CPU, if i is an executable level.

We can measure the relative effect of this exchange upon z_n as follows: as long as $EOW \neq 0$, let

A_0 = change$U$CPU * Δ * sign(EOW)/EOW,
A_L = change$U$dev$L$ * Δ * sign(EOW)/EOW,
A_K = change$U$dev$K$ * Δ * sign(EOW)/EOW,
A_i = 0, all other auxiliary devices i

and observe that an exchange of Δ * sign(EOW)/EOW words would take us from point $(y_0, y_1, \cdots y_m)$ in plane w to point $(y_0 + A_0, y_1 + A_1, \cdots, y_m + A_m)$ in plane W + sign(EOW) * Δ.

Now if the top level routine calls for movement to a higher plane $W \rightarrow W + \Delta$, we consider all those exchange quadruples (J, K, L, M) for which $y_L < \bar{y}$, $A_L \geq 0$, $y_K > \bar{y}$, $A_K \leq 0$, and $EOW > 0$, where here $\bar{y} = (W + \Delta)/(m + 1)$; for each, let

$$x(J, K, L, M) = \left(\sum_{i=0}^{m} A_i(\bar{y} - y_i) \right) - (1/2) \sum_{i=0}^{m} A_i^2$$

and note that A_i/Δ's can be precomputed from initial parameters. It is then a simple exercise in elementary algebra to show that $x(J, K, L, M) > x(J', K', L', M')$ implies the exchange (J, K, L, M) (of Δ/EOW words) would bring us closer to $(\bar{y}, \bar{y}, \cdots \bar{y})$ than would (J', K', L', M'). Similar considerations hold for moves to lower planes $W \rightarrow W - \Delta$. Note that cutting Δ directly cuts the magnitude of the exchange vectors used in the local exploration phase.

We should note here that the positivity constraints could, as in the classical pattern search, cause our routine to die prematurely on a constraint boundary $X_{ji} = 0$. Although our experimental results seem to indicate that this does not occur in practice, it is perhaps advisable to extend LLR by relaxing positivity constraints and then phasing them in through a succession of increasingly restrictive penalty functions.

Another possible source of error is a "narrow valley" which could be missed because Δ_F is too large.

In either event there is an easily computed bound on any error: for DMP = n, $z_n(y)$, where $y_0 = y_1 = \cdots = y_m = W_0/(m$

+ 1), is clearly a lower bound (although likely unobtainable, $n > 1$) on reciprocal throughput against which we can compare our results in order to determine the desirability of introducing penalty functions or cutting Δ_F (indiscriminate reduction of Δ_F can wreak havoc on computation time while returning insignificant improvement). In the special case where we do not allow any loading of executable levels, and r_j and I_j are constant (independent of j), a tighter bound can be obtained: for auxiliary i

$$1/\mu_i = a_i + c_i r$$

and

$$t_0/\mu_0 = \sum_{\text{all } i} \sum_j (f_j X_{ji}/S_j) I b_i$$

$$= \sum_{\text{aux } i} t_i I b_i.$$

Thus, we can write $z_n(y) = z_n(t)$, and since

$$\left(\sum_{i \geq 0} t_i \right) - 1 = 2 \sum_{\text{aux } i} t_i$$

$$= 2 \sum_{\text{aux } i} \sum_j f_j(X_{ji}/S_j)$$

$$= 2 \sum_{\text{all } i} \sum_j f_j(X_{ji}/S_j)$$

$$= 2 \sum_j f_j$$

$$= \text{constant},$$

we can obtain the desired bound by solving the relatively simple optimization problem

minimize: $z_n(t)$

subject to: $t_i \geq 0$ $i = 0, 1, \cdots m$

$$\Sigma t_i = \text{constant}.$$

As the final point of this section, we remark that the solution to the FA problem outlined above is sufficiently fast to render the DCFA problem trivial. We specify a minimum increment in capacity size for each device and then simply iterate over all capacity selections within the specified budget, solving the FA problem at each iteration.

IV. Extensions of the Basic Model

The basic design model presented in Section II can be augmented in many different ways, and the results of Section III can be extended for each case. Instead of further complicating the algebra of the previous sections, we present several variations on the basic design model here.

A. Locality of File References

In the basic model we have assumed that each reference to a record of a file located on an auxiliary memory requires the transfer of the record into the matching executable memory buffer. However, if we allocate a buffer of size B_j to a file j in the executable memory, then due to locality of reference only a fraction $1 - H_j(B_j)$ of all references will trigger an actual I/O transfer. Here $H_j(B_j)$ is the hit ratio of finding a record of file j in a buffer of size B_j, where function H_j and buffer size B_j are input parameters to the design problem. The only change required is to substitute $f_j * (1 - H_j(B_j))$ for f_j in each of the equations (1)–(6), (7d), (7e), (8d), and (8e) of Section II. In this manner we can also study the question of allocation of a limited buffer space among the given set of files.

In addition, we have modeled the access pattern of records using an independent reference model [6]. In practice, there is usually sequential correlation in the reference pattern, and blocking of several file records into a single device block is used to take advantage of such sequentiality. Mapping such file behavior onto a queueing network implies that the branching probabilities will not be fixed quantities anymore. However, if we assume a kth order of Markov dependence in the file access pattern, then we are able to utilize the result of Kobayashi and Reiser [17] which shows that in spite of such dependence the network has a product form solution dependent only upon the total work demand of each service center. Thus, we are able to model the sequentiality of file access pattern; details of such a model will appear in [29]. This model allows the physical block size to be device-dependent and the logical record size to be file-dependent.

B. Open Queueing Networks

We observe that all the results of Sections II and III assume that the objective function $z_n(y) = G_n(y)/G_{n-1}(y)$ is a convex and monotone increasing function of y. In these sections we chose to let $z_n(y)$ be the reciprocal throughput in a closed queueing network. We could, instead, cut open the NEW PROGRAM PATH and turn the model of Fig. 1 into an open network (Fig. 3), which is being fed from a Poisson job stream with the average arrival rate λ. The arrival rates to the nodes λ_i, and subsequently the node utilizations ρ_i, can be easily computed by using standard techniques [16] as follows:

$$\lambda_0 = \lambda t_0, \ \lambda_i = \lambda t_i,$$

$$\rho_0 = \lambda \frac{t_0}{\mu_0} = \lambda y_0, \ \text{and} \ \rho_i = \lambda y_i.$$

The average response time $R(y)$ is now given by [16] (assuming the stability condition $\rho_i < 1$ is satisfied for all i):

$$R(y) = \frac{1}{\lambda} \sum_{i=0}^{m} \frac{\rho_i}{1 - \rho_i}.$$

In [3] it is shown that $R(y)$ is a convex monotone increasing function of y, and again it is easy to establish that $R(y)$ restricted to the plane $\Sigma y_i = h$ takes on a minimum at the point of equal relative utilizations. Thus, if we let the objective function be $R(y)$ in the design models of Section II, then all of the results of Sections II and III will follow.

C. Load-Dependent Servers

Our model formulation calls for a queueing network of the BCMP class [2], [4] with the further restrictions of single job type and load-independent service at each node. These restrictions are necessary, since the convexity of the reciprocal throughput function has been shown only for this restricted class of closed queueing networks.

Our extensive experience with more general networks of the BCMP type has not yet shown any departure from unimodality. Thus, we believe that any nonconvex behavior of the reciprocal throughput function is likely to be benign. Based on this belief, we have been successfully using extended formulations of the model of Section II and the search routine of Section III for product form networks with load-dependent servers. Similarly, our procedure can be used for networks with multiple job classes. Nevertheless, the proof of convexity (or unimodality) for the general product form networks remains an open problem.

V. EXPERIMENTAL RESULTS

We have applied the results of the previous sections to systems studied by several other authors [1], [25], [9], [11]. Let us first restrict ourselves to the file-assignment problem.

1) In [25] Trivedi, Wagner, and Sigmon consider the allocation of 10 files across three auxiliary devices, a drum (IBM 2305-1) and two disks (ITEL 7330-1 and CDC 23142). No files were to be permanently stored in the single executable level, and DMP was fixed at 6.

Using a modified ZXMIN routine applied to a special case of the basic model of Section II, they obtained an optimal throughput of 51.82 jobs/s; this required 20 s of CPU time on an IBM 370/165.

Using LLR we obtained an identical throughput figure of 51.82 jobs/s; nevertheless, although considerable reassignment from the initial Vogel loading (which yielded only 41.82 jobs/s) was carried out, the total computation time required by LLR showed improvement by a factor of 125 over the 20 s mentioned above.

2) Consider the airline reservation system studied in [1], where there are 42 segments to be allocated across 5 devices; the workload specifications are reproduced in Table I, and the device parameters in Table II. Device costs and total budget were estimated by a least squares linear fit to the 10 configurations given in [1, Table IX].

Although we shall consider this system later in the context of capacity-selection problems, we can here extract an interesting collection of file-assignment problems by restricting ourselves to those capacities found to be optimal in [1]:

device 1: 128 K words (executable),
device 2: 1 M words (executable),
device 3: 1 M words (auxiliary),
device 4: 7 M words (auxiliary),
device 5: 3 M words (auxiliary).

Since the assumptions in [1] call for multiple servers at the auxiliary devices, whereas we allow, for the moment, only single-server devices, these capacities should here be termed reasonable but not necessarily optimal. (When we turn to the capacity selection problem, we shall see that these capacities are, in fact, not optimal for any DMP under either set of assumptions.)

Now for each DMP we have a file-assignment problem to which we can apply LLR. In Fig. 4 we plot the results: throughput as a function of DMP for Vogel loading and for LLR loading.

As is easily seen from these graphs, LLR becomes extremely

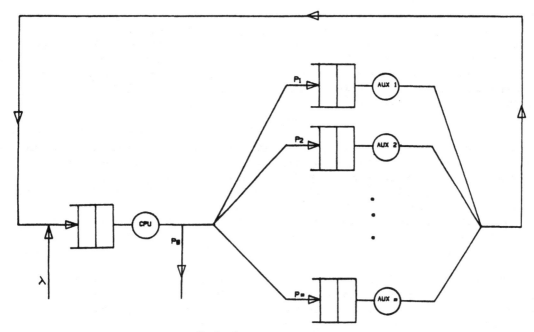

Fig. 3. Open central server network.

TABLE I
WORKLOAD PARAMETERS FOR THE AIRLINE RESERVATION SYSTEM

f[j]	l[j]	r[j]	s[j]
3.1	6000.0	2112.0	2112.0
1.2	3000.0	6000.0	6000.0
0.26	3000.0	3456.0	3456.0
0.26	3100.0	1920.0	1920.0
0.76	2900.0	254.0	254.0
0.32	2900.0	3200.0	3200.0
0.32	2400.0	2752.0	2752.0
0.14	800.0	254.0	254.0
0.176	1800.0	1088.0	1088.0
0.14	1800.0	1792.0	1792.0
0.15	1000.0	832.0	832.0
0.15	600.0	640.0	640.0
0.15	1000.0	384.0	384.0
0.296	10.0	64.0	21504.0
0.228	1700.0	1700.0	167040.0
0.268	10.0	150.0	24000.0
0.820	1.0	2.0	264000.0
1.420	304.0	304.0	516800.0
0.492	3.0	6.0	90024.0
0.176	1.0	2.0	330.0
0.492	10.0	2000.0	113154.0
0.001	20.0	462.0	462.0
0.296	27.0	27.0	216000.0
0.101	30.0	35.0	1033352.0
1.130	40.0	46.0	5630400.0
0.843	47.0	47.0	135360.0
0.180	30.0	33.0	68360.0
0.001	20.0	28.0	26032.0
0.912	30.0	33.0	600000.0
0.090	1.0	1.0	1320.0
0.560	50.0	202.0	126000.0
0.140	4.0	2.0	2112.0
0.068	1.0	1.0	4400.0
0.068	7.0	7.0	93060.0
0.0001	50.0	245.0	21102.0
0.001	100.0	209.0	30030.0
0.750	7.0	7.0	54012.0
0.0001	100.0	1000.0	60060.0
0.001	50.0	66.0	20064.0
0.001	3.0	3.0	240042.0
5.0	75.0	1056.0	3168.0
0.001	1000.0	500.0	482608.0

TABLE II
DEVICE PARAMETERS FOR THE AIRLINE RESERVATION SYSTEM

a[i]	b[i]	c[i]	cost[i]	increment[i]
0.0	.0005	0.0	13.9989	131000.0
0.0	.002	0.0	6.11732	500000.0
4.3	.0005	.0042	4.56938	500000.0
17.0	.002	.0042	2.88771	500000.0
47.5	.002	.007	.818032	3000000.0

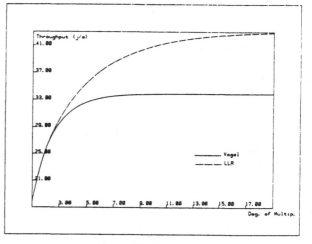

Fig. 4. Vogel versus LLR.

important as DMP increases, with a difference of more than 9 jobs/s at DMP = 20, an improvement of 27 percent. Thus, a system analysis based solely on Vogel loading, as in [1], might vastly underestimate throughput potential and hence call for new hardware, when in fact a reallocation of files would suffice.

3) In [9] Foster and Browne use a hybrid model consisting of analytic and simulation submodels to optimally allocate the 42 files of Table I across 4 memory levels (one of which is executable) in a DMP = 7 environment. Their final throughput figure (measured at the CPU) of 96.9 does not differ significantly from that we obtained using LLR, 97.2. Nonetheless, here, as in example 1), LLR showed a huge improvement in computation time, a factor of at least 110 over the 100 s (CDC 6600) required by the hybrid model.

4) In [11] Foster and Browne study the UT2D Peripheral Processor Library of the CDC 6600 system at the University of Texas. In this system there are 39 files to be allocated across three I/O devices: a central memory (CM), an extended core storage (ECS), and a CDC 808 system disk capable of holding all files. The single executable level (PPU) allows no permanent storage and consists of 4 parallel servers, so that for the DMP under consideration, 4, there is never any queueing for a processor.

Foster and Browne validate their hybrid model by setting CM = 2000, ECS = 0 (actual system values), and observing that throughput as computed by their model is reasonably close to the actual system throughput of 52. Our model passes this same validation test, as LLR returns a throughput of 54.60 for the given set of parameter values. It should be noted that since assignment of library routines is considered here, the single job class assumption seems justified.

In addition, we find a surprising and potentially important result: our model suggests that this particular system is so totally processor-bound that file-assignment is unimportant! As evidence of this, we point to the fact that increasing CM and ECS capacities beyond the validation levels given above yields no significant improvement in throughput. Further, if we select a representative case, CM=6000, ECS=6000, with LLR throughput 54.66, we find that doubling the PPU speed causes LLR throughput to jump to 109.27, almost precisely double.

We turn now to experimental results on capacity selection. As mentioned earlier, the strategy here is as follows. For each DMP we iterate over all sets of capacity choices which lie within the fixed budget, solving the FA problem for each such set; we then simply record that set of capacity choices and that associated file assignment which jointly give rise to maximal system throughput.

A priori we might expect two results.

1) There should be no globally (DMP-independent) optimal capacity selections.

2) Capacity selections based solely on the Vogel loading rule will agree with LLR selections only for DMP = 1. Neither seems to be entirely the case.

We considered two versions of the airline reservation system of [1] (parameters in Tables I and II), the first with single-servers at all devices, the second with the multiple-server structure of [1]:

Memory Level	Servers
fast executable	1
slow executable	1
fast drum	4
slow drum	4
disk	2

For each version we chose capacity increments sufficiently small to allow all 10 configurations listed in [1] to be considered:

Capacity Increments:
device 1: 128 K
device 2: 0.5 M
device 3: 0.5 M
device 4: 0.5 M
device 5: 3 M

In addition, since DMP is, realistically, limited by main memory capacity, we assumed a minimum requirement of (128K/15) words/DMP of fast executable memory, that is, device 1; note that this is consistent with [1, page 319].

For the single-server case, the optimal capacity selections found are summarized in Table III and the associated LLR throughputs are plotted in Fig. 5. These values were found in a single run of 24 min on an IBM 370/165.

Thus, expectation 1) held for DMP 1-4, but thereafter a stabilization took place and configuration 3 remained optimal until DMP = 16, at which point the externally imposed requirement of an additional increment of fast executable memory forced a change to configuration 4, which was stable thereafter.

We should also remark that the dramatic effects of LLR seen earlier in the solution to the FA problem fade rapidly as we approach optimal capacity selection; as an example, the optimal configuration 3 at DMP = 15 has an LLR-loaded throughput of 63.16 jobs/s, but this same configuration has a Vogel-loaded throughput of 61.41 jobs/s, almost as good. Note that the LLR throughput here is within 14 percent of the (likely unobtainable) upper bound of 73.54 jobs/s.

This brings us to expectation 2) and a surprise. If we solve the DCFA problem without LLR, that is, by restricting ourselves to Vogel loading alone, the capacity choices made are precisely the same as those made with LLR for DMP 1-17! After this point (beginning DMP = 18) Vogel loading called for too much fast executable memory:

device 1: 384K
device 2: 1M
device 3: 2M
device 4: 4M
device 4: 3M

The optimal capacity selections for the multiple-server case are summarized in Table IV. Here both of our *a priori* expectations come closer to being fulfilled. Optimal capacity selection appears to be more sensitive to DMP, and with the exception of DMP = 1-4 (where no queueing takes place at either drum), LLR-based capacity selections differ from those that would be made solely on the basis of Vogel loading.

Nevertheless, system tuning still provides minimal improvement for an *optimally chosen* set of capacities, and thus system designers using the technique of [1] would not lag far behind in terms of the final throughput figure. For example, in the DMP = 10 case, the technique of [1] would call for choices

DEVICE 1: 256K
DEVICE 2: 0.5M
DEVICE 3: 2.5M
DEVICE 4: 5.0M
DEVICE 5: 3.0M

on the basis of a Vogel-loaded throughput of 83.90 jobs/s, whereas the choice for DMP = 10 in Table IV was made on the basis of an LLR-loaded throughput of 84.09 jobs/s, not much better.

System tuning of suboptimal capacities, on the other hand, continues to be a major advantage of our technique over that

TABLE III
OPTIMAL CAPACITY SELECTIONS USING LLR

	CONFIGURATION		OPTIMAL FOR
1	DEVICE 1:	128K	
	DEVICE 2:	2.5M	
	DEVICE 3:	.5M	DMP = 1
	DEVICE 4:	4.5M	
	DEVICE 5:	3M	
2	DEVICE 1:	128K	
	DEVICE 2:	2M	
	DEVICE 3:	1.5M	DMP = 2-3
	DEVICE 4:	4M	
	DEVICE 5:	3M	
3	DEVICE 1:	128K	
	DEVICE 2:	1.5M	
	DEVICE 3:	2.5M	DMP = 4-15
	DEVICE 4:	3.5M	
	DEVICE 5:	3M	
4	DEVICE 1:	256K	
	DEVICE 2:	1.5M	
	DEVICE 3:	2M	DMP = 16-20
	DEVICE 4:	3.5M	
	DEVICE 5:	3M	

TABLE IV
OPTIMAL CAPACITY SELECTIONS USING LLR (MULTIPLE-SERVER CASE)

	CONFIGURATION		OPTIMAL FOR
1	DEVICE 1:	128K	
	DEVICE 2:	2.5M	
	DEVICE 3:	0.5M	DMP = 1-4
	DEVICE 4:	4.5M	
	DEVICE 5:	3.0M	
2	DEVICE 1:	128K	
	DEVICE 2:	1.5M	
	DEVICE 3:	1.5M	DMP = 5-7
	DEVICE 4:	5.0M	
	DEVICE 5:	3.0M	
3	DEVICE 1:	128K	
	DEVICE 2:	1.0M	
	DEVICE 3:	2.5M	DMP = 8
	DEVICE 4:	4.5M	
	DEVICE 5:	3.0M	
4	DEVICE 1:	256K	
	DEVICE 2:	1.5M	
	DEVICE 3:	1.5M	DMP = 9-10
	DEVICE 4:	4.5M	
	DEVICE 5:	3.0M	
5	DEVICE 1:	512K	
	DEVICE 2:	0.5M	
	DEVICE 3:	2.0M	DMP = 11 - 12
	DEVICE 4:	4.5M	
	DEVICE 5:	3.0M	
6	DEVICE 1:	512K	
	DEVICE 2:	0.5M	
	DEVICE 3:	1.5M	DMP = 13 - 20
	DEVICE 4:	5.0M	
	DEVICE 5:	3.0M	

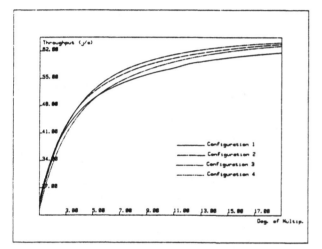

Fig. 5. LLR for optimal capacities.

of [1]. If we restrict ourselves to, say, the capacities given in configuration 2 of [1]

DEVICE 1: 128K
DEVICE 2: —
DEVICE 3: 0.5M
DEVICE 4: 9.0M
DEVICE 5: 3.0M

we find, at DMP = 15, a Vogel-loaded throughput of 41.58 jobs/s and an LLR-loaded throughput of 47.93 jobs/s, a 15 percent improvement. Even for "good" capacity selections, LLR can provide some worthwhile improvement: for configuration 1 of Table IV (optimal for DMP = 1-4!), we find at DMP = 20, a Vogel-loaded throughput of 77.96 jobs/s and an LLR-loaded throughput of 82.89 jobs/s, a 6 percent improvement.

VI. CONCLUSION

We have developed an efficient algorithm for optimal file-assignment in a storage hierarchy. Our experiments indicate that the algorithm developed in this paper executes orders of magnitude faster than existing approaches to the problem, while improving throughput substantially over the Vogel loading rule suggested in [1]. Numerical examples show the usefulness of our algorithm in system tuning. Using the efficient file loading rule as a core, optimal storage device capacities are determined by a discrete search. The result is a convenient and efficient design tool that allows the designer to experiment with many different choices without a proportionately large expense.

Extensions to include multiple job types and sequentiality of file access patterns, as well as extensive validation studies, are desired in order to make practical use of such models.

APPENDIX

Proof of Lemma 1: The level curves of $z_1(y) = \sum_{i=0}^{m} y_i$ are parallel m-planes in R^{m+1}. If we wish to evaluate $h(W_0 + \Delta)$, we can (theoretically) first proceed from the plane W_0 to the parallel plane $W_0 + \Delta$ along the straight line connecting that point at which z_1 assumes its minimum (in plane W_0) to that point at which z_n assumes its minimum (in plane W_1). Since we are moving along a straight line towards the minimum of the convex function z_n, the value of z_n obtained, upon reaching plane $W_0 + \Delta$, is no larger than the value where we started, $h(W_0)$ (see Fig. 2). (Remark: To be absolutely precise here we should say only that our starting point will be in plane W_0, not necessarily at $h(W_0)$. There is an indeterminancy in Vogel loading caused by arbitrary resolution of ties in the factors Δ_{ji}; thus, multiple Vogel loadings are possible over which we would have to minimize z_n to actually find $h(W_0)$. Nevertheless, we continue to use the term $h(W_0)$ to denote our starting point since, for realistic problems, multiple Vogel loadings are highly improbable: such would require a 16-digit tie between Δ_{ji}'s, and then, since tied segments are loaded consecutively anyway, an unfortunate split of a Δ_{ji}-tied file pair across a device boundary.) Finding $h(W_0 + \Delta)$ then amounts to a further reduction (at least no increase) obtained by moving to the minimum of $z_n(y)$ within the plane $W_0 + \Delta$, so certainly $h(W_0 + \Delta) \leq h(W_0)$. An entirely analogous argument shows $h(W_0 + 2\Delta) \leq h(W_0 + \Delta)$.

Proof of Theorem 3: The symmetry follows trivially from the definition of z_n, and since z_n is convex it remains only to show that

$$\partial\left(z_n \left| \sum_{i=0}^{m} y_i = K\right.\right)/\partial y_j = 0$$

$$\text{at } y_0 = y_1 = \cdots = y_m = K/(m+1).$$

We proceed by induction. Observe that

$$z_2 = 1/2\left[\sum_{i=0}^{m} y_i + \left(\sum_{i=0}^{m} y_i^2 \left/ \sum_{i=0}^{m} y_i\right.\right)\right]$$

and thus

$$\left(z_2 \left| \sum_{i=0}^{m} y_i = K\right.\right) = 1/2\left[K + \frac{\sum_{i=0}^{m-1} y_i^2 + \left(K - \sum_{i=0}^{m-1} y_i\right)^2}{K}\right]$$

so that

$$\frac{\partial\left(z_2 \left| \sum_{i=0}^{m} y_i = K\right.\right)}{\partial y_j} = 1/2 \frac{\left[2y_j - 2\left(K - \sum_{i=0}^{m-1} y_i\right)\right]}{K}$$

$j = 0, 1, 2, \cdots m - 1$. Setting each to 0 and solving, we find the unique solution $y_0 = y_1 = \cdots = y_m = K/(m+1)$.

Now take $n \geq 3$ and assume the result for $z_2, \cdots z_{n-1}$. Using

the recursive formula for G_n, $G_n = 1/n \sum_{j=1}^{n} \sum_{i=0}^{m} y_i^j G_{n-j}$ (see [12]

for a derivation), we can write

$$z_n = 1/n\left[\sum y_i + \frac{\sum y_i^2}{z_{n-1}} + \cdots + \frac{\sum y_i^n}{z_{n-1}z_{n-2}\cdots z_1}\right].$$

Then each summand of $z_n | \sum y_i = K$ (after the first) is of the form

$$S_t = \frac{\sum_{i=0}^{m-1} y_i^t + \left(K - \sum_{i=0}^{m-1} y_i\right)^t}{\prod_{p=1}^{t-1} (z_{n-p} \mid \sum y_i = K)} = \frac{N}{D}$$

so that

$$\frac{\partial S_t}{\partial y_i} = \frac{\left(\frac{\partial N}{\partial y_j}\right) D - \left(\frac{\partial D}{\partial y_j}\right) N}{D^2}.$$

Now using our inductive assumption and the product rule for differentiation, we can easily see that $\partial D/\partial y_j = 0$ at $y_0 = y_1 = \cdots = y_m = K/(m+1)$ (this formally requires another induction); further, it is entirely straightforward to check that $\partial N/\partial y_j = 0$ at $y_0 = y_1 = \cdots = y_m = K/(m+1)$. Thus, each summand has each partial derivative 0 at the point of equal relative utilizations, and the proof is complete.

REFERENCES

[1] S. R. Arora and A. Gallo, "Optimization of static loading of multilevel memory systems," *J. Ass. Comput. Mach.*, vol. 20, pp. 307–319, Apr. 1973.
[2] F. Baskett, K. M. Chandy, R. R. Muntz, and F. G. Palacios, "Open, closed, and mixed networks of queues with different classes of customers," *J. Ass. Comput. Mach.*, vol. 22, no. 2, pp. 248–260, 1975.
[3] K. M. Chandy, J. Hogarth, and C. H. Sauer, "Selecting capacities in computer communication systems," *IEEE Trans. Software Eng.*, vol. SE-3, pp. 290–295, July 1977.
[4] K. M. Chandy, J. H. Howard, and D. F. Towsley, "Product form and local balance in queueing networks," *J. Ass. Comput. Mach.*, vol. 24, no. 2, pp. 250–263, 1977.
[5] W-W. Y. Chiu, "Analysis and applications of probabilistic models of multiprogrammed computer systems," Ph.D. dissertation, Dep. Elec. Eng., Univ. of California, Santa Barbara, Dec. 1973.
[6] E. G. Coffman, Jr. and P. J. Denning, *Operating System Theory.* Englewood Cliffs, NJ: Prentice-Hall, 1973.
[7] P. J. Denning and J. P. Buzen, "The operational analysis of queueing network models," *Comput. Surveys*, vol. 10, pp. 225–261, Sept. 1978.
[8] D. Ferrari, *Computer Systems Performance Evaluation.* Englewood Cliffs, NJ: Prentice-Hall, 1978.
[9] D. V. Foster and J. C. Browne, "File assignment in memory hierarchies," in *Modeling and Performance Evaluation of Computer Systems,* Beilner and Gelenbe, Eds. Amsterdam, The Netherlands: North-Holland, 1976.
[10] D. V. Foster, L. W. Dowdy, and J. E. Ames, "File assignment in a STAR network," Dep. Syst. Inform. Sci., Vanderbilt Univ., Nashville, TN, Tech. Rep. 77-3, 1977.
[11] D. V. Foster and J. C. Browne, "Channel balancing in a memory hierarchy—A case study," Dep. Comput. Sci., Duke University, Durham, NC, Rep., 1976.
[12] R. Geist and K. Trivedi, "Queueing network models in computer system design," *Math. Mag.*, to be published.
[13] T. P. Giammo, "Extensions to exponential queueing network theory for use in a planning environment," in *Proc. IEEE Comput.*, Sept. 1976.
[14] *IMSL Reference Manual.* Houston, TX: IMSL, Inc., 1979.
[15] S. K. Kachhal and S. R. Arora, "Seeking configurational optimization in computer systems," in *Proc. ACM Annu. Conf.*, 1975, pp. 96–101.
[16] L. Kleinrock, *Queueing Systems, Vol. II.* New York: Wiley, 1976.
[17] H. Kobayashi and M. Reiser, "On generalization of job routing behavior in a queueing network model," IBM, Yorktown Heights, NY, Res. Rep. RC-5252, 1975.

[18] T. G. Price, "Probability models of multiprogrammed computer systems," Ph.D. dissertation, Dep. Elec. Eng., Stanford Univ., Palo Alto, CA, 1974.

[19] E. W. Pugh, "Storage hierarchies: Gaps, cliffs, and trends," *IEEE Trans. Magn.*, vol. MAG-7, pp. 810–814, Dec. 1971.

[20] C. V. Ramamoorthy and K. M. Chandy, "Optimization of memory hierarchies in multiprogrammed systems," *J. Ass. Comput. Mach.*, vol. 17, pp. 426–445, July 1970.

[21] A. J. Smith, "Algorithms and architectures for enhanced file system use," in *Experimental Computer Performance and Evaluation*, D. Ferrari and M. Spadon, Eds., SOGESTA, 1981.

[22] G. Strang, *Linear Algebra and Its Applications.* New York: Academic, 1976.

[23] K. S. Trivedi, "Prepaging and applications to the STAR-100 computer," in *High-Speed Computer and Algorithm Organization*, D. Kuck, A. Sameh, and D. Lawrie, Eds. New York: Academic, 1977.

[24] K. S. Trivedi and R. A. Wagner, "A decision model of closed queueing networks," *IEEE Trans. Software Eng.*, vol. SE-5, July 1979.

[25] K. S. Trivedi, R. A. Wagner, and T. M. Sigmon, "Optimal selections of CPU speed, device capacities, and file assignments," *J. Ass. Comput. Mach.*, July 1980.

[26] K. S. Trivedi and R. E. Kinicki, "A model for computer configuration design," *Computer*, pp. 47–54, Apr. 1980.

[27] K. S. Trivedi and T. M. Sigmon, "A performance comparison of optimally designed computer systems with and without virtual memory," in *Proc. 6th Annu. Int. Symp. Comput. Arch.*, Philadelphia, PA, 1979.

[28] ——, "Optimal design of linear storage hierarchies," *J. Ass. Comput. Mach.*, Apr. 1981.

[29] K. S. Trivedi and R. A. Wagner, "Optimal selection of CPU speed, device capacities, and file assignments—An extension," to be published.

[30] R. A. Wagner and K. S. Trivedi, "Hardware configuration selection through discretizing a continuous variable solution," in *Proc. 7th IFIP Int. Symp. Comput. Performance Modeling, Measurement, and Evaluation*, Toronto, Ont., Canada, May 1980, pp. 127–142.

Chapter 5

Disk and Disk Cache Systems

The speed of main memory and cache is determined by the speed of the logic used, while that of disks is determined by how quickly the disks can rotate and the arms move into the right position. Rotational speeds are constrained by mechanical considerations: if they are raised beyond a point, the resultant centrifugal forces can tear the disk apart. As a result, the gap between the speed of main memory and that of disks is likely to increase as time goes by.

Disks are organized into *tracks*, which are concentric circles. Each track is made up of a set of *sectors*. See Figure 5.1 for a system with eight sectors per track. In practice, there can be up to about 2,000 tracks per disk and about 32 sectors per track. Disks are usually rotated at 3,600 rpm.

Disk access time is a function of two factors. The first, called the *latency*, is the time it takes to move the arm to the right track and rotate the disk until the appropriate sector is under the disk arm so that reading can begin. This time is unlikely to be greatly reduced in the near future. The second is the time required to transfer the required data.

There has been some research done on how to schedule disk-access requests. Suppose there are multiple access requests queued at the disk controller. Should they be served in First Come First Served (FCFS) order, or should the controller choose to serve next the request which would require the least arm movement? Questions such as these are, however, of limited practical value since queues in a well-designed computer system usually do not hold more than a very small number of access requests. The reason is that any computer which has a large number of disk access requests awaiting service is likely to be heavily bottlenecked at the disk system, and have its performance gravely compromised.

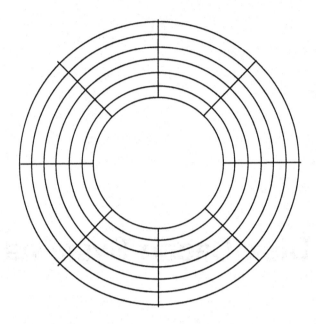

Figure 5.1. Disk Organization

Substantial decreases can be made to the transfer time through the use of disk arrays. Multiple disks can be accessed in parallel with the data interleaved among them. They also make for fault-tolerance. Whether this makes a meaningful difference to the overall performance depends on the volume of data transferred per access. This can be quantified by the following simple calculation. The time to complete an access is the sum of the latency, t_{lat} the transfer time, t_{trans}, and the disk controller overhead, t_{cont}: $t_{total} = t_{lat} + t_{trans} + t_{cont}$.[1] If we decrease the transfer time by a factor of p by using disk arrays, the time becomes $t_{total} = t_{lat} + t_{trans}/p + t_{cont}$.[2] The ratio of the two transfer times is given by

$$\frac{1 + \left(\dfrac{t_{trans} + t_{cont}}{t_{lat}}\right)}{1 + \left(\dfrac{1}{p}\right)\left(\dfrac{t_{trans} + t_{cont}}{t_{lat}}\right)}.$$

It is only if the ratio $(t_{trans} + t_{cont})/t_{lat}$ is substantial that reducing the transfer time makes a real difference. That is, it is best to move data into, and out of, disks in large blocks.

---

[1] There is also the effect of waiting for the disk to become available, if it is being used by another access operation.

[2] Actually, the use of disk arrays can also affect the latency to some extent: we shall ignore this effect in this first-order calculation.

Let us look at two types of disk arrays. The first involves *disk mirroring* by duplicating disks. That is, each disk has a mirror image of itself. The result is that any block is found in two disks, and can be read from either. When a block is written into, then both disks must be updated. Disk mirroring can speed up the read operation in two ways. First, it is possible to support two reads simultaneously. Second, if both disks are free, then the request can be directed to the disk whose seek time will be the smaller of the two. Disk mirroring also provides fault-tolerance in the form of redundancy. However, since each write operation translates into two disk writes, disk writes can be slowed down. These two writes will take place in parallel. The overall write operation will not be complete until both the disks have been written into. It will therefore be determined by the disk whose write time (due to its rotation and seek times) is the greater of the two.

A second disk array type involves *interleaving*. Data can be interleaved bitwise among multiple disks, and an additional disk provided for parity coding. Such a scheme is less expensive than disk mirroring, but also provides a modicum of fault-tolerance: it can tolerate up to one disk failure. Many other similar variations on disk arrays are possible, and have been studied.

Just as we use caches to mitigate the effects of the disparity between the speed of the processor and that of the main memory, we can use disk caches to buffer interactions with the disks. Disk caches can be implemented as part of the main memory itself. In the same way that memory caches reduce the need to access the main memory, so too disk caches reduce the number of accesses seen by the disk system. The presence of a disk cache tends to reduce the number of disk read operations seen by the disk, and thus to increase the ratio of disk writes to disk reads.

The papers that follow show how to predict the performance of disk and disk cache systems.

Carson and Setia analyze the periodic update policy for disk caches. Under this policy, writes are made to the disks periodically. The paper indicates under what conditions periodic updating is better than write-through.

Brandwajn provides models of disk systems with multiple access paths. Each disk shares the path to the CPU with several other disks. As a result, it is possible for blocking to occur when too many disks seek to transfer data at the same time. This paper models such blocking.

The next three papers deal with disk interleaving. Since, in such a system, a block is spread among multiple disks, transferring a block to and from the disk system is done in parallel. The disk system can be either synchronous or asynchronous. A group of disks is said to be synchronized if their rotation is synchronized. In other words, if we took a snapshot of the disks, each of the disks will be in the same rotational orientation. The paper by Kim models interleaving in synchronized disk systems, and those of Kim and Tantawi and Lee and Katz study the analogous problem for asynchronous systems.

Analysis of the Periodic Update Write Policy For Disk Cache

Scott D. Carson and Sanjeev Setia

Abstract— A disk cache is typically used in file systems to reduce average access time for data storage and retrieval. The "periodic update" write policy, widely used in existing computer systems, is one in which dirty cache blocks are written to a disk on a periodic basis. In this paper we determine the average response time for disk read requests when the periodic update write policy is used. Read and write load, cache–hit ratio, and the disk scheduler's ability to reduce service time under load are incorporated in the analysis, leading to design criteria that can be used to decide among competing cache write policies. The main conclusion of this paper is that the bulk arrivals generated by the periodic update policy cause a "traffic jam" effect which results in severely degraded service. Effective use of the disk cache and disk scheduling can alleviate this problem, but only under a narrow range of operating conditions. Based on this conclusion, alternate write policies that retain the periodic update policy's advantages and provide uniformly better service are proposed.

Index Terms— Disk cache, file system, mass storage, performance model, write policy.

I. INTRODUCTION

OPERATING systems typically maintain a disk cache to provide increased performance [3], [11], [10], [14], [15]. Since disk operations are slow compared to memory operations, a significant performance advantage can be realized if the hit ratio for requests is sufficiently high. Read operations are handled in a straightforward manner; upon a "cache hit," data are simply copied from the cache into a destination buffer. Write operations, on the other hand, can be handled in a number of different ways, such as "write through" (immediate update) and "write back" (update on replacement). This paper focuses on the performance of the commonly used "periodic update" write policy.

The periodic update concept arises from a need to balance the generation of I/O traffic with the potential for data loss. Write operations are accepted by the disk cache system, and modified blocks are marked as "dirty"[1] without updating the on-disk copy of the file system. To avoid data loss in the event of a system failure, dirty cache blocks are written to the

Manuscript received August 27, 1990; revised August 1, 1991. Recommended by S. S. Lam. This work was supported in part by a Grant from the Digital Equipment Corporation, and by the U.S. Army Strategic Defense Command under Contract No. DASG60-87-0066. The views, opinions, and/or findings contained in this report are those of the authors and should not be construed as an official position or policy of either the Department of Defense or the Digital Equipment Corporation, unless designated by other official documentation.

The authors are with the Department of Computer Science, University of Maryland, College Park, MD 20742.

IEEE Log Number 9104159.

[1] A dirty cache block is one that has been modified since the last time it was written to the disk.

disk on a periodic basis. Variants of this policy are used in the Sprite network file system [10] and the UNIX operating system [1], [2].

The need to understand cache write policies has become important as disk caches have become large, often consisting of many megabytes of memory space. With a small cache, the number of dirty blocks flushed from the cache at one time is limited. On the other hand, flushing a large cache can present a substantial amount of work to the disk system, all at one time [3], [7]. The need to service this backlog quickly has motivated the study of high-performance disk scheduling techniques [13]. This study addresses the more fundamental question of whether the periodic update policy should be used at all, and if so, under what circumstances.

Throughout the paper we compare the response time for read operations under the periodic update (PU) policy with that achieved using the write through (WT) policy, since the WT policy is, in effect, the "trivial" policy that makes no use of the disk cache. Intuition suggests that any write policy that takes advantage of the disk cache should perform better than WT. Surprisingly, we find that for loads that would not saturate the disk system using the WT policy, the PU policy performs worse than the WT policy unless the cache write hit ratio is in the 80–90% range, and that disk scheduling alleviates this problem only under restricted conditions. We do not, however, advocate the use of the write through policy as a solution, since it saturates the disk system at lower write loads than the PU policy. Instead, we propose alternate write policies that are based on our exposition of the specific failings of the PU policy.

The paper first presents an analytic model of the PU cache write policy, with first-come, first-served (FCFS) disk scheduling. The PU policy with FCFS disk service is compared with the WT policy, and the minimum cache write–hit ratio that makes the PU policy superior is derived. The effect of the length of the update period on cache–hit ratio requirements is described, and it is shown that increasing the update period increases the required cache–hit ratio. The relationship between the required cache–hit ratio and the disk scheduler's ability to reduce disk service time is investigated by simulation. The result is a relation that describes combinations of the cache–hit ratio and a simple measure of scheduler performance that make the PU policy superior to the WT policy. This relation defines a narrow performance envelope within which the PU policy performs better than the WT policy. Factors that mitigate the performance of the PU policy in small systems are discussed. Based on the results of this paper, write policies that avoid the PU policy's pathological behavior are described.

Reprinted from *IEEE Trans. Software Eng.*, Vol. 18, No. 1, Jan. 1992, pp. 44–54.

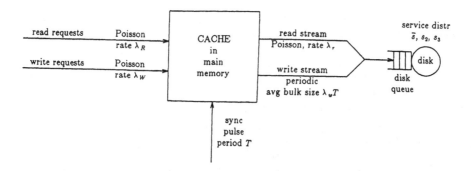

Fig. 1. Modeled request streams into and out of the disk cache.

II. ANALYSIS OF PERIODIC UPDATE POLICY

Both UNIX and Sprite use a disk cache write policy designed to postpone some writes as long as possible [10], [12], [17]. Delaying writes reduces disk traffic, since the longer a dirty block stays in the cache, the greater the chance that it will be written multiple times before the disk update occurs. Alternately, a performance improvement can result if the block is discarded before it is written to the disk [3], [10], [11]. The problem with this scheme is that there is no guarantee that a delayed block will ever be written to the disk; blocks that are updated frequently enough might never be candidates for replacement. A common solution is to provide a periodic "sync pulse" that forces dirty cache blocks to be written to the disk. In the UNIX operating system, for example, this sync pulse is generated every 30 s [1].

This section presents an analytic model of response time for read operations with the "pure" periodic update policy, in which all write operations are delayed. The pure periodic update policy is not used in any operating system, since it provides no integrity guarantee for the on-disk copy of the file system. The model, however, is readily adapted to variants of the policy used in existing operating systems by grouping nondelayed write operations with read operations.[2]

In a computer system with a large process population, the presentation of read requests to the cache can be modeled by a Poisson arrival process with a rate of λ_R requests/s. In the model, these requests enjoy a fixed-hit ratio h_r, $0 \leq h_r \leq 1$, so that the resulting disk traffic is a Poisson arrival process with a rate of $\lambda_r = (1 - h_r)\lambda_R$. Let the length of the update period, defined as the time between two sync pulses, be T. Writes arrive to the cache according to a Poisson process with rate λ_W. The write-hit ratio $h_w(T)$, $0 \leq h_w(T) \leq 1$ is the fraction of writes that are to blocks that are already dirty or those that will not be written to disk due to deletion or replacement. In other words, the write-hit ratio is defined as the fraction of writes during the update period that are not written out at the sync pulse; intuitively, the hit ratio is nondecreasing in T. At the sync pulse, those blocks that are dirty are written; the number of such blocks is Poisson distributed with mean $\lambda_w T = (1 - h_w(T))\lambda_W \cdot T$. Read and

write requests are serviced by the disk according to a general service time distribution with a mean of $\bar{s}$, and second and third moments s_2 and s_3, respectively. Fig. 1 shows a diagram of the modeled system.

In a real computer system, read cache misses can generate disk write operations, due to replacement, and write operations can generate disk read operations when cache blocks are partially modified. In both cases, processes must block until these "extra" operations complete. In the model, these operations are grouped with read operations; thus they contribute to the Poisson (sporadic) request stream. This is justified, because the focus of the analysis is on disk operations that cause processes to block.

The analytic model treats each update period independently, and this assumption is shown by simulation to hold under all but extremely high load conditions.[3] Essentially, the analytic model describes a *delay cycle* [8] that begins at the start of the update period with any remaining read work in the system, followed by the bulk service of the writes, followed by the service of reads that arrive during the service of the initial reads and writes, and so on, until the disk system becomes idle. After this delay cycle, the disk system becomes an M/G/1 server with only read work to service until the next sync pulse arrives. The update period is divided into subintervals as shown in Fig. 2. When the sync pulse arrives, it is assumed in the analytic model that with high probability, the delay cycle that started at the previous sync pulse has finished. This assumption, however, was not used in the simulations described below.

Assuming that the previous delay cycle has ended, the system is operating as an M/G/1 server when the sync pulse arrives. The interval t_r is the time required to service reads that are in the queue at the sync pulse. Since the sync pulse and the read arrival process are independent, the sync pulse occurs at a random time as far as read arrivals and service completions are concerned. Thus on average, t_r is the "virtual waiting time" of a random arrival,[4] or

$$t_r = \frac{\rho_r \bar{s}(1 + C_s^2)}{2(1 - \rho_r)} = \frac{\lambda_r s_2}{2(1 - \rho_r)}$$

where $\rho_r \equiv \lambda_r \bar{s}$ is the *read traffic intensity*, a "normalized" measure of the disk load imposed by read operations. The

---

[2]In the UNIX operating system, for example, write operations can be synchronous, asynchronous, or delayed. The model can be used in this case by grouping synchronous and asynchronous write operations together with read operations. The model then provides average response time for read, synchronous write, and asynchronous write operations.

[3]Simulations that were used to validate the model did not share the hypothesis of independent update periods.

[4]It is assumed that the reader is familiar with the results of basic queueing theory, as described in [9], for example.

squared coefficient of variation of the disk service time distribution C_s^2 is a measure of the random variability in each disk service operation.

The next interval, of length t_w, is the time required to complete the writes that are inserted when the sync pulse occurs. On average, this is the number of write arrivals during the update period, times the average service time for each, or $t_w = \rho_w T$, where $\rho_w \equiv \lambda_w \bar{s}$ is the *write traffic intensity*.

Now, following the write interval, a series of read intervals occurs before the system becomes idle. These intervals are of average length t_i, $1 \le i \le \infty$. The first read interval, of length t_1, is the time required to complete read requests that arrive during t_0, where $t_0 \equiv t_r + t_w$, so $t_1 = t_0 \rho_r$. In general, t_i is the time required to service read requests that arrive during interval $i - 1$. Thus $t_i = \rho_r t_{i-1} = t_0 \rho_r^i$. The total length of the delay cycle t_D is

$$t_D = \sum_{i=0}^{\infty} t_i = \frac{t_0}{1 - \rho_r}. \tag{1}$$

The average response time for read requests can be calculated for each of the intervals in which reads are serviced. Let R_1 be the average response time for read requests that are serviced during t_1. This is simply the average waiting time during the arrival (preceding) interval, plus the average time in the system during the service interval. The average waiting time during the arrival interval is the mean residual life of the arrival interval at a random instant, $t_0/2 + \sigma_{t_0}^2/2t_0$, where $\sigma_{t_0}^2$ is the variance of t_0. The average time in the system during the service interval includes both service time and queueing time. Let $a(\tau, k)$ be the probability that k read operations arrive during an interval of length τ; since the arrival process is Poisson, $a(\tau, k) = \exp(-\lambda_r \tau)(\lambda_r \tau)^k/k!$. The average time in the system during the service interval t_1 is then:

$$\sum_{k=1}^{\infty} (\text{average time in system given } k \text{ arrivals}$$

$$\text{during } t_0)a(t_0, k)$$

$$= \sum_{k=1}^{\infty} \sum_{i=1}^{k} \frac{1}{k} \bar{s} i a(t_0, k) = \sum_{k=1}^{\infty} \frac{\bar{s}}{k} \sum_{i=1}^{k} i a(t_0, k)$$

$$= \sum_{k=1}^{\infty} \frac{\bar{s}}{k} \frac{k(k+1)}{2} a(t_0, k)$$

$$= \frac{\bar{s}}{2} \sum_{k=1}^{\infty} k a(t_0, k) + \frac{\bar{s}}{2} \sum_{k=1}^{\infty} a(t_0, k)$$

$$= \frac{\bar{s}}{2}(\lambda_r t_0 + 1 - a(t_0, 0)) = \frac{1}{2}(t_1 + \bar{s}(1 - e^{-\lambda_r t_0})).$$

The value of the last expression lies between $t_1/2$ and $(t_1 + \bar{s})/2$. Assuming the lower value gives a slightly optimistic prediction of response time. In the interest of obtaining a closed-form expression, we will do so; numerically, assuming either bound makes little difference in the final response time calculation. The average response time for requests serviced during t_1 is thus:

$$R_1 = \frac{1}{2}\left(t_0 + \frac{\sigma_{t_0}^2}{t_0} + t_1\right).$$

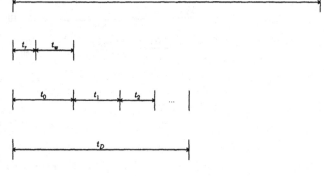

Fig. 2. Update period analysis.

The variance of the interval t_0, $\sigma_{t_0}^2$, is the variance of the M/G/1 virtual waiting time plus the variance of the time required to complete the write bulk, since the two intervals are independent. The variance of the M/G/1 virtual waiting time [9] is

$$\frac{\lambda_r^2 s_2^2}{4(1 - \rho_r)^2} + \frac{\lambda_r s_3}{3(1 - \rho_r)}$$

where s_k is the kth moment of the service time distribution. The variance of the time required to service the write bulk is expressed as the variance of the sum of a random number of random variables [9], or

$$\lambda_w T \sigma_s^2 + (\bar{s})^2 \lambda_w T = s_2 \lambda_w T.$$

Thus

$$\sigma_{t_0}^2 = \frac{\lambda_r^2 s_2^2}{4(1 - \rho_r)^2} + \frac{\lambda_r s_3}{3(1 - \rho_r)} + s_2 \lambda_w T. \tag{2}$$

For the remaining intervals $i \ge 2$, the average response time is calculated in a similar fashion. In interval $i - 1$ a random number of read operations arrive. The variance of their aggregate service time is again the variance of a random sum, or

$$\sigma_{t_{i-1}}^2 = \lambda_r t_{i-2} \sigma_s^2 + \bar{s}^2 \lambda_r t_{i-2} = s_2 \lambda_r t_0 \rho_r^{i-2}.$$

The response time for requests serviced during interval $i \ge 2$ is the sum of the waiting time during interval $i - 1$ and waiting plus service time in interval i, or

$$R_i = \frac{t_{i-1}}{2} + \frac{\sigma_{t_{i-1}}^2}{2t_{i-1}} + \frac{t_i}{2} = \frac{1}{2}\left(t_{i-1} + \frac{s_2 \lambda_r}{\rho_r} + t_i\right).$$

The probability that a read request arrives during interval $i-1$, and is therefore serviced during interval i, is t_{i-1}/T. The contribution to the average read response time of the read requests that arrive during the delay cycle is

$$\sum_{i=1}^{\infty} R_i P\{i\} = \sum_{i=1}^{\infty} \frac{1}{2}\left(t_{i-1} + \frac{\sigma_{t_{i-1}}^2}{t_{i-1}} + t_i\right)\frac{t_{i-1}}{T}$$

$$= \frac{t_D}{T}\frac{1}{2}\left(t_0 + \lambda_r s_2 + \frac{\sigma_{t_0}^2}{t_D}\right).$$

After this delay cycle, read requests are serviced by a simple M/G/1 server, which provides an average response time of

336

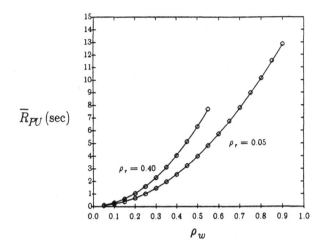

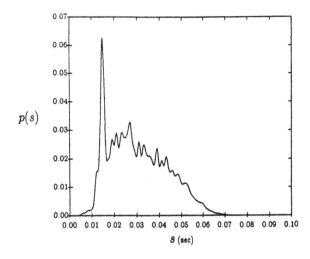

(a)

Fig. 3. Read response time as a function of write load: $\bar{R}_{PU}$(s) versus ρ_w, using the three-stage Erlang service distribution with a mean of 30 ms, $T = 30$ s. Curves are from equation (3); circled points are simulation results.

$R = \bar{s} + \lambda_r s_2/(2(1 - \rho_r))$. The probability that a read request arrives during this interval is $(T - t_D)/T$. Thus

$$\bar{R}_{PU} = \frac{t_D}{T} \frac{1}{2} \left(t_0 + \lambda_r s_2 + \frac{\sigma_{t_0}^2}{t_D} \right)$$
$$+ \frac{T - t_D}{T} \left(\bar{s} + \frac{\lambda_r s_2}{2(1 - \rho_r)} \right). \quad (3)$$

To validate the model a series of simulations was run. The service time distribution was a three-stage Erlang distribution, with a mean of 30 ms, a second moment of 0.0012 s^2, third moment of 0.00006 s^3, standard deviation of 17 ms, and squared coefficient of variation 1/3, chosen because of its similarity in the first two moments to measured disk service time distributions [18]. The update period T was 30 s, which is the value typically used in UNIX systems [1]. As shown in Fig. 3, the model predicts the response time accurately (within 1% for all but large values of ρ_r).

Simulation studies were also conducted using an empirical disk service distribution; in particular, that reported in [18]. This distribution has a mean of 30.5 ms, with a second moment of 0.0011 s^2, third moment of 0.00004484 s^3, standard deviation of 13 ms, and squared coefficient of variation 0.1811. An empirical disk service distribution is dependent on disk characteristics and the access patterns generated by the file system. In this case, the distribution was observed on a UNIX file server that provided executable files to network client workstations under low-load conditions. Fig. 4 shows that the model accurately predicts simulated performance with this distribution.

Fig. 5 illustrates the primary deficiency in the model: its reliance on the sync pulse as a regeneration point in the process. When ρ_r approaches unity, the model and the simulation diverge by as much as 20%. This is because the model treats each update period independently, while high values of ρ_r increase the variance of t_D enough that adjacent update periods affect each other. In other words, if the probability that the delay cycle does not end before the next sync pulse is

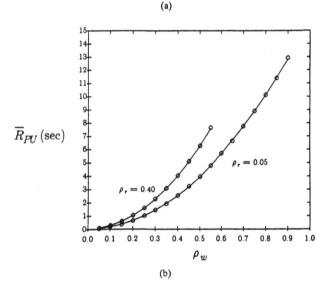

(b)

Fig. 4. (a) Empirical disk service time density function $p(s)$ versus s (s). $\bar{s} = 0.030$ s, $C_s^2 = 0.18$. (b) Read response time as a function of write load: $\bar{R}_{PU}$ (s) versus ρ_w, using the empirical disk service time distribution; $T = 30$ s. The curves are from equation (3); circled points are simulation results.

high enough, then the assumptions embodied in the model no longer hold. This effect is diminished as T becomes large. It must be noted, however, that any combination of $\rho_r + \rho_w$ near unity is uncommon in practice; computer systems are rarely, if ever, designed to operate their disk systems near saturation in the steady state.

Another potential deficiency in the model is its assumption that the M/G/1 system seen by reads after t_D operates in the steady state. For large T this is true, but when $T - t_D$ is not large relative to the mean service time, this assumption clearly does not hold. However, when t_D becomes large relative to T, $(T - t_D)/T$ becomes small, and the behavior of the M/G/1 system does not contribute significantly to the overall read response time. Thus even for ρ_w near unity, the model gives results close to those obtained by simulation.

To see how read operations are delayed, it is useful to

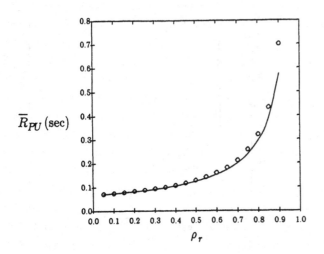

Fig. 5. Read response time as a function of read load: $\bar{R}_{PU}$(s) versus ρ_r, for $\rho_w = 0.05$, using the three-stage Erlang service distribution with a mean of 30 ms, $T = 30$ s. The curve is from equation (3); circled points are simulation results. Note that the model underestimates the average response time for high ρ_r.

examine the role of the write bulk in the delay cycle. When the read load is low, most of the delay cycle consists of the time required to service the writes. When the read load is high, however, the write bulk initiates a "traffic jam" that lasts well beyond the time required to complete the write operations, and this effect becomes increasingly pronounced as the read load grows. Consider the ratio t_w/t_D. From (1),

$$\frac{t_w}{t_D} = \frac{t_w(1 - \rho_r)}{t_w + t_r}.$$

Unless the read load approaches unity while the write load approaches zero, t_w dominates t_r, and the ratio is close to $1 - \rho_r$. Thus, for example, using the three-stage Erlang service distribution with $T = 30$ s, t_w/t_D is approximately 0.95 when $\rho_r = 0.05$ and $\rho_w \geq 0.05$. For $\rho_r = 0.75$ and $\rho_w \geq 0.05$, the ratio is approximately 0.25; the write bulk accounts for 1/4 of the total delay cycle.

III. COMPARISON WITH WRITE THROUGH POLICY

The average response times shown in Figs. 3 and 4 are on the order of several seconds. Given that these response times are high compared to the disk service time, it is natural to wonder how the PU policy compares with the simplest possible policy, write through (WT), under under load-independent (FCFS) service. Since the WT policy makes no use of the cache, it represents the "do nothing" policy. If the PU policy performs worse than WT, then it fails to meet its objective of improving performance using the cache—*it is worse than doing nothing at all.* In this section we compare the two policies in a fair manner, and show that the PU policy is not universally better than the WT policy. Further, we derive the cache write–hit ratio that must be achieved in order to make the PU policy perform at least as well as WT.

In the WT policy, all process write operations are delivered to the disk; thus the write arrival rate is λ_W, rather than λ_w. Since the read and write streams are independent and Poisson,

TABLE I
Minimum Cache–Hit Ratio Required for $\bar{R}_{PU} \leq \bar{R}_{WT}$, with $T = 30$ s

		ρ_W								
		0.05	0.15	0.25	0.35	0.45	0.55	0.65	0.75	0.85
ρ_r	0.05	0.82	0.89	0.91	0.92	0.92	0.92	0.92	0.91	0.87
	0.15	0.81	0.89	0.90	0.91	0.91	0.91	0.90	0.87	
	0.25	0.80	0.88	0.90	0.90	0.90	0.89	0.86		
	0.35	0.78	0.86	0.88	0.89	0.88	0.84			
	0.45	0.76	0.85	0.87	0.86	0.83				
	0.55	0.73	0.83	0.84	0.80					
	0.65	0.69	0.79	0.77						
	0.75	0.63	0.70							
	0.85	0.47								

the write through policy can be modeled as an M/G/1 system with a combined arrival rate of $\lambda_W + \lambda_r$. One way to compare the two policies might be to assume a particular write–hit ratio, $h_w(T)$, and to compare their read response times. This comparison, however, would be valid only for a single hit ratio, and since the hit ratio is not universally fixed, this comparison might be unfair to one of the policies. Instead, we reverse the question and determine the minimum hit ratio which makes PU perform better than WT. Determining whether or not a system can benefit from the PU policy then becomes a question of determining the write–hit ratio for that system.

Equation (3) shows $\bar{R}_{PU}$ as a function of T, λ_w, λ_r, $\bar{s}$, s_2, and s_3. Now, λ_w is a function of $h_w(T)$ and λ_W. Thus (3) can be solved for $h_w(T)$ and expressed as

$$h_w(T) = f(\bar{R}_{PU}, T)$$

where for our purposes all other variables are constant. The function $f()$ is not explicitly shown here, since it is lengthy and relatively uninteresting.

Next, we define the following:

$$h_w^{min}(T) \equiv f(\bar{R}_{WT}, T), 0 \leq \rho_r + \rho_W < 1$$

where $\bar{R}_{WT}$ is calculated from the M/G/1 response time formula with an arrival rate $\lambda_W + \lambda_r$ and service distribution moments $\bar{s}$ and s_2. In other words, $h_w^{min}(T)$ is the hit ratio that makes the response time of both policies equal as long as the system is not saturated with the WT policy. Since decreasing the hit ratio $h_w(T)$ increases the response time $\bar{R}_{PU}$, if the hit ratio is less than $h_w^{min}(T)$, then the read response time of the PU policy is greater than that achieved by the WT policy, and vice-versa.

Table I shows $h_w^{min}(30)$ for various values of ρ_r and ρ_W for the case where the system is not saturated using the WT policy. With a high read load and a low write load, the values shown are somewhat optimistic, since the model underestimates $\bar{R}_{PU}$ under these conditions. In all other cases the required hit ratio is high; with load-independent disk service, the cache must eliminate 80–90 % of all write accesses before the PU policy pays off.

The PU policy can provide better service than the WT policy in cases where the system would be saturated using WT, since the PU policy uses the cache to reduce disk write traffic. The stability condition for the system using the PU policy

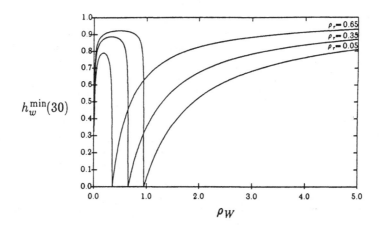

Fig. 6. Minimum cache write–hit ratio for the PU policy as a function of process write load using the three-stage Erlang distribution, $T = 30$ s. When $\rho_r + \rho_W \geq 1$, the disk system would be saturated using the WT policy. For $\rho_r + \rho_W < 1$, the PU policy gives a higher read response time than the WT policy unless $h_w(30) \geq h_w^{\min}(30)$. For $\rho_r + \rho_W \geq 1$, the system is saturated using the PU policy unless $h_w(30) > h_w^{\min}(30)$.

TABLE II
MINIMUM CACHE–HIT RATIO REQUIRED FOR STABILITY WITH THE PU POLICY WHEN THE WT POLICY IS SATURATED ($T = 30$ s)

		ρ_W				
		1.0	2.0	3.0	4.0	5.0
	0.05	0.05	0.53	0.68	0.76	0.81
ρ_r	0.35	0.35	0.68	0.78	0.84	0.87
	0.65	0.65	0.83	0.88	0.91	0.93
	0.95	0.95	0.98	0.98	0.99	0.99

is $\rho_r + \rho_w < 1$, which means that

$$h_w^{\min}(T) = \frac{\rho_r + \rho_W - 1}{\rho_W}, \rho_r + \rho_W \geq 1$$

which is independent of T. In this case, the minimum hit ratio is that for which the PU policy is saturated; with any hit ratio greater than $h_w^{\min}(T)$, the system is stable. Note that meeting this minimum hit-ratio requirement does not guarantee "good" performance in any sense - it merely guarantees finite response time. Table II shows values of $h_w^{\min}(30)$, for various combinations of read and write loads, while Fig. 6 shows how $h_w^{\min}(30)$ varies as a function of the process write load.

IV. THE EFFECT OF INCREASING T

Increasing the length of the update period T can improve performance in three ways, all of which involve reducing write traffic at the sync pulse. This effectively increases the cache write–hit ratio $h_w(T)$ as T increases. First, increasing T can increase the number of times a particular block is accessed before being written. Second, with a cache of finite size, dirty blocks that are replaced generate sporadic write traffic that becomes intermingled with read traffic. Third, as observed in [3], [11], [15], increasing T may avoid disk writes altogether for files that have short lifetimes, such as temporary files. In this light, it is appropriate to examine the behavior of $h_w^{\min}(T)$ as T grows. Note that, as in the previous section, we make no assumption about the behavior of $h_w(T)$.

From (3) it can be seen with some effort that $\bar{R}_{PU}$ grows as a function of T, if $h_w(T)$ remains constant. Since $\bar{R}_{WT}$ is

TABLE III
MINIMUM CACHE–HIT RATIO REQUIRED FOR $\bar{R}_{PU} \leq \bar{R}_{WT}$, WITH $T = 60$ s

		ρ_W								
		0.05	0.15	0.25	0.35	0.45	0.55	0.65	0.75	0.85
	0.05	0.87	0.92	0.94	0.94	0.95	0.94	0.94	0.93	0.91
	0.15	0.87	0.92	0.93	0.94	0.94	0.94	0.93	0.91	
	0.25	0.86	0.91	0.93	0.93	0.93	0.92	0.90		
	0.35	0.85	0.90	0.92	0.92	0.91	0.89			
ρ_r	0.45	0.83	0.89	0.91	0.90	0.88				
	0.55	0.81	0.88	0.88	0.86					
	0.65	0.79	0.85	0.84						
	0.75	0.74	0.79							
	0.85	0.63								

TABLE IV
MINIMUM CACHE–HIT RATIO REQUIRED FOR $\bar{R}_{PU} \leq \bar{R}_{WT}$, WITH $T = 300$ s

		ρ_W								
		0.05	0.15	0.25	0.35	0.45	0.55	0.65	0.75	0.85
	0.05	0.94	0.97	0.97	0.97	0.98	0.98	0.97	0.97	0.96
	0.15	0.94	0.96	0.97	0.97	0.97	0.97	0.97	0.96	
	0.25	0.94	0.96	0.97	0.97	0.97	0.97	0.95		
	0.35	0.93	0.96	0.96	0.96	0.96	0.95			
ρ_r	0.45	0.93	0.95	0.96	0.96	0.95				
	0.55	0.92	0.95	0.95	0.94					
	0.65	0.91	0.93	0.93						
	0.75	0.88	0.91							
	0.85	0.84								

independent of T, $h_w^{\min}(T)$ must increase with T to preserve $\bar{R}_{PU} = \bar{R}_{WT}$. Tables III–V show $h_w^{\min}(T)$ for $T = 60, 300$, and 600 s, respectively, for loads where the system would not be saturated using the WT policy. As the data show, the effect of increasing T is that the cache write–hit ratio requirement rises; when T is 10 min, the cache system must be able to eliminate between 88 and 98% of all write accesses (for the loads shown) before the PU policy pays off.

Reference [11] provides some insight into the behavior of $h_w(T)$ as T increases. In particular, examining file lifetime distributions suggests that $h_w(T)$ is nondecreasing in T, and that there are vertical "jumps" at certain values of T. These T values represent times long enough to encompass the lifetime of blocks belonging to certain classes of files, such as

339

TABLE V
Minimum Cache–Hit Ratio Required for $\bar{R}_{\mathrm{PU}} \leq \bar{R}_{\mathrm{WT}}$, with $T = 600$ s

	ρw								
	0.05	0.15	0.25	0.35	0.45	0.55	0.65	0.75	0.85
0.05	0.96	0.98	0.98	0.98	0.98	0.98	0.98	0.98	0.97
0.15	0.96	0.97	0.98	0.98	0.98	0.98	0.98	0.97	
0.25	0.96	0.97	0.98	0.98	0.98	0.98	0.97		
0.35	0.95	0.97	0.97	0.97	0.97	0.97			
ρ_r 0.45	0.95	0.97	0.97	0.97	0.96				
0.55	0.94	0.96	0.96	0.96					
0.65	0.93	0.95	0.95						
0.75	0.92	0.93							
0.85	0.88								

temporary and accounting files. There may be particular values of T for which $h_w(T) \geq h_w^{\min}(T)$. Determining whether the PU policy performs better than the WT policy in a particular system involves characterizing $h_w(T)$ and finding these T values. Alternately, if the system is saturated using the WT policy, the minimum hit ratios shown in Table II apply.

V. The Effect of Disk Scheduling

Disk scheduling can mitigate the effect of large bulk arrivals in the system by reducing disk service time as the load grows. In this section we investigate the effect of disk scheduling on the read response time $\bar{R}_{\mathrm{PU}}$, and on $h_w^{\min}(T)$. The actual numbers reported in this section are highly dependent on physical hardware configuration and disk access patterns, and are thus of limited value themselves. Nonetheless, the effects of disk scheduling on $\bar{R}_{\mathrm{PU}}$ are obvious enough that general conclusions about the resulting performance improvement are justified.

Disk scheduling allows for the selection of the next request (among many in queue) to service based on head position, rotational position, arrival time, or a combination of the three. The effect of scheduling is to reduce service time when multiple requests are in queue. Although which scheduling disciplines work "best" has been in dispute for years [5], [6], [13], [16], there is general agreement that some form of scheduling is preferable to FCFS, load-independent service.

The results presented in this section were obtained by simulation, since load-dependent service is not amenable to the mean-value analysis used in Section II. As in Section II, read requests arrive at the disk system according to a Poisson process with a rate of λ_r, and write requests arrive in bulk at the sync pulse. With load-dependent service, however, the average service time seen by a request depends on the number of requests in the disk queue when it is selected for service. Additionally, disk scheduling causes requests to be reordered; the service order is typically different from the arrival order.

The simulator used to obtain the results of this section is similar to that described in Section II, in that the assumption of independent sync periods is not used. However, two changes were made to reflect the effect of disk scheduling. First, when selecting the next request to service, the simulator chooses a request at random from among those in queue, rather than choosing the request at the "head" of the queue. This effectively reduces the average waiting time for read requests that are serviced during part of the delay cycle, since read requests that arrive behind write requests can "jump ahead" of these writes. Second, the service time distribution is no longer static; instead, the number of other requests in queue when a request is serviced is used to adjust the mean service time. This models the ability of the disk scheduler to reduce the average service time under load.

Despite differences in their particulars, all disk scheduling disciplines produce similar effects. At low load, scheduling has little or no effect and the service time seen by requests is similar to that seen with FCFS scheduling. As the load increases the average service time drops, since with a larger number of requests in queue the opportunity for optimization grows. At some (high) load the service time approaches a limiting value where seek time and/or rotational latency approach zero. With some disciplines, this limiting value is the time required to transfer the requested data, while in others the limiting value includes rotational latency.

Disk service time consists of a load-independent part, representing transfer, setup, and/or rotational delays, and a load-dependent part, representing seek and/or rotational delays. The load-dependent part of the service time is most evident at low loads, asymptotically approaching zero, on average, at high loads. In this section we model the average disk service time with an exponential function which decays as the load grows large. Although there is no evidence in the literature to either support or reject the use of an exponential function in preference to some other function with similar properties, this function allows the investigation of a continuum of decay rates by varying a single parameter.

The mean service time as seen by an arriving request is modeled as

$$\bar{s}(n) = \alpha \bar{s} + (1 - \alpha)\bar{s}e^{-kn}$$

where α, $0 \leq \alpha \leq 1$, describes the fraction of the service time that is load-independent, n is the number of requests in the system (not counting the new arrival), and k is a parameter that describes the decay rate achieved by the disk scheduling discipline. For some physical systems such as that described in [13], α is small, approximately 0.07, while for others α can be over 0.5 [16]. An intermediate value of approximately $1/3$ as reported in [4] is used in this discussion.

Choosing a value of k to use in the simulations is problematic, since it depends on both disk access patterns and the scheduling policy. One possibility is to examine an empirical curve of either utilization (typically defined for disk scheduling studies as the ratio of transfer time to the sum of transfer, seek, and rotation times) or service time as a function of queue length, finding the queue length n that provides a certain reduction, say 50%, of the load-dependent part of the service time. Let this value of n be n_{50}. Then the value of k which describes this discipline for a particular access pattern is $-\ln(0.5)/n_{50}$. From this point on we will use n_{50} in preference to k, since it has an intuitive meaning that k lacks.

The futility of choosing a particular value for n_{50} is illustrated by the results of two studies of disk scheduling. In one, n_{50} for the shortest-seek-time-first (SSTF) discipline is approximately 10 [16], while in another, n_{50} for the same

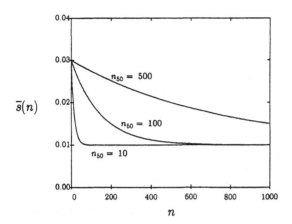

Fig. 7. Average service time $\bar{s}(n)$ (s) versus queue length for three different combinations of disk scheduling discipline and reference pattern: $n_{50} = 10,\ 100,\ 500$. In all disciplines, $\alpha = 1/3$, $\bar{s} = 0.030$, $\bar{s}(n_{50}) = 0.020$, $\alpha\bar{s} = 0.010$.

discipline is well over 1000 [13]. The reason for this disparity is that the performance of a disk scheduling policy is highly dependent on disk access patterns and disk geometry. In this study we concede that it is not possible to attach a particular value of n_{50} to a particular scheduling discipline, and vary n_{50} as a parameter. Fig. 7 shows the modeled mean service time as a function of load for various values of n_{50}.

The results were obtained using a three-stage Erlang service time distribution as in Section II. For each arriving request, $\bar{s}(n)$ was computed based on the number of requests already in the queue, then a service time was generated from an Erlang distribution with mean $\bar{s}(n)$. As in Section II, the mean service time with no load $\bar{s}(0)$ was 30 ms, and the length of the update period T was 30 s.

Figs. 8 and 9 show simulation results for $\bar{R}_{\mathrm{PU}}$ as a function of n_{50} for low- and high-load conditions, respectively. In both cases, disk scheduling mitigates the effect of the write bulk, especially when n_{50} is small, while as n_{50} grows, $\bar{R}_{\mathrm{PU}}$ asymptotically approaches the value given by (3). This effect is not surprising, since disk scheduling is most effective at high loads and since the bulk write arrival provides an artificially high load.

On the other hand, the insensitivity of the minimum cache–hit ratio required for $\bar{R}_{\mathrm{PU}} \leq \bar{R}_{\mathrm{WT}}$ to scheduler performance is remarkable. Figs. 10 and 11 show curves representing different combinations of $h_w(30)$ and n_{50} that provide the same average response time for subsaturation WT loads. Note that the write loads in these two figures are process write loads and are different than those shown in Figs. 8 and 9. In each case, the response time chosen is $\bar{R}_{\mathrm{WT}}$ with load-independent service. Thus, Figs. 10 and 11 show combinations of $h_w(30)$ and n_{50} that allow the PU policy to provide read service equal to that achieved by the WT policy with no disk scheduling. If a pair $(h_w(30), n_{50})$ falls below the constant response time curve (for a particular load), then $\bar{R}_{\mathrm{PU}} > \bar{R}_{\mathrm{WT}}$. Both graphs indicate that unless strict requirements are met, the WT policy with FCFS service provides lower average response time for read requests.

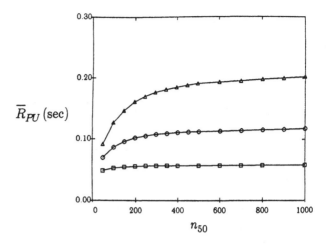

Fig. 8. Read response time as a function of disk scheduler performance: $\bar{R}_{\mathrm{PU}}$ (s) versus n_{50}; low load conditions. Note that as the independent variable n_{50} grows, the scheduler effectiveness diminishes. Curves are linearly interpolated between marked simulation points. $\bigcirc$: $\rho_r = 0.10, \rho_w = 0.10$; $\square$: $\rho_r = 0.15, \rho_w = 0.05$; $\triangle$: $\rho_r = 0.05, \rho_w = 0.15$.

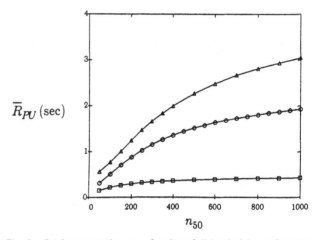

Fig. 9. Read response time as a function of disk scheduler performance: $\bar{R}_{\mathrm{PU}}$ (s) versus n_{50}; high load conditions. Curves are linearly interpolated between marked simulation points. $\bigcirc$: $\rho_r = 0.40, \rho_w = 0.40$; $\square$: $\rho_r = 0.70, \rho_w = 0.10$; $\triangle$: $\rho_r = 0.10, \rho_w = 0.70$.

In Fig. 10 the required hit ratio approaches its limit (shown in Table I) quickly. Thus scheduling does little to alleviate the need for a high cache–hit ratio. In Fig. 11, which represents higher load conditions, the required hit ratio approaches its limit somewhat more slowly, and for very effective scheduling schemes, the minimum hit ratio requirements are diminished. However, even for the high combined traffic intensity shown ($\rho_r + \rho_w = 0.8$), the scheduler must achieve at least $n_{50} = 200$ requests before the required hit ratio is significantly reduced.

For loads that would saturate the system using the WT policy, scheduling has the effect of reducing the minimum hit ratio required for stability using the PU policy. Although this effect is not quantified, it seems qualitatively clear that the PU policy can benefit substantially from disk scheduling at such high loads. However, it must be noted that the response time in such a situation is finite, but is not necessarily acceptable.

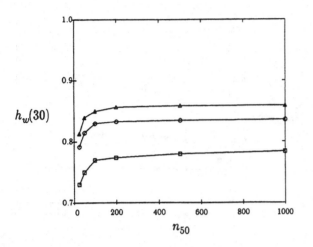

Fig. 10. Combinations of the write–hit ratio and scheduler performance that provide constant read response time: $h_w(30)$ versus n_{50} for constant $\bar{R}_{PU}$. $\rho_r + \rho_W = 0.2$. $\bar{R}_{PU} = \bar{R}_{WT} = 0.035$ s. Curves are linearly interpolated between marked simulation points. $\bigcirc$: $\rho_r = 0.10$. $\rho_w = 0.10$: $\square$: $\rho_r = 0.15$. $\rho_w = 0.05$: $\triangle$: $\rho_r = 0.05$. $\rho_w = 0.15$

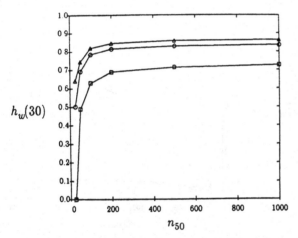

Fig. 11. Combinations of the write-hit ratio and scheduler performance that provide constant read response time: $h_w(30)$ versus n_{50} for constant $\bar{R}_{PU}$. $\rho_r + \rho_W = 0.8$. $\bar{R}_{PU} = \bar{R}_{WT} = 0.110$ s. Curves are linearly interpolated between marked simulation points. $\bigcirc$: $\rho_r = 0.40$. $\rho_w = 0.40$: $\square$: $\rho_r = 0.70$. $\rho_w = 0.10$: $\triangle$: $\rho_r = 0.10$. $\rho_w = 0.70$.

VI. Discussion

The results presented so far indicate that, given the assumptions, the performance envelope of the PU policy is narrow, and that outside this envelope the PU policy performs worse than the WT policy or causes the disk system to saturate. We believe that these results are broadly applicable, and that in general the PU policy should be avoided. However, given that these results contradict the prevailing intuition about the PU policy, it is appropriate to consider the effects of these assumptions and to discuss situations in which the assumptions may not be applicable.

The use of a stationary Poisson arrival process for read operations is reasonable for large systems, since the aggregate behavior of a sufficiently large number of merged, arbitrary arrival processes is indistinguishable from that of a single Poisson process [9]. For small systems this assumption might be violated in two ways. First, the mean might not be stationary; with a finite process population the blocking of individual processes causes the aggregate read rate to diminish. This effectively makes the delay cycle shorter and mitigates the performance of the PU policy. Second, the read operations may arrive according to a process that is "burstier" than the Poisson process.

Qualitatively, an extremely "bursty" read arrival process tends to mitigate the performance of the PU policy, compared to the WT policy, with FCFS service. When the system functions as a simple server with sporadic traffic, bursty arrivals lengthen the average response time. The delay cycle analysis, however, remains similar as long as the average number arrivals during an interval is proportional to the length of the interval. Response time is increased at all times using the WT policy, and outside the delay cycle using the PU policy. Thus bursty arrivals affect the WT policy more than the PU policy. When disk scheduling is used, individual requests in a bulk arrival generally receive faster service with both write policies. However, it would appear that disk scheduling remains more effective with the PU policy than with the WT policy.

Less important is the assumption of a Poisson write process, since the behavior of the process is only observed every T s in the PU policy. In fact, as long as the average number of writes arriving during the update period is proportional to T, the behavior predicted by the model remains similar. Thus, for example, a bulk write process that delivers groups of writes during the update period is nearly indistinguishable in the model from one that delivers fewer writes at once, but more frequently.

An assumption that affects the interpretation of the results is that cache replacement traffic is ignored. With a small disk cache, the probability that a read request causes a dirty block to be replaced may not be negligible. In the model this has the effect of decreasing the read–hit ratio, since all synchronous traffic is considered "read" traffic. Likewise, replacement traffic effectively increases the write–hit ratio, since fewer blocks are presented as part of the bulk write at the sync pulse. Thus if two systems have the same process workload, then the one with the smaller disk cache will experience less performance degradation *by the PU policy*. Overall, however, the system with the smaller cache may provide a higher average read response time due to its lower read–hit ratio. Quantifying this effect is beyond the scope of this paper.

Finally, it must be noted that the PU policy does not cause a substantial performance penalty in systems that are very lightly loaded. The effect of a low write load can be readily seen in Table I, for example, where the minimum write hit ratio for $\bar{R}_{PU} \leq \bar{R}_{WT}$ diminishes for a high read load and low write load. Even with a low read load and a low write load, the PU policy may perform worse than the WT policy, and yet the net effect may be negligible. This reflects the intuitive idea that when the I/O load is light, the choice of disk cache write policy is of little consequence.

VII. ALTERNATE WRITE POLICIES

The primary argument in favor of the PU cache write policy over one that delays writes until replacement is the need for file system integrity. Although the PU policy does not provide any real guarantee of integrity, it does ensure that the cache and the on-disk copy of the file system are never "too far" out of date. In this light, it seems reasonable to consider alternatives which provide similar write rates and preserve the minimal consistency properties of the PU policy.

One possibility is to use the WT policy with all writes operating asynchronously. Although this policy generates more disk traffic than the PU policy, for subsaturation loads it imposes an apparently smaller load on the I/O system from the point of view of read operations. However, the WT policy saturates at a lower load than write policies that take advantage of the cache.

As previously described, the WT policy behaves as an M/G/1 server, with a combined load $\rho_r + \rho_W$. Thus

$$\bar{R}_{\text{WT}} = \bar{s} + \frac{(\rho_r + \rho_W)\bar{s}(1 + C_s^2)}{2(1 - \rho_r - \rho_W)}.$$

A more attractive alternative is the "periodic update with read priority" (PURP) policy, in which nonpreemptive priority is given to read operations. The read and write arrival rates to the disk system are the same as in the PU policy: reads arrive according to a Poisson process with rate λ_r, and, on average, $\lambda_w T$ writes arrive at each sync pulse. With FCFS disk service the average response time for read operations is readily derived from results in [8] for a two-class priority queueing system:

$$\bar{R}_{\text{PURP}} = \bar{s} + \frac{(\rho_r + \rho_w)\bar{s}(1 + C_s^2)}{2(1 - \rho_r)}.$$

Note that the average response time for read operations is dependent on the write load, but is independent of the write arrival process. Thus the fact that write operations arrive in bulk does not adversely affect read response time. Further, read response time becomes infinite only if the read traffic intensity is unity; write operations cannot saturate the system.

The PURP policy preserves the principal advantage of the PU policy: reduced write traffic due to cache hits. The PURP policy is easily implemented on systems that already use the PU policy: a simple change to the disk scheduling discipline is required. However, like any fixed-priority scheduling discipline, the PURP policy introduces the theoretical possibility of indefinite postponement of low-priority (write) operations. Additionally, under heavy write load, the PURP policy may compromise the ability of the disk scheduler to reduce service time, since the service sequence is partially determined by the priority scheme.

A third alternative is the "individual periodic update" (IPU) policy. This policy, like the PU policy, accommodates write traffic that would saturate a system using the WT policy. In the IPU policy, write operations are delayed for a fixed interval T on an individual basis, rather than being presented to the disk system in bulk. On a write cache miss or a write to a clean cache block, the corresponding disk write is scheduled to occur after T s. On a write cache hit to a dirty block, data in the cache are modified, but the scheduled physical write

is unaffected. This policy provides the same cache write–hit ratio as the PU policy; thus traffic is reduced and the effect of the bulk write arrival at the sync pulse is avoided. With FCFS disk service, the system behaves as an M/G/1 server with a combined arrival rate $\lambda_r + \lambda_w$ so that the average read response time is

$$\bar{R}_{\text{IPU}} = \bar{s} + \frac{(\rho_r + \rho_w)\bar{s}(1 + C_s^2)}{2(1 - \rho_r - \rho_w)}.$$

The IPU policy avoids the problem of write starvation introduced by the PURP policy and allows the disk scheduler to reorder requests arbitrarily to reduce service time. However, this policy is slightly more difficult to implement. Essentially, a queue of disk update requests ordered by update time is maintained. At each "tick" of the system clock, the queue is consulted and physical write operations are delivered to the disk system. The overhead for the IPU policy is primarily one of space to maintain the queue; UNIX, for example, maintains a similar "callout" queue with very little CPU overhead [2].

The IPU and PURP policies never provide a higher read response time than either the PU or WT policy. When the cache write–hit ratio is zero, $\rho_w = \rho_W$, and the IPU policy degenerates to WT. The PURP policy, on the other hand, does not allow write operations to saturate the disk system. Even when the write–hit ratio is zero, the PURP policy provides a lower read response time than the WT policy. Both policies avoid the "traffic jam" effect of the PU policy, while providing the benefit of cache hits for write operations.

VIII. CONCLUSIONS

Whether or not disk scheduling is used, the performance requirements for caches using the PU policy are demanding. If a sufficiently high write–hit ratio is achieved, the PU policy can avoid saturation when the process write rate exceeds the disk service rate. For subsaturation loads, PU policy must achieve a high write–hit ratio before it offers better performance than the trivial WT policy. The latter result came as a surprise, because the PU policy provides the benefit of cache hits, while the WT policy does not. This study shows that how write requests are presented to the disk system (sporadically or in bulk) is more important than the write request rate if read response time is the most important performance metric.

A number of factors were not considered in this study, because their effects were either obvious or of secondary importance. The update period T, for example, was not varied for load-dependent service, since it appears that its behavior is similar to that shown for load-independent service. Likewise, α, the parameter that describes the access time properties of a particular physical I/O system, was not varied; the effect of making α smaller is to give disk scheduling a better opportunity to reduce access time. Given the substantial difference in mean response times between the PU and WT policies, it seemed unnecessary to study the variance in read response times, particularly since it is intuitively clear that the variance is higher with the PU policy.

The results presented in this study provide a comprehensive set of design guidelines that capture the complex relationship between cache write policy, the cache–hit ratio, and disk scheduler performance. In particular, the analytic model presented in Sections II–IV can be used to find the performance of systems that use the PU policy, and to derive requirements for cache performance. The simulation results presented in Section V give a clear picture of the relationship between the performance of scheduling policies and the required cache write–hit ratio. For a particular set of parameters the simulation methodology of Section V can be used to find a specific set of design requirements for a caching system.

The PU policy is one that performs well over a narrow range of operating conditions. If the system's workload consists largely of read operations, then the PU policy can perform competitively. Likewise, if the cache write–hit ratio is high and the disk scheduler is able to reduce service time sharply as a function of load, then the PU policy is preferred over the WT policy. Outside this envelope the performance of the PU policy degrades rapidly. In view of the continual evolutionary changes in trade-offs between CPU speed, memory size, and disk performance, it makes sense to use more robust policies such as the PURP and IPU policies described in Section VII. These policies retain the ability of PU to operate at loads which would saturate the disk system with the WT policy, while avoiding the effects of the bulk write arrivals generated by the PU policy.

REFERENCES

[1] *The UNIX Programmer's Manual*, vol. I.   New York: Holt, Rinehart, & Winston, 1983, 394pp.
[2] M. J. Bach, *The Design of the UNIX Operating System.*   Englewood Cliffs, NJ: Prentice-Hall, 1986.
[3] A. Braunstein, M. Riley, and J. Wilkes, "Improving the efficiency of UNIX file buffer caches," in *Proc. 12th ACM SOSP*, Dec. 1989, pp. 71–82.
[4] S. D. Carson, "Experimental performance evaluation of the Berkeley file system," Dept. Computer Sci., Univ. Maryland, College Park, Tech. Rep. CS-TR-2387, Jan. 1990.
[5] R. Geist and S. Daniel, "A continuum of disk scheduling algorithms," *ACM Trans. Comput. Syst.*, vol. 5, no. 1, pp. 77–92, Feb. 1987.
[6] M. Hofri, "Disk scheduling: FCFS versus SSTF revisited," *Commun. ACM*, vol. 23, no. 11, pp. 645–653, Nov. 1980.
[7] T. D. Johnson, J. M. Smith, and E. S. Wilson, "Disk response time measurements," in *Proc. Winter 1987 USENIX Conf.USENIX Assn.*, (Berkeley, CA), Jan. 1987, pp. 147–162.
[8] L. Kleinrock, *Queueing Systems*, vol. II: *Computer Applications.*   New York: Wiley, 1976.
[9] L. Kleinrock, *Queueing Systems*, vol. I: *Theory.*   New York: Wiley, 1975.
[10] M. N. Nelson, B. B. Welch, and J. K. Ousterhout, "Caching in the Sprite network file system," *ACM Trans. Comput. Syst.*, vol. 6, no. 1, pp. 134–154, Feb. 1988.
[11] J. K. Ousterhout *et al.*, "A trace-driven analysis of the UNIX 4.2 BSD file system," in *Proc. 10th ACM SOSP*, Dec. 1985, pp. 15–24.
[12] D. M. Ritchie, "The UNIX I/O System," in *The UNIX Programmer's Manual*, vol. II.   New York: Holt, Rinehart, & Winston, 1983, pp. 522–528.
[13] M. Seltzer, P. Chen, and J. Ousterhout, "Disk scheduling revisited," in *Proc. Winter 1990 USENIX Conf. USENIX Assn.* (Berkeley, CA), Jan. 1990, pp. 313–324.
[14] A. J. Smith, "Disk cache–miss ratio analysis and design considerations," *ACM Trans. Comput. Syst.*, vol. 3, no. 3, pp. 161–203, Aug. 1985.
[15] V. Srinivasan and J. Mogul, "Spritely NFS: experiments with cache-consistency protocols," in *Proc. 12th ACM SOSP*, Dec. 1989, pp. 45–57.
[16] T. J. Teorey and T. B. Pinkerton, "A comparative analysis of disk scheduling policies," *Commun. ACM*, vol. 15, no. 3, pp. 177–184, Mar. 1972.
[17] K. Thompson, "UNIX implementation," *Bell System Techn. J.*, vol. 57, no. 6, pp. 1931–1946, July-Aug. 1978.
[18] P. Vongsathorn and S. D. Carson, "A system for adaptive disk rearrangement," *Software Pract. Exper.*, vol. 20, no. 3, pp. 225–242, Mar. 1990.

Models of DASD Subsystems with Multiple Access Paths: A Throughput-Driven Approach

ALEXANDRE BRANDWAJN

Abstract—A throughput-driven approach to the performance analysis of direct access storage devices (DASD's), i.e., disks, is presented for a model of a block-multiplexor channel system with multiple transfer paths. The approach relies on a step-wise analysis of shared components within the data transfer path: head of string, control unit, channel, referred to as blocking points. In order to derive the service time of an I/O request, each blocking point is analyzed separately, using essentially a classical loss-system model. The advantages of the method are its relative simplicity and applicability to a large number of configurations. Transient and boundary effects, including the miss probability on second and subsequent reconnection attempts, and the device reconnection window (lead time), are also discussed. The inclusion of the approach in a larger system model, as well as its relationship with previous work on DASD analysis is considered. Numerical results illustrate the accuracy of the method.

Index Terms—Analytical models, block-multiplexor channels, disk subsystems, dual ports, missed reconnections, multiple transfer paths, reconnection window, shared control units, string switching, system model.

I. Introduction

IN a previous paper [3], we have presented one approach to the modeling of direct access storage device (DASD) subsystems. This approach, designed for use with the equivalence method of analysis of queueing models, results in a solution of a set of submodels, and computes the I/O request throughput as a primary performance measure. By design, it is well suited for use in a larger system model. A drawback of this approach, however, is that the number of times the submodels have to be evaluated grows with the number of users in the system. Another drawback is that extensions to other configurations may be difficult.

In this paper we propose a different approach, with different advantages and drawbacks. The approach takes the I/O request throughput as a starting point, and derives the DASD (disk) basic service time pertaining to the given throughput. By definition, the basic I/O service time is taken here to denote the average time it takes to service an I/O request from the moment it has been successfully issued. The total I/O service time is the the average time it takes to service an I/O request from the moment the CPU first attempts to issue it. The difference between the total and the basic time is viewed as a queueing delay. Having obtained the basic service time we

estimate to total I/O service time by viewing the devices as separate single-server queues.

With block-multiplexor channels—the only type considered herein—three elements in the data path between the CPU and the DASD may be shared by spindles. Devices are configured into strings where all the disks on a string may be simultaneously moving arms to the appropriate track (seek) or waiting for the read/write heads to reach the required angular position (latency). However, in most systems, only one disk may be transferring using the necessary hardware within the head of string. Several such strings may be connected to a single control unit, and several control units may share a single channel. Also, several channels may be linked to the same control unit, resulting in a more or less complex configuration. All three elements, viz. head of string, control unit and channel, are potential blocking points in that they must be available at the moment a device is about to reach the correct angular position in order for the disk to reconnect successfully and start transferring. Should any of the elements be busy with another device, a missed reconnection occurs, and the I/O request experiences the heavy penalty of a full rotation period before another reconnection attempt is possible.

In this paper, we neglect the dependence of the seek time on the load, and concentrate on missed reconnections as the principal load-dependent component of the I/O request basic service time. Each blocking point is studied separately, so that the approach taken copes easily with multiple blocking points as encountered in more complex configurations. The analysis is introduced for a model with multiple data transfer paths in control units and strings of disks. This provides a framework for modelling both existing and possibly forthcoming products.

In the next section, this approach is presented for a simplified case with balanced I/O rates and utilizations. Transient and boundary effects, such as nongeometrical distribution of the number of missed reconnections, or effect of the reconnection window (disk lead time), are also discussed in this section. Application of the approach to present-day configurations with shared channels, shared strings (string switching), and disks with dual ports (cross-call) is considered in Section III. The relationship of the method with other approaches to DASD analysis [2], [17], [10] is also discussed. Section IV briefly considers the embedding of the solution of a DASD subsystem model in that of a larger system model. Using a simple example of a DASD subsystem, a comparison of the results of the method of this paper and of [3] is presented. Finally, Section V summarizes the advantages and the drawbacks of the method.

Manuscript received March 2, 1981; revised December 21, 1981, and June 30, 1982.

The author is with the Amdahl Corporation, 1250 East Arques Avenue, Sunnyvale, CA 94086.

II. MULTIPLE ACCESS PATHS

A. Configuration Considered and Assumptions

To introduce our approach, we consider a hypothetical DASD subsystem in which every channel is connected to only one control unit, and a control unit has N_c channels connected to it. For our purpose in this section, it is irrelevant whether these channels belong to a single CPU or different CPU's. We assume that a control unit has N_r independent nondedicated data transfer paths, henceforth referred to as *routes*. We also assume that there are N_s strings of DASD's connected to the storage director, and that within every string there are N_p independent nondedicated data transfer paths shared by the disks on the string. These access paths within a string will be henceforth referred to as *paths*. For simplicity, we assume that there are N_d devices in every string attached to the control unit.

A sample configuration of a control unit is represented in Fig. 1. The control unit shown has four channels connected to it. It possesses two routes, and the single string of DASD's attached to it has two paths. Thus, a maximum of two devices may be simultaneously engaged in transfer in this example.

It is now our goal to analyze the hypothetical DASD subsystem so as to assess the impact of multiple routes and multiple paths on the I/O service time. We view the total I/O service time of a DASD as composed of the elements represented below.

Queueing	Seek	Latency	Missed Reconnection Delay	Transfer

Basic I/O Service Time

The seek time corresponds to arm movement until the correct track is reached. The latency is the time for the device to reach the required angular position in its rotation. The missed reconnection delay is that part of the basic I/O service time due to the disk finding the I/O path busy when the appropriated sector is about to be reached.

Referring to the given control unit, we denote by t_s, t_l, t_m, and t_t the average seek, latency, missed reconnection delay, and transfer time, respectively. The device rotation period is denoted by t_r.

We proceed to evaluate the basic I/O service time under the following assumptions.

1) All I/O requests are statistically identical, and are evenly distributed over channels and devices. This assumption is for exposition purposes only, and is relaxed in [4].

2) The dependence of the seek time on the load is not represented. A separate model of arm movement would have to be added if such a contention were a dominant factor determining the performance of the DASD subsystem.

3) Elongations in the basic I/O service time due to the I/O path being busy when a CPU attempts to issue the I/O request (redriven I/O's) or after the completion of a seek when the target angular position has to be forwarded to the device, are neglected.

4) The operation of count-key-data devices is implicitly represented by the transfer time. The latter, for count-key-data

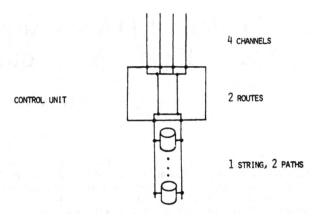

Fig. 1. A sample configuration with multiple paths and routes.

devices, is taken to include the search operation during which a key match is sought.

Additional assumptions, and departures from the above ones, are explicitly indicated where appropriate.

B. Analysis of Blocking Points

In this section we analyze the state of the data transfer path encountered by a device reconnection request. The following principal notations are used in this section.

N_d: number of DASD's (actuators) in a string.

N_s: number of strings connected to the control unit.

N_p^*: maximum number of paths which may be simultaneously active within a string.

N_r^*: maximum number of routes which may be simultaneously active at the control unit.

N_h^*: maximum total number of paths requesting reconnection to the control unit.

θ: I/O throughput of the control unit.

θ_s: I/O throughput of a string of DASD's.

λ_p: $1/\lambda_p$ is the average time between consecutive reconnection requests from a DASD not engaged in transfer.

λ_r: $1/\lambda_r$ is the average time between consecutive reconnection requests from an idle path in a string.

μ_p: rate of transfer completions of an active string path.

μ_r: rate of transfer completions of an active control unit route.

a_j: probability that an arriving device reconnection request finds the appropriate I/O path available given that j paths are found active at the device's string.

b_k: probability that the channel requested by the control unit is found available given that k routes are already busy at the control unit.

$p_s(j)$: stationary probability that j paths are busy at a string, $j = 0, \cdots, N_p^*$.

$P_s(j)$: steady-state probability that a DASD requesting reconnection finds j paths busy within its string.

$p_r(k)$: stationary probability that a k routes are busy at the control unit, $k = 0, \cdots, N_r^*$.

$P_r(k)$: probability that a reconnection request from a string finds k routes busy at the control unit.

Consider a control unit of the hypothetical DASD subsystem, and denote by θ its I/O throughput (i.e., the average number of I/O requests completed per unit time). θ is assumed to be known and is the basis for the following analysis. In order to evaluate the probability of a missed reconnection, we consider blocking points separately, starting from string paths, and moving towards the CPU. We thus most naturally follow a reconnection request as it makes its way through the I/O path. Each blocking point is viewed as a simple loss system [6]. The dependence between blocking points is taken into account via appropriate activation rates for the resources of the blocking point.

Denote also by N_r^* the maximum number of routes within the control unit that may be simultaneously engaged in transfer. We have

$$N_r^* = \min(N_r, N_c, N_s \cdot \min(N_p, N_d)).$$

Let N_p^* be the maximum number of paths within a string of DASD's which may be simultaneously transferring. We have

$$N_p^* = \min(N_r^*, N_p, N_d).$$

Having thus accounted for various awkward cases where more hardware is provided than can be actually utilized, we proceed to the analysis of the missed reconnection delay. We start with the paths at the head of string, and we denote by λ_p the rate of path reconnection requests issued by a DASD on the string, and by μ_p the rate of completions of transfers by a path. Neglecting overheads, we have $\mu_p \simeq 1/t_t$. We make the additional assumption that the path reconnection requests from a disk constitute a Poisson process. With this assumption, the equilibrium probability that j paths are simultaneously busy at the string, denoted by $p_s(j)$, is given by (cf. [6])

$$p_s(j) = \frac{1}{G_s} \prod_{i=1}^{j} \lambda_p (N_d - i + 1) a_{i-1}/(i\mu_p), \qquad (2.1)$$
$$j = 0, \cdots, N_p^*,$$

where G_s is a normalization constant, and a_j is, by definition, the probability that all other necessary elements of the I/O path (route and appropriate channel) are found available by a device requesting reconnection given that j paths are active at that string.

Let $P_s(j)$ be the steady-state probability that a DASD requesting reconnection finds j paths busy within its string. The number of reconnection requests which arrive per unit time to find such a situation is simply $(N_d - j)\lambda_p p_s(j)$. Hence,

$$P_s(j) = \frac{(N_d - j)p_s(j)}{\sum\limits_{k=0}^{N_p^*} (N_d - k)p_s(k)}, \qquad j = 0, \cdots, N_p^*. \qquad (2.2)$$

Note that (2.1) and (2.2) are valid regardless of the distribution of path busy times (see, e.g., [6]). Note also that, in order for these expressions to be useful, we must know the probability a_j and the request rate for a single device λ_p. Suppose for the moment that a_j is known. λ_p can be determined as follows. Let θ_s be the I/O throughput of the given string of DASD's. With balanced load distribution, as assumed herein, $\theta_s = \theta/N_s$. We have under equilibrium

$$\sum_{j=1}^{N_p^*} p_s(j) j\mu_p = \theta_s. \qquad (2.3)$$

Using (2.1) in (2.3) we obtain the following polynomial equation for the rate of reconnection requests λ_p

$$\sum_{j=1}^{N_p^*} \rho_p^j \left[\prod_{i=1}^{j} (N_d - i + 1)a_{i-1}/i \right](j - \rho_s) - \rho_s = 0 \qquad (2.4)$$

where

$$\rho_p = \lambda_p/\mu_p \quad \text{and} \quad \rho_s = \theta_s/\mu_p.$$

Formula (2.4) is a low degree polynomial equation so that its solution for ρ_p (and hence λ_p) may be obtined by any standard method. We note that the rate of reconnection requests from a device cannot be lower than its rate of successful reconnections

$$\rho_p \geq \rho_s/N_d.$$

Therefore, a simple bisection over the interval, say, $(\rho_s/N_d, 10\rho_s/N_d)$ has been found a satisfactory approach to the solution of (2.4).

a_i, the probability of finding a route and the appropriate channel available given that j devices are transferring at the string, is obtained by analyzing the two blocking points routes and channels. Let $p_r(k)$ be the steady-state probability that k routes are active, $k = 0, \cdots, N_r^*$. We now view the paths (at the heads of string) as sources of requests for routes. The number of such sources is denoted by N_h and is given by

$$N_h = N_s \cdot \min(N_p, N_d).$$

Denote by μ_r the rate of transfer completions for an active route. Neglecting overheads, we have $\mu_r = 1/t_t$. We make the assumption that the requests issued by each of the N_h sources constitute a Poisson process, and we denote by λ_r the corresponding rate. With this assumption $p_r(k)$ is simply given by

$$p_r(k) = \frac{1}{G_r} \prod_{i=1}^{k} \lambda_r (N_h - i + 1)b_{i-1}/(i\mu_r), \qquad (2.5)$$
$$k = 0, \cdots, N_r^*$$

where G_r is a normalization constant, and b_k is the probability that the appropriate channel is found available by a route request which is issued when k routes are already busy. Let $P_r(k)$ be the probability that a route request finds k routes engaged in transfer. The number of route requests arriving per unit time to find k routes busy is $(N_h - k)\lambda_r p_r(k)$. Hence,

$$P_r(k) = \frac{(N_h - k)p_r(k)}{\sum\limits_{j=0}^{N_r^*} (N_h - j)p_r(j)}, \qquad k = 0, \cdots, N_r^*. \qquad (2.6)$$

As before, in order for the above formula to be usable, we have to know the probabilities b_k and the request rate λ_r. Suppose b_k is known. λ_r may then be determined as follows. The I/O throughput handled by the set of routes is, of course, the total throughput of the control unit θ. Thus

$$\sum_{k=1}^{N_r^*} p_r(k)k\mu_r = \theta. \qquad (2.7)$$

Substituting (2.5) in (2.6) we get the following polynomial equation for the rate of route requests λ_r

$$\sum_{k=1}^{N_r^*} \rho_r^k \left[\prod_{i=1}^{k} (N_h - i + 1)b_{i-1}/i \right](k - \rho) - \rho = 0 \qquad (2.8)$$

where $\rho_r = \lambda_r/\mu_r$, and $\rho = \theta/\mu_r$. Since we must have

$$\rho \geq \rho/N_h,$$

formula (2.8) may be easily solved for ρ_r by simple bisection over the interval, say, $(\rho/N_h, 10\rho/N_h)$.

Assuming requests for channels from routes arrive at random with respect to the status of the appropriate channel, we readily obtain

$$b_k = 1 - k/N_c. \qquad (2.9)$$

This completes the analysis of the routes and channels, and allows us to determine a_j, the probability of finding a route and the required channel available given that j paths are busy at a string. Denote by $M(j)$ the maximum number of routes which may be simultaneously engaged in transfer when j paths are busy at the tagged string. We have

$$M(j) = \min (N_r^*, (N_s - 1) \cdot N_p + j).$$

Let $N(j)$ be the maximum number of routes which may be found active while still leaving at least one useful route available with j paths busy at the string. $N(j)$ is given by

$$N(j) = \min (N_r^* - 1, (N_s - 1) \cdot N_p + j).$$

a_j is then simply

$$a_j = \sum_{k=j}^{N(j)} P_r(k)b_k \bigg/ \sum_{k=j}^{M(j)} P_r(k). \qquad (2.10)$$

Having determined all the elements necessary to compute the state probabilities of the blocking points as seen by arriving reconnection requests, we are now ready to evaluate the probability of a missed DASD reconnection. The latter occurs if all the paths at the string are found busy, or if, at least one path being available, the remaining part of the I/O path (routes, appropriate channel) is found busy. Let p_{m_1} be the corresponding probability. We have

$$p_{m_1} = \dot{P}_s(N_p^*) + \sum_{j=0}^{N_p^*-1} P_s(j)(1 - a_j),$$

which may be rewritten as

$$p_{m_1} = 1 - \sum_{j=0}^{N_p^*-1} P_s(j)a_j. \qquad (2.11)$$

Hence, denoting the average number of missed reconnections per successful I/O request by n_m, we obtain, as a first approximation,

$$n_m \simeq n_{m_1} \triangleq p_{m_1}/(1 - p_{m_1}), \qquad (2.12)$$

and the missed reconnection delay is

$$t_m = t_r n_m.$$

Denoting by W_b the basic I/O service time, we have

$$W_b = t_s + t_l + t_m + t_t. \qquad (2.13)$$

Note that in our analysis string paths and control unit routes are taken to be nondedicated in the sense that any path and route available. Channels, however, are assumed to be conventional, and an I/O initiated on a given channel is bound to that channel until completion. If this were not the case, i.e., if the channels were "floating," we would simply have $b_k = 1$, $k = 0, \cdots, N_r^* - 1$.

We now recap the solution procedure, moving backwards as necessary in actual computation. First, the probabilities b_k are computed. Then, (2.8) is solved, and $p_r(k)$ and $P_r(k)$ are computed from (2.5) and (2.6), respectively. Next, a_j is obtained from (2.10) and used in the solution of (2.4) to compute $p_s(j)$ and $P_s(j)$ from (2.1) and (2.2), respectively. Finally, (2.11) is used to evaluate p_{m_1}. Note that from (2.11) one can easily compute the probability that a missed reconnection is caused by a given blocking point.

We have not investigated theoretically the uniqueness of the solution of the polynomial equations (2.4) and (2.8). On intuitive grounds, one would expect the I/O throughput to be a nondecreasing function of the rate of reconnection requests, and those two equations to possess a unique solution in the feasible region. In practice, in the many cases considered, the bisection has never failed to produce a solution.

C. Transient and Boundary Effects

In this section we take a brief look at a few phenomena which can affect the missed reconnection probability. The first such an effect is the nongeometrical distribution of the number of missed reconnections per transfer.

1) Correction for Missed Reconnection Probability: Our analysis of blocking points assumes that reconnection requests arrive with individual intensity independent of the status of the blocking point. This assumption of randomness is usually justified for a first reconnection attempt after initial positioning (cf. Section II-C2). It is recognized in the literature (e.g., [2], [17]) that subsequent reconnection attempts experience higher miss probabilities. Various explanations, such as disks "getting out of sync" or requests experiencing higher than average congestion spike, have been advanced for this phenomenon, and mostly empirical corrections for the miss probability have been proposed [2], [17].

We think that it is possible to view this phenomenon as a transient probability effect. For simplicity, consider a system with a single blocking point, such as one string of disks connected to a single channel. We shall refer to this blocking point as the unit. Consider also a reconnection request having experienced a first miss, i.e., having found the unit busy when the appropriate sector was reached. The next reconnection request from this device will come t_r time units later, after a full revolution of the disk. What this next request will "see" as unit busy probability is the transient probability of the unit being busy t_r time units after an initial busy condition, given that the requesting device is not contributing to the unit's utilization.

The miss probability obtained assuming that requests arrive at random with respect to the status of the unit is simply the stationary limit, independent of initial conditions, of this time-dependent probability. The importance of this transient effect must depend on the ratio of transfer to rotation times. If the rotation time is much greater than the transfer times, the transients should have dissipated and the reconnection request should "see" the stationary miss probability. If, on the other hand, the rotation period is short as compared to transfer times, transients should dominate. In the limit, with infinitely fast rotation speed, the probability of finding the unit busy again would be one.

Assume for the moment that transfer times follow the exponential distribution with mean t_t. Denote by q the probability that a transfer having caused a missed reconnection is still in progress after a full revolution. We have

$$q = \exp(-t_r/t_t). \qquad (2.14)$$

We propose to use q as an estimate for how fast the transients dissipate. Assuming that first reconnection requests do arrive at random, this yields for the probability of experiencing a missed reconnection on a second attempt

$$p_{m_2} \simeq q + (1 - q)p_{m_1}. \qquad (2.15)$$

With exponentially distributed transfers and Poisson request arrivals, subsequent attempts would experience the same miss probability as the second attempt. It is interesting to note that in a loss system with exponential service times and Poisson arrivals the probability that a request finds the unit busy again t_r time units after a previous busy condition is given by

$$p^{\cdot}_{m_2} = q^* + (1 - q^*)p_{m_1} \qquad (2.16)$$

where

$$q^* = \exp[-t_r/(t_t(1 - p_{m_1}))].$$

We believe this is a confirmation of our view of the phenomenon. In practice, (2.15) yields better results than (2.16), probably because the distributional assumptions under which (2.16) has been obtained are not met.

It has been noted in the literature [17], and confirmed by the author's observations (see the Appendix), that the average number of missed reconnections per transfer is fairly robust with respect to distributions of seeks and transfers. Hence, we use (2.15) also for nonexponentially distributed transfer times. Note that we are not implying that the higher miss probability on subsequent reconnection attempts is necessarily due to the same transfer that caused a previous miss. We simply use q as an estimate for the probability that the initially known busy condition is in effect after a full disk rotation. This approach, while still empirical, has the advantage of incorporating the dependence on the device revolution period.

From (2.15) one readily obtains for the overall miss probability, denoted by p_m,

$$p_m = p_{m_1}/(1 - p_{m_2} + p_{m_1}),$$

which may be rewritten as

$$p_m = p_{m_1}/[1 - q(1 - p_{m_1})]. \qquad (2.17)$$

From (2.17) we see that p_m is in general greater than p_{m_1}. The average number of missed reconnections per successful I/O requests is given by

$$n_m = p_m/(1 - p_m),$$

which may be expressed as

$$n_m = n_{m_1}/(1 - q) \qquad (2.18)$$

where $n_{m_1} = p_{m_1}/(1 - p_{m_1})$ is the average number of missed reconnections computed without the correction.

The average number of missed reconnections per successful I/O is thus expressed in terms of n_{m_1} and a simple corrective factor $1/(1 - q)$. It is apparent from (2.14) that the impact of this factor decreases rapidly with the ratio t_r/t_t.

2) First Reconnection Attempt: The second phenomenon, closely related to the one just discussed, concerns the miss probability experienced on a first reconnection attempt. As already mentioned, it is usually assumed [just as we did in (2.15)] that such an attempt arrives at random with respect to system state. This amounts to neglecting the fact that in most systems the I/O transfer path has to be free in order to forward the sector number to the device. In fact, the first attempt "sees" a transient unit busy probability after a latency time with an initial "path free" condition. The consensus to neglect the effects of command issuance seems to have originated from [16] where it is argued that commands have a negligible impact on total I/O time. We note that neglecting the fact that the path is free when the latency starts may result in considerable overestimation of the missed reconnection delay (the effect is more pronounced for fast spinning devices). An example is given in the Appendix. With this caveat, in the simulation results presented in the sequel, latency is allowed to start independently of the status of the I/O path. Hence, when comparing analytical results with simulation, we are assessing the accuracy of an approximate solution of a model of disk operation at a given level of abstraction. The adequacy of the level of abstraction itself can only be assessed through comparison with measurement results. (Note that the recently introduced IBM 3880 control unit can start the latency without a channel connection.)

3) Overheads and Reconnection Window: As a last point in this section, we note that in reality reconnection is requested some time (a few sectors) before the required sector is reached. This gives the time to the units within the transfer path to exchange appropriate signals. We refer to the interval between the moment reconnection is requested and the moment the correct sector is reached as the reconnection window. The latter seems to be on the order of 0.5 ms. For older disks and most applications this is negligible in comparison to the average transfer time. However, with higher transfer rates, and also for some important applications such as airlines seat reservation systems, the transfer times may be on the same order of magnitude as the reconnection window and other protocol overheads.

Note that through the use of different completion rates for various blocking points our model of Section II-B allows the inclusion of overheads for I/O path elements. While most overheads affect the missed reconnection delay by increasing the I/O path utilization "seen" by reconnection requests, the effect of the reconnection window appears more intricate.

It is clear that some load-dependent fraction of the reconnection window is added to the transfer time on every transfer, thus resulting in higher I/O path utilization than if the reconnection window was zero. In most systems, this higher utilization is apparent to a CPU attempting to initiate an I/O operation, and causes a correspondingly increased number of rejected I/O initiation attempts. The effect of the window on missed reconnections is more difficult to assess. As the window width increases, a disk requesting reconnection finds the unit busy more often at the beginning of the window. It has, however, a greater chance that the busy unit will become available within the window duration.

An analytical and simulation study of a single blocking point (see the Appendix for details) indicates that the reconnection window may have a considerable effect on I/O path utilizations, but little, if any, on missed reconnection probability. A practical conclusion from these results is that the reconnection window need not be included when evaluating missed reconnection delays. It has, however, to be taken into account, for small transfer times, to correctly assess I/O path utilizations and related quantities such as redriven I/O's. Our analytical model provides a good estimate of the average unit busy period, and hence utilization, for a system with a single blocking point.

D. Numerical Results

We have run a number of discrete-event simulations to check the accuracy of the analysis presented. As a whole, the agreement between analytical and simulation results for the number of missed reconnections per successful I/O is good. The accuracy of the analytical results tends to be excellent for medium and large transfer times (say, 8 ms and over), and slightly less so for shorter average transfer times. There is no systematic degradation of the accuracy of the results as the I/O rates are increased.

Fig. 2 shows an example of the results obtained for a configuration with three channels and three single-path strings of eight DASD's (actuators) each, connected a control unit with two routes. The device parameters indicated on the figure correspond to the IBM 3350 device with transfers of average length of 8 kbytes. The seek time has been arbitrarily set to 70 percent of the manufacturer specified average value, and thus corresponds to a situation where 30 percent of seeks find the arm already on track (zero seeks). Discrete-event simulation results have been given for comparison. The distributional assumptions used in this simulation run are: total of seek and latency—uniform, transfer—exponential. Each simulation point corresponds to 100 000 transfer completions. The agreement between analytical and simulation results is more than fair.

E. Total DASD Service Time

For completeness, we now consider the derivation of the total I/O service time. The approach used is essentially that of [2].

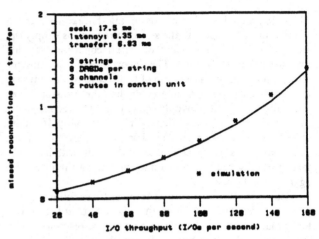

Fig. 2. Example of numerical results.

The total I/O service time for a DASD may be approximately derived as follows. Assuming I/O requests for a disk form a Poisson process and the values of basic service times are independent and identically distributed variables, we view each device as an $M/G/1$ queue. Its arrival rate is denoted by λ_d, with $\lambda_d = \lambda/(N_s N_d)$ in our case, and the average service time is the basic I/O time W_b (2.13). Denote by v_s, v_l, v_m and v_t the variance of the seek time, of the latency time, of the missed reconnection delay and that of the transfer time. Making the approximation that the above components of the disk service time are independent, we obtain for the total variance in our $M/G/1$ queue, v_b,

$$v_b \simeq v_s + v_l + v_m + v_t.$$

We assume that the variance of the seek time and of the transfer time are given. Latency times are customarily taken to be uniformly distributed between 0 and t_r, the revolution time for the disk. Hence,

$$v_l = t_r^2/12. \qquad (2.19)$$

The remaining variance of the missed reconnection delay is readily obtained as

$$v_m = t_r^2 p_{m_1}(1 + p_{m_2} - p_{m_1})/(1 - p_{m_2})^2 \qquad (2.20)$$

where p_{m_1} and p_{m_2} are miss probabilities on first and consecutive reconnection attempts, respectively. For the system considered they are given by (2.11) and (2.15).

Denote by c_b the coefficient of variation of the DASD service time, and by $\bar{n}_t$ the average number of I/O requests for the DASD (including the one in service).

We have

$$c_b = \sqrt{v_b}/W_b$$

and hence, by virtue of the Pollaczek–Khintchine formula [12]

$$\bar{n}_t = \rho_b + \rho_b^2(1 + c_b^2)/[2(1 - \rho_b)] \qquad (2.21)$$

where

$$\rho_b = \lambda_d W_b.$$

The total I/O service time, denoted by W_t, is then obtained from Little's formula [13]

$$W_t = \bar{n}_t / \lambda_d. \qquad (2.22)$$

Before closing this subject, let us note that [9] proposes a more accurate approach, taking into account the correlation between seeks.

In [4], we relax the assumption that the I/O traffic is evenly spread across strings of disks connected to a control unit and DASD's in a string. We also allow each DASD to possess its own set of characteristics of seek, latency and transfer times. Our approach is an extension of that used in Section II-B, and it proceeds as follows. First, we determine the stationary distributions of the numbers of busy paths at strings, and of the number of busy routes within the control unit. These blocking points are analyzed using loss-system models, and a simple model to estimate conditional probabilities of particular configurations of devices, strings, and channels busy given total numbers of units active. Then, missed reconnection probability is computed by analyzing numbers of requests which arrive to find various string, control unit, and channel states. The interested reader is referred to [4] for details and an example of application.

In a general case, the above solution procedure may involve a number of iterative solutions of small systems of equations. Although we do not have a theoretical convergence proof, it has been our experience that the iterative solutions involved tend to converge within just a few iterations.

In the next section, we consider the application of our approach to the analysis of present-day configurations with shared strings, shared channels and control units, and also disks with dual ports. This gives us the opportunity to compare our method with other published approaches to DASD analysis.

III. SHARED STRINGS, SHARED CHANNELS, DUAL PORTS

This section is devoted to the application of our approach to systems in which strings of DASD's are shared by several control units (referred to as string switching), channels are connected to several control units, and also, systems in which disks have two ports (referred to as cross-call). Since we do not believe that it makes much sense to have shared channels or string switching with multiple paths or routes, we restrict the scope of this section to "classical" string controllers and control units with a single data transfer path. This will give us the opportunity to discuss the relationship between our method and other approaches to the analysis of disks on block-multiplexor channels.

As a first example, consider a system of two control units sharing N_s identical strings with N_d actuators per string. Each control unit has a single channel connected to it (Fig. 3). For simplicity, we assume balanced I/O traffic distribution across control units and devices. This system with string switching can be easily analyzed using our loss-system model approach.

Denote by U_s the utilization of a single string. The probability that a DASD request finds its string controller free, denoted by f_s, is

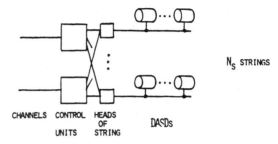

Fig. 3.   System with string switching.

$$f_s = \frac{(1 - U_s)N_d}{(1 - U_s)N_d + U_s(N - 1)} = \frac{1 - U_s}{1 - U_s/N_d}. \qquad (3.1)$$

Let $p_u(k)$ be the stationary probability that k control units are active, $k = 0, 1, 2$. Denote by λ the rate at which an idle string requests reconnection to a control unit. An I/O is bound to the control unit on which it was initiated, so that we readily obtain as the rate of control unit activations when k control units are busy

$$\lambda(N_s - k)a_k, \text{ where } a_0 = 1 \text{ and } a_1 = \tfrac{1}{2}. \qquad (3.2)$$

Hence,

$$p_u(k) = G \rho^k \prod_{i=1}^{k} (N_s - i + 1)a_{i-1}/i \qquad (3.3)$$

where G is a normalization constant. As in Section II, ρ can be determined by bisection from the condition

$$\sum_{k=1}^{2} p_u(k)k = 2U_u \qquad (3.4)$$

where U_u is the utilization of the control unit.

The probability of finding the appropriate control unit free, denoted by f_u, is given by

$$f_u = P_u(0) + \tfrac{1}{2} P_u(1) \qquad (3.5)$$

where

$$P_u(k) = (N_s - k)p_u(k) \bigg/ \sum_{i=0}^{2} (N_s - i)p_u(i).$$

Hence, the probability of a missed reconnection on a first attempt is

$$p_{m1} = 1 - f_s f_u$$

and for subsequent attempts we use the correction (2.15).

The above approach may be termed "global" in that we have determined explicitly the joint probability of the state of the two control units in our system. For many systems, a "local" approach, derived from the same basic idea of using a loss-system model, is also possible. In the system of Fig. 3, consider a string and a given control unit. The probability that the string will find the control unit free upon reconnection request, $\hat{f}_u$, may be expressed as

$$\hat{f}_u = \frac{\text{rate of string requests arriving when unit free}}{\text{total rate of requests}}.$$

$$(3.6)$$

351

Let us examine the rates of request arrivals when the given control unit is busy and free, which we denote by r_b and r_f, respectively. We have up to a proportionality constant,

$$r_b = U_u \text{ Prob \{string free|control unit busy\}}$$

and

$$r_f = (1 - U_u) \text{ Prob \{string free|control unit free\}}. \tag{3.7}$$

The local approach will work if we have a means of estimating the probability that the requestor is free given the state of the requested unit. Let

$x_f = $ Prob {string not busy with the other unit|control unit free}

and

$x_b = $ Prob {string not busy with other unit|control unit busy with another string}.

Denote by s the fraction of control unit utilization contributed by the string (in our case, $s = 1/N_s$). We have

$$r_b = U_u(1 - s)x_b, \text{ and } r_f = (1 - U_u)x_f. \tag{3.8}$$

f_u^* is given by $r_f/(r_b + r_f)$. We do not know the values of the additional probabilities, but we note that only their relative values matter in order to obtain f_u^*. We shall assume that the state of the requested control unit has little influence on the occupation of the string with the other unit. This independence assumption yields

$$x_b \simeq x_f, \tag{3.9}$$

and, hence,

$$f_u^* \simeq (1 - U_u)/(1 - sU_u). \tag{3.10}$$

Formula (3.10) may be interpreted as meaning that the string "sees" the total utilization contributed by other strings as if this contribution took place during the time the string itself does not contribute to the control unit's utilization. It is quite remarkable that the global and local approaches yield extremely close results.

The local approach applies equally easily to other systems. As an example, consider the DASD subsystem configuration depicted in Fig. 4. The system comprises two loosely coupled CPU's sharing the whole set of devices. Every channel is connected to two control units, and every control unit has two channels—one from each CPU—hooked to it. A single string of L DASD's is connected to every control unit. The CPU's spread their load evenly across all devices, but do not necessarily generate the same I/O traffic. Thus, let p_1 and p_2 be the fractions of total I/O traffic attributable to either CPU. In order to obtain the missed reconnection delay for a DASD, it suffices to analyze the simple generic subsystem represented in Fig. 5. An independence assumption analogous to (3.9) yields the simple solution given in [5].

Fig. 6 illustrates the numerical results obtained for the above model. We have plotted the expected number of missed reconnections per transfer versus the I/O rate of a single control

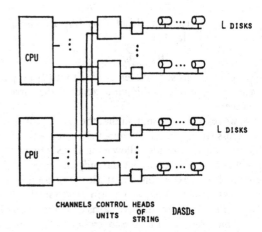

Fig. 4. Two CPU's sharing a DASD subsystem.

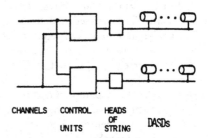

Fig. 5. Generic subsystem for analysis.

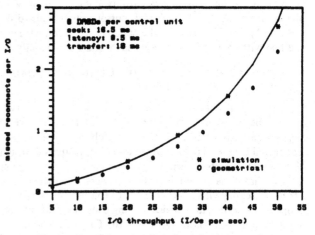

Fig. 6. Comparison of analytical and simulation results.

unit. The model parameters correspond to a configuration of 8 actuators per string. The device rotation time is 17 ms, and the average transfer time is 10 ms. The traffic split between CPU's (and channels) is 2 to 1, i.e., we have $p_1 = 2/3$ and $p_2 = 1/2$. We have also represented the results of a discrete-event simulation of the system as well as the values which would be obtained without our correction (2.15) for nongeometrically distributed numbers of missed reconnections per transfer. The simulation assumes that both the total of seek and latency, and transfer times, are exponentially distributed. Each simulation

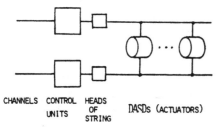

Fig. 7. System with cross-call.

point corresponds to 100 000 transfer completions. Note that the agreement between analytical results and simulation in Figure 6 holds well into prohibitively high loads and average numbers of missed reconnections per successful I/O.

Our last example in this section is a set of N_d disks (actuators) with dual ports, connected to two string controllers. Each string controller is connected to a single control unit and a single channel, as shown in Fig. 7. We consider here this system as a dual-pathing arrangement for access from the same CPU. For simplicity, we assume a homogeneous and balanced traffic across all units. We also assume that an I/O operation which starts on a given access path (channel, control unit, string controller) is bound to that path until completion. Such "cross-call" arrangements are offered by several DASD manufacturers.

The global approach for this system is quite straightforward. Let $p(j)$ be the probability that j disks are simultaneously involed in transfer, $j = 0, 1, 2$. We have

$$p(j) = G \rho^j \left[\prod_{i=1}^{j} (N_d - i + 1)a_{i-1} \right] \Big/ j! \qquad (3.11)$$

where G is a normalization constant, and

$$a_0 = 1, \text{ and } a_1 = \tfrac{1}{2}. \qquad (3.12)$$

ρ is determined from the condition

$$\sum_{j=1}^{2} p(j)j = 2U_s \qquad (3.13)$$

where U_s is the utilization of a single string. The probability of a missed reconnection on a first attempt, p_{m_1}, is readily obtained as

$$p_{m_1} = P(1)a_1 + P(2) \qquad (3.14)$$

where

$$P(j) = (N_d - j)p(j) \Big/ \sum_{i=0}^{2} (N_d - i)p(i).$$

For the local approach, we need the probability that an actuator is free given the state of a particular string. Assuming that the probability of the actuator not being busy with the other string controller is independent of the state of the tagged controller, we immediately get

$$p_{m_1} = (1 - U_s)/(1 - U_s/N_d). \qquad (3.15)$$

Again, the results of local and global approach are very close.

It is interesting to note that, as long as an I/O is bound to the channel on which it has been initiated, the cross-call arrangement of Fig. 7 is functionally equivalent to a single string

with two paths, connected to a single control unit with two routes and two channels.

Both approaches are based on the loss-system model. The global approach is well suited to the study of multipath systems in the sense of Section II. It can be extended, at the expense of increased complexity, to imbalanced systems with several classes of requests. The local approach, on the other hand, is quite simpler when applied to imbalanced configurations, and has also no trouble handling various systems with shared units. It does not appear, however, to be well suited to the general case of multiple, nondedicated transfer paths.

To the best of the author's knowledge, the number of publications dealing specifically with DASD's on block-multiplexor channels is quite limited (cf. [11]), and none of them considers multiple transfer paths in the sense of Section II. The equivalence and decomposition approach of [3] and the method of surrogate delays [10] are designed for use with closed queueing network models, and, therefore, do not lend themselves to a simple comparison with our method. Zahorjan *et al.* [17] and Bard [2] both deal, as does this paper, with directly estimating the missed reconnection probability. In Section II, we have discussed the differences in the corrections proposed to account for the miss probability on second and subsequent reconnection attempts. Here, we concentrate on the analysis of first attempts. The work by Zahorjan *et al.* is limited to a single blocking point. For such systems, the results of [17], [2] and both our global and loal approaches are all identical.

For systems with multiple blocking points, Bard's approach [2], albeit also throughput driven, is in spirit quite different from ours. He derives a set of equations for occupation probabilities of particular transfer paths with a particular device. As this set involves many more unknowns than there are equations, Bard chooses among all feasible solutions the one which maximizes a quantity called entropy. While this approach does allow "cranking out a solution" automatically, it does not, in the author's view, enhance one's intuition and understanding of the phenomena involved. Nor does it show what simplifying assumptions are introduced in the solution process. On the other hand, our approach uses a set of loss-system models with well spelled-out assumptions.

The probability of a missed reconnection is given in [2] by a formula involving a number of joint element utilizations (14). When applied to our example with string switching of Fig. 3, or to the system with shared channels of Fig. 5, this formula becomes identical to those yielded by our local analysis. Thus, for these systems, the maximum entropy principle appears to implicitly introduce independence assumptions of the type of (3.9). Unlike the maximum entropy principle, however, an independence assumption is essentially operational in nature (in the sense of operational analysis [7]) in that, when transposed into the operational domain, it relates readily measureable quantities, and can easily be tested.

Formulas like (3.10), simple and appealing, have actually been in use in the industry for some time, apparently without much theoretical justification. [8] reports on measurement campaign to validate their results. Finally, note that blind application of these formulas is not always possible. The system

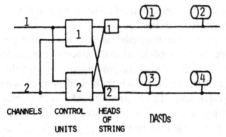

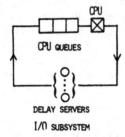

Fig. 8. System with string switching and shared channels.

CHANNELS CONTROL HEADS DASDs
          UNITS   OF
                   STRING

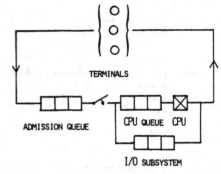

Fig. 10. Queueing model of an interactive system.

CPU

CPU QUEUES

DELAY SERVERS

I/O SUBSYSTEM

Fig. 9. CPU-I/O model.

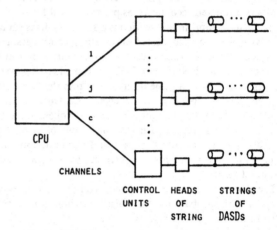

CPU

CHANNELS

CONTROL HEADS STRINGS
UNITS   OF   OF
         STRING DASDs

Fig. 11. DASD subsystem for comparison of approaches.

of Fig. 8, borrowed from [2], is a good example. Here, when one considers the reconnection of a control unit to a channel, the knowledge of the idle state of the string considerably affects the probability of the control unit being free. We show in the Appendix how the local approach can be applied to this system. The results obtained differ slightly from those of [2].

In the next section, we briefly discuss the inclusion of our DASD subsystem model in a larger system model, and also attempt a comparison with the equivalence and decomposition approach of [3].

INCLUSION IN A SYSTEM MODEL

The analysis of DASD subsystems considered in preceding sections yields the basic I/O service time for a disk at a given rate of successful I/O's directed to that device. A simple way of embedding such an analysis in a larger system model is by replacing the DASD subsystem by a set of delay servers, each delay being equal to the average total DASD time (including queueing). The latter may be approximately computed for every DASD using the Pollaczek-Khintchine formula [12] (cf. Section II), or the corresponding finite queueing room analysis when the load conditions make it necessary. The I/O throughput is then determined iteratively by analyzing a queueing network of the type shown in Fig. 9. When convergence has been reached, usually within just a few iterations, both CPU utilization and I/O service times are known. The approach described is not new and has been used by other authors, e.g., [1]. A somewhat more sophisticated approach is proposed in [4].

In a previous paper [3], the author considered a different approach to DASD subsystems, specifically designed for use with the equivalence and decomposition analysis of queueing models. It is interesting to apply the two methods to a system model, and compare their results. For the comparison we

choose the simple system depicted in Fig. 10. It represents an interactive multiprogramming system. The memory queue holds commands (jobs) awaiting admission into the multiprogramming set. The number of jobs admitted is not allowed to exceed a fixed maximum degree of multiprogramming. Upon entry into the multiprogramming set commands join the CPU queue. The only I/O devices represented are disks, and the DASD subsystem is taken to have the simple structure shown in Fig. 11, viz. a single string of disks per control unit, each connected to a single channel. A DASD reconnection request has thus a single blocking point. We consider the above model under the assumption that all the I/O requests are statistically identical with respect to their seek, latency and transfer times.

The I/O subsystem described corresponds to the basic DASD model of [3] and its equivalence and decomposition analysis may be found there. Assuming exponentially distributed CPU service times, it is not difficult to obtain an approximate solution to the overall model of Fig. 10.

The throughput-driven analysis of the system proceeds as follows. Using the results of Section II we readily obtain the basic I/O service time of a DASD, W_b. Hence, the total I/O service time (including queueing), W_t is approximately computed using the Pollaczek-Khintchine formula, as described in Section II. In the iterative analysis of the multiprogramming set model we take the simplest representation whereby the

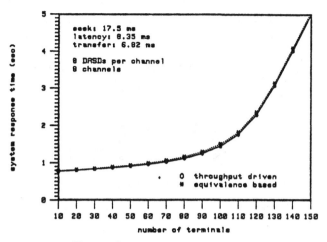

Fig. 12. Comparison of the two approaches.

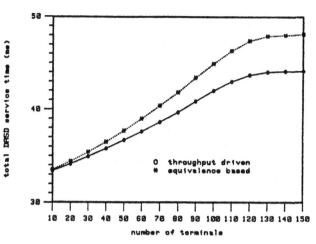

Fig. 13. Comparison of the two approaches.

DASD subsystem is viewed as a set of delay servers with service time W_t.

Numerical results obtained from both approaches are shown in Fig. 12. We have plotted there the expected system response time (time a command spends in the system)—as predicted by the two approaches, versus the total number of terminals active in the system. The following values were used for model parameters:

average user think time: 10 s
average CPU time per command: 100 ms
average number of I/O requests per command: 20
maximum multiprogramming degree: 20

The DASD subsystem comprises eight channels, two of which equally share 50 percent of the I/O traffic, the other 50% being evenly distributed across the remaining channels. All the disks at a given channel are assumed to be equally utilized.

We observe that both methods yield remarkably close results for the average system response time. It is interesting to note that these results are obtained despite differences of a few percent in total I/O service times as illustrated in Fig. 13. As regards computational time and space requirements, the throughput-driven approach appears to be superior. This statement must, however, be moderated. Due to the iterative nature of the throughput-driven approach the execution time may vary depending on the particular set of parameters. Also, the equivalence based approach lends itself nicely to parametric studies (e.g., varying the number of terminals), while this is not necessarily the case for the other method.

V. CONCLUSION

We have presented a method for analyzing disk subsystems with block-multiplexor channels. This method takes the throughput of successful disk I/O requests as basis. The seek, latency and transfer times are assumed known, and the goal of the analysis is to determine the delay due to missed device reconnections. The latter may occur at elements of the I/O transfer path which are shared by several DASD's. Such elements are referred to as blocking points, and include channels, routes (within control units) and paths (within strings of disks).

In the approach presented, conflicts at each of these blocking points are analyzed separately using essentially a loss-system model in which units demanding reconnection are viewed as sources of requests for the resources of the blocking point.

The analysis is introduced for a model with multiple transfer paths in control units and strings of DASD's. In this way a framework is provided for the evaluation of both existing configurations and those including forthcoming products with multiple routes and paths (cf. [15]).

Iteration may be involved in the solution procedure when multiple routes or paths are present. Usually, configurations with a single route per control unit and a single path per string of disks—preponderant in current systems, do not require iteration, and lead to a particularly simple solution.

A simple correction is proposed to account for the nongeometric distribution of the number of missed reconnections experienced by an I/O request. This correction is effective for longer transfer times. For very short transfer times, the effects of the device reconnection window on both missed reconnections and I/O path busy period are discussed.

The throughput-driven nature of the method makes it directly applicable to problems where one is interested in the performance of the I/O subsystem under a specified I/O traffic. Its inclusion in a system model, however, requires an iterative approach.

Numerical results obtained with the method show a good agreement, throughout wide ranges of loads, with the results of discrete-event simulations of the examples considered.

The basic idea of the method presented, viz. that of considering blocking points separately, can be successfully applied to the study of other DASD configurations, including, for example, a cache in the control unit.

APPENDIX

A. Influence of Path State at Latency Start

As an example let us take the configuration considered in Fig. 2. Table I shows the average numbers of missed reconnections per transfer observed in two sets of discrete-event

TABLE I							
I/O throughput (I/O's/second)	40	60	80	100	120	140	160
misses per transfer							
path free	0.124	0.212	0.323	0.461	0.635	0.885	1.198
any state	0.180	0.296	0.434	0.623	0.821	1.086	1.447

TABLE II							
I/O throughput (I/O's/second)	40	60	80	100	120	140	160
misses per transfer							
path free	0.122	0.210	0.313	0.450	0.630	0.873	1.160
any state	0.190	0.308	0.452	0.623	0.826	1.108	1.499

simulations of this system. In the first set, latency is allowed to start only if the I/O path is free. In the second set, latency starts independently of the status of the I/O path. The distributional assumptions are: transfer times—exponential, seek times—uniform, latency—uniform, for both sets of simulations. Each simulation point corresponds to 100,000 transfer completions. Table II shows the results obtained for a device with a shorter rotation period of 15 ms (versus 16.7 ms in Table I). We observe that neglecting the status of the I/O path at latency start can result in an overestimation of the missed reconnection delay by up to 40 percent. As expected, the overestimation is more pronounced for the faster spinning device.

B. Reconnection Window

The interested reader will find in [4] the description and derivation details of our model of the reconnection window. Numerical results obtained from this model are exemplified in Fig. 14 for an average transfer time of 0.86 ms. The rotation period, t_r, is set to 16.7 ms. We have plotted the probabilities p_{m0}: unit busy at beginning of window, g: busy unit doesn't become available and p_m: missed reconnection, as well as the average unit busy period, versus the reconnection window size. For comparison, the results of discrete-event simulation with exponentially distributed DASD transfer times are also included. Each simulation point corresponds to 500 000 transfer completions.

It is interesting to note that, within the range of values explored, the window size has little influence on the missed reconnection probability. The agreement between analytical and simulation results is good as long as the window size is not too large compared with the transfer time. The average unit busy period exhibits a remarkable robustness, even for relatively large window sizes.

C. Application to the Example of Fig. 8

Consider the system represented in Fig. 8. It consists of two control units sharing two channels and two strings of two DASD's each. Let us apply the local approach to the reconnection of device 1 along the path composed of head of string 1, control unit 1, and channel 1. For the reconnection of the device to its string, and for the reconnection of the string to the control unit, we use independence assumptions analogous to (3.9). Hence, we get for the corresponding probabilities of finding the blocking point free

$$f_s = \frac{1 - \langle S_1 \rangle}{1 - \langle D_1 \rangle}$$

and

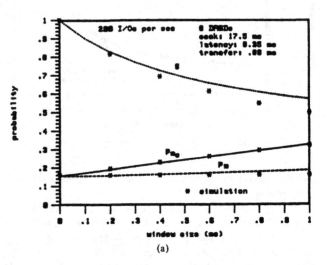

(a)

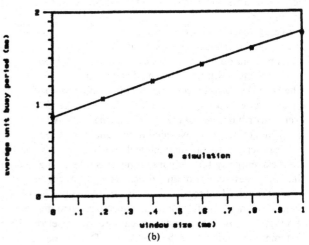

(b)

Fig. 14. (a) Effect of reconnection window. (b) Effect of reconnection window.

$$f_u = \frac{1 - \langle U_1 \rangle}{1 - \langle U_1 S_1 \rangle}$$

where, following the notations of [2], $\langle S_1 \rangle$ is the utilization of string 1, $\langle D_1 \rangle$ is the contribution of device 1 to that utilization, $\langle U_1 \rangle$ is the utilization of control unit 1, and $\langle U_1 S_1 \rangle$ is the contribution of string 1 to the latter utilization.

The probability of the control unit finding the channel free may be expressed as

$$f_c = 1 - \frac{A \cdot x_b}{A \cdot x_b + B \cdot x_f}$$

where

A = Prob {channel 1 busy|string 1 idle},
B = Prob {channel 1 idle|string 1 idle},

x_b = Prob {control unit 1 idle|channel 1 busy, string 1 idle},
x_f = Prob {control unit 1 idle|channel 1 idle, string 1 idle}.
Note that we cannot assume that the activity of the control unit with channel 2 is independent of the status of channel 1. Indeed, since string 1 is known to be idle, the control unit cannot be active with channel 2 when channel 1 is active. Therefore, we analyze the probabilities x_b and x_f in more detail. We have from the definition of conditional probabilities

$$x_b = \frac{A \cdot \text{Prob \{string 1 idle\}} - \text{Prob \{control unit 1 and chnl 1 busy, string 1 idle\}}}{A \cdot \text{Prob \{string 1 idle\}}}$$

and

$$x_f = \frac{B \cdot \text{Prob \{string 1 idle\}} - \text{Prob \{control unit 1 and chnl 2 busy, string 1 idle\}}}{B \cdot \text{Prob \{string 1 idle\}}}.$$

Hence, we readily get

$$f_c = 1 - \frac{A - \text{Prob \{control unit 1 and channel 1 busy|string 1 idle\}}}{1 - \text{Prob \{control unit 1 busy|string 1 idle\}}}.$$

The conditional probabilities in the above expression can all be estimated using independence assumptions which yield

$$A = \frac{\langle C_1 \rangle - \langle C_1 S_1 \rangle}{1 - \langle C_1 S_1 \rangle},$$

Prob {control unit 1 and channel 1 busy|string 1 idle}

$$= \frac{\langle U_1 C_1 \rangle - \langle U_1 C_1 S_1 \rangle}{1 - \langle U_1 C_1 S_1 \rangle},$$

Prob {control unit 1 busy|string 1 idle}

$$= \frac{\langle U_1 \rangle - \langle U_1 S_1 \rangle}{1 - \langle U_1 S_1 \rangle}$$

where $\langle U_1 C_1 S_1 \rangle$ denotes the utilization of channel 1 contributed by string 1 via control unit 1, $\langle C_1 \rangle$ is the utilization of channel 1, and $\langle C_1 S_1 \rangle$ is the contribution of string 1 to that utilization. Using the data of [2], we obtain

$$f_s = 0.592, \quad f_u = 0.796, \quad \text{and } f_c = 0.884,$$

i.e., a successful reconnection probability of 0.416 which is not very different from the 0.419 obtained from formula (14) in [2].

D. Influence of Transfer Time Distribution and Simulation Accuracy

As an example we show in Table III discrete-event simulation results for the configuration of Fig. 2 and constant transfer times. These results are directly comparable with those of Table I, line "any state." In order to give an idea of the accuracy of the simulation results, we also give 90 percent level approximate confidence intervals estimated from a set of independent runs.

TABLE III

I/O throughput (I/O's/second)	40	60	80	100	120	140	160
misses per transfer any state	0.168	0.283	0.412	0.584	0.801	1.092	1.456
confidence interval							
	0.169	0.279	0.413	0.582	0.793	1.077	1.428
	0.171	0.285	0.422	0.592	0.805	1.103	1.451

REFERENCES

[1] Y. Bard, "The VM/370 performance predictor," *Comput. Surveys*, vol. 10, pp. 333–342, 1978.
[2] ——, "A model of shared DASD and multipathing," *Commun. Ass. Comput. Mach.*, vol. 23 pp. 564–572, 1980.
[3] A. Brandwajn, "Models of DASD subsystems: Basic model of reconnection," *Perform. Eval.*, vol. 1, pp. 263–281, 1981.
[4] ——, "Models of DASD subsystems: multiple access paths—A throughput-driven approach," Amdahl Corp., Sunnyvale; CA, Amdahl Tech. Rep., P/N 820457-700B, available upon request.
[5] ——, "A capacity planning model of a DASD subsystem," in *Performance '81*, F. J. Kylstra Ed. Amsterdam, The Netherlands: North-Holland, Nov. 1981, pp. 401–413.
[6] R. B. Cooper, *Introduction to Queueing Theory*. New York: Macmillan, 1972.
[7] P. J. Denning and J. P. Buzen, "The operational analysis of queueing network models," *Comput. Surveys*, vol. 10, pp. 225–241.
[8] H. Hoffman, "DASD configuration analysis," in *Proc. CMG X Int. Conf.*, Dallas, TX, 1979, pp. 285–302.
[9] M. Hofri, "Disk scheduling: FCFS versus SSTF revisited," *Commun. Ass. Comput. Mach.*, vol. 23, pp. 645–653, 1980.
[10] P. Jacobson and E. W. Lazowska, "The method of surrogate delays: Simultaneous resource possession in analytic models of computer systems," *Perform. Eval. Rev.*, vol. 10, pp. 165–174, 1981.
[11] M. G. Kienzle and K. C. Sevcik, "Survey of analytic queueing network models of computer systems," in *Proc. Conf. Simulation, Measurement, Model. Comput. Syst.*, Boulder, CO, 1979; also in *Perform. Eval. Rev.*, vol. 8, pp. 113–129, 1979.
[12] L. Kleinrock, *Queueing Systems, Vol. 1: Theory*. New York: Wiley, 1975.
[13] J. D. Little, "A proof of the queueing formula $L = \lambda W$," *Oper. Res.*, vol. 9, pp. 383–387, 1961.
[14] A. Rafii, "Effects of channel blocking on the performance of shared disk pack in a multi-computer system," in *Proc. Conf. Simulation, Measurement, Model. Comput. Syst.*, Boulder, CO, 1979; also in *Perform. Eval. Rev.* vol. 8, pp. 83–87, 1979.
[15] T. Scannel, "CDC offers rival to IBM 3380 disk system," *Comput. World*, p. 14, Jan. 26, 1981.
[16] N. Wilhelm, "A general model for the performance of disk systems," *J. Ass. Comput. Mach.*, vol. 24, pp. 14–31, 1977.
[17] J. Zahorjan, J. N. P. Hume, and K. C. Sevcik, "A queueing model of a rotational position sensing disk system," *INFOR 16*, pp. 199–216, 1978.

Synchronized Disk Interleaving

MICHELLE Y. KIM

Abstract—A group of disks may be interleaved to speed up data transfers in a manner analogous to the speedup achieved by main memory interleaving. Conventional disks may be used for interleaving by spreading data across disks and by treating multiple disks as if they were a single one. Furthermore, the rotation of the interleaved disks may be synchronized to simplify control and also to optimize performance. In addition, check-sums may be placed on separate check-sum disks in order to improve reliability. In this paper, we study synchronized disk interleaving as a high-performance mass storage system architecture. The advantages and limitations of the proposed disk interleaving scheme are analyzed using the $M/G/1$ queueing model and compared to the conventional disk access mechanism.

Index Terms—Check-sum disk, interleaving, $M/G/1$ queueing model, parallel I/O transfer, simplified control, synchronous interleaving.

I. INTRODUCTION

THE speed of magnetic disk storage devices is often a major bottleneck in overall system performance. Currently, disks are at least three orders of magnitude slower than main memory. This speed gap between the disk storage and main memory may become even wider, with rapidly changing memory and processor technologies.

One might argue that by adding, say, on the order of tens of billions of bytes of main memory to a computer system, the problem of speed mismatch may become a less critical issue. Nevertheless, the fact is that no matter how large the main memory is, there will always be some programs that require more memory. Furthermore, unless the entire main memory or a substantial fraction of it is made nonvolatile, the updates made in it must be copied onto slow nonvolatile devices like disks in order to preserve data integrity. This suggests that the speed of such nonvolatile storage devices may dictate the performance of the entire system even though the system is equipped with massive amounts of main memory. Our assumption, therefore, is that there are many applications that are inevitably I/O bound, requiring either huge or frequent data transfers to and from the secondary storage devices.

There has been interest in database machines that make use of hundreds of query processors to process a database query in parallel. It has been claimed that the performance of such machines would be limited by their disk to memory transfer rates, and that unless the problem of the I/O bandwidth is tackled, building such database machines will not be justified [1], [4].

Furthermore, there is an increasing requirement for even larger storage capacity, and this demand for more capacity will continue to grow. The capacity of magnetic disk storage devices may be increased either by making the recording surfaces denser or simply by adding more disk units. The problem is that neither approach is without penalty; denser disks are more error prone [21], and adding more disk units may cause a performance interference [12]. It is safe to say that no matter how large and how dense a disk unit may be, there is always a need for more capacity, and this requirement can only be met by coupling multiple disks.

One method of disk coupling is *disk interleaving*. A group of disk units is interleaved if each data block is stored in such a way that succeeding portions of the block are on different disks. This idea of disk interleaving, or disk striping, is a known super-computer technique, which has been successfully used in the Cray operating system and has greatly improved performance on some applications such as manipulation of very large data arrays [10]. Disk interleaving has also been suggested as a means of improving bandwidth to disks for large database systems [4]. Further, this technique has been included in the recent implementation of Unix™ [19].

In this paper, synchronized disk interleaving, which allows a group of interleaved disks to operate synchronously, is studied as a high-performance mass storage system architecture. To support this architecture, we make the following claims.

I/O bandwidth may be improved: By interleaving data on multiple disks, the data may be accessed in parallel reducing data transfer time by a factor of $1/n$ where n is the degree of interleaving. Distribution of requests to disks may also become more uniform, or less skewed, as a result of interleaving. Disk skew is the observed phenomenon that accesses are not evenly distributed over the disks. An example is a system where 25 percent of the disks receive 63 percent of the total requests,[1] creating I/O bottlenecks that severely limit overall system performance. With the increasing size and number of on-line databases, the existence of these I/O bottlenecks is becoming an ever larger problem. However, the skew is dynamic in nature and as a result load balancing efforts are unlikely to be fruitful. We claim that disk interleaving offers a partial solution to this problem, and hence contributes to increased system throughput as well as to increased I/O bandwidth.

The problem of queueing control may be simplified: In conventional disk systems, each disk is treated as a unique

Manuscript received March 21, 1985; revised December 2, 1985.

The author is with IBM Thomas J. Watson Research Center, Yorktown Heights, NY 10598.

IEEE Log Number 8610929.

™ Unix is a trademark of AT&T Bell Laboratories.
[1] See the skew distribution in (3) in Section III-A-1).

entity in the main CPU with a device queue associated with it. As the number of disks increases, so does the complexity of queueing control. In interleaved disk systems, however, there is only one queueing point for a group of disks, which should simplify the control problems.

Reliability may also be improved with reduced data redundancy: Today, disk mirroring [11], or disk duplexing, is generally used to prevent critical data from being lost after failure of a disk. There are, however, several concerns with disk mirroring, although the concept is intuitively simple. First, mirroring implies full redundancy. Although disk storage has become substantially cheaper in the last few years and may become even cheaper in the future, it is still doubtful that full mirroring is a practical approach to obtaining fault tolerance. Second, performance may be severely degraded due to the overheads involved when disks are duplexed on-line. The notion of a "check-sum disk" is promising in that only a fraction of data redundancy is required compared to full mirroring and that the impact on the system performance may not be as great.

There is a wide range of possible applications that could exploit the parallelism provided by disk interleaving. In this paper, we model simple block transfers and study the performance characteristics of disk interleaving for such tasks.

Outline

In Section II, we briefly review the techniques that have been used in the past to speed up disk access time and we describe synchronized disk interleaving as an alternative. Interleaving is described as a means of achieving parallelism, and synchronization for efficiency and simplicity. A dual-mode error correcting scheme is then described as a cost-effective solution for two types of data loss: random single-bit errors and occasional massive data loss caused by failure of a disk.

In Section III, we present our model for disk systems. We first model conventional disk systems and then synchronously interleaved disk systems using the same methodology. Comparative numerical results from the analytic modeling appear in Section IV. Finally, the summary of comparison results and conclusions are presented in Section V.

II. Synchronized Disk Interleaving

Various techniques have been explored in the past to reduce the access time to disk. One class of approaches involves minimizing various mechanical delays that occur at the disks. For instance, fixed-head disks may be used to eliminate the arm movement by providing multiple READ/WRITE heads per surface, tracks-in-parallel moving head disks may be used to access an entire cylinder in parallel, or bit density along a track may be increased to reduce the data transfer time. The other class of approaches includes efforts to minimize the effects of mechanical delays rather than to decrease them directly. These include disk caching and disk scheduling techniques among others. It has been agreed, however, that none of these techniques offers in the forseeable future a satisfactory solution to the problem of maintaining large databases.

Fixed-head disks simply are not cost-effective, tracks-in-parallel moving head disks face the problem of accurate alignment of the arms as recording density increases [4]. By adopting better head technology, new recording materials, and novel recording techniques such as vertical recording [23], bit density along the track may be improved substantially. The problem, nevertheless, is that as bit density increases, reliable sensing becomes more difficult and sensing electronics become extremely complicated [21].

A disk cache may also be used to speed up the average disk access, provided that the data access pattern follows the long established principle of locality [8]. In order for a disk cache to be useful, the hit ratio, the probability of finding data in the cache, must be high [5], [24]; the ratio of READS to WRITES must also be high, because a WRITE, unlike a READ, will cause a disk access whether the data are found in the cache or not. In other words, although disk cache is a powerful means of extending the performance limits of disk systems, there still exists a lot of room for improvement. Disk scheduling (seek scheduling) techniques as described in the literature [7] do not seem very useful either. This is mainly due to the fact that the seek time is not linearly proportional to the distance the access arms travel [12].

A. Disk Interleaving for Parallelism

Disk interleaving is an attractive alternative to the techniques discussed above. Although the granularity of interleaving may be chosen to be at any level, i.e., at the attribute level, at the record level, and so on, byte-parallel interleaving is shown in this paper for its simplicity and for its capability to provide the maximal disk access concurrency. Whatever level may be chosen, whether the file is physically partitioned or semantically divided, the goal should be to utilize as well as possible the inherent parallelism provided by interleaving. With byte interleaving, byte B_i in a data block is assigned to disk unit $((B_i - 1) \bmod n) + 1$. That is, byte 1 is stored on disk 1, byte 2 of the same data block is stored at the same physical location on disk 2, and so on.

A number of database machine designs that have been proposed in the past have explored track interleaving, rather than disk interleaving, to achieve parallel reads of a single disk. SURE, a search processor for database management systems developed at the Technical University of Braunschweig, Germany, used a modified moving head disk that allowed parallel reads from all of the tracks of a cylinder [17]. In SURE, records were stored across the tracks in record-parallel, byte-serial fashion. The output of all recording surfaces was collected into a single data stream in byte interleaving mode and processed by a number of search units. The limitation with SURE was that the parallelism was achieved only in the read direction and a WRITE was done one track at a time. This was due to the difficulty, especially for a WRITE, of aligning multiple READ/WRITE heads concurrently. Disk interleaving has an advantage over track interleaving in that parallelism may be achieved using conventional moving-head disks rather than with special expensive hardware.

Intelligent Disk Controller: There are several basic tasks that a disk controller may perform in order to operate synchronized disks effectively: conversion, synchronization, and error recovery. Conversion is necessary in order to assemble parallel data streams coming from the disks into a serial data stream and vice versa [14]. As shown in Fig. 1, a subblock of data can be read from each disk into each separate column of the conversion buffer. As the buffer is filled, the columns are aligned, or converted, into the rows of a single data stream. As we shall see later, this conversion buffer may also serve as a synchronization buffer and, at the same time, as an error correction buffer.

B. Synchronized Operation for Efficiency and Simplicity

Since adjacent bytes of a data block, in byte interleaving, are stored on adjacent disks at the same place on each disk, the rotation of all disk units may now be synchronized.

Simplified Control: As the number of disk drives increases, it becomes crucial that the control scheme be simplified. By synchronizing interleaved disks, multiple disks can be treated as if they were a single disk unit. Thus, a group of disks may present a *"Single device image,"* greatly simplifying control problems that are inherent in multidisk systems.

Efficiency: As more disk units are added, if not done carefully, the performance of the system may suffer significantly from possible interferences. Synchronized operation may simplify this problem greatly; it is just like running a single device on a dedicated path. Furthermore, expected mechanical delays in synchronized systems are those of a single device. If the disks are run independently of each other, then the delay is that of the worst one.

Synchronization: A group of disk drives may be mechanically integrated and run by a single motor. Although this offers a simple solution, reliability may be a great concern in such a simple coupling. A more reliable solution is to let the disk drives be run by separate synchronous motors and control them by a central clock with a feedback control loop. With such a feedback loop, the speed and rotational position of each disk can be monitored and any necessary adjustment can be made if one of them happens to get out of synchronization.

There is a tolerance in any mechanical synchronization, however. With the use of synchronous motors, the upper bound of the phase shift, which due to varying rotational velocities between disks, can be kept under three degrees [25]. This means that in order to read out an entire track of data from a set of IBM 3380 disks, where a track contains 47K bytes, we need to allow 0.8 percent of (47×1024) bytes, or 385 bytes, of buffer space for each disk for synchronization. The fact that there is a fine tolerance in coupling the disks suggests that effective synchronization could be achieved on a block basis. The size of a block may be determined based on various parameters: disk hardware parameters, reliability requirements, as well as performance requirements.

C. Error Recovery

Error handling by the controller is an important problem for which a good solution must be found in order to operate interleaved disks. A new dual-mode error-correcting scheme, based on Reed–Solomon codes, for a large-size bubble

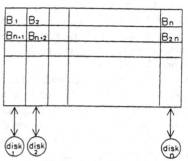

Fig. 1.   Conversion buffer.

memory was discovered by Patel and presented in [22]. This idea, when applied to interleaved disks, makes it possible to correct both random single-bit errors and occasional massive loss caused by failure of a disk, using minimum redundancy. In this section, the ECC (error correcting codes) data format for this scheme is described to provide an overview; details may be found elsewhere [13].

1) ECC Data Format: In an n-disk interleaved system, n columns of data are accessed in parallel forming m n-byte code words, or an $m \times n$ matrix, as shown in Fig. 2 where m is the size of a block discussed above.

The length of a word n, or the order of interleaving, determines the number of check bytes required in a word so that the required correcting capability may be obtained. With $n \leq 32$, only one check byte is required per word, and in this section we will show such a case although the system may easily be extended to a higher order of interleaving. As shown in the figure, the last byte in each code word is a *check byte*.

In the last word of a block, or in the mth word, there is an *end-of-block parity byte* for the block. This parity byte is used to determine if there have been errors other than random single-bit errors in the block. As shown in the figure, the end-of-block parity byte is generated first and the word check byte is generated so that the last word check byte includes a contribution from the block parity byte.

For each $(n - 1)$ bytes of data, a WRITE check byte is generated. The 8-bit check byte C is given by the modulo-2 matrix equation

$$C = \sum_{i=1}^{n-1} T^{i\lambda} B_i \qquad (1)$$

where λ is any integer such that $8 \leq \lambda < 2^8/n$, and i denotes the position of each data byte B_i in a code word. T is an 8×8 matrix such as one given below:

$$T = \begin{bmatrix} 0 & 0 & 0 & 0 & 0 & 0 & 0 & 1 \\ 1 & 0 & 0 & 0 & 0 & 0 & 0 & 1 \\ 0 & 1 & 0 & 0 & 0 & 0 & 0 & 0 \\ 0 & 0 & 1 & 0 & 0 & 0 & 0 & 1 \\ 0 & 0 & 0 & 1 & 0 & 0 & 0 & 0 \\ 0 & 0 & 0 & 0 & 1 & 0 & 0 & 1 \\ 0 & 0 & 0 & 0 & 0 & 1 & 0 & 0 \\ 0 & 0 & 0 & 0 & 0 & 0 & 1 & 0 \end{bmatrix}.$$

The matrix T represents a primitive element of $GF(2^8)$. Thus,

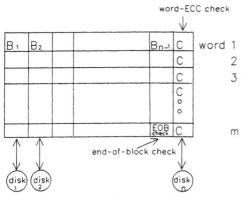

Fig. 2. An array of $n \times m$ code words.

the matrices T, T^2, T^3, T^{255} represent distinct nonzero elements of $GF(2^8)$. The matrix T^λ represents an element of the multiplicative subgroup of $GF(2^8)$, where λ is chosen, under the constraints shown above, to simplify the hardware implementation of multiplication by matrix T^λ. The matrices T^λ, $T^{2\lambda}$, $T^{3\lambda}$, $\cdots$, $T^{n\lambda}$ represent distinct nonzero elements of the subgroup, and $T^{n\lambda} = I$ where I is the 8×8 identity matrix. Thus the inverse $T^{-i\lambda}$ of the matrix $T^{i\lambda}$ is the matrix $T^{(n-i)\lambda}$. The modulo-2 sum and product operations of these matrices are closed, in the sense that the result is always one of the elements of the subfield.

A block parity byte is generated by modulo-2 summing the values of all supplied data bytes in a block of m words. Thus,

$$\sum_{j=1}^{m} \left(\sum_{i=1}^{n-1} B_i \right)_{\text{word } j} = 0. \qquad (2)$$

A READ check byte is generated for each word as data are transferred from the disks. A separate READ block parity byte is also generated at the end of all data bytes in a block, and it represents the sum of error patterns for all errors which occurred in the block. The newly generated READ check byte is EXCLUSIVE-OR'd with the previously generated check byte to produce a syndrome character [18] S for each word. An all zero syndrome byte indicates no error, while a nonzero syndrome byte indicates either a single-bit error, the location of the defective byte, or an uncorrectable error. In addition to correcting random single-bit errors in each word, this dual-function ECC scheme allows the word ECC check byte to be used to correct whole byte errors in a fixed known byte position of each word. This byte position corresponds to the failed disk. Once the failure of a disk is detected by means of an end-of-block parity byte, the location of the defective disk position is identified by summing each nonzero syndrome byte S that has been developed for each word. This summed syndrome byte $\Sigma S \neq 0$ is then used to provide an indication of the defective byte position in each word. With the defective byte position, or the failed disk position, identified, the individual syndrome bytes for each word are then employed to develop the error pattern for the defective byte position of each word.

This dual-mode error correcting scheme provides a cost-effective solution for two types of data loss: random single-bit errors and occasional massive data loss caused by failure of a disk. This scheme, in its primary mode, routinely corrects random single bit errors. In the presence of large errors caused by a disk failure, the scheme provides recovery of data lost in the failed disk. As the failing disk is detected and isolated, the interleaved disk system is reconfigured to bypass the failed disk, and operation may continue. To obtain a cost-effective solution, it is necessary to share the word check-byte to perform the two functions of correcting single-bit errors and recovering from a disk failure. The code does not have the capability to provide both functions simultaneously, although a rather expensive solution exists for the case when a random single-bit error will interfere with the processing of a disk failure. This minimum capability code may be used in a situation where high reliability and cost-competitive solution are equally important.

III. MODELING METHODOLOGY

A method for evaluating the average I/O response time is presented in this section. Queueing models that represent conventional disk systems as well as synchronously interleaved systems are then described. Conventional systems are first represented by a hypothetical, or balanced, model in which disk requests are uniformly distributed, and then by an unbalanced model in which there is a skew in disk access distribution. This unbalanced model is used throughout this paper to represent a conventional disk system, and the term "unbalanced" may be used to refer to such a system. A synchronized disk system is treated as a special case of a conventional system with a single disk.

A. Evaluating Average I/O Response Time

There are basically three sources of delay in completing an I/O request to a disk device. They are as follows.

Mechanical Delay: The time necessary for mechanical movement, i.e., arm positioning, device rotation, data transfer, etc.

Path Delay: A wait for the transfer path to and from the device to become free.

Queueing Delay: A wait for the requested device to become free.

Mechanical delays occur at the disks due to the mechanical movements of the rotating disks; these, in most cases, dominate the response time of an I/O request. *Seek* delay is the time required to position the access mechanism to the cylinder containing the data. Deriving the seek time distribution is not straightforward, because the seek time is not linearly proportional to the distance the access arms travel [3]. Moreover, empirical studies indicate that the disk arms very often, for 50 to 70 percent of requests, do not move [9]. In our model, we take 7.2 ms, the result of a simulation, as the mean seek time. Rotational *latency* is the time required for the correct data or track area of the disk to rotate under the READ/WRITE head. It can range from zero to a full revolution of the disk. Half the rotation time, 8.3 ms, is used as the average latency. *Data transfer* time is the time required to transfer data between the disk and a memory buffer either in main memory or in the control unit.

Path delays occur if the channel or the control unit to which the disk is connected is busy. Two such delays are: the delay in starting of requests and the delay due to rotational positioning sensing (RPS) misses. The RPS feature allows the rotational positioning of the disk to take place while disconnected from the channel. The penalty for this is that if the channel is not free when the disk is ready, then the device has to make a full revolution before it can reattempt a connection. We consider only the RPS miss delay in this study because it generally involves greater delay than the other type.

Queueing delay is the time a request waits for the disk to become free. This waiting time is an increasing function of load, or request rate.

1) Obtaining the Basic Service Time: We now define the basic I/O service time as the sum of the delays that occur at the disk: seek, latency, data transfer and RPS misses. Let

B	average basic service time
S	average seek time
L	average latency time
T	average data transfer time
RPS	average RPS miss delay.

Then we have

$$B = S + L + T + \text{RPS}.$$

RPS Miss Delay: The RPS miss delay, which is a load-dependent component of the basic service time, may be evaluated as follows. Let

σ_i the probability that the reconnection request from disk$_i$ is blocked, or the probability of a RPS miss, due to channel busy

λ_i the request rate for disk$_i$.

The channel is blocked for the request from disk$_i$ if any other device is transferring data on the channel. Assuming that a reconnection request "sees" the state of the channel as a random observer, we may write

$$\sigma_i = \sum_{\substack{j=1 \\ i \neq j}}^{n} \lambda_j \times T \tag{3}$$

where n is the number of devices, $\sigma_i \leq 1$ and $T = T_j$ for any j because the time to transfer data is independent of load.

If the request distribution is uniform, or the system is perfectly balanced,

$$\sigma_i = \sigma_j \text{ for any } j = 1, 2, \cdots, n.$$

In the unbalanced case, we obtain the request rate for disk$_i$

$$\lambda_i = \lambda \times \text{skew}_i \tag{4}$$

where λ is the total number of requests for the channel and skew$_i$ is the probability that a request is sent to disk$_i$; the skew distribution below is borrowed from [2].

$$\text{Skew Distribution for 8-devices} \tag{5}$$

$\text{skew}_1 = 0.388 \quad \text{skew}_2 = 0.225 \quad \text{skew}_3 = 0.153 \quad \text{skew}_4 = 0.102$

$\text{skew}_5 = 0.068 \quad \text{skew}_6 = 0.054 \quad \text{skew}_7 = 0.010 \quad \text{skew}_8 = 0.001.$

Knowing the probability that a request from disk$_i$ is blocked and assuming that the number of RPS misses per request is geometrically distributed, we may write

$$\text{RPS}_i = \frac{\text{Rev} \times \sigma_i}{1 - \sigma_i} \tag{6}$$

where *Rev* is the time for a disk rotation.

2) Estimating the Queueing Delay: Having obtained the basic service time, the queueing delay can then be estimated. Assuming that the various phases of the basic service time, seek, latency, RPS miss delay, and data transfer are mutually independent, we compute the variance of the basic service time, Var(B).

$$\text{Var}(B) = \text{Var}(S) + \text{Var}(L) + \text{Var}(\text{RPS}) + \text{Var}(T) \tag{7}$$

where Var(S), Var(L), Var(RPS), and Var(T) each denotes the variance of the seek time, latency time, missed reconnection delay, and of the transfer time, respectively. Since the RPS miss delay is load dependent, we rewrite (7) as

$$\text{Var}(B_i) = \text{Var}(S) + \text{Var}(L) + \text{Var}(\text{RPS}_i) + \text{Var}(T). \tag{7'}$$

We assume that the variance of the seek time is given, and the variance of the transfer time is 0 since the data transfer time is constant. Latency times are considered to be uniformly distributed between 0 and *Rev*, the revolution time for the disk. Hence,

$$\text{Var}(L) = \frac{\text{Rev}^2}{12}.$$

Following an assumption that the number of RPS misses per request is geometrically distributed, the variance of the RPS miss delay is therefore

$$\text{Var}(\text{RPS}_i) = \frac{\text{Rev}^2 \times \sigma_i}{(1 - \sigma_i)^2}.$$

Knowing the first moment (mean) and the variance of the service time, we obtain the second moment of the service time

$$\text{Second}(B_i) = \text{Var}(B_i) + B_i^2.$$

We now evaluate the *utilization* of each device

$$\rho_i = \lambda_i \times B_i \tag{8}$$

where λ_i is the request rate computed according to the skew rate as in (5). Modeling disk$_i$ as an $M/G/1$ queueing system, its *mean queueing delay* [16] is

$$Q_i = \frac{\lambda_i \times \text{second}(B_i)}{2 \times (1 - \rho_i)} \tag{9}$$

and its *response time* is

$$R_i = Q_i + B_i. \tag{10}$$

Finally, it follows that the average I/O response time on all connected devices R is

$$R = \sum_{i=1}^{n} R_i \times \text{skew}_i.$$

B. Queueing Models

The parameters in our disk system models are summarized as follows:

- Device parameters are set to those of the IBM 3380 disks [3]:

Transfer rate	3 Mbytes/s
Average seek	7.2 ms
Device rotation	16.6 ms
Latency	8.3 ms.

- Poisson arrival of requests is assumed, and the request rate is varied from light, 10 requests/s per channel, to heavy, 40–70 requests/s per channel.
- Service time distribution is assumed to be general.
- Block size (the amount of data to transfer) per request varies between 1 page (4096 bytes) and 60 pages (240K bytes).
- A simple I/O configuration with one channel, one control unit, and a group of n disks, where n is set to 8, is assumed.

In our model, a control unit is assumed to have only the minimum amount of storage that is necessary for disk synchronization. One might argue that by adding a disk cache in a conventional system, RPS misses may be eliminated. This is true if for each arm of the disk a cache of one track is provided. Anything less than this inevitably involves some misses, while a synchronized system, as discussed in Section II-B, requires only a small fraction of the storage that is required of a conventional system. The effect of disk cache on interleaved disks is the subject of further study, and we will not discuss it here.

We also assume that the peak transfer rate of disks is limited by their rotational speed rather than by the speed of channels or of memory systems. This is a reasonable assumption to make although today's channels certainly have a maximum speed which is not much greater than that of the disks; the bandwidths of current memory systems also have their limitations. However, it has been agreed that it is easier to increase the speed of a channel, or of a memory system, than that of a disk.

1) Balanced Conventional Disk System: A hypothetical disk system may be represented as in Fig. 3, by treating each disk as a single server queue. As shown in the figure, arriving requests are distributed over the disks with equal probability. Data transfers may occur for one disk at a time while other delays may overlap between the disks.

2) Unbalanced Conventional Disk System: There is generally a great skew of access distribution to disks, as we have stated previously. This results in an uneven utilization of devices; a few devices may be over utilized while the rest remain idle. Such conventional disk systems may be modeled as in Fig. 4.

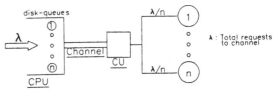

Fig. 3. Balanced conventional system.

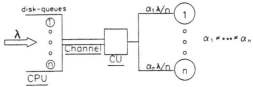

Fig. 4. Unbalanced conventional system.

Given the total request rate for a channel, the request rate for each device may be derived using the skew distribution as shown earlier. As a request arrives it is added to a disk queue, which is selected randomly according to the skewed distribution, and the request is served by the disk as it becomes free.

Data transfer may occur for one disk at a time and other delays such as seek, latency, and RPS misses may overlap between the disks.

3) Synchronized Disk System: A synchronized disk system is modeled as a special case of a conventional system with a large single disk. A conventional single disk system is shown in Fig. 5, and a synchronized disk system in Fig. 6. The difference between the two is in data transfer times. In synchronized systems, the data transfer time is reduced by a factor of $1/n$.

As shown in the figure, there is a single disk queue that represents a group of physical disks in a synchronized system. Note that a request is served by all of the disks and that the request rate for each disk is λ, the same rate as the total number of requests. Also, in this system, mean seek time and mean latency are those of a single device. Furthermore, there is no path contention such as RPS misses in this system; this is just like a single disk system.

IV. NUMERICAL RESULTS AND COMPARISONS

A synchronized system has performance advantages over a conventional system in that it provides a less skewed access distribution and that it reduces the time for data transfers by a factor of $1/n$. In this section, the results of analytic modeling are presented; various performance measures of the synchronized systems are compared to those of the conventional systems, and the advantages and limitations of each system are analyzed. Basic service times are examined first and throughput rates of the two disk systems are analyzed. Peak transfer rates of disks are then derived using the basic service time distribution. Further, mean queueing delays and response times of the two are analyzed and compared with each other. The impact of disk skew on the performance of conventional systems can be found in [12].

A. Basic Service Time

It is intuitively clear that the advantages of a synchronized system are that the access distribution is uniform, there is no

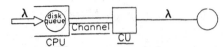

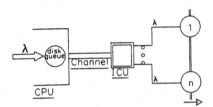

Fig. 5. Single disk system.

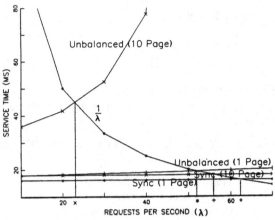

Fig. 6. Synchronized disk system.

Fig. 7. Basic service time and disk throughput.

path contention, and that the data transfer time is only a fraction of the time that is required in a conventional system. A conventional system, however, benefits from the fact that seek, latency, and RPS misses may overlap.

The average basic service time of a request may be obtained by adding up weighted averages of the basic service times on all of the connected disks. In Fig. 7, the average service times are plotted as a function of request rate for 1- and 10-page transfers. The curve $1/\lambda$ is plotted in order to derive disk throughput rates as discussed later.

In a conventional system, the time required for a 1-page transfer is 1.6 ms, and the time for a 10-page transfer is 16 ms. When the pages are read from 8 synchronized disks, it takes (1.6/8), or 0.2, ms and (16/8), or 2 ms, respectively, resulting in a difference of less than 2 ms. Note also that there is no load-dependent component in the basic service times in the synchronized systems. On the other hand, conventional systems suffer from increased data transfer times and RPS misses as block sizes become large.

At the request rate of 30 for 1-page transfers, the average service time in a conventional system is 21 ms, while that in a synchronized system is 16 ms giving a reduction of 24 percent. At the same request rate of 30, for 10-page transfers, the reduction is from 50 ms to 18 ms, or by 64 percent.

B. Device Throughput

We now compute the average service rate μ, the average number of requests that are completed per second, of each system as a function of the total request rate λ.

$$\mu = \frac{1}{B}, \quad B = f(\lambda), \quad B \text{ is the basic service time.}$$

If the request rate is greater than the service rate then there is a finite probability that the device queue may grow infinitely. Therefore, we want to have $\lambda < \mu$. The throughput, the average number of requests completed per second, is then min $\{\lambda, \mu\}$. This means that the throughput is equivalent to the request rate λ, as long as λ is less than the maximum service rate μ, beyond which the throughput is saturated at the value of μ. Then λ^* at which the throughput is saturated may be derived numerically as follows.

$$\lambda^* = \mu = \frac{1}{B}, \quad B = f(\lambda^*), \quad \frac{1}{\lambda^*} = B.$$

In a synchronized system, the throughput of disks may be derived as shown above. In a conventional system, however, the average service rate μ may no longer be used to derive the throughput rate, since the average service times vary considerably between the disks due to skew. Moreover, if any one of the disks has a probability that its queue may grow infinitely, then the system throughput rate is determined by that disk. Thus, we want to find out the request rate at which the worst case disk is saturated rather than the average case as shown above. Let B_i be the average basic service time on disk$_i$. Then, $1/B_i = \mu_i$ where μ_i is the average service rate of disk$_i$ given λ_i where $\lambda_i = \lambda \times$ skew$_i$, and we want to make sure that $\lambda_i < \mu_i$.

Since we are interested in the worst case disk, which has the lowest average service rate, or the largest average service time, we may derive the λ^* as follows:

$$\lambda^* = \min(\mu_i) = \min\left(\frac{1}{B_i}\right) = \frac{1}{\max(B_i)}.$$

Thus,

$$\frac{1}{\lambda^*} = \max(B_i)$$

where $\max(B_i)$ is the worst case average service time by which the system throughput is limited.

We can then use a graphical construct to approximate the device throughput by superimposing the plot $1/\lambda$ upon the average service times in the synchronized system and upon the worst case service times in the conventional system, as shown in Fig. 7. The intersections of these sets of curves yield the respective saturation points. Note that in the figure we have plotted the average basic service times for a conventional system rather than the worst case times for brevity; if we had plotted the worst case times and $1/\lambda_i$; where λ_i the request rate to the worst case disk, the saturation points would have been even lower than those shown in the figure.

For 1-page transfers, synchronized disks are saturated at the rate of approximately 62 requests/s and conventional disks at $\simeq 52$ requests; for 10-page transfers, synchronized disks at $\simeq 56$ requests and conventional disks at $\simeq 23$ requests. Each

364

intersection in the figure is identified by the symbols $\bigcirc$, $*$, $+$, and $\times$, respectively. Note that the device saturation point in the conventional system is very low for large block transfers, while that of the synchronized system shows a considerable improvement, an increase of 61 percent in throughput for 10-page transfers.

C. Peak Transfer Rate of Disks

We have set the disk transfer rate to 3 Mbytes/s in our model. The effective transfer rate, however, is far smaller than this. This is because there are significant delays in the service time that do not contribute to data transfers.

The peak transfer rate that can be effectively achieved from the disks may be obtained from the λ^* derived previously: peak transfer rate = $\lambda^* \times$ block size.

For 1-page transfers:

synchronized system $62 \times$ 1-page (4K bytes)

$$= 248K \text{ bytes/s}$$

conventional system $52 \times$ 1-page (4K bytes)

$$= 208K \text{ bytes/s.}$$

For 10-page transfers:

synchronized system $56 \times$ 10-page (40K bytes)

$$= 2240K \text{ bytes/s}$$

conventional system $23 \times$ 10-page (40K bytes)

$$= 920K \text{ bytes/s.}$$

Note that the rates above are the peak transfer rates on all connected disks, 8 disks in our study. In the worst case, as in the conventional system for 1-page transfers, the effective peak transfer rate per disk is (208K/8), or 26K bytes, which is two orders of magnitude smaller than the maximum rate. It is clear that we are better off with larger block transfers. By increasing the block size from 1 to 10 pages, the peak transfer rate is increased by a factor of 4 in conventional systems, and by a factor of 9 in synchronized systems. Although the improvement is substantial in the synchronized case, the rate is still far lower than the theoretical maximum. This wide gap may be narrowed down by further increasing block sizes and by carefully adding more disks (See Section IV-F). As block size changes to 20, 40, and 60 pages, peak transfer rates increase accordingly as examined later.

D. Queueing Delay

The average queueing delay on a system may be obtained by adding up weighted averages of the queueing delays on all of the connected disks.

In Fig. 8, the average queueing times in both conventional systems and synchronized systems are plotted against the request rates to the channel with varying block sizes. Two curves, $1/\lambda$ and $0.3/\lambda$ are also plotted to derive the request rates at which the queue length becomes 1 and 0.3, respectively. This will be further discussed in the section on queue length.

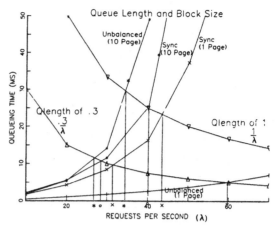

Fig. 8. Queueing delay and queue length.

We observe that with short block transfers (i.e., 1 page), the synchronized system suffers from the queueing delay significantly, while the delay is hardly noticeable in the conventional system. With larger block transfers (e.g., 10 pages), however, the synchronized system suffers less from the queueing delay than the conventional system does.

The queueing delay is an increasing function of request rate, service time, and device utilization. In synchronized systems, the service times are smaller than those in conventional systems, while the disk utilization factors are higher, especially with small block transfers. From (8) in Section III-A-2), the utilization of a disk is

$$\rho_i = \lambda_i \times B_i$$

where $\lambda_i = \lambda$ in synchronized systems. The fact that each device has to respond to every I/O request, and that the reduction in the service time is not as great for short block transfers causes heavy disk utilization of the synchronized disks; hence the high queueing delays for short block transfers. However, for larger block transfers, the opposite effect takes place. The reduction in the basic service time is no longer trivial in the synchronized systems, while the conventional systems suffer significantly from disk skew as block size increases.

Disk Utilization: In Fig. 9, disk utilization factors are plotted against the total request rate. For conventional systems, the average device utilization factors are plotted as well as the worst case situation, and their average disk utilization factors are derived by adding the weighted average utilization factors.

With small block transfers, the synchronized systems approach 100 percent utilization at a request rate of 60 requests/s, while the conventional systems, even in the worst case, stay below the 45 percent utilization mark at the same request rate. It is important to observe that in the conventional systems, the average disk throughput reaches its saturation while most of the disks are less than fully utilized. Fig. 7 shows that the disk saturation point for 1-page transfers is approximately 52 requests/s. On the other hand, in Fig. 9, we see that even the worst case disk utilization is below 45 percent at the same request rate. In other words, the disks are not fully

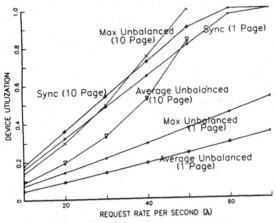

Fig. 9. Device utilization.

utilized in the conventional systems and disk saturation occurs while the average utilization factors of the disks are still low.

Large block transfers, on the other hand, narrow the gap between the two systems as far as utilization is concerned. At the request rate of 36 pages/s, a crossover occurs between the two, because the data transfer time plays a key role in this situation. That is, with large block transfers, even though every disk in the synchronized system responds to every request, the queueing delay is not as severe as in the conventional system due to the significant reduction in service time.

Queue Length: Using Little's theorem, the average queue length of each system may be obtained: $L = \lambda \times Q$ where L represents the average queue length and Q the mean waiting time in the queue. The request rates at which the queue lengths for each system become 0.3 and 1 are obtained using a graphical construct as follows:

for $L = 1$, $1 = \lambda Q$, then $\dfrac{1}{\lambda} = Q$,

and for $L = 0.3$, $\dfrac{0.3}{\lambda} = Q$.

In Fig. 8, two curves $(1/\lambda)$ and $(0.3/\lambda)$ are superimposed upon the average queueing times. The intersections of these sets of curves yield the request rates at each of which the average queue lengths in the respective system become 0.3 and 1.

Observe that in the conventional system with small block transfers the queue length is only 0.3 at the rate of 60 requests/ s. Note that the same system, as we have seen in Fig. 7, has reached disk saturation at the rate of 52. That is, disk saturation in the conventional system occurs before the average queue length reaches 0.3. The result is similar with larger block transfers; disk saturation occurs at 23, and the queue length is less than 0.3 as shown. These suggest that the disk scheduling techniques as described in the literature would hardly improve the situation in conventional systems; if not many requests have been queued, it simply does not make sense to order them.

In the synchronized systems, however, the mean queue length becomes greater than 1 before the disks reach the saturation point. Furthermore, these systems suffer greatly from queueing delays, especially with small block transfers. This suggests that various disk scheduling techniques may now be exploited to obtain further improvements in the access time.

E. Weighted Average Response Time

Having analyzed the basic service time and the queueing delay, we now add them together in Fig. 10. Note that, for small block transfers, the synchronized system actually delivers a 1-page block more slowly than the conventional system does when the request rate exceeds 25. As discussed previously, the queueing delay in the synchronized system is the predominant factor in the response times for small block transfers. For larger block transfers, however, the synchronized system outperforms the conventional system by a big margin.

F. Larger Block Sizes

So far, we have considered 1-page and 10-page transfers. We now examine the situations in which block sizes exceed 10 pages: 20, 40, and 60 pages are considered below, with the number of disks unchanged.

Basic Service Time and Throughput: The basic service times are plotted as well as the curve $1/\lambda$ against the low request rates, those of less than 20 requests/s, in Fig. 11. As before, each intersection of the curves yields the device saturation point, or the device throughput, for the respective system. Note that the service times in the synchronized systems do not intersect with $1/\lambda$ at request rates lower than 20, while the conventional systems cross $1/\lambda$ at approximately 15 requests/s for 20-page transfers, at $\simeq 9$ requests for 40-page, and at $\simeq 6.5$ requests for 60-page transfers. This means that in the conventional systems the disk saturation is the limiting factor for large block transfers.

The basic service times and the throughput at the higher request rates are plotted in Fig. 12. Here, the conventional systems do not appear at all because they had already been saturated well before the request rate reached 20. The synchronized systems intersect with $1/\lambda$ at approximately 36, 42, and 50 requests/s giving the device throughput rate for 60, 40, and 20-page transfers, respectively.

We now evaluate the peak transfer rate for each case.
For 20-page transfers:

synchronized system 50×20 pages $= 4000$K bytes/s

conventional system 15×20 pages $= 1200$K bytes/s.

For 40-page transfers:

synchronized system 42×40 pages $= 6720$K bytes/s

conventional system 9×40 pages $= 1440$K bytes/s.

For 60-page transfers:

synchronized system 36×60 pages $= 8640$K bytes/s

conventional system 6.5×60 pages $= 1560$K bytes/s.

By increasing the block size from 10 to 20 pages (see Fig. 7,

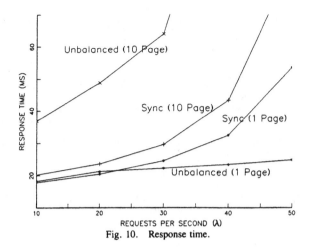

Fig. 10. Response time.

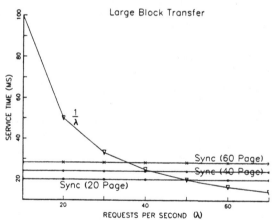

Fig. 11. Device throughput: Large block transfers at low request rates.

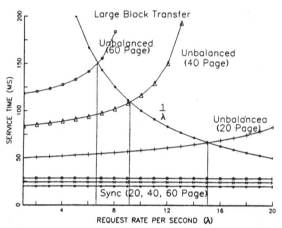

Fig. 12. Device throughput: Large block transfers at high request rates.

for the 10-page case) in the conventional system, the peak throughput rate is increased from 920K bytes to 1200K bytes, or by 30 percent; and in the synchronized system the increase is even greater, by 78 percent. By increasing the block size further from 20 to 40 pages in the synchronized system, the increase is 68 percent, and from 40 to 60 pages there is a 29 percent increase in the peak transfer rate, while the conven-

tional systems show only negligible improvements. The growth rates in the synchronized systems change by 78 percent, by 68 percent, and by 29 percent, respectively. Note that the greatest increase, by a factor of 9, is obtained by changing the block size from 1 to 10 pages. This suggests that additional disks must be used to increase further the disk throughput rate when block size exceeds 10 pages.

Average Response Time: The average response times are plotted against the request rate for 20, 40, and 60-page transfers in Fig. 13. With added queueing delay, the response times in the synchronized systems are now load dependent. At the request rate of 20 in the conventional system, 20 pages may be returned after 85 ms. In the synchronized system, the rate is 20 pages after 25 ms, 40 pages after 35 ms, and 60 pages after 48 ms. In other words, the synchronized system may deliver a block 3 times larger in half the time required in the conventional system. Again, by increasing the number of disks, the synchronized system may show even greater improvement.

V. CONCLUSIONS

The advantages of synchronized disk interleaving may be summarized as follows.

- Simplified control.
- Single logical image of interleaved disks.
- Improved performance.
- Parallelism through interleaving.
- Uniform distribution of I/O requests over the disks.
- Improved reliability with minimum redundancy.

Applications

We have modeled simple block transfers and studied the performance characteristics of interleaving for such tasks. As we have seen, the high bandwidth potential of interleaving can be exploited most efficiently with large block transfers. There are many applications that reference large address spaces and require large block transfers. To name a few: paging/swapping, database management systems, which often require the entire database to be scanned, some large engineering/scientific applications.

We have presented disk interleaving with the help of an intelligent controller. Some primitive database functions, such as search, sort/merge, garbage collection, etc., may be effectively off-loaded to such a controller, providing a backend database machine environment. Database machines can certainly benefit from the parallelism and the simple control structure provided by the interleaving. Other possibilities include the semantic paging notion [20], in which AI data may be stored in the secondary storage directly in semantic networks. This will allow us to incorporate techniques like inferencing which have been developed for artificial intelligence (AI) into an existing database management system. This may be possible by tailoring the granularity of interleaving to a level that is suitable for a specific application.

Engineering/scientific applications that deal with large-scale problems often face a serious problem due to the volume of data. Consider a seismic modeling problem that requires a 3-

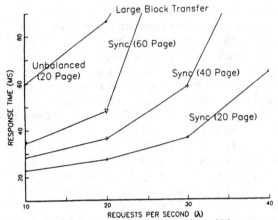

Fig. 13. Average response time: Large block transfers at high request rates.

dimensional discrete Fourier transform [6] of $512 \times 512 \times 512$ data points each of which is a complex pair of 32 bit floating point numbers. The sheer volume of data, $2^9 \times 2^9 \times 2^9 \times 8 = 1024$ Mbytes, indicates the size of the problem. More, each data point is repeatedly evaluated, $O(\log_2 (512 \times 512 \times 512))$ operations per point, requiring that the data array be passed through memory n times where $n \geq 2$ when the array does not fit in main memory. Interleaved disks, when they are used to store such partitioned data, reduce the I/O time of the algorithm. Moreover, as they are synchronized, the I/O time may be reduced even further [15].

Disk interleaving may also be used to provide the capacity of a large complex disk system using a group of small disks. Disks which are small, either in diameter or in capacity, may have advantages over a very large complex disk in that the average seek time may be reduced by reducing the storage capacity per disk, in that they can be made more reliable,[2] and in that they may spin faster thereby reducing latency, etc. A concern, nonetheless, is that the cost of moving arms generally dominates the cost of a disk system. If we only claim that a complex 1-disk system be replaced by an n-disk system to get better performance, it does not appear to be cost-effective. However, "cost" is a compound function, that of hardware cost, of system cost, of performance measures, of reliability measures, and so on. It is no longer clear that the cost of multiple small disks will be higher than that of a large disk with equivalent capacity.

ACKNOWLEDGMENT

The author is indebted to T. Bashkow, A. Tantawi, A. Patel, A. Nigam, P. Franaszek, and an anonymous referee, for their many valuable suggestions. Thanks are also due to K. Rader for many helpful editorial comments.

[2] It is relatively easier to make surfaces of small disks better, thus making them more reliable.

REFERENCES

[1] R. Agrawal and D. J. DeWitt, "Whither hundreds of processors in a database machine?" in *Proc. Int. Workshop High-Level Lang. Comput. Architect.*, 1984.

[2] T. Beretvas, "Page/swap configurations," IBM IS & TG, Poughkeepsie, NY, Tech. Rep., 1982.

[3] M. Bohl, *Introduction to IBM Direct Access Storage Devices*. Science Research Associates, Inc., 1981.

[4] H. Boral and D. J. DeWitt, "Database machines: An idea whose time has passed? A critique of the future of database machines," in *Database Machines*. Berlin: Springer-Verlag, 1983.

[5] J. P. Buzen, "BEST/1 analysis of the IBM 3880-13 cached storage controller," in *Proc. CMG 13th Int. Conf.*, 1982, pp. 156–172.

[6] J. W. Cooley and J. W. Tukey, "An algorithm for the machine calculation of complex Fourier series," *Math. Comp.*, vol. 19, no. 90, pp. 297–301, Apr. 1965.

[7] P. Denning, "Effects of scheduling on file memory operations," in *Proc. AFIPS 1967 Spring Joint Comp. Conf.*, 1967.

[8] ——, "On modeling program behavior," in *Proc. AFIPS 1972 Spring Joint Comp. Conf.*, 1972.

[9] D. Hunter, "The access time myth," IBM, Comput. Sci. Res. Rep. RC10197, Sept. 1983.

[10] O. G. Johnson, "Three-dimensional wave equation computations on vector computers," *Proc. IEEE*, vol. 72, Jan. 1984.

[11] J. A. Katzman, "A fault-tolerant computing system," *Eleventh Hawaii Int. Conf. Syst. Sci.*, 1978.

[12] M. Y. Kim, "Parallel operation of magnetic disk storage devices: Synchronized disk interleaving," in *Proc. 4th Int. Workshop Database Machines*, 1985.

[13] M. Y. Kim and A. Patel, "Error correcting codes for interleaved disks with minimal redundancy," IBM, Comput. Sci. Res. Rep. RC11185, May 1985.

[14] M. Y. Kim and R. E. Matick, "Synchronous to asynchronous conversion buffer," *IBM Tech. Discl. Bull.*, 1986.

[15] M. Y. Kim, "A synchronously interleaved disk system with its application to the very large FFT," IBM, Comput. Sci. Res. Rep., in progress, 1986.

[16] H. Kobayashi, *Modeling and Analysis: An Introduction to System Performance Evaluation Methodology*. Reading, MA: Addison-Wesley, 1978.

[17] H. Leilich, G. Stiege, and H. Zeidler, "A search processor for data base management systems," in *Proc. IEEE Fourth Very Large Data Base Conf.*, 1978, pp. 280–287.

[18] S. Lin and D. Costello, *Error Control Coding: Fundamentals and Applications*. Englewood Cliffs, NJ: Prentice-Hall, 1983.

[19] J. R. Lineback, "New features tune unix for high-end machines," *Electronics*, Aug. 1985.

[20] G. J. Lipovski, "Semantic paging on intelligent disks," in *Proc. 4th Workshop Comput. Architect. Non-Numeric Processing*, 1978.

[21] R. E. Matick, *Computer Storage Systems and Technology*. New York: Wiley-Interscience, 1977, p. 345, p. 386.

[22] A. Patel, "Error and failure-control for a large-size bubble memory," *IEEE Trans. Magn.*, vol. MAG-18, Nov. 1982.

[23] R. Rosenberg, "Magnetic mass storage densities rise," *Electronics Week*, Oct. 29, 1984.

[24] A. J. Smith, "Disk cache—miss ratio analysis and design considerations," *ACM Trans. Comput. Syst.*, vol. 3, Aug. 1985.

[25] D. Thompson, private communication, IBM T. J. Watson Research Center, Yorktown Heights, NY, 1984.

Asynchronous Disk Interleaving: Approximating Access Delays

Michelle Y. Kim, *Member, IEEE,* and Asser N. Tantawi, *Senior Member, IEEE*

Abstract—Disk interleaving, or disk striping, distributes a data block across a group of disks and allows parallel transfer of data. Disk interleaving is achieved by dividing a data block into a number of subblocks and placing each subblock on a separate disk. A subblock can be stored on an interleaved disk at a predetermined location (relative to the adjacent subblocks), or it can be stored at any location on the disk. We consider a system where adjacent subblocks are placed independently of each other, we call it an asynchronous disk interleaving system, and analyze its performance implications. Since each of the disks in such a system is treated independently while being accessed as a group, the access delay of a request for a data block in an n-disk system is the maximum of n access delays. Using approximate analysis, we obtain a simple expression for the expected value of such a maximum delay. The analytic approximation is verified by simulation using trace data, the relative error is found to be at most 6%.

Index Terms—Approximating access delays, asynchronous disk interleaving, simulation of an asynchronous system.

I. Introduction

WITH increasing processor speeds and multiprocessor organizations, the processing power of a computer system has improved greatly in recent years. This in turn has allowed the scale of computing problems to grow. Many large-scale problems require the processing of huge amounts of data. If the data array is larger than the size of main memory, it is assumed to be stored on external devices such as disks. The data rates of disks are limited by their mechanical speeds, and this has caused a huge speed mismatch between the processing power and the I/O system. Consequently, problems that were once CPU-bound are quickly becoming I/O bound. Unless the problem of I/O bandwidth is solved, the dramatically improved processing speeds will not result in a speedup of the system as desired.

Disk interleaving (also called disk stripping)[1] has been suggested as a means of improving bandwidth to disks for large database systems [2], or for scientific applications [6]. More recently, the effectiveness of disk interleaving in computing a large fast Fourier transform has been demonstrated [8]. Disk interleaving has also been studied [12], [13] as a high-performance I/O system architecture in a multiprocessor system. It has been pointed out [7] that the advantages of disk interleaving are twofold: 1) it enables parallelism and 2) it facilitates uniform distribution of requests over multiple disks. One of the major contributors to the performance problems of today's disk systems is the phenomenon that disk access requests are not uniformly distributed over the disks. Thus, only a small number of disks may be heavily utilized while the rest remain idle. This results in I/O bottlenecks, by which the performance of a disk system may be limited. By interleaving disks, it is possible to achieve a more uniform distribution of access requests, thereby improving the overall system performance.

In an interleaved disk system, a data block may be partitioned into subblocks $S_1, S_2, \cdots, S_n$. Subblock S_i is assigned to disk unit $((i - 1) \bmod n) + 1$, where n is the degree of interleaving. That is, subblock 1 is stored on disk 1, subblock 2 of the same data block is stored on disk 2, and so on. As these subblocks are placed across a group of disks, they may be stored at predetermined locations, say at the same physical location, or be stored independently of each other. The former case has been known as *synchronized interleaved disk system,* and its performance implications have been analyzed in [7]. We call the latter *asynchronous interleaved system,* and study its performance implications in this paper. In an asynchronous interleaved disk system, the disks may be treated asynchronously, or independently of each other, and those subblocks belonging to the same data block are stored independently of each other. As a result, the seek and rotational delays involved in the same transfer will be different for each disk. In order to provide an adequate error correcting scheme upon failure of a disk, checksums may be placed on separate checksum disks to improve reliability using minimizing redundancy. See [7] and [4] for a detailed discussion on reliability issues.

Evaluating Average I/O Response Time: Basically, the response time of a I/O request consists of five components: 1) queueing delay, 2) seek, 3) latency, 4) RPS (rotational positioning sensing) delay, and 5) data transfer. Queueing delay is the time that a request waits for the disk to become free. Seek delay is the time required to position the access mechanism to the cylinder containing the data. Latency is the time required for the correct data to rotate under the read/write head. The RPS feature allows the rotational positioning sensing of the disks to take place while disconnected from channel. The penalty for this is that, in the absence of a disk cache, if the channel is not free when the disk is ready, the disk has to make a full revolution before it can reattempt a connection. Data transfer time is the time required to transfer data between the disk and main memory.

Manuscript received April 11, 1988; revised February 15, 1991.

The authors are with the IBM Thomas J. Watson Research Center, Yorktown Heights, NY 10598.

IEEE Log Number 9100992.

[1] A group of disk units is interleaved if each data block is divided into portions and succeeding portions of the same block are stored on different disks.

In an asynchronous system there is one queue for each independent disk. It has been shown [7] that in a reasonably well-tuned conventional disk system, it is hard to see a disk queue growing beyond one. An n-disk asynchronous system is similar to an n-disk conventional system in that there will be one queueing point for each disk. The average number of requests that wait in a queue in an n-disk asynchronous system will be even smaller than that has been observed in a conventional system. This is because of the reduced data transfer time in an asynchronous system; queueing delay is an increasing function of the delays that occur at the disk, and the time to transfer data in an asynchronous system is a fraction of the time in a conventional system. As will be shown, a major portion of a data block access delay is the synchronization delay, by which we mean the gap between the time the first subblock is accessed and the time the last subblock is available. Although the impact of RPS misses on the performance of a disk system is great, there are implementation techniques that could be used to minimize or eliminate the problem. Hence, we shall ignore the impact of RPS miss delay. Among the remaining delays: seek, latency, and data transfer times, the latter is a constant and does not change from disk to disk. Thus, we consider seek, latency, and access delay which is defined as the sum of seek and latency.

The paper is organized as follows. In Section II, we obtain exact and approximate expressions for the expected access delay in an n-disk asynchronous system. These expressions are validated in Section III by simulating an asynchronously interleaved system. Conclusions appear in Section IV.

II. EVALUATION OF THE EXPECTED ACCESS DELAY

In this section, we evaluate the expected maximum delays of disk access requests in asynchronously interleaved disk systems with n disks. We assume that the delays at each disk are independent and identically distributed (i.i.d.) random variables. Thus, the problem is to evaluate the expected value of the maximum of a set of i.i.d. random variables. In general, it is hard to obtain a closed form expression for the expected maximum. However, for simple distributions such as the exponential and the uniform distributions one can obtain closed form expressions as we show in Section II-A. By assuming that the seek time distribution is exponential and the latency distribution is uniform, we can evaluate the expectation of their maximum delays using these expressions. We also give an approximate expression for the expected maximum and apply it to the normal distribution. This approximation method is used to evaluate the expected maximum of the access delay. Unfortunately, the access delay, which is of prime interest to us, does not have a simple distribution such as exponential, uniform, or normal, whose expected maximum can be easily evaluated using simple expressions. However, by approximating its distribution by a normal distribution, we obtain an approximation for the expected maximum value. One interesting observation, as we shall see later, is that the two extreme assumptions of exponential and uniform cases are shown to provide useful bounds on the relative error of the approximation. In Section II-B, we obtain exact expressions

for the expected maximum of the access delay for certain seek and latency distributions and evaluate the error due to our approximation.

A. Analysis

Let $\{X_i, i = 1, 2, \cdots, n\}$ be i.i.d. nonnegative random variables with distribution function F_X, mean μ_X, and standard deviation σ_X. Denote by $X_{\max}(n)$ the random variable which is the maximum of $\{X_i, i = 1, 2, \cdots, n\}$; its distribution is given by

$$F_{X_{\max}(n)}(y) = (F_X(y))^n, \qquad y \geq 0. \qquad (1)$$

Since the random variable $X_{\max}(n)$ is nonnegative, its expectation is expressed as

$$E[X_{\max}(n)] = \int_0^\infty \left(1 - (F_X(y))^n\right) dy. \qquad (2)$$

It is straightforward to evaluate the above expression for exponential and uniform distributions. Assuming that X is exponentially distributed with mean μ_X, we get

$$E[X_{\max}(n)] = H_n \mu_X \qquad (3)$$

where $H_n = \sum_{k=1}^n 1/k$ is the harmonic series. For large n, H_n may be approximated by $c + \ln(n)$, where $c = 0.5772$ is Euler's constant. Note that $E[X_{\max}(n)]$ grows logarithmically with n. As an example, if the seek times are exponentially distributed, we can obtain the expectation of the maximum seek, $S_{\max}(n)$, from (3). It is clear that seek time cannot be greater than the time it takes to move the access arm from the innermost to the outermost cylinder. Thus, we bound the value of H_n for seek on an IBM 3380 disk by $30/7.2 (= 4.2)$, where 30 ms is the time for the maximum amount of movement across cylinders and 7.2 ms the expected seek time [1].

Assuming that X is uniformly distributed in the interval $[0, 2\mu_X]$, we get

$$E[X_{\max}(n)] = 2\mu_X \frac{n}{n + 1}. \qquad (4)$$

Note that the expectation of $X_{\max}(n)$ increases slowly with n and it reaches a constant, namely $2\mu_X$, as $n \to \infty$. Let latency times be uniformly distributed between 0 and 16.6 ms, the maximum rotational latency of the disk. By substituting $2\mu_X = 16.6$ ms into (4), we obtain the expected maximum latency.

For general distribution functions F_X, the integration in (2) is not straightforward. However, $E[X_{\max}(n)]$ may be approximated by a quantity known as the characteristic maximum of the random variable X which we denote by χ_n [9], [3]; it is defined by

$$\chi_n = \min\{x : 1 - F_X(x) \leq 1/n\}.$$

For continuous functions, the characteristic maximum is obtained from the equation

$$F_X(\chi_n) = 1 - \frac{1}{n}. \qquad (5)$$

370

In terms of χ_n, $E[X_{\max}(n)]$ may be approximated by [5]

$$E[X_{\max}(n)] \cong \chi_n + \int_{\chi_n}^{\infty} n(1 - F_X(y)) \, dy$$

which has a lower bound χ_n. In other words, the expectation of the maximum of n i.i.d. random variables can be approximated by the characteristic maximum:

$$E[X_{\max}(n)] \cong \chi_n. \tag{6}$$

As an example, if X is normal with mean μ_X and standard deviation σ_X, then for $n > 4$, the characteristic maximum may be approximated by [9]

$$\chi_n \cong \mu_X + \sigma_X \sqrt{2 \log n}.$$

Therefore, from (6) we have

$$E[X_{\max}(n)] \cong \mu_X + \sigma_X \sqrt{2 \log n} \tag{7}$$

which is a good approximation for normal distributions and found to be valid for a class of general distributions. Note that $E[X_{\max}(n)]$ grows as the square root of $\log n$.

Expressions for the expectation of $X_{\max}(n)$ are given in (3), (4), and (7) for exponential, uniform, and normal distributions, respectively. We note that they all have the form

$$E[X_{\max}(n)] = \mu_X + \sigma_X G(n)$$

where $G(n)$ is a function of n which depends on the distribution F_X in an interesting fashion as illustrated in Fig. 1.

$G(n)$ may be interpreted as the expectation of the maximum of i.i.d. random variables with zero mean and unit variance. For exponential distributions, $G(n) = H_n - 1$ which grows logarithmically with n. For normal distributions, $G(n) = \sqrt{2 \log n}$ which grows at a slower rate as the square root of the logarithm. Finally, for uniform distributions, $G(n) = \sqrt{3}(n - 1)/(n + 1)$ which grows very slowly with n and goes to $\sqrt{3}$ as $n \to \infty$. A tight upper bound on $G(n)$ is given by [3]

$$G(n) \le \frac{n - 1}{\sqrt{2n - 1}}$$

which is illustrated in the figure. Note that the curve for the normal distribution is valid only for $n > 4$. Otherwise, one could use the upper bound.

B. Examples

We consider two cases: 1) exponential seek and uniform latency and 2) uniform seek and uniform latency.

The access delay Z is the sum of seek and latency, $Z = S + L$. The probability density function of Z is therefore obtained by convolving the probability density functions of seek and latency as

$$f_Z(z) = \int_0^z f_S(x) f_L(z - x) \, dx, \qquad z \ge 0. \tag{8}$$

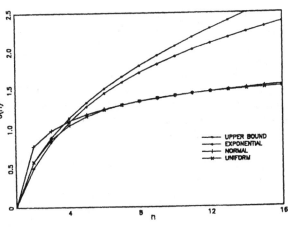

Fig. 1.

Substituting the probability density functions f_S and f_L into (8) yields the probability density function of the access delay which by integration and substitution into (2):

$$E[Z_{\max}(n)] = \int_0^{\infty} (1 - F_Z^n(t)) \, dt \tag{9}$$

gives the expected maximum access delay. Although the integration may not be straightforward and the result may not be in a closed form, the above equations can be evaluated for some simple distributions.

1) Exponential Seek and Uniform Latency:

We assume that the seek time is exponentially distributed with mean $1/\lambda$ and latency is uniformly distributed in the range $[0, a]$. Thus, we have $f_S(s) = \lambda e^{-\lambda s}$, $s \ge 0$, and $f_L(l) = \frac{1}{a}$, $0 \le l \le a$. In order to perform the integration in (8), we divide the range of z into two regions: $z \le a$ and $z > a$, and obtain

$$f_Z(z) = \begin{cases} \frac{1}{a}\left(1 - e^{-\lambda z}\right), & z \le a, \\ \frac{e^{-\lambda z}}{a}\left(e^{\lambda a} - 1\right), & z > a. \end{cases}$$

By integrating the above expression we obtain the distribution function of Z, which we denote by $F_Z(t) = \int_0^t f_Z(z) \, dz$; it is given by

$$F_Z(t) = \begin{cases} \frac{t}{a} - \frac{1}{\lambda a}\left(1 - e^{-\lambda t}\right), & t \le a, \\ 1 - \frac{e^{-\lambda t}}{\lambda a}\left(e^{\lambda a} - 1\right), & t > a. \end{cases} \tag{10}$$

Substituting (10) into (9) yields

$$E[Z_{\max}(n)] =$$
$$a\left\{1 + \frac{1}{\lambda}\left[H_n(1) - H_n\left(1 - \frac{1 - e^{-\alpha}}{\alpha}\right) - \frac{Y_n(\alpha)}{\alpha^n}\right]\right\} \tag{11}$$

where $\alpha = \lambda a$, $H_n(x) = \sum_{i=1}^{n} \frac{x^i}{i}$, $E_n(x) = \sum_{i=0}^{n} \frac{x^i}{i!}$

$$Y_n(x) = (-1)^n \left\{x + \sum_{i=1}^{n} (-1)^i \frac{n!}{(n - 1)!} Q\right\},$$

and

$$Q = \frac{x^{i+1}}{(i + 1)!} + \sum_{j=1}^{i} \frac{e^{-jx}}{j! j^{i-j+1}} \left(E_\infty(jx) - E_{i-j}(jx)\right).$$

371

We note from (11) that the exact expression for $E[Z_{\max}(n)]$ is given in terms of finite sums and is easily evaluated numerically for various values of n. In Fig. 2 we plot $E[Z_{\max}(n)]$, the expected maximum access delay, against n, the number of disks. We assume that the mean values of seek and latency are 7.09 and 8.333 ms, respectively. Also, we plot the approximate expression for the expected maximum access delay which we obtained by approximating the distribution of the access delay by a normal distribution, as given in (7). Note that the approximation is valid only for $n > 4$. The relative error of the approximation is plotted in Fig. 3. From Fig. 3, the relative error for $n = 8$ is approximately 7.6%.

2) Uniform Seek and Uniform Latency: Assume that both S and L are uniformly distributed in the ranges $[0, b]$ and $[0, a]$, respectively. Their probability density functions f_S and f_L are given by $f_S(s) = \frac{1}{b}$, $0 \le s \le b$, and $f_L(l) = \frac{1}{a}$, $0 \le l \le a$, respectively. By substituting these equations into (8) we obtain the probability density function f_Z of the access delay:

$$f_Z(z) = \begin{cases} \frac{z}{ab}, & 0 \le z \le a, \\ \frac{1}{b}, & a \le z \le b, \\ \frac{a+b}{ab} - \frac{z}{ab}, & b \le z \le a + b. \end{cases}$$

By integrating $f_Z(z)$ we obtain the distribution function of Z as

$$F_Z(t) = \begin{cases} \frac{t^2}{2ab}, & 0 \le t \le a, \\ \frac{1}{b}\left(t - \frac{a}{2}\right), & a \le t \le b, \\ 1 - \frac{((a+b)-t)^2}{2ab}, & b \le t \le a + b. \end{cases}$$

Substituting the above equation into (9) yields

$$E[Z_{\max}(n)] = \int_0^{a+b} (1 - F_Z^n(t))\, dt = A + B + C,$$

where

$$A = \int_0^a 1 - \left(\frac{t^2}{2ab}\right)^n dt = a - \frac{a}{2n+1}\left(\frac{a}{2b}\right)^n,$$

$$B = \int_a^b 1 - \left(\frac{1}{b}\left(t - \frac{a}{2}\right)\right)^n dt$$

$$= b - a - \frac{b}{n+1}\left[\left(1 - \left(\frac{a}{2b}\right)\right)^{n+1} - \left(\frac{a}{2b}\right)^{n+1}\right],$$

and

$$C = \int_a^{a+b} 1 - \left[\frac{(1-(a+b)-t)^2}{2ab}\right]^n dt$$

$$= a - b\sqrt{\frac{a}{2b}} \sum_{i=0}^n (-1)^i \binom{n}{i} \left(\frac{a}{2b}\right)^{i+\frac{1}{2}} \frac{1}{i+\frac{1}{2}}.$$

By summing we get

$$E[Z_{\max}(n)] = a + b - \left[\begin{array}{c} \frac{a\alpha^n}{2n+1} + \frac{b}{n+1}\left((1-\alpha)^{n+1} - \alpha^{n+1}\right) \\ + a\sum_{i=0}^n (-1)^i \binom{n}{i}\frac{\alpha^i}{2i+1} \end{array}\right] \tag{12}$$

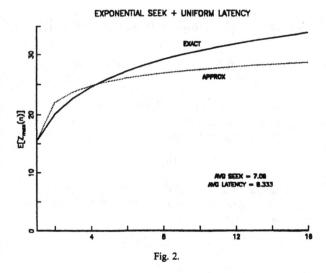

EXPONENTIAL SEEK + UNIFORM LATENCY

EXACT

APPROX

AVG SEEK = 7.09
AVG LATENCY = 8.333

Fig. 2.

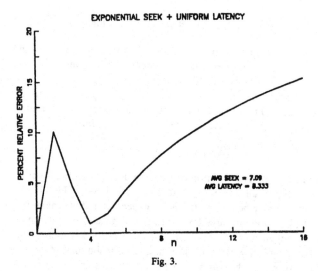

EXPONENTIAL SEEK + UNIFORM LATENCY

AVG SEEK = 7.09
AVG LATENCY = 8.333

Fig. 3.

where $\alpha = \frac{a+b}{2}$.

In Fig. 4 we plot $E[Z_{\max}(n)]$ for various values of n, with mean values of seek and latency equal to 25 and 8.333 ms, respectively. Note that the device parameters are those of an IBM 3350 disk system. As previously, we compare the exact $E[Z_{\max}(n)]$ obtained from (12) to the normal approximation discussed in Section II-A. The relative error of the approximation is computed and plotted in Fig. 5. For $n = 8$, the relative error is approximately 0.89%. For all n that are shown in Fig. 5, the relative errors are very small, almost negligible. In the case where the seek time distribution is exponential, we have shown that the relative error is 7.6%, which is still very low. We can, therefore, safely conclude that the normal approximation is a good approximation for a wide class of seek time distributions.

III. Experiments and Results

In the previous section, we have obtained an approximation to the expected access delay in an asynchronous interleaved

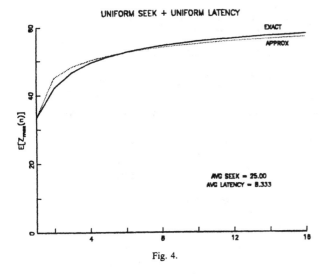

UNIFORM SEEK + UNIFORM LATENCY

AVG SEEK = 25.00
AVG LATENCY = 8.333

Fig. 4.

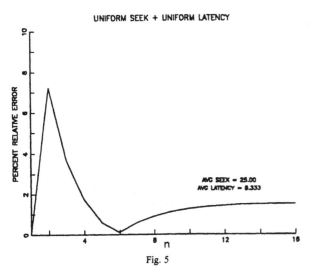

UNIFORM SEEK + UNIFORM LATENCY

AVG SEEK = 25.00
AVG LATENCY = 8.333

Fig. 5

system. Experiments were run to validate our method, and we summarize the results in this section.

A. Traces Used

Two types of trace data are used for the experiments: real reference traces and synthetic traces, as described below.

1) Real Traces: The disk reference traces that were available for our experiments originated at the data processing center of a major manufacturing company. The company has large IMS (information management system) databases, which are accessed interactively. Our traces are of IMS database references from 32 of the company's 430 IBM 3350 DASD's (direct access storage devices). A more detailed description of the traces can be found elsewhere [11]. The traces have been filtered to eliminate all but sequences of seek addresses, or cylinder addresses, on the disk, we are interested in. Once the seek activities have been grouped by disk, we compute their displacements, or the distance the access arms travel. We assume that the access arms are initially positioned at

the cylinder where the required data are. The number of displacements is then one smaller than the number of original seek addresses.

Seek times are calculated using the mechanical characteristics of the actuator.[2] For high-performance voice coil actuator, the seek time is given by [14]

$$S = a + b\sqrt{\Delta}, \qquad \Delta \geq 1$$

where Δ is the displacement in cylinders, a is the mechanical setting time, and b is related to track density and the acceleration of the actuator. For 3350 devices seek times are obtained from

$$S = 7.8 + 1.8\sqrt{\Delta}, \qquad \Delta \geq 1,$$

whereas for 3380 devices, they are given by

$$S = 2.1 + 0.9\sqrt{\Delta}, \qquad \Delta \geq 1.$$

In our experiments, the seek times of both device types have been considered and our methods have been shown equally valid in both cases. Our methods are based on certain assumptions, about the distribution of seeks, and their resulting distributions are similar, although the magnitudes of the seek times on the two device types are quite different. Since the traces were taken from 3350 DASD's, we will base our discussion on the 3350 seek times in this section.

From the above process we have obtained a sequence of seek times for each of the disks that were monitored. Note that from the traces, we have obtained only seek information. As for latency, we assume that it is uniformly distributed between 0 and 16.6, the maximum rotational delay.

We examine in our experiments four of the most active disks among the 32 which were monitored. Their seek time distributions are depicted in Figs. 10–13. The seek activities exhibit commonly a significant number of zero seeks, and vary widely otherwise.

2) Synthetic Traces: Real reference streams are complicated and variable. From a limited number of traces, there is always uncertainty associated with drawing a general conclusion. In order to experiment with other seek distributions which are certainly conceivable, we create two reference streams for seek time: uniform and exponential. Having generated seek times, we generate a sequence of latency times, which are uniformly distributed. These two sequences are then merged to form a sequence of (seek, latency) pairs. In fact, having a uniform seek time distribution implies that the seek times are independent of where data are stored. Although this is not conceivable given today's storage technology, it is theoretically interesting, and worth investigating. More importantly, this uniform distribution of seek times, as we shall see shortly, is shown to provide a lower bound on the relative error of the approximation, while exponential distribution provides an upper bound.

---

[2] An arm mechanism that moves the read/write heads and attached heads form an actuator.

Seek	Disk-1	Disk-2	Disk-3	Disk-4	Disk-E	Disk-U
(Measured)						
Mean	7.3337	14.9320	23.7070	19.7737	7.0916	24.8910
Std dev	7.0629	13.7520	15.1140	13.9850	6.9143	14.3240
Max	20.1402	45.6860	49.0824	47.6450	47.8950	49.9371
Exp max	16.4092	35.1879	42.2031	37.0035	18.5752	44.3544

Fig. 6. For each disk, mean, standard deviation (std dev), maximum (max), and expected maximum (exp max) seek times are measured.

3) Redistribution of Trace Data: The disk references from a single disk may be redistributed over n disks so as to simulate an asynchronous n-disk system. Note that our goal is to preserve the original access pattern so that each of the interleaved disks, after the references have been redistributed across them, still maintains the same access pattern as the original disk. While the access pattern is being preserved on each disk, the disks must at the same time be treated independently of each other. This may be accomplished by splitting a sequence of (seek, latency) pairs originally obtained from a single disk into eight, $n = 8$ in our experiments, subsequences. This split is done by assigned the first $\frac{1}{8}$th references to $disk_1$, the second $\frac{1}{8}$th to $disk_2$, and so on. In this manner, the original access pattern on each disk is preserved on all of the interleaved disks, and yet at any point of reference the references across them are independent of each other.

B. Measurements

Having regrouped the original trace sequence for each disk, and split each group into eight subsequences of (seek, latency) pairs, each of length k, we take measurements of the trace data as follows. Let $S_{i,j}$ and $L_{i,j}, i = 1, 2, \cdots, n$ and $j = 1, 2, \cdots, k$, denote the jth seek and latency for $disk_i$, respectively. Furthermore, let $Z_{i,j} = S_{i,j} + L_{i,j}$ be the access delay. The sample average values of seek, latency, and access delays are therefore obtained from

$$E[S] = \frac{1}{nk} \sum_{i=1}^{n} \sum_{j=1}^{k} S_{i,j},$$

$$E[L] = \frac{1}{nk} \sum_{j=1}^{n} \sum_{j=1}^{k} L_{i,j},$$

and

$$E[Z] = \frac{1}{nk} \sum_{i=1}^{n} \sum_{j=1}^{k} Z_{i,j},$$

respectively. Define the sequences of maximum values of seek, latency, and access delays as

$$\hat{S}_j = \max_{1 \leq i \leq n} \{S_{i,j}\},$$

$$\hat{L}_j = \max_{1 \leq i \leq n} \{L_{i,j}\}, \text{ and}$$

$$\hat{Z}_j = \max_{1 \leq i \leq n} \{Z_{i,j}\},$$

$j = 1, 2, \cdots, k$, respectively. In order to obtain the sample average values of the maximum, we simply evaluate the

(Measured)	
Mean	8.2921
Max	16.6230
Exp max	14.8177
(Estimated)	
*exp max	14.7779
Relative error	0.0027

Fig. 7. Latency. Measured values and estimated expected maximum (*exp max).

following expressions:

$$E\left[\hat{S}_{\max}(n)\right] = \frac{1}{k} \sum_{j=1}^{k} \hat{S}_j,$$

$$E\left[\hat{L}_{\max}(n)\right] = \frac{1}{k} \sum_{j=1}^{k} \hat{L}_j, \text{ and}$$

$$E\left[\hat{Z}_{\max}(n)\right] = \frac{1}{k} \sum_{j=1}^{k} \hat{Z}_j.$$

Having computed the sample average values of the maximum, we now compute the corresponding estimated values:

$$E[S_{\max}(n)] = H_n E[S],$$

where S is exponentially distributed,

$$E[L_{\max}(n)] = \frac{n}{n+1} \text{ Rev},$$

where Rev is the time for a disk revolution, 16.6 ms, and L is considered to be uniformly distributed, and

$$E[Z_{\max}(n)] = E[S + L] + \sigma \sqrt{2 \log_{10} n},$$

where σ the standard deviation of the access delay and is given by

$$\sigma = \sqrt{\frac{1}{nk} \sum_{i=1}^{n} \sum_{j=1}^{k} ((S_{i,j} + L_{i,j}) - E[S + L])^2}.$$

Note that for $n = 8$, $H_8 \simeq 2.7$, and $\sqrt{2 \log_{10} 8} \simeq 1.34$. In order to determine the goodness of an estimated value, we compute the percent relative error as follows.

• Seek:

$$\varepsilon_S = \frac{\left| \left(H_8 E[S] - E\left[\hat{S}_{\max}(n)\right] \right) \right|}{E\left[\hat{S}_{\max}(n)\right]}$$

	Disk-1	Disk-2	Disk-3	Disk-4	Disk-E	Disk-U
$(E[S + L])$						
Estimate	15.645	23.225	31.924	28.06	15.394	33.221
Lower	15.268	22.504	30.857	27.161	15.032	32.3700
Upper	16.028	23.945	32.99	28.959	17.757	34.073
(Std dev)						
Estimate	8.5378	14.491	15.898	14.564	8.1085	19.029
Lower	8.2813	14.003	15.188	13.962	7.8619	18.45
Upper	8.8156	15.023	16.7	15.236	8.3757	19.655
(Sample)						
Mean	15.645	23.225	31.924	28.06	15.394	33.221
Median	15.371	21.661	34.68	30.275	14.401	33.282
Std dev	8.5379	14.491	15.898	14.564	8.1085	19.029
(Fitted)						
Mean	15.645	23.225	31.924	28.06	15.394	33.221
Median	15.645	23.225	31.924	28.06	15.394	33.221
Std dev	8.5379	14.491	15.898	14.564	8.1085	19.029

Fig. 8. Analysis of normal distribution fit. Confidence intervals (95%).

Access Delay	Disk-1	Disk-2	Disk-3	Disk-4	Disk-E	Disk-U
(Measured)						
Mean	15.6344	23.2140	31.9130	28.0490	15.3944	33.2210
Max	36.5523	61.3470	63.7150	62.7720	57.2641	66.5760
Exp max	27.6528	45.3925	51.4120	47.1228	28.1765	53.7402
(Estimated)						
*exp max	27.1480	43.2678	52.9328	47.9321	26.4484	53.4761
Relative error	.0183	.0468	.0296	.0172	.0613	.0049

Fig. 9. Summary of experiments. For each experiment, measured access delays are summarized. Estimated maximum values (*exp max) are compared to the measured expected maximum delays.

- Latency:

$$\varepsilon_L = \frac{\left| \left(\frac{n}{n+1} \operatorname{Rev} - E\left[\hat{L}_{\max}(n) \right] \right) \right|}{E\left[\hat{L}_{\max}(n) \right]}$$

- Access delay:

$$\varepsilon_Z = \frac{\left| \left(E[S + L] + \sigma\sqrt{2\log n} - E\left[\hat{Z}_{\max}(n) \right] \right) \right|}{E\left[\hat{Z}_{\max}(n) \right]}.$$

C. Results of Measurements and Comparisons

We first examine the latency, seek, and access delay distributions for each of the original trace sequences. We then give the expected maximum values which have been measured on the simulated systems. These measured values are then compared to the corresponding estimated values, and the relative error for each estimated value is computed.

1) Seek: We first inspect the real trace data from the four most active disks, and study the synthetic data which we have created. The seek time distributions found from the four disks from the real trace data are illustrated in Figs. 10–13 for Disk-1–Disk-4, respectively. A summary of the seek time distributions on all the six disks, including Disk-U with a uniform seek and Disk-E with an exponential seek, is provided in Fig. 6.

Note that each of the seek time distributions from the real trace has a significant number of zero seeks. Disk-1 as in

Fig. 10 has approximately 50% of zero seeks with the mean of 7.3337 ms. The maximum seek time observed on the disk is 20.14 ms. Disk-2 as in Fig. 11 shows almost the same ratio of zero seeks as in Disk-1, but the maximum seek time is more than twice as much, that of 45.68 ms. Consequently, its mean value and also the standard deviation are almost doubled. Disk-3 as in Fig. 12, on the other hand, shows fewer zero seeks, only 25%. Note that not counting the zero seeks, the nonzero seek time distribution has the well-known bell-shaped curve which characterizes the normal density function. Finally on Disk-4 as in Fig. 13, zero seeks are again not as much, $\simeq 32\%$, but this time, the mean and standard deviation are considerably smaller than those found on Disk-3.

As discussed previously, the seek time distribution is complicated. None of the four disks from the real trace data has a simple seek time distribution. We will show in the next section that the sum of seek and latency can be rather accurately approximated by a normal distribution.

On Disk-E, where the seek times have been generated by the exponential number generator, the expected maximum seek that has been measured is 18.5752 ms, as shown in Fig. 6. The expected maximum value that has been estimated by the method described previously, $H_8 E[S]$, is 19.143 ms. The relative error is approximately 3%. The reason for this somewhat higher error rate is as follows. As we generate the exponential numbers using the formula shown previously, there will be a small number of seek times that are larger than the maximum time required for seek. The probability that the number X generated is larger than the maximum

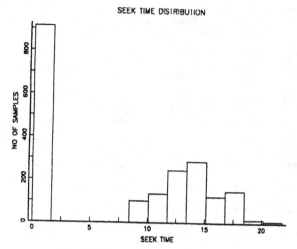

Fig. 10. Seek time distribution of Disk-1.

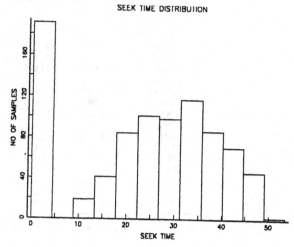

Fig. 12. Seek time distribution of Disk-3.

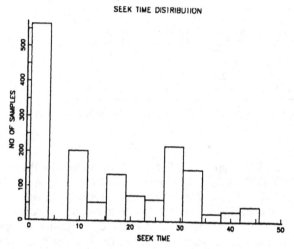

Fig. 11. Seek time distribution of Disk-2.

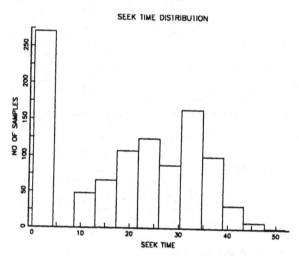

Fig. 13. Seek time distribution of Disk-4.

M, $\Pr[X > M]$, is $\left(e^{\frac{-M}{\mu}}\right)$, where μ is the mean value of X. As a result of generating 2000 random variates, four of them were larger than 50 ms, the maximum seek time on an IBM 3350 disk system. Although the number is small, we discard such numbers and experiment only with the remaining ones. Hence, the resulting distribution was not exactly an exponential one. As we include all such large numbers, the relative error naturally becomes smaller; it was 0.9% with our experiment.

2) Latency: The latency time distribution is straightforward. Given a sequence of uniformly distributed latency times, the sequence was then split into eight subsequences, and a measurement was taken to obtain the expected value of the maximum latency. Its corresponding estimated value was then computed. As summarized in Fig. 7, the measured expected maximum is 14.8177 ms, and its estimated value, which is denoted by (*exp max), is 14.7779 ms. Note that this estimated value of the expected maximum has been computed using the exact method. Thus, the estimation is very accurate with a small error of 0.27%. This error, although very small, is due to the fact that the size of the trace data we have used was limited. As the size of the trace data grows, it is likely that the estimated value and the measured value will converge.

3) Access Delay: Each seek time sequence we have obtained is now paired with a latency sequence which has been generated by the random number generator. The distribution of the sum (seek + latency) for each of the four sequences from the real trace data is plotted in Figs. 14, 15, 16, and in 17. The two synthetic sequences, one with the exponential seek distribution and the other with the uniform distribution, are also plotted in Figs. 18 and 19. By examining the six figures each of which has its own seek time distribution, we can say that for a wide range of seek time distributions the sum of seek and latency may be approximated by a normal distribution. To show this, each of them is fitted to a normal distribution as shown in the figures, and the fit is summarized in Fig. 8.

Each sequence of (seek + latency) times is then split into eight subsequences as if we were simulating an eight-disk asynchronous system. As we have done previously, expected

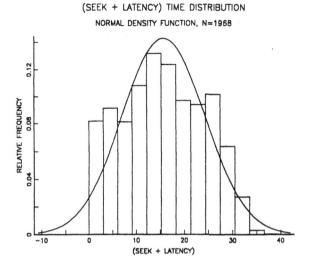

Fig. 14. (Seek + latency) time distribution of Disk-1.

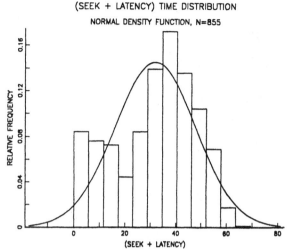

Fig. 16. (Seek + latency) time distribution of Disk-3.

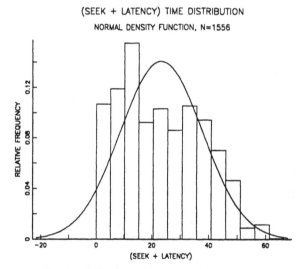

Fig. 15. (Seek + latency) time distribution of Disk-2.

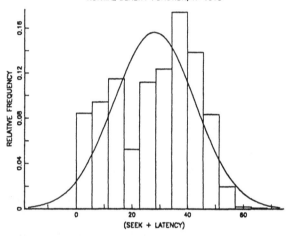

Fig. 17. (Seek + latency) time distribution of Disk-4.

maximum values are measured. These measured values are then compared to the estimated values. A summary of our experiments is presented in Fig. 9.

Note that the mean and maximum values have been measured from the original sequences, treating each sequence as a reference stream per disk. The expected maximum values, both measured and estimated, however, have been obtained after splitting each sequence to eight subsequences.

On the four disks whose traces have been taken from the real trace data, the estimated maximum values vary from 1.72% to 4.68%. Disk-U with the uniform seek shows the smallest relative error of 0.49% providing a lower bound, and Disk-E with the exponential seek showing the largest relative error of 6.13%.

We repeated the same experiments using the IBM 3380 seek times. The results were not significantly different. Therefore, we can say that for a wide range of the seek time distributions,

the sum of seek and latency can be approximated by a normal distribution. Consequently, as we preserve the same distribution on the asynchronous disk system which has been simulated by the trace sequence we have at hand, we can estimate its expected maximum using the formula $E[S + L] + \sigma\sqrt{2\log_{10} n}$.

IV. CONCLUSIONS

We have studied the performance implications of asynchronous disk interleaving. We have used approximate analysis to develop simple expressions for various expected delays and demonstrated that they are good for a wide range of seek time distributions.

Disk interleaving is a useful technique in computing large-scale problems that require huge amounts of data. Disk interleaving may be achieved synchronously or asynchronously. Synchronous interleaving may be best suited for algorithms whose reference patterns are regular and structured and whose

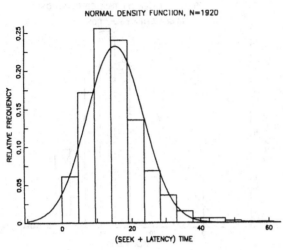

Fig. 18. (Experimental seek + latency) time distribution on Disk-E.

(UNIFORM SEEK + LATENCY) TIME DISTRIBUTION

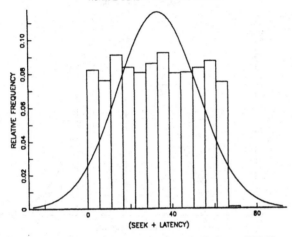

Fig. 19. (Uniform seek + latency) time distribution on Disk-U.

block sizes are large [8]. Nevertheless, a fully synchronized disk system may no longer be an option as the number of disks in a disk system reaches beyond a certain point [12]. A suitable combination of the two may provide an effective I/O system architecture that can also scale well according to the size of the disk system. In particular, asynchronous interleaving can be used to group clusters of synchronously interleaved disks. Each cluster of synchronous disks can be treated as if it were a single disk and it can then participate to form yet another level of interleaving.

REFERENCES

[1] M. Bohl, *Introduction to IBM Direct Access Storage Devices*, Science Research Associates, Inc., 1981.
[2] H. Boral, and D. J. DeWitt, "Database machines: An idea whose time has passed? A critique of the future of database machines," in *Database Machines*. Berlin, Germany: Springer-Verlag, 1983.
[3] H. A. David, *Order Statistics*. New York: Wiley, 1981.
[4] H. Garcia-Molina and K. Salem, "Disk stripping," Computer Research Report, Princeton Univ., 1988.
[5] A. Gravey, "A simple construction of upper bound for the mean of the maximum of N identically distribution random variables," *J. Appl. Probability*, vol. 22, pp. 844–851, 1985.
[6] O. G. Johnson, "Three-dimensional wave equation computations on vector computers," *Proc. IEEE*, vol. 72, no. 1, Jan. 1984.
[7] M. Y. Kim, "Synchronized disk interleaving," *IEEE Trans. Comput.*, vol. C-35, no. 11, Nov. 1986.
[8] M. Y. Kim, A. Nigam, G. Paul, and R. J. Flynn, "Disk interleaving and very large fast Fourier transforms, *Int. J. Supercomput. Appl.*, vol. 1, no. 3, pp. 75–96, 1987.
[9] C. Kruskal and A. Weiss, "Allocating independent subtasks on parallel processors," *IEEE Trans. Software Eng.*, vol. SE-11, no. 10, Oct. 1985.
[10] J. R. Lineback, "New features tune Unix for high-end machines," *Electronics*, Aug. 19, 1985.
[11] C. May, "LARGQ: A study in the design and evaluation of a memory management algorithm," IBM Computer Sci. Res. Rep. RC10048, July 1983.
[12] A. L. N. Reddy and P. Banerjee, "An evaluation of multiple-disk I/O systems," *IEEE Trans. Comput.*, Dec. 1989.
[13] ——, "Design analysis and simulation of I/O architectures for hypercube multiprocessors," *IEEE Trans. Parallel Distributed Syst.*, 1990.
[14] R. A. Scranton, D. A. Thompson, and D. W. Hunter, "The access time myth," IBM Res. Rep. RC10197, Sept. 1983.

An Analytic Performance Model of Disk Arrays

Edward K. Lee
University of California
571 Evans Hall
Berkeley, CA 94720
eklee@cs.berkeley.edu

Randy H. Katz
University of California
571 Evans Hall
Berkeley, CA 94720
randy@cs.berkeley.edu

Abstract

As disk arrays become widely used, tools for understanding and analyzing their performance become increasingly important. In particular, performance models can be invaluable in both configuring and designing disk arrays. Accurate analytic performance models are preferable to other types of models because they can be quickly evaluated, are applicable under a wide range of system and workload parameters, and can be manipulated by a range of mathematical techniques. Unfortunately, analytic performance models of disk arrays are difficult to formulate due to the presence of *queueing* and *fork-join synchronization*; a disk array request is broken up into independent disk requests which must all complete to satisfy the original request. In this paper, we develop and validate an analytic performance model for disk arrays. We derive simple equations for approximating their utilization, response time and throughput. We validate the analytic model via simulation, investigate the error introduced by each approximation used in deriving the analytic model, and examine the validity of some of the conclusions that can be drawn from the model.

1 Introduction

Disk arrays provide high I/O performance by striping data over multiple disks. High performance is achieved by servicing multiple I/O requests concurrently and by using several disks to service a single request in parallel. Given the increasing importance of disk arrays as high-performance secondary storage systems [7, 8, 12, 14, 15, 17], tools for understanding their performance become increasingly important. In particular, perfor-

mance models, combined with a thorough understanding of an installation's workload, will be invaluable in both configuring and designing disk arrays. In general, accurate analytic performance models are preferable to other types of models, such as empirical and simulation, because they can be quickly evaluated, are applicable under a wide range of system and workload parameters, and can be manipulated by a range of mathematical techniques. Even when analytic models are not directly applicable to a particular system or workload, they are frequently useful for quickly analyzing general properties of the system, stimulating intuition and furthering understanding.

Unfortunately, analytic performance models of disk arrays are difficult to formulate due to the presence of queueing and fork-join synchronization; a disk array request is broken up into independent disk requests, all of which must complete to satisfy the disk array request. While systems with only of queueing *or* fork-join synchronization are frequently tractable given certain reasonable approximations, the combination of the two result in systems that are very difficult to analyze analytically. Exact analytic solutions for the two server fork-join queue given Poisson arrivals and independent service times currently exist [1, 4] but the *k*-server fork-join queue remains unsolved. Other related work in the field of disk array performance falls into four primary categories: (1) simulation studies [3, 12, 16], (2) analytic models that ignore queueing effects [2, 9, 17], (3) analytic models that ignore fork-join synchronization [8] and (4) restricted queueing models that deal with fork-join synchronization using specialized techniques not easily extended to modeling disk arrays [5, 13]. Most analytic queueing studies deal with general queueing systems rather than disk arrays in particular.

In this paper, we develop and validate an analytic performance model for asynchronous disk arrays. Our model is different from previous analytic models of disk arrays mentioned above for the following reasons. First, we use a closed queueing model with a fixed number of processes whereas previous analytic models of disk

"An Analytic Performance Model of Disk Arrays" by E.K. Lee and R.H. Katz from *Proc. 1993 ACM SIGMETRICS Conf. Measurement and Modeling of Computer Systems*, ACM Press, New York, N.Y., 1993, pp. 98–109. Copyright © ACM, Inc., 1993. Reprinted by permission.

arrays have used open queueing models with Poisson arrivals. A closed model more accurately models the synchronous I/O behavior of scientific, time-sharing and distributed systems. In such systems, processes tends to wait for previous I/O requests to complete before issuing new I/O requests, whereas in transaction based systems, I/O requests are issued randomly in time regardless of whether the previous I/O requests have completed. Second, to the best of our knowledge, we present the first analytic model for disk arrays that handles both the queueing at individual disks and the fork-join synchronization introduced by data striping. Previous analytic models handling both queueing and fork-join synchronization cannot easily be applied to disk arrays; these assume service times across servers (disks) are independent whereas in disk arrays, service times are very much dependent.

We have found the analytic model useful for comparative studies that focus on the relative performance of various disk array configurations. Lee [10] uses the analytic model presented here to derive a formula for the optimal size of data striping in disk arrays, providing an important application of the model. We are currently using the model to calculate quantitative price/performance metrics for disk arrays under a range of system and workload parameters. The model is also useful in identifying important factors in the performance of disk arrays and presents insights that are useful in characterizing the performance of real disk arrays. The model, of course, is not without limitations. Although the analytic model can be used to model both read and write requests to non-redundant disk arrays and read requests to a subclass of RAID's (Redundant Arrays of Inexpensive Disks) identified in Section 2, it currently does not model parity updates which occur during write requests to a RAID. Another limitation is that the workload model is not expressive enough to easily model real workloads. Thus, although the model can be used to accurately predict the performance of real disk arrays under many of the synthetic workloads used in this paper, its prediction of performance under real workloads may be highly approximate. A final limitation is that we only model the disk components of a disk array system. Real disk array systems have many other components such as strings, I/O controllers, I/O busses and CPU's that affect the performance of the system. We are currently addressing the above limitations in a work in preparation.

In the following sections, we first derive an exact expression for the utilization of the model system. Because the exact expression contains parameters that are difficult or impossible to compute, we analytically approximate the difficult parameters to make the expression more tractable. From the resulting approximate

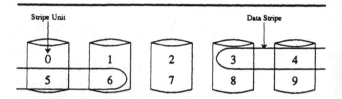

Figure 1: Data Striping in Disk Arrays.

Stripe unit is the unit of data interleaving, that is, the amount of data that is placed on a disk before data is placed on the next disk. Stripe units typically range from a sector to a track in size (512 bytes to 64 kilobytes). The figure illustrates a disk array with five disks with the first ten stripe units labeled.

Data stripe is a sequence of logically consecutive stripe units. A logical I/O request to a disk array corresponds to a data stripe. The figure illustrates a data stripe consisting of four stripe units spanning stripe units three through six.

---

equation for utilization, we derive equations for response time and throughput. We then validate the analytic model via simulation and investigate the error introduced by each approximation made in deriving the analytic model. Next, we empirically verify certain conclusions that can be drawn from the analytic model and present an alternative empirical derivation of the analytic model. Finally, we derive and validate a simple extension to the basic analytic model which allows the modeling of variable sized request distributions.

2   The Modeled System

Our primary focus is on modeling non-redundant asynchronous disk arrays. Figure 1 illustrates the basic disk array of interest and the terms *stripe unit* and *data stripe*.

For readers who are familiar with the RAID taxonomy, we mention that the analytic model we develop can also be used to model reads for RAID level 5 disk arrays using the left-symmetric parity placement [11]. This is because the left-symmetric parity placement has the property that it does not disturb the *data* mapping illustrated in Figure 1.

3   The Analytic Model

In this section, we derive equations that approximate the read/write performance of non-redundant asyn-

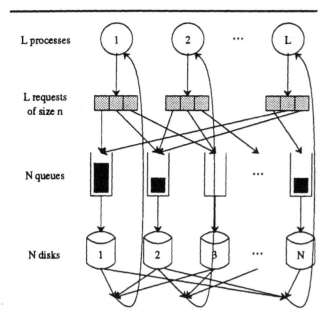

Figure 2: Closed Queuing Model for Disk Arrays. The parameters of the above system are as follows:

$$L \equiv \text{Number of processes issuing requests.}$$
$$N \equiv \text{Number of disks.}$$
$$n \equiv \text{Request size in disks } (n \leq N).$$
$$S \equiv \text{Service time of a given disk request.}$$

chronous disk arrays. Our approach is to derive the expected utilization of a given disk in the disk array. Because we are modeling a closed system where each disk plays a symmetric role with respect to each other, knowing the expected utilization of a given disk will allow us to compute the entire system's throughput and response time.

For the sake of convenience and clarity, we present the complete derivation of the analytic model before presenting the empirical validation of the model. However, the actual development of the model followed an iterative process consisting of an alternating sequence of analytical derivations and empirical validations. While some of the approximations made in this section, when separately presented from their empirical validation, may appear arbitrary, the approximations and results of the model are justified in Section 4.

3.1 The Model System

Consider the *closed* queueing system illustrated by Figure 2. The system consists of L processes, each of which

issues, one at a time, an *array request* of size n stripe units. Each array request is broken up into n *disk requests* and the disk requests are queued round-robin starting from a randomly chosen disk. Each disk services a single disk request at a time in a FIFO manner. When all of the disk requests corresponding to an array request are serviced, the issuing process generates another array request, repeating the cycle. Note that two or more array requests may partially overlap on some of the disks, resulting in complex interactions. We sometimes refer to array requests simply as *requests*. In the derivation of the analytic model, we will assume that L and n are fixed. We will also assume that the processes do nothing but issue I/O requests. Later, we will extend the model to allow variable sized requests.

3.2 The Expected Utilization

In deriving the expected utilization of the model system, the following definitions will prove useful:

$$U \equiv \text{Expected utilization of a given disk.}$$
$$R \equiv \text{Response time of a given array request.}$$
$$W \equiv \text{Disk idle (wait) time between disk requests.}$$
$$Q \equiv \text{Queue length at a given disk.}$$
$$p_0 \equiv \text{Probability the queue at a given disk is empty when the disk finishes a disk request.}$$
$$p \equiv n/N,$$
$$\text{probability of a request accessing a given disk.}$$

If we visualize the activity at a given disk as an alternating sequence of busy periods of length S and idle periods of length W, the expected utilization of a given disk is,

$$U = \frac{E(S)}{E(S) + E(W)}. \tag{1}$$

Idle periods of length zero can occur and imply that another disk request is already waiting for service, $Q > 0$, when the current disk request finishes service.

Let r_0 denote the time between the end of service of a given disk request and the issuing of a new array request into the system. Let $r_i, i \in \{1, 2, \ldots\}$, denote the successive time intervals between successive issues of array requests numbered relative to r_0. Let M denote the number of array requests issued after a given disk finishes a disk request until, but excluding, the array request that accesses the given disk. Since each array request has probability p of accessing a given disk and disk requests are issued one at a time, M is a modified geometric random variable with $E(M) = 1/p - 1$. Figure 3 illustrates the above terms.

By conditioning on the queue length at the time a

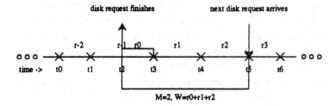

Figure 3: Time-line of Events at a Given Disk.
After the disk request finishes service at time t_2, $M = 2$ array requests that do not access the given disk are issued at times t_3 and t_4 before an array request that accesses the given disk is issued at time t_5. The disk remains idle for a time period of $W = r_0 + r_1 + r_2$.

disk request finishes service, we can write,

$$
\begin{aligned}
E(W) &= P(Q > 0)E(W|Q > 0) + \\
      &\quad P(Q = 0)E(W|Q = 0), \\
E(W) &= (1 - p_0)0 + p_0 E(\textstyle\sum_{i=0}^{M} r_i), \\
E(W) &= p_0(E(r_0) + E(\textstyle\sum_{i=1}^{M} r_i)).
\end{aligned}
$$

Substituting into Equation 1 we have,

$$
U = \frac{E(S)}{E(S) + p_0(E(r_0) + E(\sum_{i=1}^{M} r_i))} \tag{2}
$$

Equation 2 is an exact, though not directly useful, equation for the expected utilization of the model system.

3.3 Approximating the Expected Utilization

In the previous section, we formulated an exact equation, Equation 2, for the expected utilization of the model system. Unfortunately, the exact equation consists of terms which are very difficult if not impossible to compute. In this section, we approximate components of Equation 2 to make it analytically tractable.

To simplify Equation 2, the first approximation we make is $E(\sum_{i=1}^{M} r_i) \simeq E(M)E(r_i) = (1/p - 1)E(R)/L$. From Little's Law, we know that the average time between successive issues of array requests is $E(R)/L$. Note also that M is a *stopping time*, that is, the event that the mth request misses the given disk, $M > m$, is independent of the random variables $r_{m+1}, r_{m+2}, \ldots$. Thus, from Wald's Equation, the above approximation would be exact if $r_i, i \in \{1, 2, \ldots\}$ <u>were</u> independently distributed with a common mean of $E(R)/L$. For the moment, we will take the above approximation as given,

but later show via simulation that the above is an extremely good approximation.

The second approximation we make is to assume that $E(r_0) \simeq 0$. As motivation, we present the following observations concerning $E(r_0)$:

- $E(r_0) = 0$ implies that disk requests associated with the same array request finish at the same time and thus an array request is issued immediately whenever *any* disk request finishes.

- $E(r_0) = 0$ when $n = 1$, that is, when each array request consists of a single disk request, the completion of each disk request corresponds to the completion of the corresponding array request and, thus, the process that issued the disk request will immediately issue another array request.

- $E(r_0) \simeq 0$ when $n = N$, that is, when an array request always uses all the disks, disk requests associated with the same array request will tend to finish at close to the same time because all of the disks will be in very similar states and operate in a lock step fashion since disk service times are deterministic and disk requests across disks will be almost identical.

- Hopefully, $E(r_0)$ will not deviate too far from zero for values of n other than one or N.

The third and final approximation is $p_0 E(R)/E(S) \simeq 1$. This equation is true for $M/M/1$ systems and approximately holds at low to moderate loads for $M/G/1$ systems but the primary motivation for the approximation comes from empirical observations. Incorporating the three approximations, we can rewrite Equation 2 as,

$$
U \simeq \frac{1}{1 + \frac{1}{L}(1/p - 1)}. \tag{3}
$$

Note that under the approximations we have made, *the expected utilization is insensitive to the disk service time distribution, S.*

The expected throughput in bytes per second can be written as,

$$
T = \frac{UNB}{E(S)}, \tag{4}
$$

where B is the size of the stripe unit. Since this is a closed system, the expected response time can be expressed as,

$$
E(R) = \frac{LnB}{T}, \tag{5}
$$

where $T/(nB)$ is simply the throughput in array requests per second. Future references to a specific analytic model will refer to the above equations and to Equation 3 in particular.

To briefly motivate the usefulness of the analytic model, consider the following applications of the model. An equation for the stripe unit size, B, that maximizes throughput can be computed from Equation 4 by differentiating it with respect to B and solving for local maxima. Another simple application is to solve Equation 5 with respect to N to get a feel for the number of disks needed to achieve a certain response time for a given workload.

4 Empirical Validation

In this section, we examine via simulation the accuracy of the analytic model and the error introduced by each approximation in the derivation of the analytic model. We also empirically examine the validity of the conclusions that can be drawn from the model. In particular, we will show that utilization is insensitive to the disk service time distribution and that utilization can be accurately represented by an equation of the form $U = 1/(1 + \frac{1}{L}f(p, N))$ where $f(p, N)$ represents an arbitrary function of p and N. Finally, we will extend the basic analytic model to handle variable sized requests and validate the result. Our basic approach is to compare the results of the analytic model to simulation using aggregate statistics which summarize errors and graphs which plot the analytic model versus the simulated data points.

4.1 Metrics for Error Analysis

When analyzing the errors in an analytic model versus simulation over a wide range of inputs, we must use aggregate statistics summarizing the errors because it is infeasible to compare directly the error resulting from each and every data point. The following defines standard statistical terms [6] and metrics that will be used in the rest of this paper. Note in particular the definitions of the three error metrics R^2, *max error* and *90% error* which will be used to characterize errors in the analytic model.

response The result of a simulation run.

parameter A simulation variable that can influence the response.

factor A parameter that is being varied in a simulation study. In most studies, certain simulation parameters are held constant.

factor level A possible value for a factor. For example, the factor *request size* may have factor levels 4 KB, 8 KB, or 16 KB.

design An experimental design is constructed by specifying the factors, the factor levels used at each simulation run and the number of times the simulation is repeated with the same factor levels (usually using a different seed in the random number generator).

design point The factor levels for a single simulation run. For example, (number of disks = 8, request type = read, request size = 4 KB).

design set The set of design points used in an experimental design. For example, a design set can be constructed by taking a cross product of the following factor levels: number of disks $\in \{8, 16\}$, request type $\in \{$read, write$\}$, request size $\in \{4, 8, 16\}$ KB.

The following defines the metrics R^2, *max error* and *90% error*.

y_i	The ith simulated response.
$\hat{y_i}$	The ith analytically predicted response.
e_i	$y_i - \hat{y_i}$ (error of the ith input)
$\overline{y}$	Arithmetic mean of y_i's.
SSE	$\sum e_i^2$ (sum of squared errors)
SST	$\sum (y_i - \overline{y})^2$ (sum of squares total)
R^2	$(SST - SSE)/SST$ (coefficient of determination)
max error	max e_i (maximum error)
90% error	The 90th percentile of e_i.

The coefficient of determination, R^2, is a measure of how closely the analytic model predicts the simulated response. A simple model predicting that the response is equal to the mean, $\overline{y}$, for all design points would have $R^2 = 0$. A model that perfectly predicts the simulated response would have $R^2 = 1$. R^2 can be interpreted as the fraction of "total variation" that is explained by a model. Although R^2 is a good measure for checking the overall accuracy of a model, it may be highly dependent upon the choice of the design set and may vary significantly for certain subsets of the design set. That is, an analytic model that is wildly inaccurate for a significant collection of design points can still have $R^2 \simeq 1$ if the model is accurate for the other design points. Because R^2 can be insensitive to large errors in the analytic model, the *max error* metric is useful as an indication of the worst predictions made by the model. The *90% error* metric is a compromise between R^2 and *max error* which compensates for the extreme sensitivity of *max error* to outliers.

4.2 Experimental Design

We are interested in the following factors to validate our analytic model.

$diskModel$ Disk type.
N Number of disks in the disk array.
L Number of processes issuing I/O requests.
B Size of the stripe unit (block size).
p Request size as a fraction of the disk array.

The design set consists of the complete cross product of the following factor levels.

Factor	Factor Levels
$diskModel$	Lightning, Fujitsu, FutureDisk
N	2, 3, 4, 8, 16
L	1, 2, 4, 8, 16, 32
B	$(1, 4, 16, 64)\,$KB
p	$(1, 2, \ldots, N)/N$

The parameters for the three disk models listed above are described in Table 1. Note that the number of factor levels for p depend upon N and are expressed as multiples of $1/N$. This means, for example, that there are twice as many design points with $N = 4$ relative to $N = 2$. Thus, although we do not intrinsically value disk arrays with $N = 4$ more than disk arrays with $N = 2$, the design set implicitly assigns the former twice the importance of the latter. To compensate for this effect, we weigh all design points by the factor $1/N$ when calculating statistics.

We simulate each design point in the design set twice with two different random seeds to quantify the experimental error which intrinsically cannot be explained by any model. Thus, the total number of simulation runs is $2(3 \times 4 \times 6 \times (2 + 3 + 4 + 8 + 16)) = 4,752$. In each simulation run, the disks are rotationally synchronized, requests to the disk array are aligned on stripe unit boundaries, and L and p are held constant.

4.3 Validation of the Analytic Model

In this section, we examine via simulation the accuracy of the analytic model and the error introduced by each of the three approximations in the model of Section 3. Recall that the three approximations are as follows:

1. $E(\sum_{i=1}^{M} r_i) \simeq (1/p - 1)E(R)/L$,

2. $E(r_0) \simeq 0$,

3. $p_0 E(R)/E(S) \simeq 1$.

Consider the following definitions:

$$\hat{U} \equiv \frac{1}{1 + \frac{1}{L}(1/p - 1)}$$

$$\hat{U}_1 \equiv \frac{E(S)}{E(S) + p_0(E(r_0) + (1/p - 1)E(R)/L)}$$

$$\hat{U}_2 \equiv \frac{E(S)}{E(S) + p_0(\sum_{i=1}^{M} r_i)}$$

$$\hat{U}_3 \equiv \frac{1}{1 + \frac{1}{E(R)}(E(r_0) + \sum_{i=1}^{M} r_i)}$$

The variable $\hat{U}$ represents the analytic model derived in Section 3 by applying approximations 1, 2 and 3. The variables $\hat{U}_1$, $\hat{U}_2$ and $\hat{U}_3$ are submodels derived by applying only one of approximations 1, 2 or 3, respectively. By examining the errors in $\hat{U}_1$, $\hat{U}_2$ and $\hat{U}_3$, we can approximately study the errors introduced by each of the corresponding approximations.

The table below tabulates the error metrics discussed in Section 4.1 for the *best* empirical model, $\hat{U}$, $\hat{U}_1$, $\hat{U}_2$ and $\hat{U}_3$. The best empirical model is that model which minimizes the sum of squared errors or, equivalently, maximizes R^2 and is computed by averaging the responses of data points with the same design point. The error metrics for the best empirical model are useful for comparison purposes and give a feel for the magnitude of experimental errors that can not be explained by any model. The metric $1 - R^2$ is included for easier comparisons of models that have values of R^2 very close to one. Because we are more interested in relative rather than absolute errors, the error metrics are calculated for the logarithm of utilization rather than utilization directly. This means that for small errors, less than approximately 20%, the *max error* and *90% error* metrics can be interpreted as percentage deviations. For example, a *max error* of 0.0430 represents a 4.30% deviation from the *predicted* utilization.

Model	R^2	$1 - R^2$	$max\ err$	$90\%\ err$
BEST	0.9995	0.0005	0.0430	0.0133
$\hat{U}$	0.9814	0.0186	0.1863	0.0987
$\hat{U}_1$	0.9990	0.0010	0.0834	0.0192
$\hat{U}_2$	0.9888	0.0112	0.1676	0.0742
$\hat{U}_3$	0.9808	0.0192	0.1807	0.0951

The above table shows that 0.05% of the variation in response is due to experimental errors which can not be explained by any model. The maximum experimental error is 4.30%, and 90% of all experimental errors are less than 1.33%. The maximum error for the analytic model, $\hat{U}$, derived in Section 3 is 18.63% with 90% of errors less than 9.87% of the predicted utilization. Finally, approximations 2 and 3 introduce most of the experimental errors, while approximation 1, as expected, introduces very few errors.

Figure 4 plots the response predicted by the analytic model $\hat{U}$ together with the 90 percentile intervals as a

	Lightning	Fujitsu	FutureDisk
bytes per sector	512	512	512
sectors per track	48	88	132
tracks per cylinder	14	20	20
cylinders per disk	949	1944	2500
revolution time	13.9 ms	11.1 ms	9.1 ms
single cylinder seek time	2.0 ms	2.0 ms	1.8 ms
average seek time	12.6 ms	11.0 ms	10.0 ms
max stroke seek time	25.0 ms	22.0 ms	20.0 ms
sustained transfer rate	1.8 MB/s	4.1 MB/s	7.4 MB/s

Table 1: Disk Model Parameters. Average-seek-time is the average time needed to seek between two equally randomly selected cylinders. Note that sustained-transfer-rate is a function of bytes-per-sector, sectors-per-track and revolution-time. *Lightning* is the IBM 0661 3.5" 320 MB SCSI disk drive, *Fujitsu* is the Fujitsu M2652H/S 5.25" 1.8 GB SCSI disk drive and *FutureDisk* is a hypothetical disk of the future created by projecting the parameters of the Fujitsu disk approximately three years into the future based on current trends in disk technology. The most dramatic improvements are in the bit and track density of the disks rather than in mechanical positioning times. Thus, disks in the future will have much higher sustained transfer rates but only marginally better positioning times. The seek profile for each disk is computed using the following formula:

$$seekTime(x) = \begin{cases} 0 & \text{if } x = 0 \\ a\sqrt{x-1} + b(x-1) + c & \text{if } x > 0 \end{cases}$$

where x is the seek distance in cylinders and a, b and c are chosen the satisfy the single-cylinder-seek-time, average-seek-time and max-stroke-seek-time constraints. The square root term in the above formula models the constant acceleration/deceleration period of the disk head and the linear term models the period after maximum disk head velocity is reached. If cylinders-per-track is greater than approximately 200, a, b and c can be approximated using the following formulas:

$$a = (-10\, minSeek + 15\, avgSeek - 5\, maxSeek)/(3\, \sqrt{numCyl})$$
$$b = (7\, minSeek - 15\, avgSeek + 8\, maxSeek)/(3\, numCyl)$$
$$c = minSeek$$

where *minSeek, avgSeek, maxSeek* and *numCyl* correspond to the disk parameters single-cylinder-seek-time, average-seek-time, max-stroke-seek-time and cylinders-per-track, respectively. We have compared the model to the seek profile of the Amdahl 6380A published by Thisquen [18] and have found the model to closely approximate the seek profile of the actual disk. In practice, we have found the model to be well behaved, although care must be taken to check that a and b evaluate to positive numbers.

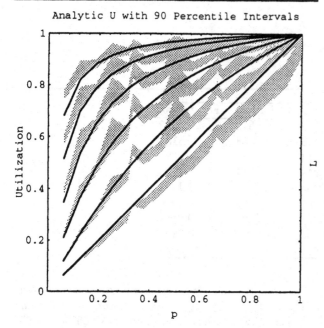

Analytic U with 90 Percentile Intervals

Figure 4: Analytic U with 90 Percentile Intervals as a Function of L and p. Each line and shaded region represents the analytically predicted response and empirically determined 90 percentile intervals, respectively, for a different value of L. From bottom to top the values for L are 1,2,4,8,16 and 32, respectively.

function of L and p, the only two factors considered important by the analytic model. In the figure, each 90 percentile interval encloses 90 % of the weighted simulated responses for the given values of L and p. We have elected to give percentile intervals rather than confidence intervals because standard methods for calculating confidence intervals require that errors be normally distributed with a constant standard deviation. Certain transformations can be made on responses to satisfy the requirement but these transformations are often artificial. Percentile intervals, on the other hand, do not require any assumptions in the distribution of errors but do require a larger number of data points to calculate. Figure 4 shows that the analytically predicted utilization approximately passes through the 90 percentile intervals determined by simulation. As we will see later, the jaggedness of the percentile intervals is caused by the fact that the factor N, which is ignored by the analytic model, is significant in explaining variations in the response.

4.4 Validation of Model Properties

The previous section examined the errors in the analytic model, but regardless of the accuracy of the model, certain properties of the model may be valid where the model itself is not. This section will investigate the model's prediction that the utilization is independent of the disk service time distribution, S, or more specifically is dependent only on the factors L and p. We will also examine whether, as implied by the model, the utilization can be accurately modeled by an equation of the form $U = 1/(1 + \frac{1}{L} f(p, N))$ where $f(p, N)$ represents an arbitrary function of p and N. Recall that $f(p, N)$ is equal to $1/p - 1$ in the analytic model.

4.4.1 Significance of Factors

The following table tabulates the error metrics for the best empirical models—models that maximize R^2—when certain factors are excluded. The first entry labeled *NONE* corresponds to the best empirical model that can be constructed when no factors are excluded and is identical to the model identified as *BEST* in the previous section. If the exclusion of a factor results in error metrics that are only slightly different from the error metrics of the *NONE* entry, this provides strong evidence that the factor can be safely ignored by the analytic model, at least over the range of factor levels investigated. The last two entries in the table illustrate the effects of excluding more than one factor at a time. As before, the metrics are calculated for the logarithm of utilization rather than for utilization directly.

Deleted Factors	R^2	$1 - R^2$	max err	90 % err
NONE	0.9995	0.0005	0.0430	0.0133
diskModel	0.9990	0.0010	0.0570	0.0205
N	0.9936	0.0064	0.1653	0.0525
L	0.4238	0.5762	1.4311	0.4835
B	0.9986	0.0014	0.0789	0.0252
p	0.4285	0.5715	1.8733	0.5018
diskModel B	0.9983	0.0017	0.0843	0.0269
diskModel B N	0.9926	0.0074	0.1678	0.0577

As predicted by the analytic model, the above table illustrates that utilization is insensitive to the disk service time distribution, S, or more specifically to the two principle factors, *diskModel* and B, that determine S. Excluding both the factors *diskModel* and B result in error metrics *max error* = 8.43 % and *90 % error* = 2.69 % which compare favorably with the error metrics of the best case when no factors are excluded of *max error* = 4.30 % and *90 % error* = 1.33 %. Thus, we conclude that utilization is insensitive to the disk service time distribution, S.

The insensitivity of utilization to the disk service time distribution is hardly surprising given that we have a closed queueing system where processes perform nothing but I/O. Consider the following thought experiment. If we replaced all the disks with devices twice as fast but the same in other respects, we would expect throughput to exactly double but utilization to remain the same. Real systems are more complicated because changing disks or stripe unit sizes not only changes the mean of the service time distribution but also its shape. However, this simple thought experiment provides a valuable insight as to why utilization is insensitive to the disk service time distribution. It also provides a reason to believe that this is a generalizable property that also holds under a wide range of factor levels that we have not investigated in this paper.

Unlike excluding the factors *diskModel* and B, excluding factor N introduces significant errors. The errors, however, are not large enough to say that it is never acceptable to ignore N. Whether N can be ignored depends on the actual use of the model. If one is primarily interested in the effects of varying N, it may not be acceptable, but otherwise, it is probably acceptable. The table shows that the remaining factors, L and p, are clearly important and cannot be ignored.

4.4.2 Relationships Between N, L and p

The previous section identified the factors N, L and p as significant in formulating a model for the utilization of the modeled system. In this section, we empirically investigate the relationships between these factors. In particular, we examine whether, as implied by the model, the utilization can be accurately modeled by an equation of the form $U = 1/(1 + \frac{1}{L}f(p, N))$ where $f(p, N)$ represents an arbitrary function of p and N. We then search for values of $f(p, N)$ that result in accurate analytic models.

Figure 5 plots $\log(1/\overline{U} - 1)$ versus $\log_2 L$ for the different factor levels of N and p where $\overline{U}$ is the geometric mean of the utilization over all design points with the same values of N, L and p. We use $\overline{U}$ rather than arbitrarily selecting design points with a specific value for *diskModel* and B to reduce experimental error. If $U \simeq 1/(1 + \frac{1}{L}f(p, N))$, a plot of $\log(1/\overline{U} - 1)$ versus $\log_2 L$ should result in straight lines with a slope of -1. As is evident from the figure, this is approximately the case.

Now that we have verified that $U \simeq 1/(1 + \frac{1}{L}f(p, N))$, it remains to determine a good approximation for $f(p, N)$. Since f is a function only of p and N and not L, we can theoretically determine f by fixing L to any particular value. In particular, if $L = 1$, the resulting system has no queueing and it is evident that

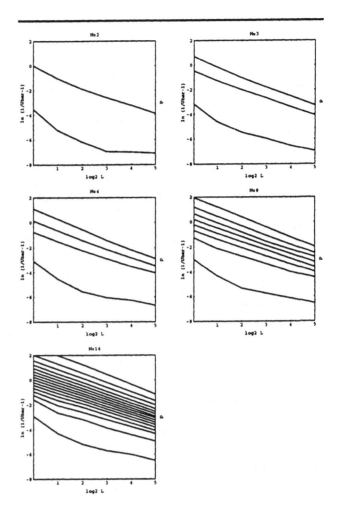

Figure 5: Plots of $\log(1/\overline{U} - 1)$ vs. $\log_2 L$. Each plot corresponds to a different value of N. Within each plot, each line represents a plot of $\log(1/\overline{U} - 1)$ versus $\log_2 L$ for a different value of p. From top to bottom the values for p are $1/N, 2/N, \ldots,$ and N/N, respectively.

$U \simeq p$. Substituting, we have $p \simeq 1/(1 + \frac{1}{L}f(p, N))$ and solving for $f(p, N)$ we have $f(p, N) = 1/p - 1$. Note that this results in the same analytic model, $U \simeq 1/(1 + \frac{1}{L}(1/p - 1))$ derived in Section 3. The reader can look upon the above result as an alternative derivation of the analytic model based on empirical techniques.

Having rederived the analytical model above, two questions immediately arise:

1. Can we get a more accurate model by solving for utilization with $L = 2$ rather than $L = 1$? Theoretically, a solution to such a model would take into account a greater amount of the interaction between processes and should result in a more accurate model.

2. How good is the best model of the form $U \simeq 1/(1 + \frac{1}{L}f(p, N))$?

The second question is easily answered empirically; we simply calculate the values of $f(p, N)$ which maximizes R^2 and examine the errors of the resulting model. The first question is more difficult to answer. Even for $L = 2$, we must take into account both queueing and fork-join synchronization. We approximately model the system with $L = 2$ as a discrete-time discrete-state Markov chain. If we assume that disk service times are constant, the number of states required to model the system is equal to the number of disks in the system. That is, the queue length at each disk is either zero or one, disks with a queue length of one are always consecutively located in the disk array, and the state where every disk has a queue can be merged with the state where no disk has a queue. We have formulated and solved such a model for arbitrary N. The solution is complex enough and would require sufficient explanation that it is not presented here. The model will be presented in a dissertation currently in preparation.

Let $\hat{U}_L$ represent the best empirical model of the form $U \simeq 1/(1 + \frac{1}{L}f(p, N))$, let $\hat{U}_{L1} \equiv 1/(1 + \frac{1}{L}(1/p - 1))$, and let $\hat{U}_{L2}$ represent the approximate solution for utilization derived by assuming $L = 2$. The table below tabulates the error metrics for $\hat{U}_L$, $\hat{U}_{L1}$ and $\hat{U}_{L2}$.

Model	R^2	$1 - R^2$	max err	90 % err
$\hat{U}_L$	0.9929	0.0071	0.1299	0.0642
$\hat{U}_{L1}$	0.9814	0.0186	0.1863	0.0987
$\hat{U}_{L2}$	0.9814	0.0186	0.2176	0.0920

The error metrics of $\hat{U}_{L1}$, the analytic model derived in Section 3, compares favorably with the error metrics of $\hat{U}_L$, the best empirical model of the form $U \simeq 1/(1 + \frac{1}{L}f(p, N))$. Somewhat surprisingly, The max error for $\hat{U}_{L2}$ is larger than that for $\hat{U}_{L1}$ although the 90 % error is smaller. Although not visible from the table due to roundoff, R^2 for $\hat{U}_{L2}$ is slightly larger than that for $\hat{U}_{L1}$. We conclude that the additional complexities of $\hat{U}_{L2}$ does not, in general, merit its use over $\hat{U}_{L1}$.

4.5 Modeling Variable Request Sizes

In this section, we extend our model to handle variable sized workloads. Although we derived Equation 3 assuming a constant request size, it can be easily extended by noting that the parameter p is just the probability that a given request will access a given disk. Thus, given a workload which is f_1 fraction requests of size p_1 and $f_2 = 1 - f_1$ fraction requests of size p_2, $p = f_1 p_1 + f_2 p_2$. In general, if x is the size of requests as a fraction of the disk array and $F(x)$ its corresponding cumulative distribution function. Then,

$$p = \int_0^1 x \, dF(x) = \overline{p} \qquad (6)$$

where $\overline{p}$ is the average request size as a fraction of the disk array.

To validate the above result, consider the design set consisting of the following parameter and factor levels:

Parameter	Parameter Value
$diskModel$	Fujitsu
N	8
B	32 KB

Factor	Factor Levels
L	1, 2, 4, 8, 16, 32
p_1	$(2, \ldots, N)/N$
p_2	$(1, \ldots, p_1 N - 1)/N$
f_1	0.20, 0.40, 0.60, 0.80

Since we have shown in Section 4.4.1 that utilization is insensitive to $diskModel$, N and B, we hold them constant. In each simulation run, L processes randomly issue requests of size p_1, f_1 fraction of the time, and requests of size p_2, $1 - f_1$ fraction of the time. Each design point in the design set is simulated twice with two different random seeds in order to quantify the experimental error. Thus, the total number of simulation runs is $2(6 \times 28 \times 4)) = 1344$. In each simulation run, the disks are rotationally synchronized, requests to the disk array are aligned on stripe unit boundaries and L is held constant.

The following are the error metrics from the experiment where $\hat{U} \equiv 1/(1 + \frac{1}{L}(1/\overline{p} - 1))$.

Model	R^2	$1 - R^2$	max err	90 % err
BEST	0.9986	0.0014	0.0801	0.0192
$\hat{U}$	0.9969	0.0031	0.0934	0.0300

As can be seen from the table, the analytic model which only uses the factors L and $\overline{p}$ compares favorably with the best empirical model which uses all of the factors L, p_1, p_2 and f_1.

Figure 6 plots the response predicted by the analytic model $\hat{U}$ together with the maximum error intervals and individual data points as a function of L and $\overline{p}$. As can be seen from the figure, the analytically predicted response approximately passes through the simulated data points.

5 Summary and Future Work

We have derived and validated an analytic performance model for disk arrays. We initially modeled disk arrays as a closed queueing system consisting of a fixed

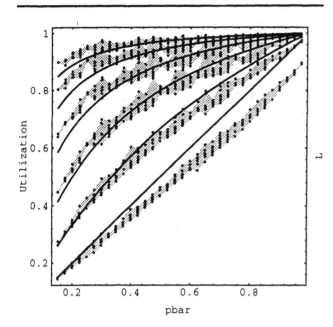

Figure 6: Analytic U with Maximum Error Intervals and Individual Data Points. In the above plot, *diskModel* = Fujitsu, $N = 8$ and $B = 32\,KB$. Each line, shaded region and set of datapoints corresponds to a different value of L. From bottom to top the values for L are 1,2,4,8,16 and 32, respectively.

number, L, of processes continuously issuing requests of a fixed size, p, to a disk array consisting of N disks. We then extended the model to handle variable sized requests. The resulting model predicts the expected utilization of the model system, U, as approximately $\frac{1}{1+\frac{1}{L}(1/\bar{p}-1)}$ where $\bar{p}$ is the average size of requests as a fraction of the number of disks in the disk array. We then directly derived the expected response time and throughput as a function of utilization. We showed via simulation that the simulated utilization is generally within ±10% of the utilization predicted by the analytic model. We also examined the error introduced by each approximation made in the derivation of the analytic model to better understand the validity of the approximations. Finally, we validated two results of the analytic model, namely that utilization is insensitive to the disk service time distribution and that utilization can be accurately represented by an equation of the form $U = 1/(1 + \frac{1}{L}f(p, N))$ where $f(p, N)$ represents an arbitrary function of p and N.

There are several major areas for future work with respect to the analytic model presented here. First, we plan to extend the workload model to handle something similar to CPU think time, where the processes, instead of simply issuing I/O requests, would alternate between computation and I/O. Second, we plan to extend the model to handle write requests to RAID's. Finally, we will apply the analytic model to solve problems in the design and configuration of disk arrays such as determining the optimal size for data striping, computing the price/performance ratios for various disk array and workload parameters, and quantifying tradeoffs between the performance and reliability of disk arrays.

6 Acknowledgements

We would like to thank our government and industrial affiliates, Array Technologies, DARPA/NASA (NAG2-591), DEC, Hewlett-Packard, IBM, Intel Scientific Computers, California MICRO, NSF (MIP 8715235), Seagate, Storage Tek, Sun Microsystems and Thinking Machines Corporation for their support. This material is based in part upon work supported by the National Science Foundation under Infrastructure Grant No. CDA-8722788.

References

[1] Francois Baccelli. Two parallel queues created by arrivals with two demands. Technical Report 426, INRIA—Rocquencourt France, 1985.

[2] Dina Bitton and Jim Gray. Disk shadowing. In *Proc. Very Large Data Bases*, pages 331–338, August 1988.

[3] Peter M. Chen and David A. Patterson. Maximizing performance in a striped disk array. In *Proc. International Symposium on Computer Architecture*, pages 322–331, May 1990.

[4] L. Flatto and S. Hahn. Two parallel queues created by arrivals with two demands i. *SIAM J. Appl. Math.*, 44:1041–1053, October 1984.

[5] Philip Heidelberger and Kishor S. Trivedi. Queueing network models for parallel processing with asynchronous tasks. *IEEE Trans. on Computers*, C-31:1099–1109, November 1982.

[6] Raj Jain. *The Art of Computer Systems Performance Analysis*. John Wiley & Sons, Inc., 1991.

[7] R. H. Katz, G. A. Gibson, and D. A. Patterson. Disk system architectures for high performance computing. In *Proc. IEEE*, volume 77, pages 1842–1858, December 1989.

[8] Michelle Y. Kim. Synchronized disk interleaving. *IEEE Trans. on Computers*, C-35:978–988, November 1986.

[9] Michelle Y. Kim and Asser N. Tantawi. Asynchronous disk interleaving. Technical Report RC12497, IBM, January 1987.

[10] Edward K. Lee and Randy H. Katz. An analytic performance model of disk arrays and its application. Technical Report UCB/CSD 91/660, University of California at Berkeley, November 1991.

[11] Edward K. Lee and Randy H. Katz. Performance consequences of parity placement in disk arrays. In *Proc. ASPLOS*, pages 190–199, April 1991.

[12] Miron Livny, S. Khoshafian, and H. Boral. Multi-disk management algorithms. In *Proc. SIGMETRICS*, pages 69–77, May 1987.

[13] R. Nelson and A. N. Tantawi. Approximate analysis of fork/join synchronization in parallel queues. *IEEE Trans. on Computers*, 37:739–743, June 1988.

[14] David A. Patterson, Peter M. Chen, Garth Gibson, and Randy H. Katz. Introduction to redundant arrays of inexpensive disks (RAID). In *Proc. IEEE COMPCON*, pages 112–117, Spring 1989.

[15] David A. Patterson, Garth Gibson, and Randy H. Katz. A case for redundant arrays of inexpensive disks (RAID). In *Proc. ACM SIGMOD*, pages 109–116, June 1988.

[16] A. L. Narasimha Reddy and Prithviraj Banerjee. An evaluation of multiple-disk I/O systems. *IEEE Trans. on Computers*, 38:1680–1690, December 1989.

[17] K. Salem and H. Garcia-Molina. Disk striping. In *Proc. IEEE Data Engineering*, pages 336–342, February 1986.

[18] J. Thisquen. Seek time measurements. Technical report, Amdahl Peripheral Products Division, May 1988.

About the Author

C.M. Krishna received his B.Tech in 1979 from the Indian Institute of Technology (Delhi), his MS in 1980 from Rensselaer Polytechnic Institute, and his PhD in 1984 from the University of Michigan, all in electrical engineering. Since 1984, he has been a faculty member of the University of Massachusetts Department of Electrical and Computer Engineering at Amherst. His research interests include distributed processing, real-time systems, and fault tolerance.